CHRONOLOGY

OF

AMERICAN

HISTORY

VOLUME II

★ ★ ★

Expansion and Civil War
1789 to 1865

CHRONOLOGY OF AMERICAN HISTORY

CHRONOLOGY

OF

AMERICAN HISTORY

VOLUME II

★ ★ ★

Expansion and Civil War
1789 to 1865

JOHN C. FREDRIKSEN

☑ Facts On File

An imprint of Infobase Publishing

Chronology of American History

Facts On File, Inc.
An imprint of Infobase Publishing
132 West 31st Street
New York NY 10001

Library of Congress Cataloging-in-Publication Data
Fredriksen, John C.
    Chronology of American history / John C. Fredriksen.
        v.   cm.
    Includes bibliographical references and indexes.
    Contents. v. 1. Colonization and independence, beginnings to 1788–
v. 2. Expansion and Civil War, to 1865–v. 3. Industry and modernity, to 1920–
v. 4. Challenges at home and abroad, to the present.
    ISBN 978-0-8160-6800-5 (set : hc : alk. paper)   1. United States–History–
Chronology.   2. United States–Civilization–Chronology.   3. United States–
Biography.   I. Title.
E174.5.F74 2008
973–dc22   2007033964

Facts On File books are available at special discounts when purchased in bulk quantities for businesses, associations, institutions, or sales promotions. Please call our Special Sales Department in New York at (212) 967-8800 or (800) 322-8755.

You can find Facts On File on the World Wide Web at http://www.factsonfile.com

Text design by Kerry Casey
Cover design by Salvatore Luongo

Printed in the United States of America

VB BVC 10 9 8 7 6 5 4 3 2 1

This book is printed on acid-free paper and contains 30 percent postconsumer recycled content.

CONTENTS

INTRODUCTION

H aving secured independence, the nascent United States adopted a new, more centralized system of governance under the Constitution in 1789, and George Washington was sworn in as the nation's first chief executive. The ensuing seven decades proved a period of unprecedented growth and internal consolidation, although not without intermittent bumps along the way. In a military parlance, the American polity struggled with its acceptance of standing professional forces, army and navy alike, in the many conflicts with Native Americans, Tripolitan pirates, revolutionary France, a second showdown with Great Britain, and a war of conquest against Mexico. The military and political institutions survived this repeated buffeting, which left the United States thriving and on the cusp of becoming a two-ocean power. Concurrent with national expansion was a similar boom in the economic and population sectors, both of which experienced steady growth due to the industrial revolution and unprecedented waves of immigration. Millions of new citizens from a dozen nations added to the patchwork ethnic diversity already extant, contributing to the energy and innovations of a young country on the rise. This period also witnessed the rise of a native intelligentsia, which sought out higher vistas by declaring their cultural independence from Great Britain and crafting a uniquely American strain of philosophy, literature, and art. The nation also witnessed the rise of "Jacksonian democracy," whereby the common man, freed from the restraints of property qualifications, participated in increasingly larger numbers and thereby shaped both politics and parties. Religion itself likewise underwent a resurgence during the so-called Second Awakening, which, in turn, occasioned the rise of numerous and significant reform movements such as temperance, women's rights, and abolitionism. In sum, self-determination in all its forms took root and flourished for the vast majority of Americans and ushered in a period of unbridled prosperity and freedom.

The decades leading up to 1860 also promulgated escalating sectionalism and stridency over the issue of slavery. Perpetuation of that "peculiar institution," along with its threatened expansion into newly acquired territories, set the stage for an armed confrontation between North and South, and the ensuing civil war, 1861–65, proved a trial by fire for American institutions. Victory here insured that the high ideals espoused by the Declaration of Independence and the Constitution, Enlightenment products of the previous century, would finally apply to all Americans. The demon of human bondage was only exorcised by force and at great cost in blood and treasure. It was also an epic struggle, one ushering in the age of "total war" toward noncombatants, along with "modern war"–the rise of technologically sophisticated, mass-produced weaponry. For all the carnage and suffering this entailed, however, the United States once again emerged united, tempered by its fiery rite of passage, and ready for its next stage of evolution as a global power.

This volume covers the growth and maturation of the United States from the accession of George Washington to the presidency in 1790 to the end of the Civil War in 1865. Chronologies of American history are standard fare in reference collections but, in a major oversight, these tend to stress social and political events at the expense of military affairs; this volume goes to great lengths to address such deficiencies with a more balanced approach. It also affords treatment of numerous and salient topics of interest to researchers, students, and laypersons alike. Even a simple perusing of the text calls to the reader's eye such wide-ranging concerns as art, business, diplomacy, literature, medicine, military, politics, publishing, religion, science, slavery, society, and technology in a simple to use and easily accessed format. Space constrains restrict most entries to a single line, but highly important events can command up to a paragraph in coverage. Wherever possible, entries are also assigned an exact year, month, and day for organizational purposes. The text is further buttressed by inclusion of 100 capsule biographies throughout the text denoting individuals of singular import to their passage in time. These are uniform in composition and touch upon birth and death dates, background, education, and other facets in addition to their most obvious concern. The volume is finally rounded out with a 5,000-word bibliography of the very latest scholarship pertaining to most events represented therein, including dissertations and master's theses, where applicable. Furthermore the pages are replete with numerous and relevant illustrations, which function both as embellishments and visual points of reference.

From perusing these pages one can hopefully grasp the imposing pageantry of American history, and all its threads of continuity and points of departure. Nothing or no one has been overlooked in making editorial choices and, while degrees of coverage may vary in length, the author cast the widest possible net for purposes of inclusion. I am deeply indebted to my editor, Owen Lancer, for suggesting this project to me. It was an arduous, nearly exhausting sojourn at times, but I am a better historian for it.

——John C. Fredriksen, Ph.D.

CHRONOLOGY

☆ ☆ ☆ ☆ ☆ ☆ ☆ ☆ ☆ ☆ ☆ ☆ ☆ ☆ ☆

1789

BUSINESS: German immigrant John Jacob Astor purchases real estate in New York City's Bowery, his first step toward creating the nation's first commercial empire.

LITERATURE: William Hill Brown's *The Power of Sympathy; or The Triumph of Nature* is the first American novel published. It ponders the consequences of seduction along with the advantages of female education.

PUBLISHING: Christopher Colles compiles and publishes *A Survey of Roads of the United States of America* in New York City, being the nation's first comprehensive set of road maps.

Adam Smith's seminal book *The Wealth of Nations* is published in the United States; its laissez-faire approach to economics wields enormous influence on the course of national development.

RELIGION: The Methodist Church establishes the Methodist Book Concern in New York City; this is the first religious publishing house for the advancement of Christian education.

SOCIETAL: A group of 200 Litchfield, Connecticut, farmers organize the nation's first temperance group, forswearing any use of alcohol during the farming season.

January

PUBLISHING: Bishops Thomas Cooke and Francis Asbury of Philadelphia edit and publish the *Arminian Magazine,* the nation's first religious magazine.

The *Children's Magazine,* the first juvenile publication in the United States, starts publication at Hartford, Connecticut; it survives only three issues.

January 7

POLITICS: The first presidential electors are elected either by state legislatures or the direct vote of citizens or, as in the case of Massachusetts, by both. Said individuals, once appointed, are free to cast their vote for whomever they like.

January 9

INDIAN: General Arthur St. Clair, presently governor of the Old Northwest, concludes the Treaty of Fort Harmar with the Indians. This pact reaffirms the previous Treaty of Fort McIntosh.

January 23
EDUCATION: The Academy of Georgetown (Georgetown University), the first Catholic institution for higher learning in the United States, is founded by Father John Carroll on the future site of the District of Columbia. It also serves as a seminary for future Catholic clergy.

February 2
POLITICS: In Virginia, James Madison defeats rival James Monroe for a seat in Congress.

February 4
POLITICS: All presidential electors cast their ballots, which will not be counted until April 6. Various states then go about electing their senators and representatives.

March 2
ARTS: The Pennsylvania state legislature votes to allow the performance of plays, signaling a liberalization of attitudes toward the performing arts along the eastern seaboard.

March 4
POLITICS: Eight senators and 13 representatives of the first Constitutional Congress convene in New York City, although they are unable to achieve a quorum until more politicians arrive.

April 1
POLITICS: The House of Representatives is off to an early start by cobbling together 30 members, enough for a quorum, and Frederick A. Mühlenberg of Pennsylvania becomes the first speaker under the Constitution.

April 6
POLITICS: New Hampshire Senator John Langdon gains appointment as that body's first presiding officer, although only nine senators are present out of 22. He nonetheless begins tabulating the presidential ballots previously cast in February. Not surprisingly, George Washington is unanimously elected president with 69 votes and John Adams, who receives 39 votes, becomes vice president.

April 8
POLITICS: The House of Representatives wades into the important issue of raising revenues for the government.

April 14
POLITICS: George Washington, residing in his home at Mount Vernon, Virginia, is informed by congressional secretary Charles Thomson of his election as president.

April 15
JOURNALISM: John Fenno begins publishing the *Gazette of the United States* in New York City; it is Federalist in orientation and serves as the government's de facto mouthpiece. The paper is also backed by Alexander Hamilton.

1789

Hamilton, Alexander   (1757–1804)
Politician

Alexander Hamilton was born in the West Indies on January 11, 1757, the illegitimate son of a Scottish merchant and a planter's daughter. He was well-educated locally and sent to a private academy in New Jersey in 1772 to complete his studies. Hamilton subsequently gained entrance into King's College (Columbia University) to study law when the Revolutionary War broke out in 1775. He quickly joined a militia company, fought well at the battles of Long Island, White Plains, and Princeton, where he garnered the attention of General George Washington. Hamilton subsequently became a lieutenant colonel of Washington's staff but yearned for military glory and

Alexander Hamilton. Engraving *(Library of Congress)*

accepted a command position in the field. He particularly distinguished himself at Yorktown on October 14, 1781, by carrying out a spectacular nighttime charge on the British fortification. Shortly afterward Hamilton married into the wealthy and powerful Schuyler family of New York and parleyed his considerable energy and genius into a viable career in politics. By 1785 Hamilton had opened a law office on Wall Street, helped to found the Bank of New York, and won a seat in the Confederation Congress. In this last capacity he decried the weakness of the Articles of Confederation and, at the ill-fated Annapolis Convention, agitated for a new Constitutional Convention. He then functioned in Philadelphia as a delegate, but his biggest role was in championing the new document. In concert with James Madison, John Jay, and Thomas Jefferson, he helped write the *Federalist Papers*, an erudite collection of essays favoring more centralized governance.

Once the new Constitution had been ratified and George Washington inaugurated as the first president, Hamilton gained appointment as secretary of the treasury. He immediately distinguished himself in various reports to Congress, advocating creation of a national bank, the assumption of state and national debts at face value, and establishing the new nation's credit abroad. These positions formed the heart of the then emerging Federalist Party, which called for strong central intervention in and regulation of the economy, and were vehemently opposed by Madison and Jefferson of the new Democratic-Republicans. The growing list of personal enemies finally

(continues)

(continued)

forced Hamilton from office in 1795. After 1796 Hamilton continued to intrigue against President John Adams, whom he considered as weak and vacillating in the face of the French Revolution. His opposition consequently split the Federalists, although he lent his political support to Jefferson as president to keep Aaron Burr from winning. In 1804 Hamilton also opposed Burr for his role in the *Essex Junto*, which threatened to detach New England from the Union and led to Burr's loss as governor. Burr then angrily challenged Hamilton to a duel, mortally wounding him. He died on July 12, 1804, one of the most brilliant and accomplished members of the Revolutionary generation, who single-handedly established the modern economic outlook of the young nation.

April 16
POLITICS: George Washington departs Mount Vernon, Virginia, and begins his eight-day journey to New York to be sworn in as president.

April 21
POLITICS: John Adams, arriving in New York from Braintree, Massachusetts, is sworn in as vice president and then sits as president pro tempore of the Senate.

April 23
JOURNALISM: America's first Catholic newspaper, the *Courrier de Boston*, begins publication.

April 30
POLITICS: Amid much pomp and excitement, a sullen and grim-faced George Washington takes his oath of office from Robert Livingston on the balcony of Federal Hall in New York City. Once inaugurated, Washington walks into the Senate chamber and delivers his inaugural address, urging "preservation of the sacred fire of liberty."

May 7
POLITICS: The nation's first inaugural ball, honoring George and Martha Washington, is held at New York City.
RELIGION: The Protestant Episcopal Church is organized in Philadelphia from the American branch of the Church of England.

May 12
POLITICS: The Society of Saint Tammany, an amalgam of anti-Federalist laborers, tradesmen, and political activists, is founded in New York City under William Mooney, the first grand sachem. They derive their name from the Indian Chief who originally greeted William Penn in Pennsylvania, and they gradually evolve into a powerful political lobby.

June 1
POLITICS: The first act passed by Congress entails the administering of oaths for public office.

July 4
BUSINESS: Congress, eager to generate money for the cash-strapped government, passes its first Tariff Act. This applies to an enumerated list of imported goods by

Washington, George   (1732–1799)
President

George Washington was born in Westmoreland County, Virginia, on February 22, 1732, where he pursued surveying. He joined the militia, was forced to surrender Fort Necessity to the French in 1754, and the following year accompanied General Edward Braddock's ill-fated expedition against Fort Dusquesne. He sided with the Patriots during the approach to the Revolutionary War and on June 15, 1775, Washington was appointed commander in chief of the new Continental Army. After several hard defeats he finally bested the British and Hessians at Princeton and Trenton in the winter of 1776–77 and thereafter managed to keep the war effort alive with increasing skill and determination. After 1778 he was able to take to the field and threatened British armies garrisoning New York, but he lacked the strength to attack them directly. Therefore, Washington greatly benefited from the military alliance with France, and in October 1781 he and French general Comte de Rochambeau captured the British army of General Charles Cornwallis at Yorktown, Virginia. This for all intents and purposes ended the Revolutionary War for the United States, a fact confirmed by the Treaty of Paris signed in 1783. In a very real sense Washington was the indispensable man of the revolution, possessing both the strategic grasp and indomitable will to see it through to a successful conclusion. At this juncture several conservatively minded officers on his staff urged him to seize control from Congress and establish himself as king, but

Washington refused. He remained deferential to civilian authority and on December 23, 1783, formally surrendered his sword to Congressional President Thomas Mifflin and retired from the military a private citizen.

Washington sought to live the rest of his life in anonymity, but politics and his stature as the nation's most trusted figure brought him back into the limelight. In 1787 he attended the Constitutional Convention in Philadelphia and threw his weight behind more centralized governance. When the constitution was finally ratified, Washington was sworn in as America's first president in February 1789 and was easily reelected three years later. In this capacity he ruled well and moderately, distancing himself from the mounting ideological discord between Alexander Hamilton and Thomas Jefferson. In 1796 he refused to serve a third term and was succeeded by John Adams. Before leaving he bid his fellow citizens to strive for political unanimity, pursue neutrality in international affairs, and avoid entangling alliances with Europe. Washington then resumed his life as a private citizen until the war scare with France in 1798 required him to come out of retirement and serve as commander in chief once again. Washington died of illness on December 14, 1799, and was widely mourned by fellow citizens. His moderation, common sense, and unimpeachable integrity set the tone for the new American government, thereby insuring its ultimate success. In poll after poll Washington still remains the most admired chief executive.

imposing an 8.5 percent protective duty, although imports arriving in American vessels are assessed at a lower rate.

July 14
DIPLOMACY: American minister to France Thomas Jefferson is on hand in Paris to witness the fall of the Bastille and the opening shots of the French Revolution.

July 20

BUSINESS: To raise additional funding, Congress passes the Tonnage Act, which assesses foreign cargo entering American ports at a rate of 50 cents per ton.

July 27

DIPLOMACY: The Department of Foreign Affairs is created by Congress and staffed by John Jay, pending the return of Thomas Jefferson. It is eventually renamed the Department of State.

August 7

MILITARY: The War Department is created by Congress with Henry Knox to be appointed secretary of war a month later. The army at this time consisted of less than 1,000 men who guarded public property and garrisoned the Indian frontier.

September 2

POLITICS: Congress established the Treasury Department with Alexander Hamilton destined for appointment as first secretary of the Treasury.

September 15

DIPLOMACY: The Department of Foreign Affairs is renamed the Department of State under Thomas Jefferson.

September 22

POLITICS: Congress founds the office of postmaster general under the Treasury Department with Samuel Osgood slated to become the first postmaster general.

September 24

LAW: Congress passes the Federal Judiciary Act, which establishes a six-man Supreme Court, an attorney general, 13 district courts, and three circuit courts. This is undertaken to establish one part of the system of checks and balances between the three branches of government.

September 25

POLITICS: Congress votes to submit 12 proposed constitutional amendments to the states; the first 10 are approved as the Bill of Rights in 1791. It is hoped that such measures will calm fears about the power of central governance, for the amendments clearly delineate the rights of individuals and states alike.

September 26

POLITICS: Congress appoints Edmund J. Randolph and John Jay as attorney general and chief justice of the Supreme Court, respectively. Samuel Osgood becomes postmaster general.

September 29

MILITARY: Mindful of the dangers posed to liberty by a standing professional military, Congress fixes the size of the U.S. Army at 1,000 men, which are divided into eight infantry and four artillery companies. This is all that remains of the once impressive Continental Army, which fought and won the American Revolution. Its work completed, Congress votes to adjourn.

October

RELIGION: Members of the Protestant Episcopal Church convene in Philadelphia for the purpose of declaring their independence from the Church of England; they also revise the *Book of Common Prayer*.

October 15
POLITICS: President George Washington begins a successful tour of New England.

November 20
POLITICS: New Jersey is the first state to ratify the Bill of Rights.

November 21
POLITICS: The North Carolina legislature, finally persuaded by the addition of a Bill of Rights, becomes the 12th state to ratify the U.S. Constitution on a vote of 184 to 77.

November 26
POLITICS: Congress establishes the first national Thanksgiving Day, intended to offer thanks for the Constitution. Anti-federalists protest that a national holiday violates states' rights.

December
GENERAL: Virginia yields a tract of land along the Potomac River to the government for the purpose of constructing a new federal district and a national capital. Maryland had previously ceded land in the same region.

December 11
EDUCATION: The North Carolina legislature charters the University of North Carolina at Chapel Hill; its first class graduates in 1798.

December 18
POLITICS: After considerable wrangling, Virginia finally agrees to relinquish its claims to the Kentucky territory.

December 21
SETTLEMENT: Three Yazoo land companies arise in Georgia and purchase from the Georgia legislature 25.4 million acres of land along the Yazoo River. They pay $207,580 for the land, despite the fact that it is also claimed by Spain.

December 22
SETTLEMENT: The North Carolina legislature deeds all its western holdings to the United States government.

1790

BUSINESS: Duncan Phyfe begins manufacturing exquisitely rendered cabinets at his workshop in New York City, establishing industry and artistic standards for their fine workmanship.

PUBLISHING: *Dobson's Encyclopedia*, an 18-volume American variant of the already famous *Encyclopædia Britannica*, begins production and continues over the next seven years. With its unique typefaces and engravings, this is considered a landmark national publication.

RELIGION: Matthew Carey publishes the first Catholic Bible in the United States at Philadelphia; he continues on as a major publisher of Catholic texts.

SOCIETAL: The Society for Alleviating the Miseries of the Public Prisons, spearheaded by Tenche Coxe, William Howard, and Dr. Benjamin Rush, pushes for changes and improvements in the Pennsylvania penal system. Specifically, they help institute changes in clothing, privacy, religious instruction, and better regulation of guards to avoid abuse. These reforms are first instituted at

This detailed rendering of an iron gag is an attack on the cruelty in Pennsylvania's Eastern Penitentiary, a prison notorious for its abuses and atrocities against prisoners, 1835. (*Library of Congress*)

Philadelphia's Walnut Street Prison and eventually adopted throughout the state.

TRANSPORTATION: The initial part of Philadelphia-Lancaster turnpike begins operating and ultimately stretches for 61 miles. Its success spurs development of similar roadways throughout New England and the Mid-Atlantic states.

January 14
BUSINESS: Secretary of the Treasury Alexander Hamilton delivers his first report of public credit to Congress, announcing foreign debt of $12 million and domestic debts of $40 million. Still, he argues that the United States should assume all debts at face value, even through speculators may profit. Hamilton also maintains that the federal government should absorb all state debts accruing from the Revolutionary War in order to bind their allegiance to the new government. All told, it is a bold and far-sighted approach to national finance.

February 11
SLAVERY: The Society of Friends presents Congress with the first-ever petition calling for the abolition of slavery.

March
SETTLEMENT: A group of French expatriates, driven from home by the revolution, establish a settlement at Gallipolis along the Ohio River. They do so at the behest of Joel Barlow, agent and land speculator for the Scioto Company; when the company subsequently fails, the newcomers are stranded.

March 1
SOCIETAL: Congress authorizes the Census Act, which calls for a census of the inhabitants of the United States every 10 years.

March 22
POLITICS: Thomas Jefferson arrives back in New York to assume his post as secretary of state; John Jay is thus enabled to turn his full attention to matters at the Supreme Court.

March 26
POLITICS: The Naturalization Act is passed by Congress, requiring prospective citizens to establish residency for at least two years.

March 29
GENERAL: John Tyler, 10th president, is born at Greenway, Virginia.

April 10
BUSINESS: Congress enacts legislation for the protection of patents. It also empowers a three-man board consisting of the secretaries of state and war and the attorney general to award them.

April 12
POLITICS: The House of Representatives defeats a proposal for the assumption of debts as proposed by Secretary of the Treasury Alexander Hamilton.

April 17
SOCIETAL: Benjamin Franklin, doyen of his age, dies in Philadelphia at the age of 84; three days later his funeral draws 20,000 attendees, then the largest–ever public gathering in America.

May 25
RELIGION: Universalists gather in Philadelphia at the behest of Reverend Elhanan Winchester and Dr. Benjamin Rush. They then promulgate an anti-Trinitarian doctrine declaring that Jesus was a human intermediary between man and God, not his son.

May 26
SETTLEMENT: Congress appoints William Blount to head a government for frontier territory ceded by North Carolina south of the Ohio River (Tennessee). This same region was previously known as the "State of Franklin," a self-governing entity under John Sevier which lasted from 1785 to 1788.

May 29
POLITICS: Despite anti-Federalist agitation at home and a boycott by other New England states, Rhode Island becomes the 13th and last state to ratify the U.S. Constitution. They do so by a margin of only two votes.

May 31
LAW: Congress, bowing to the lucid agitation of Noah Webster, passes the Copy Right Act for the protection of plays, books, and maps, against infringement. Rights are accorded for 14 years with an option to renew for another 14.

June 20
POLITICS: Alexander Hamilton strikes a deal with James Madison to secure his support for establishing a national federal capital on the banks of the Potomac River in exchange for passage of the Assumption Act. This enables the federal government to absorb state debts dating back to the Revolutionary War.

July 26
POLITICS: The House of Representatives passes Alexander Hamilton's plan for assuming states' Revolutionary War debts on a vote of 34 to 28.

July 31
BUSINESS: The first government patent is issued to Samuel Hopkins of Vermont for using potassium carbonate compounds ("pot and pearl ashes") while manufacturing glass.

August 1
SOCIETAL: The government completes the first federal census, which reveals an overall population of 3,929,625; of these, 697,624 are African-American slaves.

August 4
BUSINESS: The Funding Act is passed by Congress, which authorizes the Treasury Department to issue bonds at six percent interest in exchange for Revolutionary War bonds to fund the national debt. Moreover, the bonds are funded at face value.

1790

Webster, Noah   (1758–1843)
Lexicographer

Noah Webster was born in West Hartford, Connecticut, on October 16, 1758, the son of farmers. He enrolled at Yale College in 1774, interrupted his studies briefly to serve in the Continental Army, and finally graduated in 1779. Webster then taught school at Hartford, Litchfield, and Sharon, becoming dissatisfied with the British-style teaching aids of the day. Determined to institute a new and distinctly American form of the English language, Webster compiled and published *The American Spelling Book* in 1783 and followed up two years later with a grammar book and a reader. These titles were aimed at a juvenile audience but enjoyed amazing success and longevity; by 1830 it is estimated that 15 million copies were in print. Thanks to Webster there are still noticeable differences in spellings between American English and British English to the present day, and the changes were widely embraced by the ardent nationalism then sweeping the nation. In 1782 he also began touring the nation state by state to press for better copyright protection for writers, and in 1790 Congress complied. Webster was also an ardent Federalist, and he became caught up in the political fervor of that decade. He established the short-lived *American Magazine* in New York City to lessen the dependency on British publications, and also edited *American Minerva*, the city's first daily newspaper, and the *Herald*, a semiweekly. However, Webster gradually became disillusioned by partisan bickering in the press, and in 1803 he abandoned journalism and retired to New Haven to continue his work on language.

In 1806 Webster scored another triumph by introducing *A Compendious Dictionary of the English Language*. This slim volume contained 5,000 words, including vernacular "Americanisms" not found elsewhere, along with standard spellings. Then, over the next two decades, he worked assiduously on his masterpiece, which was released in 1828 as *An American Dictionary of the English Language*. This landmark publication incorporated both formal words and those used in everyday speech and listed several definitions and etymologies for the user's enlightenment. At the time it appeared this was the largest dictionary of its kind and listed over 70,000 words. In 1841 a second, enlarged edition was released as *Webster's Unabridged Dictionary*. These endeavors gained Webster national recognition as an original American lexicographer. Webster was also active in the realm of education, and in 1821 he helped establish Amherst College in addition to writing and publishing books on a wide variety of scientific, political, and moral topics. He died at New Haven on May 28, 1843, renowned for helping establish a national system of grammar and spelling. This information was transmitted to generations of students through his "blue-backed speller" of which 1 million copies were in circulation by 1850.

NAVAL: The Revenue Marine Service is formally established with the purchase of 10 small boats; it gradually evolves into the U.S. Coast Guard in 1915.

August 7
INDIAN: Secretary of War Henry Knox and Creek Chief Alexander McGillivray sign the Treaty of New York, in which the Creek recognize United States sovereignty over parts of tribal territory. McGillivray is also commissioned a brigadier general but soon after he intrigues with the Spanish to resist American expansion.

1790

August 10
BUSINESS: The ship *Columbia* under Captain Robert Gray becomes the first American vessel to circumnavigate the globe by departing Boston for Canton, China, and returning three years later. The entire voyage covers 42,000 miles. Gray departs with a cargo of furs and returns with a shipment of tea.

August 12
POLITICS: Philadelphia becomes the temporary national capital of the United States.

August 15
RELIGION: Father John Carroll is consecrated as the first Roman Catholic bishop of the United States at the behest of Pope Pius VI. Baltimore, Maryland, is chosen as the site of the first American cathedral see while Carroll emerges as an early leader of note in church history.

September 25
BUSINESS: The Massachusetts legislature repeals its state excise tax in the wake of federal assumption of Revolutionary War debts.

September 30
MILITARY: General Josiah Harmar leads an expedition of 353 soldiers and 1,100 Kentucky militia out of Fort Washington (Cincinnati), Ohio, on a punitive expedition against hostile Shawnee and Miami Indians.

October 19
MILITARY: Miami and Shawnee under Little Turtle and Blue Jacket defeat an American militia force under General Josiah Harmar near Fort Wayne, Indiana. Harmar had previously dispatched his men into a large Indian village and then marched out in search of the warriors. Little Turtle then attacked, routing the militia from the field and massacring the regulars where they stood.

October 28
DIPLOMACY: The Nookta Sound Convention between Spain and Great Britain strengthens British claims to the Oregon territory, a fact disputed by the United States.

December 6
POLITICS: Congress formally shifts from New York to Philadelphia until the new federal district becomes available.

December 14
BUSINESS: Secretary of the Treasury Alexander Hamilton makes a second appearance before Congress and promulgates his plan for a Bank of the United States. This institution is envisioned as an instrument to fund the assumption of debts and also help establish national credit.

December 16
POLITICS: Patrick Henry drafts the Virginia Resolutions in opposition to Alexander Hamilton's debt assumption plan. Henry, like many others, feels that the scheme caters to monied interests, places commercial interests above agriculture, and cannot pass constitutional muster.

1790

Little Turtle   (ca. 1752–1812)

Miami chief

Little Turtle (Michikinikwa) was born near the Eel River in the vicinity of present-day Fort Wayne, Indiana, around 1752. His father was a Miami chief but, because his mother was from the Mahician, tribal custom dictated that he could not inherit a leadership position. Nonetheless, Little Turtle displayed fine qualities as a warrior and he was eventually made a Miami chief by tribal elders. He was also pro-British by nature and in 1780 his warriors attacked a French-Illinois expedition under Colonel Augustin de la Balme. After the Revolutionary War Little Turtle became a leading spokesman for resistance to white encroachment north of the Ohio River and, in concert with noted Shawnee chief Blue Jacket, formed an anti-American coalition. In 1787 Congress assured the tribes that their hunting grounds would be respected, but within three years a rash of illegal settlements precipitated a fierce frontier war. In 1790 the American government dispatched an armed expedition of 1,400 militia under Colonel Josiah Harmar to punish the tribes for their resistance. However, Little Turtle lured the invaders deeper and deeper into Indian land then ambushed and defeated Harmar in October. His success served as a rallying point for other tribes, and soon the Miami and Shawnee were joined by the Pottawatomie and Ojibwas. Little Turtle had become unquestioned leader of the Native American resistance in the Old Northwest, much in the manner that his predecessor, Pontiac, tried to be, and President George Washington ordered that an even larger military effort be mounted against him.

In September 1791 General Arthur St. Clair marched into the Ohio territory with 2,600 soldiers and militia. As the raw Americans advanced, their poorly disciplined force was weakened by desertion and dwindled to around 1,500 men. Little Turtle observed these developments closely and decided to attack the Americans directly in their camp. This was a dangerous tactic, rarely attempted by Native Americans, but under Little Turtle's excellent leadership the Americans were surprised on November 4, 1791, and completely routed. More than 600 soldiers were killed and 260 wounded, making this the largest defeat ever suffered at the hands of Native Americans. Within three years the Americans had rebuilt their army under the aegis of veteran General Anthony Wayne, who defeated the Indians at Fallen Timbers on August 20, 1794. Little Turtle had previously cautioned the tribes to make peace with this new invader and was relieved of command, but the following year he submitted to the Treaty of Greenville and thereafter swore his allegiance to the United States. In 1797 he traveled to Washington, D.C., to confer with President Washington, and Indiana territorial governor William Henry Harrison also built a home for him on the Eel River. When the War of 1812 commenced the aged chief offered to fight on behalf of the United States but he died at the Indian agency at Fort Wayne on July 14, 1812. Little Turtle was one of the most accomplished Indian leaders.

December 21

TECHNOLOGY: Samuel Slater introduces Arkwright spindle mill machinery at his cotton mill in Pawtucket, Rhode Island. He had previously seen such technology in England, then a closely guarded trade secret, came home and

1790

was able to reproduce the device from memory. Its simplicity of operation allows children as young as 10 to operate it safely and helps stimulate the Industrial Revolution in the United States. Slater also pioneered the practice of breaking down the production process into simple procedures to facilitate manufacturing.

1791

EDUCATION: Historian Reverend Jeremy Belknap establishes the Massachusetts Historical Society as an institution dedicated to the collecting and preservation of documents relevant to American history. This is the first and thus oldest such institution in America.

PUBLICATIONS: John Adams codifies his aristocratic vision of society by publishing his *Discourses on Davalia*, which envisions a utopian society ruled by a rich, powerful, and talented elite. It is understandably not well-received by the American public at large and, furthermore, taints him as an elitist.

William Bartram publishes his *Travels*, which describes botanizing expeditions in the Carolinas, Georgia, and Florida. His accounts are highly popular in Europe and stimulate interest in America's natural landscape.

SOCIETAL: Andrew Jackson, a hotheaded Tennessee state prosecutor with a penchant for dueling, endures a spate of controversy after marrying Rachel Robards, only to discover that her divorce from husband Lewis Robards has not yet been finalized.

January 1
POLITICS: George Washington establishes the custom of a presidential reception every New Year's Day.

January 5
LAW: A petition by free African Americans to end the practice of banning black-initiated lawsuits and refusing to allow blacks to testify in court against whites is rejected by the South Carolina legislature.

January 10
POLITICS: Vermont, though still not a state, ratifies the U.S. Constitution.

January 28
BUSINESS: Secretary of the Treasury Alexander Hamilton testifies before Congress concerning the organization of a national mint and the coining of money.

February 15
POLITICS: Secretary of State Thomas Jefferson testifies that the bill chartering the Bank of the United States is unconstitutional by the simple explanation that Congress has been delegated no such authority. His dissent ultimately gives rise to a political party based upon strict interpretation of the Constitution, the Democratic-Republicans.

February 23
POLITICS: Secretary of the Treasury Alexander Hamilton goes before Congress insisting that charting the Bank of the United States is fully constitutional, falling under congressional authority to collect taxes and regulate trade. Hamilton's

stance reflects a political constitutional philosophy based upon "loose construction," or implied powers. President George Washington supports Hamilton less from being convinced of the correctness of his belief than from a need to support a cabinet official.

February 25
BUSINESS: President George Washington approves legislation chartering the Bank of the United States, lending credence to Alexander Hamilton's "loose construction" of implied powers in the U.S. Constitution. Hamilton does so to provide the new nation with a steady source of capital to fund new industries and to insure a sound money supply. The bank itself functions as a depository of government funds and is run by a board of 25 directors, with five of these appointed by the president, the rest by the states.

March
MUSIC: "The Death Song of an Indian Chief" is printed in an issue of *The Massachusetts Magazine*, becoming the first published orchestral score in the United States.

March 3
BUSINESS: Congress passes the Whiskey Act at the behest of Alexander Hamilton, which creates 14 revenue districts and fixes an excise tax on distilled liquors. However, it is widely resented in backwoods areas while the legislatures of North Carolina, Maryland, and Virginia pass resolutions in protest.

March 4
POLITICS: Vermont, boasting a population of 85,000, gains admittance into the union as the 14th state. Previously, $30,000 had to be paid to the state of New York for lands it long claimed in Vermont.

March 9
ARCHITECTURE: French engineer Pierre-Charles L'Enfant arrives in Maryland with preliminary designs for the proposed national capital.

March 30
POLITICS: President George Washington chooses the site of the new federal district on land along the Potomac River, which straddles the settlements of Georgetown, Maryland, and Alexandria, Virginia. This is a 70-square-mile tract that will house the new White House in 1792 and the United States Capitol in 1793.

TRANSPORTATION: The Knoxville Road, linking Virginia's Wilderness Road to the frontier community of Knoxville (Tennessee), commences construction. In time it serves as a major conduit for settlement.

April 7
POLITICS: President George Washington begins a tour of the southern states.

April 23
GENERAL: James Buchanan, the 15th president, is born at Cove Gap, Pennsylvania.

April 26

INDIAN: The Cherokee sign the Treaty of Holston with the United States, whereby they cede land holdings along the upper Tennessee River in exchange for undisputed control of their remaining lands elsewhere.

May

POLITICS: Continuing disputes over the direction of the U. S. government induces Thomas Jefferson and James Madison to tour New York and New England and help organize anti-Federalist factions within those states. This opposition constitutes the origins of the Democratic-Republican (or Democratic) Party, which favors an agrarian-based society dominated by individual landholders.

June

RELIGION: St. Mary's, the first Roman Catholic seminary in America, is founded by French Suplicans in Baltimore, Maryland.

June 12

SLAVERY: African-American slaves in Spanish Louisiana, taking inspiration from recent events in Haiti, stage a brief and unsuccessful revolt of their own; 23 slaves are hanged in consequence.

July 4

BUSINESS: The Bank of the United States, newly chartered, starts raising capital through a subscription drive.

July 16

SOCIETAL: Benjamin Banneker, an African-American mathematician of note, becomes one of three commissioners directed to survey the new federal district along the Potomac River. He performs exceptionally well in this capacity and also introduces the first edition of his successful almanac.

September 6

EDUCATION: The University of Vermont is founded at Burlington.

September 17

MILITARY: General Arthur St. Clair, governor of the Northwestern Territory, commands a large expedition from Fort Washington, Cincinnati, in order to establish a chain of fortifications in and around hostile Indian land. In time these are christened Forts Hamilton, St. Clair, Jefferson, Greenville, and Recovery. His force consists of 320 soldiers and 1,100 poorly trained militia.

September 29

TRANSPORTATION: A canal linking the Schuylkill and Susquehanna Rivers is chartered by the Pennsylvania legislature.

October

DIPLOMACY: George Hammond, the first British minister to the United States, presents his credentials to the government.

October 31

JOURNALISM: The fires of political partisanship are fueled when poet Philip Freneau edits a pro-Jeffersonian piece in the *National Gazette* in Philadelphia.

November 3
EDUCATION: The University of Vermont is chartered at Burlington; the first class graduates in 1804.

November 4
MILITARY: General Arthur St. Clair and 1,400 militia and soldiers are disastrously defeated by the Miami under Chief Little Turtle near Fort Wayne, Indiana. Sensing indecision on St. Clair's part, Little Turtle takes the extraordinary tactic of charging directly into the American camp, scattering the defenders. The Americans withdraw with a loss of 637 dead and 261 wounded in the worse defeat ever suffered at the hands of Native Americans.

November 26
POLITICS: President George Washington begins the practice of meeting regularly with his inner circle to discuss a variety of military, diplomatic, and political issues. This is the origin of the president's "cabinet."

December 5
POLITICS: Alexander Hamilton lectures Congress on the need for a tariff system to protect the fledgling American industries. He also seeks an agricultural bounty system and direct federal funding for such publicly oriented works as roads and canals to help stimulate the growth of national industry and agriculture.

December 12
BUSINESS: The Bank of the United States opens its first branch in Philadelphia and is soon followed by other branches in most major cities. The gold and silver owned by this institution is the bulwark of the American currency system.

December 15
POLITICS: The Virginia legislature ratifies the Bill of Rights and, having brought the number of states so disposed to 10—three-quarters—allows them to go into effect as part of the U.S. Constitution.

1792

ARCHITECTURE: Ewel Hale constructs the first wooden truss bridge in America at Bellows Falls, Vermont. It consists of two 175-foot spans joined together at an island in midstream.

ARTS: American-born Benjamin West becomes president of the Royal Academy of London, which affirms his reputation as among the foremost painters of his day.

JOURNALISM: The nation's first political contretemps erupts between dueling columns in the *National Gazette*, a supporter of Thomas Jefferson, and the *Gazette of the United States*, a partisan of Alexander Hamilton.

MEDICAL: After a smallpox outbreak, 8,000 inhabitants of Boston volunteer for inoculation.

POLITICS: The Democratic-Republican Party begins coalescing nationally around opposition to Alexander Hamilton's fiscal policies. They are headed by Thomas Jefferson, the leading democrat of his day.

PUBLISHING: Henry Marie Brackenridge publishes *Modern Chivalry*, a pointed satire on the manners of his contemporaries. A popular work, it is revised several times and is enlarged for a new edition in 1815.

Robert Bailey Thomas edits and publishes the first edition of *The Farmer's Almanac* at Grafton, Massachusetts. It is a useful compendium of dates, facts, information on weather, and is leavened throughout with homespun information about New England life.

SCIENCE: James Woodhouse establishes the Chemical Society of Philadelphia, one of the earliest scientific societies in the nation.

SLAVERY: Virginia political pundit George Mason spearheads the opposition to slavery in his state, denouncing it as an affront to mankind. Furthermore, he views the "peculiar institution" as a slow-acting poison that will ultimately corrupt future generations of politicians.

January

PUBLISHING: Thomas Paine unleashes his controversial *Rights of Man* (in support of the French Revolution), an unvarnished attack upon monarchy and an endorsement of revolution and democracy. He espouses the seemingly radical view that political power rests solely with the will of the majority.

January 12

DIPLOMACY: South Carolina Federalist Thomas Pinckney is appointed the first American minister to Great Britain and departs with instructions to secure better terms for American trade. Gouverneur Morris, then in France, also gains appointment as minister to that nation.

February 21

POLITICS: Congress approves of the Presidential Succession Act, which allows for the president pro tempore of the Senate and then the speaker of the House of Representatives to replace the president and vice president in the event of death or removal. Federalists manage to defeat Thomas Jefferson's attempt to have the Secretary of State placed in line of succession, although this is eventually adopted in 1886.

March 5

MILITARY: General Arthur St. Clair is replaced by General "Mad Anthony" Wayne as military commander of troops in the Northwest Territory.

April

SLAVERY: Presbyterian clergyman David Rice unsuccessfully tries to have slavery excluded from Kentucky during the constitutional convention there.

April 2

BUSINESS: The Coinage Act is passed by Congress, whereby a national mint is founded in Philadelphia and a decimal system is instituted. David Rittenhouse, a noted mathematician, becomes the first director of the mint. This establishes a decimal system of coinage with both silver and gold as legal tender; the ratio of silver to gold coins is set at a ratio of 15 to one.

April 24

ARTS: A farce, *The Yorker's Strategem, or Banana's Wedding*, is staged in New York; it is the first production to feature non-stereotyped West Indian (African) characters on the stage.

May 8

MILITARY: Faced with a protracted Indian war and endemic manpower shortages for the U.S. Army, Congress passes the Militia Act, which authorizes states to draft eligible males aged 18 to 45 into state service as needed.

1792

May 11

EXPLORATION: Captain Robert Gray, completing his second circumnavigation of the globe, discovers the Columbia River in the Washington-Oregon Territory. This 1,214-mile-long waterway remains unexplored until 1805.

May 17

BUSINESS: A meeting of 24 brokers at the Merchants Coffee House results in establishment of the New York Stock Exchange. Within months it mounts formidable competition to the nation's first stock exchange, founded at Philadelphia in 1791.

June 1

POLITICS: Kentucky enters the Union as the 15th state; its constitution reflects the democratizing influence of the frontier and calls for male suffrage and a bill of rights but also allows slavery. Revolutionary War hero Isaac Shelby is elected the first governor.

July 13

BUSINESS: The U.S. Mint begins coining a five-cent silver piece, or "half dime," one of the earliest American coins.

July 18

NAVAL: Revolutionary war hero John Paul Jones dies at Paris, France, in relative obscurity. His body lays in an unmarked grave until being rediscovered in 1905.

August 21

POLITICS: A political convention in Pittsburgh, Pennsylvania, gathers to protest imposition of the whiskey excise tax. A committee headed by Swiss émigré Albert Gallatin then drafts a resolution condemning the tax and seeks a legal remedy to circumvent it. Resistance to the measure is exceptionally profound in frontier regions where surplus grain has traditionally been distilled into liquor.

September 29

POLITICS: President George Washington, cognizant of mounting resistance to the whiskey excise tax, issues a proclamation that the levy will be collected in full compliance with the law and warns against possible avoidance.

October 2

POLITICS: President George Washington arranges a meeting between Secretary of State Thomas Jefferson and Secretary of the Treasury Alexander Hamilton at his home in Mount Vernon, Virginia. The chief executive tries unsuccessfully to smooth ruffled feathers arising from differing interpretations of the Constitution. Hamilton, furthermore, bluntly accuses Jefferson of opposing the Washington administration and attempting to undermine the government.

October 11

RELIGION: The first African-American Catholic sisterhood is founded by Antonine Blanc.

October 12

GENERAL: The Society of St. Tammany orchestrates the first recorded celebration of Columbus Day in New York City; it does not become a national holiday until 1892. The first memorial to Columbus also rises on this day in Baltimore, constructed of English brick.

1792

October 13
ARCHITECTURE: President George Washington lays the cornerstone for the new chief executive office, or President's Palace, subsequently known as the White House. This is the first public building constructed in the new federal district and has been designed by architect James Hoban, inspired by the duke of Leinster's Irish mansion.

November 1
POLITICS: A general election unfolds to select presidential electors for the second presidential election; incumbents George Washington and John Adams are expected to win handily.

November 5
POLITICS: The Second Congress reconvenes in Philadelphia for its second session.

December 5
ARTS: Sheriffs arrest manager Joseph Harper and Boston's first theater, The New Exhibition Room, is forced to close. The city still rigidly enforces ordinances against theaters.

POLITICS: George Washington is convincingly reelected to a second term as president of the United States with 132 electoral votes. John Adams is also returned as vice president by 77 votes while anti-Federalist George Clinton of New York amasses 50 votes. Curiously, Washington did not originally intend to seek a second term in office; it was only after the conflict between Alexander Hamilton and Thomas Jefferson arose, along with current difficulties with France, that he felt obliged to be a stabilizing influence in a sea of discord.

1793

ARTS: Noted poet Philip Freneau composes "On the Anniversary of the Storming of the Bastille" in honor of the French Revolution, although the ongoing excesses there have caused support elsewhere to wane.

EDUCATION: Industrialist Samuel Slater institutes a Sunday school to impart reading, writing, and computational skills to his young factory workers in Pawtucket, Rhode Island.

JOURNALISM: Federalist Noah Webster founds the *American Minerva*, the nation's first daily newspaper, in New York City.

LAW: Town trustees in Lexington, Kentucky, outlaw the practice of horse racing down city thoroughfares for fear of frightening pedestrians.

LITERATURE: Elihu Hubbard Smith publishes *American Poems, Selected and Original* at Litchfield, Connecticut. This work showcases the writings of the so-called Connecticut Wits, including Joel Barlow, Timothy Dwight, Lemuel Hopkins, and John Trumbull, and is a celebration of American literary distinctiveness.

PUBLISHING: Jedidiah Morse illustrates and publishes the *American Universal Geography,* a significant compendium of global geographical information and charts for a curious nation.

The first American edition of J. Hector St. John Crevecoeur's *Letters from an American Farmer* is published in Philadelphia. This is a collection of poignant and insightful observations on American life by a studious French observer.

SOCIETAL: Quaker minister John Woolman composes his *A Word of Remembrance and Caution to the Rich*, a humanitarian tract calling for social reforms, especially abolition of slavery.

TRANSPORTATION: The Middlesex Canal, linking Boston to the Merrimack River, 27 miles away, is constructed.

January 9

AVIATION: Frenchman Jean-Pierre François Blanchard conducts the first successful balloon flight in America, rising to 5,800 feet over Philadelphia. His ascent is witnessed by President George Washington.

January 21

DIPLOMACY: The execution of King Louis XVI and Queen Marie Antoinette stuns Europe and forces anti-Federalists in America to reevaluate their sympathy for the ongoing revolution in France.

January 23

POLITICS: Congress passes a set of resolutions calling on Secretary of the Treasury Alexander Hamilton to answer charges of corruption and mismanagement in his department.

February 12

SLAVERY: A Fugitive Slave Act is approved by Congress outlining the rights of slave owners to recover their property. It also forbids harboring fugitive slaves and assisting in their flight.

February 18

LAW: The U.S. Supreme Court decides the case of *Chisholm v. Georgia*, whereby a citizen of one state may sue another state in federal court.

February 22

EDUCATION: Williams College is chartered in Massachusetts, distinct in allowing fluency in French to be substituted for traditional Greek and Latin.

February 28

POLITICS: A motion to censure Secretary of the Treasury Alexander Hamilton fails to pass the House of Representatives. His detractors nonetheless maintain he is the pawn of monied interests.

March 4

POLITICS: George Washington is sworn into office for a second term as president while John Adams begins his second term as vice president. The only change to the cabinet is the appointment of Timothy Pickering as postmaster general.

April 8

DIPLOMACY: Edmond-Charles-Édouard Genet ("Citizen Genet"), the new French minister to the United States, arrives at Charleston, South Carolina, seeking American aid in the war against Great Britain. There he violates American neutrality by issuing French letters of marque (thus commissioning) to four privateers to raid English shipping in the Caribbean.

April 16

TECHNOLOGY: Eli Whitney publicly demonstrates his cotton gin; in time this device proves instrumental in preserving slavery and making it profitable.

Whitney, Eli   (1765–1825)
Inventor

Eli Whitney was born in Westborough, Massachusetts, on December 8, 1765, into humble circumstances. Mediocre as a student, he displayed great aptitude for tinkering in his father's workshop, and in 1781 he opened a business for manufacturing nails. Whitney used his profits to attend Yale College, from which he graduated in 1782 and then ventured to Georgia to work as a tutor. There he encountered the widow of General Nathaniel Greene, who introduced him to her plantation manager, Phineas Miller. Whitney also experienced his first encounter with slavery, which he disliked and sought technical ways of ending it. He then observed that it took each slave an entire day to separate short-staple upland cotton from its seeds, a laborious process that had to be accomplished by hand. In April 1793 Whitney conceived and built the so-called cotton gin, a hand-cranked device that would eliminate seeds from cotton in a matter of minutes. This dramatically improved cotton productivity and, far from eliminating slavery, actually made it profitable. For example, in 1790 cotton production amounted to only 4,000 bales; by 1840 that figure had risen exponentially to 1,347,640. Considering the profits to be made exporting cotton to textile markets like England and France, slavery now became a valuable economic lifeline for the South. Worse for Whitney and Miller, although they received a patent for their invention in 1794, it was never enforced by Southern courts and many counterfeit machines were manufactured and sold. The inventors were then forced into protracted legal disputes, and it was not until 1807 that Whitney's claim could be validated after spending roughly $100,000 in legal fees.

A potential war with France was also looming in 1798, and that year Whitney assured the government that he could easily manufacture 10,000 muskets in only two years instead of the usual 10. He then received a contract from the War Department and proceeded to construct his own factory outside New Haven, Connecticut (Whitneyville), from the ground up. Always the innovator, Whitney insisted on making his own special tools for the task, as well as employing the first water-powered milling machine used in the United States. He also conceived the ingenious idea of interchangeable parts for his weapons. Prior to this, muskets and rifles were individually manufactured by hand and the parts so fashioned would not fit other weapons, a fact that militated against easy repairs in the field. Under Whitney's system, identical parts were turned out in quantity and could be interchanged on any individual weapon, quickly and easily. Ultimately, it took him 10 years to fulfill his contract, although the government remained highly pleased with his interchangeable concept. Whitney died in New Haven on January 8, 1825, one of the most significant inventors of American history. His cotton gin and musket factory introduced modern manufacturing to America and laid the foundations for its burgeoning industrial revolution.

April 18

DIPLOMACY: Citizen Genet departs Charleston, South Carolina, and makes his way north to present his credentials to the government in Philadelphia. He receives an enthusiastic welcome from most Americans.

POLITICS: President George Washington discusses the prospects of declaring neutrality during the ongoing war between France and Great Britain. His

1793

cabinet is in agreement, but Thomas Jefferson openly sympathizes with the French revolutionaries.

April 22
POLITICS: President George Washington declares the neutrality of the United States in the ongoing war between Great Britain and revolutionary France and warns American citizens against involvement. Both Alexander Hamilton and Thomas Jefferson support Washington's decision, although the former sympathizes with England and the latter with France.

May 9
DIPLOMACY: The government of the French republic intends to seize all neutral shipping entering the ports of England, Holland, or the Netherlands. Such a move holds dire implications for the United States which lacks a standing naval force to protect its own commerce.

May 18
DIPLOMACY: French ambassador Citizen Genet is coolly received by President George Washington, angered by the latter's unauthorized arming of privateers and other violations of American neutrality.

May 25
RELIGION: Father Stephen Theodore Badin, a refugee from the French Revolution, becomes the first Roman Catholic priest ordained in the United States.

June 5
DIPLOMACY: Secretary of State Thomas Jefferson advises French minister Citizen Genet not to transgress upon American neutrality by offering military commissions and arming private vessels as privateers. Genet initially agrees to halt such practices, then promptly arms a fifth vessel and orders it out to sea.

June 8
DIPLOMACY: Great Britain responds to French depredations at sea by threatening to seize all neutral shipping entering French ports.

July 31
BUSINESS: Captain Robert Gray of the ship *Columbia* reaches Boston after a second circumnavigation of the globe.

August
MEDICAL: A yellow fever epidemic strikes Philadelphia, killing more than 4,000 inhabitants. The African-American community, organized by Reverend Absalom Jones and Dr. Benjamin Rush, distinguish themselves in assisting their neighbors.

August 23
DIPLOMACY: The radical and violent Jacobin regime of France dispatches Joseph Fauchet to the United States as its new minister, and he arrives carrying papers for the arrest of Citizen Genet. Genet then receives political asylum and ultimately marries the daughter of Governor George Clinton of New York.

September 18
ARCHITECTURE: President George Washington lays the cornerstone for the new United States Capitol (Congress House) in the planned federal district. The new

structure is designed by William Thornton and James Hoban with distinctly classical overtones.

October 7
MILITARY: General "Mad Anthony" Wayne marches into the Ohio Territory at the head of 2,600 soldiers and militia, determined to crush Indian resistance.

October 28
BUSINESS: Inventor Eli Whitney applies for a patent on his new cotton gin. He does so in the mistaken belief that, by making cotton more productive, the new device will make slavery unprofitable; sadly, it has the opposite effect.

November 6
DIPLOMACY: An Order in Council issued by the government of Great Britain mandates the seizure of any neutral vessels trading with France in the West Indies. Consequently, American crews become subject to seizure and impressment onboard Royal Navy vessels.

November 25
SLAVERY: Albany, New York, is the scene of a slave uprising and several destructive fires.

December 31
POLITICS: Thomas Jefferson resigns as secretary of state, feeling that his opinions and council are no longer valued or heeded in the present administration. He then begins agitating for an opposition party to counter the policies of Alexander Hamilton. This is the genesis of the Democratic Republicans, or Democrats.

1794

ARCHITECTURE: Charles Bullfinch initiates the Classic Revival in American architecture by designing and constructing houses on Tontine Crescent, Boston, in a manner soon designated the Federal style.
ARTS: Noted painter Charles Willson Peale opens his museum in Philadelphia to promote mass education among the American public. The scientific, historical, and ethnological displays are usually accompanied by a realistically painted background.
MUSIC: Supply Belcher publishes *The Harmony of Maine*, a collection of simple hymns and fugues that were popular among rural audiences on the New England frontier.
SOCIETAL: Powdering men's hair is finally passé in all but the stuffiest social circles; henceforth, men's locks are usually tied with black ribbon into a queue.
TRANSPORTATION: In Pennsylvania, the Philadelphia–Lancaster Turnpike, a 61-mile long, macadam-covered roadway, is finished. Its success as a toll road inspires the construction of similar routes elsewhere.

January 2
POLITICS: Attorney General Edmund Randolph is appointed the new secretary of state by President George Washington. He replaces Thomas Jefferson but is subsequently found to be working against the administration.

Bullfinch, Charles　(1763–1844)
Architect

Charles Bullfinch was born in Boston, Massachusetts, on August 8, 1763, the son of a wealthy physician. He graduated from Harvard in 1781 and four years later ventured to England to study architecture, especially the neoclassical designs of Robert Adams. Bullfinch came home in 1787, married into a wealthy family, then began working as an architect for his native city. His first assignment was to design a new Massachusetts State House, plans for which were completed and approved in 1798. Another early endeavor was the Beacon Street column, a Revolutionary War monument rising 60 feet and topped with a metal eagle that doubled as a weather vane. As a designer, Bullfinch incorporated the classic tenets of Greek and Roman design, although making them heavier and more robust to render them longer lasting. As his reputation spread, he received other commissions elsewhere, such as the Connecticut state house in Hartford. In 1793–94 Bullfinch grew ambitious, designed and built Tontine Crescent, an expensive row of elegantly designed Boston townhouses for an upscale clientele, but when buyers failed to materialize he went bankrupt. He then served as chairman of the city's board of selectmen and superintendent of police to supplement his income while designing other buildings. He also functioned as Boston's chief administrator for two decades, which allowed him to influence design decisions, and left his personal stamp on the city through construction of dozens of public buildings and scores of private homes. Having recouped his losses,

Bullfinch entered his most prolific stage by designing significant buildings throughout the state. In this respect, he became the best known of America's "colonial" or first-generation architects.

Proof of Bullfinch's popularity occurred in 1817 when President James Monroe, then touring New England, was highly impressed by his work and invited him to Washington, D.C. There Bullfinch was to complete the design of the U.S. Capitol building using drawings originally crafted by Benjamin Henry Latrobe, another outstanding draftsman. In practice, Bullfinch left the wings of the capitol as drawn, but he modified the dome by making it taller and more impressive. He also took it upon himself to enlarge the original plan for the capital rotunda, much to the satisfaction of those utilizing it. The structure was finally completed in 1830 and remains the best tribute to his classical innovations. Amazingly, Bullfinch also found time to draw up plans for the Federal Penitentiary and the Unitarian Church before returning to Boston and entering retirement. Prior to that he also designed the capitol building at Augusta, Maine, along with a long list of private dwellings. Bullfinch died in Boston on April 4, 1844, the most accomplished draftsman and architect of his generation. Throughout his lengthy career he was content to approach his task like an aristocratic gentleman of taste, rather than a professional artist. In many respects Bullfinch set the architectural tone for his native town and indelibly defined city architecture as no designer before or since.

January 3
Politics: In light of the British orders in council to seize American shipping carrying French West Indian exports, James Madison proposes seven retaliatory measures in the House of Representatives; none of them are passed but the issues of seizure and impressment remain volatile ones.

1794

January 13
GENERAL: Congress mandates the addition of two stripes and two stars to the American flag, signifying the addition of Vermont and Kentucky.

February
ARTS: Boston finally repeals its 1750 law prohibiting plays, and the new Boston Theater opens under the auspices of Charles Stuart Powell.
DIPLOMACY: Governor-General Sir Guy Carleton of Canada promises Native American tribes living in northwestern Ohio to return their lands taken if they should support Great Britain in a war with the United States.

February 14
ARTS: Samuel Arnold's opera *The Castle of Andalusia* is the opening performance for the New Theater in Philadelphia, following lengthy delays caused by the yellow fever epidemic of 1793.

February 28
POLITICS: Federalists in the U.S. Senate erect a residential technicality to keep Swiss-born Jeffersonian Albert Gallatin from taking his elected seat. Gallatin had apparently failed to fulfill the nine-year residency requirement for the Senate; the Federalists also apparently resent his strident opposition to the Whiskey Tax.

March 5
LAW: Congress submits the 11th Amendment to the U.S. Constitution to the states for ratification. This measure repeals the Supreme Court's ruling in *Chisholm v. Georgia* and restricts federal judicial authority over the states.

March 14
BUSINESS: A patent is issued to Eli Whitney for his cotton gin.

March 22
SLAVERY: Congress outlaws the slave trade with other nations, especially Haiti, then in the throes of a major slave uprising. Southern lawmakers fear that the contagion of rebellion may be exported to their own backyard.

March 27
NAVAL: The Naval Act of 1794 authorizes the construction of four 44-gun frigates and two 36-gun frigates; these vessels form the nucleus of the nascent U.S. Navy. This is undertaken to stop depredations committed against American commerce by the pirates of Algiers.

April 19
DIPLOMACY: Supreme Court Chief Justice John Jay gains Senate confirmation as envoy to Great Britain. He is sent there on a mission to secure a favorable commercial treaty.

April 22
LAW: The death penalty is abolished by the Pennsylvania legislature for all crimes except murder.

May 1
LABOR: The Federal Society of Journeymen Cordwainers (shoemakers) is organized in Philadelphia as America's first trade union.

May 6
TECHNOLOGY: English mechanic John Hewitt sets up the first steam engine assembled in the United States for the waterworks at Belleville, New Jersey.

1794

May 8
POLITICS: Congress creates the Post Office Department.

May 27
DIPLOMACY: James Monroe is appointed minister to France to replace Gouverneur Morris, whose royalist sympathies have angered the revolutionary French government. John Quincy Adams also gains appointment as minister to the Netherlands.

June 1
NAVAL: British Admiral Lord Richard Howe attacks a French fleet escorting numerous American cargo ships bound for France. The French are handily defeated in this encounter, celebrated as the "Glorious First of June," but the American ships escape damage and make landfall.

June 5
POLITICS: Congress passes the Neutrality Act, forbidding American citizens from joining the army or navy of foreign powers. Foreign vessels are also forbidden from arming or provisioning themselves in American ports.
SCIENCE: Noted English scientist Joseph Priestley, fearing persecution in Great Britain, arrives at Philadelphia.

June 24
EDUCATION: Bowdoin College is chartered at New Brunswick, Maine, under the direction of Congregationalists; its first class graduates in 1806.

June 28
NAVAL: Congress appoints the first six captains of the new U.S. Navy; John Barry, Samuel Nicholson, Silas Talbot, Joshua Barney, Richard Dale, and Thomas Truxton.

June 30
ARTS: The drama *Slaves in Algiers*, written by Susanna Haswell Rowson, is performed at a theater in Philadelphia. Rowson herself is in the audience in this, its opening performance.

July
POLITICS: The Whiskey Rebellion breaks out in the Monongahela Valley of Western Pennsylvania to protest the federal excise tax on liquor and stills. Consequently tax officials have their houses burned while revenue officials are tarred and feathered. Alexander Hamilton is eager to use the rebellion as a test of the power of the federal government.
RELIGION: The first African-American congregation forms in Philadelphia with the opening of the African Protestant Episcopal Church of St. Thomas under the leadership of Reverend Absalom Jones. It is founded because white parishioners badly mistreated blacks attending St. George's Methodist Church.

August 7
MILITARY: President George Washington issues a proclamation ordering the so-called Whiskey Rebels to return home. He also mobilizes 13,000 militia from Maryland, New Jersey, Pennsylvania, and Virginia to suppress the uprising.

August 20
MILITARY: General Anthony Wayne and 3,000 well-drilled soldiers and militia crush a 2,000-man Indian coalition under Blue Jacket at the Battle of Fallen Tim-

bers in northwest Ohio. The battle is fought in an area devastated by tornados and the Americans attack the milling warriors in a well-executed bayonet charge that routs them. Wayne's losses were 33 killed and 140 wounded; Indian losses are presumed to be lighter but still significant. Previously, Miami chief Little Turtle, who pronounced the energetic Wayne as "the Chief who does not sleep," urged his fellow tribesmen to seek peace with the Americans, and he was removed from command. This victory clears the way for continued and unobstructed migration into the Old Northwest. The Indians were also embittered that, despite pledges of support, the British did not assist and even locked them out of nearby Fort Miami.

September 10

EDUCATION: Blount University (University of Tennessee) is chartered by Presbyterians at Knoxville, Tennessee.

September 24

MILITARY: President George Washington instructs General Henry Lee to march against the tax rebellion in western Pennsylvania. Ultimately 200 rebels are detained, 25 are tried, and two are convicted of treason but subsequently pardoned.

November 1

ARTS: Boston lifts its ban on staged plays (in effect since 1750), and the new Boston Theater opens for business.

November 19

DIPLOMACY: Special envoy John Jay negotiates and signs a commercial treaty with Great Britain, the so-called Jay's Treaty, which mandates a withdrawal of British forces from the Old Northwest in exchange for payment of pre-Revolutionary War debts. The agreement opens British ports in the British East and West Indies to American shipping while also granting Britain most-favored nation status. Furthermore, joint commissions are to be assembled to resolve the question of illegal seizures at sea, but the question of impressment of American crewmen for service in the Royal Navy is unaddressed.

1795

ARCHITECTURE: Noted architect Charles Bullfinch designs the Massachusetts State House, hailed as an exemplary example of post-Revolutionary War construction.

EDUCATION: Judge Nathaniel Chipman of Vermont advocates a view of history that promotes the understanding of social forces rather than military events.

INDIAN: In an attempt to encourage Indian trade and ensure fairer treatment of Native Americans, the Federal government establishes the factory system which will supervise trading activities.

RELIGION: In Philadelphia, Richard Allen is ordained as the first African-American minister in the Methodist Church.

TECHNOLOGY: A primitive railroad is first constructed in Boston employing wooden tracks for running up the slopes of Beacon Hill.

January 2

MILITARY: Federalist Timothy Pickering, former postmaster general, replaces Henry Knox as secretary of war.

Jay, John   (1745–1829)

Diplomat, Supreme Court justice

John Jay was born in New York City on December 12, 1745, the scion of wealthy merchants. As such he was afforded a splendid education and graduated from King's College (Columbia University) in 1760, with fluency in French, Greek, and Latin. He then clerked several years in a law firm before being admitted to the bar and forming a partnership with his friend Robert R. Livingston. The onset of the Revolution induced Jay to side with the patriots despite his conservative leanings, and in 1774 he served as a delegate at the First Continental Congress. He subsequently sat with the Second Congress before coming home to help author a new state constitution for New York with Gouverneur Morris. After serving as chief justice of New York's Supreme Court, he returned to Congress in 1778 and was elected president. Then, in 1782, Jay was dispatched as American minister to Spain, where he failed to secure diplomatic recognition for the United States. He then proceeded on to Paris and helped convince ministers John Adams and Benjamin Franklin to seek a peace treaty without French approval. In 1783 he signed the ensuing Peace of Paris and returned home a national hero. Jay was then appointed secretary of state under the Articles of Confederation, but he actively agitated for adoption of more centralized governance. In concert with Alexander Hamilton and James Madison, he contributed several essays to the pro-Constitution series *The Federalist* and proved instrumental in having the new document approved in New York. In light of his conspicuous contributions to the nation and his reputation as a sound and prudent jurist, President George Washington appointed him the first chief justice of the U.S. Supreme Court in 1789.

Jay's tenure as chief justice proved unremarkable for very few cases of import were brought before him. However, at one point he refused to council Washington and Hamilton on questions of public policy, thereby affirming the separation of powers. His greatest legal contribution came in 1793 when he decided the case of *Chisholm v. Georgia*. Here he ruled that Georgia could be sued by an individual from another state in federal court, reflecting his Federalist beliefs in strong central governance. Jay's decision was widely condemned by members of Congress, who passed the Eleventh Amendment to the Constitution to curtail what they perceived as an assault upon state's rights. Jay's most challenging work fell in the diplomatic arena, however. In 1795 Washington dispatched him as a special envoy to Great Britain to resolve several trade issues. The resulting Jay's Treaty did secure the removal of British troops from the Old Northwest and partially opened up the British Caribbean to American goods, but it failed to address preservation of American neutrality at sea during the French Revolution, which caused a political firestorm that also gave rise to the new Democratic-Republican faction under Thomas Jefferson. Jay served two terms as governor of New York before retiring from politics and dying on May 17, 1829, an accomplished public servant.

January 7

BUSINESS: A corrupt Georgia legislature sells 35 million acres of land along the Yazoo River (Alabama and Mississippi) to four land companies. In return the state receives a nominal sum.

January 29
Politics: The Naturalization Act passes Congress, mandating a five-year residency to meet the requirements of citizenship. The renunciation of previous allegiances and titles of nobility are also required.

January 31
Politics: Oliver Wolcott succeeds Alexander Hamilton as secretary of the treasury. Hamilton, however, continues on as an unofficial adviser to President George Washington.

February 25
Education: Union College is chartered at Schenectady, New York, by the Presbyterians; the first class graduates in 1800.

March
Politics: Word of the Jay Treaty reaches Philadelphia and triggers a fierce national debate between those already favorably disposed toward France or England.

March 3
Settlement: French immigrants living in the Ohio territory, having been falsely lured there by the Scioto Company, finally obtain the title to their lands at Gallipolis.

April
Diplomacy: Thomas Pinckney, then minister to Great Britain, is appointed a special commissioner to Spain.

May
Law: Two of 200 "Whiskey rebels" captured are convicted of treason and sentenced to hang; both are subsequently pardoned.

May 22
Arts: A play, *The Triumphs of Love* by John Murdock, features "Sambo," the first role for an African American, and also debuts the first Quaker characters. For the first time blacks are not being portrayed as comic, shiftless servants.

June 24
Diplomacy: Jay's Treaty is ratified by the Senate following a rancorous debate. Its passage has been marred by opposition between Federalists and Republicans, both of whom represent their own specific interests. The latter group is outraged that British seizure of American shipping has not been addressed.

July 19
Settlement: The Connecticut Land Company obtains rights to land in the Northwest along the southern bank of Lake Erie. This is the future site of Cleveland, Ohio, named after company director Moses Cleaveland.

July 22
Journalism: Alexander Hamilton, writing under the nom de plume Camillus, waxes eloquently in favor of the Jay Treaty.

August 3
Indian: General Anthony Wayne and numerous chiefs of the Delaware, Shawnee, Wyandot, and Miami conclude the Treaty of Greenville, whereby they

1795

cede the eastern portion of their lands to the United States in return for a fixed boundary. The Old Northwest is now ready for expanded white settlement.

August 14

DIPLOMACY: President George Washington signs Jay's Treaty into law over objections from the House of Representatives, which previously tried to scuttle the agreement by voting against funding for its enforcement. This constitutes an important precedent for executive prerogatives over legislative ones.

August 19

POLITICS: Secretary of State Edmund Randolph resigns from office, officially for corruption but unofficially under allegations that he was in collusion with France in an attempt to scuttle Jay's Treaty. He is replaced by Timothy Pickering for the time being.

September 5

DIPLOMACY: The United States concludes a treaty of peace and amity with the Dey of Algiers. Henceforth the Americans will pay $1 million for the release of 115 captive seamen who had been held for 10 years, followed by an annual series of tribute payments. The lack of naval power makes American shipping vulnerable to such coercion.

October 27

DIPLOMACY: Thomas Pinckney, commissioner to Spain, concludes the Treaty of San Lorenzo to resolve the western and southern boundaries of the United States. He also obtains free navigational rights on the Mississippi River and the ability to deposit cargo at the port of New Orleans.

November 2

GENERAL: James Knox Polk, the 11th president, is born at Pineville, North Carolina.

December 10

POLITICS: Secretary of War Timothy Pickering resigns from office and succeeds Edmund Randolph as secretary of state; President George Washington's cabinet now consists solely of Federalists.

December 15

POLITICS: The Senate scuttles John Rutledge's nomination to succeed John Jay as chief justice of the supreme court, ostensibly over his recent opposition to Jay's Treaty.

1796

ARTS: Noted painter Gilbert Stuart completes his famous portrait of George Washington as the first president, which consists solely of his face. In this manner viewers were calculated to gauge the tremendous depth and character of the sitter. After being displayed at the Boston Athenaeum, it has been placed on permanent loan to the Boston Museum of Fine Arts.

Stuart, Gilbert   (1755–1828)
Painter

Gilbert Stuart was born in North Kingston, Rhode Island, on December 3, 1755, and raised in Newport. There he took an interest in art at an early age and was partly tutored there by the Scottish artist Cosmo Alexander. He subsequently accompanied his instructor to Edinburgh in 1771, where Alexander died the following year, and Stuart was forced to subsist on a sailor's wages. He managed to return home just as the Revolutionary War was about to commence, and in 1775 he fled with his Loyalist-leaning family to Nova Scotia. Stuart then continued on to London, determined to make his living painting portraits. He eventually came to the attention of the great American expatriate artist Benjamin West, who took him in as an apprentice. Unlike West, however, Stuart evinced no interest in the historically themed paintings of West and remained a strict devotee of portraiture. In this he displayed a demonstrable genius for capturing on canvas the vitality and personality of his sitters with remarkably few colors. Within a few years his work was being compared to British masters such as Sir Joshua Reynolds and Sir Thomas Gainsborough. Stuart was allowed to exhibit his work at the Royal Academy, and in 1782 his noted painting of William Grant entitled "The Skater" garnered him great recognition and secured several lucrative commissions. Stuart, however, was careless with money, lived recklessly, and accumulated great debts. In 1787 he fled to Ireland to escape creditors and continue painting until 1792, when his profligacy forced him to return home once again. This time he finally emerged as the foremost American portraitist of his day.

After a brief stay in New York City, Stuart relocated to Philadelphia and gained national renown painting America's first generation of leaders. Foremost of these was George Washington, who sat for him three times, and the resulting works, depicting the president as stern, remote, yet dignified, remain the most easy identifiable images of that elder statesman. As Stuart's reputation grew, he also painted portraits of Thomas Jefferson, John Adams, James Madison, and Horatio Gates, all exquisitely captured on canvas. In 1805 Stuart moved to Boston to continue his work and, by concentrating strictly upon portraits, he ended up executing almost 1,000 works. This sheer volume of work insured that his paintings would be widely seen and admired around the nation for years to come. Stuart, however, squandered his fortune, lived in debt, and was struck by partial paralysis in 1825. He nonetheless continued working up to the time of his death on July 9, 1828, making him one of the most prolific artists of his day. Stuart's passing was thus greatly lamented in artistic circles because he set the tone and the standards for American portraiture that lasted through the first half of the 19th century. In fact an entire generation of young artists, including Thomas Sully, John Wesley Jarvis, Samuel F. B. Morse, Chester Harding, John Neagle, Ezra Ames, Matthew Jouett, and Mather Brown were all heavily influenced by his effective techniques.

William Dunlap and Benjamin Carr write and stage *The Archers, or the Mountaineers of Switzerland*, an early American opera, in New York City. It is a variation of the William Tell story.

BUSINESS: Robert Morris, a highly-respected financier, organizes a syndicate for land speculation; when it eventually collapses he will serve three years in debtor's prison.

LAW: The Virginia legislature reforms the state criminal code, reducing the number of crimes eligible for the death penalty. This is indicative of a national trend to de-emphasize or eliminate capital punishment.

LITERATURE: "Connecticut Wit" Joel Barlow publishes his poem *The Hasty Pudding* as a mock epic celebrating the virtues of cornmeal mush, a uniquely American dish.

POLITICS: Albert Gallatin leads a successful effort in the House of Representatives to establish the ways and means committee.

PUBLISHING: Amelia Simmons publishes *American Cookery*, the first American cookbook.

TECHNOLOGY: Experiments with the use of gas for illumination are orchestrated in Philadelphia.

January
POLITICS: The House of Representatives issues standards that any individual attempting to coerce or influence Congressmen for their personal gain rather than the public good is to be charged with contempt. The ruling stems from the efforts of Robert Randall who was lobbying Congress on behalf of Great Lakes fur traders.

January 1
POLITICS: Oliver Ellsworth is appointed Chief Justice of the U.S. Supreme Court to succeed John Jay.

January 27
MILITARY: Maryland Federalist James McHenry succeeds Timothy Pickering as secretary of war.

February 15
DIPLOMACY: The French government informs minister James Monroe that the ratification of Jay's Treaty with Great Britain negates all previous agreements with France.

February 18
BUSINESS: The newly elected Georgia legislature voids the Yazoo land sales of 1795.

February 29
DIPLOMACY: President George Washington announces that the Jay Treaty is officially in effect, a fact that deeply antagonizes France and brings the former allies to the brink of warfare.

March 8
LAW: The U.S. Supreme Court settles *Hylton v. United States*, ruling that a carriage tax imposed in 1794 is an indirect levy and, hence, constitutional. This sets an important precedent as, for the first time, the court had weighed the constitutionality of a congressional act.

March 15
DIPLOMACY: The Treaty of San Lorenzo between the United States and Spain is unanimously ratified by the U.S. Senate.

April 22
LAW: The U.S. Supreme Court rules that all pacts made by the government under the Constitution are, in effect, federal law and supercede all conflicting state laws.

April 30
DIPLOMACY: Despite heated opposition from the Democratic-Republicans, the Federalist-dominated House of Representatives votes to enforce provisions of Jay's Treaty.

May 18
SETTLEMENT: A new Land Act passed by Congress requires both the surveying of all acreage in the Northwest Territory, and the sale of the same at a public auction for a minimum price of $2 per acre. A credit system is also instituted, allowing prospective purchasers one year to pay. Federal land offices are also established at Pittsburgh and Cincinnati to facilitate sales. However, the greatest beneficiary of this new law are land companies and speculators, as most settlers cannot afford the minimum purchasing price.

June 1
POLITICS: Tennessee is admitted into the Union as the 16th state with Revolutionary War hero John Sevier serving as the first governor. However, Federalists in Congress restrict the number of members sent from Tennessee to the House of Representatives to one until 1800.

July
DIPLOMACY: Revolutionary France declares that it will try to seize all neutral shipping headed for British ports.

July 11
SETTLEMENT: British forces evacuate Fort Detroit in accordance with the Jay Treaty, and the post is reoccupied by Captain Moses Porter and a company of soldiers.

August 17
SOCIETAL: The Boston African Society is established as a benevolent group for African Americans.

August 22
DIPLOMACY: The French government informs Minister James Monroe that he will be replaced for failing to adequately explain the recent Jay's Treaty between the United States and Great Britain.

August 29
DIPLOMACY: Minister James Monroe, having made conciliatory statements to the French government, is informed by Secretary of State Timothy Pickering that he is being replaced by Charles C. Pinckney.

September 17
JOURNALISM: President George Washington delivers his farewell address to Congress, outlining his decision not to run for a third term in office. In it he warns against entangling alliances with foreign nations, large, standing military forces,

1796

the divisiveness of factions (political parties), and he stresses the importance of stable public credit. In reality, James Madison and Alexander Hamilton are the actual authors of the address.

September 30
SETTLEMENT: Moses Cleaveland, director of the Connecticut Land Company, purchases 3 million acres of land from the so-called Western Reserve (Ohio) and begins surveying high ground where the nearby Cuyahoga River empties into Lake Erie. This is the site of the future city of Cleveland.

October 29
BUSINESS: The ship *Otter* under Captain Ebenezer Dorr sails into Monterey Bay, marking the first time that an American vessel has skirted the coast of California.

November
POLITICS: Andrew Jackson is selected as Tennessee's first delegate to the U.S. House of Representatives.

November 4
DIPLOMACY: The United States concludes a treaty with the Pasha of Tripoli whereby ongoing capture of American crews and vessels ceases in exchange for ransom and an annual tribute. Similar agreements are already in play with the Barbary states of Algiers and Morocco.

November 15
DIPLOMACY: The government of revolutionary France declares its suspension of diplomatic relations with the United States over the Jay Treaty and other issues.

December 7
DIPLOMACY: Charles C. Pinckney, the new American minister to France, presents his credentials to the revolutionary government and is as quickly rejected until French grievances have been addressed. He then returns home.
POLITICS: The third presidential election is decisively and bitterly won by sitting Vice President and Federalist John Adams with 71 electoral votes while Democratic-Republican Thomas Jefferson secures the post of vice president with 68 votes. Jefferson's close defeat is indicative of rising national dissatisfaction with the Jay Treaty and the Federalists. Adams is also the last Federalist to hold office.
SETTLEMENT: British forces evacuate Fort Michilimackinac, Michigan Territory, consistent with the terms of the Jay Treaty.

1797

ARCHITECTURE: Mexican stonemason Isidoro Aguilar designs and begins construction of the main church at San Juan Capistrano, California, which includes a 120-foot bell tower. This imposing structure is subsequently destroyed by an earthquake in 1812.
ART: Noted historical painter John Trumbull finishes his monumental Declaration of Independence in Congress at Independence Hall, which ultimately adorns the halls of Congress itself.
BUSINESS: The firm O'Hare and Craig founds the first frontier glassworks at Pittsburgh.

LITERATURE: The novel *Alcuin* by Charles Brockden explores the notion that men and women have far more in common than they realize and, for that reason, ought to enjoy equal rights.

MEDICAL: Samuel Latham Mitchell publishes the *Medical Repository* in Boston; it is the first American medical publication.

PUBLISHING: Dr. James Woodhouse, a noted scientist, publishes the first handbook in experimental chemistry at Philadelphia.

SOCIETAL: Isabelle Graham and a group of 15 Protestant women found the Society for the Relief of Poor Widows with Small Children in New York City.

TECHNOLOGY: Eli Terry receives the first clock patent for his wooden timekeeping devices. These are sold inexpensively and are rather reliable despite their lack of metal parts. Terry also pioneers the use of waterpower to cut and finish his parts.

January 1

POLITICS: The seat of New York government relocates from New York City to Albany.

January 23–30

SLAVERY: Congress receives the first-ever petition by fugitive slaves, four of whom had fled North, to ask for their freedom. However, their plea is rejected following a vigorous debate.

February 8

TECHNOLOGY: The first coal-fired glass-making plant is built at Pittsburgh, Pennsylvania.

February 27

BUSINESS: Secretary of State Timothy Pickering reports before Congress on the commercial losses arising from French hostility toward American shipping.

March 4

POLITICS: John Adams takes the oath of office as the second chief executive of the United States with Thomas Jefferson as his vice president. The cabinet, including Timothy Pickering, Oliver Wolcott, James McHenry, are holdovers from the Washington administration.

May 10

NAVAL: The new 44-gun frigate USS *United States* is launched in Philadelphia, becoming the first official warship of the new U.S. Navy. It is also the largest warship of its class in the world and command is awarded to Revolutionary War hero Captain John Barry.

May 15

POLITICS: President John Adams summons a special session of Congress for the first time to discuss ongoing tensions with France, the recent expulsion of American minister Charles C. Pinckney, projected diplomatic initiatives, and military preparations.

May 31

DIPLOMACY: In an attempt to avert military confrontation, President John Adams appoints a three-man commission to secure a new treaty of commerce and amity with France. The members are Charles C. Pinckney, Elbridge Gerry, and John Marshall.

1797

Adams, John   (1735–1826)
President

John Adams was born in Braintree, Massachusetts, on October 19, 1735, the son of a farmer. An excellent student, he graduated from Harvard College in 1755, studied law, and was accepted to the bar in the wake of the Stamp Act crisis of 1765. Adams became increasing identified with a radical clique of pro-independence politicians. To that end he served as a delegate to the Continental Congress and lobbied vociferously and effectively on behalf of the Declaration of Independence, which was signed on July 4, 1776. Adams was then dispatched to Europe where he served as minister to France. After a brief return home in 1779 to help write the new Massachusetts constitution, he returned to France to begin secret peace negotiations with Great Britain. Adams, distrusting the French, prevailed upon John Jay and Benjamin Franklin to disregard Congressional instructions and negotiate with the English without informing their allies. In 1780 he served capably as minister to the Netherlands, securing a large loan for the American government. After independence had been secured, Adams relocated to London as the first American minister to that nation. In this capacity he sought normalized relations with England but was continually vexed by Great Britain's refusal to honor the terms of the Treaty of Paris until all prewar debts were paid in full. He came home in 1788 and was elected vice president under the newly adopted constitution.

Adams's tenure at the center of executive leadership proved an unhappy one, simply because he determined to be strictly guided by philosophical principles and remain nonpartisan for the national good. At the time national polity was wracked by growing political discord arising from the monetary and governmental policies of arch-Federalist Alexander Hamilton, but Adams dutifully supported the administration of President George Washington. In 1796 he was himself elected the second president of the United States and endured four years of controversy and rising national acrimony over foreign affairs. The French Revolution became a catalyst for the Democratic-Republic opposition of Thomas Jefferson to emerge, and Adams also had to contend with dissent within his own Federalist party. Despite French provocation and Hamilton's bellicosity, Adams refused to allow the country to slide into war and sought a diplomatic solution. However, he also signed the Federalist-inspired Alien and Sedition Acts of 1798 to silence political opposition, which further exacerbated national tensions. He ran again for the presidency in 1800, barely supported by fellow Federalists, and was narrowly defeated by Jefferson. Adams, taking the political upset personally, withdrew from public life altogether and moved back to Braintree, where he engaged in a lucid and furious publishing campaign to defend his term in office. He was not personally reconciled with Jefferson, his ideological adversary, until 1812 but gradually rehabilitated his reputation as an elder statesman. Adams died in Braintree on July 4, 1826, the fiftieth anniversary of the Declaration of Independence.

June 1
POLITICS: Secretary of State Timothy Pickering declares that French warships and privateers have seized 300 American vessels.

June 24
MILITARY: Congress, anticipating an outbreak of war with France, authorizes recruitment of 80,000 militia as a national contingency.

June 26
TECHNOLOGY: Inventor Charles Newbold of New Jersey patents a cast-iron plow; he had spent his entire fortune developing the device but farmers resist the invention out of a misplaced fear of contaminating the soil.

July 8
POLITICS: The House of Representatives impeaches Senator William Blount of Tennessee on charges that he was conspiring to instigate the Cherokee to attack both the American and Spanish holdings in the Southwest. The Native Americans would obviously lose such an encounter, along with additional lands ripe for speculators. This is the first instance of the House utilizing its powers to remove an elected official.

August 28
DIPLOMACY: The United States and the Barbary kingdom of Tunis reach an agreement to cease piratical acts against American shipping in exchange for an annual payment of tribute. However, the terms are deemed so offensive that the treaty is not ratified until January 1800.

September 7
NAVAL: The 36-gun frigate USS *Constellation* is launched at Baltimore, Maryland, as the new U.S. Navy begins acquiring real combat capabilities.

October 4–18
DIPLOMACY: In Paris, the XYZ Affair unfolds as American commissioners Charles C. Pinckney, Elbridge Gerry, and John Marshall confront three French negotiators named "X," "Y," and "Z," who rather undiplomatically insist on a $240,000 bribe as a precondition to any treaty negotiations. Pinckney and Marshall eventually depart in a huff while Gerry remains behind to deal with French minister Talleyrand. A naval confrontation is in the offing, the so-called Quasi War.

October 21
NAVAL: The 44-gun frigate USS *Constitution* is launched at Boston. This is the second vessel of its class to be acquired by the nascent U.S. Navy and will become America's most famous and celebrated warship.

1798

ARTS: Joseph Hopkinson's patriotic poem "Hail, Columbia" is published as an indication of anticipated hostilities with France.

BUSINESS: The 30-ton schooner *Jemima* is constructed near Rochester, New York, for the trade on Lake Ontario.

LITERATURE: Charles Brockden Brown, the nation's first professional author, publishes his novel *Wieland*, an early Gothic romance reflecting a strong European influence.

MEDICAL: Dr. Valentine Seaman pioneers the first professional instructions in nursing and subsequently publishes them in outline form as an early medical textbook.

SETTLEMENT: Frontier icon Daniel Boone receives an 850-acre grant from the Spanish government in the Femme Osage District, Louisiana Territory (Missouri).

TECHNOLOGY: At New Haven, Connecticut, Eli Whitney introduces his revolutionary concept of interchangeable parts while constructing firearms for the U.S. Army. It greatly facilitates factory production and repairs in the field and is a sign of America's burgeoning role in the nascent Industrial Revolution. However, Whitney, who has promised the government to construct 10,000 muskets in only two years, lacks a factory and misses his deadline by several years.

January 8

LAW: The Eleventh Amendment to the U.S. Constitution, which restricts federal judicial authority over the states, is ratified by the states. Specifically, it forbids lawsuits against a state by citizens of other states or foreign nations.

January 17

DIPLOMACY: In Paris, American commissioner John Marshall formally rejects French attempts to solicit a bribe as a precondition for treaty negotiations. Marshall gives the French until March 18 to reply satisfactorily, then departs.

March 19

DIPLOMACY: President John Adams informs Congress that a diplomatic solution to French depredations at sea has failed.

April

ARTS: John Daly Burk's powerful play, *Female Patriotism, or the Death of Joan d'Arc*, is staged at the Park Theater in New York City.

April 3

POLITICS: Details of the XYZ Affair are released to the public by President John Adams with a corresponding outbreak of indignation and anti-French sentiments nationally. America begins girding for the eventuality of war with France.

April 7

SETTLEMENT: Congress creates the Mississippi Territory, carved out of parts of present-day Alabama and Mississippi.

April 30

NAVAL: To further strengthen the defensive capability of the nation, President John Adams prevails upon Congress to create the Department of the Navy under a Secretary of the Navy. This new entity oversees naval administration previously handled by the Department of War.

May 21

NAVAL: Benjamin Stoddert is appointed the first Secretary of the Navy, and he oversees a tiny naval establishment hovering on the cusp of war with France.

May 28

MILITARY: Congress passes a bill mandating recruitment of a 10,000-man army for three years.

NAVAL: Congress authorizes President John Adams to order naval commanders to engage any French vessel attempting to seize or interfere with American commerce at sea.

1798

June 6
LAW: In a major step, Congress abolishes the practice of imprisoning debtors.

June 13
DIPLOMACY: Congress votes to suspend commercial activities with France and its colonies.

June 18
POLITICS: The Federalist-dominated Congress votes to enhance national security through passage of the first of the Alien and Sedition Acts, which effectively clamps down on political opposition to their policies. The first is an amendment to the Naturalization Act, which increases mandatory residency from five to 14 years.

June 25
POLITICS: Congress passes the Alien Friends Act, which authorizes the president two years to deport any foreigner deemed sufficiently treasonous or dangerous to national defense to warrant removal.

July 2
MILITARY: Former president George Washington gains appointment as commander of the three-year provisional army; Alexander Hamilton is made his second in command and inspector general. Washington, a thoroughly trusted figure, is the only man that the American polity would be comfortable with while leading such a force.

July 6
POLITICS: Congress passes the Enemy Alien Act to facilitate the wartime arrest and banishment of any resident formerly associated with an enemy power.

July 7
DIPLOMATIC: Treaties of France dating back to 1788 are repealed by Congress; this is the first time that the United States has abrogated a prior commitment.
NAVAL: Lieutenant Stephen Decatur, commanding the 20-gun sloop USS *Delaware*, captures the 14-gun French privateer *La Croyable* off New Jersey; this is the first prize of the Quasi-War and is recommissioned at Philadelphia as the USS *Retaliation*. This victory also signifies the start of Decatur's impressive career as a naval officer.

July 11
NAVAL: The U.S. Marine Corps is established by Congress, an outgrowth of the Continental Marines raised during the Revolutionary War.

July 14
POLITICS: Congress passes the Sedition Act, which stipulates that the author of any published item deemed seditionist to the president, Congress, or government is subject to arrest, imprisonment, and fines. Intended to curb political dissent, it stimulates membership in the Democratic-Republican opposition and politically damages the Federalists.

July 16
MEDICAL: The Marine Hospital Service is established by Congress; it gradually evolves into the U.S. Public Health Service.

August 8
NAVAL: The secretary of the Navy forbids the service of African Americans from U.S. Navy warships, reversing a trend in effect since the Revolutionary War.

1798

September 12

JOURNALISM: Benjamin Franklin Bach, Benjamin Franklin's grandson, is arrested under the Sedition Act for essays he published in the Philadelphia *Aurora* "libeling" President John Adams. His detention sparks widespread outrage and protest against the Alien and Sedition Acts.

October 12

SETTLEMENT: The newly designated Mississippi Territory receives firm boundaries while its capital is fixed at Natchez.

November 16

NAVAL: British warships accost the 20-gun American frigate *Baltimore* on the high seas and remove part of its crew, suspected British deserters, for impressment purposes.

POLITICS: Thomas Jefferson drafts the Kentucky Resolutions protesting the Alien and Sedition Acts as unconstitutional, which are then passed by the Kentucky legislature. According to Jefferson, states have a right unto themselves to determine the constitutionality of the acts. This is the origin of the "compact theory" of governance, whereby the United States is a compact between otherwise sovereign states.

November 20

NAVAL: The schooner USS *Retaliation* under Lieutenant William Bainbridge is seized by French forces at the Caribbean Island of Guadalupe; the 250-man crew remains in captivity until February 1799.

December 14

TECHNOLOGY: David Wilkinson of Rhode Island receives a patent for his screw-threading machine.

December 24

POLITICS: The Virginia Resolutions, penned by James Madison, are adopted by the Virginia legislature to oppose the unconstitutionality of the Alien and Sedition Acts permitting states to declare null and void any illegal Congressional act.

December 31

LAW: The Supreme Court decides the case of *Calder v. Bull*, ruling that prohibitions against laws enacted after the commission of a crime apply solely to criminal, not civil, law.

1799

ARCHITECTURE: Benjamin H. Latrobe's design for the Bank of Pennsylvania anticipates what becomes known as the Greek Revival movement. It incorporates an Ionic-style portico later commonly found on most large public buildings.

ARTS: Johann Graupner wears blackface for the first time during the performance of *Oroonoko,* one of the earliest minstrel shows.

BUSINESS: The Russian American Company receives from the government of Czar Paul I a monopoly of trade in the northern Pacific region, with headquarters at Sitka, Alaska.

EDUCATION: Child prodigy Timothy Dwight passes through Rhode Island College (Brown University) at the age of 14; reputedly, he could read the Bible at four.

JOURNALISM: The *Baltimore American* becomes the first newspaper outside Washington, D.C., to grant regular coverage to congressional reports and debates.

LABOR: The Federal Society of Cordwainers initiates the nation's first labor action by striking for nine days until they receive a wage increase.

MEDICAL: Dr. Benjamin Waterhouse creates the first viable vaccination against smallpox at Cambridge, Massachusetts.

RELIGION: Seneca wastrel Handsome Lake, recovering from an alcoholic bout, experiences strange visions that lead him to seek purity through a nativist revival.

Handsome Lake   (ca. 1735–1815)
Seneca prophet

Handsome Lake (Skaniadariio) was born at the village of Conwagas along the Genessee River (Avon, New York) around 1735, a member of the Wolf clan of the Seneca tribe. The Seneca then constituted part of the powerful Six Nations Iroquois Confederation and he counted among his family and near relatives noted chief Cornplanter and the distinguished orator Red Jacket. Little is known of Handsome Lake's childhood or early years other than that he was raised among the Turtle Clan. Like many contemporaries he undoubtedly sided with Great Britain during the American Revolution after which the tribe was punished by the United States by appropriating large tracts of land. The formerly far-ranging Seneca then found themselves hemmed into cramped reservations which began playing havoc upon traditional patterns of tribal, family, and individual behavior. Shortly after the death of his daughter, Handsome Lake took to drinking and became severely alcoholic. He continued degenerating mentally and physically until August 7, 1799, when he experienced the first of four spiritual visions. During these spiritual sojourns Handsome Lake was purportedly instructed by various messengers to stop drinking, oppose all forms of witchcraft as practiced by his people, and embrace traditional tribal lifestyles and values. The "messengers" underscored their lessons with a warning that the Seneca would be visited by destruction if they did not reform their ways. Struck by the intensity of his visions, Handsome Lake cured himself of his addiction, assumed the role of a tribal prophet, and began preaching among his people.

Commencing in 1800 Handsome Lake addressed his conflict-ridden tribe with his unique call for nativist renewal. In fact, he did not hesitate to insist that while change was inevitable, the Seneca did not have to sacrifice their identity. After 1801 and further refinement he expounded upon the concept of Gaiwiio or "Good Word" to reject alcohol, embrace spirituality, and also adopt European-style agriculture to enhance the Seneca's traditional ties to the land. The new creed also featured coopted Christian features such as silent prayer and confession of one's sins. He found a ready audience willing to listen and absorb his message although his strident insistence on the persecution of suspected witches caused a major disruption in his conversion efforts. Handsome Lake was nevertheless considered

(continues)

(continued)

an important tribal figure, and he gained election to the Seneca tribal council. In that capacity he ventured to Washington, D.C., in 1801 to confer with President Thomas Jefferson over the acquisition of additional tribal lands and discontinuing the sale of alcohol to his people. By the time Handsome Lake died on the Onondaga Reservation on August 10, 1815, he had managed to halt the sad slide of the Seneca and other tribes into debauchery. Moreover, the tenets of his religion were codified by Blacksnake in 1850 and are still practiced in their present form as the "Longhouse Religion."

January 30

POLITICS: The Logan Act, which expressly forbids private citizens to engage in unauthorized diplomatic activities, is approved by Congress. This is enacted in response to Dr. George Logan, a Philadelphia Quaker, who sought to venture to Paris as a private citizen in an attempt to avert war with France.

February 7

POLITICS: John Fries is arrested by Federal marshals in Bethlehem, Pennsylvania, for leading a revolt against federal property taxes in Bucks and Northampton Counties, Pennsylvania. He is tried, convicted, and sentenced to death for treason but is ultimately pardoned by President John Adams.

February 9

NAVAL: In a smart action off the island of Nevis, Captain Thomas Truxton of the 38-gun frigate USS *Constellation* captures the French frigate *L'Insurgent* ; losses in this lopsided affair are three Americans wounded to 29 French dead and 41 injured. Lieutenant John Rodgers and Midshipman David Porter are subsequently detailed to sail the prize into St. Kitts with 173 prisoners. This is a significant victory for the U.S. Navy during the so-called Quasi-War with France.

POLITICS: Congress forbids trade with France and also stops American vessels from entering French ports.

February 18

DIPLOMACY: Despite the pro-war urgings of Alexander Hamilton, President John Adams appoints William Vans Murray as the new American minister to France. He does so upon the advice of the French foreign minister, Talleyrand, now receptive to American overtures.

February 23

MEDICAL: Congress passes its first national quarantine act, whereby federal officials will assist state authorities in matters respecting medical quarantines.

February 25

DIPLOMACY: President John Adams, reacting to pressure from arch-Federalist Alexander Hamilton, appoints William K. Davie and Oliver Ellsworth to accompany William Vans Murray to France as ministers plenipotentiary.

Patrick Henry had originally been selected but then declined on account of age. The three men are charged with reopening peace negotiations with the French republic.

March 29
SLAVERY: New York approves an emancipation law for the gradual abolition of slavery.

April 1
PUBLISHING: The *American Review and Literary Journal* commences publication under the aegis of Charles Brockden Brown.

May
BUSINESS: The American vessel *Franklin* under Captain James Devereaux drops anchor at the Dutch-controlled island of Deshima in Nagasaki harbor, Japan. He then barters his cargo of cotton, sugar, tin, pepper, and cloves in exchange for the first Japanese mats, lacquered goods, and pans brought back to the United States.

June 6
GENERAL: Revolutionary War icon Patrick Henry dies in Charlotte County, Virginia.

June 15
POLITICS: New Hampshire's Federalist-dominated legislature passes the New Hampshire Resolutions to rebut the antigovernment Kentucky and Virginia Resolutions.

November 9–10
DIPLOMACY: Napoleon Bonaparte overthrows the French Directorate and installs himself as First Consul; obsessed by expansionist ambitions in Europe, he proves much more amenable to diplomacy toward the United States.

November 22
POLITICS: Thomas Jefferson drafts another Kentucky Resolution, passed by the Kentucky legislature, which repudiates the assertion that the federal judiciary alone can determine the constitutionality of acts passed by Congress. Once again, he insists that states have the right to nullify federal laws.

December 12
POLITICS: The sixth Congress convenes its first session, being the last to boast a Federalist majority.

December 14
GENERAL: The new nation suffers its first major loss when George Washington, the most trusted military and political figure of his times, and a beloved national icon, dies at Mount Vernon. His renown is such that even France and England render honors on his passage.

December 26
POLITICS: Henry Lee, a distinguished Revolutionary War veteran, delivers a famous eulogy to George Washington and proclaims him as "first in war, first in peace, first in the hearts of his countrymen."

1800

AGRICULTURE: John Chapman, a Pennsylvania horticulturist, begins his 50-year career of spreading appleseeds around the region of the Ohio River Valley. For this reason he enters into folklore as Johnny Appleseed.

MEDICAL: Dr. Benjamin Waterhouse performs the first cowpox vaccination in America in Cambridge, Massachusetts.

MUSIC: Benjamin Carr commences printing his weekly *Musical Journal*, the first publication devoted to the dissemination of popular music from Europe and the United States.

POPULATION: The 1800 census reveals a national population of 5.3 million, including 896,849 African American slaves. Virginia, boasting 900,000 inhabitants, is the most populous state.

PUBLISHING: Mason Locke Weems, a Episcopal parson, publishes his celebrated panegyric *The Life and Memorable Actions of George Washington*, within months of the president's death. It is an immediate best seller and endures through 87 printings to 1927. "Parson Weems" is best remembered for including his fictional account of a young Washington cutting down the cherry tree.

Isaiah Thomas of Worcester, Massachusetts, is the nation's foremost publisher, with 400 titles in print since the end of the Revolutionary War. His latest is a rendition of the New Testament in Greek.

RELIGION: The Church of the United Brethren in Christ is organized with Philip William Otterbein and Martin Boehm as bishops. It is an outgrowth of the Mennonite community in Pennsylvania.

January 2
SLAVERY: Free African Americans in Philadelphia petition Congress to end slavery, halt the slave trade, and to allow the Fugitive Slave Act of 1793 to expire. Not surprisingly, the petition is allowed to die in committee.

January 7
GENERAL: Millard Fillmore, the 13th president, is born at Locke (Summerville), New York.

January 10
DIPLOMACY: Congress ratifies the recent treaty with Tunis, signed the previous August.

February 1
NAVAL: The American frigate USS *Constellation* under Captain Thomas Truxton defeats the French frigate *La Vengeance* off Guadalupe, but the French vessel escapes after Truxton's ship loses its mainmast.

February 22
SOCIETAL: Philadelphia is the scene of a grand parade in honor of George Washington's birthday; this is the first public observance of what becomes a national holiday.

March 8
DIPLOMACY: First Consul Napoleon Bonaparte of France cordially receives American commissioners William Vans Murray, Oliver Ellsworth, and William

R. Davie. Napoleon, who is planning wars of expansion in Europe, wants to settle his matters with the United States beforehand.

April

POLITICS: The nation's first political party caucuses for presidential and vice presidential candidates take place over the following two months. In time John Adams and Charles C. Pinckney are selected by the Federalists while Thomas Jefferson and Aaron Burr will represent the Democratic Republicans.

April 3

BUSINESS: Congress extends a franking privilege to Martha Washington, in effect to allow mail sent and received by her to be done so for free. It is gradually extended to all Revolutionary War veterans.

April 4

BUSINESS: Congress passes the first Federal Bankruptcy Law pertaining to merchants and bankers; its net result is the release from Debtor's Prison of financier Robert Morris.

April 24

GENERAL: The Library of Congress is founded by a congressional act for the purpose of informing and enlightening members of that body.

April 29

BUSINESS: A British court rules on the case of the American vessel *Polly*, establishing the principle of a "Broken voyage." Henceforth, American vessels can travel from the French West Indies to France if their cargos are landed at an American port and duties paid on them.

May 6

POLITICS: President John Adams, convinced that Secretary of War James McHenry is working in collusion with Alexander Hamilton for his defeat in the upcoming presidential election, demands and receives McHenry's resignation.

May 7

SETTLEMENT: Congress carves up the Northwest Territory by imposing a boundary between the Kentucky and Ohio Rivers. The area west of this is christened the Indiana Territory under Governor William Henry Harrison, with its capital at Vincennes. The eastern region (Ohio) remains known as the Northwest Territory with a capital at Chillicothe.

May 10

SETTLEMENT: The Public Land Act, sponsored by Governor William Henry Harrison of the Indiana Territory, passes Congress. It creates district public land offices, liberal credit terms for purchasing land, and engenders a surge of land speculation throughout the territory. The minimum purchase is 320 acres, usually beyond what the average settler could afford.

May 11

NAVAL: In a startling action, Lieutenant Isaac Hull and 100 U.S. Marines hide themselves on board the vessel *Sally* and sail alongside the French privateer *Sandwich* off Santo Domingo. They quickly sortie and capture that vessel without a loss, then storm ashore and also take a nearby Spanish fort. Hull then triumphantly sails off without loss.

1800

May 12

POLITICS: President John Adams dismisses Secretary of State Timothy Pickering out of a belief that he is secretly conspiring against him in the 1800 presidential election.

May 13

POLITICS: Virginia Federalist John Marshall replaces Timothy Pickering as Secretary of State at the behest of President John Adams.

May 23

LAW: In Richmond, Virginia, James T. Callender is tried and convicted of seditious libel and sentenced to nine months' imprisonment. This is among the most celebrated cases arising from the Alien and Sedition Acts.

June

POLITICS: The American government begins moving from Philadelphia to the new federalist district recently christened Washington, District of Columbia. This is the first planned capital city in history.

June 12

POLITICS: Massachusetts Federalist Samuel Dexter is appointed by President John Adams to serve as the new secretary of war.

July 9

ARTS: Mount Vernon Gardens, the nation's first summer theater, opens on Broadway in New York.

August 30

SLAVERY: A planned rebellion led by African-American slave Gabriel Prosser is revealed to white authorities; Prosser is subsequently hanged along with 36 suspected cohorts.

September 30

DIPLOMACY: The United States and a new French regime, the Consulate under Napoleon Bonaparte, formalize the Treaty of Morfontaine (or Convention of 1800), which ends the Quasi-War between the two nations while also restoring regular diplomatic relations. The agreement also annuls the alliance of 1778 while leaving the question of compensation for seized American vessels open to future negotiations.

October 1

DIPLOMACY: France and Spain conclude the secret treaty of San Ildefonso, whereby the colony of Louisiana is transferred back to its former owner, France. Apparently, the ambitious Napoleon Bonaparte, distracted by the outbreak of peace in Europe, now aspires for a revival of French colonial fortunes in North America.

October 12

NAVAL: The frigate USS *Boston* under Captain George Little engages and captures the 24-gun frigate *Le Berceau* off the Massachusetts coast.

October 19

DIPLOMACY: In an egregious national insult, Captain William Bainbridge is ordered by the Dey of Algiers to convey his emissary to Constantinople aboard the warship USS *George Washington*. There he is forced to present gifts to the Ottoman government and also fly the Ottoman flag from his masthead.

November 17
POLITICS: The seat of government is formally transferred to the new District of Columbia; President John Adams and his wife Abigail occupy the soon-to-be-named White House while Congress convenes its first session there.

December 3
POLITICS: The presidential election of 1800 pits the Federalist ticket of John Adams and Charles C. Pinckney against Democratic-Republican Thomas Jefferson and Aaron Burr. It will be decided largely around issues surrounding the Alien and Sedition Act, higher taxes to support a large defense establishment, the reduction of trade with France, and British impressment of American seamen.

1801

ARCHITECTURE: The first large suspension bridge is erected over Jacob's Creek, Pennsylvania, to link the settlements of Uniontown and Greensborough. It was inspired by a suspension system pioneered by James Finely of Fayette County in that state.
EDUCATION: South Carolina College (today's University of South Carolina) is chartered in Columbia, South Carolina; its first class graduates in 1806.
JOURNALISM: The *New York Evening Post* commences publication as a Federalist mouthpiece.
PUBLISHING: Noted Philadelphia publisher Matthew Carey organizes the American Company of Booksellers in New York City, which promotes the latest publications through book fairs.
RELIGION: The second Great Revival commences with the evangelical camp meetings of Presbyterian minister James McGready, who began preaching in Logan County, Kentucky, in 1797. The movement of frontier Protestantism, replete with hellfire and damnation sermons, soon sweeps the upper mid-west.
Yale president Timothy Dwight leads a religious revival in Connecticut.
TECHNOLOGY: Legendary engraver Paul Revere manufactures the first cold, rolled copper in Boston, Massachusetts.

January 1
POLITICS: Samuel Dexter is confirmed by the U.S. Senate as secretary of the Treasury.

February 4
POLITICS: John Jay having refused to hold public office again, President John Adams appoints Virginia Federalist John Marshall as the new chief justice of the U.S. Supreme Court. This is one of his last official acts in office and, as events prove, among the most influential legal appointments in American history.

February 11
ARTS: The play *Abaellino, the Great Bandit* by William Dunlap commences its amazing 25-year run.

February 11–16
POLITICS: Once the presidential elector ballots are counted, Thomas Jefferson and Aaron Burr tie at 73 votes apiece with John Adams, the first incumbent to be defeated, with 65 votes, while Charles C. Pinckney receives 64 votes. To end the impasse the process reverts to the House of Representatives for the first time, as provided by the Constitution.

Marshall, John   (1755–1835)

Supreme court justice

John Marshall was born in Fauquier County, Virginia, on September 24, 1755, the son of a surveyor. He was imperfectly educated by the time he joined the Continental Army in 1775 as a captain and fought well in several battles. While still in service he enrolled at William and Mary College in 1779, easily mastered law, and was admitted to the bar in 1780. Soon Marshall gained a well-deserved reputation as one of Virginia's foremost legal authorities. After several terms in the legislature, he served with the state constitutional convention in 1788, lending his support to ratification. In time Marshall, by dint of keen judicial and political insight and a driven personality, emerged as leader of the Federalist party in Virginia. He soon came to the attention of President George Washington, a fellow Virginian, who appointed him a minister to France in 1797. He emerged from the infamous XYZ Affair with a national reputation, and in 1800 President John Adams offered him the position of secretary of war, which Marshall declined. That year Adams was defeated by the Democratic-Republicans of Thomas Jefferson, the first time that one party was about to replace another. Adams, realizing the Federalists had lost control of the government politically, now sought to wield influence over it judicially through the courts. A spate of "midnight appointments" ensued in January 1801 before he left office and Marshall was appointed chief justice of the U.S. Supreme Court when John Jay declined. From the standpoint of shaping the tone of Constitutional law, this proved one of the most significant appointments in American history.

As a Federalist, Marshall was determined to preserve strong central governance and check what he viewed as the excesses of democracy. He also wished to render the Supreme Court, heretofore a relatively benign branch of the government, into a first among equals. He had his chance in 1803 by ruling in the famous case *Marbury v. Madison*, which established the principle of "judicial review." Thanks to Marshall's brilliant maneuvers, the Supreme Court would unilaterally determine the constitutionality of all laws passed by Congress, dismissing them if they failed to meet constitutional standards. He also strengthened the court by insisting that each ruling be rendered by a single opinion–his–while dissent was removed from the public forum. A series of important cases followed through which Marshall inevitably sided with the federal government over the states. Another significant ruling, *McCulloch v. Maryland*, upheld the rechartering of the Bank of the United States, thus reaffirming Alexander Hamilton's policy of implied powers, or "loose construction," in the Constitution. Marshall closely directed the judicial and constitutional direction of the United States for 35 years before dying in office on July 6, 1835. Philadelphia's famous Liberty Bell acquired its celebrated crack while tolling in his memory.

February 17

POLITICS: The House of Representatives endures an all-night session of 36 deadlocked ballots before Thomas Jefferson is finally elected president and Aaron Burr vice president. Apparently, Alexander Hamilton uses his influence among Federalist delegates to have them cast blank ballots, thereby electing Jefferson. Hamilton sees his old adversary as the "lesser of two evils" when compared to the brilliant but erratic Burr. The Federalists also lose control of Congress but now make strident attempts to retain control of the judiciary.

February 27

POLITICS: The Judiciary Act is passed by Congress; it reduces the number of Supreme Court justices from six to five and also establishes 16 circuit courts nationwide. Administering the federal District of Columbia also becomes a jurisdiction of Congress. Moreover, outgoing President John Adams uses it as a convenient pretext to make several last-minute appointments to the court. Congress this day also assumes control over the District of Columbia.

March 3

POLITICS: The Judiciary Act enables President John Adams to make several last-minute appointments (midnight judges) to the circuit court, on literally his last day in office, to ensure Federalist domination of the courts. Opposition to these appointments by the Democratic-Republicans under President Thomas Jefferson leads to the landmark judicial ruling in *Marbury v. Madison.*

March 4

POLITICS: Thomas Jefferson, the tall, gangling, red-headed philosopher, becomes the first president inaugurated into office in the new national capitol of Washington, D.C. He is also the first Democratic-

Aaron Burr *(Library of Congress)*

Republican to hold high office. In his inaugural address, Jefferson sounds the case for limited government, fiscal frugality, states' rights, and preserving civil liberties. Aaron Burr is also sworn in as vice president.

March 5

POLITICS: Revolutionary War hero Henry Dearborn becomes secretary of war while Levi Lincoln is appointed attorney general.

May 2

DIPLOMACY: James Madison is appointed secretary of state.

May 14

DIPLOMACY: Pasha Yusuf Karamanli of Tripoli, wishing to increase his tribute demands on the United States, threatens war and cuts down the American flag in at the consulate in Tripoli City. President Thomas Jefferson, determined to protect America's freedom of the seas, authorizes the outfitting of several naval expeditions against the North African pirates.

POLITICS: Swiss born Albert Gallatin becomes the new secretary of the treasury.

June 2

NAVAL: Commodore Richard Dale leads the first American naval expedition of four vessels and a complement of U.S. Marines from New York against the Barbary pirates.

1801

Jefferson, Thomas   (1743–1826)
President

Thomas Jefferson was born in Albemarle County, Virginia, on April 13, 1743, son of a plantation owner. He proved adept as a student, passed through William and Mary College in 1762, and joined the colonial bar in 1767. Jefferson subsequently developed an affinity for politics and public service, so he was elected to the House of Burgesses in 1769, remaining there until 1775. Throughout the period leading up to the American Revolution he agitated on behalf of the patriots against Great Britain and served as a delegate to the Second Continental Congress. In this capacity he made indelible contributions to the American cause by drafting the memorable Declaration of Independence, which was adopted on July 4, 1776. He then returned to Virginia to serve with the House of Delegates before becoming governor in 1779. After the war ended in 1783 Jefferson served the government in various capacities, most notably as minister to France in 1784, where he witnessed the outbreak of the French Revolution. He then favored adoption of the new U.S.

Thomas Jefferson. Painting by Thomas Sully *(National Archives)*

June 10
DIPLOMACY: The Dey of Tripoli declares war against the United States over its cessation of tribute payments.

July
RELIGION: An early Methodist camp meeting unfolds near the Gaspar River Church in Logan County, Kentucky. Soon this practice becomes a common occurrence along the frontier.

July 17
NAVAL: The squadron of Commodore Richard Dale arrives off Tripoli and imposes a blockade. Meanwhile, the American consul there, James Cathcart, tries in vain to have Pasha Yusuf Karamanli reduce his new tribute demands of a one-off payment of $250,000 and annual payments of $20,000 thereafter.

August
NAVAL: In France, American inventor Robert Fulton creates his viable submarine *Nautilus* and offers it to Napoleon, who remains skeptical and uninterested.

Constitution, but only if it contained a Bill of Rights. President George Washington appointed him secretary of state in 1789, but he was increasingly drawn into an ideological struggle with Alexander Hamilton and other Federalists as to the nature of American governance. He finally broke with them over the issue of Jay's Treaty in 1795 and went on to help found an opposition party, the Democratic-Republicans. In this capacity he increasingly criticized President John Adams and the oppressive Alien and Sedition Acts before running for the presidency in 1800. He was elected to the office through the House of Representatives, although this required the help of Hamilton to conclusively defeat Aaron Burr.

As chief executive, Jefferson set the government down a new path. He sought to reduce the size and influence of government so as to assist yeoman farmers and deflect an overly ambitious merchant class. Jefferson, a pacifist by nature, was nonetheless determined to protect the American flag at sea, and in 1801 he sent several naval expeditions into the Mediterranean to combat the Tripolitan pirates of North Africa. In 1803 he authorized creation of the U.S. Military Academy, West Point, to scientifically train the officer corps and secured the Louisiana Purchase from France, which doubled the size of the nation. In 1804 he also dispatched the expedition of Captains Meriwether Lewis and William Clark to explore this vast region. When British warships attacked American ships at sea in 1807 he launched a complete embargo on foreign trade to punish the offenders; in the end this nearly ruined the economy and had to be repealed. Jefferson left office in March 1809 still a popular public figure, and he retired to his estate at Monticello, Virginia, to write and conduct scientific research. He was not personally reconciled with his former friend John Adams until 1812 and remained a respected elder statesman until his death at Monticello on July 4, 1826–the 50th anniversary of his Declaration of Independence.

August 1
NAVAL: In an early naval encounter, the brig USS *Enterprise* under Lieutenant Andrew Sterett engages and captures the 14-gun North African vessel *Tripoli*, killing 30 Algerians and taking 30 captive.

August 7
RELIGION: The Great Revival of the West increases with a Presbyterian camp meeting at Cane Ridge, Kentucky. Presbyterian minister Barton W. Stone presides over a gathering estimated at 25,000.

August 21
SCIENCE: The first mastodon bones are unearthed in Newburgh, New York, causing a popular sensation.

September
ENGINEERING: The Cayuga Bridge, a wooden structure more than a mile long and broad enough for four wagons to traverse abreast, is opened in central New York. It is considered one of the technical marvels of its day.

1801

Camp meetings, such as the one shown here, helped to spread Protestantism to the scattered frontier population. *(Library of Congress)*

October 16
DIPLOMACY: Robert R. Livingston, newly appointed minister to France, departs for Europe.

October 19
TECHNOLOGY: Benjamin H. Latrobe designs and builds the nation's first freshwater aqueduct system at Philadelphia, which supplies the city year round.

November 1
EDUCATION: Middlebury College is chartered at Middlebury, Vermont; its first class graduates in 1802.

November 16
JOURNALISM: Federalists Alexander Hamilton and John Jay join forces to found and publish the Federalist-oriented *New York Evening Post.* They do so in response to the recent loss of Federalist Stephen Van Rensselaer in his race for the governorship.

December 7
POLITICS: The Seventh Congress convenes in Washington, D.C., with the Democratic-Republicans in firm control of both the Senate and the House of Representatives for the first time.

December 8
POLITICS: President Thomas Jefferson, disliking ceremony, renders his first annual message to Congress on paper, a practice that continues until 1913.

1802

ARTS: The New York Academy of Arts is founded in New York City; it is organized and run like a business, with shares of stock bought and sold.

BUSINESS: Colonel David Humphreys brings back the first shipment of 100 merino sheep from Spain. Soon the fine wool of this animal becomes a staple of the growing textile industry.

SPORTS: New York public law forbids horse racing in public and the sport remains restricted to private organizations, the so-called jockey clubs.

TECHNOLOGY: In New York, noted inventor John Stevens develops the first screw (propeller) driven steamboat.

January 7
EDUCATION: The American Western University is founded at Athens, Ohio, becoming the first higher education institution in the Northwest Territory. It is also part of the Ohio Company of Associates and is renamed Ohio University in 1804.

January 8
DIPLOMACY: Consistent with the terms of Jay's Treaty, a commission determines that the United States owes $2.6 million in pre-Revolutionary war debts, based both on English and Loyalist claims.

January 15
EDUCATION: Jefferson College (today's Washington and Jefferson College) is chartered in Canonsburg, Pennsylvania.

January 29
GENERAL: John James Beckley, former clerk of the House of Representatives, is appointed the first Librarian of Congress by President Thomas Jefferson.
POLITICS: President Thomas Jefferson approaches Congress for a repeal of the Judiciary Act, which he regards as nothing more than a partisan legislation by the Federalists to control the courts.

February 6
DIPLOMACY: Congress authorizes the arming of merchant vessels in light of a declaration of war by the Pasha of Tripoli. The United States is thus preparing to enter a state of limited war without a congressional declaration.
BUSINESS: Secretary of the Treasury Albert Gallatin begins a new government policy of fiscal retrenchment to reduce the national debt. However, he does propose federal aid for the purpose of national road construction to facilitate commerce and frontier settlement. Gallatin, consistent with President Thomas Jefferson's wishes, outlines a plan for severe military reductions and the repeal of all internal taxation.

March 8
POLITICS: The Democratic-Republican dominated Congress repeals the Judicial Act of 1801 at the behest of President Thomas Jefferson.

March 16
MILITARY: A bill authorizing the United States Military Academy at West Point, New York, passes Congress. In promoting its creation, President Thomas Jefferson has two goals for this school: to train professional military engineers whose talents in surveying and road building will greatly facilitate frontier settlement, and to afford political indoctrination for an officer class, rendering them favorably disposed toward democratic republicanism. The site had previously been selected by George Washington.

March 27
DIPLOMACY: The Treaty of Amiens between France, England, the Netherlands, and Spain brings a temporary halt to harassment of American shipping in Europe.

April 6
BUSINESS: The Democratic-Republican controlled Congress repeals all excise taxes, including the hated whiskey tax.

April 14
POLITICS: The Naturalization Act is restored by Congress to mandate a five-year residency requirement for citizenship; this ends the 14-year tenure stipulated under the Alien and Sedition Acts of 1795.

April 24
BUSINESS: Georgia requests help in sorting out the legal entanglement caused by the fraudulent Yazoo land sales of 1795 and the state's 1796 invalidation of the same. The land in question is then ceded to the federal government, for $1.2 million, which ultimately engenders a landmark Supreme Court decision in 1810.

April 29

POLITICS: The Judiciary Act of 1801 is amended by Congress to increase the number of Supreme Court justices to the original number of six, while the court will hold one session per year. Moreover, a system of six circuit courts is established, down from 16, each presided over by a Supreme Court justice.

April 30

SETTLEMENT: The Enabling Act is passed by Congress that allows any territory organized from the Ordnance of 1787 to strive for statehood. The Northwest Territory (Ohio) subsequently begins electing delegates for a state constitutional convention, a precedent followed by other territories similarly disposed.

May 1

DIPLOMACY: President Thomas Jefferson is apprised of and alarmed by Spain's recent sale of the Louisiana Territory to France. He therefore authorizes his minister in Paris, Robert R. Livingston, to negotiate for land on the Mississippi River to use as a port and thereby preserve American navigation rights. Moreover, Livington is to inquire if France would be willing to sell the land in question.

May 3

GENERAL: Washington, D.C., is incorporated as a city and the president is authorized to appoint a mayor.

June 19

BUSINESS: French refugee Éleuthère Irénée du Pont opens up his first gunpowder factory at Wilmington, Delaware.

July 4

MILITARY: The U.S. Military Academy at West Point, New York, is officially opened. This marks the genesis of professionalism in the U.S. Army.

August 11

DIPLOMACY: Spain and the United States agree to a convention which creates a special commission to settle any claims of one nation's citizens against the other.

October 2

BUSINESS: The U.S. Patent Office becomes a new bureau within the Department of State.

October 16

DIPLOMACY: In an alarming development, France forbids the United States from depositing cargo at New Orleans, Louisiana, thereby negating an earlier arrangement reached with Spain, the previous owner. President Thomas Jefferson, anxious to preserve American navigation rights along the Mississippi, begins negotiations to purchase New Orleans and West Florida.

November 29

SETTLEMENT: At Chillicothe, Ohio, a state convention adopts a new constitution, this being the first step in applying for statehood. This is accomplished over the protests and obstructionism of territorial governor Arthur St. Clair, an aristocratically inclined former soldier. The new document closely mirrors the Northwest Ordinance of 1787 and forbids slavery.

1802

December 6
POLITICS: President Thomas Jefferson reemphasizes the necessity of balanced governmental economy in his annual message to Congress. He also declares his intention to further reduce the power of the federal government.

1803

ARCHITECTURE: New York City Hall is designed and built by John McComb; it is considered today one of the nation's best surviving examples of Georgian style.
DIPLOMACY: The resumption of warfare between France and Great Britain in Europe leads to continuing attacks upon neutral shipping at sea. Both sides prove equally rapacious towards American commerce, but the new spate of impressment of American seaman by the British leads to escalating national anger over the practice.
RELIGION: The Albrights, professing a combination of Methodist and Lutheran doctrines, is formed when Jacob Albright is ordained in Lebanon County, Pennsylvania. After 1816 they are known as the Evangelical Association.
SOCIETAL: The first tax-supported public library is founded in Salisbury, Connecticut.

January
EXPLORATION: President Thomas Jefferson, desirous of securing friendly relations with Native American tribes in the interior and expanding the nation's internal commercial boundaries, prevails on Congress to fund a small western exploratory expedition led by two army officers.

January 11
DIPLOMACY: President Thomas Jefferson appoints fellow Virginian James Monroe as minister plenipotentiary to France and orders him to Paris to join American minister Robert R. Livingston. Monroe is instructed to offer $2 million for the purchase of New Orleans and West Florida—he is authorized to spend upwards of $10 million.

February 4
ARTS: William Dunlap, the nation's first professional playwright, adapts his play *The Voice of Nature* from a contemporary French work of the same name. This is the earliest example of melodrama for the stage in America, having been pioneered in France, and features starkly drawn villainous and virtuous characters, with the latter usually prevailing.

February 24
LAW: The landmark *Marbury v. Madison* case is dramatically decided by Chief Justice John Marshall of the U.S. Supreme Court. Henceforth the Court declares its implied power to render null and void any action by Congress which is deemed unconstitutional. This is also the first time that the high Court has voided a congressional act. The process of judicial review is thereby established, making the Supreme Court first among equals in the balance of power among the three branches of government.

March 1
POLITICS: Ohio enters the union as the 17th state; because it is carved from territory established by the Northwest Ordnance of 1787, slavery was already excluded and is never an issue.

March 3
SETTLEMENT: Congress authorizes the sale of all uncommitted land within the Mississippi Territory.

April

SCIENCE: Naturalist John James Audubon is the first American to practice banding birds for scientific observation.

April 12

DIPLOMACY: James Monroe, minister plenipotentiary to France, arrives in Paris to assist American minister Robert R. Livingston in an attempt to purchase New Orleans and West Florida from the First Consulate of Napoleon Bonaparte. By this time, Napoleon's attention has shifted back to warfare on the European continent and he readily abandons prior notions of resurrecting a French empire in the New World. His foreign minister, Talleyrand, inquires how much the United States would be willing to offer for the entire Louisiana Territory.

April 19

BUSINESS: With French prodding, Spain reinstitutes the right to deposit stores at New Orleans, an economic essential for American traders there.

May

TECHNOLOGY: Benjamin H. Latrobe gives a less-than glowing assessment of the current state of steam technology in his report to the American Philosophical Society in Philadelphia. This is only four years before Robert Fulton's spectacularly successful steamboat *Clermont*.

May 2

DIPLOMACY: In Paris, James Madison and Robert R. Livingston arrange to purchase the entire Louisiana Territory (828,000 square miles) for $11 million. This purchase literally doubles the size of the United States and encompasses a region that will eventually give rise to the states of Arkansas, Colorado, Iowa, Kansas, Louisiana, Minnesota, Missouri, Montana, Nebraska, North Dakota, Oklahoma, South Dakota, and Wyoming. The Americans also conclude a convention to assume claims by French citizens against the United States worth $3.7 million. Napoleon Bonaparte, eager to embark on a war of conquest in Europe and already saddled with a costly rebellion in Haiti, sells the land at a bargain price in exchange for a quick infusion of cash.

May 23

NAVAL: Captain Edward Preble, a stern, no-nonsense disciplinarian, is appointed commodore of the Mediterranean Squadron. His aggressive brand of leadership proves infectious to all ranks.

June 7

DIPLOMACY: Indiana territorial governor William Henry Harrison concludes a treaty with representatives of nine Native American tribes, whereby the latter cede land along the Wabash River. This constitutes the first white intrusion beyond the fixed barriers established by the 1795 Treaty of Greenville and sparks the rise of nativist resistance throughout the Old Northwest.

August 17

MILITARY: Captain John Whistler marches his company of infantry to the site of present-day Chicago, Illinois, and commences construction of Fort Dearborn.

August 31

EXPLORATION: The first government-sponsored exploratory expedition, headed by army captains Meriwether Lewis and William Clark, departs down the Ohio River. They will not return from their epic voyage for three years, and their

Lewis, Meriwether   (1774–1809)
Explorer

Meriwether Lewis was born in Albemarle, Virginia, on August 18, 1774, son of a Continental Army officer. He was attracted to military life and in 1794 he joined the militia to help suppress the Whiskey Rebellion in western Pennsylvania. Lewis subsequently served with the U.S. Army in 1794 and fought under General Anthony Wayne at the Battle of Fallen Timbers. At that time he also befriended Lieutenant William Clark and the two became lifelong friends. Lewis then completed several tours of duty along the western frontier and served as regimental paymaster at Detroit. However, his fortunes dramatically shifted in 1801 when President Thomas Jefferson invited him to Washington, D.C., to serve as his personal secretary. After the Louisiana Purchase of 1803, Jefferson sought to outfit a small but professional scientific expedition to explore the new region. His goal was to facilitate western migration and also learn more about new furbearing regions to expand trade. He consequently selected Lewis, who was highly adept at astronomy, navigation, and mapmaking, to head the expedition. Once Congress granted approval for the endeavor both Lewis and his friend Clark were commissioned captains in the new "Corps of Discovery." The two departed St. Louis in May 1804, assisted by the Shoshone woman Sacagawea, and gradually wended their way as far west as Oregon on the Pacific coast. En route they met and befriended numerous tribes of Native Americans who had never heard of the United States. After wintering at Astoria, Oregon, the party commenced the return leg of its journey, with Lewis and Clark taking separate routes. The expedition finally ended at St. Louis on September 23, 1806, after covering more than 4,000 miles with the loss of only one man through illness. Lewis's minute observations did much to enhance the geographical, botanical, and scientific knowledge of the region, and President Jefferson appointed him governor of the new Louisiana Territory.

Lewis had acquired national renown for his explorations, but temperamentally he was unsuited for political office. Sullen and inflexible, he argued incessantly with local officials and became unpopular with the inhabitants. He was also uncommunicative with superiors back in Washington, D.C., and failed to consult with them in advance about his plans. After only a year and a half in office, Lewis was summoned back to the national capital to explain his boorish behavior to superiors. He was also going east to push for publication of his detailed journals under the aegis of Nicholas Biddle of Philadelphia. Lewis proceeded along the celebrated Natchez Trace—the "Devil's Backbone"—to a point near Nashville, Tennessee, where he checked into an inn on October 11, 1809. He died there suddenly at the age of 35. It has never been ascertained if Lewis's death was the result of murder, suicide, or natural causes, and speculation remains rife. Despite a sometimes stormy disposition, his sound leadership proved essential to the conduct of a daring expedition that opened the western frontier to the American nation.

endeavors greatly enhance the scientific and geographical knowledge of the American interior. President Thomas Jefferson, intending to lessen the influence of commercial elites along the east coast, feels that settlement of the frontier will lead to a dominant, agrarian-based, yeoman farmer class, hence the region they inhabit becomes "the bulwark of Liberty."

1803

Clark, William   (1770–1838)
Explorer

William Clark was born in Caroline County, Virginia, on August 1, 1770, a younger brother of Revolutionary War hero George Rogers Clark. He was raised in Kentucky, exposed to the nuances of frontier life, and also inculcated with the habits and mannerisms of Native American tribes. He joined the U.S. Army as an ensign in 1791 and served under General Anthony Wayne at the Battle of Fallen Timbers, 1794. Around this time he struck up a close acquaintance with fellow officer Ensign Meriwether Lewis, the two becoming fast friends. Clark then returned home in 1796 to manage his plantation in Kentucky, but in 1803 he was contacted by Lewis to join the "Corps of Discovery" established by President Thomas Jefferson to explore the vast reaches of the Louisiana Purchase. In May 1804 Lewis and Clark departed Pittsburgh in keelboats and wended their way westward, greatly assisted by the Shoshone woman Sacajawea. Clark himself was well-versed at dealing with Native Americans, and his tact and diplomacy while encountering numerous tribes insured a peaceful transit. Over the next two years Clark artfully mapped the terrain they covered up as far as the Pacific Northwest and back, which greatly contributed to American knowledge of the interior. Reputedly his draftsmanship was so accurate that the maps required only minor alterations 50 years later. Clark also compiled a military journal of events which was published in 1807, became an instant best seller, and greatly stimulated interest in western migration.

Clark resigned from the military again in February 1807 to become Indian agent of the Louisiana Territory and brigadier general of militia. For the next six years he labored ceaselessly to cultivate better relations with nearby Indians, then stressed by the tide of white encroachment, and conducted several chiefs to Washington, D.C., to confer with President James Madison. He became a familiar fixture at many Indian councils, and they relied upon him for fair and honest advice. Moreover, Clark believed that the best way of promoting good relations between whites and Native Americans was through commerce and feared that unscrupulous traders would incite unrest and violence. When the War of 1812 broke out Clark was tasked with guarding the thinly populated Missouri region from attack, and he was appointed the first territorial governor. Here he was hampered by scanty resources and manpower, but in 1814 he conducted an expedition up the Mississippi River to Prairie du Chien, Wisconsin, constructed Fort Shelby, and raised the American flag there. After the war Clark was authorized to conclude several peace treaties with the remaining hostile tribes, and in 1821 he lost his sole bid to become governor of Missouri. He then served as superintendent of Indian affairs at St. Louis for the next 16 years and facilitated their eventual removal to new homelands in the Kansas Territory. Clark died in St. Louis on September 1, 1838, receiving the lavish state funeral usually accorded a national hero.

September 29
RELIGION: Boston formally dedicates its first Roman Catholic Church.

October 20
POLITICS: The Senate ratifies the purchase of the Louisiana Territory on a vote of 24 to seven. This had proved something of a thorny issue, ideologically, to the

Democratic-Republicans, as there was no provision for such an acquisition in the Constitution. President Thomas Jefferson and his followers had no recourse but to backpedal and adopt the Federalist "broad constructionist" interpretation of that document, based on the concept of implied powers.

October 31
NAVAL: Disaster strikes when the frigate USS *Philadelphia* under Captain William Bainbridge grounds in Tripoli Harbor while chasing an enemy vessel and is captured; plans are then made by Commodore Edward Preble to destroy the vessel at its berth.

November 12
NAVAL: The American naval squadron under Commodore Edward Preble establishes a blockade of Tripoli Harbor and warns neutral vessels to steer clear.

December 9
POLITICS: The Twelfth Amendment to the Constitution is passed by Congress; this mandates that candidates for president and vice president must be on separate ballots to avert tie votes, as happened to Thomas Jefferson and Aaron Burr in 1800.

December 19
BUSINESS: Congress repeals the Bankruptcy Act of 1800.

December 20
SETTLEMENT: President Thomas Jefferson, Mississippi Territory governor William C. Claiborne, and General James Wilkinson attend ceremonies at New Orleans, Louisiana, marking the formal transfer of that territory from France to the United States. This fortuitous acquisition literally doubles the size of the United States and pushes it closer to a two-ocean power.

December 24
SOCIETAL: American Elizabeth Patterson, daughter of wealthy businessman William Patterson, marries Jerome Bonaparte, younger brother of Napoleon, in Baltimore.

1804

AGRICULTURE: The first agricultural fair is held in Washington, D.C., and soon becomes a common sight in rural and frontier communities.

EDUCATION: Rhode Island College is renamed Brown University in honor of a wealthy benefactor, Nicholas Brown.

LAW: Despite its incorporation into the United States, the new Louisiana Territory maintains the Code Napoleon as its legal basis, which is subsequently carried on into statehood. This is in direct contrast to the rest of the country, which utilizes English-based common and statutory laws.

PUBLISHING: John Marshall publishes the first volume of his *Life of George Washington,* with the remaining four volumes appearing up through 1807. It remains the most authoritative biography of this seminal figure for half a century.

RELIGION: Charles Bulfinch designs St. Stephen's Catholic Church in Boston; it is also known as the New North Church.

January 5

POLITICS: Samuel Chase, a federal associate justice of the U.S. Supreme Court, is investigated by the House of Representatives for allegedly biased conduct in cases involving publisher James T. Callender for sedition and John Fries for his role in a tax rebellion.

February 15

SLAVERY: The New Jersey legislature adopts laws mandating the gradual emancipation of African-American slaves.

February 16

NAVAL: In a stunning naval upset, Lieutenant Stephen Decatur leads a cutting-out expedition that recaptures the 38-gun frigate USS *Philadelphia* in Tripoli Harbor, then burns it under the city's cannon. Decatur had sailed into the harbor with only 75 sailors on board a captured Tripolitan ketch, pulled alongside, then quickly stormed his objective without loss of life. British Admiral Horatio Nelson declares it the boldest act of his day, and it establishes Decatur as the doyen of the naval officer corps for the next two decades.

POLITICS: Alexander Hamilton publicly slurs Aaron Burr during the New York gubernatorial election, dismissing him as "a dangerous man."

February 25

POLITICS: The Democratic-Republicans, holding their first regular party caucus, unanimously nominate Thomas Jefferson for president and George Clinton of New York for vice president.

March 12

LAW: The U.S. Senate impeaches John Pickering, a federal district judge from New Hampshire, on the grounds of intoxication, profanity, and other offenses judged detrimental to his performance on the bench. This is the latest manifestation of President Thomas Jefferson's ongoing strife with the Federalist-dominated courts.

March 26

SETTLEMENT: The Land Act of 1804 is passed by Congress to amend the Harrison Land Law of 1800; this lowers the price of public lands to $1.64 an acre and allows the sale of 160 acre units called quarter sections. Credit terms are also liberalized and payments extended for a period of 10 years.

Congress establishes the Territory of Orleans in the southern Louisiana Territory, comprising land west the Mississippi River. The remaining land constitutes the new District of Louisiana.

April 25

POLITICS: Aaron Burr is defeated in his bid for the New York governorship and correctly blames Alexander Hamilton for slandering him in the state press.

April 29

NAVAL: The Mediterranean Squadron under Commodore Edward Preble captures two Tripolitan warships.

May 14

EXPLORATION: The Lewis and Clark expedition of 33 men departs St. Louis, Missouri Territory, in a keelboat and two pirogue boats, and begins paddling up

1804

Decatur, Stephen (1779–1820)
Naval officer

Stephen Decatur was born in Sinepuxent, Maryland, on January 5, 1779, part of a seafaring family. After briefly attending the University of Pennsylvania, he joined the merchant marine at an early age and in 1798 received a midshipman's commission in the U.S. Navy. Decatur distinguished himself in this capacity throughout the Quasi War with France, 1798–1800, and rose to lieutenant in 1803. That year Decatur accompanied the American squadron dispatched to the Mediterranean to combat the Barbary pirates of North Africa. During the night of February 16, 1804, he led a cutting-out expedition which boarded the captured frigate USS *Philadelphia,* burned it at its moorings, and safely escaped with the loss of only one man wounded. This singular act captured the American public, established Decatur's reputation as a daring naval officer, and resulted in his promotion to captain at the age of 24. Until hostilities ceased in 1804, Decatur subsequently distinguished himself in other hand-to-hand actions off Tripoli and furthered his reputation. When the War of 1812 commenced, Decatur was commanding the large, 44-gun frigate USS *United States,* and on October 12, 1812, he confronted the slightly smaller British 38-gun warship HMS *Macedonian.* Using superb sailing skills, Decatur expertly devastated his opponent with 70 broadsides, gaining the second surprise victory over the heretofore unbeatable Royal Navy. However, the British fleet soon enveloped the American coastline in a blockade, and Decatur proved unable to get to sea for two years. On January 15, 1815, he managed to slip the large frigate USS *President* out of New York harbor but the ship then struck a sandbar during a gale and was badly damaged. He was then set upon by a squadron of British warships, defeated the nearest of these, then surrendered to the remaining two.

Defeat did not diminish Decatur's stature as a national hero, and in the summer of 1815 he commanded a new, nine-ship squadron tasked with stopping Algerian depredations against American shipping. In a short and brilliant campaign he captured two warships and forced the beys of Algiers, Tunisia, and Tripoli to sign peace treaties and pay indemnities. His activity finally ended the scourge of Mediterranean piracy and he sailed home to additional laurels. In November 1815 Decatur won a position on the Board of Navy Commissioners to modernize the administration of that service. He also gained renown by proffering the oft-quoted toast, "Our country! In her intercourse with foreign nations may she always be in the right, but right or wrong—our country!" He performed well for six years but entered into a fatal controversy in 1820 by voting to deny Captain James Barron his promotion. Barron had earlier been disgraced by the 1807 *Chesapeake-Leopard* affair and he blamed Decatur for conspiring against him and then challenged Decatur to a duel. Decatur readily accepted the challenge and was fatally wounded near Bladensburg, Maryland, on March 22, 1820. He remains the most accomplished naval officer of his age.

the Missouri River toward the interior of the continent. Among them is the 16-year-old Shoshone girl, Sacagawea, who has been hired to act as a guide with her French fur-trader husband.

1804

Sacagawea (ca. 1790–ca. 1884)

Indian woman guide

Boinaiv ("Grass Maiden") was born among the Lehmi band of the Shoshone (Snake) nation in central Idaho around 1790, the daughter of a prominent chief. At the age of 11 she was kidnapped by a band of hostile Hidatsa warriors and taken to their village. There she received the name Sacagawea ("Bird Woman") and lived among the people, traveling with them. At some time in her journeys, Sacagawea encountered the French trader Toussaint Charbonneau, who bought her from captivity and eventually married her. The couple was residing at a Mandan Indian village in present-day North Dakota when an American expedition headed by captains Meriwether Lewis and William Clark arrived to spend the winter of 1805 there. Lewis and Clark, realizing they needed experienced capable guides and translators, hired both Charbonneau and his wife to accompany them on their sojourn to the Pacific coast. Sacagawea's fluency in the Shoshone dialect was considered essential to this task because the expedition would have to obtain horses and other supplies from that tribe in order to cross the Continental Divide. Prior to departing Sacagawea gave birth to a son named Jean Baptiste Charbonneau on February 11, 1805, although this latest addition to the expedition was simply strapped to her back and she marched on with the others that April.

As the journey unfolded, Lewis and Clark came to highly value Sacagawea's linguistic and navigational skills, along with her skills as a botanist. Invariably, at each campsite, she would go off into the bushes to procure various kinds of edible roots to supplement the soldiers' meager rations. This teenage guide was apparently quite fearless and on one occasion she dove into a river to rescue many artifacts that had spilled over when a canoe capsized. At length Sacagawea led the party into the heart of the Shoshone homeland, which she recognized but had not visited for many years. The Native Americans of this region believed that a party of men led by a woman invariably came in peace, and their extended their hospitality to the strangers. At this juncture Lewis and Clark were introduced to Chief Cameahwait, whom Sacagawea instantly recognized as her older brother and a tearful reunion ensued. She then explained the need for horses to her hosts, which were provided, and she remained with the expedition as they wintered at the present location of Astoria in Oregon. Sacagawea subsequently accompanied the expedition back east at which point she disappears from the historical record. Certain accounts place her death at Fort Lisa, Nebraska, on December 20, 1812, while tribal traditions maintain she lived among the Wild River Shoshone in Wyoming until 1884, when she died at the age of around 100 years. Regardless of her fate, the youthful Sacagawea made invaluable contributions to the Lewis and Clark expedition, who valued her presence and wrote favorably of her in their journals. Several statues have been erected in her memory in St. Louis, Portland, and other locations.

May 21

EXPLORING: The Lewis and Clark expedition arrives at the home of frontier legend Daniel Boone in Missouri.

1804

July 11–12

POLITICS: Aaron Burr challenges Alexander Hamilton to a duel for his role in derailing the former's political aspirations in New York. The two men confront each other at Weehawken, New Jersey. Hamilton deliberately misfires his gun while Burr takes deliberate aim and fatally wounds his antagonist. This act effectively ends Burr's political career.

August 3–4

NAVAL: Commodore Edward Preble takes the unprecedented step of arranging his Mediterranean Squadron in bombardment positions and shelling the port city of Tripoli. His nine ships and nine gunboats engage nine Tripolitan shore batteries, yet the Americans manage to sink three gunboats and capture four more at a cost of 54 casualties.

August 13

DIPLOMACY: Indiana territorial governor William Henry Harrison arranges the purchase of additional land from the Delaware Indians, this time encompassing the region between the Wabash and Ohio Rivers.

August 18–27

DIPLOMACY: Indiana territorial governor William Henry Harrison signs two treaties at Vincennes for lands north and south of the Ohio River.

September 4

NAVAL: The captured brig *Intrepid*, manned by Lieutenant Richard Somers and 13 sailors, explodes in Tripoli Harbor after its cargo of gunpowder is accidentally detonated, killing everyone on board.

September 25

POLITICS: The Twelfth Amendment to the Constitution is ratified; hereafter presidential and vice presidential candidates run separately on their own ballots.

October

EXPLORATION: A government expedition headed by scientists William Dunbar and Dr. George Hunter departs Natchez, Mississippi, and paddles down the Red and Ouachita Rivers into present-day Arkansas.

October 1

POLITICS: Jeffersonian stalwart William C. Claiborne is appointed governor of the Territory of Orleans, with his seat of government at the city of New Orleans. The United States is finally in control of the mouth of the Mississippi River, which proves to be a major economic conduit for the interior of the country.

November 2

EXPLORATION: The Lewis and Clark expedition winters near the site of present-day Bismarck, North Dakota. They encamp at a village of friendly Mandan Indians along the banks of the Upper Missouri River, having successfully negotiated treacherous waters on the Missouri River and an encounter with hostile Sioux Indians.

November 3

DIPLOMACY: Indiana territorial governor William Henry Harrison strikes an accord with the Sac and Fox Indians to acquire five million acres in present-day Wisconsin for the United States. The natives retain the right to remain on the land.

1804

November 29
EDUCATION: The New York Historical Society is founded in New York City by John Pintard, Mayor DeWitt Clinton, Judge Egbert Benson, and Dr. David Hosack. This institution is dedicated to the collection and preservation of important documents relating to American history.

December 5
POLITICS: In the first presidential election under the Twelfth Amendment, Thomas Jefferson decisively outpolls Charles C. Pinckney with 162 votes to 14 while vice president George Clinton eclipses Rufus King by the identical margin. Moreover, the Democratic-Republicans maintain their large majorities in the Congress and thus completely control the political agenda of the nation.

1805

ART: Painter Charles Willson Peale opens America's second public art gallery, the Pennsylvania Academy of Fine Art, in Philadelphia. The first such institution, the New York Academy of Fine Arts, folded the previous year.
BUSINESS: The first known shipment of ice is carried by merchant captain Frederick Tudor to the French island of Martinique; thereafter it becomes a valuable export to the tropics and other warm climes.
DIPLOMACY: As warfare escalates in Europe, Napoleon issues the Berlin and Milan Decrees and Great Britain invokes the Orders in Council; both have the effect of barring neutral shipping from entering each other's harbors at the risk of confiscation. However, the continuing British practice of impressing American seamen for service on Royal Navy warships leads to increasing resentment against that nation.
EDUCATION: Georgetown College, founded in 1789 as the first Catholic institution of higher learning, is transferred to the Society of Jesus (Jesuits).
EXPLORING: Scientists William Dunbar and Dr. George Hunter conclude their exploration down the Red and Ouachita Rivers and return to Natchez, Mississippi. One result of this government-sponsored endeavor is the first glimpse of mineral wells at Hot Springs, Arkansas.
PUBLISHING: Female historian Mercy Warren Otis publishes her *Rise, Progress, and Termination of the American Revolution*, based on her firsthand knowledge of events and major players. However, her biased treatment of John Adams for aristocratic pretensions leads to a breakdown to their former friendship.

January 11
SETTLEMENT: The Michigan Territory is created from a division of the Indiana Territory; William Hull, a distinguished soldier of the Revolutionary War, is appointed the first governor with his seat of government at Detroit.

February 15
SOCIETAL: A German-speaking utopian community is created by George Rapp at Harmonie in western Pennsylvania. The 600 inhabitants agree to surrender all their worldly possessions for the betterment of the community.

February 17
SETTLEMENT: In Louisiana, New Orleans is incorporated as a city.

March 1

LAW: Supreme Court Justice Samuel Chase, having been impeached by the House of Representatives for inappropriate behavior, is tried and acquitted in the Senate. He then resumes his seat on the bench with a somewhat tarnished reputation, but his survival discourages future administrations from attempting to remove judges for political reasons.

March 3

SETTLEMENT: Congress establishes the Louisiana Territory from the Louisiana District and enacts legislation confirming all French and Spanish land grants extant. The capital is then designated at St. Louis.

March 4

POLITICS: Thomas Jefferson is inaugurated for his second term as president while George Clinton is sworn in as vice president, replacing Aaron Burr. In his address the chief executive notes the passing of internal taxation in favor of consumption taxes on luxury items and also speaks favorably about publicly funded public works such as roads.

March 6

MILITARY: A remarkable and improbable military campaign unfolds as American Consul William Eaton and U.S. Marine Lieutenant Presley O'Bannon march from Alexandria, Egypt, with seven marines and 400 Arab and Greek mercenaries. They are determined to storm the Tripolitan city of Derna on the North African coast.

April 7

EXPLORING: The Lewis and Clark expedition decamps from its Mandan Indian village and resumes paddling up the Missouri River, assisted by the 16-year-old Shoshone guide, Sacagawea. The Corps of Expedition consists of 26 men in six canoes and two large pirogues.

April 26

EXPLORING: The Lewis and Clark expedition arrives at the mouth of the Yellowstone River.

April 27

MILITARY: A small American expedition commanded by U.S. Consul William Eaton and Marine Corps Lieutenant Presley O'Bannon captures the port city of Derna from Tripolitan forces, assisted by gunfire from the brigs USS *Nautilus, Hornet,* and *Argus* under Captain Isaac Hull. The victors suffer 14 casualties, including one dead Marine. Hamet Karamanli, brother of Pasha Yusuf, is then placed on the throne as an opposition figure. This is the first real victory in the war against the Barbary pirates and also the first time the American flag flies over an enemy fortification.

May 1

SLAVERY: The Virginia legislature enacts a law ordering all free African Americans to leave the state or face imprisonment.

May 25

LABOR: Members of the Federal Society of Cordwainers (shoemakers) are arrested by law enforcement authorities and charged with striking for an increase of wages, a violation of English common law. This marks the first time that the judicial system has intervened on behalf of an employer to settle a work dispute. It also denotes a hostile attitude of the judiciary toward labor, which lasts several decades.

May 26
EXPLORING; The Lewis and Clark expedition attempts crossing the Rocky Mountains down the Jefferson River but is thwarted. They then elect to proceed on foot through the Lemhi Pass and thence across the continental divide.

June 4
DIPLOMACY: A peace agreement is reached between the United States and the Barbary state of Tripoli; the Americans pay a one-time $60,000 ransom to release Captain William Bainbridge and 306 sailors of the captured USS *Philadelphia*, but thereafter commerce is assured free passage throughout the Mediterranean Sea without further tribute.

June 11
EXPLORING: The Lewis and Clark expedition catches its first glimpse of the Great Falls of the Missouri River.
GENERAL: The newly acquired settlement of Detroit, Michigan, is nearly destroyed in a fire.

July 1
SETTLEMENT: Congress carves the Michigan and Indiana Territories from the remaining Northwest Territory.

July 23
DIPLOMACY: In a case regarding the American vessel *Essex*, an English court decides that any neutral ship visiting an enemy port can be subject to seizure unless the captain can demonstrate that his final voyage was to an American port. This action, based on the Rule of 1756, clears the way for additional maritime seizures by British warships plying the French West Indies, where most of the trade occurs.

July 25
POLITICS: Former vice president Aaron Burr arrives at New Orleans, allegedly to help plot a separatist state with that city as its capital.

July 27
EXPLORING: The Lewis and Clark expedition reaches the three forks of the Missouri River, at which point the exhausted explorers go ashore to rest.

August 9
EXPLORING: Lieutenant Zebulon M. Pike is ordered by General James Wilkinson to seek out the source of the Mississippi River within territory acquired by the Louisiana Purchase. This day he departs St. Louis with 20 men into the region of present-day Minnesota.

October 1
EXPLORING: The Lewis and Clark expedition concludes a harsh overland trek through the Bitterroot Mountains and then places its canoes in the waters of the Clearwater River.

October 10
EXPLORING: Tramping overland from the continental divide, the Lewis and Clark expedition encounters the Snake River, which flows westward. They then paddle downstream and enter the Columbia River a week later.

Pike, Zebulon M.   (1777–1813)

Explorer

Zebulon Montgomery Pike was born in Trenton, New Jersey, on January 5, 1777, son of a Continental army officer. He entered his father's company of the 2nd Infantry at the age of 15 and served with General Anthony Wayne in the Northwest Indian War, 1790–94. Pike's education to this point had been meager; nonetheless, he possessed considerable drive to excel and studied mathematics, science, and Spanish on his own. Afterward he served in the garrison at Kaskaskia, Illinois, coming to the attention of General James Wilkinson, commanding general of the Louisiana Territory. This huge expanse had been acquired in 1803 and remained largely unexplored. Therefore Wilkinson ordered Pike to outfit a small overland expedition for the purpose of establishing friendly contacts with native Americans living there, invite their chiefs to St. Louis, report on the activities of British traders, identify the source of the Mississippi River, and provide detailed geographic and geological information. Pike departed St. Louis on August 9, 1805 with 20, men and ascended the Mississippi River in a 20-foot keelboat. He ventured far upstream and established contacts with the Sioux tribe, wintered on the future site of Fort Snelling, Minnesota, and explored the adjacent region on sled. Pike also encountered Leech Lake, which he wrongly believed was the source of the Mississippi. He then warned British traders off American territory before returning to St. Louis on April 30, 1806. Pike covered 5,000 miles in nine months, contributing greatly to the knowledge of the American interior.

In July 1806 Wilkinson ordered Pike on another foray, this time along the southwestern fringes of the Louisiana Purchase to locate the source of the Red River. He was also to gather military intelligence as to the Spanish army in the region. Pike departed, entered the area known as Colorado and identified the 14,000-foot mountain known today as Pike's Peak. In January 1807 the expedition turned south toward the Red River and accidentally entered Spanish territory, where Pike and his men were arrested by Spanish authorities and brought to Mexico for questioning. He was then released and arrived back at Natchitoches, Louisiana, a hero. There he was apprised of the arrest of Aaron Burr and Wilkinson's possible complicity in a conspiracy, but Pike was cleared of any participation. Furthermore, his endeavors, along with that of Meriwether Lewis and William Clark, made possible the wave of western immigration that followed in subsequent decades. Pike remained in the military, rising to brigadier general by March 1813 and tasked with outfitting an amphibious expedition on Lake Ontario. His objective was to capture the Canadian town of York (Toronto), Ontario, which was successfully stormed on April 27, 1813. However, a British magazine exploded after the town's surrender, whereby Pike was mortally wounded by a falling rock. He died later that same day, an enterprising officer and accomplished explorer.

November 7

EXPLORING: The Lewis and Clark expedition arrives at the source of the Columbia River and catches their first glimpse of the Pacific Ocean from present-day Astoria, Oregon. They also construct Fort Clatsop over the winter, having covered 4,000 miles in 18 months.

1805

December 4
POLITICS: In his annual message to Congress, President Thomas Jefferson strikes a untypically bellicose tone, apparently intending to intimidate the Spanish.

December 9
POLITICS: The Ninth Congress assembles with the Democratic-Republicans enjoying a clear ascendancy over the Federalists by a margin of 27 to seven in the Senate and 116 to 25 in the House of Representatives.

1806

ARCHITECTURE: Asher Benjamin designs and builds the Old West Church in Boston as a stirring example of the Federal style.

ART: Charles Willson Peale depicts the retrieval of fossilized mastodon bones in a painting called *Exhuming the Mastodon*, quite possibly the first time paleontology has been displayed as art. When the bones are recovered in New York, they are brought to Philadelphia, assembled, and displayed in Peale's museum of scientific curiosities.

TECHNOLOGY: David Melville designs and builds the first gas-powered streetlamps in Newport, Rhode Island.

January
BUSINESS: President Thomas Jefferson orders the U.S. Mint to stop issuing silver dollars; production will not resume until 1836.

EXPLORING: The Lewis and Clark expedition winters at Fort Clatsop (Astoria, Oregon), spending their time organizing copious notes taken and numerous maps drawn during the previous year. The information they have recorded touches upon science, geography, ethnology, and meteorology.

PUBLISHING: Noah Webster, grammarian and lexicographer, compiles his *Compendius Dictionary of the English Language,* intended to impart standardized American English. He has since abandoned earlier attempts to completely "Americanize" the English language and make it distinct from its European counterpart. Still, his retention of such Americanisms as *lengthy, sot, spry, gunning, belittle,* and *caucus* are denounced in certain quarters as "wigwam words" and he is charged with coarsening the language.

TRANSPORTATION: Congress votes funding to construct the Natchez Road, running 500 miles from Nashville, Tennessee, to Natchez, Mississippi.

January 25
POLITICS: Secretary of State James Madison delivers a blistering condemnation of British harassment of American shipment on the high seas, including the impressment of American seamen. His report stokes the rising tide of anti-English sentiments.

February 12
POLITICS: The Senate passes a resolution roundly condemning high-handed British behavior on the open seas as a violation of America's neutral rights. The British ignore the proceedings entirely.

March 29
TRANSPORTATION: Congress votes to authorize federal funding to construct the Cumberland Road from Cumberland, Maryland, to Wheeling, West Virginia, for

the economic benefits it will confer. This route ultimately reaches as far west as Vandalia, Illinois.

April

EXPLORING: A 40-man expedition under Captain Richard Sparks and noted astronomer Thomas Freeman depart Natchez, Louisiana Territory, to search for the source of the Red River.

April 5

BUSINESS: In Spanish-occupied San Francisco, authorities decide to allow trade relations with new Russian settlements in Alaska. This principally entails the sale of food to keep the settlers from starving over their long winter.

April 18

BUSINESS: The Nicholson Act is passed by Congress which forbids the importation of enumerated British products such as brass, hemp, flax, tin, and certain woolen textiles to protect nascent American industries. This is in response to continued harassment of American ships and crews at sea.

April 30

EXPLORING: The expedition headed by Lieutenant Zebulon M. Pike returns to St. Louis after unsuccessfully searching for the source of the Mississippi River in present-day Minnesota.

May

DIPLOMACY: President Thomas Jefferson instructs William Pinkney to serve as a special envoy to England. Once in London he is to assist American minister James Monroe in seeking a diplomatic end to the British practice of impressment, indemnity for American ships and cargos seized, and a safe resumption of the West Indian trade.

May 19

EDUCATION: The Lancastrian system of education, which employs pupil-teachers to instruct less advanced students, debuts in a New York City school. This approach to teaching is considered desirable owing to the lower costs involved in employing students.

May 30

SOCIETAL: Andrew Jackson, one-time supreme court justice of Tennessee, enraged over a personal insult, kills lawyer Charles Dickinson in a duel.

June 2

EXPLORING: Captain Richard Sparks, 2nd U.S. Infantry, departs his camp in Natchitoches, Louisiana, in search of the source of the Red River.

June 5

SPORT: In New York City, the horse Yankee is the first animal to trot a mile in two minutes, 59 seconds, breaking the three-minute mile.

June 15

EXPLORING: The Lewis and Clark expedition ascends the Rocky Mountains to begin its return voyage back to St. Louis. Once across, they divide into three smaller parties to cover and explore as much terrain as possible.

1806

July 15

EXPLORING: Lieutenant Zebulon M. Pike departs Fort Bellfontaine, Missouri Territory, to explore and chart parts of the Old Southwest (New Mexico and Colorado). He is officially instructed to avoid violating Spanish territory.

July 20

POLITICAL: Brilliant and disgruntled politician Aaron Burr meets on Blenderhasset's Island in the Ohio River with Irish adventurer Harman Blenderhasset. They are prepared to engage in some kind of private military expedition, possibly in the West, for the purpose of establishing an independent republic.

August

RELIGION: The Brethren is founded by five students at Williams College, Massachusetts, as the first American society to conduct missionary work in foreign countries.

August 3

EXPLORING: Captain William Clark and his small detachment of explorers reaches the Yellowstone River and begins a descent downstream toward the Missouri River. He is joined there by Captain Meriwether Lewis's detachment three days later.

August 27

DIPLOMACY: American minister James Monroe and special envoy William Pinkney meet in London with Lord Holland in an attempt to stop the British practice of impressment and arrange indemnity for property seized on the high seas. Failure to reach an accord may result in reimposition of nonimportation, a position that fails to change British attitudes.

September 23

EXPLORING: The Lewis and Clark expedition reaches its successful conclusion at St. Louis, two years after it commenced. They cover 7,000 miles of rugged wilderness with the loss of only one man to disease. Beyond the scientific bounty reaped, their labors also demonstrate the viability of reaching the Pacific coast by an overland route.

October 21

MILITARY: In light of continuing tensions with Great Britain, Congress authorizes a new organizational and legal framework for the U.S. Army.

November 15

EXPLORING: Lieutenant Zebulon M. Pike sees a large mountain, soaring 14,000 feet in height, in the distance while exploring the Southwest; it is subsequently christened Pike's Peak in his honor. Shortly afterward he is arrested by Spanish authorities for trespassing, then released.

PUBLISHING: The Yale University *Literary Cabinet* debuts as America's first college magazine.

November 27

POLITICAL: General James Wilkinson, a spy for Spain, reveals to President Thomas Jefferson Aaron Burr's plan for carving out an independent republic from Spanish territory—he does so without implicating himself. Jefferson responds by warning American citizens not to become involved in any illegal military actions against Spain.

1806

December 12
SLAVERY: President Thomas Jefferson asks Congress to approve a ban on all slave imports after January 1, 1808.

December 31
BUSINESS: Trappers and fur traders around the upper Great Lakes form the Michilimackinac Company in an attempt to mount better competition against the British-owned North West Company, operating in the same region.

DIPLOMACY: American minister James Monroe and special envoy William Pinkney sign a treaty with Great Britain, securing a negligible compromise of the issue of West Indian trade. Insofar as the pressing issues of impressment and compensation remain unaddressed, their efforts are a significant failure.

1807

GENERAL: The Boston Athenaeum is founded as a significant source for promoting scholarship and learning among the subscribers. It merges the functions of a library with a social meeting place for the city's commercial, professional, and scientific elite.

January 22
POLITICS: President Thomas Jefferson informs Congress of Aaron Burr's apparent conspiracy; when Burr is informed that his plot has been revealed he attempts to flee the country.

February 10
EXPLORING: Congress authorizes a complete survey of the U.S. coastline, which is then delegated to the Coast Survey within the Treasury Department.

February 19
POLITICS: Aaron Burr is arrested in the Mississippi Territory (Alabama) and charged with conspiring to lead an armed expedition into Spanish territory.

March
DIPLOMACY: When President Thomas Jefferson reviews the newly signed Monroe-Pinckney Treaty, which fails to address either the issue of impressment or indemnifications, he refuses to submit it to the Senate for ratification. As such the effort is a failure for American diplomacy.

March 2
SLAVERY: Following President Thomas Jefferson's plea, Congress prohibits the further importation of African slaves into the United States after January 1, 1808.

March 20
DIPLOMACY: President Thomas Jefferson instructs American minister James Monroe and special envoy William Pinckney to resume negotiations to halt British harassment of American shipborne commerce, using their failed 1806 treaty as a starting point.

March 30
POLITICS: A captive Aaron Burr appears before a federal circuit court headed by Chief Justice John Marshall.

June 22

NAVAL: The 52-gun British warship HMS *Leopard* under Captain Salisbury P. Humphreys, cruising the American coast in search of British deserters, accosts the smaller 39-gun American frigate USS *Chesapeake* of Commodore James Barron, three miles off Norfolk, Virginia. The British captain demands the right to search Barron's vessel for deserters and, when he refuses, the British pour several broadsides into the unprepared Americans. Three American sailors are killed and 18 wounded, while four alleged deserters are removed; one is subsequently hanged. Word of the affair triggers intense anti-British activity nationwide, and Commodore Barron is court-martialed and suspended for five years for failing to order his crew to battle stations.

July

EXPLORING: John Colter enters the Bighorn and Yellowstone basins of the Louisiana Territory (Montana and Wyoming).

July 2

NAVAL: In light of the *Chesapeake-Leopard* incident, President Thomas Jefferson orders all Royal Navy warships in American waters to depart immediately. Jefferson still hopes that peaceful coercion will avert war and result in improved British behavior.

August 3–September 14

POLITICS: Aaron Burr, having been arrested on a misdemeanor, is tried for treason in Richmond, Virginia.

August 17–21

TECHNOLOGY: Inventor Robert Fulton makes a successful passage upon the Hudson River in his steamboat, *Clermont*. This 150-foot-long vessel is powered by a Watt steam engine driving large paddle wheels on either side and can reach a top speed of five miles per hour. Fulton then successfully completes a 62-hour round-trip voyage from New York City to Albany and back, inaugurating the age of steamboat navigation. Commercial operations begin on September 4.

September 1

LAW: Aaron Burr is acquitted of treason at his trial in Richmond, Virginia, principally because presiding Judge John Marshall interprets the law of treason strictly. Burr was not present personally when the alleged treason took place, so he is found innocent by default.

October 1

LITERATURE: The Knickerbocker School of American Literature debuts with the publication of *Salmagundi; or the Whim-Whams and Opinions of Launcelot Longstuff, Esq., and Others*, a collection of satirical jottings by New York writers Washington Irving, William Irving, and James Kirk Paulding. Their writing concentrates on American subject material, rendered in either a realistic or humorous light.

October 17

DIPLOMACY: The British government announces its decision to enforce even harder its policy to arrest British deserters at sea, even if American seamen are impressed into the Royal Navy.

Fulton, Robert   (1765–1815)

Inventor

Robert Fulton was born near Lancaster, Pennsylvania, on November 14, 1765, a son of farmers. While growing up he displayed an aptitude for art and mechanical tinkering and as early as 1779 he was employed by gunsmiths. By 1782 Fulton had established himself as a painter in Philadelphia, but he remained fascinated by the world of engineering. He ventured to England in 1786 to study art under noted expatriate Benjamin West but also beheld a nation in the earliest throes of the Industrial Revolution. Fulton was particularly interested in the promise of new forms of inland transportation, particularly canals, and he developed a double incline system of locks to allow boats to pass through uneven land. He also found the time to secure patents for a marble saw, a flax spinner, and a hemp rope maker. In 1796 Fulton gathered national attention by publishing his booklet *A Treatise on the Improvement of Canal Navigation* and confidently predicted their close integration with another revolutionary transport system, railroads. However, the onset of the French Revolution prompted him to focus on naval matters, and he spent several years perfecting a practical submarine, the *Nautilus,* in 1800. This innovative device enjoyed successful trial runs in both England and France, and actually sank a large frigate during a test, but the admiralties of neither country expressed any interest in what they considered a dangerous novelty.

Fulton returned to the United States around 1802 where he had the good fortune of meeting Robert L. Livingston, minister to France and a wealthy potential investor. At that time he had formalized his plans to invent a practical steamship for river travel and through English contacts managed to obtain a working steam engine from the firm of Boulton and Watt. This represented state-of-the-art technology and was a closely guarded secret, but Fulton secured his engine and began designing a ship around it. The first steamship had been successfully built and demonstrated by John Fitch in 1787, but he failed to attract public interest. Fulton, backed by Livingston, now possessed money for both perfecting the design and marketing it. In 1807 this vessel, christened the *Clermont,* made a successful passage up the Hudson River and back in only 62 hours, initiating regular steamboat service in the United States. Because Livington secured a monopoly, the venture proved extremely lucrative for both men. In the War of 1812 Fulton was also called upon to apply steam technology to military use, and in December 1814 he launched the USS *Demologos* ("Voice of the People") at New York, a heavily armored, steam-driven catamaran and predecessor to the modern warship. Fulton died in New York on February 24, 1815, and the vessel was promptly rechristened *Fulton the First* in his honor. He was America's first civil and military technologist, pioneering both the new ideas and nascent technology of the rapidly industrialized world. He also helped usher in a revolution in transportation systems, which directly facilitated the growth of America's economic infrastructure.

October 26

POLITICS: The Tenth Congress assembles in Washington, D.C., with the Democratic-Republicans still in firm control of both chambers; 28 to six Federalists in the Senate, 118 to 24 in the House.

November 15

DIPLOMACY: The Non-Importation Act against British goods becomes law until the persistent harassment of American commerce at sea ends. However, the government of Great Britain remains quite willing to endure such commercial measures to successfully prosecute their war against Napoleon in Europe.

December 14

BUSINESS: President Thomas Jefferson declares that the Non-Importation Act against England and France is in force.

December 18

BUSINESS: President Thomas Jefferson, faced with continuing seizures of Americans boats and cargos by both France and England, requests a complete embargo on all foreign trade. That same day Congress complies with a 22 to 6 vote in the Senate.

December 21

BUSINESS: The House of Representatives approves President Thomas Jefferson's suggested embargo against all foreign trade, 82 to 44. However, this constitutional right of Congress to control and regulate foreign commerce has disastrous consequences for the American economy and is repealed in 1809.

December 22

BUSINESS: President Thomas Jefferson signs the Embargo Act into law, through which he sought to economically punish France and England for their harassment of neutral American shipping. In the end, it has little effect on the belligerents, greatly stimulates smuggling between New England and Canada, and causes considerable harm to the American economy. Still, Jefferson preferred it to war.

1808

ARTS: New Orleans constructs an opera house costing $100,000, making it the opera capital of the nation. The New York Academy of Fine Arts also opens with former diplomat Robert R. Livingston serving as president. This act also establishes New York City as a leading center for the arts.

American painter John Vanderlyn exhibits his painting *Marius* in France; the Emperor Napoleon I comments on it favorably.

PUBLISHING: The *American Law Journal*, one of the earliest legal magazines in the United States, begins publishing in Baltimore and is edited by Professor John Elihu Hall of the University of Maryland.

RELIGION: Congregationalist Reverence Jedediah Moore founds the Amherst Seminary in Massachusetts to counter Harvard College's increasing liberalism.

SCIENCE: Alexander Wilson publishes the first volume of his attractively illustrated *American Ornithology*, which runs to nine volumes and is finally completed in 1814.

January 1

SLAVERY: As of this date the importation of African slaves into the United States is banned. Violators risk having their vessel confiscated, but all slaves captured become property of the states involved and put up for sale.

January 9

BUSINESS: The existing Embargo Act is expanded by a new, broadened act.

February 11

TECHNOLOGY: Judge Jesse Fell conducts an early experiment with anthracite coal in his home at Wilkes-Barre, Pennsylvania. The material is judged too hot for conventional stoves used in the home but might have minor applications in manufacturing and forging.

April 6

ARTS: James N. Barker's play *The Indian Princess, or La Belle Sauvage* is staged in Philadelphia; this is the first play drawn upon Native American themes and purports to represent incidents in the life of Pocahontas.

BUSINESS: The New York legislature incorporates John Jacob Astor's latest enterprise, the American Fur Company, his attempt to pry domination of the fur trade from foreign hands. Within two decades it acquires a near monopoly on the fur trade.

Astor, John Jacob   (1763–1848)

Businessman

John Jacob Astor was born in Waldorf, Baden (Germany) on July 17, 1763, the son of a butcher. He moved to England at the age of 13 to learn the construction of musical instruments but subsequently migrated to the United States in 1783 and entered the fur trade. A penniless immigrant, Astor clerked for several years in a fur shop in New York, acquired business knowledge firsthand, and slowly tested the lucrative waters of this field. Astor proved so adept at buying and selling furs that by 1786 his business was firmly established and doing a brisk trade in Canada and England. The Jay Treaty of 1794 opened up new venues for trapping in the Old Northwest, and Astor quickly dispatched his agents to acquire furs from American, French, or Canadian trappers, Native Americans, or anyone willing to sell to him. In 1792 he also sponsored the first American commercial vessel to trade with China, where American furs commanded fabulous prices, and brought back the first shipment of Chinese teas, silk, and lacquerware for the burgeoning American market. Astor proved successful in both endeavors and by 1800 he dominated the fur trade throughout North America. In 1808 he capitalized on this by forming the American Fur Company with Ramsey Crooks, through which he aspired to control new fur-bearing lands discovered by Lewis and Clark. In 1811 Astor took the very big risk of establishing a frontier outpost on the Columbia River, Oregon, christened Astoria, in order to monopolize the China fur trade. The following year one of his far west expeditions discovered the South Pass in the Rocky Mountains. Astor subsequently lost Astoria to the British in the War of 1812 but reaped another windfall by offering to finance the war effort by lending the government money at high interest rates.

In addition to fur, Astor was one of the first businessmen to recognize the potential in real estate. Early on he parleyed part of his wealth into acquiring hundreds of acres of land in New York City, and by the 1820s he collected an annual sum of $100,000 in rents. He also operated a fleet of eight ships which invariably visited China with furs and brought back valuable and expensive cargos of Oriental exotica, still in demand. By 1834 the fur trade was declining and Astor

(continues)

(continued)

sold off his company to a partner and spent the rest of his life attending to real estate matters. By the time he died in New York on March 29, 1848, Astor enjoyed a net worth of $10 million, making him the richest man in America—and allegedly the very individual for which the term *millionaire* was coined. Shrewd and ruthless in business, he also had a generous streak, and his will stipulated a specific amount of funding for the Astor Library, which now functions as part of the New York City Public Library system. To this day Astor is still held up as the epitome of the American dream, whereby modest immigrants, through hard work and diligence, can acquire fortunes and happiness deemed unattainable in their native lands.

April 17

BUSINESS: The Emperor Napoleon I issues the Bayonne Decree in response to Jefferson's Embargo Act; this mandates the seizure of all American ships and their cargos in French waters. The resulting losses amount to $10 million.

May 6

TECHNOLOGY: Noted inventor John Steven takes his steam-powered ship *Phoenix* on the first oceanic cruise for a vessel of this type by sailing from Hoboken, New Jersey, to Philadelphia.

July 12

JOURNALISM: The *Missouri Gazette* begins circulating in St. Louis, the first newspaper available west of the Mississippi River.

July 16

BUSINESS: The Missouri Fur Company is founded by trader Manuel Lisa, Pierre Choteau, and William Clark; this arises as a direct result of the Lewis and Clark expedition and knowledge it revealed of new fur-bearing regions.

October

DIPLOMACY: The British government, in an attempt to smooth over ruffled feathers resulting from the *Chesapeake-Leopard* Affair of 1807, dispatches special envoy George Rose to the United States to discuss the matter of reparation payments. However, the British also insist on retraction of President Thomas Jefferson's ordering of their warships out of American waters as a precondition.

October 30

GENERAL: When Captain Benjamin Ireson of the schooner *Betty* refuses to assist a sinking vessel out of fear of losing his own, he is tarred, feathered, and run out of Marblehead, Massachusetts, by angry sailors' wives. In 1857 his plight is recapitulated in a story by John Greenleaf Whitter called "Skipper Ireson's Ride."

November 10

BUSINESS: John Jacob Astor activates the American Fur Company in New York City, wherein he is the sole stockholder; this is the first step in establishing the nation's first business empire. His first goal is to compete successfully with the long established North West Company of Canada for the lucrative fur trade.

1808

DIPLOMACY: The Osage sign the Osage Treaty with the United States, whereby they cede all lands north of the Arkansas River (present-day Arkansas and Missouri) and will be relocated to a reservation in nearby Oklahoma. This sets a precedent that will subsequently be applied to the Cherokee and tribes in the Southwest.

TRANSPORTATION: Secretary of the Treasury Albert Gallatin reports to Congress on the status of roads and canals.

December 7

POLITICS: Thomas Jefferson, declining to run for a third term in office, throws his political support behind Secretary of State and fellow Virginian James Madison in his bid for the presidency. However, the Democratic-Republicans are wracked by dissent as James Monroe and Vice President George Clinton also vie for the nomination. The Federalists again nominate their previous candidates, Charles C. Pinckney and Rufus King; Madison wins the contest handily with 122 electoral votes to 47 for Pinckney and six for Clinton. Clinton nevertheless defeats King for the vice presidency, 113 to 47. However, mounting opposition to the Embargo leads to Federalist gains in the House of Representatives and at the state level.

December 12

RELIGION: The first American Bible Society is founded in Philadelphia by the Reverend William White for promoting the Scriptures.

December 29

GENERAL: Andrew Johnson, 17th president, is born in Raleigh, North Carolina.

1809

ART: Charles Willson Peale executes his painting *Family Group*, made important by his application of careful observation and objective rendering of its subject. This is the first time American art has been rendered through the prism of techniques better associated with science.

Aspiring painter Thomas Sully studies in London under celebrated American expatriate Benjamin West.

BUSINESS: The Boston Crown Glass Company is incorporated, a status freeing it from taxes, and allows its employees exemption from military service. This particular organization has gained renown for producing glass products deemed superior to its European counterparts.

SCIENCE: William Maclure's *Observations on the Geology of the United States* is published and contains the first geological survey map of the nation.

January 9

BUSINESS: The Enforcement Act is passed by Congress to halt smuggling and other illegal trade activities, particularly in New York and New England. The new law mandates strict penalties and confiscation of suspected goods, which only further increases the Embargo's unpopularity.

February 9

POLITICS: Arch-Federalist Timothy Pickering of Massachusetts seeks a New England convention to nullify the policy of embargo, which is seriously depressing the regional economy based largely on shipping.

February 12
GENERAL: Abraham Lincoln, 16th president, is born in Hodgenville, Kentucky.

February 17
EDUCATION: Miami University is chartered at Oxford, Ohio, although classes will not actually begin until 1824.

February 20
LAW: The Supreme Court decides the case of *United States v. Peters*; Chief Justice John Marshall sides firmly with federal power and declares that Pennsylvania cannot nullify the results of federal court cases.

February 23
POLITICS: In his address to the state legislature, Connecticut governor John Trumbull chastises the Embargo as unconstitutional and illegally infringing upon states rights and personal liberties. As more and more New England assemblies question the Embargo's legality, their governors are emboldened to withhold the use of state militias in its enforcement.

March 1
BUSINESS: President Thomas Jefferson, facing mounting criticism of the Embargo Act, finally replaces it with the Non-Intercourse Act. This expedient allows resumption of trade with all nations except France and England, until the latter cease their depredations upon American shipping. The net effect of the Embargo Act is to ruin the American economy and establish smuggling patterns into Canada that flourish during the War of 1812.
SETTLEMENT: The Territory of Illinois is formed by Congress by dividing the Indiana Territory; the new region encompasses the present-day states of Illinois, Wisconsin, and eastern Minnesota.

March 4
POLITICS: The diminutive, cerebral James Madison is inaugurated as the fourth president, and George Clinton continues on as vice president. Thomas Jefferson, meanwhile, concludes 44 years of public service by retiring to his home at Monticello in Charlottesville, Virginia. There he immerses himself in science, philosophy, and architecture.

March 6
POLITICS: Robert Smith replaces James Madison as the new secretary of state.

April 19
DIPLOMACY: President James Madison suspends the Non-Intercourse Act and allows trade with Great Britain. He does so upon the advice of British minister David M. Erskine, who assures Secretary of State Robert Smith that the hated Orders in Council are going to be repealed in June. This is a goodwill gesture to Madison but, unfortunately, Erskine lacks any authority to make this assertion.

April 29
SETTLEMENT: Congress approves territorial status for the Illinois region to facilitate migration and possibly shore up its defenses against British-inspired Indian hostilities.

1809

Madison, James   (1751–1836)
President

James Madison was born at Port Conway, Virginia, on March 16, 1751, son of an affluent planter. Well-educated at home and possessing a lucid, engaging intellect, he attended the College of New Jersey (Princeton) in 1771 before being gradually drawn into the revolutionary politics of his day. Madison, short at five feet six inches in height, ironically exuded the persona of someone both spirited and brainy. In 1776 he joined the Virginia convention tasked with drawing up a new state constitution, befriending another keen intellectual, Thomas Jefferson, in the process. His greatest work here was in disestablishing the Church of England as an official creed, thereby paving the way for complete freedom of religion. In 1779 Madison also gained a seat in the Second Continental Congress in Philadelphia, and after 1781 he began railing against the inherent weakness of the Articles of Confederation. In 1788 Madison became a delegate to the Constitutional Convention in Philadelphia to facilitate the quest for more centralized governance. Here he promulgated the so-called Virginia Plan, which ultimately served as the basis for the new constitution. He joined fellow nationalists John Jay and Alexander Hamilton in penning erudite essays for *The Federalist*, a collection of pro-constitutional newspaper articles. He spent the rest of the year arguing in favor of its adoption and overcoming formidable resistance from such political stalwarts as Patrick Henry.

Once the Constitution was adopted, Madison was appointed minister to France by President George Washington in 1794, and he also served as secretary of state under President Jefferson, 1801–09. His tenure here was marred by America's continuing ensnarement in European wars, principally through the British practice of seizing American ships and impressing their crews. In 1808 he was elected to the presidency himself and watched helplessly as the nation began its four-year descent toward renewed conflict with Great Britain. Feeling he had no recourse, Madison asked Congress for a declaration of war in June 1812 to preserve American republicanism and gain respect on the high seas. However, this was undertaken despite the nation's general unpreparedness for armed conflict. The first year of fighting proved disastrous

(continues)

James Madison *(Library of Congress)*

(continued)

to the United States, but Madison was easily reelected in the fall of 1812, even though the Republican Party was split and Northerners advanced Governor George Clinton of New York to oppose him. Madison then weathered two more years of hardship before the Treaty of Ghent was signed in December 1814. He was finally succeeded by fellow Virginian James Monroe in 1816, third member of the so-called Virginia Dynasty. Madison then retired to his estate at Montpelier, Virginia, lived quietly with his celebrated wife Dolley Madison, and died there on June 28, 1836. As "father of the Constitution," Madison was a little man whose political career had great importance for the United States.

May 22
POLITICS: The 11th Congress assembles in Washington, D.C., with the Democratic-Republicans still firmly in control of both the House of Representatives and the Senate. However, unease arising from the Embargo Act has doubled the number of Federalists in the House to 48, and they have also made gains at the state level.

May 30
DIPLOMACY: George Canning, British foreign secretary, disavows the Erskine Agreement of April 19 and orders minister David M. Erskine back to London. The Orders in Council authorizing the seizure of American ships and crews remain in force.

June
RELIGION: Elizabeth Seton, a Roman Catholic nun, forms her own religious charitable order based on the Sisters of Charity of St. Vincent de Paul. This is also the first Catholic order organized in the United States.

June 27
DIPLOMACY: President James Madison appoints John Quincy Adams to be American minister to the Russian court in St. Petersburg.

July 2
DIPLOMACY: Shawnee statesman Tecumseh, backed by his religious brother Tenskwatawa, begins an intertribal effort to form a defensive alliance against the United States. He is motivated by a burning desire to stop the sale of Indian land and the inevitable influx of American settlers that follows. No less than 30 million acres have been lost by native Americans in the past seven years alone.

July 5
RELIGION: The African American Abyssinian Baptist Church is organized in New York City.

August 9
DIPLOMACY: In the latest turn of events, President James Madison reimposes the Non-Intercourse Act against England following that government's rescinding of the Erskine Agreement of the previous April.

August 17
RELIGION: Thomas Campbell, representing a dissident Presbyterian group from Scotland, with a small group of followers founds the Christian Association of

1809

Tecumseh   (ca. 1768–1813)
Shawnee chief

Tecumseh ("Shooting Star"), member of the Shawnee Panther clan, was born near Piqua, Ohio, around 1768. His father was apparently killed during Lord Dunmore's War in 1774 and from that time on Tecumseh expressed his undying hatred for whites. He soon proved himself an able warrior and distinguished himself in fighting against Colonel Josiah Harmar and Arthur St. Clair in 1790–91. Tecumseh was later present at the defeat of Fallen Timbers against General Anthony Wayne in 1794 but refused to sign the Treaty of Greenville and left Ohio for Indiana. After a decade of peace William Henry Harrison was appointed governor of the new Indiana Territory and began forcing Indians to sell their land to the United States. Tecumseh, backed by his religiously inspired brother Tenskwatawa ("The Prophet"), cobbled together a coalition of Native Americans to oppose future sales without the consent of all. Harrison, who conferred with the chief on several occasions, remarked how he was struck by the former's bearing, eloquence, and dignity. However, relations between the two groups deteriorated, and in November 1811 Harrison defeated the Prophet at Tippecanoe Creek while Tecumseh was recruiting among the Creek. Afterward he felt he had no choice but to solicit aid from the English in Canada, and his repeated trips there were held by American politicians as proof that the British were behind Indian unrest in the Old Northwest. In June 1812 this perception was a major cause of the next round of military confrontation with Great Britain in the War of 1812.

Tecumseh again fought with distinction in several battles, and he joined forces with celebrated General Isaac Brock in the capture of Detroit. However, he usually tried in vain to have his warriors spare the lives of captured Americans. He was particularly angered at British Colonel Henry Procter for failing to protect American captives during the siege of Fort Meigs, a turning point in the war. Shortly after, a large American army under General Harrison began pursuing the British and Indians across Lake Erie and into western Ontario. Unwilling to retreat further, Tecumseh berated Procter for timidity and forced him to make an ill-fated stand along the River Thames. On October 5, 1813, Harrison's cavalry routed the British and nearly captured Procter but met much stouter opposition from Indians positioned in the woods. Combat proved intense and forced the Kentuckians to dismount and fight on foot, at which point Tecumseh was apparently slain. His body was then spirited off by several warriors and buried in an unmarked grave. For the time he lived, this eloquent Shawnee mounted the most effective resistance to white encroachment since the days of Pontiac, a cause that would not be taken up again until the Black Hawk War of 1832. Tecumseh's cause ultimately failed, but he remained admired by friends and enemies alike for his bravery, vision, and strength of character.

Washington, Pennsylvania. This movement is the genesis of the Disciples of Christ, which rejects all beliefs and practices not specifically mentioned in the Bible.

September 30
DIPLOMACY: Indiana territorial governor William Henry Harrison concludes the Treaty of Fort Wayne with Indian tribes of southern Indiana. The United

1809

Campbell, Thomas (1763–1854)

Theologian

Thomas Campbell was born in County Down, Ireland, on February 1, 1763. Though raised an Anglican, he joined the "seceder" branch of Presbyterianism, which had strong Congregationalist tendencies. He was then educated at the University of Glasgow and trained for preaching within the Antiburgher faction of the church. Campbell began working in 1798 from the pulpit of the Ahorey Church but was disillusioned by the rampant factionalism he encountered. By 1807 he grew thoroughly discouraged and immigrated to the wilds of Pennsylvania to review and hone his religious precepts. In 1808 he accepted work with the presbytery at Chartiers, where he expressed doubts as to the legitimacy of creeds, confession, fast days, and other facets he ascribed to human authority. Such apostasy resulted in his dismissal from the Presbyterian church that September, but he continued on as an itinerant preacher. After continuing reflection, Campbell founded the Christian Association in Washington, Pennsylvania, which served as the pulpit for his new Restorationist program. Here he formally denounced creeds and confessions as divisive and espoused a primitive form of Christianity basely solely upon New Testament scripture. Campbell further enunciated his principles by publishing *A Declaration and an Address* (1809), which held that perfect comprehension of the Bible, being the revealed word of God, is within the grasp of any rational person. Furthermore, any church practices not specifically mentioned by the Scriptures are human and not divine in origin, hence irrelevant. Campbell next took the bold step of proclaiming that the New Testament alone forms the sole basis for uniting all Christians. Doctrinal, creedal, or hierarchical practices unmentioned in Scripture were simply irrelevant at best and un-Godly at worst, he maintained.

By 1812 Campbell was joined by his son Alexander, and together they preached and established small academies throughout the Old Northwest. He also published and edited an early religious newsletter, the *Christian Baptist*, which later gave way to the *Millennial Harbinger*. Reaction proved mixed: Although the laity responded favorably to calls for unity, the Presbyterian community looked askance at this very notion of Restorationism. In 1812 Campbell enjoyed a brief liaison with the Redstone Baptist Church Association, but he became a pariah for attacking Baptist emotionalism at the expense of rationality and was expelled. Eventually his followers, known as "Campbellites," merged with dissident Methodists, Baptists, and Presbyterians under Barton W. Stone to form an entirely new entity, the Disciples of Christ. Campbell continued working closely with his son and successor Alexander until his death at Bethany College, (West) Virginia, on January 4, 1854. His advocacy of unity and rationality among Christians renders him a significant frontier theologian, whose tenets found their greatest expression in the forthcoming Fundamentalist movement.

States now obtains additional land along the Wabash River, a reality underscoring the urgency of Tecumseh's call for Indian unity in the face of continual white encroachment.

1809

December 6
LITERATURE: The writer Washington Irving publishes his *History of New York*, a parody of Dutch New Amsterdam that also lampoons, among others, Thomas Jefferson, Republicans, Yankees, Swedes, and himself. It becomes a best-selling book and elevates Irving to a writer of international repute, both at home and in Europe.

December 25
MEDICAL: At Danville, Kentucky, Dr. Ephraim McDowell successfully removes a 20-pound ovarian tumor from a female patient for the first time.

1810

ARCHITECTURE: The Newburyport Bridge is designed and built by John Templeman to span the Merrimack River in Massachusetts. At 224 feet in length, it is considered one of the most famous American suspension bridges of the century. It is not rebuilt until 1909.
ARTS: The Society of American Artists is organized.

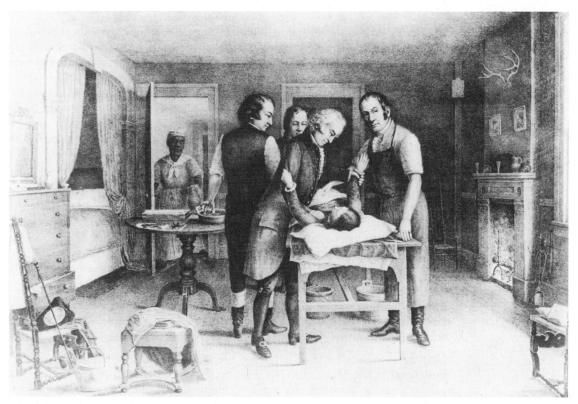

This lithograph depicts the first ovariotomy (removal of an ovary) being performed by Dr. Ephraim McDowell in 1809 in Danville, Kentucky. During the operation, McDowell successfully removed a 20-pound tumor from his 45-year-old patient—without anesthesia. *(National Library of Medicine)*

1810

Cornelius Vanderbilt (*Library of Congress*)

The first road companies begin offering a theater season in Lexington, Kentucky, the first such presentations west of the Appalachian Mountains.

AVIATION: Balloonists A. R. Hawley and Augustus Post complete a 1,117-mile sojourn from St. Louis, Missouri, before landing in Canada.

BUSINESS: Cornelius Vanderbilt, 16 years old, commences a ferry service between New York City and Staten Island, the humble beginning of a vast transportation empire.

MILITARY: King Kamehameha I of Hawaii unites the many surrounding islands into a single kingdom under his reign. He does so with ships and cannon provided by the British.

MUSIC: The Boston Philharmonic Society, America's first resident orchestra, is founded by former Prussian army musician Johann Christian Gottlieb. The 12-member band, including Gottlieb's wife, plays to the public on Saturdays.

POPULATION: The 1810 census reveals the United States with a population of 7,239,881, including 1,378,110 African Americans, overwhelmingly held in bondage. The total number of states is 17.

RELIGION: Congregationalists found the American Board of Commissioners for Foreign Missions to facilitate the dispatch of religious missionaries abroad, especially to India and Asia.

A New York law mandates that all slave children be taught to read the Bible.

March 16

LAW: The Supreme Court under Chief Justice John Marshall renders an important verdict in *Fletcher v. Peck*, whereby the Yazoo lands sales orchestrated by the Georgia legislature were subsequently negated by that same body. Marshall rules such a move is unconstitutional according to the law of contracts. This is also the first instance where a state law is judged annulled on constitutional grounds. Consequently the purchasers of Yazoo land under the initial deal are to receive $4 million in federal money for land the government obtained from Georgia in 1802.

March 23

DIPLOMACY: Napoleon I issues his Rambouillet Decree, which authorizes the additional seizures of American shipping in French ports.

May 1

DIPLOMACY: The Macon Bill No. 2 passes Congress, which authorizes President James Madison to commence trade with either England or France if American shipping is respected. Failing that, the president is permitted to reimpose nonintercourse upon either nation. French and Royal Navy warships are also forbidden from entering American waters.

June 23
BUSINESS: John Jacob Astor creates the new Pacific Fur Company to exploit the rich and untapped fur-bearing lands of the Pacific Northwest and expand his business empire further west.

July 4
AGRICULTURE: The *Agricultural Museum*, America's first farming magazine, debuts at Georgetown, D.C.

July 12
LABOR: Members of the Journeymen Cordwainers are tried and found guilty of conspiracy to strike for higher wages in New York City; the violators are then assessed $1 and court costs. This decision reflects the prevailing legal notion that strikes are illegal if supported by a conspiracy, an interpretation that remains in effect until 1842.

August 5
DIPLOMACY: In a continuing spate of diplomatic subterfuge, the French foreign minister Duc de Cadore informs American minister John Armstrong in Paris that Napoleon's Milan and Berlin decrees against American shipping will be withdrawn if the United States declares non-intercourse against Great Britain. Napoleon, meanwhile, signs the Trianon Decree to seize any American vessel docked at French ports from May 1809 to May 1810.

September 26
SETTLEMENT: American settlers in West Florida rebel against Spain, seize the fort at Baton Rouge, then declare themselves the "Independent Republic of West Florida." Their ultimate intention is annexation by the United States.

October 1
SOCIETAL: Elkanah Watson orchestrates the first Berkshire Cattle Show in Pittsfield, Massachusetts, which sets a precedent for country fairs around the nation. It also coincides with his founding of the Berkshire Agricultural Society to promote crop rotation and use of fertilizer.

October 27
SETTLEMENT: President James Madison orders the military occupation of Spanish West Florida, which is then annexed to the Territory of Orleans (southern Louisiana). This region falls between the Perdido and Mississippi Rivers with its capital at Baton Rouge.

November 2
DIPLOMACY: President James Madison, acting upon the devious actions of the Duc de Cadore, reinstates trade with France and imposes non-importation against Great Britain until the Orders in Council are withdrawn. However, the French fully intend to continue seizing American ships and cargos. The net result of this duplicity is to increase diplomatic tensions between the United States and England.

December 10
SPORTS: Tom Molineaux, a freed African-American slave from Virginia, is the first American heavyweight boxer. On this day he loses a 40-round match in London to England's Tom Cribb.

1811

LITERATURE: Eaglesfield Smith's novel *William and Ellen* is published, an early American imitation of Sir Walter Scott's romanticism.

MILITARY: In a major armament breakthrough, inventor John H. Hall designs and builds the first American breech-loading carbine with a higher rate of fire than conventional, muzzle-loading muskets. However, the conservatively minded U.S. Army displays little interest in the weapon and only a handful are procured prior to the War of 1812.

TRANSPORTATION: Inventor John Stevens designs and builds the *Juliana*, the first steamboat ferry to ply the waters between Hoboken, New Jersey, and New York City. However, because Robert Fulton and Robert L. Livingston own a monopoly on steamboat operations in New York State, Stevens is forced to close his operation.

January 10
SLAVERY: A large revolt by African Americans occurs in Louisiana when 400 slaves kill a plantation owner's son then march en masse to New Orleans. U.S. Army troops are called in to suppress the uprising, and 75 slaves are killed; their heads are then placed along the road from New Orleans to the plantation as a warning to prospective rebels.

January 15
SETTLEMENT: A secret congressional session authorizes the United States to seize Spanish East Florida if either the inhabitants desire annexation or a foreign power attempts to occupy it. The statue is not publicly revealed until 1818.

February 2
SETTLEMENT: Russian settlers establish a fort at Bodega Bay, north of San Francisco, California, around which rises an agricultural and fur-trading colony. It is subsequently known as Fort Ross.

February 11
DIPLOMACY: President James Madison again suspends all trade with Great Britain for failing to halt the harassment of American commerce at sea. This is the third such imposition in four years yet elicits no change in British behavior towards neutral shipping.

February 20
BUSINESS: The Democratic-Republican controlled Congress votes to allow the first Bank of the United States to expire, despite pleas by Secretary of the Treasury Albert Gallatin to recharter it. The institution is opposed by an influential group of "Old Republicans" who feel it a Federalist imposition on the country, by those alarmed by the fact that two-thirds of the stock is owned by British subjects, and by lobbyists who advocate state-chartered banks. Nonetheless, the vote in the Senate is a tie until broken by Vice President George Clinton.

March 2
DIPLOMACY: Congress, taken in by the deception of French foreign minister Duc de Cadore, authorizes reimposition of non-intercourse against Great Britain unless it rescinds its Orders in Council against American shipping. The British counter by enacting harsher measures to impress American seamen.

March 4

BUSINESS: The Bank of the United States is allowed to expire, an unwise move considering that the nation is on the cusp of renewed hostilities with Great Britain.

April 2

DIPLOMACY: President James Madison names his heretofore political competitor, Virginian James Monroe, as the new secretary of state.

April 12

BUSINESS: A group of colonists sails aboard the vessel *Tonquin* and lands at Cape Disappointment, Washington, to establish the fur-trading outpost of Astoria. This is accomplished at the instigation of John Jacob Astor, who seeks to ship furs to the lucrative Chinese market directly from the Columbia River. Astoria is also the first American settlement in the Pacific Northwest region.

May

DIPLOMACY: American minister William Pinkney departs England for home, having failed to mitigate the ongoing impasse between the two nations.

May 1

NAVAL: The 38-gun British frigate HMS *Guerriere* accosts the American merchant brig *Spitfire* off Sandy Hook, New Jersey, and impresses an American seaman. A public outcry ensues and prods the government into action.

May 16

NAVAL: The 44-gun frigate USS *President* under Captain John Rodgers, cruising off Sandy Hook, New Jersey, to protect American commerce from British depredations, encounters an unidentified vessel in the dark. Shots ring out and broadsides are exchanged before his antagonist is identified as the 22-gun corvette HMS *Little Belt* under Commander Arthur B. Bingham. The British suffer 13 killed and 19 wounded in the one-sided exchange and are allowed to limp off. The action is hailed throughout the nation as revenge for the British attack on the USS *Chesapeake* in 1807.

July 8

INDIAN: Shawnee chief Tecumseh travels south to solicit Creek help in his Indian coalition. Before departing he warns his brother, Tenskwatawa, not to seek a fight with the Americans.

July 31

MILITARY: Frontier settlers in the region of Vincennes, Indiana Territory, call upon federal authorities to uproot an Indian community established along Tippecanoe Creek by the Shawnee Prophet, Tenskwatawa.

September 11

TRANSPORTATION: Robert Fulton's sidewheeler steamboat *New Orleans* sails down the Ohio River from Pittsburgh, Pennsylvania, until it reaches New Orleans, Louisiana, via the Mississippi River. Thereafter it commences the first regular service on inland waters by steaming between Natchez, Mississippi, and New Orleans.

September 19

DIPLOMACY: American minister Joel Barlow arrives at Paris, France, demanding clarification of the alleged nullification of the Berlin and Milan decrees. French

1811

foreign minister Duc de Bassano shows him the Decree of St. Cloud, supposedly signed by Napoleon and dated April 28, 1810, which has never been published or given to the American embassy.

September 26

MILITARY: Indiana territorial governor William Henry Harrison leads a force of 1,000 soldiers and militia from Vincennes, Indiana, toward the Indian encampment at the confluence of the Wabash and Tippecanoe Rivers. He does so taking advantage of the absence of Tecumseh, who has ventured south to solicit Creek membership in his anti-American coalition.

October 20

TRANSPORTATION: Robert Fulton's steamboat *New Orleans* arrives at Louisville, Kentucky, from Pittsburgh, Pennsylvania, having covered 700 miles of treacherous waters in two weeks.

November 1

DIPLOMACY: In light of the *Little Belt* Affair of the previous May, the American government notifies British minister Augustus John Foster of the nation's willingness to offer compensation if Great Britain will stop harassing American shipping and rescind the Orders in Council. The British decline but counter with a offer of compensation for victims of the 1807 *Chesapeake-Leopard* Affair.

November 4

POLITICS: Elections for the 12th Congress result in a large number of "War Hawks" who seek military confrontation with Great Britain rather than ongoing appeasement. Among their ranks are John C. Calhoun, William Lowndes, Langston Cheves, Peter B. Porter, Richard M. Johnson, Henry Clay, Felix Grundy, and John Sevier. Significantly, while the northern militants agitate for the conquest of Canada, the southerners among them seek annexation of Florida.

November 5

POLITICS: President James Madison's annual message to Congress calls for increased spending on national defense and military preparation in the face of French and British predation upon American shipping.

November 7

MILITARY: The Battle of Tippecanoe, Indiana Territory, unfolds as the army of General William Henry Harrison encamps near the makeshift Indian village. At dawn Indians under the Tenskwatawa, the Shawnee Prophet–Tecumseh's brother–storm into the American camp, nearly overrunning it, but are gradually repulsed by accurate musketry. The victorious Americans then occupy and burn Tippecanoe before withdrawing to safety. Harrison's losses are 39 killed and 151 wounded; Indian losses are unknown but presumed equally heavy.

November 12

DIPLOMACY: Secretary of State James Monroe accepts the British offer to compensate victims of the 1807 *Chesapeake-Leopard* affair.

November 18

JOURNALISM: The *Niles Weekly Register* is founded at Baltimore by editor Hezekiah Niles; it soon becomes a recognized national newspaper.

November 20

TRANSPORTATION: The Cumberland Road (or Old National Road) commences construction with federal funding; this is one of the earliest and largest public works projects in American history. Ultimately, the road will stretch from Cumberland, Maryland, as far west as Vandalia, Illinois, by 1840 and will serve as a major conduit for western expansion. Parts still exist as modern-day U.S. Route 40.

December 16

GENERAL: A huge earthquake rattles New Madrid, Missouri, causing the Mississippi River to flow backward and flooding parts of Tennessee. At its height parts of the river were raised or lowered as by much as 15 feet.

1812

ART: John Vanderlyn exhibits a nude painting, *Adriane,* which shocks contemporary critics at home and nearly ends his artistic career but is favorably received in Paris.

BUSINESS: The Pennsylvania Company for Insurance on Lives and Granting Annuities is the first such institution to employ actuarial tables.

LITERARY: James Kirke Paulding, writing under the pseudonym *Hector Bull-us,* publishes *The Diverting History of John Bull and Brother Jonathan,* which excoriates British attitudes and policies.

MEDICAL: Dr. Benjamin Rush publishes *Medical Inquiries and Observations upon the Diseases of the Mind,* the first national treatise to address mental illness, its probable causes, and cures.

SCIENCE: The Academy of Natural Sciences of Philadelphia is established and attracts a wide public following.

SOCIETAL: Noted printer Isaiah Thomas founds and endows the American Antiquarian Society in Worcester, Massachusetts; it remains dedicated to the collection and preservation of early American manuscripts and historical artifacts.

TECHNOLOGY: William Monroe of Concord, Massachusetts, uses native graphite to manufacture the first lead pencils sold in America.

January 12

TRANSPORTATION: Robert Fulton's steamship *New Orleans* sails down the Mississippi River from Pittsburgh, Pennsylvania, and reaches the city of New Orleans, Louisiana. The four-month transit is the first of its kind and demonstrates the viability of steam technology on western waters.

January 22

SETTLEMENT: Louisiana draws up its first constitution prior to attaining statehood; though a slave state, it still allows French-speaking African Creoles to bear arms and serve in the militia. Many of these are also slave owners.

February 11

POLITICS: Governor Elbridge Gerry of Massachusetts begins the time-honored practice of artfully drawing state election districts to ensure the supremacy of his Democratic-Republican Party in the U.S. House of Representatives. Because this results in a district somewhat shaped like a salamander, the practice enters the political lexicon as "Gerrymandering."

1812

February 15

EXPLORING: William Hunt, having blazed an overland trail from St. Louis, Missouri Territory, arrives at Astoria, Oregon. His trail closely follows what eventually emerges as the Oregon Trail.

March 3

DIPLOMACY: Congress passes the nation's first foreign aid bill by authorizing $50,000 to assist survivors of a severe earthquake in Venezuela.

March 12

MILITARY: Georgia militia under Colonel Lodowick Ashley occupy Amelia Island off the Florida Coast to prevent its occupation by British forces.

March 14

BUSINESS: With war clouds gathering, Congress authorizes an $11 million bond issue to finance military preparations outlined by President James Madison in the previous November. Five more bonds are issued over the next two and a half years, but the nation remains fiscally handicapped by the lack of a central banking apparatus.

March 18

MILITARY: U.S. Army troops and militia under Colonel Thomas Adams Smith move down the St. Mary's River, Florida, and gradually besiege Spanish-held St. Augustine, in a halfhearted attempt to capture that province. The ensuing fiasco, conducted with shoestring forces, is known as the "Patriot War" and ends in failure.

April

MILITARY: After their defeat at Tippecanoe the past November, Native Americans in the Old Northwest commence an undeclared border war against American settlements in Missouri, Indiana, and Illinois. Both sides fear that a war with Great Britain will lead to all-out conflict in the region.

April 1

POLITICS: To underscore his dissatisfaction with Great Britain, President James Madison requests a 60-day embargo of British goods. This move is viewed by many of the "War Hawks" as a prelude to armed confrontation.

April 4

BUSINESS: Congress approves a 90-day embargo of British goods, while many politicians hope that differences between American and England can be settled peacefully.

April 10

DIPLOMACY: Great Britain informs the United States that, since Napoleon has failed to retract his Milan and Berlin Decrees, the Orders in Council against neutral shipping remain in effect.

MILITARY: In a sign of growing bellicosity, Congress authorizes President James Madison to mobilize up to 100,000 state militia for up to six months. Recruitment goals for the regular U.S. Army, however, remain much more modest as the polity still distrusts standing professional forces.

April 13

ARTS: James N. Barker's play *Marmion*, adapted from a poem by Sir Walter Scott, is successfully staged in New York City; not surprisingly, its anti-English sentiments resonate with a wartime American audience.

April 20
GENERAL: Vice President George Clinton dies; he is the first vice president to die in office.

April 30
POLITICS: Louisiana enters the union as the 18th state with its capital at New Orleans and a population of 75,000. Slavery is legal but free, mostly French-speaking citizens of African descent can still bear arms and enlist in the militia. The remaining part of the Louisiana Territory is subsequently renamed the Missouri Territory by Congress.

May 14
POLITICS: Congress orders the incorporation of the Republic of West Florida into the state of Louisiana.

May 18
POLITICS: The Democratic-Republican congressional caucus renominates James Madison for the presidency and John Langdon for vice president.

May 26
EDUCATION: Presbyterian interests charter Hamilton College in Clinton, New York; its first class graduates in 1814.

May 29
POLITICS: In Albany, New York, a coalition of disgruntled Democratic-Republicans and Federalists nominates Lieutenant Governor DeWitt Clinton for the presidency. He is distinctly an antiwar candidate.

June 1
POLITICS: President James Madison dispatches his war message to Congress, citing British intransigence on harassment of trade, impressment of American citizens, blockading of American ports, and agitation of Native Americans—the latter a supposed point deeply angering western politicians.

June 3
DIPLOMACY: Feeling that war with the United States is inevitable, Governor General Sir George Prevost of Canada arranges a meeting with Shawnee chief Tecumseh at Amherstburg, Ontario.

June 4
POLITICS: The House of Representatives votes in favor of renewed war with Great Britain, 79 to 49, much to the delight of the "War Hawk" faction.

June 8
POLITICS: After John Langdon refuses the nomination for vice president, he is replaced by Massachusetts governor Elbridge Gerry.

June 16
DIPLOMACY: British Prime Minister Lord Castlereagh suspends the Orders in Council against neutral shipping in order to improve the national economic climate at home. This has also been a prime factor in the American movement toward war, but word arrives too late to alter the outcome of events.

June 18
NAVAL: The harrowing prospect of war with Great Britain pits the young U.S. Navy of 17 warships, 447 guns, and five thousand men against the veteran and

1812

haughty Royal Navy of Great Britain boasting 1,048 vessels, 27,800 guns, and 151,500 men.

POLITICS: The U.S. Senate votes 19 to 13 for renewed war with Great Britain, unaware that England has recently suspended the offending Orders in Council. However, the country is badly split by dissent, with New England largely opposing the conflict, and to dissenters it becomes derided as "Mr. Madison's War." The ensuing War of 1812 is also the first declared conflict under the Constitution; a declaration of war against France, which has been equally rapacious toward American shipping, fails by only two votes.

June 19

POLITICS: President James Madison announces that a state of war exists between the United States and Great Britain.

June 26

DIPLOMACY: President James Madison instructs American envoy Jonathan Russell to negotiate an armistice only on the basis of suspending the Orders in Council and halting the practice of impressment.

POLITICS: Federal Governor Caleb Strong of Massachusetts strongly denounces the War of 1812 and declares a statewide fast in protest.

June 30

BUSINESS: Treasury notes amounting to $5 million are authorized by Congress to help finance the war effort.

July 1

BUSINESS: To raise additional capital for the war effort, Congress increases the tariff on imported items.

NAVAL: British and Indian forces in the Detroit River capture a transport carrying General William Hull's personal papers. These are then forwarded to General Isaac Brock, who now knows the exact strength, composition, and strategy of the American invaders.

July 2

MILITARY: Federalist Governor John Cotton of Connecticut declares his intention not to provide the federal government with militia forces, which removes a relatively well-trained pool of manpower from the war effort.

July 12

MILITARY: A force of 1,500 militia and regulars under General William Hull crosses the Detroit River from Michigan and occupies Sandwich, Ontario. The American are counting on Canadian discontent with Great Britain to produce a large number of deserters, but few are forthcoming.

July 15–17

NAVAL: The frigate USS *Constitution* under Captain Isaac Hull endures a harrowing chase by a five-vessel British squadron off New York but, by dint of splendid seamanship, he manages to escape undamaged to New York.

July 17

MILITARY: A surprise British raid by 600 British, Canadians, and Indians under Captain Charles Roberts upon the 61-man American garrison of Lieutenant Porter Hanks at Fort Mackinac, Michigan, results in their surrender. Hanks, unaware that war had been declared, surrendered without a shot. This bloodless victory encourages increasing numbers of Native Americans to join the British, and their activity further unnerves General William Hull.

July 19

NAVAL: Ships of the Canadian Provincial Marine attack the American port of Sackets Harbor, New York, only to be driven off by artillery from the USS *Oneida*, commanded by Lieutenant Melancthon T. Woolsey. Among his cannon is a 32-howitzer nicknamed "Old Sow," which fires spent British cannonballs back at the enemy.

July 23

RELIGION: Pacifistic minister William Ellery Channing gives a sermon opposing the War of 1812 and all attempts to stifle opposition in the name of patriotism.

August 5

POLITICS: Federalist Governor Caleb Strong of Massachusetts joins Connecticut in declaring its refusal to provide the federal government with militia forces necessary to invade Canada, then declares a day of prayer and fasting. Furthermore, public hostility has been openly directed at Major General Henry Dearborn, tasked with defending Boston and the New England coastline.

August 8

MILITARY: General William Hull, feeling threatened by the approach of British reinforcements under General Isaac Brock, abandons Canada and retreats to Detroit. This surrenders the initiative to Brock, who intends to make effective use of it.

Mexican revolutionary Bernardo Gutierrez de Lara, assisted by 150 American filibusters (adventurers) under Augustus W. Magee, crosses the Sabine River from Louisiana into Texas, intending to overthrow the Spanish regime.

August 15

MILITARY: A force of 400 Potawatomie Indians massacres the small American garrison of Captain Nathan Heald at Fort Dearborn (Chicago), Illinois Territory, after they are ordered to evacuate that post by General William Hull. The Americans lose 53 soldiers, women, and children, including the noted scout Captain William Wells, who had been raised by Chief Little Turtle. The victorious Indians then burn the fort.

August 16

MILITARY: Convinced he is outnumbered and fearing an Indian massacre, General William Hull timorously surrenders Detroit and 1,200 men to smaller forces under General Isaac Brock and Tecumseh. Victory here gives heart to Native American tribes throughout the region and they begin flocking to the British standard. Brock has also managed to extend British influence and prestige throughout the Great Lakes region. Detroit remains the only American settlement captured by an enemy and its loss shocked the public.

August 17

POLITICS: A secret Federalist convention in New York City decides to throw its weight behind DeWitt Clinton of New York, a Democratic-Republican.

August 19

NAVAL: In a startling naval upset off Nova Scotia, the 44-gun American frigate USS *Constitution* under Captain Isaac Hull defeats the 38-gun frigate HMS

Guerriere of Captain James R. Dacres in a half-hour battle. Losses are seven Americans killed and seven wounded to 15 British dead and 64 wounded. The British vessel is so shattered by *Constitution's* firepower that it has to be sunk. Hull is the nephew of defeated General William Hull, and his victory does much to restore American morale.

August 23

MILITARY: British General Isaac Brock makes a quick transit from Detroit to Fort George on the Niagara frontier, in preparation for repelling another American invasion. Across the Niagara River, General Stephen Van Rensselaer struggles to assemble a mixed force of untrained soldiers and equally raw militia.

August 29

DIPLOMACY: Prime Minister Lord Castlereagh declines to accept the peace proposal of American envoy Jonathan Russell, who sought an end to impressment and payment of indemnities for past seizures.

September 11

MILITARY: Native Americans, assisted by escaped African-American slaves, ambush a supply detachment of U.S. Marines at Twelve Mile Creek outside St. Augustine, Florida. Captain John Williams is mortally injured and six of his marines are wounded.

September 17

MILITARY: Former Indiana territorial governor William Henry Harrison is commissioned a brigadier general and tasked with retaking Detroit, Michigan, at the earliest possible opportunity.

September 21

DIPLOMACY: Czar Alexander I of Russia offers to mediate the dispute between Great Britain and the United States; he does this in order to strengthen the combined British/Russian effort against Napoleon.

September 30

DIPLOMACY: Admiral Sir John Borlase Warren, commanding at Halifax, Nova Scotia, offers an armistice and peace negotiations to the U.S. government.

October 4

MILITARY: A surprise attack by British forces ousts a small American garrison at Ogdensburg, New York; this removes a threat to British navigation along the St. Lawrence River, the principal British line of communication.

October 9

NAVAL: Navy Lieutenant Jesse D. Elliot, assisted by army Captain Nathan Towson, attacks and captures the British vessels *Detroit* and *Caledonia* as they lay anchored near the Niagara River close to Buffalo, New York.

October 13

MILITARY: The Battle of Queenstown Heights transpires when a mixed force of 1,300 U.S. Army troops and New York militia under General Stephen Van Rensselaer attempt to cross the Niagara River. General Isaac Brock meets the invaders head-on with 1,000 troops and Indians and is killed in action, but the Americans fail to receive promised reinforcements from the New York side. When General Roger Hale Sheaffe arrives with British reinforcements, the invaders under Lieutenant Colonel Winfield Scott are forced to surrender. American losses are 300 killed and wounded and 1,000 captured; British losses are 14 killed, 77 wounded, and 21 missing, including the irreplaceable Brock.

Scott, Winfield (1786–1866)
General

Winfield Scott was born in Petersburg, Virginia, on June 13, 1786, son of a Revolutionary War veteran. He attended William and Mary College briefly in 1806, then dropped out to study law. The following year Scott enlisted in the U.S. Army as a captain where he proved capable but extremely sensitive toward matters of rank and honor. In 1810 he was court-martialed for criticizing his superior, General James Wilkinson, and endured a year's suspension. He passed the time studying European military literature so that when the War of 1812 commenced, he was among the most professional officers in his grade. Scott was one of a handful of leaders to garner any recognition, and in July 1814 he joined General Jacob Brown's Niagara Campaign as a brigadier general. In this capacity he fought well at the bloody battle of Chippewa and Lundy's Lane, being severely wounded but gaining a national reputation. After the war he remained in service and translated several European drill manuals for army use. By this time his reputation as "Old Fuss and Feathers," arising from his insistence on proper military decorum, was also well-established. After fighting in the Florida Second Seminole War and helping resolve a tricky border dispute between Maine and Canada, Scott became the army's senior general in 1841. In this capacity he commanded an army during the War with Mexico and in 1847 conducted one of military history's most decisive campaigns. Commencing with a large amphibious landing at Veracruz, Scott marched inland, repeatedly defeated larger Mexican forces, and finally occupied the capital of Mexico City. This act forced the government of General Antonio Lopez de Santa Anna to sue for peace and Scott became a national hero again.

Success on the battlefield whetted Scott's appetite for politics, and in 1852 he sought the Whig Party nomination. However, he lost the general election to Democrat Franklin Pierce and resumed his military interests. Though Southern-born, Scott proved an ardent nationalist and he unflinchingly sided with the North during the approach

(continues)

Winfield Scott *(National Archives)*

(continued)

of civil war. He was President Abraham Lincoln's senior military adviser before being replaced by General George B. McClellan in 1861 and as Lincoln's adviser he promulgated the so-called Anaconda Plan. This was a brilliant strategic expedient calling for a military offensive down the Mississippi River valley to cut the Confederacy in half, while a naval blockade throttled its economy. The plan was initially derided as far too cautious by officers who sought to end the war in a single decisive blow, despite Scott's warnings that the newly recruited army was too raw for combat. After the defeat at Bull Run in August 1861, Union strategists gradually came to adopting Scott's overarching strategy. Scott himself retired from the military in the fall of 1861 and relocated to the U.S. Military Academy, West Point. He died there on May 29, 1866, having bequeathed to the U.S. Army tradition of professionalism and the goal of victory it had heretofore lacked.

October 18

NAVAL: Captain Jacob Jones of the 18-gun sloop USS *Wasp* engages and captures the 18-gun British brig *Frolic* with a loss of 10 Americans to 90 Britons. Both vessels are dismasted in combat and subsequently recaptured by the 74-gun ship of the line HMS *Poictiers*.

October 25

NAVAL: In the war's second naval upset, Captain Stephen Decatur and the 44-gun frigate *United States* capture the 38-gun frigate HMS *Macedonian* under Captain John S. Carden off the Madeira Islands. The heavier American vessel pounds its adversary into submission in only 30 minutes. Decatur's losses are five killed and seven wounded to a British tally of 36 dead and 68 injured. The prize is then towed intact to New London, Connecticut, where it enters American service as USS *Macedonian* and serves until 1828.

October 27

DIPLOMACY: Secretary of State James Monroe informs Admiral John Borlase Warren at Nova Scotia that the United States will readily enter peace negotiations with Great Britain once it halts the practice of impressment.

NAVAL: Captain David Porter and the 32-gun frigate USS *Essex* depart the Delaware Capes on a voyage around Cape Horn and into the Pacific. The enterprising Porter is determined to destroy the British whaling fleet operating there.

November

NAVAL: Royal Navy warships begin a blockade of the Delaware River and Chesapeake Bay.

November 19–23

MILITARY: General Henry Dearborn leads a force of barely trained U.S. troops and raw militia north form Plattsburg, New York, intending to capture the strategic city of Montreal. Once they reach the Canadian border, Dearborn's militia refuses to cross, pursuant to their legal rights, and the invasion is canceled. The only fighting occurs when two columns of troops mistake each other for the enemy and open fire, causing several casualties. It is another ignominious display of incompetence.

November 27
NAVAL: Buoyed by the surprising string of victories at sea, Congress authorizes construction of six new 44-gun frigates—none of which are completed in time for the war.

December 1
MILITARY: American forces under General Alexander Smyth make a failed attempt to cross the Niagara River and then withdraw. Anger and disorder breaks out in Smyth's camp in consequence, and he is soon struck from the army rolls.

December 2
POLITICS: James Madison, despite the disasters and humiliations of the previous summer, is reelected president over fellow Democratic Republican DeWitt Clinton by an electoral vote of 128 to 89. Elbridge Gerry also defeats Jared Ingersoll for the vice presidency, 131 to 86. However, Federalists in the northeast score an impressive election victory, doubling their number in Congress.

December 24
DIPLOMACY: American minister and former Connecticut poet Joel Barlow dies in Paris, France, ending all American negotiations with Napoleon.

December 26
NAVAL: The British admiralty declares Chesapeake Bay and the Delaware River under a state of blockade; as the war continues, the blockade will extend from Maine to Georgia.

December 29
EDUCATION: The University of Maryland is chartered in Baltimore and organized around the College of Medicine of Maryland, which had functioned since 1807.
NAVAL: The Americans score a third naval upset when the 44-gun frigate USS *Constitution* under Captain William Bainbridge engages and defeats the 38-gun British frigate HMS *Java* off Brazil. The Americans sustain nine dead and 25 wounded to a British tally of 48 killed and 102 wounded. The *Constitution*'s hull proves so impervious to British cannonballs that it acquires the nickname "Old Ironsides."

1813

JOURNALISM: Nathan Hale begins editing the *Boston Daily Advertiser*, which runs until 1917.
RELIGION: Reverend William Ellery Channing begins editing and publishing the *Christian Disciple*, a liberal Protestant magazine to counter more conservative publications already extant.
TECHNOLOGY: Nathaniel Stevens of Andover, Massachusetts, builds a woolen broadcloth mill and begins manufacturing the first flannels.

January 13
POLITICS: Disgraced Secretary of War William Eustis is replaced by ambitious John Armstrong, author of the 1783 Newburgh Addresses against Congress and a former minister to France.

January 22–23
MILITARY: The Battle of Frenchtown (or River Raisin), Michigan Territory, occurs when 1,000 Americans, mostly half-frozen Kentucky militia under General James

Winchester, are overrun by a similar force of British and Native Americans commanded by Colonel Henry Procter. Winchester's entire force was captured at a loss of 24 British dead and 158 wounded. The Indians, greatly emboldened by the easy victory, take to drinking and massacre around 60 wounded prisoners. Thereafter, "Remember the Raisin!" becomes the battle cry of the Kentuckians.

February 20
POLITICS: Brigadier General Lewis Cass becomes governor of the Michigan Territory, serving for nearly two decades.

February 14
NAVAL: The frigate USS *Essex* under Captain David Porter rounds Cape Horn at the tip of South America, becoming the first American warship operating in the Pacific Ocean.

February 24
NAVAL: The 18-gun American sloop USS *Hornet* under Master Commandant James Lawrence captures the 20-gun British sloop HMS *Peacock* off Guiana, South America. The Americans lose four killed and four wounded to a British tally of five dead and 33 wounded.

March 4
POLITICS: James Madison is inaugurated for his second term in office as president while Elbridge Gerry replaces the late George Clinton as vice president.

March 8
DIPLOMACY: President James Madison appoints Swiss-born Secretary of the Treasury Albert Gallatin and Delaware Senator James A. Bayard to a special peace commission slated to join American minister John Quincy Adams at St. Petersburg, Russia. They are there at the invitation of Czar Alexander I, who wishes to mediate the dispute between England and America. However, the British will reject the czar's offer of help.

March 11
DIPLOMACY: President James Madison accepts the Russian offer of mediation to end the current war.

March 15
GENERAL: At New Orleans, Governor William C. C. Claiborne of Louisiana places a bounty on the head of French pirate Jean Laffite; the flamboyant buccaneer counters by offering an even larger one for the governor's.

March 27
NAVAL: Captain Oliver Hazard Perry arrives at Presque Isle (Erie, Pennsylvania) to oversee construction of an American fleet on Lake Erie. This will ultimately consist of two brigs, a schooner, and three gunboats constructed from nearby woods and materials hauled overland from Pittsburgh. To do so he supercedes Captain Jesse Duncan Elliott, gaining his lasting enmity.

April 15
MILITARY: American forces under General James Wilkinson seize and occupy Mobile, Alabama, displacing the Spanish garrison there. Soon the region between the Pearl and Perdido Rivers are under U.S. control.

1813

April 27
MILITARY: York, Ontario, (Toronto), the provincial capital of Upper Canada, falls to a combined amphibious force of 1,700 men under Commodore Isaac Chauncey and General Henry Dearborn. The actual fighting is accomplished by General Zebulon M. Pike, the noted explorer, who expels 700 British defenders under General Roger Hale Sheaffe, only to die in a British magazine explosion. American losses are 54 dead and around 200 wounded; the British tally is 62 dead, 34 wounded, and 50 missing. Afterward discipline breaks down and the Americans, assisted by Canadian prisoners, burn and loot the settlement. This is the first joint operation by the respective services.

May 1–9
MILITARY: British and Indian forces under General Henry Procter and Shawnee chief Tecumseh besiege Fort Meigs, (Toledo) Ohio. However, the 1,000-man garrison under General William Henry Harrison is determined to resist.

May 4–5
MILITARY: General William Henry Harrison, once reinforced by Kentucky militia under General Green Clay, sorties from Fort Meigs, Ohio, and captures the British siege battery. The militia, however, are lured inland by the Indians, who then surround and massacre them. Chief Tecumseh roundly castigates General Henry Procter for failing to stop the atrocities. The siege will be lifted in four days and Procter returns to Upper Canada.

May 24
POLITICS: The 13th Congress assembles in Washington, D.C., with the Democratic Republicans still in firm control. However, the Federalists have made gains in recent elections as, of 36 new seats granted to the House of Representatives, 32 of them are Federalist.

May 26
NAVAL: The British Admiralty extends their blockade of the American coast from Chesapeake Bay as far south as the Mississippi River, including the ports of Charleston, South Carolina, and Savannah, Georgia. They also begin systematically raiding along the coastline.

May 27
MILITARY: The Battle of Fort George, upper Canada, unfolds when a combined amphibious force under General Henry Dearborn and Commodore Isaac Chauncey attacks and captures the noted post. The British under General John Vincent resist handily but are smothered by American firepower and chased inland by General Winfield Scott until Dearborn erroneously halts the pursuit. Vincent consequently escapes in the direction of Burlington Heights to fight another day.

May 29
MILITARY: The Battle of Sackets Harbor, New York, occurs when Governor-General Sir George Prevost and Commodore Sir James Lucas Yeo make a surprise attack on this strategic American port while Commodore Isaac Chauncey is at Fort George. The 1,200 British initially scatter 500 militia commanded by General Jacob Brown, but prove unable to carry the main works garrisoned by 250 regulars. Once Brown rallies the militia in Prevost's rear, the governor-general is

1813

unnerved and sounds the retreat. The British fall back intact to their fleet and sail away, although considerable damage has been inflicted on American naval stores. Prevost's losses are about 260 men; Brown sustains around 100 casualties, mostly militia. For his role in the victory, he is also commissioned a brigadier general in the regular army.

June 1

NAVAL: The 38-gun American frigate USS *Chesapeake* under Captain James Lawrence, with a new and largely inexperienced crew, engages the crack British frigate HMS *Shannon* under Captain Philip B. V. Broke outside Boston. In spite of great bravery and sacrifice, the Americans are defeated in a bloody, 15-minute engagement in which Lawrence is mortally wounded and Broke critically. American losses are 62 killed and 58 injured to a British tally of 33 killed and 42 wounded–making it one of the bloodiest encounters in the Age of Sail. Lawrence's dying command of "Don't give up the ship!" subsequently passes into U.S. Navy tradition as a battle cry.

June 6

MILITARY: The Battle of Stoney Creek, Upper Canada, unfolds when 700 British troops under General John Vincent and Colonel John Harvey attack an American force of 2,000 encamped nearby. Both American generals, John Chandler and William H. Winder, are taken prisoner in the darkness but the British are gradually driven off by daylight. Still, this marks the end of the American offensive on the Niagara peninsula and the surviving troops fall back to Fort George. American losses are 17 dead, 30 injured, and 99 missing while the British sustain 23 killed, 136 wounded, and 55 captured.

June 24

MILITARY: An American military expedition of 600 men under Colonel Charles G. Boerstler comes to grief at Beaver Dams, Ontario, when it is surrounded by British light troops and Indians under Lieutenant James Fitzgibbon. Fitzgibbon then convinces Boerstler that he in fact commands 1,700 men, demands his surrender, and the Americans timidly comply.

July 6

MILITARY: On the Niagara frontier, General Henry Dearborn, whose slow movement and lethargic activity bequeathed him the nickname "Granny," is replaced by the scheming General James Wilkinson. Meanwhile, Wilkinson's archenemy, General Wade Hampton, assumes command of troops at Plattsburgh, New York.

July 14

NAVAL: Lieutenant John M. Gamble becomes the first Marine Corps officer to captain a vessel when he takes charge of the captured British whaler *Greenwich* in the Pacific Ocean.

August 2

MILITARY: General Henry Procter, goaded into attacking Fort Stephenson, Ohio, by Shawnee chief Tecumseh, is roundly repulsed by a smaller garrison under Major George Croghan. Previously the defenders had masked their only cannon, "Old Betsey," and allowed the British to approach to within point-blank range before firing. Procter's failure disheartens his Indian allies and he falls back into

Canada. British losses are 90 killed and wounded to an American tally of one dead and seven injured.

August 4

NAVAL: The British Lake Erie squadron under Captain Robert H. Barclay momentarily abandons its blockade of Presque Isle (Erie), Pennsylvania. During his absence, Commodore Oliver Hazard Perry rapidly disarms his vessels, passes them over the sandbar blocking the harbor, then painstakingly rearms. He then begins cruising Lake Erie in search of the enemy with three brigs and five schooners.

August 9

MILITARY: The town of St. Michaels, Maryland, conducts the first American blackout following the approach of a British squadron at night. By extinguishing all city lights and placing lamps in trees and on the masts of vessels, the British gunners fire too high and miss the town.

August 7–11

NAVAL: The American Lake Ontario squadron under Commodore Isaac Chauncey engages a British force under Commodore Sir James Lucas Yeo in a protracted running fight. However, Chauncey loses two small vessels to stormy weather and another two when they are cut off and captured.

August 14

NAVAL: The 20-gun American sloop USS *Argus* under Captain William H. Allen is captured by the 21-gun British brig HMS *Pelican* under Captain John F. Maples; Allen is mortally wounded in combat. American losses are 10 dead and 14 injured to two dead British and five wounded. Prior to its loss, *Argus* had captured 27 British vessels in a matter of weeks.

August 18

MILITARY: In Texas, Spanish forces under General Joaquin de Arrendondo attack and scatter a mixed Mexican/American force of 1,300 irregulars at the Medina River. The rebels are quickly pursued back to San Antonio and Spanish control is reasserted over the entire province.

August 30

MILITARY: Disgruntled Upper Creek Indians under Chief William Weatherford (Red Eagle) attack and surprise Fort Mims, Alabama Territory, massacring nearly 500 inhabitants. This is the start of the Creek War which catapults General Andrew Jackson to national fame.

September 4

RELIGION: John W. Scott begins editing and publishing the *Religious Remembrancer* in Philadelphia, the nation's first religious weekly.

September 5

MILITARY: Secretary of War John Armstrong arrives at Sackets Harbor, New York, to confer with General James Wilkinson about his forthcoming St. Lawrence Campaign against Montreal.

NOVAL: The 14-gun brig USS *Enterprise* under Lieutenant William Burrows defeats the 14-gun British brig HMS *Boxer* commanded by Captain Samuel Blyth off Portland, Maine. Both Burrows and the British commander are killed in action and are buried in Portland with honors of war. American losses are 13 wounded to a British tally of 28 dead and 14 injured.

September 7

JOURNALISM: The expression "Uncle Sam" to denote the U.S. government first appears in an issue of the Troy *Post* in New York. It is apparently drawn from the practice of having all government property stamped "U.S." as well as from the name of a local military supplier, "Uncle Sam" Wilson.

September 10

NAVAL: The Battle of Lake Erie transpires when an American squadron of 10 vessels under Commodore Oliver Hazard Perry seeks out and engages a smaller British force of six warships under Commodore Robert H. Barclay. As Perry closes, his flagship USS *Lawrence* becomes separated from his main body and bears the brunt of the entire British squadron. At length his ship is forced to strike its colors but Perry then heroically transfers his command to the USS *Niagara* under fire and resumes the fight. At length Barclay, seriously wounded, is forced to surrender—the first time in history that an entire British squadron is captured. "We have met the enemy," Perry wrote laconically, "and they are ours." Casualties in this three-hour slugfest are 27 Americans killed and 96 wounded to 41 British killed and 94 injured. This is one of few decisive encounters in the War of 1812 and leads to an American invasion of Upper Canada.

September 18

MILITARY: General Henry Procter, reacting to the recent loss of Lake Erie to the Americans, orders an evacuation of Detroit, Michigan, and Malden, Ontario. He begins withdrawing his force back to the Niagara frontier over the protests of Chief Tecumseh and his Indian allies.

September 28

NAVAL: In a second encounter, the Lake Ontario squadron of Commodore Isaac Chauncey gets the better of Commodore James Lucas Yeo's British force, driving them headlong into Burlington Bay, Ontario, but failing to destroy them.

October 5

MILITARY: The Battle of the Thames unfolds after 3,000 Americans under General William Henry Harrison overtake fleeing British and Indians under General Henry Procter and Tecumseh. Vengeful Kentuckian cavalry easily disperses the 900-man 41st Regiment in a spirited charge, but they have a harder time dislodging 1,000 Indians from nearby woods. In the fight Colonel Richard M. Johnson is toppled from his horse and wounded but Tecumseh is killed and resistance dwindles. Harrison, facing expiring enlistments, then orders his victorious army back to Detroit. Harrison loses only 12 dead and 22 wounded to a British tally of 12 killed, and 600 captured; Indian losses are unknown but presumed heavy.

October 26

MILITARY: The Battle of Châteauguay occurs when a division of 4,000 Americans under General Wade Hampton advances up the Lake Champlain corridor against Montreal and encounters a force of 1,700 entrenched British, Canadians, and Indians under Lieutenant Colonel Charles De Salaberry. The Americans make a halfhearted attempt to flank the defenders through a swamp and suffer a handful of casualties, then Hampton calls off the entire invasion and falls back to New York, covered by General George Izard's brigade.

November 3

MILITARY: A force of 900 Tennessee cavalry under General John Coffee attacks and destroys the Creek Indian village of Tallasahatchee. The victorious Americans kill 186 warriors and take 86 captives at a cost of five killed and 40 wounded. Among the participants is a very young scout named Davy Crockett.

Crockett, Davy (1786–1836)
Frontiersman

Davy Crockett was born near Greeneville, Tennessee, on August 17, 1786, the son of a Revolutionary War veteran. He ran away at the age of 12 and ventured to Baltimore, then returned on his own to the frontiers of his native state. Barely educated, he proved unsuited for farming but was a crack shot with a rifle and an expert tracker. Crockett married and was living near the Alabama border when the Creek War erupted in August 1813. He joined the militia and served under General Andrew Jackson in several pitched battles, including the bloody encounter at Tallasahatchee on November 3, 1813. He then marched to Fort Strother and nearly mutinied with the garrison when they were not discharged as promised. Crockett subsequently joined a mounted battalion and campaigned in Florida, thereby missing Jackson's spectacular victory at New Orleans in January 1815. His first wife died, and he hired a substitute to finish out the remainder of his enlistment. After the war Crockett served as a justice of the peace in Giles County, Tennessee, and he gradually developed a taste for frontier politicking. In 1821 he gained a seat in the state legislature, serving several terms. His natural charm and homespun humor held him in good stead with constituents in 1827, when he was elected to the U.S. House of Representatives as a Jacksonian Democrat. In fact, in an age of increasing sophistication, Crockett was one of the first politicians to actively flaunt his rural origins and lack of education. Two years later he switched over to the Whigs and was finally defeated in 1831. He returned to Congress two years later and

(continues)

David "Davy" Crockett *(Library of Congress)*

(continued)

toured the Northeast as a frontier celebrity on behalf of other Whig candidates. Crockett also strongly opposed President Jackson's Indian removal policy, but enemies in the Democratic Party managed to defeat his bid for reelection in 1835. In fact, Crockett was sadly out of touch with the Tennessee political establishment, which was totally controlled by Jackson and his cronies.

Tiring of politics, Crockett found himself drawn to events in the Mexican province of Texas. The American settlers there had declared their independence from General Antonio López de Santa Anna, who then marshaled his troops against them. Crockett, meanwhile, arrived at Nacogdoches on January 18, 1836, received a hero's welcome, and took his oath to the Texas provisional government. He then continued on to San Antonio with 12 other Tennesseeans and joined the garrison defending the old mission known as the Alamo. The Mexican army under Santa Anna deployed nearby and a costly 13-day siege unfolded. On March 6, 1836, the Mexicans successfully carried the mission, putting the 186 defenders to the sword, including Crockett. Death in no way diminished his stature as a quintessential American hero and, in fact, elevated him to near mythic proportions. Enshrined in numerous books and motion pictures, Crockett remains an embodiment of the rough-hewn Tennessee frontiersman.

November 4

DIPLOMACY: Foreign Secretary Lord Castlereagh of England writes Secretary of State James Monroe and offers direct negotiations for an end to hostilities. When informed, President James Madison acquiesces and appoints a peace commission consisting of John Quincy Adams, James A. Bayard, Henry Clay, Albert Gallatin, and Jonathan Russell.

November 9

MILITARY: General Andrew Jackson, leading a force of Tennessee militia, attacks and destroys the Indian village of Talladega. The Indians are surrounded and nearly destroyed before they escape through gaps in Jackson's lines. Creek losses are 299 warriors left dead on the field while the Americans incur 95 killed and wounded. Food shortages then force Jackson back to his main base at Fort Strother.

November 11

MILITARY: The Battle of Crysler's Farm transpires when General James Wilkinson takes 2,400 men from his St. Lawrence expedition, advances inland, and attacks an 800-man British force shadowing his advance. Their commander, Colonel Joseph Morrison, proves tactically astute and manages to skillfully repulse several uncoordinated American thrusts against his line. General Leonard Covington is killed before Wilkinson finally calls off the battle and withdraws back to the river to embark. The much-vaunted American attempt to capture Montreal has ended in defeat and disaster. British losses are 22 dead, 148 wounded, and nine missing to an American tally of 102 killed, 237 wounded, and 100 missing. This concludes operations in Lower Canada, and Wilkinson enters winter quarters.

November 13
MILITARY: General James Wilkinson lands his chastened force at the Salmon River, New York, where they will spend an uncomfortable winter at French Mills.

November 16
NAVAL: The British Admiralty extends the blockade northward from Chesapeake Bay and the Delaware River up to Long Island. Only the New England ports still conduct commercial activity.

November 19
NAVAL: In the Pacific, Captain David Porter of the USS *Essex* claims the Marquesas island chain for the United States, renaming the biggest island Madison Island.

November 29
MILITARY: A detachment of 950 Georgia militia under General John Floyd and 400 allied Creek under Chief William McIntosh engages and defeats a large party of hostile Creek at Autosee, Mississippi Territory. Both sides sustain considerable losses after hard fighting; Floyd suffers 11 killed and 54 wounded to an Indian loss estimated at 200. After burning the nearby village the Americans withdraw back to the Chattahoochee River.

December 9
POLITICS: President James Madison addresses Congress on the subject of illegal trade with the enemy, especially along the Canadian border with New York and New England. He then requests a war embargo on such activity.

December 10
MILITARY: General George McClure of the New York militia hastily evacuates Fort George, Ontario, in the face of a possible British attack; before doing so he burns the Canadian village of Newark to deny it to the enemy.

December 17
BUSINESS: Congress imposes an embargo on all British goods; this measure is apparently aimed at New England merchants who have been supplying British forces in Canada with food.

December 18
MILITARY: British forces under newly arrived General Gordon Drummond surprise and capture Fort Niagara, New York, setting the stage for intense retaliatory action along the American side of the Niagara River. Captain Nathaniel Leonard is captured, and his command suffers 65 dead, 15 wounded, and 350 captured; British losses are negligible with six dead and five wounded.

December 23
MILITARY: A mixed force of militia and army troops under General Ferdinand L. Claiborne attacks and defeats the Creek at Econochaca (Holy Ground), Mississippi Territory. They manage to kill 30 Indians and almost capture Chief William Weatherford, who jumps off a high bluff and into the waters of the Tallapoosa River below. American losses are one killed and 20 wounded.

December 29–30
MILITARY: British and Indian forces under General Phineas Riall systematically burn American settlements along the Niagara River region, including Black

1813

Rock and Buffalo, New York. The militia under General Amos Hall are unable to mount effective resistance and flee the battlefield. For a loss of 112 of his men, Riall inflicts 30 dead, 40 wounded, and 69 captured. The entire Niagara frontier is now systematically laid to waste.

December 30
DIPLOMACY: The British vessel *Bramble* arrives under a flag of truce at Annapolis, Maryland, bringing peace dispatches from the English government.

1814

ARTS: William Rush, the first noted American sculptor, carves a full-length statue of George Washington in wood. He had previously made a name for himself by sculpting realistic wooden figureheads for vessels.

BUSINESS: At Waltham, Massachusetts, Francis Cabot Lowell establishes the first factory to house powered cotton spinning and weaving machines in the same building, which greatly enhances efficiency and production. Lowell is also known for a paternalistic attitude toward his work force and a nearby city is named after him.

MILITARY: Secretary of War John Armstrong initiates badly needed reforms by establishing military districts and purging the senior officer corps of its deadwood. Younger, more energetic officers like Jacob Brown, George Izard, Winfield Scott, and Eleazer W. Ripley are promoted to command positions in an attempt to revive the flagging war effort.

RELIGION: Reverend Richard Allen establishes the African Methodist Episcopal Church in Philadelphia.

SOCIETAL: The first functioning library network west of the Allegheny Mountains emerges in Pittsburgh when several circulating libraries merge.

TECHNOLOGY: Francis Cabot Lowell constructs the first American factory capable of processing raw cotton with powered machinery. Lowell had previously observed such equipment functioning in Great Britain, then a closely guarded trade secret, yet managed to smuggle out carefully rendered sketches. The town of Lowell, Massachusetts, is named in his honor.

January 3
DIPLOMACY: President James Madison receives an invitation from Lord Castlereagh for direct peace negotiations and he accepts.

January 22
MILITARY: Tennessee militia under General Andrew Jackson decides to attack a large Indian encampment at Emuckfau Creek, Alabama Territory. However, the Indians strike first and rout his left flank commanded by General John Coffee. After severe fighting, Jackson extricates his command with a loss of 25 dead and 75 wounded and falls back upon Fort Strother.

January 24
MILITARY: General Andrew Jackson's rear guard is roughly handled and withdraws in a panic from Enitachopco Creek. American losses are considerable but Jackson manages to keep his command intact. The Tennessee militia are suffering from low morale, food shortages, and the general's insistence upon rigid discipline.

January 25

BUSINESS: The embargo outlawing trade with the British is modified by Congress when the inhabitants of Nantucket Island off Massachusetts are threatened with famine.

January 27

MILITARY: Congress raises the U.S. Army manpower ceiling to 67,773 men, although only half that amount is ever recruited. However, they defeat a proposal by President James Madison to raise 100,000 men.

General John Floyd and 1,300 Georgia and Carolina militia, backed by 400 allied Creeks, encamps at Calabee Creek in the Alabama Territory. That evening they are assailed by Chief William Weatherford, who commands as many as 1,800 braves and the Americans are hard-pressed to maintain their position. The Creeks are finally driven off by artillery fire at dawn; enemy losses are estimated at around 200 while Floyd loses 17 dead and 132 wounded. The extent of losses induce the American to withdraw back to Fort Mitchell, Georgia.

February 9

DIPLOMACY: Secretary of State Albert Gallatin, en route to Europe for peace talks, is replaced by George W. Campbell.

March 24

MILITARY: Although acquitted by a court-martial, General James Wilkinson is sacked as senior commander along the Northern frontier, and replaced by General George Izard, who assumes command of troops at Plattsburg, New York. Meanwhile, General Jacob Brown is ordered to take charge of affairs along the Niagara frontier.

March 26

MILITARY: Former general William Hull is court-martialed for treason, found guilty, and sentenced to death for his August 1812 surrender of Detroit; in light of his prior service in the Revolutionary War, the sentence is commuted by President James Madison.

March 27

MILITARY: The Battle of Horseshoe Bend, Alabama Territory, is won by 2,500 American troops under General Andrew Jackson. Jackson confronts a large Creek force of 1,300 men and women dug in behind the bend of the Tallapoosa River and attacks with the 39th U.S. Infantry. Resistance is fierce and Lieutenant Sam Houston is severely wounded, but the Indians are gradually crushed and driven into the river. This victory decisively ends the Creek War and renders Jackson a national hero. American losses are 47 dead and 159 wounded while allied Creek and Cherokee lose an additional 23 killed and 47 wounded.

March 28

NAVAL: The 38-gun American frigate USS *Essex* under Captain David Porter is attacked and defeated by British warships HMS *Phoebe* and *Cherub* off Valparaiso, Chile. American losses are 58 dead, 31 drowned, and 66 wounded to five British killed and 10 injured. Prior to this lopsided engagement, Porter was the first American naval officer to scour the Pacific Ocean for British commerce, and he captured or destroyed nearly 40 whaling vessels. One of the battle's survivors, 13-year-old midshipman David Farragut, subsequently rises to the rank of admiral during the Civil War.

1814

March 30

MILITARY: General James Wilkinson and 4,000 of his soldiers brave freezing weather to attack the stone fortification at La Colle Mill, Quebec. The small British garrison refuses to budge, and the Americans incur a loss of 254 casualties before Wilkinson calls off the action. This is one of the most demoralizing setbacks of the war and leads directly to Wilkinson's dismissal.

March 31

BUSINESS: President James Madison declares the Embargo and Non-Importation Acts failures and urges their repeal by Congress.

April 1

DIPLOMACY: The British and American governments agree to the site of Ghent, Belgium, for their upcoming peace negotiations.

April 6

MILITARY: Emperor Napoleon I is overthrown by an allied coalition; his defeat releases 14,000 veteran British soldiers, "Wellington's Invincibles," for service in America.

April 14

BUSINESS: Congress repeals the Embargo and Non-Importation Acts although, to protect nascent American industries, war duties are imposed on certain imports for two years after peace arrives.

April 25

NAVAL: Eager to increase economic pressure upon the United States, the British Admiralty extends its blockade to include all of New England. All told, the Royal Navy is a major factor in the near-collapse of the American economy, which finds itself suffering from high inflation, severe shortages, and virtual bankruptcy.

April 29

NAVAL: The American sloop USS *Peacock* under Master Commandant Lewis Warrington defeats the British brig HMS *Epervier* of Captain Richard W. Wales off Cape Canaveral, Florida. The British, then conveying $120,000 in specie, lose eight dead and 15 injured to two American wounded.

May 1

MILITARY: At Plattsburgh, New York, the efficient, spit-and-polish General George Izard assumes command of the Right Division. Izard is unique among American senior field commanders for being the only one to have received professional military instruction in France. He immediately begins reconstructing an army from the demoralized rabble he inherits.

May 6

NAVAL: A quick raid by British land and naval forces under Commodore Sir James Lucas Yeo and General Gordon Drummond captures the American depot at Oswego, New York. The port is stormed with heavy loss, but the British goal, heavy cannon intended for the American fleet at Sackets Harbor, had been previously moved upstream.

May 22

MILITARY: For his outstanding successes in the Creek War, Andrew Jackson is commissioned a major general in the U.S. Army and receives command of all military forces in the South. This proves one of the most fateful appointments in all American military history.

June 28
NAVAL: The 18-gun sloop USS *Wasp* under Master Commandant Johnston Blakely engages and defeats the 18-gun British brig HMS *Reindeer* under Captain William Manners in a 19-minute action. The Americans sustain five dead and 21 wounded to a British tally of 25 killed and 42 wounded. *Reindeer* is so badly damaged that it is deliberately sunk by the victors.

July 3
MILITARY: The Left Division under General Jacob Brown crosses the Niagara River and captures Fort Erie, Ontario.

Brown, Jacob J.   (1775–1828)
General

Jacob Jennings Brown was born in Bucks County, Pennsylvania, on May 9, 1775, a son of Quaker farmers. He was by turns a teacher, a surveyor, and one-time secretary of Alexander Hamilton before moving to upstate New York to farm and serve as a county judge. After President Thomas Jefferson declared an embargo in 1808, Brown took readily to smuggling potash into Canada. However, he also displayed genuine interest in military affairs and in 1809 gained appointment as colonel of the Jefferson Country militia. In this capacity he spent the first months of the War of 1812 guarding a 200-mile strip of land stretching from Lake Ontario to the St. Lawrence River. Brown, unlike many contemporaries, proved himself an active and energetic leader. On October 4, 1812, he assembled his militia and cannon to defeat a British amphibious raid against Ogdensburg, New York. A year later he surmounted a more serious situation when a British fleet under Governor-General Sir George Prevost made an amphibious attack against Sackets Harbor, New York, home port of the Navy's Lake Ontario squadron. Brown's militia were routed in the initial charge but he rallied them further inland and led them back against the British rear. His activity so unnerved Prevost that he ordered the attack upon the harbor canceled and quickly sailed back to Canada. As a reward for his dramatic victory Brown was commissioned a brigadier in the U.S. Army effective July 19, 1813. He subsequently accompanied the ill-fated St. Lawrence expedition of General James Wilkinson commanding a brigade, handled his affairs competently, and was one of few senior officers to escape disgrace. For this reason Secretary of War John Armstrong promoted him to major general on January 24, 1814, and tasked him with leading an invasion of the Niagara Peninsula that summer.

Brown, assisted by noted leaders Winfield Scott and Eleazar W. Ripley, crossed the Niagara River on July 3, 1814, and two days later his forces won the Battle of Chippewa against veteran British forces. However, his offensive stalled when the fleet under Commodore Isaac Chauncey failed to rendezvous as promised, and British reinforcements under General Gordon Drummond arrived to confront the invaders. Brown and Drummond clashed heavily at Lundy's Lane on July 25, 1814, in the hardest fought battle of the war, with each side incurring 900 casualties. Brown was wounded and spent several

(continues)

(continued)

weeks recuperating before resuming command at Fort Erie. On September 17, 1814, he orchestrated a surprise sortie that nearly routed Drummond's besieging army. In light of his good conduct, Brown was one of two major generals retained in active service after the war. In 1821 he was appointed commanding general of the Army and acted in concert with a vigorous new secretary of war, John C. Calhoun, to institute badly needed reforms and also advised President James Monroe and John Quincy Adams on military affairs. Brown died in office on February 24, 1828, an important military figure of the early republic.

July 5

MILITARY: The Battle of Chippewa is won by the Americans when British forces under General Phineas Riall attack General Jacob Brown's encampment behind Chippewa Creek, Ontario. He encounters the crack brigade of General Winfield Scott, who happens to be exercising his men, and a formal engagement unfolds. Riall, noticing that Scott's men are dressed in gray cloth, assumes they are militia, but the Americans quickly outmaneuver and outflank their veteran adversaries. The Americans lose 60 dead and 235 wounded to a British tally of 148 killed and 321 wounded. This is also the first triumph of American forces over the British on an open field and proof of their growing military professionalism.

July 22

DIPLOMACY: The United States signs the Treaty of Greenville with representatives of the Miami, Delaware, Shawnee, and Wyandot Indians, which not only secures the peace but also mandates that they go to war against England.

July 25

MILITARY: The Battle of Lundy's Lane is fought between the divisions of General Jacob Brown (2,800 men) and General Sir Gordon Drummond (3,200). The engagement commences when the brigade of General Winfield Scott attacks Lundy's Lane, driving back the force of General Phineas Riall but running afoul of reinforcements brought up by Drummond. The Americans then take a pounding until Brown brings up the rest of his force, the regular brigade of General Eleazar W. Ripley, and militia under General Peter B. Porter. Ripley manages to storm the British battery at the top of the lane and a swirling fight continues around it. At length both sides withdraw with heavy losses although Drummond manages to return in the night and claims the victory. The Americans lose 171 dead, 571 wounded, and 110 missing to a British tally of 84 killed, 559 injured, and 235 captured. Lundy's Lane is another fine performance by the Americans, but they cannot replace their losses as readily as Drummond. Brown, seriously wounded, orders a withdrawal back to Fort Erie.

August 8

DIPLOMACY: An American peace commission consisting of John Quincy Adams, James A. Bayard, Henry Clay, Albert Gallatin, and Jonathan Russell arrives at Ghent, Belgium, to negotiate peace with British representatives Lord Gambier, Henry Goulburn, and William Adams. Each side changes its demands according to news received from across the ocean.

August 9

INDIAN: The defeated Creek nation submits to the Treaty of Fort Jackson, whereby they cede 23 million acres—two-thirds of their territory in south Georgia, southern Alabama, and east Mississippi—to the United States. This effectively removes one of the last obstacles to white colonization of the South.

August 14

MILITARY: British forces under General Gordon Drummond besiege Fort Erie, Ontario. The Americans, commanded by General Edmund P. Gaines, are alert for such a move and decisively repulse the attacking columns. Disaster strikes when a British force storms the fort, then accidentally touches off a magazine, which explodes. British losses are nearly 1,000—the Americans suffer less than 100 killed and wounded.

August 19

MILITARY: A British army of 4,000 men under General Robert Ross lands at Benedict, Maryland, before proceeding overland to Washington, D.C. His first goal is to attack and destroy the gunboat flotilla of Commodore Joshua Barney presently anchored in the Patuxent River.

August 22

NAVAL: Commodore Joshua Barney blows up his flotilla of gunboats on the Patuxent River, Maryland, to prevent its capture by British forces.

August 24

MILITARY: At the Battle of Bladensburg the Americans under General William H. Winder are disastrously defeated. Winder possesses 7,000 poorly trained and positioned militia which crumple under an assault by 4,000 of General Robert Ross's veteran troops. Only a small contingent of U.S. Marines under Commodore Joshua Barney makes effective resistance before being overrun. Losses are 160 Americans dead, wounded, and missing, to 249 for the British. The result is so disgraceful that the conflict becomes derided as the "Bladensburg Races," and the American capitol now lays at the mercy of the invader.

August 25

MILITARY: British forces under General Robert Ross burn all public buildings in Washington, D.C., ostensibly to avenge the destruction of York, Ontario, in April 1813. They then withdraw unmolested to Admiral George Cockburn's waiting fleet.

August 27

POLITICS: President James Madison and some of the American government drifts back into the burned-out remains of Washington, D.C. Secretary of War John Armstrong, who is largely blamed for the debacle, is forced from office and replaced by James Monroe.

August 31

MILITARY: Governor-General Sir George Prevost leads 10,000 crack British troops from Canada and down the Lake Champlain Valley. This is the largest military endeavor of the northern frontier, and the Americans are ill-prepared to contain it.

September 1

MILITARY: British forces land and occupy at the mouth of the Castine River, Maine, then march overland to capture Castine and Bangor. They easily brush

1814

aside local militia upstream and force Captain Charles Morris to burn the frigate USS *Adams* to prevent its capture.

NAVAL: The USS *Wasp* under Captain Johnston Blakely engages and sinks the 18-gun British brig HMS *Avon* at sea, losing two dead and one wounded. British losses are 10 killed and 12 wounded.

September 11

MILITARY: A force of 1,500 regulars and a similar number of militia under General Alexander Macomb make a gallant stand at Plattsburg, New York, against 10,000 Peninsula veterans under Governor-General Sir George Prevost. The Americans put up fierce resistance but are on the verge of being outflanked when Prevost, informed of his defeat upon Lake Champlain, cancels the attack.

NAVAL: The Battle of Lake Champlain unfolds as a large British squadron under Commander George Downie rounds Plattsburgh Bay and sails directly into a clever ambush set by Master Commandant Thomas Macdonough. Downie is killed early on and Macdonough is twice knocked unconscious by falling debris before he orders his entire force rotated by springs, which brought the undamaged sides of the warships to bear. For the second time in the war an entire British squadron has been captured. American losses are 52 dead and 59 wounded to a British tally of 84 killed and 10 wounded. Downie's loss is also a considerable strategic victory for the United States in that it forces Governor-General Sir George Prevost to withdraw his large army back into Canada.

September 13–14

MILITARY: The Battle of Baltimore begins as General Robert Ross is shot by snipers while advancing upon the city and the British attack is commanded by Colonel Arthur Brooke. American militia under General John Stricker then make a determined stand at North Point for several hours before being driven into the city's field works, but the 4,500 British, badly outnumbered by 15,000 defenders under General Samuel Smith, decline to press the attack. Disheartened, Brooke orders his army withdrawn back to their fleet.

MUSIC: Francis Scott Key, a lawyer visiting the British fleet to release a prisoner, was so moved by the naval bombardment of Fort McHenry that he composes the "Star Spangled Banner," a stirring hymn, on the back of an old envelope. It is eventually adopted as the national anthem.

NAVAL: Warships of Admiral Sir George Cockburn's armada slip into bombardment positions off Baltimore and pour a heavy fire into Fort McHenry, garrisoned by 1,000 troops and militia under Major George Armistead. The attack proves ineffectual, however, and by dawn of the next day the garrison's huge American flag is seen waving defiantly in the distance. Despite having more than one thousand rounds fired at him, Armistead loses only four killed and 20 wounded.

September 17

MILITARY: The sortie from Fort Erie occurs when General Jacob J. Brown, having recovered from wounds received at Lundy's Lane, decides to attack the British siege positions. He details several columns of regulars and militia under General Peter B. Porter to move forward under the cover of a rainstorm, and they successfully seize three of four British batteries. General Sir Gordon Drummond then counterattacks and drives the Americans back into the fort, but the damage is done. The British make preparations to abandon their siege.

September 25–26
NAVAL: British forces en route to New Orleans decide to attack the American privateer *General Armstrong* in the neutral Azores. Captain Samuel Chester Reid, however, is well prepared and repulses several boat attacks with heavy losses. Hopelessly outnumbered, Reid scuttles his ship rather than surrender. The damage inflicted detains the British force for several weeks, hindering their offensive against New Orleans.

October 17
POLITICAL: The Massachusetts legislature requests a convention of New England delegates to discuss their grievances against the government. They suggest convening at Hartford, Connecticut, on December 15.

October 19
MILITARY: The 900-man brigade of General Daniel Bissell advances down Chippewa River as far as Lyon's Creek, Ontario, where it is attacked by 750 British commanded by Lieutenant Colonel Christopher Myers. Bissell, by dint of adroit maneuvering, forces his opponent back, burns nearby Cook's Mills, and retires back to Fort Erie. American losses are 12 dead and 55 wounded to a British tally of one dead and 35 injured. Significantly, this is the last clash between regular forces in Canada and a modest American victory.

October 21
GENERAL: Thomas Jefferson sells his entire 7,000-volume book collection to the government to replace those lost in the recent burning of the Library of Congress by British forces. Congress pays out $23,950 for the purchase.

October 29
NAVAL: Robert Fulton launches the USS *Demologos* ("Voice of the People"), history's first armored, steam-powered warship, at New York City. It is 153 feet long, 56 feet across the beam, and weighs 2,475 tons. The formidable vessel is actually a catamaran with two hulls and a steam paddle mounted between them. It also mounts 30 32-pound cannon, two 100-pound Columbiads (super-heavy cannon), and is subsequently christened *Fulton the First* in his honor after he dies the following spring. This visionary vessel remains on the navy list until June 1829, when it is destroyed by a fire.

November 5
MILITARY: General George Izard orders captured Fort Erie, Ontario, blown up and evacuated. This formally signals the end of campaigning in Canada.

November 7
MILITARY: Acting against the wishes of Secretary of War James Monroe, General Andrew Jackson attacks and captures Pensacola, Florida, from Spanish forces. Resistance is timorous and the Americans sustain only five killed and 11 wounded. Jackson's victory forces British warships in the harbor to immediately put to sea.

November 26
NAVAL: A British fleet conveying 7,500 Peninsula veterans under General Thomas Pakenham, the Duke of Wellington's brother-in-law, departs Jamaica for New Orleans, Louisiana. Capturing this city will insure British control of the Mississippi River.

December 1
MILITARY: American forces under General Andrew Jackson, marching hastily from Pensacola, Florida, arrive at New Orleans, Louisiana, slightly ahead of the British.

December 13
MILITARY: General Andrew Jackson declares martial law in Louisiana upon learning of the British approach through Lake Borgne.

December 14
NAVAL: Combined British land and naval forces attack a force of six American gunboats under Lieutenant Thomas ap Catesby Jones at Lake Borgne, Louisiana, capturing them. The American resist tenaciously but are gradually overwhelmed with a loss of six dead, 35 wounded, and 86 captured. British losses were 17 killed and 77 wounded; moreover the effort further delays the British approach upon New Orleans by nine days.

December 15
POLITICS: The Hartford Convention assembles at Hartford, Connecticut, with 26 Federalist delegates from all six New England states. The meeting is presided over by two Massachusetts delegates, George Cabot and Harrison Gray Otis.

December 23
MILITARY: An American force of 2,000 regulars and militia under General Andrew Jackson, assisted by the 14-gun schooner USS *Carolina*, attacks 1,600 British encamped along Villiere's Plantation at night. The attack is fiercely pressed, but darkness, confusion, and a prompt British response force the Americans back. British General John Keane is nonetheless convinced that he is outnumbered and suspends this advance upon New Orleans until reinforcements can arrive. This respite allows Jackson to perfect his defenses below New Orleans and await their approach. Losses are 215 Americans and 275 British killed, wounded, and captured.

December 24
DIPLOMACY: American and British commissioners sign the Treaty of Ghent which ends the War of 1812. Henceforth all prisoners are to be released and all territory to be restored, save for West Florida, which remains in American hands. Both sides also pledge themselves to a series of commissions to end border disputes between the United States and Canada and disarmament on the Great Lakes. Heretofore pressing issues such as impressment, indemnity, rights of search, and a neutral Indian buffer state are not addressed. Considering the relative military weakness of the United States, the terms are extremely generous and a reflection of Britain's preoccupation with threatening events in Europe.

1815

EDUCATION: Georgetown College, founded in 1789 by Charles Carroll as an early Catholic institution, is chartered as a university by Congress.
RELIGION: The Boston Society for the Moral and Religious Instruction of the Poor is founded in Boston to promote Sunday school education.
TRANSPORTATION: The venerable Connestoga Wagon, in service for over half a century and subject to continual refinements, remains the preferred vehicle of

choice for long trips from the East to regions of the Mid-West. These stout "prairie schooners" are drawn by teams of four to six horses and can carry several tons of cargo in addition to people.

January 1

MILITARY: At New Orleans, British forces under General Sir Edward Pakenham begin probing American defenses under General Andrew Jackson. They are heavily repulsed by accurate artillery fire and then withdraw.

January 5

POLITICS: The Hartford Convention, meeting at Hartford, Connecticut, approves various states' rights proposals, then elects to disband. However, the strident Federalist antiwar stance meets with public derision and leads to the eventual demise of that party.

January 8

MILITARY: The Battle of New Orleans unfolds when British forces under General Sir Edward Pakenham attack the entrenched American position under General Andrew Jackson and are bloodily repulsed. Pakenham is killed and 2,000 of his men become casualties in a few minutes while Jackson incredibly suffers only 13 killed, 39 wounded, and 19 missing. This is the largest battle of the War of 1812, although actually transpiring two weeks after the Treaty of Ghent has been signed. The British are allowed to withdraw through the swamps unmolested.

January 13–15

NAVAL: The 44-gun American frigate USS *President* under Captain Stephen Decatur is accosted by a British squadron 50 miles off Sandy Hook, New Jersey. Previously, Decatur's ship had been damaged after a storm at sea repeatedly battered it against a sandbar. He nonetheless manages to defeat and damage the HMS *Endymion* before finally succumbing to three additional warships. Decatur's losses are 24 dead and 56 wounded; the British sustain 25 casualties.

January 20

BUSINESS: President James Madison vetoes a congressional bill intended to recharter the Bank of the United States. He does so less out of ideological concerns than undercapitalization and inadequate powers accorded that institution.

February 6

TRANSPORTATION: Inventor John Stevens of New Jersey receives the first railroad charter in America, intending to cover the route from Trenton to New Brunswick. However, the project never materializes.

February 7

NAVAL: A three-man board of naval commissioners is created by Congress to assist the secretary of the Navy in administering his charge.

February 11

DIPLOMACY: Word of the Treaty of Ghent, signed the previous Christmas eve, finally reaches the United States and causes wild outbursts of celebration.

February 17

DIPLOMACY: The Treaty of Ghent is formally ratified by the Senate, leaving President James Madison to declare that the War of 1812 is over.

1815

February 20

NAVAL: Unaware of peace, the 44-gun American frigate USS *Constitution* under Captain Charles Stewart engages and artfully defeats and captures the British warships HMS *Cyane* and *Levant* off Portugal. American losses are three dead and 12 wounded while the British lose 19 killed and 42 wounded.

February 27

NAVAL: As part of peacetime entrenchment, Congress orders the U.S. Navy's gunboat flotilla sold off while all warships on the Great Lakes are docked and placed in storage.

March 3

BUSINESS: Congress adopts a policy of trade reciprocity with all nations.

MILITARY: President James Madison had previously requested a peacetime establishment of 20,000 men, but Congress only approves a new force half that size, 10,000, under two major generals and four brigadier generals. Still, this is twice the authorized manpower of Thomas Jefferson's day and signals increased political acceptance of an army.

POLITICS: Congress, angered by depredations against American commerce by the Dey of Algiers, authorizes the use of naval force against that kingdom. Apparently the Dey felt he had not been receiving adequate levels of tribute from the United States and resumed seizing ships and crews.

March 23

NAVAL: The American sloop USS *Hornet* under Captain Thomas Biddle attacks and captures the British sloop HMS *Penguin* off the Cape of Good Hope, South Africa. Word of peace had yet to reach the combatants. American losses are one dead and one injured to 10 British killed and 28 wounded.

May

PUBLISHING: The first issue of the *North American Review* is published in Boston. It has been founded by William Tudor, Edward T. Channing, and Richard Henry Dana and is intended to raise the scholarly and literary level of American periodicals.

May 10

NAVAL: Commodore Stephen Decatur assumes control of a 10-ship armada tasked with ending piratical raids by the rulers of Algiers. His mission is to establish peace in the Mediterranean with force, if need be.

June 17

NAVAL: The American squadron of Commodore Stephen Decatur captures the 44-gun Algerian frigate *Mashouda*, killing Admiral Hammida in the process.

June 19

NAVAL: The 22-gun Algerian brig *Estido* falls prey to the American Mediterranean squadron under Commodore Stephen Decatur.

June 30

DIPLOMACY: The Dey of Algiers, awed by the aggressive action of Commodore Stephen Decatur, signs an agreement which ends depredations at sea, releases all hostages without ransom, and ceases all tribute payments.

NAVAL: The last action of the War of 1812 unfolds when the 18-gun sloop USS *Peacock* under Master Commandant Lewis Warrington engages and defeats the 14-gun HMS *Nautilus* in the Straits of Sunda. However, once Warrington is informed that hostilities had ceased he releases the *Nautilus*; British losses are six killed and eight injured.

July

INDIAN: The United States and Native American tribes sign the Treaty of Portage des Sioux, which finally removes all Indian resistance to American settlement of lands below Lake Michigan. This is the price the Indians pay for siding with Great Britain in the War of 1812.

July 3

BUSINESS: The United States and Great Britain sign a commercial convention eliminating discriminatory duties and also allows Americans to trade in the British East Indies.

July 4

ARCHITECTURE: Construction begins on the mammoth Washington Monument in Washington, D.C., when the first cornerstone is laid. The structure has been designed by Robert Mills and reflects the Greek revival movement then prevalent in American architecture.

July 26

DIPLOMACY: The Mediterranean Squadron of Commodore Stephen Decatur drops anchor at Tunis Harbor, where he forces the leaders to sign an agreement to stop harassment of American commerce at sea. Tunis is also forced to pay restitution for allowing the British to seize American vessels in its waters during the War of 1812.

August 5

DIPLOMACY: Commodore Stephen Decatur and his Mediterranean Squadron make a port call at Tripoli and make the leadership sign a treaty which stops attacks on American shipping, frees all hostages without ransom, and ends all tribute payments. Tripoli also pays compensation for vessels it allowed Great Britain to seize in its waters during the War of 1812.

December 4

POLITICS: The 14th Congress assembles with the Democratic-Republicans still in firm control of both the House and Senate. Ironically, while still championing agrarian and states' rights positions, the party of Jefferson has co-opted Federalist positions of protective tariffs, national roads, and a national bank. The Federalists, for their part, have begun to embrace heretofore heretical positions such as states' rights and protection of civil liberties.

December 5

POLITICS: In his address to Congress, President James Madison reiterates the call for a national public works program and urges that the Bank of the United States be rechartered, the military be strengthened, and a national university be founded. In many respects the Democratic-Republicans have co-opted many programs previously championed by their Federalist opposition.

1816

POLITICS: The antiwar sermons of Reverend William Ellery Channing inspire the founding of the Peace Society of Massachusetts. Curiously, Channing was not against waging war in self-defense or for defending a moral principle.

PUBLISHING: The *Vocabulary* is published by John Pickering; this is a compilation of 500 words unique to America, including Native Americans terms in use, and is part of the ongoing effort to nationalize the English language. However, American English still remains closely tied to the mother tongue.

RELIGION: The American Bible Society arises in New York City, whose sole purpose is to increase the distribution of holy scripture. It ultimately prints and distributes the Bible in more than 1,000 languages, worldwide.

SPORTS: Jacob Hyer becomes America's first boxing champion by defeating Tom Beasley in a bare-knuckles brawl moderated by London Prize Ring Rules.

January 1

GENERAL: The national debt is calculated at $127,335,000, roughly $15 per citizen.

POLITICS: Columbus replaces Chillicothe as the capital of Ohio.

January 11

BUSINESS: Democratic-Republican leaders Henry Clay and John C. Calhoun, dropping their prior constitutional opposition to a Bank of the United States, call for a 20-year reconstitution with a $50 million capitalization. They also press the case for a strong and uniform national currency to assist in the postwar economic chaos and depression following the War of 1812. They are roundly opposed by Daniel Webster, who wishes congressional laws against banknotes issued by suspended state banks.

January 15

SETTLEMENT: The first American to reach California is Thomas Doak, who settles near Santa Barbara.

March 14

BUSINESS: Congress approves the Second Bank of the United States with a capitalization of $35 million, including $7 million contributed by the government. The bank is chartered for a period of 20 years, and President James Madison will select five of the 25 directors. The central office is designated for Philadelphia, and William Jones, former secretary of the Navy, is appointed the first president. Significantly, this is the first debate to feature Henry Clay, John C. Calhoun, and Daniel Webster as active participants.

March 16

POLITICS: The Democratic-Republican congressional caucus chooses James Monroe to be its presidential candidate, having defeated Georgia senator William C. Crawford by a vote of 65 to 54. New York Governor Daniel D. Tompkins is chosen for the vice presidency.

March 20

LAW: The Supreme Court decides the case of *Martin v. Hunter's Lessee*, a case originating in a Virginian appellate court. They rule that the Supreme Court is granted the ability to review state court decisions based upon the 1789 Judiciary Act.

April 10

BUSINESS: Congress charters the second Bank of the United States with a lease of 20 years; it begins with a capitalization of $35 million, mostly to be sold in $100 shares to stockholders.

1816

April 11
RELIGION: The African Methodist Church is created in Philadelphia under the leadership of Reverend Richard Allen, its first bishop. This is the first independent black church in America.

April 27
BUSINESS: The Tariff Act of 1816 is passed by Congress, with the urging of Henry Clay and John C. Calhoun, to extend protective duties previously imposed during the War of 1812. This legislation is aimed primarily at the nascent textile and iron manufacturing sector and imposes rates of between 15 and 30 percent on foreign imports of cotton, textiles, leather, wool, and pig iron among others. It is also the first duty levied for protection purposes, not simply to raise revenue.

April 29
NAVAL: Congress passes a naval appropriations bill that authorizes construction of nine 84-gun ships of the line, the first in American naval history, along with 12 44-gun frigates. From a design standpoint, the U.S. Navy has finally reached parity in firepower with Royal Navy warships.

May 10
MILITARY: Soldiers construct Fort Howard at Green Bay, Illinois (Wisconsin) Territory; in time it functions as a major center of the fur trade.

May 20
POLITICS: The inhabitants of Maine vote to cede from Massachusetts and form their own state, but they are derided by the legislature as "childish and irresponsible."

June
POLITICS: A constitutional convention meets at Corydon, Indiana Territory, for the purpose of gaining statehood.

June 11
TECHNOLOGY: The Gas Light Company of Baltimore, Maryland, is contracted to light streets through the use of coal gas, becoming the first American city so illuminated.

June 16
SCIENCE: A major disruption in the usual weather pattern occurs when 10 inches of snow drops in Vermont, New Hampshire, and western Massachusetts. This aberration is attributed to volcanic activity in Indonesia and severely disrupts the agricultural season in New England.

June 22
SOCIETAL: DeWitt Clinton becomes grand master of the newly created Grand Encampment of Knights Templar in New York City.

July 9
INDIAN: The Cherokee reach an agreement with the U.S. government to cede all of their land in northern Alabama.

July 27
MILITARY: American troops and gunboats attack Fort Apalachicola in Spanish East Florida that is garrisoned by fugitive slaves and hostile Seminole Indians. A cannon shot ignites their powder supply, killing 270 defenders.

1816

August
NAVAL: Commodore Stephen Decatur toasts the United States at a banquet held in his honor by thundering, "Our country! In her intercourse with foreign nations may she always be in the right; but right or wrong, our country!"

September 14
INDIAN: The Chickasaws cede all their land south of Tennessee to the United States.

October 22
POLITICS: Secretary of the Treasury Albert Gallatin is appointed minister to France by President James Madison; he is replaced by the current secretary of war, William C. Crawford.

December 4
POLITICS: Democratic-Republican James Monroe is elected president over Federalist Rufus King by 183 electoral votes to 34, while former New York governor Daniel Tompkins becomes vice president. Federalist political fortunes continue to wane nationally, and they only retain sizable influence in Delaware, Connecticut, and Massachusetts.

December 11
POLITICS: Indiana gains admittance as the 19th state with its new capital at Corydon; slavery is outlawed.

December 13
BUSINESS: The Provident Institution for Savings, the first savings bank in America, opens for business in Boston.

December 20
BUSINESS: Congressman John C. Calhoun proposes that $1.5 million paid to the U.S. government by the Bank of the United States be utilized as a public works fund for internal improvements. President James Madison, however, opposes such spending on constitutional grounds.

December 28
SLAVERY: The American Colonial Society is founded in Washington, D.C., by Presbyterian minister Robert Finley. Its goal is to encourage free African Americans to resettle back in Africa; a direct result of their efforts leads to founding the African republic of Liberia.

1817

ART: After studying in London under Benjamin West, John Trumbull establishes himself as America's foremost painter of historical scenes. His canvas *Signing of the Declaration of Independence* presently adorns the U.S. Capitol.
MEDICAL: The nation's first insane asylum is established at Frankfort, Pennsylvania.
RELIGION: The American Tract Society begins delivering religious literature nationally principally through Methodist circuit riders.
TECHNOLOGY: Thomas Gilpon manufactures the first machine-made paper near Wilmington, Delaware.

Trumbull, John (1756–1843)
Painter

John Trumbull was born in Lebanon, Connecticut, son of a future governor of that state. As a child he demonstrated a considerable knack for art and briefly studied under John Singleton Copley before attending Harvard College. Trumbull graduated in 1773 and worked as a surveyor in western Connecticut, where his ability to draw accurate maps assisted land claims. However, when the Revolutionary War broke out two years later he enlisted in the Continental Army as an officer, ultimately serving as an aide to generals George Washington and Horatio Gates. Trumbull had risen to a colonel at the age of 21 by the time he mustered out in 1777, but he subsequently served as a volunteer in the Rhode Island campaign of 1778. That year he also resumed his artistic studies in Boston, and in 1780 Trumbull obtained special permission to visit London to study under noted American expatriate artist Benjamin West. However, once there, Trumbull was seized and charged with treason, probably in retaliation for the hanging of British Major John André, and suffered imprisonment. He was finally released through the agency of Edmund Burke and sailed to the Netherlands. There he completed the first full-length study of General George Washington, which was engraved and distributed throughout Europe. In 1783 Trumbull returned to the United States but visited London the following year to study with West, who specialized in large historical depictions. Trumbull thus was enabled to make his own detailed works like *The Battle of Bunker Hill* and *The Death of General Montgomery,* which established him as a significant painter of American historical events.

Trumbull returned to America in 1789, whereupon Thomas Jefferson sought to make him a personal secretary. Trumbull declined and the two men had a serious falling-out that was never reconciled. He then spent several years painting historical art and individual portraits which, while well-rendered, failed to sell in the postwar depression. Again seeking employment, Trumbull returned to London to work as secretary to Minister John Jay while painting on the side. He remained there until 1804 and then came home, painted for several years waiting for President Jefferson to offer him a lucrative commission which never came, and returned to London in 1808. Trumbull supported himself with portraiture for nearly a decade before coming home in 1816 and establishing a studio in New York. The following year Congress commissioned him to do a series of large-scale historical paintings for the new rotunda of the Capitol in Washington, D.C. He then rendered the *Signing of the Declaration of Independence, The Surrender of Cornwallis at Yorktown,* and others which remain on permanent display. His fame now assured, Trumbull returned to New York in 1817, where he founded the American Academy of Fine Arts and served as its president until 1835. He died in New York on November 10, 1843, a noted national artist.

January 7
BUSINESS: The reconstituted Bank of the United States opens its doors for business in Philadelphia with William Jones as president. Ultimately it possesses 25 offices to augment its operations. However, Jones, its first president, proves himself to be less than a competent appointment.

February 8

POLITICS: Congress votes to appropriate $1.5 million from the Bank of the United States to begin public works programs. However, President James Madison opposes the move on constitutional grounds.

February 18

TRANSPORTATION: Congress approves John C. Calhoun's suggestion to spend the $1.5 million bonus from the Bank of the United States for federally financed public works projects, especially roads and canals. Such emphasis on "internal improvements" are expected to boost the national economy. As a rule New England Federalists oppose the move, fearing it would accelerate the trend toward Western expansion and diminish the commercial importance of their region.

March 1

POLITICS: The Mississippi Territory is authorized by Congress to hold a constitutional convention as a preliminary to applying for statehood.

March 3

POLITICS: President James Madison vetoes the so-called Bonus Bill to expand public works projects; he does so out of a belief that the Constitution does not permit the Federal government to be engaged in public works without a constitutional amendment. This is his last official act in office.

SETTLEMENT: The Alabama Territory is organized from the eastern portion of the Mississippi Territory, with its capital at Fort St. Stephens (Mobile).

TRANSPORTATION: Henry M. Shreve's steamboat *Washington* begins a regularly scheduled commercial route up and down the Ohio and Mississippi Rivers between Louisville, Kentucky, and New Orleans, Louisiana.

March 4

POLITICS: James Monroe is inaugurated as the fifth president while Daniel D. Tompkins becomes vice president. Monroe is the last member of the so-called Virginia Dynasty, which has dominated national politics since 1801. However, in this period the Democratic-Republican Party has co-opted many principles of their Federalist opponents, hence Monroe, in his address, declares his support for adequate military and naval forces and the protection of American manufacturing.

March 15

TRANSPORTATION: The New York legislature, with enthusiastic support from Governor DeWitt Clinton, votes to construct the landmark Erie Canal that reaches from the Hudson River in Albany all the way to Buffalo in the west. This $7 million investment is expected to produce a windfall of profit by opening up Western markets to the state and negate Canadian trade advantages in the Great Lakes region.

March 24

EDUCATION: Allegheny College is chartered at Meadville, Pennsylvania.

April 7

SOCIETAL: A large riot by African-American slaves in St. Mary's Country, Maryland, injures several white passersby until rioters are suppressed by police and militia.

Monroe, James   (1758–1831)
President

James Monroe was born in Westmoreland County, Virginia, on April 28, 1758, part of the minor gentry. He attended William and Mary College for two years but left to join the Continental Army as a junior officer to fight in the Revolutionary War. He distinguished himself in several sharp battles, was wounded at the Battle of Princeton in 1777, and returned to college to study law under Governor Thomas Jefferson. Monroe then entered politics in 1782 by winning a seat in the state legislature and then served in Congress from 1783 to 1786. The following year he attended the Virginia constitutional convention to oppose adoption of the new government, and in 1788 he was defeated by James Madison for a seat in the new Congress. In 1790 he was tapped to serve out a term in the U.S. Senate as an anti-Federalist, but President George Washington nevertheless appointed him minister to France in 1794. His tenure there proved unsuccessful so he came home to successfully run as governor of Virginia in 1799. Four years later President Thomas Jefferson appointed him minister to France to assist Robert R. Livingston in negotiations that secured the Louisiana Purchase in 1803. He ran for the presidency as a Democratic-Republican in 1808, lost again to Madison, then was asked to serve as his secretary of state. Monroe held this position for eight years without much distinction, but in the fall of 1814 he replaced the disgraced Secretary of War John Armstrong and performed capably. The Federalist opposition having destroyed themselves by opposing the War of 1812, Monroe had little trouble being elected the fifth president in 1816.

As chief executive, Monroe adopted many of the Federalist positions he had previously opposed, like a national bank and a strong military. He also displayed an uncanny knack for assembling a brilliant circle of politicians in his cabinet, including John C. Calhoun and John Quincy Adams, who remained with him throughout his two terms. Adams was particularly efficient as secretary of state, and in 1819 he arranged for the peaceful acquisition of Florida from Spain. Monroe also enjoyed the luxury of inheriting a nation at peace and basking in the afterglow of newfound nationalism. In fact his eight-year tenure in office was popularly hailed as the "Era of Good Feelings." However, he faced serious challenges in regard to the expansion of slavery and signed the Missouri Compromise of 1820 while doubting its constitutionality. That year Monroe was easily reelected president with all but one electoral vote. In 1823 he

(continues)

President James Monroe *(Library of Congress)*

(continued)

also accepted Secretary of State Adams's suggestion that the United States formally preclude future European colonization in the Western hemisphere, a policy known as the Monroe Doctrine. Monroe left the White House in 1825 and returned to his native state, where he served as a regent of the University of Virginia. In 1829 he also served as presiding officer at the Virginia constitutional convention. Monroe, a taciturn individual who wore his hair queued as in the days of the Revolutionary War, died in New York on July 4, 1831.

April 15
EDUCATIONAL: Thomas Hopkins Gallaudet, who was trained at the Paris Institute, founds The American Asylum, the first free public school for deaf students, in Hartford, Connecticut. He is assisted there by Laurett Clerc, who is himself deaf, and the two begin devising a comprehensive sign language for English.

April 28–29
DIPLOMACY: In Washington, D.C., Secretary of State Richard Rush and British minister Charles Bagot sign the Rush-Bagot Agreement, which limits both sides to possessing eight warships and begins the process of demilitarizing the Great Lakes region. In this manner a very expensive naval arms race is avoided and eventually leads to the world's longest undefended border.

May
POLITICS: President James Monroe begins a celebrated tour of the Northeast and Middle West; his friendly reception in previously Federalist territory indicates that the "era of Good Feeling" is in full play.

July 4
TRANSPORTATION: Governor DeWitt Clinton breaks ground for the new Erie Canal at Rome, New York; this massive project is intended to link the Hudson River Valley with the Great Lakes, thereby bringing the Great Lakes trade directly to New York City.

July 12
JOURNALISM: The Boston *Columbian Sentinel* first proclaims President James Monroe's administration "The Era of Good Feelings," a euphemism for the surge of nationalism experienced after the War of 1812. As proof, it points to the popular reception of President Monroe as he toured New England and the Northwest that summer. However, as the decade plays out, the American polity is increasingly polarized by sectional differences.

August 29
SLAVERY: Abolitionist Charles Osborne begins publication of the *Philanthropist*, unique in demanding the immediate emancipation of all African-American slaves.

September
LITERATURE: William Cullen Bryant's poem "Thanatopsis" appears in the *North American Review* and is widely praised by British critics. It pioneered serious reflection on nature and death, spawning an entirely new school of American poetry.

October 8
MILITARY: Congressman John C. Calhoun is appointed secretary of war; although not considered a prestigious appointment, especially considering the disarray the military establishment finds itself in, Calhoun functions as one of the most effective and efficient secretaries in American history. He performs competently while putting U.S. Army administration back on an even keel.

November 20
MILITARY: The First Seminole War commences as Indian warriors, upset over the loss of life at the destruction of Fort Apalachicola in 1816, begin raiding American settlements along the south Georgia border. Many Americans believe that Spanish authorities have also been inciting the Indians' hostility.

November 30
MILITARY: Vengeful Seminoles ambush a boatload of U.S. Army troops on the Apalachicola River, Florida, killing 36 soldiers, six women, and four children.

December 1
POLITICS: The 15th Congress assembles with the Democratic-Republicans firmly controlling both the Senate and the House of Representatives.

December 2
POLITICS: President James Monroe, in his annual address to Congress, differs from his predecessor by supporting the notion that the U.S. Constitution does, in fact, grant authority to fund public works projects. He goes to great length to assure their constitutionality.

December 10
POLITICS: Mississippi enters the union as the 20th state; slavery is declared legal.

December 26
MILITARY: General Andrew Jackson supercedes General Edmund P. Gaines as commander of American forces combating hostile Seminoles in northern Florida. Secretary of War John C. Calhoun authorizes him to use whatever force he deems necessary to bring the contest to a speedy conclusion.

1818

ARTS: Noted artist and mezzotint engraver Bass Otis renders the first known lithograph, etched on stone, for publication in religious magazines.

Painter Washington Allston, having studied in London with Benjamin West, returns to the United States and settles at Boston.
BUSINESS: Englishman Peter Duran introduces the tin can to the United States as a practical method of preserving food.
MILITARY: General Andrew Jackson writes President James Monroe through Tennessee Congressman John Rhea that he is able to capture all of Spanish Florida in only two months if granted permission. When Monroe fails to respond to the missive, Jackson interprets his silence as approval to proceed.
TECHNOLOGY: The West Point Foundry, a small forge capable of producing cannonballs and other military ordinance, opens at Cold Spring, New York. By the time of the Civil War it will manufacture more than 1.6 million shells and 3,000 artillery pieces.

1818

January
TRANSPORTATION: The Black Ball Line, consisting of four steamships, commences regularly scheduled service between New York City and Liverpool, England.

January 1
GENERAL: The former executive mansion, burned by the British in August 1814 and rebuilt, formally reopens with a new name: the White House.
PUBLISHING: Noted scientist Benjamin Silliman becomes publisher and editor of the *American Journal of Science and Arts* at New Haven, Connecticut, the first such publication in the United States.

January 5
TRANSPORTATION: The vessel *James Monroe* departs New York for Liverpool, England, initiating the Black Ball Line's transatlantic service.

January 6
MILITARY: General Andrew Jackson, anticipating favorable orders, attacks Seminole Indians in Spanish-held Florida. Previously he had written to President James Monroe that he could secure the area within two months, then proceeds without proper authorization.

January 8
POLITICS: The first petitions calling for Missouri statehood begin arriving at Congress.

March 18
POLITICS: The Pension Act is passed by Congress, which provides lifetime pensions for surviving veterans of the Revolutionary War.

March 25
DIPLOMACY: Henry Clay harangues members of Congress to recognize the emerging revolutionary governments of South America; his resolution for the same is defeated as the government, already embroiled with Spain in a dispute over Florida, does not seek to confuse matters further.

April 4
GENERAL: Congress limits the number of red and white stripes added to the American flag at 13; henceforth new states will be signified by additional stars.

April 7
MILITARY: General Andrew Jackson's first foray against the Seminole Indians at St. Marks, Florida, results in the capture of two English traders, Alexander Arbuthnot and Robert Ambrister. Jackson has both men tried for arming and inciting the Seminole toward violence.

April 16
DIPLOMACY: The Rush-Bagot Agreement for demilitarizing the American-Canadian border is passed by the Senate.

April 29
MILITARY: British traders Alexander Arbuthnot and Robert Ambrister are executed by General Andrew Jackson at St. Marks, Florida, for agitating the Seminole into violence against the United States. His harsh treatment triggers a public

outcry from Great Britain but, in light of his popularity at home, no action is taken to censure him.

May 24

MILITARY: American forces under General Andrew Jackson seize the Spanish-held town of Pensacola, effectively ending the First Seminole War.

May 30

TRANSPORTATION: Scheduled packet ship service between New York City and Liverpool, England, commences; recent improvements in hull design and other refinements reduce the time spent during an Atlantic transit to 33 days.

June 20

POLITICS: Connecticut becomes the first state to liberalize its voting franchise by doing away with strict property qualifications.

July 4

SOCIETAL: A new U.S. flag is designed with 20 stars, five more than the last revision, although the number of stripes remains fixed at 13.

August 19

NAVAL: Captain James Biddle of the sloop USS *Ontario* arrives at Cape Disappointment on the Columbia River and claims the Oregon Territory for the United States.

August 23

TRANSPORTATION: The 338-ton steamboat *Walk in the Water* departs Buffalo, New York, and heads for Detroit, Michigan, with 29 passengers. This is the first such vessel on the Great Lakes to afford regularly scheduled service.

September 20

BUSINESS: Seth Boyden manufactures the first patent leather in Newark, New Jersey, for use in the production of expensive furniture.

October

MILITARY: U.S. troops found Cantonment Martin on the Isle du Vache, Kansas Territory, the first military post in that region.

October 19

INDIAN: The Chickasaw Indians sign a treaty with the United States whereby they cede all their holdings between the Mississippi River and northern parts of the Tennessee River, a move which opens western Kentucky up to new settlement. In return they receive $300,000 over 15 years.

October 20

DIPLOMACY: American minister to England Richard Rush and minister to France Albert Gallatin appear in London to conclude the Convention of 1818 with Great Britain. This documents fixes the boundary between the United States and Canada at the 49th Parallel as far west as the continental divide, so the region of Oregon remains open to traders and shipping from both nations for a decade. Moreover, the United States retains fishing rights off Labrador and Newfoundland.

November 28

DIPLOMACY: Secretary of State John Quincy Adams explains to the government of Spain that General Andrew Jackson's recent invasion of Florida was in response to Indian raids and runaway slaves. Moreover, he suggests that if the

Spanish are incapable of properly administering the territory they should sell it to the United States.

December 3
POLITICS: Illinois enters the union as the 21st state with its capital at Kaskaskia; slavery is prohibited.

1819

ARCHITECTURE: Engineer Benjamin H. Latrobe designs the building to be used as the second Bank of the United States and is the latest example of the Greek revival in American architecture. Latrobe draws his inspiration directly from the Parthenon by incorporating a Doric portico (entrance).

ARTS: Chester Harding paints Daniel Boone at his home in St. Charles County, Missouri; this is the only known portrait from life.

BUSINESS: Ezra Daggett and Thomas Kensett begin one of the earliest food canning enterprises by canning fish products in New York City.

LITERATURE: Washington Irving publishes his *Sketchbook*, which proves a best seller and among the most significant American books of the century. This book seals his reputation as the foremost American writer of his day.

MILITARY: Former army officer and West Point commandant Alden Partridge establishes Norwich University at Northfield, Vermont, as the first private military college in the country. Partridge, fearing that an elite officer corps constituted a danger to democracy, wishes to impart military skill across a broad cross section of American society. This is the origin of Reserve Officer Candidate Training (ROTC).

January
BUSINESS: The American economy endures its first financial panic owing to congressional insistence on curtailing credit and requiring payments in hard currency. Consequently, throughout the "panic of 1819," a number of state banks will collapse with numerous foreclosures on large tracts of western real estate.

January 12
POLITICS: Henry Clay's report on events in Florida, whereby he condemns General Andrew Jackson's conduct in the First Seminole War, fails to pass in Congress.

January 26
POLITICS: The Arkansas Territory is created by Congress by separating it from the Missouri Territory. An attempt to forbid slavery in the region by New York Congressman John W. Taylor is defeated.

February 2
LAW: The Supreme Court under Chief Justice John Marshall decides the case *Trustees of Dartmouth College v. Woodward*, which reaffirms that a private corporate charter is a contract and cannot be voided or revised by a state. This is a Federalist, pro-business decision that stimulates the growth of corporations, free of state control.

February 8
POLITICS: The House of Representatives repudiates Speaker Henry Clay and rejects his motion to censure General Andrew Jackson for his role in the First Seminole War on a vote of 107 to 63.

Irving, Washington (1783–1859)
Author

Washington Irving was born in New York City on April 3, 1783, the son of a wealthy merchant. Though raised in an affluent atmosphere, he proved uninspired as a student before settling upon a law career. Irving subsequently abandoned this to embark on a six-year tour of Europe after which he began writing genteel satirical pieces for his brother's newspaper, *Morning Chronicle*. He then continued experimenting as a writer and contributed many popular and erudite essays to the publication *Salmagundi* (1808) in concert with James Kirke Paulding. Success here finally prompted Irving to try a book-length work, and in 1809 he published *A History of New York* under the pseudonym Diedrich Knickerbocker. This pretentious parody of New York history was roundly praised for its wit and insights and led to Irving's appointment as editor of the *Analectic Magazine*, 1813–14. Following a brief stint in the militia during the War of 1812, Irving then ventured to England in 1815 to confer with noted writer Sir Walter Scott and toured the continent until 1832. There he took various notes of his observations abroad, which were collected into a volume, *The Sketch Book of Geoffrey Crayon, Gent*, published in London in 1820. This proved to be Irving's most celebrated endeavor, was widely praised on both sides of the Atlantic, and contains the famous short stories "Rip Van Winkle" and "The Legend of Sleepy Hollow." Its success brought Irving recognition as America's first man of letters, as did a subsequent

volume, *Bracebridge Sketch Book* (1822). The significance of his work at this juncture was in defining the short story format with an engaging dialogue and interweaving of American folklore into the central theme.

In 1826 Irving's career took a different turn altogether when he gained appointment as U.S. Minister to Spain. There he switched over to writing historical biographies of Christopher Columbus and various books concerning Spanish folklore and his travels within that peninsula. He then came home in 1832 and settled at Tarrytown, New York, before conducting several forays to the western frontier in search of new material. The result was *A Tour on the Prairies* (1835) and *The Adventures of Captain Bonneville* (1837) which, while competently executed, lacked the sparkle of earlier works. Irving returned to Spain in 1842 and remained there four more years as minister, where his writing principally revolved around biographies. His most significant effort along these lines was a five-volume set entitled *George Washington* (1855–59), the first serious biography of the noted leader in five decades. Irving died at Tarrytown on November 28, 1859. Few of his later works enjoyed the celebrity of earlier efforts, but these were unique enough to secure his reputation as the first American writer to garner praise from his English counterparts. In a strictly literary sense, Irving helped pioneer and refine the short descriptive story for the generation of writers following in his wake.

February 13
POLITICS: The Missouri Bill is introduced into Congress, allowing that territory to apply for statehood. Attempts to outlaw slavery in the region by New York Congressman James Tallmadge are passed in the House but subsequently defeated in the Senate. The reason for this is that Missouri will upset the balance between slave and free states, and constitutes the first, real national divide over the issue.

1819

February 17

LAW: The Supreme Court decides the case of *Sturges v. Crowninshield*, which declares that state bankruptcy laws passed after the signing of a contract are in violation of the contract clause of the Constitution.

February 18

SLAVERY: Representative John W. Taylor of New York introduces an amendment to the House of Representatives which would bar the importation of slaves to Arkansas once it is admitted as a state; the move is rejected.

February 22

DIPLOMACY: Secretary of State John Quincy Adams and Spanish minister Luis de Onís conclude the Adams-Onís Treaty in Washington, D.C., whereby Spain cedes East Florida to the United States in return for $2 million. The Americans also renounce any claims to the region of Texas and pledge to pay $5 million in debt owed to Spain by various citizens while a firm boundary is established between American and Spanish territories along the Sabine River.

February 28

EDUCATION: Former president Thomas Jefferson founds the University of Virginia at Charlottesville, and he also designs the first buildings constructed there.

March 2

IMMIGRATION: Congress instructs ships' captains to provide descriptive lists of passengers brought to the United States. This is the first attempt to control and regulate immigration.

SETTLEMENT: The Arkansas Territory is organized from the Missouri Territory with its capital at Arkansas Post.

March 3

SLAVERY: Congress passes a law providing a $50 reward per slave for anyone reporting the illegal importation of Africans into the United States. Any such slaves apprehended are to be promptly returned to Africa.

March 6

LAW: The U.S. Supreme Court under Chief Justice John Marshall decides the seminal case of *McCulloch v. Maryland*, ruling that it is patently unconstitutional for any state to impose a tax on an agency of the United States government. This thwarts an attempt by Maryland to tax a branch of the Bank of the United States and also reaffirms the Federalist-generated "implied powers" clause of the Constitution.

RELIGION: In his noted sermon "Unitarian Christianity," Liberal Protestant preacher William Ellery Channing delineates the basic theological points of Unitarianism—which underscores the schism with more conservative Protestant faiths.

April 2

PUBLISHING: John Stuart Skinner edits and publishes the *American Farmer*, the first successful agricultural journal in the United States, which remains in print until 1897.

April 23

JOURNALISM: The *Missouri Intelligencer* takes root at Franklin, Missouri; this is the first newspaper published west of St. Louis.

1819

Channing, William Ellery   (1780–1842)
theologian

William Ellery Channing was born in New-port, Rhode Island, on April 7, 1780, the scion of a prominent New England family. He graduated from Harvard College in 1798 and then served as a household tutor in Virginia for several months. His firsthand experiences with slavery seared him and thereafter he was firmly against continuation of that institution. He did, however, respect slave owners and always sought to engage them, not condemn them. Channing returned to Harvard in 1802 to study theology and in June 1803 he became minister of the Federal Street Congregationalist Church in Boston, a position he held for the rest of his life. At the onset of his career, Channing was regarded as a powerful, persuasive speaker, but a relatively minor religious thinker. At this time the prevailing strains of New England theology fell into two distinct camps. The first was a conservative and very strict Calvinist persuasion that promulgated a jealous God, human depravity, and the absence of free will. The second school of thought, the anti-Calvinists, advocated a merciful deity, potential redemption of all mankind, and absolute free will. Channing, at the inception of his career, leaned toward the more liberal end of the argument and espoused broadly liberal sympathies and a profound understanding of human nature and its frailties. It was not until 1815, however, when the struggle between Calvinists and anti-Calvinists spilled heatedly into the public arena, that he was enabled to refine his religious stance.

The turning point for Channing's career happened in Baltimore in 1819, at the ordination of Jared Sparks. There he delivered his landmark oration, "Unitarian Christianity," which crystallized the liberal movement and served as a template for the new Unitarian creed. In 1820 he helped arrange a conference of Unitarian ministers, which led directly to the founding of the American Unitarian Association in 1825. To this end Channing also began editing and publishing the newsletter *Christian Disciple*, which proffered Unitarianism as a rational system of belief, one catering to human intellect. In sum, this was a unique blend of traditional Christian mysticism with renewed emphasis on and respect for human reasoning. The emerging New England intelligentsia found Channing's message appealing and counted among its adherents such local luminaries as Ralph Waldo Emerson, Henry Wadsworth Longfellow, and Oliver Wendell Holmes. Outside of theological matters, Channing also paid considerable attention to the state of American literature, commented on it widely in various erudite journals, and entreated prospective writers to establish a national school of writing to distinguish itself from that of much-copied England. Toward the end of his life Channing also increasingly dabbled in politics, being at the forefront of both the abolition and temperance movements, although he always sought national harmony through innate goodness. Channing died in Bennington, Vermont, on October 2, 1842, the reluctant founder of a new religious movement.

April 26
SOCIETAL: The Independent Order of Odd Fellows takes root in America following establishment of Washington Lodge No. 1 in Baltimore, Maryland, through the efforts of Englishman Thomas Wildey.

1819

May 8

SOCIETAL: Seventy-one-year-old King Kamehameha, unifier of the Hawaiian islands, dies in his palace. He is succeeded by his son Liliohilo, who is enthroned as Kamehameha II.

May 24

TRANSPORTATION: The 330-ton vessel *Savannah*, a sailing ship partially powered by steam propulsion, departs Savannah, Georgia, and wends its way toward Liverpool, England.

June 6

EXPLORING: Army topographical engineer Major Stephen H. Long is commissioned by Secretary of War John C. Calhoun to lead an expedition from Pittsburgh, Pennsylvania, to the region south of the Missouri River. The effort lasts two years and thoroughly examines the eastern Rocky Mountains and the area known as the "Great American Desert."

June 19

POLITICS: The District of Maine successfully petitions the Massachusetts legislature for statehood.

June 20

TRANSPORTATION: The steamer *Savannah* under Captain Moses Rogers crosses the Atlantic and completes the transit from Savannah to Liverpool in only 27 days.

July 23

NAVAL: Captain Oliver Hazard Perry, hero of the Battle of Lake Erie in 1813, dies of yellow fever while on a diplomatic mission to Trinidad.

September 1

TECHNOLOGY: Jethro Wood receives a patent for a plow with interchangeable parts.

September 24

INDIAN: The United States concludes the Treaty of Saginaw with the Chippewa Indians of Michigan, gaining the land in and around Saginaw Bay.

October 22

TRANSPORTATION: A steamboat makes its way from the Hudson River to Utica, New York, being the first vessel to employ that waterway.

December 8

SETTLEMENT: The Territory of Maine formally petitions Congress for statehood.

December 14

POLITICS: Alabama gains admittance to the union as the 22nd state with its capital at Huntsville; slavery is permitted.

1820

LITERATURE: Henry Wadsworth Longfellow publishes his first poem, entitled "The Battle of Lovell's Pond," in the *Portland Gazette*.

MEDICAL: Lyman Spalding publishes the *U. S. Pharmacopoeia*, the first list of government-approved drugs.

POLITICS: The so-called Relief Party is formed during the panic of 1819 for the assistance of debtors. Henry Clay and his followers in the Democratic-Republican

Party oppose it while Andrew Jackson and his supporters embrace it; their respective factions form the basis for the Whig and Democratic parties.

POPULATION: A total of 9,638,453 inhabitants is reported by the fourth U.S. Census.

RELIGION: The general synod of Lutheran churches is established.

SLAVERY: Quaker convert Elihu Embree begins publication of his abolitionist newspaper *Emancipator* at Jonesboro, Tennessee.

SOCIETAL: New York and New Hampshire pioneer the first state-supported public libraries.

January 23

POLITICS: The Maine Bill, granting statehood to that region, passes the House of Representatives, but inasmuch as it is a free state, Maine will upset the delicate balance between free and slave states. The matter is then referred to the Senate for resolution.

January 25

POLITICS: The Illinois state capital is transferred from Kaskaskia to Vandalia.

February

MILITARY: The U.S. Army officially refuses to enlist African Americans.

February 6

SOCIETAL: The ship *Mayflower of Liberia* departs New York with 86 free African Americans on board who have elected to return to Africa. They intend to resettle at the British West African colony of Sierra Leone, a refuge for freed slaves over the past three decades.

February 17

POLITICS: Rather than upset the balance between slave and free states, the Senate crafts the Missouri Compromise, which allows Maine and Missouri to join the union as free and slave states respectively. An amendment proposed by Senator Jesse B. Thomas of Illinois also prohibits slavery in northwestern portions of the Louisiana Territory.

March 3

POLITICS: The Missouri Compromise passes both houses of Congress following protracted wrangling over the issue of slavery. Maine and Missouri thus enter the Union as free and slave states respectively, although the latter is not admitted until 1821. Because Southern states lag behind their Northern counterparts in population, therefore with fewer members in the House of Representatives, it is essential to maintain parity of slave and free numbers in the Senate. If this becomes a de facto policy to allow one slave state in the Union for every free state, the balance at present stands at 12 apiece.

March 15

POLITICS: Maine gains admission to the Union as the 23rd state, with its capital at Portland. The region had been administered by Massachusetts since the 1690s, but the influx of new arrivals stimulates calls for independence. The new constitution extends suffrage and educational rights to all.

March 22

NAVAL: Commodore Stephen Decatur, hero of the War of 1812, dies in a duel with fellow officer Captain James Barron over recriminations dating back to the 1807 *Chesapeake-Leopard* Affair.

March 30
RELIGION: King Kamehamea II of Hawaii greets a number of New England missionaries who arrive on the vessel *Thadeus.*

April 24
SETTLEMENT: The Public Land Act passes Congress, mandating a reduction of the minimum price per acre from $2.00 to $1.25 and a reduction in the size of minimum purchases from 160 to 80 acres. The use of credit to acquire land is also abolished.

May 15
POLITICS: The Tenure of Office Act passes in Congress, which limits the time in office for specific appointed offices to four years.
SLAVERY: Congress brands any participation in the slave trade as an act of piracy, and punishments include both confiscation of the vessel and a possible death penalty.

June 6
EXPLORING: Major Stephen H. Long's expedition departs Pittsburgh and makes for the Missouri River.

July 14–15
EXPLORING: Major Stephen H. Long's exploring expedition reaches the eastern Rocky Mountains (Colorado), and a team under Edwin James ascends Pike's Peak for the first time.

July 19
SOCIETAL: At St. Louis, the new Missouri Territory constitution bars the presence of free African Americans and mulattos once statehood is achieved.

September 26
GENERAL: Daniel Boone, the iconic frontiersman of his generation, dies in St. Charles County, Missouri, aged 85 years.

November 18
SCIENCE: The Connecticut sloop *Hero* under Captain Nathaniel B. Palmer, while on a seal-hunting expedition south of Cape Horn, South America, sights the Antarctic landmass for the first time.

November 27
ARTS: Actor Edwin Forrest debuts on stage for the first time at the age of 15; though critics seem singularly underwhelmed by his performance, he is destined to emerge as one of the nation's first stage idols.

December 6
POLITICS: James Monroe easily sails to victory in his bid for reelection as president, swamping John Quincy Adams by 231 electoral votes to 1; Daniel D. Tompkins of New York also remains as vice president with 218 votes.

December 26
SETTLEMENT: Moses Austin asks Spanish authorities for permission to settle 300 American families in Texas.

1821

ARTS: The African Company, consisting solely of African-American actors, begins performing the classics in New York City.

LITERATURE: James Fenimore Cooper publishes his novel *The Spy*, which establishes him as a romantic writer specializing in uniquely American themes. It undergoes three printings in its first year.

PUBLISHING: The *Saturday Evening Post* is founded in New York City.

Cooper, James Fenimore   (1789–1851)
Author

James Fenimore Cooper was born in Burlington, New Jersey, on September 15, 1789, the son of a successful landowner and developer. He matured at Cooperstown, New York, and in 1802 attended Yale College but three years later was expelled for raucous behavior. Cooper then tried his hand as a seaman, serving with the merchant marine in 1806 and then joining the U.S. Navy as a midshipman in 1808. He left the service in 1811 to marry a wealthy landowner's daughter and settled at Cooperstown to live the life of a country gentleman. It was not until 1820 that Cooper evinced any interest in writing, principally through his wife's dare to compose something better than the British novels of the day. His first attempt, *Precaution*, basically copied most English literary conventions, but his subsequent effort, *The Spy* (1821), pioneered a new character, the so-called Cooper Hero, who was invariably a solitary and brave frontier figure. Having found a ready market for his American-oriented novels, Cooper proceeded to compose the *Leatherstocking Tales*, featuring the archetypical character Natty Bumpo, who was invariably struggling to maintain his love of nature, closeness to Native Americans, and independence in a world of encroaching civilization. In this respect his most famous novel, *The Last of the Mohicans* (1826), set new standards for establishing the literary connection between Americans and their wilderness heritage. Cooper was the first writer to view nature as a gift from God and therefore to be enjoyed, not plundered. He invariably sought to balance the needs of society with responsibility toward the environment.

Cooper's success as the first great American novelist led him to tour Europe for many years, where he continued writing and vigorously defended the country's nascent national literature. However, after returning to Cooperstown in 1833, he was struck by the sweeping change in attitudes brought on by Jacksonian democracy, which he characterized as anarchical. His political treatise, *The American Democrat* (1838), and his next two novels, *Homeward Bound* (1838) and *Home as Found* (1838), which basically reflected his own aristocratic leanings, were badly received by critics and Cooper was roundly abused in the press. He responded with several successful law suits against his detractors, many of which set prevailing standards for libel in the courts, but these only deepened public apathy toward his writings. Nonetheless, Cooper compiled a very useful *History of the Navy of the United States* (1839) and the final two installments of the *Leatherstocking* series, *The Pathfinder* (1840) and *The Deerslayer* (1841), which were better received. Cooper died at Cooperstown on September 14, 1851, the nation's first significant author of novels. Despite his somewhat condescending attitude toward the lower orders of society, he indelibly established a distinctly novel format, employing both American themes and American environments, which finally set it apart from British contemporaries.

SLAVERY: The American Colonization Society establishes the nation of Liberia for the resettlement of African-American slaves and freed men. Its capital is Monrovia, named after President James Monroe.

SPORTS: A relaxation of limitations on horse racing in New York results in the construction of tracks in Queens County and on Long Island.

January

SLAVERY: Quaker editor Benjamin Lundy begins publication of *The Genius of Universal Emancipation*, an early abolitionist journal, at Mt. Pleasant, Ohio.

January 17

SETTLEMENT: The Spanish government grants lead mine operator Moses Austin a grant to settle 300 American families on a tract along the lower Brazos River, Texas. He dies soon after and his son, Stephen Austin, subsequently assumes control of the colony.

February 6

EDUCATION: Columbian College (present George Washington University) is chartered in the District of Columbia sponsored by Baptist interests.

February 19

DIPLOMACY: The Senate ratifies the Adams-Onís Treaty for the acquisition of Florida.

February 24

DIPLOMACY: Mexico declares itself independent from Spain.

March 2

POLITICS: A second Missouri Compromise vote unfolds in Congress as a compromise arranged by House Speaker Henry Clay admits Missouri into the union but only if it does not discriminate against free African Americans there. The new Missouri legislature will have no choice but to adopt this condition.

March 3

LAW: The Supreme Court decides the case of *Cohens v. Virginia,* which reaffirms the earlier decision in *Martin v. Hunter's Lessee,* affirming the Court's right to review state court decisions.

March 5

POLITICS: President James Monroe and Vice President Daniel D. Tompkins are inaugurated for their second terms in office. This is also the first time that an inauguration day had been rescheduled so as not to fall on a Sunday.

April 15

MILITARY: President James Monroe appoints General Andrew Jackson as governor of the new Florida Territory.

May

EDUCATION: English Classical School, the first, free, publicly supported secondary school, opens in Boston. It is subsequently dubbed the English High School, denoting the first use of that term in an educational context.

May 31

RELIGION: The Cathedral of the Assumption of the Blessed Virgin, the nation's first Catholic cathedral, opens its doors to the faithful in Baltimore, Maryland. It has been under construction since 1806.

1821

June 1
EDUCATION: The Troy Female Seminary is founded at Troy, New York, by Emma Hart Willard; it serves as America's first institution of higher education for women. Willard is determined to advance the state of female education, a fact reflected in her curricula of mathematics, history, and philosophy.

July 17
SETTLEMENT: General Andrew Jackson, now acting in the capacity of territorial governor, formally receives control of Florida from Spanish authorities.

August 10
POLITICS: Missouri enters the union as the 24th state with its capital at Jefferson City; its addition brings the total number of slave states to 12, equaling the number of free states.

September 1
BUSINESS: A wagon train of goods departs Independence, Missouri, under the command of William Becknell, and threads its way to Santa Fe, New Mexico. This venture is the origin of the famous Santa Fe Trail.

September 4
DIPLOMACY: Czar Alexander I claims the Pacific coast of North America as far south as the 51st Parallel, including the Oregon Territory already jointly claimed by the United States and Great Britain. Furthermore, the waters of Alaska, previously open to American and British whaling, are now restricted.

October 18
MUSIC: A music book published by Lowell Mason, which includes the noted hymn "Nearer, My God, to Thee," eventually goes through 22 editions and 50,000 copies.

November 1
TRANSPORTATION: The noted early steam vessel *Walk in the Water* sinks in a storm on the Great Lakes.

November 10
POLITICS: The so-called Albany Regency under Martin Van Buren, a radical faction of the Democratic-Republican Party, dominates a constitutional convention in New York. They manage to liberalize voter suffrage by abolishing all property qualifications; however, these provisions are not extended to free African Americans.

December
SLAVERY: The Maryland supreme state court, in *Hall v. Mullin*, frees an African-American slave whose master has bequeathed him property, since slaves, by definition, are not allowed to own property.

December 18
EDUCATION: The University of Alabama is chartered at Tuscaloosa, although classes do not commence until 1831.

1822

BUSINESS: Full-scale manufacturing of cotton cloth begins at the mills in Lowell, Massachusetts, one of America's earliest industrial centers. The largely female

Becknell, William   (ca. 1790–1865)
Trader

William Becknell was probably born in Amherst County, Virginia, around 1790, and he settled in Saline County, Missouri, just prior to the War of 1812. From his few letters that have survived he was apparently barely literate and obtained a scanty education in his youth. In 1814 he served as an ensign in the U.S. Rangers, then resigned the following year. In September 1821, to help mitigate the effects of a national depression, Becknell and four companions took a small convoy of pack animals from Franklin, Missouri, to Colorado. They originally intended to trade with Comanche tribesmen along the southern Rocky Mountains but, after encountering a group of Mexican soldiers who informed them of Mexico's newly won independence from Spain, they turned south to Santa Fe, New Mexico. Prior to this, Spanish authorities had rigorously arrested all American traders found trespassing on their territory, so Becknell gladly altered his destination. There he found a ready new market for American goods and resolved to return the following year with even more supplies. The new expedition departed Missouri in August 1822, becoming the first western expedition to utilize wagons. Becknell also employed a new route across the Kansas Plains and then followed the Cimarron River south into New Mexico to avoid the treacherous passes of the Colorado mountains. This route facilitated the transit of large wagons directly into Santa Fe but also imposed great hardships on men and animals owing to its arid climate and lack of water. The Americans nonetheless profited considerably from their exertions, and this is the first recorded use of what later became known as the Santa Fe Trail. It subsequently served as a major avenue of trade and migration into the Old Southwest, and within a few years hundreds of wagons made the trek. Becknell's pioneering efforts also stimulated the first major trade arrangements between the United States and Mexico. Furthermore, the sheer volume of traffic along the trail prodded the American government to begin using routine military escorts to protect the traders from bands of hostile Indians. These constituted the first American military presence on the southern plains.

In 1824 Becknell personally conducted an even larger expedition of 25 wagons and 81 men to Santa Fe, with a considerable profit of $190,000 in gold and furs. He is also known to have explored the region around the Green River Valley, Colorado, but this was to prove his final overland venture. By 1828 he contented himself with operating a small ferry service on the Missouri River, although he subsequently developed a taste for politics and was twice elected to the Missouri state legislature representing Saline County. He briefly served as a captain of Missouri militia during the Black Hawk War. In 1835 he forsook politics to command a ranger company in the Texas War for Independence against Mexico. He eventually settled at Clarksville, Texas, and died there on April 30, 1865. For his success in trading and exploring he remains known as the "Father of the Santa Fe Trail."

workforce is strictly regulated under paternalistic conditions and receives many benefits missing in more common agrarian settings.

John Jacob Astor acquires a near-total monopoly on the fur trade by buying out the few remaining companies still functioning once Congress shuts down the Indian factory system.

1822

LITERATURE: James Fenimore Cooper's fourth novel, *The Pilot*, is an immediate hit with the public. This is also his first attempt to write a maritime novel which surpasses those of Sir Walter Scott.

MUSIC: The popular song "The Hunters of Kentucky," a patriotic paean to the War of 1812, is first sung by Noah Ludlow at New Orleans.

PUBLISHING: Noted printer and author Mathew Carey of Philadelphia weighs in on the national economy with his *Essays on Political Economy*, which stresses the "American System" of high tariffs and internal improvements subsidized by the federal government.

SPORTS: President of Yale Reverend Timothy Dwight outlaws a sports that roughly resembles modern day football; transgressors are to be fined half a dollar.

January

JOURNALISM: In a glimpse of things to come, the *Nashville Gazette* endorses General Andrew Jackson for president.

January 23

POLITICS: Le Fleur, Mississippi, is renamed Jackson and functions as the new state capital.

March 8

DIPLOMACY: President James Monroe addresses Congress, imploring them to extend recognition to the new Latin American republics of South America, including La Plata (Argentina), Brazil, Chile, Peru, Colombia, Mexico, and the Federation of Central American States. He delays his decision until the acquisition of Florida has been secured.

March 22

BUSINESS: William Henry Ashley, a noted fur trader, places an advertisement in the *St. Louis Missouri Republican* for 100 volunteers to venture down the Missouri River with him and develop the fur trade; he gets more than 200 applicants. This is the genesis of the successful Rocky Mountain Fur Company.

March 30

SETTLEMENT: Congress orders the union of East and West Florida into a single entity, the Florida Territory, led by General Andrew Jackson. This superimposes a territorial organization on the region to replace Jackson's military arrangements.

April 10

EDUCATION: Geneva College (present-day Hobart College) is chartered at Geneva, New York, uniquely offering many nonclassical courses for practical knowledge.

April 27

GENERAL: Ulysses S. Grant, the 18th president, is born at Point Pleasant, Ohio.

May 4

DIPLOMACY: Congress appropriates $100,000 to establish diplomatic missions in several new South American nations.

TRANSPORTATION: President James Monroe vetoes the Cumberland Road Toll Bill, which mandates the levying of state tolls in order to finance repairs along that transportation system. The president feels such authority is not found in the Constitution and recommends passing an amendment to that effect.

Ashley, William Henry (1778–1838)
Fur trader

William Henry Ashley was born around 1778 in Powhatan County, Virginia, although he migrated to the Louisiana Territory sometime before it was acquired by the United States in 1803. He settled at St. Louis and engaged in the saltpeter and gunpowder manufacturing trade essential for this frontier region. During the War of 1812 Ashley served as a lieutenant colonel of militia, which also did much to enhance his political reputation. Consequently, when Missouri joined the Union in 1820 he served as the first lieutenant governor. The postwar depression afflected his business fortunes severely, however, and Ashley was forced to seek alternative sources of income. He did so by forming the Rocky Mountain Fur Company in concert with fellow investor Andrew Henry. The fur trade was a century-old occupation on the American frontier, but Ashley proved brilliantly innovative in his business techniques. In 1821 he bought out newspaper advertisements eeking "enterprising young men," and more than 200 responded. From these he selected 100 of the most capable hunters and trappers and occasionally accompanied them into the field on various forays. In this capacity Ashley acquired firsthand knowledge of what his "mountain men" needed in the bush to succeed. He also instituted the celebrated practice of the "rendezvous," a yearly frontier gathering by frontiersmen to swap tales, fraternize, and conduct business matters. In this manner Ashley was able to dispatch organized teams of trappers, or "brigades," further and longer into the most remote corners of the far west. In 1824 a party of his men under Jedediah Strong Smith discovered the South Pass, which subsequently served as an important conduit for frontier migrations to California and Oregon. Ashley himself headed a large expedition which sailed down the Green River for the first time as far as the fort at Henry's Fork, contributing to the knowledge of that remote region.

In all his frontier endeavors Ashley proved highly successful and mounted the only real competition to the Hudson Bay Company in Canada and John Jacob Astor's American Fur Company in New York. In 1826 Ashley, now a very wealthy man, sold his interest in the company to Jedediah Smith to reenter the world of frontier politics. He ran failed campaigns for the governorship and the U.S. Senate in 1824 and 1829, but in 1836 he won a seat in the House of Representatives as a Whig. He was elected three times over continual opposition to the antibusiness Jacksonians in Missouri before declining to run a fourth time in 1837. Following another failed attempt to run for governor, in which his highly probusiness leanings militated against him in this preponderantly agrarian state, Ashley retired from public life to attend to his business ventures. He died near Boonville, Missouri, on March 26, 1838, a frontier legend and a very successful entrepreneur. His farsighted leadership completely changed the direction of the fur trade in America and assisted its subsequent expansion westward.

May 30
SLAVERY: A planned slave uprising by free African-American Denmark Vesey collapses when the plot is revealed to white authorities. A ship's carpenter by profession, he had previously won his freedom by winning a lottery. Vesey and 34

other blacks will hang in consequence, and stricter control of slaves throughout the South results.

June 6

MEDICAL: Dr. William Beaumont makes medical history when he tends Alexis St. Martin, who is wounded by a shotgun blast and has a small hole on the side of his stomach. Beaumont uses this access to study his subject's stomach fluids and conducts the first ever experiments and observation of the human digestive tract.

June 19

DIPLOMACY: The United States extends formal recognition to the republic of Gran Columbia (Colombia, Venezuela, Ecuador, and Panama) under the leadership of noted liberation hero Simón Bolívar.

July

SLAVERY: The South Carolina legislature adopts regulations restricting the movement of free African Americans in the state; the measure even applies to black seamen on shore leave.

July 2

SLAVERY: Denmark Vesey, a free African American, is hanged in Charleston, South Carolina, for his role in plotting a slave insurrection.

July 7

BUSINESS: Missouri trader William Becknell completes the 800-mile journey to New Mexico and arrives at Santa Fe with three wagons of wares.

July 20

POLITICS: Andrew Jackson is chosen by the Tennessee state legislature to serve as its presidential nominee for the 1824 election. This action dispenses with the previous method of choosing candidates through a congressional caucus and offers greater popular participation, an indication of the onset of Jacksonian democracy.

July 24

DIPLOMACY: The United States strongly protests Czar Alexander I's claim of the Pacific northwest coast and threatens war if the Russians attempt to take control.

September 3

SOCIETAL: The Sac and Fox Indians conclude a treaty with the United States which allows them to live and hunt on land ceded to the government in Wisconsin and Illinois.

September 15

BUSINESS: The Rocky Mountain Fur Company of William Henry Ashley and Andrew Henry commences business operations by employing a select group of "Mountain Men" like Jedediah Smith and Jim Bridger to hunt and trap in the northern Rocky Mountains. They remain a lucrative enterprise until John Jacob Astor surpasses them with his American Fur Company.

October 4

GENERAL: Rutherford B. Hayes, the 19th president, is born at Delaware, Ohio.

1822

October 27
TRANSPORTATION: The initial 280-mile section of the Erie Canal, linking Albany, New York, to Rochester, is opened.

November 18
POLITICS: Henry Clay is nominated to run for the presidency by the Kentucky state legislature.

November 29
POLITICS: Luis Antonio Arguello is appointed the first governor of the new republic of California, now a part of Mexico.

December 12
DIPLOMACY: The United States extends official recognition to Mexico, headed by former royalist Agustín de Iturbide, who has assumed the title of "emperor."

December 22
NAVAL: In an effort to combat a rising tide of piracy in the Caribbean, Congress establishes the West Indies Squadron under Commodore James Biddle. Over the next eight years more than 50 pirate vessels are either captured or destroyed.

1823

ARTS: The Hudson River School is formed by a group of American painters who reject classical artistic school of naturalism and embrace the more romantic approach of contemporary Europe.

EDUCATION: In Vermont, Samuel R. Hall founds the nation's first school for teachers.

RELIGION: The American Tract Society is founded for the purpose of publishing religion and moral literature.

SLAVERY: The Mississippi legislature approves ordinances which forbid gathering of more than five African Americans in any one place; its also forbids their learning to read and write.

January
BUSINESS: Nicholas Biddle, a wealthy financier from Philadelphia, gains appointment to head the Bank of the United States. In this capacity he serves with considerable success and the bank prospers until its charter expires in 1836.

PUBLISHING: Charles J. Ingersoll rushes to the defense of American culture in his *Discourse Concerning the Influence of America on the Mind*. He publishes it to silence English critics and maintains that the nation's greatest contribution is the notion and exercise of self-government.

SCIENCE: Benjamin Silliman of Yale is the first American scientist to concoct hydrofluoric acid.

January 27
DIPLOMACY: The United States extends formal recognition to the new nations of Argentina and Chile.

February
LAW: The Supreme Court, in deciding the case of *Green v. Biddle*, rules that a contract between two states is as valid as that between two individuals and subject to the same legal standards.

Biddle, Nicholas   (1786–1844)
Banker

Nicholas Biddle was born in Philadelphia, Pennsylvania, on January 8, 1786, a son of Quaker parents. He proved himself a child prodigy by gaining admittance to the University of Pennsylvania at the age of 10, transferring to the College of New Jersey (Princeton University), and graduating as a class valedictorian at 13. Biddle then returned to Philadelphia to study law and in 1804 relocated to France to serve as secretary of American Minister John Armstrong. In 1806 he shifted over to London to serve on the staff of Minister James Monroe and in this capacity absorbed many nuances about national finance and banking. Biddle returned home the following year to resume his legal studies and was admitted to the bar, but he preferred working as editor of the *Port Folio*, a leading literary magazine. A learned man of letters, Biddle also commenced editing the journals of explorers Lewis and Clark for publication, but in 1814 he won a seat in the state legislature and concentrated on politics. One of his principal endeavors here was defending the first Bank of the United States, which President James Madison allowed to expire with disastrous economic consequences in the War of 1812. The Democratic Republicans soon rechartered the bank after the peace to restore order to the American economy, and in 1819 President Monroe appointed Biddle to its board of directors. He performed capably in this role and in 1822, following the resignation of Langdon Cheves as director, Biddle was appointed in his place. He held this position for 14 years, longer than any appointee.

Biddle proved himself a brilliant financier, and he used the Bank of the United States to orchestrate a flexible money supply that would rise and contract as the economy demanded. Consequently, the American marketplace experienced a period of great stability owing to the pursuit of conservative fiscal policies. Under Biddle's aegis, the bank also expanded nationally, opening offices in major cities across the nation. The economy thrived, but the notion of central banking and business-oriented policies rankled the new Jacksonian democrats, who attacked it as a bastion of wealth and privilege. Furthermore, Biddle's aristocratic demeanor and lack of tact in politics played directly into their hands. President Andrew Jackson, who assumed the presidency in 1829, routinely assailed both Biddle and his bank for the elite business clique they represented. Knowing that the bank charter would expire in 1836, Biddle pushed Henry Clay, his ally in Congress, to renew it in 1832, four years ahead of schedule. Jackson, always eager for a political brawl, vetoed the bill and basically terminated the bank. Once the charter expired, Biddle gave it a new lease on life as the Bank of the United States in Pennsylvania and helped restore the American economy during a steep depression, but he finally retired from public life in 1839. The United States thus lacked any central bank until the 20th century. Biddle died in Philadelphia on February 27, 1844.

February 18
SETTLEMENT: The Mexican emperor Augustin I reconfirms the Rio Brazos land grant made earlier to Moses Austin, soon to be home to 300 American families led by his son, Stephen Austin.

1823

742 Chronology of American History

March 3

TRANSPORTATION: Congress authorizes the construction of numerous lighthouses and beacons around the nation's coastline to facilitate safety and trade.

May

SPORTS: The first competition between racehorses from the North and South is run at the Union Course on Long Island, New York. Northern entry American Eclipse beats out Sir Henry, winning a purse of $20,000 before an audience estimated at 100,000.

May 8

MUSIC: John Howard Payne's sentimental "Home Sweet Home" became one of the most popular tunes in American history to that date; it is first performed in an obscure play of his.

TECHNOLOGY: Gas lighting is employed for the first time at the American theater in New Orleans.

July 14

GENERAL: King Kamehameha II dies of measles while onboard a British vessel to visit King George IV in England. He is succeeded by his nine-year-old son Prince Kauikeaouli, but the actual reins of government will be held by Dowager Queen Kaahumanu until he reaches 18.

July 17

DIPLOMACY: Secretary of State John Quincy Adams tells the Russian minister to the United States that North America is no longer subject to colonization by European or other powers. This directly confronts Czar Alexander I's claims on the Pacific coast, including Alaska and Oregon and the Holy Alliance's intention to help Spain reconquer its rebellious colonies in Central and South America.

August 20

DIPLOMACY: George Canning, the British foreign secretary, suggests to American minister in London Richard Rush that their two nations should cooperate militarily if any countries of the Holy Alliance (France, Austria, Prussia, Russia) attempt to reconquer South America for Spain. Rush's initial response is favorable.

September 4

POLITICS: Father Gabriel Richard is elected to the U.S. House of Representatives as a nonvoting delegate from the Michigan Territory; he is the first Catholic priest to serve in Congress.

September 10

TRANSPORTATION: The Champlain Canal connecting Lake Champlain to the Hudson River, New York, formally opens for business.

September 21

RELIGION: Eighteen-year-old Joseph Smith apparently has a vision in Palmyra, New York, wherein the angel Moroni appears and tells him where to find a buried religious book made of gold.

November 5

RELIGION: In a move that must have sent Puritans spinning in their graves, Father William Taylor, a Roman Catholic priest, delivers the prayer invocation during the opening session of the Massachusetts General Court.

1823

November 7
DIPLOMACY: Secretary of State John Quincy Adams prevails upon President James Monroe to reject any British offers of alliance to counter European intervention in the New World, warning that they would "come in as a cockboat in the wake of a British man-of-war." Instead, he champions the idea that the United States ought to act alone in that regard and police the Western hemisphere on its own.

December 1
POLITICS: Recent elections mark the return of Daniel Webster to the House of Representatives, in which Henry Clay continues serving a speaker.

December 2
DIPLOMACY: In his message to Congress, President James Monroe outlines the Monroe Doctrine, whereby the United States will not tolerate the colonization of the New World by Europe or any other power. Moreover, he pledges not to become involved in any dispute with existing colonies in Latin America and also declines to participate in European wars. This speech becomes the cornerstone of American diplomacy in the Western Hemisphere.

December 23
ARTS: The anonymous poem "A Visit from St. Nicholas" ("Twas the Night before Christmas") appears in the *Troy Sentinel,* New York. It originates from the lucid pen of Clement Clarke Moore, a professor of Greek and Oriental literature.

1824

INDIAN: The Cherokee educator Sequoyah develops the first written alphabet for a Native American language. The ensuing system has a syllabary of 85 characters reflecting the spoken sounds of the Cherokee dialect.
LABOR: The first strike involving female factory workers occurs in Pawtucket, Rhode Island, when the owners of textile mills proposes a cut in wages and longer hours.

January 24
EDUCATION: The Theological Seminary of the Protestant Episcopal Church (today's Kenyon College) is chartered at Gambier, Ohio; the first class graduates in 1829.

February 10
POLITICS: Congress approves the General Surveys Bill, which empowers the president to authorize surveys for the construction of roads and canals.

February 14
POLITICS: William H. Crawford of Georgia is nominated for the presidency by the last congressional caucus despite the fact that only 66 of 216 Democratic Republican delegates are present. Other candidates will be nominated by their state legislatures.

February 15
POLITICS: The Massachusetts legislature nominates John Quincy Adams for the presidency.

March 1
TRANSPORTATION: Construction begins on the Morris Canal, New Jersey, intending to link New York City with the Delaware River.

Sequoyah (ca. 1770–1843)
Cherokee linguist

Sequoyah ("Sparrow") was born in the Cherokee village Taskigi (Fort Loudoun), Tennessee, around 1770, a member of the Paint Clan. His mother, Wurtee, was apparently related to several important chiefs, while his father is suspected to have been American soldier and trader Nathaniel Gist. The two apparently never married, and she relocated with part of her tribe to present-day Willstown, Alabama, where Sequoyah learned to tend cattle and hunt. However, during one hunting foray he apparently sustained a leg injury that left him permanently lame and thus outside of the usual tribal activities. Sequoyah took to drink in consequence and nearly died before embarking on a life of abstinence. He then gained renown as a silversmith, actively traded with white settlers and traders in the region, and developed a fascination with their "talking leaves" (books). Being intellectually inclined, he then envisioned the advantages Cherokee could enjoy if they had their own alphabet and could transmit and preserve important information on paper. He began experimenting with an Indian syllabary around 1809 by using pictorial symbols but abandoned this approach because of the sheer number of symbols required. The Creek War of 1813–14 then interrupted his studies and he joined a noted Cherokee battalion that served under General Andrew Jackson. In 1818 Sequoyah departed Alabama with his family and settled down in present-day Pope County, Arkansas, with the first wave of Cherokee to move westward. Around this time he resumed his work creating a Cherokee alphabet despite the taunts of fellow tribesmen and accusations that he was engaging in witchcraft. On one occasion his home was burned down but he persevered.

By 1821 Sequoyah had finally perfected his system, which utilized 87 characters to represent all the sounds of the Cherokee dialect. He arrived at this solution by closely studying English, Greek, and Hebrew characters depicted in mission schoolbooks. Then he faced a gathering of elders in the tribal assembly and tested his system with his six-year-old daughter. They were amazed when she answered all written questions perfectly and the Tribal Council authorized adoption of his syllabary. Formal instruction began and within a few months large numbers of Cherokee could communicate over vast distances by the written word. White missionaries also availed themselves of Sequoyah's system by translating parts of the Bible into Cherokee. Tribal literacy was firmly established in 1828 with the founding of the *Cherokee Phoenix and Indian Advocate*, the first Native American newspaper, which was written partly in English and partly in the native dialect. For his role in becoming the only person to ever single-handedly invent a viable alphabet, Sequoyah was awarded a silver medal by his tribe and also became the first Native American voted a pension. In 1843 he departed his new home in Oklahoma to search for a missing band of Cherokee supposedly further west and died of dysentery in Tamaulipas, Mexico.

March 2
LAW: The U.S. Supreme Court under Chief Justice John Marshall decides the case of *Gibbons v. Ogden*, which strikes down a New York State monopoly on steamboat navigation between that state and New Jersey. In his latest, Federalist-

inspired ruling, he declares such enterprises unconstitutional for only the federal government can regulate interstate navigation and commerce.

March 4
POLITICS: A nominating convention held at Harrisburg, Pennsylvania, seconds Andrew Jackson for the presidency and also selects John C. Calhoun for vice president.

March 19
LAW: The U.S. Supreme Court decides the case of *Osborn v. Bank of the United States,* and under Chief Justice John Marshall decrees that Ohio, a state, cannot tax the bank of the United States, a federal institution.

March 22
INDIAN: An all-white jury convicts four men of brutally murdering nine Indians at Fall Creek, Indiana; they are the first whites to suffer the death penalty for crimes against Native Americans.

March 30–31
BUSINESS: U.S. House Speaker Henry Clay delivers a noted speech defending the practice of protective tariffs and internal improvements to expand domestic economic growth and trade. He defines such policies outlined in the new Tariff Act of 1824 as tantamount to an "American system."

April 17
DIPLOMACY: The United States and the Russian government reach an accord on limiting the extent of Russian expansion in the Pacific northwest and removing all commercial restrictions relative to shipping in those waters. This is an early triumph for the Monroe Doctrine, although the Americans are backed by British sea power.

April 30
TRANSPORTATION: The General Survey Bill passes Congress, whereby federal surveys for proposed road and canal routes, with military, commercial, and postal application, are paid for by the government. This act follows President James Monroe's contention that Congress ought to establish its authority in matters pertaining to internal improvements. Among the most notable routes covered is the Great Sauk Trail between Detroit and Chicago.

May 12
ARTS: The play *Superstition* by James N. Barker is successfully staged at the Chestnut Theater, Philadelphia. This is one of the earliest attempts to incorporate American history and themes in theatrical drama, in this instance Indian warfare and witch trials.

May 22
BUSINESS: Congress adopts Henry Clay's much-touted Tariff Act of 1824, which raises existing levies on wool, cotton, and iron to 33 percent in an attempt to protect American industry from European competition. However, the South rails against its application to finished cotton used in slave clothing, which now is at an artificially high price.

Clay, Henry   (1777–1852)
Politician

Henry Clay *(Library of Congress)*

Henry Clay was born in Hanover County, Virginia, on April 12, 1777, and raised in a log cabin environment. Poorly educated, he nonetheless clerked for a local lawyer and was admitted to the bar in Lexington. Clay won his first election in 1803 when he gained a seat in the state legislature, and six years later he was chosen to complete an unexpired term in the U.S. Senate. In 1810 his constituents sent him back to the U.S. House of Representatives where, by dint of his oratory and political skills, he became speaker. In this capacity Clay, a vocal "War Hawk," became a driving force behind renewed war with Great Britain in 1812. Two years later he accompanied John Quincy Adams to Ghent, Belgium, to help draw up the peace treaty signed there. He then resumed his role as speaker in 1815 and began promulgating his "American System," a closely linked policy of high protective tariffs, vast internal improvements, and central banking through a national bank. He

May 24
BUSINESS: President James Monroe signs a bill authorizing the U.S. Army Corps of Engineers to build dams, dredge harbors, and engage in other construction with civilian applications.

May 25
RELIGION: The American Sunday School Union is organized to promote Sunday School across the nation.
SETTLEMENT: Tallahassee becomes the capital of the Florida Territory.

May 26
DIPLOMACY: The United States extends recognition to the newly independent nation of Brazil.

May 27
ARTS: John Howard Payne's successful comedy, *Charles the Second, or the Merry Monarch*, which he wrote with Washington Irving, begins its run in New York City.

June 17
INDIAN: Congress establishes the Bureau of Indian Affairs and places it under the jurisdiction of the War Department.

pursued this agenda with varying luck over the next 30 years but was constantly deflected by other pressing issues arising from slavery. In 1819 Clay proved instrumental in crafting the Missouri Compromise of 1820, whereby slavery was not permissible north of a specific latitude. He also ran unsuccessfully for president in 1824, finished fourth, then used his influence in the house to elect John Quincy Adams over Andrew Jackson. Clay became secretary of state in consequence, and a furious Jackson, who received more popular and electoral votes, accused them of a "corrupt bargain." Clay strenuously denied any such arrangement, although in 1826 he fought a bloodless duel with John Randolph because of it.

The rest of Clay's career was marked by frustration and rising antagonism with other political leaders. He bitterly opposed Jackson's decision to veto rechartering of the Second Bank and censured him for withdrawing federal funds and placing them in so-called pet banks. He also denounced Jackson's political adviser and vice president Martin Van Buren's scheme for independent treasuries but declined to run against him in 1836 owing to Jackson's overwhelming popularity. However, in 1832 he proved instrumental in helping diffuse the "Nullification Crisis" with South Carolina by adopting a gradual approach to lowered tariffs. In 1840 Clay was eager to run again for the presidency as the Whig candidate and was bitterly disappointed when the nod went to the neophyte William Henry Harrison. He also endured tense relations with Harrison's successor, John Tyler, who continually vetoed part of Clay's "American system." Clay ran again in 1844 and lost to Democrat James K. Polk over the issue of Texas annexation. Clay's most valuable work was in arranging the "Compromise of 1850," which allowed slavery to be decided by territorial legislatures, or "popular sovereignty." Clay died in Washington, D.C., on June 29, 1852, an artful politician widely hailed as the "Great Compromiser."

June 26
LAW: The U.S. Supreme Court decides the case of the *United States v. Planter's Bank of Georgia*, ruling that whenever a bank becomes a party to a business venture it remains liable to a legal suit as a result of that venture.

August 1
POLITICS: In one of the earliest state-level nominating conventions, New Yorkers gather at Utica to select candidates for governor and lieutenant governor. Here, electors for candidates are chosen directly by popular vote.

August 2
SLAVERY: The state of Illinois ushers in Emancipation Day to celebrate the anniversary when slavery was abolished within its confines.

August 4
DIPLOMACY: The United States extends formal diplomatic recognition to the Empire of Brazil under Emperor Dom Pedro.

August 14
GENERAL: The aged marquis de Lafayette, French hero of the American Revolution, arrives at New York City to begin a sentimental tour of the nation he helped to found. He is greeted by booming cannon while hundreds of boats lay in the harbor,

and an old friend, Vice President Daniel D. Tompkins, boards his ship to personally greet him. This is the start of a triumphant return for the 67-year-old veteran.

August 18

EXPLORING: A group of explorers led by Jedediah Strong Smith of the Rocky Mountain Fur Company crosses the Rocky Mountains through the South Pass, Wyoming. This route eventually forms a basis for the famous Oregon Trail.

September

RELIGION: Reverend Benton Pixey and his family establish a mission among the Osage Indians of Kansas; this is the first endeavor sponsored by the United Foreign Missionary Society.

September 11

POLITICS: Henry Clay is nominated for the presidency by a political gathering in Philadelphia.

September 20

EXPLORATION: Noted scout and trapper Jim Bridger discovers the Great Salt Lake, in present-day Utah.

October 3

EDUCATION: The Rensselaer School of Theoretical and Practical Science (today's Rensselaer Polytechnic Institute) is founded at Troy, New York, and proves itself unique in possessing an innovative curriculum stressing science and innovation rather than the usual classical studies. This is also the first private technical school in the nation.

November

RELIGION: The first Reform branch of Judaism is founded by 20 members of Congregation Beth Elohim in Charleston, South Carolina. The new institution, the Reformed Society of Israelites, includes a weekly sermon delivered in English in its service.

November 24

NAVAL: Commodore David Porter, responding to an alleged Spanish insult to the American flag a few weeks previously, lands a force of U.S. Marines and sailors at Farjardo Bay, Puerto Rico, and storms a Spanish battery without loss. The defenders then offer the requisite apology, at which point Porter embarks and leaves, but he is subsequently suspended and court-martialed for his actions.

December 1

POLITICS: The presidential election ends in a draw with no candidate receiving a majority of electoral votes: Andrew Jackson, 99, John Quincy Adams, 84, William H. Crawford, 41, Henry Clay, 41. The matter is then referred to the House of Representatives for resolution, but it remains a bitterly contested matter. However, John C. Calhoun is a clear winner for the vice presidency with 182 electoral votes.

1825

EDUCATION: John Pierpont pioneers a series of grade school readers which gain wide acceptance in schools throughout New England.

MEDICAL: The practice of homeopathy, whereby a person suffering from a given disease can be cured by medicine that produces similar symptoms in healthy people, is introduced by Dr. Hans Burch Gram of Germany.

POLITICS: The Albany Regency, an influential clique of liberal Democrats headed by Martin Van Buren, begins asserting its dominance over state politics. It will dominate New York affairs for 20 years before losing power.

SCIENCE: Amasa Holcomb begins manufacturing the first American telescopes at Southwick, Massachusetts.

SPORTS: The New York Trotting Club is organized at a race course on Long Island, New York.

TECHNOLOGY: Mechanical pressing of glass, the first real innovation in glass production since antiquity, is introduced at several American factories and gains wide acceptance.

January 3

SOCIETAL: Scottish industrialist Robert Owen purchases a 20,000-acre estate in Harmony, Indiana, to erect 'Harmonie,' one of the earliest utopian communities in America. It will fail two years later, costing him most of his fortune.

January 31

TRANSPORTATION: The Chesapeake and Ohio Canal Company is established in Maryland.

February

INDIAN: President James Monroe, upon the urging of Secretary of War John C. Calhoun, begins the process of transporting Native Americans across the Mississippi River and resettling them in the west.

February 9

POLITICS: John Quincy Adams is elected president of the United States by the House of Representatives with 13 votes to Andrew Jackson's seven and William H. Crawford's four. Apparently, Henry Clay's supporters were told to throw their weight behind Adams so that Clay would be considered for the post of Secretary of State. Jackson, who won a majority of popular votes and a plurality of electoral votes, angrily remonstrates against what he considers a "corrupt bargain." The ensuing schism consequently divides the Democratic Republicans in two with Clay's faction forming the National Republicans (Whigs) and Jackson's supporters the Democrats.

February 12

INDIAN: Creek Chief William McIntosh signs the Treaty of Indian Springs, surrendering all tribal land in Georgia to state authorities; he is subsequently murdered by angry Indians. The treaty is also repudiated by the government.

March 3

TRANSPORTATION: Congress authorizes a federal survey of the Santa Fe Trail, linking New Mexico to the Missouri River.

March 4

POLITICS: John Quincy Adams is inaugurated as the sixth president of the United States, becoming the first son of a prior president to serve as chief executive. His idealistic inaugural address outlines his stance against using political patronage, a stance that will deprive him of valuable allies.

March 7

DIPLOMACY: Henry Clay gains appointment as secretary of state, and Joel R. Poinsett becomes the first American minister to Mexico. He is best known for introducing a shrub now called the poinsettia.

1825

Adams, John Quincy   (1767–1848)
President

John Quincy Adams was born in Braintree, Massachusetts, on July 11, 1767, the son of attorney John Adams, the future second president. As a youth he accompanied his father abroad, was well-educated at leading schools throughout Europe, and in 1787 he graduated from Harvard College. Adams was subsequently admitted to the Massachusetts bar, but a series of essays defending President George Washington's neutral policies won him an appointment as minister to the Netherlands in 1794. This was followed by a stint of diplomatic service in Europe, after which he returned home and gained a seat in the U.S. Senate as a Federalist. Like his father, Adams was a dour and strident moralist, completely above partisanship, which gained him the ire of fellow Federalists. Therefore, in 1809 he switched over to the Democratic-Republicans under Thomas Jefferson and became U.S. Minister to Russia at St. Petersburg. In this capacity he served diligently and in 1814 Adams relocated to Ghent, Belgium, to conduct peace negotiations with Great Britain. With skill and tact he formulated the Treaty of Ghent that December, which ended the War of 1812 and granted no territorial concessions to the English. He came home a hero and was appointed secretary of state under President James Monroe. Adams's flare for diplomacy was never more apparent when he arranged the Rush-Bagot Agreement with England in 1818, which demilitarized the Great Lakes and drew the U.S. Canadian border along the 49th Parallel.

The following year he concluded the Adams-Onís Treaty, which secured the province of Florida for the United States, but his biggest contribution was in rejecting a British proposal for providing joint security for the New World, in favor of the United States solely assuming such responsibility–the so-called Monroe Doctrine.

In 1824 Adams was one of four candidates running for the presidency and, when no one individual was a clear majority, the issue was decided in the House of Representatives. Adams became president with the help of Henry Clay, while the popular Andrew Jackson accused the two men of a "corrupt bargain." His tenure in office was an extremely unhappy one, vexed by the Jacksonian faction of the party that controlled Congress and defeated all proposals for internal improvements on a lavish scale. In 1828 Adams heavily lost his reelection bid to Jackson, but two years later he made history by becoming the first former executive to win a seat in the House of Representatives. Over the next 17 years Adams gained a reputation as "Old Man Eloquence" for his articulate stances on many divisive issues such as nullification, the tariff, and–above all–slavery. In this capacity he introduced so many abolitionist petitions that the House adopted a gag rule to forbid all debate on the subject. In 1841 Adams found the time to appear before the Supreme Court to help free slaves taken in the celebrated Amistad Case. He died while still serving in Congress on February 23, 1848.

March 24
SETTLEMENT: The new Mexican state of Coahuila-Texas announces that American settlers are welcome.

April 10
GENERAL: Aged hero the marquis de Lafayette arrives at New Orleans where he is greeted by enthusiastic crowds and showered with gifts.

1825

July 4
TRANSPORTATION: Extending the Cumberland Road from Wheeling, (West) Virginia, through Ohio is discussed; from this point forward it is known as the National Road.

June 17
POLITICS: Daniel Webster's oration at the Battle of Bunker Hill celebration gains him renown for oratorical brilliance.

July 19
RELIGION: The liberal wing of the New England Congregational community founds the American Unitarian Association in Boston. Members have been inspired by an oration delivered by William Ellery Channing in 1819.

August 19
INDIAN: The U.S. government brokers a peace treaty among competing Chippewa, Iowa, Potawatomi, Sioux, Sac, and Fox Indians at Prairie du Chien, Wisconsin. It is hoped that by establishing firmer boundaries between the tribes the frontier violence many be averted.

September 6
SETTLEMENT: General Simon Perkins helps to establish the city of Akron, Ohio, an important stop along the projected Ohio and Erie Canal. Its name is Greek for "City on the Hill," so-called from being located on the highest point of the projected canal system.

October
POLITICS: The Tennessee state legislature again nominates Andrew Jackson as its presidential candidate in the 1828 election—three years hence.

October 26
TRANSPORTATION: Construction on the Erie Canal is finished, and New York City is now linked to the Great Lakes region via the Hudson River, the Mohawk River, and Lake Oneida. Governor DeWitt Clinton is on hand to symbolically dump two kegs of Lake Erie water into New York Harbor. The final waterway is 550 miles in length at its terminus of Buffalo. The economic importance of the canal cannot be overstated—its reduces travel time into the interior by one-third and shipping costs by nine-tenths of previous rates. Consequently, New York emerges as the major Atlantic port and the principle conduit for New England emigration and settlement out west. For this reason the strategic Middle West is gradually dominated by a Northern culture and political outlook, rather than a Southern one.

November 8
ARTS: Samuel F. B. Morse becomes the first president of the New York Drawing Association, founded by dissenters attending the New York Academy of Arts.

November 19
ARTS: New York is introduced to grand Italian opera when *Il barbiere di Siviglia* ("The Barber of Seville"), debuts in all its costumed glory, replete with a cast of several well-known Italian singers.

1825

December 1
EDUCATION: Queen's College, New Brunswick, New Jersey, is renamed Rutgers College in honor of a benefactor, Colonel Henry Rutgers. It becomes a university in 1924.

December 5
POLITICS: The 19th Congress assembles in Washington, D.C., with the Democratic-Republicans still in firm control; the Federalists are no longer a political factor at the national level. However, the ruling party is split into factions both supporting and opposing President John Quincy Adams, who now enjoys tenuous support at best.

December 6
POLITICS: President John Quincy Adams makes his first annual address to Congress, a sweeping declaration of his support for continuing internal improvements, creation of a national university, a national astronomical observatory, and federal support for the arts and sciences. However, this approach wins few friends among states' rights Southerners in Congress.

December 26
DIPLOMACY: At the urging of the president, Congress appoints two envoys to attend the Panama Congress proposed by Simón Bolívar to promote a pan-Latin American confederation. Resistance to the suggestion is one cause of the growing rivalry between John C. Calhoun and Martin Van Buren.

1826

JOURNALISM: William Cullen Bryant, a noted poet, is appointed editor of the *New York Evening Post.*
MUSIC: Noted Italian tenor Manuel del Popolo Vincente Garcia performs for a season at the Park Theater in New York, where he also aspires to organize a permanent Italian opera company for the city.
PUBLISHING: The *National Philanthropist* becomes the first journal entirely dedicated to the promotion of temperance.
RELIGION: Congregationalists found the American Home Missionary Society, which reaches its peak activity during the Civil War years.
SCIENCE: Joseph Henry begins experiments with electricity, inventing insulated wires, magnets, and other devices essential for the invention of telegraphs.
TECHNOLOGY: The first experimental steam locomotive is constructed in Hoboken, New Jersey, by John Stevens, and is run along a circular track.

January 6
JOURNALISM: The newspaper *United States Telegraph,* edited by Duff Green, debuts in Washington, D.C., beginning as a stridently anti-Adams mouthpiece of the Andrew Jackson political clique. Its arrival signifies the growing factionalism that will ultimately tear the Democratic-Republican party into Democrats and Whigs.
LAW: James Kent, law professor at Columbia College in New York, begins publishing his *Commentaries on American Law,* which becomes a standard canon for understanding constitutional and common law.

January 24
INDIAN: The Creek and the United States sign the Treaty of Washington, whereby the tribe surrenders most of its land in western Georgia, but less than what had

been previously negotiated in the 1827 Treaty of Indian Springs. They are thus allowed to remain on their lands until January 1, 1827.

February 4
LITERATURE: James Fenimore Cooper publishes *The Last of the Mohicans*, a phenomenal best seller on both sides of the Atlantic with two million copies ultimately sold.

February 7
EDUCATION: Presbyterian and Congregational denominations unite to found Western Reserve University in Hudson, Ohio, with its first class graduating in 1830.

February 13
SOCIETAL: The American Society for the Promotion of Temperance (modern-day American Temperance Society) is founded in Boston by a mixed group of clergymen and lay people. They have been motivated by the preaching of Lyman Beecher.

February 17
MILITARY: Governor George M. Troup of Georgia, determined to prevent the arrival of federal troops in the western part of his state, calls up the state militia.

March 3
SOCIETAL: Radical reformer Fanny Wright establishes her model commune in Nashville, Tennessee, which she christens Nashoba. She quickly gains the ire of locals by allowing blacks and whites to associate closely.

March 9
EDUCATION: Lafayette College, named after the Revolutionary War hero and affiliated with the Presbyterian Church, is chartered at Easton, Pennsylvania.

March 14
DIPLOMACY: Congress votes to send only two observers to the projected congress of Latin American republics to be held in Panama in the summer. As it turns out, neither is able to reach the conference in time.

March 30
POLITICS: John Randolph of Roanoke, Virginia, a master of political invective, stridently denounces President John Q. Adams and Secretary of State Henry Clay as "The combination of the puritan with the blackleg." Clay, taking the insult personally, challenges Randolph to a duel.

April 8
POLITICS: Secretary of State Henry Clay and Jacksonian partisan John Randolph of Roanoke wage a bloodless duel over the latter's accusation that Clay made a "corrupt bargain" by supporting the candidacy of John Quincy Adams.

April 26
DIPLOMACY: The United States concludes a treaty of amity and commerce with Denmark.
TECHNOLOGY: Samuel Morely of Orford, New Hampshire, receives the first patent for a two-chambered, internal combustion engine.

1826

May 2
DIPLOMACY: The United States extends formal recognition to the newly independent nation of Peru.

July 4
GENERAL: This day, two preeminent founding fathers, Thomas Jefferson and John Adams, die at Monticello, Virginia, and Braintree, Massachusetts, respectively.

August 2
POLITICS: Daniel Webster movingly eulogizes both John Adams and Thomas Jefferson in a major address at Faneuil Hall, Boston. Their nearly simultaneous passing concludes a seminal period of American history.

August 22
EXPLORING: Jedidiah Strong Smith departs the Great Salt Lake, Utah, and makes for California through the Cajon Pass of the Rocky Mountains.

September 3
NAVAL: The frigate USS *Vincennes* under Captain F. B. Finch sails from New York on a four-year mission to *circumnavigate* the globe for the first time under the American flag.

September 12
POLITICS: The Anti-Masonic Party is founded in New York following the alleged abduction and murder of former Freemason William Morgan for revealing the organization's secrets; this is the first third party in American history.

October 7
TRANSPORTATION: The Quincy Tramway, America's first railroad, consisting of steel tracks and horse-drawn wagons, is constructed at Quincy, Massachusetts. It is designed to transport stone from a quarry to the Neoponset River, three miles distant, for transportation to the new Bunker Hill Monument.

October 23
ARTS: The Bowery Theater, boasting the largest stage in New York City, opens; it remains a center for vaudeville and minstrel-type performances for nearly a century.

October 26
RELIGION: Newly ordained Ralph Waldo Emerson delivers his first sermon in Boston, Massachusetts.

November
POLITICS: Congressional midterm elections result in marked gains for the anti-Adams, Jacksonian faction of the Democratic-Republicans, who now control both houses of Congress.

November 11
SETTLEMENT: A Royal Navy vessel under Captain Frederick Beechey maps San Francisco Bay.

November 27
EXPLORING: A wagon train headed by Jedidiah Strong Smith arrives at San Diego, California, having utilized the Rocky Mountain Cajon Pass (South Pass) for the first time.

1827

LITERATURE: Edgar Allan Poe publishes *Tamerlane and Other Poems* anonymously in Boston; it barely garners attention from the literary world.

PUBLISHING: The *American Quarterly Review* is founded in Philadelphia by Robert Walsh, who counts among his contributors noted writers George Ticknor, George Bancroft, and James Kirke Paulding.

The *Journal of Commerce* begins publishing in New York City under Arthur Tappan.

Francis Lieber, a German political philosopher and refugee, begins compiling his *Encyclopedia Americana*, and organizes it along German lines of research and scholarship.

Sarah Josepha Hale publishes her first novel, *Northwood*, which is also the first antislavery novel.

January 10
BUSINESS: The House of Representatives passes a bill calling for imposition of even higher duties than imposed by the Tariff Bill of 1824, which has thus far failed to eliminate British textile competition. A sectional split develops over its passage, with the North favoring it and the South opposing it.

February 2
LAW: The U.S. Supreme Court decides the case of *Martin v. Mott*, ruling that the president alone has the constitutional power to mobilize the state militias. These actions cannot be negated by state authorities.

February 7
ARTS: The art of toe dancing (ballet) is introduced by ballet dancer Francisque Hutin at the Bowery Theater, New York. Her scantily clad appearance so shocked American sensibilities that every woman in the lower tier of the theater reputedly left the theater in a huff. The rest responded with calls for an encore.

February 17
MILITARY: U.S. Army troops are dispatched to Creek lands in Georgia to prevent premature surveying of tribal lands, yet Governor George M. Troup mobilizes the state militia to oppose them. The transfer of land stipulated in the Treaty of Washington, signed the previous January, has not yet occurred.

February 28
POLITICS: The Senate defeats an attempt to impose higher tariffs on textiles, the Woolens Bill, when Vice President John C. Calhoun casts the decisive, tie-breaking vote against it. High tariffs become a matter of increasingly shrill sectional discord in national politics from this point on.

TRANSPORTATION: The Baltimore and Ohio Railroad is chartered by the state of Maryland; it is the first business of its kind licensed to carry both passengers and freight.

March 13
LAW: The U.S. Supreme Court decides the case of *Ogden v. Saunders*, ruling that any contract signed after the passage of a bankruptcy law is governed by all provisions of the same.

March 16

JOURNALISM: John Russworm and Samuel Cornish edit and publish *Freedom's Journal*, the first newspaper by and for African Americans.

March 29

SOCIETAL: The utopian community of New Harmony, Indiana, is disbanded, having cost founder Robert Owen an estimated $125,000 after a tumultuous two years.

May

TRANSPORTATION: The Mauch Chunk railroad, a descending nine-mile track powered by gravity, connects the Carbondale, Pennsylvania, coal mines to the Leigh River.

May 8

SETTLEMENT: The site for Cantonment Leavenworth is fixed in the Kansas Territory; this is the future site of Fort Leavenworth, erected to provide protection for commerce along the Santa Fe Trail. It is constructed and named for Colonel Henry H. Leavenworth, a noted War of 1812 soldier who had been dispatched there by Brigadier General Henry Atkinson, another significant frontier administrator.

May 14

BUSINESS: The declining price of wool induces farmers and manufacturers to convene in Philadelphia to discuss their options.

July 2

POLITICS: In an early dispute over economic policy, Thomas Cooper, president of South Carolina College, declares that the high tariff policy of the government favors the industrial North at the expense of the agricultural South. Thanks to this moving presentation, resistance to high tariffs begins to coalesce statewide.

July 4

SLAVERY: New York formally abolishes slavery, granting freedom to 10,000 former slaves, now new citizens.

July 23

SPORTS: The first public swimming pool opens in Boston and is frequently attended by 61-year-old John Quincy Adams, who enjoys using the six-foot diving board.

July 26

INDIAN: The Cherokee Nation, with its capital at New Echota, Georgia, adopts a constitution patterned after the American model.

July 30

BUSINESS: Following the failure of congressional action, a convention of 100 delegates from 13 states convenes at Harrisburg, Pennsylvania, and calls for higher tariffs to protect the wool industry and producers of hemp, flax, and iron products.

August 6

DIPLOMACY: The United States and Great Britain renew their 1818 commercial treaty and also resolve to continue joint occupation of the Oregon Territory.

August 14
LABOR: Journeyman tailors in Philadelphia mount a strike.

September 19
GENERAL: Legendary frontier figure Jim Bowie kills a sword-armed man in a duel at Vidalia, Louisiana, with a knife purportedly of his own design. Thus the "Bowie Knife" passes into legend.

September 22
RELIGION: At Palmyra, New York, Joseph Smith claims to have received instructions to dig up a mysterious book with golden pages. He is then assisted in translating its passages, which reveal a story of the lost tribes of Israel.

October 10
SCIENCE: Scientist Joseph Henry delivers a paper at the Albany Institute which discusses early experiments with electromagnetism; this is an essential first step in the development of devices such as the telegraph.

October 17
WOMEN: Methodist minister Salome Lincoln becomes the first American woman to conduct a public lecture tour, delivering the first address at her church in Raynham, Massachusetts.

November 15
INDIAN: The Creek sign an additional treaty with the United States, finally ceding their remaining land in western Georgia.

December 3
POLITICS: The midterm congressional elections result in additional gains for the anti-Adams, pro-Jacksonian faction of the Democratic-Republican Party, with 26 to 20 Senators and 119 to 94 Representatives. This leaves President John Quincy Adams with fewer friends in Congress.

December 24
POLITICS: The pro-Jacksonian majority in Congress refuses to endorse the protectionist, high tariff proposals from the memorial of a recent convention in Harrisburg, Pennsylvania.

1828

ARTS: One of the earliest debuts of blackface minstrels occurs in Louisville, Kentucky, in the form of "Jim Crow," a character invented by white comedian Thomas Dartmouth Rice. In this rapidly flourishing form of entertainment, African Americans are invariably stereotyped as ignorant knaves and perform various song and dance routines.

LABOR: The first recorded strike by textile workers unfolds in Paterson, New Jersey; the affair lasts 10 days and fails to win participants their desired 10-hour day.

LITERATURE: Nathaniel Hawthorne debuts with the publication of his first novel *Fanshawe*, written anonymously.

POLITICS: William Ladd founds the American Peace Society, and he also edits and publishes its periodical.

1828

Hawthorne, Nathaniel   (1804–1864)
Writer

Nathaniel Hawthorne *(Library of Congress)*

Nathaniel Hawthorne was born in Salem, Massachusetts, on July 4, 1804, son of a sea captain and descended from several lines of distinguished Puritans. His father died in Hawthorne's youth, and he absorbed from his reclusive mother a tendency toward reflective isolation. Hawthorne subsequently attended Bowdoin College in Maine, performing well academically, and counted among his classmates such future luminaries as Henry Wadsworth Longfellow and Franklin Pierce. Thereafter he returned to Salem to work in various odd jobs and city positions while aspiring to be a writer. His first novel *Fanshawe* (1828) was published anonymously and garnered no favorable notice. Hawthorne enjoyed better success with a collection of short stories, *Twice-Told Tales* (1837) and *Mosses from an Old Manse* (1846) before switching over to historical romances. In the interim he was forced to hold down several positions in the local customshouse but in 1850 finally triumphed with the publication of *The Scarlet Letter*

Publishing: John James Audubon, a noted painter and naturalist, publishes the first volume of his epic *Birds of America*; this seminal series of five volumes, will be completed in 1838 and artfully depicts 1,065 species in their natural habitats.

Sarah Josepha Hale becomes one of the earliest female editors by taking charge of *Godey's Lady's Book*.

Sports: A group of famous artists founds the United Bowman of Philadelphia, the nation's first archery club.

Technology: Scientist Joseph Henry invents insulation for copper wire in Albany, New York, an essential step toward the transmission of electricity.

January 12
Diplomacy: The United States and Mexico agree to establish their mutual border along the Sabine River, identical to the terms established for Spain in 1819.

January 24
Education: The Indiana legislature charters Indiana College at Bloomington; it awards its first degrees in 1830.

1828

(1850), since regarded as an American literary masterpiece. He then demonstrated his mastery of the genre with *The House of Seven Gables* (1851) and *The Blithedale Romance* (1852), both of which are representative of Hawthorne's gift for darkly themed stories and sweeping allegories of good and evil. He was also adept at employing Puritan history as a vehicle for commenting upon contemporary American life. He then backpeddled completely to produce two highly popular children's titles, *A Wonder-Book for Girls and Boys* (1852) and *Tanglewood Tales for Girls and Boys* (1853). Success here finally granted him the financial security so conspicuously missing in his earlier days.

Despite his penchant for solitude, Hawthorne associated with the influential writer's circle of the Transcendentalist Club and enjoyed cordial relations with Ralph Waldo Emerson, Henry David Thoreau, and Bronson Alcott. However, he remained a marginal figure within that larger body of contemporary talent, obsessed by the allure and power of evil to eclipse the greatest optimism. In 1842 Hawthorne married Sophia Peabody of Salem, from one of that city's most prominent families, yet was so embarrassed over informing his family of the engagement that reputedly none of them attended the wedding. In 1852 Hawthorne's college friend Pierce ran for the presidency and Hawthorne composed a campaign biography for him. Once Pierce was elected he appointed Hawthorne U.S. Consul in Liverpool, England, and then Italy. Back home at Concord in 1860, he found the time and inspiration to pen *The Marble Faun* and *Our Old Home*, his last major works. Hawthorne died in Plymouth, New Hampshire, on May 19, 1864, while en route to visit his friend Pierce. By dint of effective prose and captivating imagery, he had become one of the most accomplished American writers of this or any other age.

January 30

TRANSPORTATION: In Charleston, the South Carolina Canal and Railroad Company is chartered to construct what will become known as the Charleston-Hamburg Line.

January 31

POLITICS: The antiadministration Jacksonians in Congress, determined to embarrass President John Quincy Adams, pass an excessively high tariff bill on several protected items, while repealing those on the New England wool industry. They fully expect the president, who agrees with protectionist legislation, to veto the move.

February 21

JOURNALISM: At Echota, Georgia, Cherokee linguist Sequoyah and editor Elias Boudinot begin publishing the *Cherokee Phoenix*, the first newspaper written in a Native American language. The paper employs a system of characters, each denoting a unique Cherokee utterance or sound.

March 24

TRANSPORTATION: The Pennsylvania legislature appropriates funding to construct a railroad from Philadelphia to Columbia; this is the first publicly funded venture of its kind in the nation.

1828

Audubon, John James (1785–1851)
Naturalist

John James Audubon was born in San Domingo (Haiti) on April 26, 1785, the illegitimate son of a French naval officer. He was raised and well-educated in France and served as a cadet in the French navy, 1796–1800, before immigrating to the United States in 1803. Audubon initially worked managing an estate at Norristown, Pennsylvania, where proximity to nearby woods piqued his interest in nature. There he first discovered his fascination for wildlife, especially birds. Audubon had always been interested in animal behavior and he became the first individual to scientifically "band" the legs of birds to identify them in their yearly migrations. After marrying a local woman in 1808, he relocated to Louisville, Kentucky, to operate a general store with a business partner and take in the rough, frontier nature of his new abode. His closeness to the natural world inspired him to take up a brush and he began painting birds in their natural habitats. In fact, Audubon had been a gifted artist ever since childhood and his preoccupation with ornithology brought him hours of delight and a source of additional income. In 1810 he moved again to the frontier region of Henderson, Kentucky, selling goods and painting birds until his a business failure forced him back to Louisville. During the Panic (depression) of 1819 he was forced into bankruptcy and moved to Cincinnati, Ohio, to work as a taxidermist in the Western Museum there. It was at this period that he decided to sever his business connections and paint birds full time.

For six years Audubon and his artist partner Joseph Mason traveled the Ohio and Mississippi Rivers looking for appropriate subjects to capture on canvas and by 1826 had amassed a considerable body of work. He tried publishing his work in America, meeting only with scorn, then ventured to England to find a sponsor. Surprisingly, his labors were enthusiastically received in London and Edinburgh, and so highly regarded were his renditions that he was inducted into the Royal Society. More important, he secured financial support to publish his mammoth series *Birds of America* over the next 11 years by offering it on a subscription basis to wealthy collectors and naturalists. The final product boasted 435 hand-colored aquatint engravings that depicted 1,065 species of birds. The result was an instant success on both sides of the Atlantic, and Audubon returned to America in 1839 to continue his work. He subsequently wrote the equally impressive five-volume set *The Ornithological Biography* (1831–39) and an illustrated catalog, *Synopsis of Birds of North America* (1839). Audubon's success propelled him to the front rank of famous American naturalists, and all his books have been continually republished. His last work, *The Viviparous Quadrapeds of North America* (1852–54) dealt with mammals and was partially finished by his son. Audubon died at Hudson, New York, on January 27, 1851, among the earliest and most influential of American naturalists.

April 21

PUBLISHING: At Amherst, Massachusetts, Noah Webster finishes his *An American Dictionary of the English Language*, a seminal reference book two decades in the making. The final product contains 70,000 entries, more than any other such

Boudinot, Elias (ca. 1803–1839)
Cherokee editor

Galagina (Male Buck) was born near Rome, Georgia, around 1803, into the Cherokee nation. He belonged to a prominent tribal family as his father, David Oowatie, was an individual of some repute, and his younger brother, Stand Watie, was a future Confederate general. The Cherokee by this time had been partly acculturated by their exposure to American civilization and Galagina was sent north to attend a missionary school at Cornwall, Connecticut. His benefactor in this regard was the retired New Jersey philanthropist Elias Boudinot and Galagina adopted his name as a token of respect. Boudinot performed well in his studies but incurred a measure of controversy when he fell in love with a local white girl, Harriet Ruggles Gold, and married her over parental objections. This act led to the closing of the Indian school at Cornwall, and Boudinot returned home to his tribe in Georgia. Well-educated by Cherokee standards, he gained appointment as editor of the tribal newspaper *Cherokee Phoenix*, thereby becoming the first Native American editor of a major publication. The Cherokee at that time were being buffeted by increasing demands by Georgia authorities to sell their lands and migrate west. Boudinot, printing in both English and the Cherokee alphabet developed in 1828 by Sequoyah, argued strenuously against the sale of any tribal holdings. In 1833 he also published a novel entitled *Poor Sarah; or, The Indian Woman* in the Cherokee language. However, the tribe was increasingly torn by factions both for and against relocating to the west. The major shift in Boudinot's career occurred in 1832, after returning from a fund-raising event in Boston, when he switched sides and advocated selling traditional land under the best possible terms before it was seized by whites. This brought him in direct conflict with Chief John Ross, who vigorously condemned the practice of selling land with consent of the entire tribe, and Boudinot was forced out as editor.

By 1835 the so-called Treaty Party within the Cherokee nation had evolved and were willing to sell their land to the American government. That year Boudinot, accompanied by John Ridge, Major Ridge, Stand Watie, and others, visited Washington, D.C., and signed the Treaty of New Echota for the tribes' removal to the Indian Territory. This was accomplished without the consent of Ross and other senior chiefs, but on May 23, 1836, the treaty was ratified by the U.S. Senate by a single vote. This act set in motion the notorious "Trail of Tears," whereby one-fourth of the Cherokee died in transit to new homes out west. Boudinot established himself there in September 1837 and resumed his publishing activities, principally through the translation of the New Testament and other religious tracts into Cherokee. However, tribal loyalists never forgave him for his role in signing the relocation treaty, and on June 22, 1839, Boudinot, the Ridges, and others associated with it were assassinated at Park Hill, Arkansas. His fate is indicative of the cultural conflict of tribes caught between two worlds.

dictionary, and includes many immigrant and Native American words specific to the New World and the United States. Curiously, he completed it while living in Cambridge, England, where most of the research was performed.

1828

April 28

DIPLOMACY: The U.S. Senate ratifies the agreement with Mexico to fix their mutual boundary along the Sabine River.

May 19

POLITICS: President John Quincy Adams, not to be outwitted by Jacksonian adversaries in Congress, slyly signs the so-called Tariff of Abominations into law. New Englanders in Congress, against whom the bill was aimed, also strongly support it for the protection of American industry it affords. This proves a major Machiavellian triumph for the beleaguered executive.

May 24

BUSINESS: The Reciprocity Act passes Congress, whereby discriminatory duties are abolished on trade with favorable, reciprocating nations.

July 4

TRANSPORTATION: Aged Charles Carroll, the only surviving signer of the Declaration of Independence, assists in groundbreaking ceremonies for the new Baltimore and Ohio Railway. The first operational section of track will be utilized by horse-drawn trains, but by 1830 the conversion to steam will be complete.

July 14

EXPLORING: A small expedition headed by noted scout Jedediah Smith comes to grief near the Sacramento River, California, when hostile Indians attack and kill 18 men.

July 21

JOURNALISM: The *Mechanic's Free Paper* gives exclusive coverage to the first strike by textile workers in Paterson, New Jersey—and the ensuing use of militia to end it.

August 11

LABOR: A group of small businessmen form the first labor-oriented party in Philadelphia by gaining temporary control of the city council; in this capacity they agitate for a 10-hour working day, abolishing debtor's prison, and universal education. Their success establishes a trend, and similar organizations rise in New York and Boston.

October 16

TRANSPORTATION: The Delaware and Hudson Canal, running from Honesdale, Pennsylvania, to Kingston, New York, opens for business. Its primary function is to permit shipments of anthracite coal from Pennsylvania coalfields to industrial centers in the Northeast.

December 3

POLITICS: A blistering presidential campaign concludes with Andrew Jackson defeating John Quincy Adams by a vote of 178 electoral votes to 83; John C. Calhoun remains in office as vice president after defeating Richard Rush by similar margins. Jackson won the crucial state of New York thanks to the adept machinations of Martin Van Buren.

December 12

DIPLOMACY: The United States concludes a treaty of peace and navigation with Brazil.

1828

December 19

POLITICS: The recently passed "Tariff of Abominations" is condemned by the South Carolina legislature as unconstitutional, unjust, and oppressive. Vice President John C. Calhoun also contributes an anonymous essay entitled "South Carolina Exposition and Protest" extolling state sovereignty and nullification by a single state. This is the genesis of what becomes known as the "Nullification Crisis," and a precursor to the events of 1861.

December 20

INDIAN: The Georgia legislature passes a bill which declares all laws passed by the Cherokee nation null and void after June 1, 1830.

December 30

POLITICS: The Georgia legislature condemns the new Tariff of 1828.

1829

LABOR: The Fellenberg Manual Labor Institution is established at Greenfield, Massachusetts; this is the first official labor school in the nation.

PUBLISHING: German philosopher and refugee Francis Lieber published the first volume of his seminal *Encyclopedia Americana*, which runs 13 volumes and is finished in 1833. This is the first reference work to be erudite, yet written for a general audience.

RELIGION: Political agitation against Roman Catholics and immigrants, resulting in street violence and several blatantly anti-Catholic publications eventually give rise to the Native American Party, better known as the "Know-Nothings."

January 9

SETTLEMENT: The House of Representatives defeats a bill mandating construction of a military fort in the Oregon Territory and establishment of a territorial government there.

February 4–5

POLITICS: The Virginia and Mississippi legislatures denounce the "Tariff of Abominations" on constitutional grounds.

February 24

POLITICS: The Virginia legislature votes to find the new Tariff of 1828 unconstitutional.

March 2

SOCIETAL: Dr. John Dix Fisher founds the New England Asylum for the Blind in Boston; this is the nation's first such institution.

March 4

POLITICS: Andrew Jackson is inaugurated seventh president of the United States. His inaugural address mentions frugal governance, support of states' rights, a fair Indian policy, and reorganizing the federal civil service. The pressing issues of tariffs, the Bank of the United States, and public works go unaddressed. He also introduces the so-called spoils system (political patronage) on a larger scale than previously practiced. Moreover, the ensuing boisterous celebrations by rough-hewn frontiersmen and onlookers suggest that Jacksonian "democracy" has arrived with a vengeance.

Jackson, Andrew   (1767–1845)
President

Andrew Jackson *(National Archives)*

Andrew Jackson was born in the Waxhaw settlement, South Carolina, on March 15, 1767. Though young, Jackson served in the American Revolution and was slashed by a British officer for refusing to polish his boots. Thereafter he expressed an inveterate hatred of England. Afterward he studied law in North Carolina, was admitted to the bar, and relocated to Tennessee to commence his practice. In 1796 he was elected to the U.S. House of Representatives as the state's sole congressional member, and the following year gained appointment to the U.S. Senate. He returned home soon after and served many years on the state supreme court, gaining the reputation as a tough, single-minded individual. When the Creek War erupted in August 1813, Jackson was commissioned a major general of militia and he commenced a series of successful battles against the Indians. In March 1814 he crushed the Creeks at Horseshoe Bend, then proceeded to Pensacola and captured it from the Spanish for

March 23

INDIAN: President Andrew Jackson writes to the Creek and orders them to either conform to the laws of Alabama or remove themselves across the Mississippi River.

April 15

POLITICS: Once in office, President Andrew Jackson comes to rely exclusively on his unofficial "kitchen cabinet" consisting of lawyers Amos B. Kendall and William B. Lewis and editor Duff Green.

May 17

GENERAL: John Jay, revolutionary diplomat and first chief justice of the Supreme Court, dies in Bedford, New York.

May 29

TRANSPORTATION: Construction begins on the Chesapeake and Ohio Canal at Georgetown.

June 4

NAVAL: The USS *Demologos*, the world's first steam warship, better known as *Fulton the First*, catches fire and burns in New York Harbor. So strong was the

aiding the Indians. At that time Great Britain was launching a major invasion against New Orleans to take control of the Mississippi River, but Jackson reached the city ahead of them and entrenched. On January 8, 1815, he bloodily repelled them in the largest land battle of the War of 1812, ironically fought two weeks after the Treaty of Ghent had been signed. Now a national hero, he was next tasked with subduing hostile Seminole Indians in 1818, invaded Spanish-held Florida, and executed two English traders found assisting them. Though widely criticized in political circles, Jackson's actions proved popular with the public and he was not officially castigated. Budget cuts forced him from the army in 1821, and he parleyed his immense popularity into national politics.

Jackson ran for the presidency in 1824, winning the most popular and electoral votes, but the election went to John Quincy Adams thanks to Henry Clay's activity in the House of Representatives. He angrily remonstrated against what he considered a "corrupt bargain" and ran again in 1828.

That year he handily defeated Adams and was sworn in as the seventh president. His ascent heralded the trend toward "Jacksonian democracy" in which the plight of the common man was widely addressed. Jackson came down hard on South Carolina for its nullification of high tariffs and also allowed the charter of the Bank of the United States to expire. To a man of his frontier sensibilities, the bank represented a bastion of elite commercial interest at the expense of average citizens. Jackson also agitated for the removal of the Cherokee and other native Americans to designated area beyond the Mississippi to acquire their land. Jackson was roundly reelected in 1832, at which point he authorized the withdrawal of all federal money from the Bank of the United States and its redistribution among state institutions. Jackson left office in March 1837 a highly popular and successful executive who did much to expand the power and prestige of the presidency. He died at his home, The Hermitage, in Tennessee, on June 8, 1845, a singularly willful leader.

prejudice against steam power in the sail-dominated U.S. Navy that for many years the vessel performed only minor service as a receiving ship.

July 23

TECHNOLOGY: William Austin Burt of Detroit, Michigan, receives the first patent for a mechanical typewriter; this proves a somewhat crude device, quickly supplanted by machines featuring a keyboard.

July 29

INDIAN: A treaty signed between the United States and the Chippewa, Ottawa, and Potawatomi results in the loss of Indian land in the Michigan Territory.

August

SPORTS: John Stuart Skinner founds the first sports periodical, *American Turf Register and Sporting Magazine,* in Baltimore, Maryland.

August 8

TRANSPORTATION: The *Stourbridge Lion,* America's first steam locomotive, runs on tracks owned by the Delaware and Hudson Canal Company. This British-built device runs at 10 miles per hour for the entire distance between Carbondale to Honesdale, Pennsylvania. However, at seven tons, it is considered far too

1829

heavy for tracks designed to be used with horses, and the entire route must be reinforced.

August 25

DIPLOMACY: Secretary of State Martin Van Buren instructs American minister to Mexico Joel R. Poinsett to purchase the states of Texas and Coahuila from that government. However, the Mexicans spurn President Andrew Jackson's offer to purchase these territories, home to several thousand American settlers and squatters.

September 15

SLAVERY: The Republic of Mexico, through its Guerrero Decree, abolishes slavery throughout the country, including Texas.

October 16

BUSINESS: The Tremont Hotel in Boston becomes America's first luxury hotel and pioneers such innovations as private bedrooms with locks, soap and a pitcher of water in every room, indoor water closets (toilets), clerks and bellboys. Its success inspires many imitators across the nation.

DIPLOMACY: The Mexican government dismisses Joel R. Poinsett, the American minister, and he is called back to Washington, D.C.

October 17

DIPLOMACY: Anthony Butler becomes chargé d'affaires in Mexico and is instructed to continue with negotiations for purchasing land.

TRANSPORTATION: The Chesapeake and Delaware Canal, a 14-mile artificial waterway funded by a combination of private investors, the federal government, and state governments, opens between Chesapeake Bay and the Delaware River.

November 7

LABOR: Ebenezer Ford, president of the New York City Carpenter's Union, wins a seat to the New York State Assembly; he is the first labor union member to hold public office.

November 13

SPORTS: Diver Sam Patch is killed when he attempts to dive 125 feet headfirst into the Genesee River, New York.

December 2

SLAVERY: Perhaps as a sop to prospective American settlers, Mexican President Guerrero exempts Texas from a national antislavery decree.

December 8

POLITICS: In his first message to Congress, President Andrew Jackson broaches the issue of sharing surplus federal revenue with the states. He also questions the constitutionality of the Bank of the United States, probably a result of learning that the institution worked actively against his election.

December 22

TRANSPORTATION: The Baltimore and Ohio Railroad commences service along the 13-mile strip of track from the main city to Ellicott's Mills. However, the initial cars are pulled by horses, not locomotives, although they reach and sustain speeds of up to 12 miles an hour along metal tracks.

December 29
SETTLEMENT: Senator Samuel A. Foot of Connecticut authors a resolution calling for a moratorium on public land sales out west.

1830

BUSINESS: Lowell, Massachusetts, is the site of a new woolen mill operated along the lines of the Waltham system. This entails women living in closely managed dormitories and attracts the daughters of rural farmers.

EDUCATION: Francis Wayland, president of Brown University, becomes head of the American Institute of Instruction, the nation's oldest educational association.

POPULATION: The latest U.S. Census records a population of 12,866,020.

PUBLISHING: In Philadelphia, *Ladies' Magazine*, published by John Lauris Blake, is becoming the first successful woman's magazine in America. It is eventually edited by Sarah Josepha Hale, one of the earliest and most successful women editors. By concentrating on features of interest to women such as fashion and morality, it eventually builds a readership of 150,000.

RELIGION: Alexander Campbell and his followers establish the Disciples of Christ, which rejects all

Woman and girl in fashionable clothing, 1862 *(Library of Congress)*

creeds and confessions in favor of New Testament beliefs and practices. They are also known as "Campbellites."

SETTLEMENT: Plans are drawn up for the city of Chicago; it rises on the site of old Fort Dearborn, which has been an army post for 27 years.

TRANSPORTATION: The relatively slow start of railroads can be gauged by the fact that this year only 73 miles of track exist as opposed to 1,277 miles of canals. However, this ratio will dramatically reverse itself as railroad technology, particularly as it relates to the design and construction of tracks, is perfected.

January 17
POLITICS: Senator Thomas Hart Benton of Missouri accuses the author of the Foot Resolution as opposing the continuing political and economic growth of the West, a charge he then levels at the northeastern political establishment. However, the issue of land sales is soon lost over the bigger issue of the nature of the American government under the Constitution.

January 19–27
POLITICS: Senator Robert Y. Hayne of South Carolina engages Daniel Webster of Massachusetts in a debate over what appears on the surface to be land sales in the west but actually touches upon the more serious issue of states' rights versus federal power–especially in regard to nullification. This debate ominously arrays Northerners and Southerners against one another, and Webster delivers one of

Hale, Sarah (1788–1879)
Editor

Sarah Josepha Buell was born in Newport, New Hampshire, on October 24, 1788, into a modest household. At this time girls were denied the educational opportunities afforded boys, but she was carefully tutored by her parents and brother, a student at Dartmouth. In 1813 she married attorney David Hale, raised a family, and received additional education and encouragement from her husband. Hale had previously dabbled in publishing poems and various short pieces in regional newspapers, but after her husband died in 1822 she took to publishing as a vocation. This was an unusual career decision for a woman at the time, but Hale was well-trained and motivated. Her first novel, *Northwood, a Tale of New England*, received critical acclaim in 1827, and the following year she accepted publisher John Lauris Blake's invitation to serve as editor of his *Ladies' Magazine*. In this capacity, Hale quickly distinguished herself as a first-rate editor with keen insights as to the female reading audience. Completely devoted to enhancing female education, Hale insisted that the magazine be enlightening and entertaining in equal measure. She also resisted commercial pressures to include elaborate plates of the latest fashion in favor of erudite discussions of politics, domestic practices, morality, and history. Moreover, at a time when most American magazines simply reprinted materials from their British counterparts, Hale actively cultivated original pieces from such noted women writers such as Lydia Sigourney, Sarah Whitman, and Maria Fuller. She was also acutely interested in dispensing advice for the rearing of children, and in 1830 her book *Poems for Our Children* contained the endearing "Mary Had a Little Lamb." Interestingly, Hale distanced herself from the feminism and insisted that men and women exist in different spheres and ought to confine their respective talents to the same. She also favored the colonization of African Americans rather than abolition and assimilation.

The panic of 1837 forced the *Ladies' Magazine* into receivership and it was acquired by Philadelphia publisher Louis Godey. A new publication, *Godey's Lady's Book*, was the result, and he invited Hale to continue on as editor from Boston. Here she was forced to accept the inclusion of fashion-orientated materials which she considered superfluous but continued lacing her issues with useful and informative columns. Hale remained in Boston until 1841, when she moved her entire operation to Philadelphia. She continued functioning capably in this capacity until 1877, at which time the publication enjoyed a circulation of 150,000—the nation's largest. She also found the time to pen numerous books on cooking and household management, mastery of which she considered a moral imperative for all women as housewives and mothers. Hale finally retired from the editor's desk at the age of 89 and she died at Philadelphia on April 30, 1879. She enjoyed a remarkable 50-year stint as one of the nation's most successful editors, an accomplished writer, and the first domestic diva.

the great speeches of American history by declaring, "Liberty and Union, now and forever, one and inseparable!" The original issue of public land sales is entirely overlooked in this struggle to define the Federal union.

1830

Webster, Daniel (1782–1852)

Politician

Daniel Webster was born in Salisbury, New Hampshire, on January 18, 1782, the son of an impoverished Revolutionary War veteran. He attended the noted Phillips Exeter Academy and subsequently graduated from Dartmouth College in 1801 before studying law and opening a successful practice. In 1813 he gained election to the U.S. House of Representatives as a Federalist and in this capacity roundly opposed the War of 1812. Webster then quit Congress in 1816 to practice law in Boston, gaining national renown for arguing before the U.S. Supreme Court on three occasions. In 1819 he won the celebrated *Dartmouth College v. Woodward* when the Court under Chief Justice John Marshall upheld the nature of contract law. That year Webster also helped win *McCulloch v. Maryland* on behalf of the Second Bank of the United States, and in 1824 he successfully argued the case of *Gibbons v. Ogden* in favor of unfettered interstate commerce. He then was elected to the U.S. Senate from Massachusetts as a northern Whig and functioned as an exemplary spokesman. In 1830 he particularly distinguished himself in a constitutional debate with Robert Y. Hayne of South Carolina, declaring "Liberty and Union, now and forever, one and inseparable." Two years later he sided with President Andrew Jackson in the Nullification Crisis, despite his strong affiliation with the anti-Jacksonian Whig Party. He then opposed the president over his refusal to recharter the Second Bank of the United States. Webster apparently felt that Jackson's removal of federal deposits to "pet banks" could be an issue propelling him to the White House.

In 1836 Webster was one of several Whig candidates to seek the party nomination, but in the end they split the vote and Democrat Martin Van Buren won. Webster functioned several more years in the opposition until 1840, when he became a strong supporter of a new Whig candidate, William Henry Harrison. After Harrison won he appointed Webster secretary of state and continued in that position after John Tyler succeeded Harrison a month later. In this capacity Webster negotiated the Webster-Ashburton Treaty of 1843 to settle a boundary dispute with Canada then resigned to run for the Senate when Tyler vetoed a new national bank. In 1844 Webster failed to receive the Whig nomination for president, so he campaigned on behalf of Henry Clay, who then lost to James K. Polk. Afterward Webster stridently opposed the war with Mexico,

(continues)

Daniel Webster *(Library of Congress)*

(continued)

the expansion of slavery into the new territories, and supported the Wilmot Proviso. However, in March 1850 he outraged his constituents by defending the Fugitive Slave Act as essential for the Union at that point. In July 1850 he served again as secretary of state under President Millard Fillmore and two years later was bitterly disappointed when he was again passed over for the Whig nomination in favor of General Winfield Scott. Webster died at Marshfield, Massachusetts, on October 24, 1852, an outstanding orator and the major spokesman for the North during a period of rising sectional tensions. He, along with Clay and John C. Calhoun, helped define the national agenda.

February 4
TRANSPORTATION: The Camden and Amboy Railroad, New Jersey's first such business, is chartered.

March 12
LAW: The U.S. Supreme Court settles the case of *Craig v. Missouri,* ruling that state loan certificates, intended for circulation, are bills of credit and patently unconstitutional.

March 15
POLITICS: The Louisiana legislature votes to endorse the Tariff of 1812.

March 28
DIPLOMACY: The United States and Denmark conclude a treaty for the adjustment of indemnity claims.

March 31
POLITICS: The Pennsylvania legislature endorses Andrew Jackson for the presidency.

April 6
DIPLOMACY: A postrevolutionary government in Mexico adopts laws to halt American immigration into Texas and also prohibits the importation of African-American slaves. American settlers living there under prior arrangements consider this a violation of their "rights."
RELIGION: Joseph Smith founds the Church of the Latter-day Saints (Mormons) at Fayette, New York; he draws inspiration from religious visions and translations of messages on golden tablets. These were reputedly revealed to him by the angel Moroni. He then goes on to publish his influential *The Book of Mormon*, setting the stage for one of America's most powerful religious sects. Mormonism is a uniquely American creed which holds that the country was colonized by a lost tribe of Israel, and that God has special message—and mission—for the United States.

April 10
BUSINESS: A covered wagon train departs Missouri for the Rocky Mountains under the leadership of Jedediah Strong Smith and William Sublette. This year they also sell their holdings to what emerges as the Rocky Mountain Fur Company.

1830

Smith, Joseph   (1804–1844)
Mormon prophet

Joseph Smith was born in Sharon, Vermont, on December 23, 1805, a son of poor farmers. He endured a hardscrabble existence while maturing along the frontiers of western New York, and around 1820 Smith began experiencing a series of religious visions. Here both God and Jesus Christ appeared to him and revealed the location of several golden plates buried in the ground and allegedly deposited by the Indian descendants of lost Hebrew tribes. Smith was then enabled to decipher the plates through magic and published his treatise, *The Book of Mormon*, in 1830. This is the genesis of a uniquely American sect, the Mormons, who derive their name from a supposed American prophet. Smith began preaching to his neighbors, winning many converts. He then formally organized the Church of Jesus Christ of Latter-day Saints on April 6, 1830, which was distinguished by its insistence of church ownership of all property, placing all political power in the church, and recognition of Smith as the sole prophet. As the Mormon community grew it experienced friction with more traditionally minded Christians, and in 1838 Smith relocated his church and its followers to western Missouri. This led to further strife with other communities and an outbreak of violence in which Smith was arrested and detained for several months. Ultimately, he was forced to relocate church and followers alike to a new abode in Illinois, christened Nauvoo. Though viewed with suspicion, Smith gained respectability among state politicians for his ability to deliver 12,000 Mormon votes to whomever he pleased. He was thus able to achieve considerable autonomy in running church affairs, and also recruited, trained, and equipped his own militia force, the Nauvoo Legion.

While at Nauvoo, Smith continually updated and refined church doctrine and his role as prophet. In 1844 he pronounced his community as independent of the United States while church elders crowned him king of this kingdom of God on Earth. Smith also began harboring political aspirations and at one point proffered himself as a presidential candidate on a platform of establishing a "theodemocracy" and the abolition of slavery. A breaking point occurred around this time when he apparently also introduced the practice of multiple wives, or polygamy, among church leaders. This struck dissidents within the Mormon ranks as antithetical to proper religion and also outraged

(continues)

Joseph Smith, Jr. *(Library of Congress)*

(continued)

more traditional Protestant communities that practiced monogamy. The final break occurred when a breakaway newspaper, *The Nauvoo Expositor*, openly criticized Smith for polygamy and exposed him as a false prophet. Church loyalists then attacked and destroyed the press upon Smith's orders, at which point he was arrested and charged with disorderly conduct. He was then lodged in the Carthage jail for his own safety, but a mob stormed in, killing Smith and his brother. Smith was only 38 years old at the time, but his reputation as one of the 19th century's most charismatic religious figures was assured. He was replaced by a new leader, Brigham Young.

April 13

POLITICS: In a sign of continuing political and sectional tension, President Andrew Jackson toasts a dinner held in honor of Thomas Jefferson by thundering, "Our Federal Union—it must be preserved!" Vice President John C. Calhoun then offered a Southern riposte, declaring, "The Union—next to our liberty, the most dear."

May 7

DIPLOMACY: The United States and Turkey conclude a treaty of commerce which opens up the Black Sea region to American commerce.

May 20

BUSINESS: Import duties on tea, coffee, salt, and molasses are reduced by Congress.

May 21

POLITICS: The Foot Resolution, calling for restrictions on western land sales, is tabled in the Senate.

May 24

TRANSPORTATION: The first 13-mile section of the Baltimore and Ohio Railroad opens between Baltimore and Ellicott's Mills.

May 27

TRANSPORTATION: The Maysville Road Bill, which would have funded construction of a 60-mile road in Kentucky, is vetoed by President Andrew Jackson—his first use of executive authority in that regard. He opposes federal subsidies for public works projects that are confined to one state and not part of a larger system of overall national improvement.

May 28

INDIAN: The Indian Removal Act is signed by President Andrew Jackson, mandating the forced relocation of several Eastern Indian tribes to reservations located across the Mississippi River. Through this expedient, the government can acquire thousands of square miles of pristine Indian land east of the river. In return the tribes receive $500,000 in compensation and an annuity. Debate over the bill is marked by intense acrimony, with opponents insisting it is the best alternative to gradual annihilation and by detractors insisting it is both cruel and inhumane.

Calhoun, John C. (1782–1850)
Politician

John Caldwell Calhoun was born in Abbeville District, South Carolina, the son of an affluent judge and slave owner. He graduated from Yale in 1804, began a successful law practice, and in 1808 commenced a long career in politics by winning a seat in the state legislature. Calhoun, intense, reserved, and profound, successfully stood for a seat in the U.S. House of Representatives in 1811 where he functioned as a prominent "War Hawk" agitating for war with England. As such he voted for an increased military establishment and became closely associated with Henry Clay. Afterward Calhoun's political career bore all the trappings of an ardent nationalist through his vocal support for a strong military, internal improvements, and protective tariffs to assist industry. In 1817 President James Monroe appointed him secretary of war, a disgraced office since the disasters of the recent conflict, yet he applied himself with such energy, diligence, and foresight in this capacity that in 1824 he was enabled to run for the vice presidency with John Quincy Adams. His name was frequently mentioned as a possible presidential contender, but in 1828 he deferred to Andrew Jackson and once served as his vice president. His tenure with Jackson proved unhappy, owing to conflicting personalities, Calhoun's prior criticism of Jackson's behavior during the First Seminole War in Florida, and the rising tide of sectionalism occasioned by high tariffs. The breaking point occurred in 1832 when South Carolina threatened to "nullify" high tariffs and Calhoun penned an anonymous pamphlet defending the practice. When Jackson threatened military force to collect the tariff, Calhoun broke precedence by resigning from office and he was replaced by Martin Van Buren. He then gained elec-tion to the U.S. Senate from his home state and spent nearly two decades as the South's leading political intellect and spokesman.

The remainder of Calhoun's career was buffeted by the rise of strident abolitionism in the North, which called for an immediate end to slavery. He was quick to defend that "peculiar institution" and argued that the Congress had no constitutional ability to thwart its continued existence anywhere in the nation. To this end he supported the annexation of Texas as a slave state but also opposed the war with Mexico as an unnecessary evil. He particularly railed against the Wilmot Proviso on constitutional grounds for outlawing slavery in territory acquired from Mexico. Calhoun subsequently found himself working both with

(continues)

John C. Calhoun *(Library of Congress)*

(continued)

and against two other fine minds, Henry Clay and Daniel Webster, in a failed attempt to accommodate rising national hostility over sectionalism and secession. His health failing, Calhoun nonetheless remained a strident Southern nationalist to the end and opposed the Compromise of 1850 for failing to ensure the continued existence of slavery. He died in Washington, D.C., on March 31, 1850, having been spared from witnessing the very civil war that would destroy his beloved South.

May 29
SETTLEMENT: Congress passes the Preemption Act to protect squatters from land speculators and claim jumpers; henceforth any settler established on public land in the past year is entitled to purchase up to 160 acres at $1.25 an acre. Duties on molasses and salt are also reduced.

May 31
TRANSPORTATION: President Andrew Jackson vetoes federal subscription to stock in the Washington Turnpike Company, considering it a local and state project.

June 5
NAVAL: The frigate USS *Vincennes* under Captain F. B. Finch returns to New York, being the first U.S. warship to successfully circumnavigate the globe.

July 15
INDIAN: The United States and representatives from the Sac, Fox, and Sioux conclude a treaty that cedes all Indian land encompassing present-day Iowa, Missouri, and Minnesota. This transpires over the objections of a principal chief, Black Hawk.

August 4
SETTLEMENT: Civil engineer James Thompson begins laying out the town of Chicago, Illinois.

August 28
TRANSPORTATION: The *Tom Thumb*, the first steam-powered locomotive made in America, successfully runs along the Baltimore and Ohio Railroad from Baltimore to Ellicott's Mills. Prior to this, American steam trains had been acquired from the English.

September 11
POLITICS: The Anti-Masonic Party demonstrates its political viability by holding its first convention in Philadelphia, attracting numerous delegates.

September 15
INDIAN: The Choctaw and the United States conclude the Treaty of Dancing Rabbit Creek, whereby the tribe transfers eight million acres of land east of the Mississippi to the government. They are then entitled to resettle on land set aside for them in present-day Oklahoma.

September 16
LITERATURE: In an attempt to prevent the aged frigate USS *Constitution*, "Old Ironsides," from being sold and broken up, Oliver Wendell Holmes writes and pub-

lishes the poem "Old Ironsides" in the *Boston Daily Advertiser*. His effort proves so popular that the Navy Department rescinds its order to mothball the vessel.

September 18
TRANSPORTATION: On its return leg of a trip to Baltimore, the locomotive *Tom Thumb* races a horse and loses owing to mechanical failure.

September 27
INDIAN: The United States and the Choctaw nation conclude the Treaty of Dancing Rabbit Creek, whereby the tribe's remaining land east of the Mississippi is ceded in exchange for new homes in the designated Indian Territory (Oklahoma).

September 30
POLITICS: The Kentucky legislature nominates Henry Clay as its presidential candidate.

October 5
DIPLOMACY: Secretary of State Martin Van Buren discusses opening trade with the West Indies with British minister Sir Charles Vaughan.
GENERAL: Chester A. Arthur, the 21st president, is born at Fairfield, Vermont.

November 2
TRANSPORTATION: Another early locomotive, the *Best Friend of Charleston*, completes its first sojourn down the Charleston-Hamburg Railroad; its becomes the first train to complete regularly scheduled runs.

November 26
TECHNOLOGY: During a visit to England, Robert Stevens invents the improved "T-rail" rail track, which is still employed to present times.

December
SLAVERY: Once the American schooner *Comet* is wrecked on the Bahamas, British authorities declare that the slaves it was carrying are now free.
WOMEN: Robert Dale Owen publishes *Moral Physiology*, the first American manual to touch upon the sensitive issue of birth control. Most newspapers refuse to carry advertisements promoting it, but the book nonetheless sells 25,000 copies.

December 6
POLITICS: President Andrew Jackson delivers his annual address to Congress, reiterating his opposition to the Bank of the United States and proposing internal improvements financed by distributing federal surpluses back to the states.

December 7
JOURNALISM: Supporters of President Andrew Jackson choose Francis P. Blair to edit a pro-administration newspaper, the *Washington Globe,* as a semiofficial mouthpiece. Jackson relies on this new paper as his old ally, Duff Green of the *U.S. Telegraph*, has become a supporter of Henry Clay.

1831

ARTS: Yale University establishes the Trumbull Gallery in honor of alumnus and artist John Trumbull.
MEDICAL: Dr. James Guthrie successfully synthesizes chloroform, an early and effective anesthetic, in his laboratory at Sackets Harbor, New York.

SLAVERY: A resolution in the Georgia senate offers a $5,000 reward for the arrest and conviction in a state court of abolitionist William Lloyd Garrison.

TECHNOLOGY: Inventor Joseph Henry creates the first practical electric bell using primitive magnets and copper wire; it becomes one of the first electrical devices with domestic applications.

TRANSPORTATION: The steamboat *Yellowstone* of the American Fur Company is the first such vessel to ascend the Missouri River.

January

RELIGION: To escape violence and persecution, Joseph Smith and 70 Mormon followers relocate from New York to Kirtland, Ohio. This is the site of what they hope will be New Zion.

SLAVERY: Free African Americans in the Washington, D.C., area are arrested and whipped for owning copies of William Lloyd Garrison's abolitionist newspaper *The Liberator*.

January 1

SLAVERY: William Lloyd Garrison, radical abolitionist, begins publication of his newspaper *The Liberator* in Boston, vowing "I will not retreat a single inch, and I will be heard." He also intends to remain in print until the last of African Americans is released from bondage; Garrison keeps his word and does not fold until 1865.

January 15

TRANSPORTATION: The steam locomotive *Best Friend of Charleston* becomes the first American train to actually haul passengers, in this instance on a run between Charleston and Hamburg, South Carolina, as part of the South Carolina Railroad. Soon Isaac Dripps invents the trademark grill eventually seen on all locomotives, nicknamed the "Cowcatcher."

February 2

POLITICS: Senator Thomas Hart Benton, a nominal Jacksonian ally, frames the debate on the National Bank by attacking it as "too great and powerful to be tolerated in a Government of free and equal laws."

February 3

BUSINESS: Congress passes a new Copyright Act which extends the rights and benefits of the original 1790 act from 14 to 28 years. An additional 14 years is permitted if asked for by the author's wife or children.

February 15

POLITICS: In a move indicative of the breech between President Andrew Jackson and Vice President John C. Calhoun, the latter publishes letters critical of the president's behavior during the First Seminole War of 1818. In consequence, an angry Jackson chooses New York's Martin Van Buren as his running mate.

March 4

POLITICS: Former president John Quincy Adams, whom many believed was ruined as a political figure, becomes the first former executive to win a seat in the U.S. House of Representatives, representing Plymouth, Massachusetts.

March 5

TRANSPORTATION: The *West Point*, the first locomotive utilizing a four-wheeled truck, debuts on the South Carolina Railroad.

March 18

INDIAN: The U.S. Supreme Court decides the case *Cherokee v. Georgia,* ruling that the Cherokee are not a sovereign nation but rather a "domestic dependent" and cannot sue in federal court. The Indians were trying to stop Georgia from applying its laws on their land, where gold had recently been discovered.

April 5

DIPLOMACY: The United States and Mexico conclude a commercial treaty.

April 7

POLITICS: Secretary of War John H. Eaton resigns from the cabinet of President Andrew Jackson to protest the snubbing of his wife, Peggy O'Neale, a former barmaid, whom administration wives consider unacceptable. This act leads to a spate of resignations and by a day later all cabinet officials have either left or been replaced.

April 18

EDUCATION: The University of the City of New York is chartered; it becomes New York University after 1896.

April 26

LAW: The New York legislature decriminalizes indebtedness and abolishes prison terms for it.

May 26

EDUCATION: The Methodists charter Wesleyan University at Middletown, Connecticut, becoming the oldest institution of higher learning associated with that sect.

June 11

SOCIETAL: The Annual Convention of People of Color, the first large gathering of free African Americans, convenes at the Wesleyan Church in Philadelphia. There they approve measures to study the conditions of blacks in America overall, weigh the possibility of resettling in Canada, and oppose efforts of the American Colonization Society.

June 27–30

INDIAN: Black Hawk, head chief of the Sac and Fox and a distinguished warrior from the War of 1812, reluctantly agrees with General Edmund P. Gaines to move his people from their traditional homeland in Illinois across the Mississippi River and into new lands in Iowa. They nearly starve there over the winter, which occasions an unexpected return to their former abodes.

July 4

DIPLOMACY: American minister in Paris William C. Rives presses damage claims against France dating back to the Napoleonic Wars. The French have been dragging their feet, citing counterclaims by their own citizens. Ultimately France pays out $5 million in claims, the Americans $300,000.

GENERAL: Former President James Monroe dies in New York City at the age of 73.

MUSIC: The song "America," written to the traditional British tune "God Save the King," is arranged and played by Dr. Samuel Francis Smith for the first time in Worcester, Massachusetts.

1831

Black Hawk (ca. 1767–1838)

Sac and Fox chief

Black Hawk (Makataimeshekikiak) was born near Rock Island, Illinois, around 1767, into the Thunder Clan of the Sac and Fox Indian nation. He matured into an outstanding warrior and by 1788 was functioning as a minor chief. By this time the tribe had established friendly relations with the United States, although these soured after 1804 when efforts accelerated to have the Indians sell their traditional hunting grounds. Black Hawk, in particular, refused to move from his village at Saukenuk and continually declined Indiana territorial governor William Henry Harrison's offers of compensation. When the War of 1812 erupted, Black Hawk readily joined Tecumseh's pan-Indian coalition against the United States, defeating American troops in several actions. His most successful battle occurred in September 1814 when his braves attacked Major (and future president) Zachary Taylor's small force on the Rock River, Illinois, forcing them to retreat. It was not until 1816, a year after the Treaty of Ghent had been signed, that Black Hawk finally and sullenly made peace with his hated adversaries. An uneasy truce prevailed for the next two decades, but in 1829 the Illinois state government under Governor John Reynolds began pressing Black Hawk's tribe to migrate west across the Mississippi River. The old chief refused and in 1831 the local militia was assembled to evict them by force. Black Hawk, wishing to avoid hostilities, then slipped quietly across the river into Iowa, which seemed to diffuse the emergency for the moment.

The Sac and Fox spent a desperate winter in Iowa, nearly starving to death. To circumvent further suffering, on April 5, 1832, Black Hawk ordered his 1,400 tribesmen back across the Mississippi to reoccupy their old homeland. A party of two Indians was sent ahead under a white flag to assure the whites they meant no harm, but when militiamen killed the messengers, Black Hawk went to war. Several costly skirmishes ensued over the intervening weeks while General Henry Atkinson collected a force of militia and soldiers to deal with the intruders. On May 12, 1832, the Indians were soundly defeated by Atkinson at the Battle of Bad Ax, principally by the armed steamboat *Warrior*. Black Hawk's band scattered and he was eventually captured and taken to Fort Monroe, Virginia, by Lieutenant Jefferson Davis. He was also introduced to President Andrew Jackson before being released into the custody of Keokuk, a rival chief far more amicably disposed toward Americans. While in captivity Black Hawk dictated his memoirs to Indian agent Antonine LeClaire, which were published in 1833 and became a best seller. In them the old chief excoriates the whites for their injustice against Native Americans, and he carefully recounts his many victories over them in the field. Black Hawk continued to live quietly at Keokuk's village in Iowa until his death on October 3, 1838. Significantly, the so-called Black Hawk War to which his name is indelibly associated was the last act of Native American resistance east of the Mississippi River.

July 20

POLITICS: President Andrew Jackson appoints Roger B. Taney of Maryland to serve as attorney general.

1831

July 26

POLITICS: Vice President John C. Calhoun elaborates on the doctrine of nullification in his "Fort Hill Letter," reiterating that states possess the right to both accept and reject actions taken by the federal government at their own discretion.

August

RELIGION: Mormon founder Joseph Smith selects Independence, Missouri, to serve as his Holy City of Zion.

William Miller, a Baptist preacher, founds the Seventh-Day Adventist movement in American Protestantism and predicts the imminent return of Jesus Christ between 1843 and 1844 based on his interpretation of the books of *Daniel* and *Revelation*.

August 1

POLITICS: Lewis Cass of Ohio gains appointment as the new secretary of war.

August 8

POLITICS: Louis McLane of Delaware becomes the new secretary of the treasury.

August 9

POLITICS: A political gathering in New York City nominates John C. Calhoun for the presidency.

TRANSPORTATION: New York's first steam locomotive, the *De Witt Clinton*, initiates service on the Mohawk and Hudson Railroad.

August 10

GENERAL: The first reference to the U.S. Flag as "Old Glory" occurs in a toast by sea captain William Driver of Salem, Massachusetts. The expression gains widespread use by the middle of the century.

August 13–23

SLAVERY: Reverend Nat Turner, a radical slave preacher, leads a bloody rebellion in Southampton, Virginia, killing 70 whites. The rebellion is then speedily crushed by local militia and Turner is captured. He and 12 others are hanged for their participation, while an additional 100 slaves are killed in fighting.

August 28

NAVAL: In response to the attacks by Sumatran pirates on American shipping in the Far East, President Andrew Jackson orders Captain John Downes of the frigate USS *Potomac* to undertake punitive actions against them.

September 26

ARTS: Robert Montgomery Bird's abolitionist play *The Gladiator*, set in Roman times during the days of Spartacus, begins a successful run in New York City. It stars noted actor Edwin Forrest in one of his earliest roles as a romantic hero.

POLITICS: The Anti-Masonic Party, which appeared suddenly as the third national party and now has chapters in 13 states, holds its first national convention. Attorney William Wirt of Maryland is nominated as its presidential candidate with Amos Ellmaker of Pennsylvania as vice president.

September 30

POLITICS: A gathering of free trade advocates in Philadelphia drafts a message to Congress, written by Albert Gallatin.

1831

Cartoon illustrating Nat Turner's uprising against southern whites *(Library of Congress)*

October 13
SOCIETAL: Riots break out at the Park Theater in New York City when English actor Joshua R. Anderson, who publicly criticized Americans, emerged on the stage.

October 26
POLITICS: Advocates of protective tariffs gather at a convention in New York City.

November 11
SLAVERY: Radical preacher Nat Turner is hanged at Jerusalem, Virginia, for his role in the violent slave uprising of the previous August.

November 12
TRANSPORTATION: *John Bull*, an English-built locomotive, begins clacking down the tracks on the Camden and Amboy Railroad, New Jersey.

November 19
GENERAL: James A. Garfield, 20th president, is born at Orange Township, Cleveland, Ohio.

1831

December 5
POLITICS: National elections keep the Democrats in control of Congress. John Quincy Adams is elected to the House of Representatives from Massachusetts; he is the first former chief executive returned to Congress.

December 12
POLITICS: The new National Republican Party convenes its first nominating convention in Baltimore, Maryland, and selects Henry Clay for president and John Sergeant of Pennsylvania for vice president. The party platform attacks President Andrew Jackson for patronage and abuses of veto power, supports Clay's "American system" and seeks to recharter the Bank of the United States.

SLAVERY: Former president John Quincy Adams, now holding a seat in the House of Representatives, presents 15 Pennsylvania petitions calling for the abolition of slavery in the District of Columbia.

December 26
GENERAL: Stephen Girard, one of the nation's wealthiest men, dies and leaves his fortune to the founding of Girard College, dedicated to the education of poor, white male orphans.

1832

ARTS: Richard Brinsley Sheridan's play *Pizarro* is staged in Columbus, Georgia, with genuine Creek Indians playing the role of Native Americans and performing authentic Indian dances to an amazed audience.

EDUCATION: The Perkins Institute, the first school dedicated to teaching the deaf, is opened in Boston by Samuel Gridley Howe.

LITERATURE: The collected poems of William Cullen Bryant are published and hailed by the *North American Review* as the best American verse to have been written.

MEDICAL: New Orleans is ravaged by epidemics of cholera and yellow fever which kill 5,000 inhabitants.

MUSIC: The Boston Academy of Music opens, being the first American institution to offer advanced musical instruction.

PUBLISHING: William A. Alcott authors *The Young Man's Guide* as a directory of proper manners and morality in a variety of social settings and situations. It is widely read and accepted.

RELIGION: Evangelical preacher Charles G. Finney establishes the Second Presbyterian Church in New York City.

SCIENCE: The pseudoscience of phrenology is brought to America by Austrian Johann Kaspar Spurnzhiem; it holds that the moral character and intellectual capacity of an individual can be gauged by the shape of his skull.

SOCIETAL: Oranges and lemons begin arriving in large shipments from Sicily and gain popularity as part of the national diet; previously, such delicacies were reserved for the very wealthy.

SPORTS: William Trotter becomes the nation's first sportswriter by contributing a column to the newspaper *The Traveler*.

January 6
SLAVERY: The New England Anti-Slavery Society is founded in Boston; it strongly opposes the resettlement of African Americans in Africa.

Finney, Charles G.   (1792–1875)
Theologian

Charles Grandison Finney was born in War-ren, Connecticut, on August 29, 1792, the son of farmers. He matured on the frontier of Jefferson County, New York, where he studied law with a view toward opening a practice. However, 1820 marked the begin-ning of the Second Great Awakening, a profound religious revival movement among frontier communities, and Finney found himself increasingly drawn into biblical stud-ies. The turning point in his life occurred in October 1821 when he underwent a dra-matic conversion experience and committed his life to Christ as an evangelical minister. Finney was particularly gifted in this capac-ity, being flamboyant, physically imposing, and—thanks to his legal training—a fine ora-tor. He began attending and preaching at frontier revival meetings through western New York and in 1824 was ordained as a Presbyterian minister. His fiery sermons, in which he challenged parishioners to step forward and accept Jesus as their personal savior, gained in popularity and won thou-sands of converts. Finney even took his message to the factories of the northeast by visiting Boston, New York, and Philadel-phia, where a newly emergent middle class readily accepted his message of salvation. In 1832 he established the Second Pres-byterian Church in New York, again with considerable success. The secret to Finney's persuasiveness was his insistence that all people are sinners, that hell was very real, and that only a personal relationship with God through direct prayer could save them

from eternal damnation. However, strict adherents of Calvinism, who insisted that most people are preordained for hell, found his message heretical and he was forced from the Presbyterian assembly.

Undaunted, Finney established the Broadway Tabernacle in 1836 and then associated himself with the Congregational-ist Church. In 1835 he also accepted the position of teacher of theology at Oberlin College, Ohio, and he alternated between the two positions. In 1837 Finney relocated to Ohio as pastor of the First Congregational Church in Oberlin, where he continued to teach and preach with little interrup-tion. In 1849–50 and 1859–60 he carried his message of hope to England, and he also served as president of Oberlin College after 1851. In this capacity he championed social causes such as temperance and urged abstention from alcohol, tobacco, and other stimulants. Furthermore, as an evangelical Christian, Finney stridently opposed slavery as a sin. He was upset with President Abra-ham Lincoln's moderate accommodation of it during the early period of the Civil War and criticized him for failing to pursue the matter of civil rights for African Americans. Finney continued successfully preaching at Oberlin well past his retirement, and he died there on August 16, 1875. He is a significant figure of the Second Great Awakening for his emotional innovations in preaching, which have since become hallmarks of mainstream evangelical Prot-estantism in America.

January 9
BUSINESS: Congress begins agitating to extend the Bank of the United States' charter three years ahead of its expiration date. This is despite heavy political criticism from westerners and others who view it as a symbol of aristocracy and corporate privilege.

1832

January 21
POLITICS: President Andrew Jackson enacts a "reform" program by rewarding numerous governmental positions to his circle of political friends. New York Democrat William Marcy summarizes the practice when he declares "To the victor go the spoils of the enemy."
SLAVERY: Thomas Jefferson Randolph, grandson of the former president, presses the Virginia legislature to adopt his grandfather's plan for the gradual abolition of slavery.

February 2
EDUCATION: Denison Literary and Theological Institution (Denison University) is chartered in Granville, Ohio, by the Baptists; its first class graduates in 1840.

February 6
NAVAL: Captain John Downes of the USS *Potomac* launches a landing party against pirates at Qualla Battoo, Sumatra. The Americans destroy four forts, kill 150 pirates, along with Rajah Po Mohamoet, their leader, suffering only two killed and 11 wounded. The surviving Malays agree not to harass American vessels.
TRANSPORTATION: An essay in the Ann Arbor, Michigan, newspaper *Emigrant* is the first to suggest the possibility of a transcontinental railroad.

February 10
BUSINESS: Henry Clay, seeking to embarrass President Andrew Jackson with a useful campaign issue, convinces Nicholas Biddle, director of the Bank of the United States, to press for rechartering four years before the original grant expires.

March 3
LAW: The U.S. Supreme Court decides the case of *Worcester v. Georgia*, ruling that the federal government enjoys jurisdiction over Indian affairs in a state. For this reason, Georgia laws have no relevance on Indian land. The state legislature, appreciably upset, refuses to acknowledge the court's decision. Moreover, President Andrew Jackson, a firm states' right supporter, bellows, "John Marshall has made his decision, now let him enforce it!"

March 19
SOCIETAL: Mrs. Francis Trollope publishes her book, *The Domestic Manners of the Americans*, which excoriates them as a bunch of unsophisticated bumpkins. Not surprisingly, her work is itself savagely lampooned throughout the country as an example of British upper-class snobbery.

March 24
INDIAN: The Creek sign a treaty with the United States which cedes that last of their territory east of the Mississippi. Shortly after they are to be relocated to new lands in present-day Oklahoma.

April 6
MILITARY: Chief Black Hawk suddenly moves his Sac and Fox tribe back across the Mississippi River to traditional hunting grounds in Illinois. Frightened farmers then fire on a group of Indians bearing a white flag and Black Hawk orders them killed. The so-called Black Hawk War ensues, and among those called to serve in this brief conflict are Abraham Lincoln and Jefferson Davis.

1832

April 7

EDUCATION: Pennsylvania College is chartered in Gettysburg, Pennsylvania, under Lutheran auspices; its first class graduates in 1834.

May 1

SETTLEMENT: Army captain Benjamin Bonneville leads a large wagon train from Fort Osage, Missouri, as far as the Columbia River, Oregon. He then goes off on his own to explore the West for an additional three years.

May 9

INDIAN: Seminole chiefs conclude the Treaty of Payne's Landing with the United States, which cedes their land in exchange for new homes west of the Mississippi River. However, many chiefs are angry over the settlement and begin coalescing around Osceola, a quasi-religious figure.

May 16

DIPLOMACY: The United States and Chile conclude a treaty of peace and commerce.

May 21–22

POLITICS: The new Democratic Party convenes its first national convention at Baltimore, Maryland. In a newly adopted rule that endures until 1936, candidates Andrew Jackson and Martin Van Buren need two-thirds of the delegates to win the party nomination but both are chosen unanimously. Van Buren also replaces John C. Calhoun, who intends to run for a senate seat in South Carolina.

May 23

BUSINESS: John Quincy Adams reports a tariff bill to lower rates from the Tariff of 1828 but still retains some protectionist features.

June

MEDICAL: A cholera epidemic sweeps through New York City, killing 4,000 inhabitants.

June 11

BUSINESS: A bill to recharter the Bank of the United States passes through the Senate 28 to 20.

June 26

MILITARY: A skirmish between Mexicans and Texans in the Battle of Velasco results in the first bloodshed between the opposing groups.

June 28

MEDICAL: The first appearance of Asiatic cholera in the United States occurs in New York, leading to 2,225 deaths in that city alone. It is eventually spread by human contact to the frontiers and has a devastating impact on many Indian tribes.

July 3

BUSINESS: The National Bank bill passes the House of Representatives on a vote of 107 to 85.

July 9

RELIGION: Henry Clay's proposal for a National Fast Day is defeated in the U.S. Senate after a bitter debate. He makes his plea for divine assistance to help combat an ongoing cholera epidemic.

1832

July 10
Business: With great relish, President Andrew Jackson vetoes a bill intending to recharter the Bank of the United States. He does so to oppose the conservative policies of its chief officer, Nicholas Biddle, which apparently favor corporations and the wealthy. He is also alarmed that the largest group of stock owners are also foreigners. Jackson thereby accepts Henry Clay's challenge to use the institution as a campaign issue in the upcoming contest.

July 13
Exploring: Henry R. Schoolcraft, leading an exploration party, discovers that Lake Itasca, in Minnesota, is the source of the Mississippi River.
Politics: As anticipated, the U.S. Senate fails to muster the two-thirds vote necessary to override President Andrew Jackson's veto of the Bank of the United States. This sets the stage for its second disbandment in 1836.

July 14
Business: The Tariff Act of 1832 is signed into law by President Andrew Jackson; while it lowers duties, many Southerners still view it as favoring the rapidly industrializing North at their expense.

August 2
Military: General Henry Atkinson, assisted by a fleet of steamships, decisively defeats the Sac and Fox Indians under Chief Black Hawk at the Battle of Bad Axe, Michigan. This engagement concludes the final episode of Native Indian resistance east of the Mississippi River.

September 21
Indian: After Chief Black Hawk surrenders himself to American authorities, the surviving Sac and Fox Indians under Chief Keokuk sign a treaty obliging them to remain on land west of the Mississippi River. This reaffirms a treaty first signed in 1804, since denounced by Black Hawk as fraudulent.

October
Arts: Painter George Catlin, determined to capture on canvas the rapidly vanishing Indian way of life, continues painting various chiefs and tribes along his 2,000-mile sojourn up the Missouri River.

October 14
Indian: In light of recent events, the Chickasaw agree to cede all their land east of the Mississippi River to the United States.

October 26
Politics: A new state constitution adopted by Mississippi allows many state officials to be elected, not appointed.

November 14
General: Charles Carroll, last surviving signer of the Declaration of Independence, dies in Baltimore at the age of 95.

November 19–24
Politics: In a major escalation of political tension, a special convention in South Carolina adopts an ordinance which nullifies the Tariffs of 1828 and 1832. They also declare their right to secede from the Union if state authority is challenged

Atkinson, Henry   (1782–1842)
General

Henry Atkinson was born in North Carolina in 1782, and in 1808 he joined the U.S. Army as a captain in the Third Infantry. He served in various capacities throughout the War of 1812, rising to colonel of the Sixth Infantry by 1815. Atkinson remained at Plattsburgh, New York, until 1819, when Secretary of War John C. Calhoun ordered him on an expedition to the Great Plains for the purpose of impressing Native Americans living there with the power of the United States. This was the first military expedition outfitted with new steamboats and much was expected of it. In July of that year Atkinson shepherded nearly 1,000 men up the Missouri River from St. Louis, but mechanical difficulties forced him to stop for the winter at Council Bluffs, Nebraska. He nonetheless received command of the Ninth Military district, headquartered at St. Louis, from which he helped orchestrate the construction of roads and forts to facilitate frontier exploration and migration. In 1820 Atkinson dispatched Major Stephen H. Long on his noted exploring expedition to the Rocky Mountains and across the great "American desert." In 1825 he advanced to brigadier general and conducted a second foray to the mouth of the Yellowstone River (Wyoming), there to conclude the first treaties with several tribes inhabiting that region. In this manner trade relations and exploration were greatly facilitated. That same year Atkinson chose the site for the celebrated Jefferson's Barracks in St. Louis, the army's only school for infantry. In 1827

he next dispatched Colonel Henry Leavenworth into the Kansas Territory to establish a post there, which later evolved into Fort Leavenworth, another important frontier post.

The western frontier at this time could be a violent, dangerous place, and in 1827 Atkinson was required to accompany troops in Wisconsin to contain a revolt by the Winnebago Indians. Affairs became more violent in 1832 when a dissident band of Sac and Fox Indians under Chief Black Hawk abrogated an earlier agreement to relocate across the Mississippi River and returned to their homelands in Illinois. Atkinson then formed an army out of state militia and army troops pursued and then engaged Black Hawk at the Battle of Bad Axe on August 2, 1832. The Americans vigorously pursued the fleeing Indians to the banks of the Mississippi and used the steamship *Warrior* to bombard them. The tribesmen were completely defeated in this, the last gasp of Native American resistance east of the Mississippi River, with Black Hawk captured and his tribesmen forcefully relocated. President Andrew Jackson was thus empowered to accelerate his timetable for Indian removal. In 1837 and 1840 Atkinson was tasked with removing the Potawatomi and Winnebago tribes, respectively, to new homes before dying at Jefferson Barracks on June 14, 1842. He was an important military and administrative figure throughout the middle plains region, and Fort Atkinson, Iowa, is named in his honor.

by Federal force. Once the South Carolina legislature passes the ordinance, the state is on an eventual collision course with the federal government.

November 26
Transportation: New York City begins employing the first horse-drawn street cars operated by the New York & Harlem Railroad.

Mathias Baldwin's new locomotive *Old Ironsides* makes its debut run in Philadelphia.

November 27
POLITICS: The South Carolina legislature unhesitatingly adopts the nullification ordinance, even if it provokes a military response from the federal government. President Andrew Jackson places Federal troops in Charleston Harbor on the alert.

December 4
POLITICS: President Andrew Jackson makes his annual address to Congress, calling for tariff rates to be lowered. To many it appears he is trying to mollify radical elements in South Carolina.

December 5
POLITICS: In his bid for reelection Andrew Jackson overwhelmingly defeats Henry Clay, accruing 219 electoral votes to 49. A major factor in Jackson's victory is his continuing opposition to rechartering the national bank, which secure him scores of votes from the frontier and farmlands of America. Meanwhile, Vice President John C. Calhoun is successfully elected to the Senate from South Carolina and resigns from office. His native state casts 11 electoral votes for John Floyd of Virginia rather than give them to Jackson.

December 10
POLITICS: President Andrew Jackson, having ordered federal forts in Charleston, South Carolina, reinforced, sternly warns that no state will be allowed to secede and "disunion by armed force is treason." He determines to fiercely suppress any attempt to leave the Union—by force, if necessary.

December 12
POLITICS: Henry Clay introduces a bill to distribute surplus federal revenue accruing from federal lands back to the states; the measure is vetoed by President Andrew Jackson.

December 13
POLITICS: Robert Y. Hayne, a strident defender of states' rights, is elected governor of South Carolina.

December 18
DIPLOMACY: The United States and Russia conclude a commercial treaty.

December 20
POLITICS: Governor Robert Y. Hayne of South Carolina issues a declaration defying President Andrew Jackson's opposition to nullification and secession. Throwing down the gauntlet here incites Jackson to invoke whatever means are necessary to preserve the Union.

December 27
POLITICS: Gulian Verplanck of New York introduces a measure to further reduce tariffs into Congress.

December 28
EDUCATION: St. Louis College University is chartered in Missouri; it is the only Roman Catholic institution of higher learning west of the Appalachian Mountains.

1832

1833

ARTS: Swiss painter Karl Bodmer accompanies Prince Maximilian of Germany on an extended tour of the Missouri River region and begins painting numerous Indian tribes and chiefs in great detail. For many now extinct tribes such as the Mandan, this is the only record of their daily existence. Curiously, the explorers are guided by maps first drawn in 1804 by the Lewis and Clark expedition.

EDUCATION: The Haverford School Association (Haverford College) is founded at Haverford, Pennsylvania as the first Quaker institute for higher learning.

LABOR: The General Trades Union is formed by all the trade unions in New York City while their president, Ely Moore, is elected to Congress.

LITERATURE: Edgar Allan Poe's short story "MS Found in a Bottle" wins a $50 prize sponsored by the *Baltimore Saturday Visitor*. John Pendleton Kennedy subsequently arranges for Poe to publish additional works as editor of the new *Southern Literary Messenger*.

MUSIC: Lowell Mason founds the Boston Academy of Music to educate children and music instructors.

POLITICS: The 18-year-old Kauikeouli is crowned king of Hawaii under the name Kamehameha III.

RELIGION: The Congregational Church is disestablished in Massachusetts, finally severing the final connection between church and state.

SLAVERY: Former president James Madison becomes president of the American Colonization Society to convince free African Americans to migrate back to the Dark Continent.

SOCIETAL: Peterborough, New Hampshire, founds the nation's first tax-supported public library at the behest of Reverend Abiel Abbot. This is the oldest public library in the United States, save for the Library of Congress, which was founded in 1800.

TRANSPORTATION: The vessel *Ann McKim* is launched at Baltimore; this is the first of the long, slim "clipper ships" that are designed for speed rather than cargo. This class of ships establishes many world speed records that are not broken until long after the Civil War period. However, as a class it remains subject to continual refinement in design and reaches its highest expression of beauty and efficiency in the ships of Donald McKay of Boston.

January 1

PUBLISHING: The *Knickerbocker Magazine* debuts in New York City; within a few years it will be the nation's most popular and influential literary magazine.

January 16

POLITICS: The South Carolina state convention denounces President Andrew Jackson as "King Andrew" for his stance against nullification and begins raising volunteers to defend the state by force if need be. Jackson, determined to keep South Carolina in the fold, asks Congress for a "Force Bill" to enforce compliance of the tariff law.

February 5

EDUCATION: Newark College (University of Delaware) is chartered in Newark, Delaware, by Presbyterians; it graduates its first class in 1836.

February 12
POLITICS: Henry Clay, ever a moderating influence, introduces a bill that gradually lowers tariffs over a 10-year period to 20 percent. This move mollifies most Southern states and leaves South Carolina out on a limb.

February 15–16
POLITICS: President Andrew Jackson, having asked Congress for a "Force Bill" to enforce the Tariff Acts of 1828 and 1832, is criticized in the Senate by John C. Calhoun.

February 16
LAW: The Supreme Court decides the case of *Barron v. Baltimore*, ruling that state governments are not subject to the Bill of Rights, as this is a strictly federal jurisdiction.

February 20
POLITICS: The Senate passes both President Andrew Jackson's "Force Bill" and Henry Clay's Compromise Tariff Bill, both of which the president signs. Only John Tyler of Virginia opposed the former. This ends the nullification crisis and confrontation is averted.

February 25
TECHNOLOGY: Samuel Colt successfully patents his six-shot revolving pistol, the first marketable rapid-fire weapon in history. It is also the first gun to be handled effectively while on horseback and wields an indelible impact on events along the western frontier.

March 2
BUSINESS: A resolution by the U.S. House of Representatives approves continuing use of the Bank of the United States, but President Andrew Jackson demands that all funds be withdrawn and redistributed to state institutions. This move causes considerable dissent in the president's cabinet.
POLITICS: The Nullification Crisis continues as President Andrew Jackson signs the "Force Bill" to authorize military use to collect tariffs in South Carolina. He also signs Henry Clay's compromise tariff, which gradually reduces the rates imposed.

March 4
POLITICS: Andrew Jackson is inaugurated for his second term as president of the United States and Martin Van Buren is sworn in as vice president, replacing John C. Calhoun, who has resigned from office to successfully stand for a Senate seat in his home state.

March 15
POLITICS: Aware that Andrew Jackson follows through on his threats to use force, the South Carolina state convention rescinds its Ordinance of Nullification in light of Henry Clay's Compromise Bill; however, three days later it defiantly votes to nullify the now superfluous "Force Bill."

March 19
POLITICS: President Andrew Jackson decides to remove all government deposits from the Bank of the United States; considerable debate ensues within his own cabinet as to the legality and expedience of the move.

1833

Colt, Samuel   (1814–1862)
Manufacturer

Samuel Colt was born in Hartford, Connecticut, the son of a textile mill owner. He worked in his father's mill in Ware, Massachusetts, until 1830, and then went to sea. There, on a voyage to India, Colt conceived the idea of a rapid-fire handgun utilizing a revolving cylinder that stored the bullets. Firing the device would advance the cylinder, placing the next loaded chamber in line with the hammer and barrel. Thus configured, such a weapon could load and discharge at much higher rates of fire than the muzzle-loading ordnance extant. After touring the country to raise money while demonstrating "laughing gas" (nitrous oxide), Colt built several functioning prototypes and applied for a patent. He then established the Patent Arms Manufacturing Company in Paterson, New Jersey, and commenced production on his new Colt "revolver," but the military was uninterested. He was then forced to liquidate his assets and spent several years tinkering with underwater mines and telegraph cables. Fortunately for Colt, the United States declared war on Mexico in 1846 and the army finally realized the military potential of his weapon. To this end General Zachary Taylor dispatched Texas Ranger Captain Samuel Walker to confer with Colt and further refine the weapons. The resulting "Walker Colt" was the first real production model, which became a standard sidearm throughout this conflict. However, insomuch as Colt no longer owned a factory, he forged a partnership with Eli Whitney, Jr., to manufacture the guns in Whitneyville, Connecticut.

Over the next few years Colt continually refined his weapon, selling more than 200,000 to civilians and military personnel alike. In combat the Colt handgun's good accuracy and rapid fire proved instrumental in allowing frontiersmen and armed groups like the Texas Rangers to defeat and subdue fierce nomadic tribes like the Comanche. Mass production also brought the price down so that even lowly settlers, alone and wandering the frontiers, could effectively defend themselves. By 1856 Colt had established a new manufacturing plant at Hartford which employed the very latest assembly techniques, interchangeable parts, and a highly skilled and educated work force. He also pioneered the use of new, precision lathes, specialized cutting and stamping machines, and gas-fed lighting. In 1860, when the Civil War seemed imminent, Colt received and fulfilled an order for 200,000 of the New Model Army Pistols for the U.S. Army. Colt, a multimillionaire, died at Hartford on January 10, 1862 at the age of 47; he was estimated to have a net worth of $10 million. Having become the most important arms manufacturer in American history, his efforts also wielded an enormous impact on the field of early mass production techniques. It was his simple, deadly Colt .45 pistol, however, that made the biggest impact of all, becoming an iconic symbol of the rough and tumble Wild West. His efficient manufacturing, coupled with low pricing, made it possible for the average settler to afford the luxury of self-defense.

March 20
DIPLOMACY: The United States and the Kingdom of Siam conclude a treaty of commerce; this is the first agreement reached between America and an Oriental nation.

1833

April 1
BUSINESS: U.S. Attorney General Roger B. Taney upholds the legality of removing federal deposits from the Bank of the United States.

April 1–13
SETTLEMENT: At San Felipe de Austin, American settlers living in Texas assemble and vote to separate Texas from Mexico. They are angry over the government's refusal to recognize their "right" to own slaves.

May
EDUCATION: Oberlin College, Ohio, becomes the first coeducational college by enrolling both men and women; two years later it is the first higher learning institution to matriculate African Americans.

June 1
POLITICS: Continuing dissent over the issue of withdrawing funds from the Bank of the United States and redistributing them to the states forces President Andrew Jackson to reorganize his cabinet. Secretary of the Treasury Louis McLane is reappointed Secretary of State while William J. Duane occupies the former office.

June 6
POLITICS: President Andrew Jackson begins a tour of the states, starting in Virginia and proceeding up to New Hampshire.

August
LABOR: The General Trades Union of New York begins agitation for a National Trade Union, a general labor federation incorporating all crafts. Ely Moore, a New York printer, is elected the first president and is subsequently sent to Congress.
POLITICS: John Quincy Adams declines to confer a honorary degree upon President Andrew Jackson from Harvard College, decrying the chief executive as an "illiterate barbarian."

August 1
LABOR: Shoemakers in Geneva, New York, successfully strike for a wage increase.

August 20
GENERAL: Benjamin Harrison, the 23rd president, is born in North Bend, Ohio.

August 28
SLAVERY: Great Britain outlaws slavery in its empire leaving the United States increasingly isolated regarding its perpetuation.

September 1
JOURNALISM: Benjamin H. Day edits the *New York Sun*, the country's first penny newspaper; its smaller size and lower price is expected to attract a wider readership. It foregoes the usual discussion of politics in favor of human-interest stories, outlandish crimes, and police court news. The tabloid press had arrived.

September 10
POLITICS: President Andrew Jackson declares that the government will no longer deposit money with the Bank of the United States, but Secretary of the Treasury William J. Duane hotly contests such a move.

1833

September 18

POLITICS: President Andrew Jackson has Attorney General Roger B. Taney submit a brief to his cabinet regarding the legality of removing funds from the Bank of the United States. In it he signals that the role of the presidential cabinet is as his personal organ.

September 21

DIPLOMACY: The United States concludes a commercial treaty with the Sultan of Muscat (Oman).

September 23

POLITICS: After Secretary of the Treasury William J. Duane refuses to remove government funds from the Bank of the United States, he is sacked and replaced by Roger B. Taney of Maryland.

September 26–October 1

BUSINESS: The so-called "Bank War" begins once Secretary of the Treasury Roger B. Taney orders federal money withdrawn from the Bank of the United States as per President Andrew Jackson's executive order. The funds are then transferred to 23 state institutions, soon derogated as "pet banks."

November 15

POLITICS: Massachusetts Democrat and future Civil War general Benjamin F. Butler gains appointment as attorney general.

November 13

SCIENCE: The inhabitants of Alabama are treated to a spectacular astronomical display as Earth passes through the Leonid Shower, resulting in 10,000 streaking lights per hour.

November 16

MUSIC: The Italian Opera House opens its door at Leonard and Church Streets in New York City. It caters to the city's cultural elite, and season boxes are available for as much as $6,000.

December

SLAVERY: The Female Anti-Slavery Society is organized in Philadelphia under the aegis of Lucretia C. Mott, seeing that the male-dominated American Anti-Slavery Society will not allow women.

December 3

POLITICS: In his annual address to Congress, President Andrew Jackson defends his decision to withdraw federal funds from the Bank of the United States. He justifies his action by declaring that the bank took a partisan stance against him during the 1832 election.

December 6

SLAVERY: The American Anti-Slavery Society is organized in Philadelphia by Theodore Weld, an abolitionist minister, and Arthur and Lewis Tappan, wealthy New York merchants.

December 11

POLITICS: The Senate demands to see a copy of the papers presented by then Attorney General Roger B. Taney to the cabinet of President Andrew Jackson in September, but Jackson refuses, citing the executive branch's independence of the legislature.

1833

Mott, Lucretia Coffin   (1793–1880)
Reformer

Lucretia Coffin was born in Nantucket, Massachusetts, on January 3, 1793, the daughter of a whaling captain. During her father's absences she was raised and educated by her mother, who instilled in her a sense of self-sufficiency and discipline. Her family then converted to Quakerism, a sect that generally granted women equal rights and responsibilities, and she subsequently attended a Quaker school in Poughkeepsie, New York. She taught there many years and eventually married James Mott, a fellow teacher, in 1811. In 1827 she and her husband sided with the more liberal Hicksite faction of the Society of Friends and both became more actively involved in the nascent abolitionist movement upon relocating to Philadelphia. Women at this time were discouraged from voicing their opinions publically but Mott, never one to be silenced, organized the Female Anti-Slavery Society of Philadelphia. Five years later she expanded her efforts to help establish the Anti-Slavery Convention of American Women. While acting in this capacity she was frequently harassed and her meeting halls were sometimes burned by angry mobs, but, for this reason, Mott became known for her calmness and grace under duress, as well as her engaging delivery. In 1840 she ventured to London with William Lloyd Garrison to attend the World Anti-Slavery Convention, where she and other female delegates were turned aside. However, there she also encountered a young and impressionable Elizabeth Cady Stanton, another pioneering feminist, who became a protégée. At this time they began planning a national conference to address the gross inequities suffered by women at the hands of society.

In 1848 Mott, assisted by Stanton and others, orchestrated the first women's rights convention at Seneca Falls, New York. This was the genesis of the women's rights movement in the United States and a springboard for the careers of many young feminists in attendance. Mott, however, felt that the convention's resolution for immediate suffrage rights was far in advance of public opinion at that time. Mott followed up this success in 1850 with her publication *Discourses on Women*, which portrayed female subordination as artificial and based more on laws, customs, and lack of education than biological necessity. In the decade approaching the Civil War Mott and her husband became actively involved in the Underground Railroad and opened their house up to fugitive slaves. Deeply pacifistic, she was disillusioned by conflict when it erupted in April 1861 but found solace in the fact that the abolition of slavery was now inevitable. After 1865 Mott became active in the antiwar movement as well as her usual commitments to the Society of Friends. She remained a familiar speaker at many such events until her death in Philadelphia on November 11, 1880. In an age of growing stridency and militance among the feminist movement, Mott invariably came across as a kindly mother figure, a calculated image which belied her otherwise steely resolve.

December 26
POLITICS: Henry Clay introduces motions to censure President Andrew Jackson and Secretary of the Treasury Roger B. Taney for their role in removing funds from the Bank of the United States.

Shown here is *The Anti-Slavery Almanac*, published yearly by the American Anti-Slavery Society. *(Library of Congress)*

December 31
TECHNOLOGY: Obed Hussey patents the first successful, horse-drawn grain reaper; this makes him a direct competitor with Cyrus H. McCormick, who has also invented a similar device.

1834

EDUCATION: The Wabash Manual Labor College is founded at Crawfordsville, Indiana, by the Presbyterians; its first class graduates in 1838.

PUBLISHING: Historian George Bancroft writes and publishes the first volume of his seminal *History of the United States from the Discovery of the American Continent*; the final volume appears 40 years later in 1874.

The *Southern Literary Messenger*, a significant regional journal, begins publication in Richmond, Virginia, with Edgar Allan Poe as its foremost editor.

RELIGION: Anti-Catholic protesters burn an Ursuline Convent in Boston, Massachusetts.

SOCIETAL: The Adelphi Club is founded in Philadelphia, Pennsylvania; this is the oldest association for gentlemen in the country and subsequently renames itself the Philadelphia Club.

January 3
SETTLEMENT: When Stephen F. Austin ventures to Mexico City with a petition from American settlers requesting independence from Mexico, he is arrested and imprisoned for eight months by General Antonio López de Santa Anna. This act leads to continuing deterioration of Mexican-American relations.

TECHNOLOGY: Thomas Davenport of Vermont constructs the world's first electric motor, which incorporates the basic design still utilized today. He died in 1851 without ever finding a practical application for his device.

January 29
LABOR: When Irish laborers working on the Chesapeake and Ohio Canal riot, President Andrew Jackson orders Secretary of War Lewis Cass to contain the violence with army troops. This is the first instance when federal forces intervene in a labor dispute.

February 14
DIPLOMACY: The United States and Spain sign the Van Ness Convention in Madrid to settle any continuing claims between them.

March 28
POLITICS: The Senate votes 26 to 20 to pass Henry Clay's censure of President Andrew Jackson and Secretary of the Treasury Roger B. Taney for removing fed-

eral funds from the Bank of the United States. This move is ultimately expunged from the records on January 16, 1837.

April 4

POLITICS: The House of Representatives passes four resolutions in favor of General Andrew Jackson's banking policies.

April 14

POLITICS: The evolving National Republican Party adopts the new name of Whigs (an English political term), while Henry Clay and Daniel Webster serve as its most prominent members. They are extremely anti-Jacksonian in tenor and outlook.

April 15

POLITICS: President Andrew Jackson protests the motion to censure in the Senate and claims he has not been given an opportunity to defend himself, despite the fact that he is charged with an impeachable offense.

May 7

POLITICS: An angry Senate votes 27 to 16 to not include President Andrew Jackson's remarks in their official record.

June 15

SETTLEMENT: Fur trader Nathaniel J. Wyeth founds Fort Hall on the Snake River, Idaho, soon a major stopover along the Oregon Trail.

June 20

INDIAN: An act of Congress denotes all land west of the Mississippi River, minus populated regions of Missouri, Louisiana, and Arkansas, as "Indian Country."

June 21

TECHNOLOGY: Cyrus McCormick secures a patent for his first horse-drawn mower and reaper, an invention soon to revolutionize agricultural production. This device cuts grain and it moves along then gathers it in sufficient quantities for a sheaf to be quickly tied. This device not only increases production, but its also lowers a farmer's dependency on high-priced seasonal labor for harvesting purposes.

June 24

POLITICS: In their latest political confrontation with President Andrew Jackson, the U.S. Senate refuses to confirm Roger B. Taney as his secretary of the treasury.

June 28

BUSINESS: The Second Coinage Act increases the ratio of silver to gold coins by 16 to 1, which undervalues silver coins and drives them from circulation on account of hoarding.

TRANSPORTATION: In New York, the Harlem Railroad's first engine explodes shortly after completing a run; many view its destruction as divine intervention against this new technology.

June 30

INDIAN: The Department of Indian Affairs is established by Congress to administer Native American policies west of the Mississippi River. It also sets aside

1834

McCormick, Cyrus H.   (1809–1884)
Inventor

Cyrus Hall McCormick was born in Rockbridge County, Virginia, on February 15, 1809, the son of stern Presbyterian farmers. He was imperfectly educated but always displayed a talent for tinkering and inventing, particularly as it related to agriculture. In 1831 McCormick created a hillside plow that allowed cultivation of uneven ground and then went on to develop his famous horse-drawn mechanical reaper. This device was pulled across an area full of ripened wheat and then would cut it and automatically bundle it for harvesting. As interest developed in his device, McCormick acquired the Cotopaxi Iron Works to begin mass production although the panic of 1837 soon drove him into bankruptcy. McCormick was also engaged in a bitter lawsuit with Obed Hussey, who had invented a similar machine and, ultimately, the patent for McCormick's reaper entered into the public domain. By 1843 he realized that the small-scale farms of Virginia and New England did not represent the best market for his product, so he licensed production of the device to factories in New York and Ohio. When these products proved of inferior design and construction to his own, McCormick relocated his thriving business to Chicago in 1847, much closer to a region heralded as the "breadbasket of the nation." In time he adopted modern, mass-production techniques and stocked his workplaces with the latest time-saving technology. His 1,500-man workforce was also among the most educated and highly paid in the nation, but with his patent in the public domain, McCormick faced stiff competition from other firms and he decided to counter them by possessing the best organization available.

By 1860 McCormick was building and selling 5,000 reapers annually, and his business endeavors were enhanced by a scheme of centralized regional offices to handle promotion, sales, and repairs efficiently. His company was also unique in offering generous credit arrangements for customers and offered one of the first money-back guarantees in business history. The presence of an estimated 80,000–90,000 of his reapers in Northern fields throughout the Civil War also paid dividends by ensuring that the Union and its armies enjoyed a readily available surplus of food, in contrast with the slowly starving South. In sum, the McCormick reaper was also a significant but frequently overlooked contributor to the ultimate Union victory. McCormick himself took an interest in politics and in 1864 he ran for Congress on the Peace Ticket and lost handily. He was also closely involved with doctrinal matters within the Presbyterian Church and helped found and finance the McCormick Theological Seminary of Chicago. McCormick himself largely personified the strict Calvinistic approach to life, being hardworking, pious, and abstentious toward smoking and drinking. He died in Chicago on May 13, 1884, one of the most successful and farsighted entrepreneurs of American history.

the Indian Territory (Oklahoma) as a reservation for tribes displaced from tribal lands in the East.

July 4
SLAVERY: In Philadelphia, the Annual Convention of People of Color adopts a resolution making July 4 a day of prayer and contemplation for all African Americans. Abolitionists and pro-slavery crowds riot in New York City.

1834

July 4–12
SLAVERY: The Chatham Street Chapel in New York City is the scene of an eight-day riot between pro- and anti-slavery advocates. Several adjoining homes and churches are destroyed or damaged in the process.

August 1
SLAVERY: The British Empire under Queen Victoria formally abolishes slavery.

August 11
RELIGION: An anti-Catholic riot at Charlestown, Massachusetts, results in the destruction of an Ursuline Convent; nobody was injured in the attack.

October
SLAVERY: Pro-slavery advocates riot in Philadelphia, damaging or destroying 40 African-American homes and two churches.

October 14
TECHNOLOGY: Henry Blair receives a patent for his corn harvester; he is also the first African American so rewarded.

October 28
INDIAN: The United States government insists that the Treaty of Payne's Landing be observed by all Seminole Indians living in Florida, with many tribal leaders under Chief Osceola refusing to comply.

November 1
TRANSPORTATION: A new railroad is completed between Philadelphia, Pennsylvania, and Trenton, New Jersey.

December 1
POLITICS: Abraham Lincoln, a little-known frontier lawyer, is seated for the first time in the Illinois House of Representatives.

December 2
DIPLOMACY: Three years after France signed the spoliation treaty with the United States, agreeing to pay restitution for abuses during the Napoleonic wars, no payments have been made. President Andrew Jackson, in his annual message to Congress, suggests seizing French property in retaliation. He also mentions that the national debt will be paid off by New Years' Day.

1835

LABOR: A New York court decides the case of *The People v. Fisher*, whereby labor strikes for higher wages are judged conspiratorial, hence illegal.

LITERATURE: A noted compilation, *The Collected Works of James Kirke Paulding*, is published and well-received.

PUBLISHING: French political observer Alexis de Tocqueville publishes his *Democracy in America* in Belgium; it is soon translated into English to become a classic analysis of national politics. As a whole, the author is favorably impressed by the American quest to secure both liberty and equality and is pleased with the balance struck thus far.

Catherine Martha Sedgwick, soon to be one of the most popular female authors in America, publishes her first novel, *The Linwoods*, a romantic piece set in the waning days of the American Revolution.

SLAVERY: Influential Unitarian leader William Ellery Channing begins publishing antislavery pamphlets with his first title, simply called *Slavery*.

TECHNOLOGY: Gas lighting for guests and hallway lighting debuts at the American House in Boston.

January

POLITICS: The Whig Party of Massachusetts elects Daniel Webster to be its presidential candidate while those in Tennessee nominate Hugh L. White. The Whigs hope to deny the Democrats a majority of electors and thus force the election into the House of Representatives.

The national debt is finally paid off, leading to political bickering as to how surplus revenue is to be allocated and spent.

SOCIETAL: Lucius Manlius Sargent begins publishing his stories about temperance, and he becomes the most popular writer on the subject over the next 25 years.

TECHNOLOGY: Samuel F. B. Morse demonstrates an early version of his new communications device, the telegraph. It is initially limited to a range of 40 feet but improves with continual refinement.

January 30

CRIME: President Andrew Jackson survives an assassination attempt when house painter Richard Lawrence fires two pistols at him which misfire. The transgressor is subsequently found insane and committed to an asylum.

February 14

EDUCATION: Marietta College is founded at Marietta, Ohio, by the Congregationalists; its first class graduates in 1838.

March 3

BUSINESS: Congress establishes branches of the U.S. Mint in New Orleans, Louisiana, Charlotte, North Carolina, and Dahlonega, Georgia.

March 17

SETTLEMENT: The town of Milwaukee, long used as a gathering point for regional Native Americans, is formally incorporated as a town within the Michigan Territory.

April 25

DIPLOMACY: France finally begins payments on American spoliation claims but also demands that President Andrew Jackson apologize for calling for reprisals; Jackson angrily refuses.

May 6

JOURNALISM: The *New York Herald* begins as a penny paper, edited by James Gordon Bennett; it is pro-slavery and also a mouthpiece for the Tammany Hall Democratic machine.

May 1–June 29

POLITICS: A constitutional convention meeting in Detroit adopts guidelines that specifically outlaw slavery.

May 20

POLITICS: The Democratic National Convention, meeting at Baltimore, nominates Martin Van Buren of New York for the presidency and Richard M. Johnson of Kentucky for the vice presidency.

June 5
SLAVERY: A National Negro Convention in Philadelphia objects to the use of "African" or "Colored" and seeks to remove them from the black vernacular.

June 30
SETTLEMENT: The attempts at greater centralization by Mexican dictator Santa Anna leads to increasing friction between that ruler and American settlers in Texas. Colonel William B. Travis and a group of armed colonists take control of a Mexican fort at Anahuac in protest while other Texans skirmish with Mexican cavalry near Gonzales.

July
DIPLOMACY: President Andrew Jackson wishes to purchase the region known as Texas, but Mexican president Santa Anna refuses.

July 6
GENERAL: John Marshall, the influential chief justice of the U.S. Supreme Court, dies in Philadelphia. President Andrew Jackson then nominates his friend Roger B. Taney to succeed him. Two days later the famous Liberty Bell in Philadelphia develops its celebrated crack while tolling for Marshall. Taney, meanwhile, weathers a storm of criticism in the Senate and will not be confirmed until 1836.

July 29
SLAVERY: A mob in Charleston, South Carolina, burns antislavery literature sent there by abolitionists in New York. The city postmaster, Alfred Huger, requests the postmaster general to forbid such materials to be mailed to the state.

August
SLAVERY: The American Anti-Slavery Society mails 75,000 tracts to inhabitants throughout the South, excoriating slave owners.

August 10
SOCIETAL: A crowd of antiblack citizens in Canaan, Connecticut, attacks and burns the Noyes Academy after it enrolls a number of African-American children.

August 26
JOURNALISM: The Democrats publish their first party platform in the *Washington Globe*.

October 2
MILITARY: A party of Texas volunteers defeats a detachment of Mexican cavalry near the Guadalupe River in central Texas; this is the opening round of the Texas Revolution.

October 21
SLAVERY: A pro-slavery mob drags abolitionist William Lloyd Garrison through the streets of Boston with a rope around his neck to protest his views—he spends the night at the city jail for his own safety. His assailants apparently became distraught when he declared that "all men are created equal." Another mob heckles and interrupts English abolitionist George Thompson as he addresses the Female Anti-Slavery Society in Boston.

Garrison, William Lloyd   (1805–1879)
Abolitionist

William Lloyd Garrison *(Library of Congress)*

William Lloyd Garrison was born in New-buryport, Massachusetts, on December 10, 1805, the son of a poor family. He worked as a printer's apprentice at 13 to help his family and subsequently entered the profession of journalism. Garrison, who inherited from his mother an intense religiousness, next became coeditor of the *National Philanthropist*, a temperance newspaper, at 21 and began circulating within various reform movements. Foremost among these was the abolitionists headed by Quaker publisher Benjamin Lundy, who convinced Garrison to edit his paper *Genius of Universal Emancipation* in 1828. However, Garrison's views gradually became radicalized and he broke with Lundy over the latter's demand for forced repatriation back to Africa. Thereafter he vociferously insisted on immediate emancipation of all African-American slaves without compensation to their owners. Such a stance established Garrison on the radical fringes

October 29
POLITICS: An extreme wing of Jacksonian Democrats, known locally as the Equal Rights Party, meets at Tammany Hall, New York, to oppose the mainstream candidates chosen by their party. The radicals then acquire the nickname "Loco Focos" after the newly developed friction matches used to light candles once the gaslights had been turned off to silence them.

November 1
INDIAN: Large portions of the Seminole tribe under Chief Osceola steadfastly refuse to be relocated from Florida and threaten to resist by force; this defiance precipitates the Second Seminole War.

November 23
TECHNOLOGY: Henry Burden of Troy, New York, receives a patent for his horseshoe-making machine; this device can churn out horseshoes at the rate of 60 a minute. Much later it functions as a major source of horseshoes for Union cavalry during the Civil War.

November 24
LAW: In an attempt to enforce order along its frontiers, the Texas Provincial Government establishes a new mounted constabulary, the Texas Rangers.

1835

of abolitionism, elevated him to leadership within the movement, and in 1831 he began publishing his own newspaper, *The Liberator*. "On this subject I do not wish to think, speak, or write with moderation," he declared in the first issue, "I am in earnest—I will not equivocate—I will not excuse—I will not retreat a single inch—and I WILL BE HEARD." His uncompromising stance against slavery coincided with a rising tide of abolitionism in the Northeast, and in 1833 Garrison established the American Anti-Slavery Society. Beyond his radical stance, this was unique in allowing women to participate fully, along with African Americans. In fact, Garrison became an outspoken advocate of women's suffrage, temperance, and other social causes.

Garrison's strident radicalism soon caused a rift within his own organization. He openly condemned Christianity and the U.S. Constitution for their toleration of slavery, which lost him many supporters. He also steadfastly refused to work within the political system for change, calling instead for pacifism and moral suasion to achieve an end to slavery. Garrison's strident agitation led to confrontation with pro-slavery mobs, and in 1835 he was dragged through the streets and nearly killed before being rescued by police. By 1840 his tactics caused the American Anti-Slavery Society to break into warring factions, but he remained true to his own precepts. Garrison was sympathetic toward radicals like John Brown but completely disagreed with their methods. It was not until the advent of the Civil War in April 1861 that he finally accepted the notion that war can sometimes be used for the eradication of evil, and he finally abandoned his pacifism. Following adoption of the Thirteenth Amendment to the Constitution in 1865, which abolished slavery, Garrison finally folded his tent, ceased publication of the *Liberator*, and withdrew from public life altogether. He died at Roxbury, Massachusetts, on May 24, 1879, a driving force behind abolitionism—if at times its own worst enemy.

November 30

GENERAL: Samuel Clemens, better known by his pseudonym Mark Twain, is born as Halley's Comet makes its scheduled appearance; ironically he dies in 1910 during the comet's return.

December

TRANSPORTATION: The Carrollton Railroad opens for business in New Orleans, replacing its horse-drawn passenger cars with steam engines.

December 2

POLITICS: In his message to Congress, President Andrew Jackson, cognizant of antiabolitionist violence in Charleston, South Carolina, recommends that the U.S. Mail be forbidden from distributing antislavery publications there.

December 7

POLITICS: The 24th Congress convenes with a strong Whig presence—they hold 25 seats to 27 Democrats, and James K. Polk is voted the new speaker of the House of Representatives.

December 8–9

MILITARY: Texan forces drive a Mexican force under General Martin Perfecto Cos out of San Antonio after three days and nights of intense fighting.

1835

December 15

SETTLEMENT: American settlers in Texas, determined to resist Mexican president Santa Anna's new centralized government—including its sweeping antislavery regulations—declare their intention to secede from Mexico rather than abandon their "right" to own slaves.

December 16

POLITICS: A gathering of Whigs and Anti-Masons at Harrisburg, Pennsylvania, nominates William Henry Harrison to run for the presidency. They also select Francis Granger of New York for the vice presidency.

December 16–18

GENERAL: New York City is ravaged by a huge fire that damages more than 600 buildings and inflicts $20 million in damages.

December 21

EDUCATION: Oglethorpe College is chartered at Milledgeville, Georgia, by the Presbyterians; its first class graduates in 1839.

December 28

MILITARY: In opening skirmishes of the Second Seminole War, Indian Agent Wiley Thompson is murdered at Fort King, Florida, by a war party headed by Chief Osceola while Major Francis L. Dade is ambushed outside Fort Brooke, losing 110 men.

December 29

INDIANS: The Cherokee sign another treaty at New Echota, ceding all their lands east of the Mississippi River for $5 million, for new homes in the newly designated Indian Territory (Oklahoma).

Osceola (ca. 1804–1838)

Seminole chief

Osceola was probably born around 1804 along the Tallapoosa River on the Georgia-Alabama border, a part of the Lower Creek Nation. This group had been under duress in the face of white encroachment and parts had relocated to Florida in concert with escaped African-American slaves and became part of the related Seminole nation. Little is known of his youth, but Osceola's name is most likely a corruption of the phrase asi yohola or "black drink crier," a term with religious connotations. He apparently matured into a fine warrior with a commanding presence and around 1832 was noted as a tustenugge, or war chief. In this capacity Osceola railed against the continuing loss of land to the United States. Two years earlier Congress approved the Indian Removal Bill, which mandated the forced relocation of Native Americans across the Mississippi River to new homes in Arkansas. However, this was done in violation of an earlier treaty signed in 1823, which granted the Indians the right to existing lands until 1832. Moreover, that year the government forced tribal elders to conclude the Treaty of Payne's Landing, whereby the Seminole were to surrender all their holdings in Florida and move to Arkansas. It also stipulated the surrender of all African-American refugees who had since been absorbed into the tribe. Because one of Osceola's two wives was a mulatto he refused to comply. In 1833 Indian Agent Wiley Thompson arrived in Florida with

1836

Arts: James N. Baker's play *Court Of Love*, adapted in 1817 from a French play, is staged at the Arch Street Theater in Philadelphia to popular reviews.

Education: William Holmes McGuffey publishes the *First Reader* and *Second Reader*, which become widespread and standard schoolbook texts. These booklets imparted literature, morality, and selected writings from famous English-language authors.

Educational reformer William A. Alcott publishes *The Young Woman's Guide and the Young Mother*, which proffers practical advice and upholds traditional norms of morality.

Journalism: No less than 500 abolitionist societies are functioning throughout the North as the movement gains momentum.

Literature: Ralph Waldo Emerson publishes a book entitled *Nature*, the first example of a literary and philosophical movement known as Transcendentalism. In it he expresses a profound regard for the natural world and the attitude that spirituality and self-awareness are essential for proper living. He also proffers it to counter the tenants of Unitarianism, which he regards as a religious orthodoxy.

Medical: German immigrant Constantine Hering is licensed to found the North American Academy of the Homeopathic Healing Art in Allentown, Pennsylvania. This is the first such institution in the world.

Religion: Noted Unitarian minister William Ellery Channing publishes *The Abolitionist*, a stinging indictment on the moral implications of slavery.

Slavery: The Massachusetts Supreme Court declares that any slave brought within state borders is declared free.

the Treaty of Fort Gibson, intending to enforce earlier agreements, but Osceola reputedly drew his knife and defiantly stabbed the parchment in front of the Americans. He was then arrested and held in shackles for several days until, feigning a change of heart, Osceola was released.

Once free Osceola made immediate preparations to go to war. On December 28, 1835, he attacked the Indian Agency at Fort King, killing Thompson, while other Seminoles massacred the army patrol of Major Francis L. Dade near Wahoo Swamp. This violence precipitated the Second Seminole War, one of the costliest guerrilla conflicts ever waged by the United States. For seven years America dispatched hundreds of troops and militia, waged several skirmishes, large and small, but failed to awe the Indians into surrendering. Osceola, for his part, was tricked into a parley by General Thomas S. Jesup and then treacherously captured on October 21, 1837. He was transported to Fort Moultrie, South Carolina, where he was interned and had his portrait painted by George Catlin. Despite public outrage over the manner in which the chief was taken, Osceola remained behind bars and died there of illness on January 30, 1838. He was buried with full military honors but his Seminole compatriots waged an incessant partisan war until 1842, when a truce was signed. At that time the exhausted tribesmen decided to allow the government to deport 3,000 members to new homes in Arkansas, but at least 300 holdouts, inspired by Osceola's example, defiantly refused. The fact that Seminole still reside in Florida to this day is his greatest legacy.

Emerson, Ralph Waldo   (1803–1882)
Philosopher

Ralph Waldo Emerson *(Library of Congress)*

Ralph Waldo Emerson was born in Boston, Massachusetts, on May 25, 1803, the son of a Unitarian minister. His father died during his infancy and he endured a hardscrabble existence but still won admission to Harvard College at the age of 14. Emerson proved himself adept intellectually, and after graduating he enrolled at the college's divinity school to study theology. He began his career as a Unitarian minister in 1826 at Boston's famous Second Church and also served on the Boston School Committee. Emerson also fell deeply in love with and married Ellen Tucker in 1829, but when she suddenly died a year and a half later he underwent a period of personal crisis. He then dejectedly left the ministry and went to Europe to reevaluate his life. There Emerson encountered noted British philosopher Thomas Carlyle, whose ideas prompted a new perspective on spirituality. He then returned to Concord intending to serve as a lecturer and essayist, remaining there the rest of

TRANSPORTATION: Work starts on the Illinois and Michigan Canal, designed to connect Chicago with the Illinois and Mississippi Rivers.

WOMEN: Ernestine L. Rose submits to the New York legislature the first petition for married women to own their own property.

January
SLAVERY: Radical abolitionist James G. Birney publishes the first issue of his journal *Philanthropist* in New Richmond, Ohio.

January 4
POLITICS: A convention gathers at Little Rock, Arkansas Territory, and draws up a constitution for approaching statehood; in accordance with the Missouri Compromise, slavery is accorded legal status.

January 9
EDUCATION: Spring Hill College arises at Spring Hill, Alabama, under Roman Catholic auspices; the first class graduates in 1837. This is also the first Catholic institute of higher learning in the Deep South.

1836

his life. His efforts coincided with the rising popularity of the public lyceums, or lecturing circuit, which gave him an immediate and well-heeled audience eager for his ideas. It was through this medium that Emerson established himself as the nation's foremost transcendentalist philosopher, a school of thought and spirituality which opposed formal religion, materialism, and slavery–hallmarks of American life in the 1840s. His two publications, *Nature* (1836) and *Essays* (1844), are considered brilliant examples of the genre, and in 1840 he also lent his writing skills to the new publication *The Dial*, edited by Margaret Fuller. In 1837 Emerson gained national notoriety for delivering an address called "The American Scholar," which called for breaking all intellectual ties with Europe in pursuit of a new, nativist philosophy.

Emerson was by nature rather detached and cerebral, but the onset of Civil War brought him fully into the abolitionist movement. He lectured widely and effectively against the evils of slavery, arguing that the system must be destroyed. In addition to excoriating Southerners, he also castigated Northerners for their complicity for tolerating the system as long as they had. For this reason he hailed the notorious raid of John Brown and welcomed the onset of hostilities to expunge servitude from American society. When the Civil War erupted in April 1861 Emerson evinced little faith in President Abraham Lincoln, who had campaigned on the basis of containing slavery–not eliminating it–but he gradually came over to the president's side. Emerson publicly rejoiced at the Emancipation Proclamation in January 1863 and openly hailed Lincoln as a national martyr following his assassination. After the war Emerson resumed writing several erudite booklets such as *Society and Solitude* (1870) and *Letters and Social Aims* (1876) while continually combating the onset of senility. He died in Concord on April 27, 1882, one of the most original transcendental thinkers, essayists, and lecturers in American history, and certainly the most influential.

January 11

SLAVERY: Petitions are presented to Congress by Senator James Buchanan for the abolition of slavery in the District of Columbia; these are immediately denounced by Senator John C. Calhoun as slanderous toward the South.

January 15

DIPLOMACY: President Andrew Jackson reiterates his demand for reprisals against France for failing to make payments on spoliation claims; behind the bluster he also delivers a conciliatory message to the French government, which stops short of the apology they demanded.

January 20

DIPLOMACY: The United States and Venezuela conclude a treaty of peace, amity, and commerce.

January 27

DIPLOMACY: The government of Great Britain offers to mediate the spoliation dispute between the United States and France.

January 30
EDUCATION: The Indiana Baptist Manual Labor Institute (today's Franklin College) is founded in Franklin, Indiana.

February 18
BUSINESS: The Bank of the United States, whose charter expired and was not renewed by Congress, receives a state charter to be reinstated as the Bank of the United States of Pennsylvania.

February 23–March 6
MILITARY: General Antonio Lopez de Santa Anna leads a force of 3,000 soldiers against a motley garrison of 187 Texans under Colonel William B. Travis at the Alamo, in San Antonio, Texas.

March 1
BUSINESS: The now defunct Bank of the United States is brought back with a state charter as the Bank of the United States of Pennsylvania.

March 2–4
POLITICS: Texan settlers convene in Washington, Texas, to draw up and pass a declaration of independence from Mexico; they also appoint Sam Houston to command their tiny army. However, when their agents George Childress and Robert Hamilton are dispatched to Washington, D.C., they are considered *persona non grata* because the American government declines to grant Texas recognition. March 2 is henceforth celebrated as Texas Independence Day.

March 6
MILITARY: In a final rush, Mexicans under General Antonio Lopez de Santa Anna capture the American outpost at the Alamo, San Antonio, Texas. Among the defenders is the noted frontiersman Davy Crockett, who was apparently taken alive then executed by firing squad. Instead of cowing Texan resistance, the martyrdom of the Alamo further galvanized resistance.

March 9
SLAVERY: In the Senate, John C. Calhoun moves that abolitionist petitions be barred from presentation; his effort is defeated.

March 11
SLAVERY: Senator James Buchanan's motion that the Senate both consider and then reject abolitionist petitions easily passes.

March 13
MILITARY: Alamo survivor Susanna Dickinson is released by General Antonio Lopez de Santa Anna and she returns to Gonzalez, Texas, with a message that further resistance "is hopeless."

March 15
POLITICS: Roger B. Taney is confirmed as Chief Justice of the Supreme Court by the Senate.

March 16
POLITICS: A new constitution is adopted by Texas delegates at Washington, Texas; thus is born the Independent Republic of Texas; slavery is formally legalized.

1836

Taney, Roger B. (1777–1864)
Supreme court justice

Roger Brooke Taney was born in Calvert County, Maryland, on March 17, 1777, into a slave-owning family associated with the minor gentry. Tutored at home, he entered Dickinson College at the age of 15 and graduated with honors in 1795. He then pursued law successfully and gained admission to the state bar in 1799. Politically, Taney was a Federalist although he broke with his party over the War of 1812 and subsequently realigned himself with the Democratic-Republicans. In 1816 he was elected to the state senate, where he served five years, and in 1827 accepted the position as state attorney general. Taney was widely regarded as an outstanding lawyer and legal scholar, and also outspoken in his support for the Democratic Party under Andrew Jackson. As such he came to the president's attention through party officials and in 1831 he joined Jackson's cabinet as the new attorney general. In this capacity he always upheld the president's political agenda as a strict loyalist. In 1832 Taney authored the legal reasoning behind the president's veto of extending the charter of the Second Bank of the United States. The following year he supported the constitutionality of Jackson's decision to withdraw federal money from the Second Bank of the United States and was ultimately appointed Secretary of the Treasury when no other individual was willing to perform the task. As a Southerner, Taney also upheld the notion of African-American slavery, supporting South Carolina's decision to legally forbid free blacks from entering that state. Despite his pre-dictable opinion about blacks, which was consistent with a man of his breeding and background, Taney still enjoyed a reputation for possessing one of the country's best legal minds.

The biggest turn in Taney's career came on December 28, 1835, when President Jackson appointed him U.S. Supreme Court justice to succeed the late John Marshall. His succession changed the overall tenor of the court from Marshall's consistent pro-federal government outlook and replaced it with one more favorably disposed toward states' rights. Proof of this was manifested in the landmark case of *Charles River Bridge v. Warren Bridge*, which Taney decided in favor of the state of Massachusetts over a company enjoying monopoly rights. His refusal to recognize the doctrine of implied contract allowed states greater latitude in matters of public interest. However, Taney's most notorious decision came with *Dred Scott v. Sanford* in 1857, which determined that slaves were property and could be moved across state lines with impunity. This had the effect of not only negating the Missouri Compromise, which restricted slavery from northern area of the nation, but also called for increased enforcement of the Fugitive Slave Law. The negative reaction to Taney's reasoning soured opinions of him, and during the Civil War he functioned far less effectively. He died in Washington, D.C., on October 12, 1864, reviled by contemporaries as a pro-slavery judge, but subsequently regarded as one of the most effective chief justices of American history.

March 17

POLITICS: American settlers meeting in Washington, Texas, adopt a new constitution; slavery is officially adopted.

1836

March 23

TECHNOLOGY: A steam-powered press designed by inventor Franklin Beale produces its first coins for the U.S. Mint.

March 27

MILITARY: Mexican forces under General Antonio Lopez de Santa Anna capture a detachment of 350 Americans under Captain James W. Fannin, then massacre them. The Mexicans continue devastating American settlements on their march to Galveston Bay.

April 20

SETTLEMENT: The Wisconsin Territory is carved out of the western Michigan Territory by Congress; frontier figure Henry Dodge is appointed as the first governor.

April 21

MILITARY: A Texan force of 900 men under General Sam Houston attacks and routs the 1,300-strong Mexican army under General Antonio Lopez de Santa Anna at the Battle of San Jacinto. A surprise attack catches the Mexicans off guard and the Texans completely overrun their camp to the fierce battle cry of "Remember the Alamo!" Santa Anna is captured and he suffers 630 killed and

Houston, Sam   (1793–1863)
Politician

Sam Houston *(Library of Congress)*

Sam Houston was born near Lexington, Virginia, on March 2, 1793, and he matured on the Tennessee frontier. Possessing little formal education, he ran away to escape farm life and spent several years among the nearby Cherokee Indians. When the Creek War erupted in 1813 he joined the U.S. Army as an ensign in the 39th Infantry, fought with distinction at General Andrew Jackson's bloody victory of Horseshoe Bend on March 28, 1814, and was severely wounded. Thereafter Houston functioned as an government agent to the Cherokee nation and assisted their removal to the Indian Territory set aside for them across the Mississippi River (Oklahoma). He finally resigned from the military in 1818 and returned to Tennessee to study law. Houston then embarked upon a successful political career, winning several terms in the U.S. House of Representatives and also winning the governorship. He also served as a major general of militia until an unexplained separation from his wife in 1829 prompted his resignation.

1836

730 captured. Texan losses are nine dead and 30 injured. This startling upset virtually assures Texas independence from Mexico.

April 27–28
SLAVERY: The nation's first antislavery convention transpires outside of Granville, Ohio, and is attended by 192 delegates.

May 10
DIPLOMACY: Having been assisted by Viscount Palmerston, the British foreign secretary, President Andrew Jackson declares that the last of four spoliation payments has been received from France.

May 11
JOURNALISM: The *Dubuque Visitor* becomes the first newspaper printed in the Wisconsin Territory.

May 14
DIPLOMACY: General Antonio Lopez de Santa Anna signs two Treaties at Velasco, Texas, both recognizing the Independent Republic of Texas and withdrawing all Mexican forces beyond the Rio Grande River; the Mexican Congress subsequently repudiates them.

Houston then withdrew from polite society altogether, and he moved back among the Cherokee, where he took a Native American wife and was inducted into the tribe. Thereafter Houston acted constantly for the Cherokee and made several trips to Washington, D.C., on their behalf. In 1832 President Jackson dispatched him to the Mexican province of Texas to negotiate with the Comanche for the safe conduct of American goods. This trip proved a major turning point in his career.

While in Texas, Houston became caught up in the emerging war for independence and in 1833 attended the San Felipe Convention that outlined statehood and promulgated a constitution. This act brought upon them the wrath of General Antonio Lopez de Santa Anna, who marched north from Mexico City to crush the insurgents in the spring of 1836. By this time Houston had been appointed commander in chief of all Texas forces, and he withdrew in the face of superior Mexican numbers until reaching San Jacinto. There,

on April 21, 1836, he launched a surprise counterattack that routed Santa Anna's army and captured him. With Texas independence now assured, Houston was elected the first president of the republic as of September 1836, serving two years. He then fulfilled two terms in the Texas legislature before becoming president again in 1841–44. After the war with Mexico, 1846–48, Texas was formally annexed to the United States and Houston served as a U.S. Senator for the next 14 years. Though Southern-born, he was an ardent nationalist and always voted as a pro-Union Democrat. In this capacity he railed against the Kansas-Nebraska Act of 1854, which made slavery legal in the new territories, and his pro-Union stance finally led to his defeat in 1859. Houston then served another term as Texas governor. He roundly condemned secession and was finally forced from office in March 1861. He died at Huntsville, Texas, on July 26, 1836, out of touch with his now Confederate constituents but still acknowledged as the "Father of Texas."

1836

May 25

DIPLOMACY: John Quincy Adams hoping to prevent war with Mexico opposes the possible annexation of Texas. The entire issue has set anti-slave Northerners against pro-slave Southerners. Furthermore, hereafter the House ponders "gag rules" to table any or all slavery-related petitions for the remainder of the session.

May 26

POLITICS: Pro-slavery Southerners in the House of Representatives enact a "gag" rule to prevent the discussion of abolitionist petitions presented before Congress; the new measure prevents the issue of slavery from being discussed on the floor. Another resolution states that Congress has no business debating slavery or interfering with it in the District of Columbia. John Quincy Adams, dubbed "Old Man Eloquence" because of his doggedness, bitterly condemns the rule.

May 31

BUSINESS: Tycoon John Jacob Astor opens up the luxurious Astor Hotel in New York City. It sets new standards for high-fashion accommodations and rapidly becomes the most fashionable meeting place in town.

June 15

POLITICS: Arkansas joins the Union as the 25th state; it also legalizes slavery. Its statehood bill had been introduced three years earlier but it took three years to gain admission until a free state, Michigan, also joined.

June 23

BUSINESS: Congress passes the Deposit Act, whereby specified banks in each state will hold public deposits. It also requires all surplus government revenue over $5 million to be distributed as a loan to the states based on their population.

June 28

GENERAL: James Madison, founding father, author of the U.S. Constitution, and fourth president of the United States, dies at his estate at Montpelier, Virginia.

July 1

DIPLOMACY: Even through Congress votes in favor of recognizing the Texas Territory, President Andrew Jackson, seeking to avoid war with Mexico, declines all moves toward annexation and maintains a strict policy of neutrality.

July 2

POLITICS: Congress votes to punish any postmaster who deliberately withholds the delivery of mail; this negates any attempts to keep abolitionist materials from being sent to the South by post. The Post Office is also directed to accept newspapers and pamphlets as deliverable items.

July 11

BUSINESS: To halt skyrocketing inflation accompanying an onslaught of paper money then in circulation, President Andrew Jackson imposes a Specie Circular which requires all sales involving federal land be conducted with gold and silver. The legislation also intends to deprive speculators of financial power but actually places all the credit in their hands, a major cause of the ensuing panic of 1837.

July 12

JOURNALISM: A pro-slavery mob in Cincinnati, Ohio, destroys a factory which manufactures the type used by James Birney's abolitionist newspaper *Philanthropist*.

September

POLITICS: The inhabitants of newly independent Texas petition the United States government for annexation.

September 1

WOMEN: A wagon train full of missionaries advances through the South Pass and arrives at Walla Walla, Washington, with Protestant missionaries Dr. Marcus Whitman and H. H. Spaulding. They also include Narcissa Whitman and Eliza Spaulding, who become the first American women to cross the Rocky Mountains and settle in Oregon. The party has been dispatched there by the American Board of Commissioners for Foreign Missions.

September 16

DIPLOMACY: The United States and Morocco conclude a treaty of peace and friendship.

September 19

LITERATURE: Boston's noted Transcendental Club begins its first unofficial and loosely structured meetings. It acts as a magnet for such like-minded writers and philosophers as Emerson, William Ellery Channing, Nathaniel Hawthorne, Henry David Thoreau, Margaret Fuller, and others.

October 22

POLITICS: Sam Houston becomes the first president of the new Republic of Texas, having defeated Stephen F. Austin; Mirabeau B. Lamar becomes vice president. A colorful frontier character, Houston is known as "The Raven."

November

LITERATURE: Noted satirist Washington Irving complains about the apparent obsession with materialism among his fellow Americans, coining the phrase "the almighty dollar."

November 30

DIPLOMACY: The United States signs a commercial treaty with the Peru-Bolivian Confederation.

December 5

POLITICS: In his annual message to Congress, President Andrew Jackson reiterates his reasons for issuing the Specie Circular.

December 7

POLITICS: Martin Van Buren defeats Whig candidate William Henry Harrison by a vote of 170 electoral votes to 73; competing Whig candidates Daniel Webster and Hugh L. White fared even poorer. However, when none of the four vice presidential candidates garner a majority, the issue is referred to the Senate for resolution.

December 10

EDUCATION: Emory College is chartered in Oxford, Georgia, by the Methodists; the first class graduates in 1841.

1836

December 12
Politics: Senate Whigs issue a resolution calling for the repeal of the Specie Circular.

December 27
General: Stephen F. Austin, a founder of both the American colony in Texas and the Independent Republic established there, dies at the age of 43 at Columbia, Texas.

1837

Arts: Painter Thomas Cole produces a landmark work of the Hudson River school of landscape artists entitled "In the Catskills," which incorporates visually romantic themes in a rural setting.

Business: John Deere starts his company at Grand Detour, Illinois, and manufactures steel-faced plows; in time they trigger an agricultural revolution as "the plow that broke the plains."

Literature: Nathaniel Hawthorne publishes his second volume, *Twice-Told Tales*, which chronicles historical nuggets drawn from New England's colorful past and presents several as moral allegories.

Medical: Dr. William W. Gerard of Philadelphia performs the first clinical tests of typhus and typhoid fever, scientifically concluding that they are entirely different ailments.

Politics: The American Peace Society condemns war and all warlike activities.

Religion: The Quaker-dominated American Moral Reform Society is founded in Philadelphia; among its tenets are to refrain from wearing mourning clothes for the dead and restricting elaborate funeral services as this imposes hardships upon the less fortunate.

Societal: Norwegian immigrant Ole Rynning publishes *True Account of America for the Information and Help of Peasant and Commoner*, which triggers a wave of Scandinavian immigration over the next two years.

January 1
Economics: The Distribution Bill, designed to relieve the federal government of all surplus monies, is enacted. Henceforth, governmental books are to be balanced, $5 million is to be set aside as working capital, and all remaining funds are to be redistributed to the states.

January 25
Journalism: The *New Orleans Picayune* is founded; its takes its name from the small coin, or "picayune," that each issue costs.

January 26
Politics: Michigan joins the union as the 26th state; slavery is outlawed to balance off the admission of Arkansas. Prior to this a long-standing border dispute with Ohio also required resolution, and the new state acquires the 470-square-mile area known as the Toledo Strip in consequence.

February
Law: The U.S. Supreme Court upholds the case of *New York v. Miln*, whereby a state court requires all ship captains to keep lists of immigrants coming into the country.

Deere, John   (1804–1886)
Inventor

John Deere was born in Rutland, Vermont, on February 7, 1804, and he received scanty education. He was nevertheless apprenticed to a blacksmith at 17 and acquired a reputation for high-quality metalwork. Deere subsequently owned his own blacksmith shop but lost it in the panic of 1837 and migrated to Grand Detour, Illinois, to start anew. Here he encountered farming conditions radically different from those in New England and envisioned a self-cleaning plow that would facilitate work in the sticky soil conditions. That year Deere designed a new plow that worked far more efficiently in the clays and sods of the mid-west. This device was made of the finest stainless steel and was distinctly wedge-shaped for better cutting power. Sales proved slow at first, but by 1848 Deere was among the leading manufacturers in Illinois. He established his factory at Moline, Illinois, to be adjacent to the Mississippi River and enjoy easier access to larger markets. Further refinements led to better plows and a wider variety of designs, and by 1857 the John Deere Company was making and selling 13,000 plows a year. Moreover, his constant flow of technical innovations to assist farmers greatly enhanced agricultural output through his region, with commensurate profits to farmers and their attendant markets. The "plow that broke the plain" was born.

In addition to improving farm technology, Deere also pioneered aggressive marketing and advertising techniques. He continually built up a surplus of inventory while dispatching an army of company representatives through the countryside and Canada to actively hawk his wares, rather than wait for orders. Deere products were thus a common sight at country fairs nationwide, and he also advertised heavily in publications like the *Prairie Farmer* to reach as wide a consumer base as possible. By 1860 he was experimenting with metal plows that featured interchangeable parts, seed drills, and steam-powered tractors. The onset of the Civil War in 1861 afforded Deere additional outlets for business through the construction of thousands of wagons, carriages, and harnesses for army use. His steady supply of steel plows to innumerable farmers also insured that the North had a considerable abundance of food supplies to fuel the war effort. By 1868 his company was incorporated as Deere & Company, although actual leadership had been handed down to his son. Deere, freed from administrative concerns, poured his energy and talents into the development of new agricultural equipment. By the time he died in Moline on April 16, 1886, his firm was the unquestioned leader with respect to sales, distribution, marketing, and service organizations nationwide. By enabling farmers to greatly enhance food production at relatively little cost, Deere made indelible contributions to the growth and maturation of the American agricultural sector. His innovative devices also allowed the first wave of migrants to the mid-west to successfully populate and thrive in their new environment.

Congress is petitioned by 56 British authors requesting that national copyright protection be extended to their works.

February 6
SLAVERY: The U.S. House of Representatives passes a resolution denying slaves the right to petition Congress.

1837

February 8

POLITICS: The Senate elects Democratic Richard M. Johnson to serve a second term as vice president.

February 11

LAW: The Supreme Court decides the case of *Briscoe v. Bank of Commonwealth of Kentucky*, ruling that all banks owned by states can issue bills of credit for public circulation.

February 12

LABOR: A mob of unemployed workers, demonstrating against the high costs of rent and food in New York City, ransacks a flour warehouse.

February 14

BUSINESS: The Supreme Court decides the case of *Charles River Bridge v. Warren Bridge*, ruling that one company cannot claim a monopoly on transportation routes. Chief Justice Roger B. Taney rules that the interests of the community outweigh those of a single corporation, a complete reversal of perspective from the Marshall Court.

March

BUSINESS: As proof of an impending economic downturn, the Herman Briggs Company of New Orleans, a major cotton firm, goes bankrupt. The price of cotton has plunged to nearly half its former value.

March 1

BUSINESS: Congress adopts a bill to rescind President Andrew Jackson's Specie Circular of July 11, 1836, mandating the purchase of public land with gold and silver; the president kills it with a pocket veto.

March 3

DIPLOMACY: On his last day in office, President Andrew Jackson finally recognizes the independence of the Republic of Texas and appoints Alcee La Branche as chargé d'affaires.

LAW: A congressional bill increases the number of Supreme Court Justices from seven to nine.

March 4

POLITICS: Democrat Martin Van Buren is inaugurated as the eighth president and Richard M. Johnson is also sworn in as his vice president. Van Buren is also the first chief executive born after the Declaration of Independence was signed. Outgoing Andrew Jackson, meanwhile, publishes his *Farewell Address*, implores fellow citizens to place loyalty to the union above all else, and attacks the practices of speculation, monopolies, and paper currency.

March 17

GENERAL: Andrew Jackson departs the political limelight of Washington, D.C., and heads for his home in Tennessee, reputedly with only $90 in his pocket. He leaves behind the legacy of an expanded voting franchise, but deep divisions between the business community, farmers, and laborers.

March 18

EDUCATION: The University of Michigan is chartered at Ann Arbor, Michigan; its first class graduates in 1841.

1837

Van Buren, Martin   (1782–1862)

President

Martin Van Buren was born in Kinderhook, New York, on December 5, 1782, the son of a tavern keeper. Though poorly educated, he clerked at a law office while young and was admitted to the bar in 1803. Van Buren was a vivacious character, and in 1813 he gained election to the state senate as a Democratic-Republican and opposed Governor DeWitt Clinton's canal policy. He spent several years in and out of political office before establishing a political clique called the "Albany Regency" and was then appointed to the U.S. Senate in 1821. In this capacity Van Buren opposed the Federalist policies of President John Quincy Adams and threw his support behind a new contender, Andrew Jackson, while also opposing internal improvements. After Jackson became president in 1828, Van Buren quit the governorship of New York to serve in his cabinet as secretary of state. Van Buren achieved several positive accomplishments by opening American trade with the British West Indies and acquiring French compensation for abuses during the Napoleonic wars. He then resigned from the cabinet at Jackson's request to serve as minister to England, although the vote was blocked in the Senate by John C. Calhoun. In 1832 he was tapped to run as Jackson's vice president and loyally supported his anti-bank, hard money policies over the next four years. Though a Northerner, Van Buren was also vocal in his support of the rights of slaveholding states. In 1836 he was nominated as Jackson's heir apparent, faced down a badly divided Whig opposition, and won the presidency by reaching out to both Northern and Southern Democrats. His ability to cobble together such an alignment earned Van Buren a reputation as "The Magician."

Van Buren had no sooner taken power than the hard currency policies of his predecessor resulted in the panic of 1837, a very deep and prolonged economic depression. The best Van Buren was willing to do to counter this malaise was creation of an independent treasury to deposit the federal funds that had been withdrawn from the now defunct Bank of the United States. His popularity was also diminished by the outbreak of a civil war in Canada and tensions along the Maine border with the province of New Brunswick. Van Buren lost much of his southern support by failing to support the annexation of Texas, which he feared would cause a war with Mexico. By 1840 the Whigs had united behind William Henry Harrison, and Van Buren was soundly defeated in the celebrated "Log Cabin Campaign" in which

(continues)

President Martin Van Buren *(Library of Congress)*

(continued)

he was successfully portrayed as a wealthy elitist. In 1844 Van Buren sought the Democratic party nomination, but his wavering over Texas allowed the expansionist James K. Polk to win it instead. Feeling betrayed by Southerners, he ran as a third-party candidate in 1848, which allowed Whig Zachary Taylor to win New York and the White House at the expense of Lewis Cass. Van Buren remained interested in national politics while in retirement, and he died at Kinderhook on July 24, 1862, both admired and reviled as "The Old Fox."

GENERAL: Grover Cleveland, the 22nd and 24th president, is born at Caldwell, New Jersey.

March–May

BUSINESS: The supply of credit shrinks nationally, ushering in the panic of 1837. This is one of the largest economic disruptions in American history.

April 20

EDUCATION: Horace Mann, a determined reformer, is appointed the first secretary of the newly created Massachusetts Board of Education, and he serves until 1848. He subsequently wields an indelible influence in terms of modernizing curricula and opening public education to all American children.

May 10

BUSINESS: New York banks stop making specie payments, triggering the panic of 1837, in which 618 banks fail nationwide. This is on account of President Andrew Jackson's Specie Circular, mandating the sale of federal land in gold and silver, which drained the valuable metals to the West. The ensuing inflation

This engraving shows a white teacher barring African-American children from entering a school. *(Library of Congress)*

1837

Mann, Horace (1796–1859)
Educator

Horace Mann was born in Franklin, Massachusetts, on May 4, 1796, the son of farmers. Disliking farm work, he was well-educated by private tutors and gained admittance to Brown University in 1816, graduating with honors three years later. Mann joined the Massachusetts bar in 1823 and won a seat in the state legislature. In Boston he encountered noted reformer Dorothea L. Dix. They cooperated on creating the state's first mental hospital, penal reforms, and other social matters, and Mann developed an abiding interest in education. At that time public education was practically nonexistent and affluent families generally sent their children through private academies. In 1837 Mann advanced legislation creating the Massachusetts School Board of Education, from which he resigned his legislative seat to serve as secretary. He always believed that common schools could be a great equalizer for all classes, especially in imparting morality and social mobility. Mann thereby successfully pushed for creation of three normal schools specifically designed to train teachers, and he was also the first educator to stress the need for personal hygienics and physical fitness. He also compiled and published the first annual education reports that statistically reflected progress and anticipated problems statewide. Most important of all, Mann extended the school year to six months and made attendance compulsory for all Massachusetts children. No mere bureaucrat, he also toured educational facilities throughout his charge and also founded the *Common School Journal*, among the earliest educational magazines, and served as its editor for a decade. During his tenure, no less than 50 new schools were constructed statewide, replete with new textbooks and school libraries. In all these capacities, Mann single-handedly revolutionized both the concept and quality of public education, with dramatic and sustainable results. His methods were then exported to other states and countries, granting him considerable renown.

In 1848 Mann resigned from the educational board to win a seat in the U.S. House of Representatives as a Whig. In this capacity he proved a vocal opponent to the extension of slavery into the territories, although the animosity he encountered induced him to abandon politics after 1852. That year he made an unsuccessful bid to become governor of Massachusetts as the Free-Soil Party candidate and quit politics altogether. Mann subsequently accepted the position as president of Antioch College, Ohio, where he proved instrumental in updating the curricula and also created a teaching program. He also further distinguished himself by insisting on equal treatment for female students. However, the college ultimately failed and was sold. Mann died of exhaustion in Ohio on August 2, 1858, only two weeks after exhorting Antioch's graduating class to win "some kind of victory for humanity." His strong belief in the virtues of public education, coupled with an unyielding determination to enhance it for the benefit of all citizens, establishes him as one of the leading American social reformers of the 19th century.

and speculation were major causes of the depression that followed and lasted until 1841.

June 10

BUSINESS: The Connecticut legislature adopts the first general incorporation law.

1837

July 4

LITERATURE: On the 62nd anniversary of the Battle of Concord in 1775, Reverend Ralph Waldo Emerson first pens the lines to a poem that includes the phrase, "The shot heard round the world."

August

MEDICAL: The outbreak of smallpox in North Dakota claims 1,500 Native Americans of the Mandan, Hidatsa, and Arikara tribes.

August 4

POLITICS: The newly independent Republic of Texas petitions Congress for immediate annexation as a slave state; the move is supported by Southerners and opposed by Northerners. In the end the issue of slavery prevents any action on the request.

August 25

POLITICS: The U.S. government formally notifies the Republic of Texas that their request for annexation has been denied. The move was defeated in the U.S. Senate by the Whigs, who oppose admission of another slave state; the vote of 35 to 16 is short of the necessary two-thirds majority.

August 31

EDUCATION: Ralph Waldo Emerson delivers his landmark "American Scholar" speech for the Harvard Phi Beta Kappa Society. In it he calls for a philosophical basis to create and perpetuate uniquely American schools of art, literature, and thought.

September 4

TECHNOLOGY: Inventor Samuel F. B. Morse files for a patent to cover his newly invented device, the telegraph, before seeking government and private investment to allow production.

September 5

POLITICS: President Martin Van Buren addresses a special session of Congress to promote specie currency and he also criticizes state-chartered banks. He feels it necessary to have federal funds kept in depositories which are independent of state banks.

September 12

MILITARY: Mexican forces invade the province of New Mexico and brutally crush a rebellion against authority there.

October 2

BUSINESS: The succession of bank failures leads to a suspension of paying surplus federal revenues to the states.

October 12

BUSINESS: Congress, eager to ameliorate the panic of 1837, authorizes the use of short-term treasury notes, not to exceed $10 million. This major economic contraction follows a decade of unprecedented economic growth and speculation.

October 14

POLITICS: A bill to secure the annexation of the Republic of Texas, having passed the Senate, is tabled by the House of Representatives.

1837

October 21
MILITARY: American forces under General Thomas S. Jesup treacherously seize Seminole Chief Osceola under a flag of truce in Florida.

October 31
BUSINESS: William Procter and James Gamble begin their famous firm with an initial investment of $7,102.

November 7
SLAVERY: Abolitionist editor Elijah Lovejoy is killed by a mob in Alton, Illinois; now a martyr, his death causes an outcry and a resurgence in the antislavery movement nationwide.

November 8
EDUCATION: Mary Lyon opens Mount Holyoke Seminary in South Hadley, Massachusetts, to afford women educational benefits similar to those received by men at college. It initially enrolled 80 students and within a year had to turn down 800 applicants for want of living space. The first class graduates in 1838.

December 4
POLITICS: In the face of renewed attempts to introduce antislavery petitions into Congress, Northern and Southern Democrats impose an even more stringent "gag rule" to squelch the endeavor. The move is roundly criticized by former president John Quincy Adams.

December 8
SLAVERY: Wendell Phillips, an outstanding orator, publicly eulogizes the murdered editor Elijah Lovejoy; this is his first abolitionist speech, "The Murder of Lovejoy," and commences a distinguished career as an agitator.

December 19
POLITICS: The U.S. House of Representative adopts a strengthened "gag rule" requiring all petitions or papers concerning slavery to be automatically tabled without discussion.

December 25
MILITARY: A force of 1,000 soldiers and militia under General Zachary Taylor attack and defeat Seminoles at Okeechobee Swamp, Florida. An intense three-hour struggle ensues in knee-deep water and the Americans suffer 26 dead and 112 wounded before the Indians finally quit. Seminole losses are lighter but they cannot afford such attrition and revert back to guerrilla warfare.

December 29
POLITICS: A group of Canadians, angered by American support for rebels under William Lyon Mackenzie, attacks and burns the American steamer *Caroline* on the American side of the Niagara River. Apparently the vessel had been chartered by Canadian rebels to run arms and ammunition to Navy Island in the Niagara River. The death of American Amos Durfee triggers an outbreak of anti-British sentiments nationwide.
TECHNOLOGY: Hiram Avery and John Avery Pitts of Winthrope, Maine, receive a patent for a combination thresher/fanning mill they had invented. It becomes the most popular brand of machine for nearly half a century.

1837

1838

MUSIC: Lowell Mason becomes the nation's first superintendent of music instruction in a public school system thanks to the Boston School Committee.

PUBLISHING: James Fenimore Cooper, recently arrived from an extended stay in Europe, publishes his nonfiction work *The American Democrat*, which criticizes the excesses of democracy from a purely aristocratic perspective. The book is unfavorably reviewed and diminishes the author's once stellar popularity with the reading public.

RELIGION: Unitarian leader William Ellery Channing, intent upon promulgating a creed of self improvement, publishes his philosophical tract *Self Culture*. He proffers it as an alternative to strict Calvinist theology.

SLAVERY: The so-called Underground Railroad is started by abolitionists to provide runaway African-American slaves with an escape route to the North. Abolitionist Robert Purvis of Philadelphia becomes its unofficial president.

TECHNOLOGY: Standardized brass clocks are created by John and Lyman Hollingsworth of South Braintree, Massachusetts; they sell for only $2.00 as opposed to $40 for a wooden version.

January 3–12
SLAVERY: John C. Calhoun introduces a resolution that legitimizes slavery in the district of Columbia. The motion passes but the Senate declines to annex any slaveholding regions and expand the potential number of slave states.

January 5
POLITICS: President Martin Van Buren issues a neutrality proclamation and warns American citizens not to become embroiled in the ongoing Canadian revolution, especially by assisting the rebels fighting Great Britain. He also orders General Winfield Scott to command troops and militia along the northern border to stop arms-smuggling to the rebels.

January 26
LAW: Tennessee posts the first prohibition law outlawing the sale of alcohol in taverns and stores.

February 14
SLAVERY: John Quincy Adams introduces 350 antislavery petitions into the House of Representatives to protest the new "gag rule," and all the petitions are promptly tabled.

February 16
WOMEN: The Kentucky legislature extends suffrage to widows whose children are of school age.

March 26
BUSINESS: The Senate passes legislation to create an independent treasury so that the government may administer its own monies.

March 31
BUSINESS: The first commercial silk mill opens at South Manchester, Connecticut.

April 19
SOCIETAL: The Massachusetts legislature, eager to bring alcohol consumption under control, mandates that hard liquor can be sold only in lots of 15 gallons or more.

April 23

TRANSPORTATION: Transatlantic steamship service commences at New York when the British steamship *Sirus* docks in the harbor after a transit of only 17 days. That same day the large, 1,340-ton American steamship *Great Western* begins plying the Atlantic on regularly scheduled voyages between New York and Bristol, England; it reaches New York in only 15 days. British engineers are concurrently developing new techniques of converting wood-powered steam engines to far hotter coal-generated devices, but the eclipse of the speedy, beautiful clipper ship, in which the Americans enjoy a decided edge, is still not at hand.

April 25

TECHNOLOGY: The peril of new technology is underscored when the steamer *Moselle* explodes on the Ohio River near Cincinnati, killing 100.

May 17

SLAVERY: A pro-slavery mob burns Philadelphia's Pennsylvania Hall to the ground after it has been extensively used by the Female Anti-Slavery Society for abolitionist meetings. Quaker leader Lucretia Mott is undeterred by the violence and presses ahead with her agenda.

May 18

EXPLORING: Lieutenant Charles Wilkes, a capable, hot-tempered martinet, receives command of the U.S. Exploring Expedition in Washington, D.C. This is the first government-funded attempt to acquire scientific knowledge around the globe.

May 21

BUSINESS: President Andrew Jackson's Specie Circular of July 11, 1836, now largely blamed for the panic of 1837, is revoked by Congress.

May 29

POLITICS: Americans outraged by the Canadian burning of the steamship *Caroline* in American waters attack and burn the Canadian vessel *Sir Robert Peel* in the St. Lawrence River. Anti-British sentiment also flares in the form of secret "Hunter's Lodges" to assist rebels trying to overthrow the Canadian government.

June 12

SETTLEMENT: The Iowa Territory is separated from the Wisconsin Territory by Congress; it includes much of the Dakotas and Minnesota.

June 14

TECHNOLOGY: At least 140 people are killed when the steamer *Pulaski* explodes off the North Carolina coast.

June 25

BUSINESS: The House of Representatives defeats an attempt to create an independent treasury due to a split between Democrats; the "Loco-Focos" agree with President Martin Van Buren about the move but more conservative elements side with the Whigs in opposing it.

July 4

SETTLEMENT: Congress establishes the Territory of Iowa with Robert Lucas as the first governor.

1838

July 7
TRANSPORTATION: The rapidly expanding railroad network is designated by Congress as a postal route.

August 13
BUSINESS: Banks in New York are finally able to resume payment in gold and silver specie.

August 18
EXPLORATION: U.S. Navy Lieutenant Charles Wilkes leads a six-ship exploring expedition from Hampden Roads, Virginia, into the Pacific and Antarctic oceans. This is a large and impressive four-year endeavor and the first scientific expedition funded entirely by the federal government. The numerous scientists and specialists on board will make reports on hydrography, geology, botany, geography and related fields.

September 3
SLAVERY: Using the identity papers of an African-American sailor, Frederick Douglass slips out of bondage in Baltimore, Maryland, and embarks on his career as an outspoken abolitionist.

Douglass, Frederick   (ca. 1817–1895)
African-American abolitionist

Frederick Augustus Bailey was born a slave in Tuckahoe, Maryland, around 1817; he never knew his father and scarcely saw his mother. At the age of eight he was sent to Baltimore to work as a domestic, where he learned to read and write from his mistress until her husband stopped her. As a young man Bailey was sent to a plantation in the countryside and made several escape attempts. In 1838 he borrowed a free African-American sailor's papers and sailed to New York and freedom. Bailey eventually settled in New Bedford, Massachusetts, where he married and adopted the surname Douglass, but found his new abode only slightly less hostile. He had no recourse but to work as a low-paid laborer until 1841, when he was asked to speak at an abolitionist meeting at Nantucket. Douglass, with power and eloquence, transfixed the crowd, many of whom began to doubt that he was ever a slave. He countered by writing and publishing *The*

Frederick Douglass (*National Archives*)

1838

October
INDIAN: U.S. soldiers under General John E. Wool rounds up and begins relocating the few remaining Cherokees from their tribal homes in Georgia; this exodus becomes known in Indian lore as the "Trail of Tears."

October 12
POLITICS: The Republic of Texas, having failed to be annexed by the United States, elects Mirabeau B. Lamar president to succeed Sam Houston. Thereafter Texas pursues an independent foreign policy and establishes diplomatic relations with various European countries.

October 30
EDUCATION: Oberlin College, Oberlin, Ohio, becomes the first institution of higher learning to admit women as full-fledged students.
RELIGION: Governor Lilburn Boggs decrees that Mormons living in Missouri are to be treated as enemies and mobs attack them, killing 17 members. This violence triggers a mass migration to Illinois under Brigham Young; prophet Joseph Smith is imprisoned at the time.

Narrative of the Life of Frederick Douglass in 1845, at the instigation of students from Harvard College. The book proved an immediate best seller and made Douglass a celebrity in abolitionist circles, but, as a former slave, he also feared being recaptured and sailed to England for two years. In 1847 he resettled at Rochester, New York, where he published and edited the newspaper *North Star* for many years. A year later he also declared his support for women's rights and was a featured speaker at the Seneca Falls convention. Douglass by this point had befriended many white abolitionists, but he gradually broke with William Lloyd Garrison over the latter's refusal to become engaged in active politics. In 1858 Douglass was also approached by radical abolitionist John Brown for help in his planned attack on Harper's Ferry, but Douglass diplomatically declined, citing the plan's futility.

The onset of the Civil War in 1861 gave Douglass a new platform upon which he could advocate emancipation and equal rights. He met twice with President Abraham Lincoln and pressed hard for him to allow the widespread use of African-American volunteers in the army as combat soldiers. Lincoln, fearing a white backlash, did so only reluctantly but after 1863 black regiments were commonly raised and deployed. Ultimately, half a million African Americans served in the army and navy, acquitting themselves with distinction. After the war, Douglass was the only African-American leader with any national stature, and he remained a ceaseless spokesman for civil rights and an end to violence against former slaves during the Reconstruction period. A staunch Republican, he supported the administration of Ulysses S. Grant and became consul-general to the Republic of Haiti. In 1870 he began publishing *The New National Era*, and two years later President Rutherford B. Hayes appointed him U.S. Marshal for the District of Columbia. Douglass, a man of great intelligence, integrity, and purpose, died in Washington, D.C., on February 20, 1895. He was the leading African-American spokesman of his day.

November
POLITICS: In midterm congressional elections, the Whigs wrest control of Congress away from the Democrats, leaving President Martin Van Buren unsupported in the national legislature.

November 7
POLITICS: Noted Whig William H. Seward is elected governor of New York.

November 21
POLITICS: President Martin Van Buren issues a second proclamation warning American citizens not to assist rebels in Canada under the pain of severe penalties.

November 26
DIPLOMACY: The United States and the Kingdom of Sardinia conclude a treaty of commerce.

December
INDIAN: Escorted by U.S. troops under generals Winfield Scott and John E. Wool, the last of 14,000 Cherokee are forcibly relocated from their tribal homelands in Georgia and marched overland to Oklahoma. Around 4,000 Indians die en route, and the ensuing hardship and struggle come to be known as the "Trail of Tears."

December 3
SLAVERY: Whig Joshua Giddings becomes the first avowed abolitionist member of the U.S. House of Representatives.

December 11
POLITICS: The new "Atherton Gag" rule, promulgated by Representative Charles G. Atherton of New Hampshire, is adopted by the House of Representatives to preclude any discussion of slavery. The measure is adopted by every new session until 1844.

December 26
EDUCATION: Wake Forest College is chartered at Wake Forest, North Carolina, by the Baptists; its first class graduates in 1839.

December 28
EDUCATION: The Greensborough Female College is chartered by Methodists at Greensborough, North Carolina.

1839

BUSINESS: In New York, *Hunts' Merchant Magazine* becomes the nation's first business periodical.

EDUCATION: Horace Mann, Secretary of the Massachusetts Board of Education, institutes the first public normal schools for all children; attendance is mandatory.

Jared Sparks is installed at Harvard as the nation's first professor of American history.

LITERATURE: Henry Wadsworth Longfellow publishes *Voices of the Night*, his first volume of poems; however, his work languishes without public or critical recognition until 1847.

RELIGION: Mormon leader Brigham Young moves his adherents to Nauvoo, Illinois, where they establish a town. Previously, they had been violently ejected from the settlements in Missouri while leader Joseph Smith was imprisoned.

Longfellow, Henry Wadsworth   (1807–1882)
Poet

Henry Wadsworth Longfellow was born in Portland, Maine, on February 27, 1807, into an established New England family. He was well-educated at the Portland Academy before attending Bowdoin College in 1821, where Nathaniel Hawthorne was his classmate. Longfellow proved himself adept as a student and enjoyed a facility for foreign languages, so upon graduating in 1825 the college trustees took the unusual step of proffering their young charge a teaching position. Longfellow, who determined early on to work as a writer, readily accepted, although he was required to travel to Europe for additional study. He came home in 1829, was happily married to Mary Storer Potter, and in 1833 published his first picturesque travel sketches, *Outre-Mer: A Pilgrimage Beyond the Sea.* The book was well-received and the following year Longfellow accepted a teaching position at Harvard. He also undertook another extensive literary tour of Europe, although his life was tempered by tragedy when his wife suddenly died. Longfellow consoled himself by becoming engrossed with moody and mystical German romanticism, which left its mark on his subsequent writings. In 1839 he wrote both his first romantic novel, *Hyperion,* and his first volume of poetry, *Voices of the Night.* The latter established him as an American original and sold 43,000 copies. He then furthered his national reputation with the publication of *Evangeline* (1847), a sentimental narrative poem concerning the French exodus from Acadia.

By 1854 Longfellow was financially secure enough to resign from Harvard and pursue writing full time. A year later he produced *The Song of Hiawatha*, an epic narrative poem about an Indian chief that was partly inspired by a Finnish epic. In 1858 he scored another popular work with *The Courtship of Miles Standish*, another historically oriented epic poem. However, the death of his second wife in a fire in 1861 profoundly affected Longfellow and he turned to translating European works to console himself. His treatment of *Dante's Divine Comedy* appeared in three volumes, 1865–67, and is regarded as a definitive translation. By this time Longfellow basked in an international reputation as America's most adept poet, and in 1868 he received honorary degrees from both Cambridge and Oxford. However, he shunned publicity and preferred to work in solitude in his home at Cambridge, Massachusetts. Longfellow remained extremely active in his final years, producing such varied and well-regarded works as *The Christus: A Mystery* (1872), which examined Christianity at various points in its evolution as a creed. Longfellow died in Cambridge on March 24, 1882, long heralded an American sage. His poetry closely mirrored his own life, exhibiting sweetness, gentleness, and romanticism, yet unmistakably tinged with melancholy. In homage to his renown, a memorial bust was placed in his honor at the Poet's Corner of Westminister Abbey; Longfellow was the first American writer so honored.

SETTLEMENT: Sacramento, California, is founded as a Swiss settlement by John Sutter.

SLAVERY: Abolitionist Theodore Dwight Weld publishes a book entitled *American Slavery as It Is*, a scathing expose gathered from eyewitness accounts and other sources. One avid reader, Harriet Beecher Stowe, is so moved by its sordid tale of woe that she is inspired to write *Uncle Tom's Cabin*.

1839

TECHNOLOGY: Inventor Charles Goodyear discovers the vulcanizing process for creating rubber when he accidentally drops a mixture of rubber and sulfur on a hot surface.

WOMEN: Mississippi is the first state to allow women to control their own property without legal guardians.

January

POLITICS: Governor John Fairfield of Maine empowers land agent Rufus McIntire to expel Canadian loggers from land claimed by his state.

January 1–2

NAVAL: A landing force from the warships USS *Columbia* and *John Adams* attacks pirate forts on Quallah Battoo, Sumatra, in retaliation for new attacks on American commerce. The survivors pay reparations and promise to halt all harassment.

January 7

BUSINESS: The Washington Silver Mine, the nation's first, is chartered in Lexington, North Carolina.

January 12

TECHNOLOGY: Anthracite coal is used to smelt iron for the first time in Mauch Chunk, Pennsylvania.

January 19

DIPLOMACY: The United States and the Netherlands conclude a treaty of commerce and navigation.

February 7

SLAVERY: Henry Clay, intent upon running for the presidency as a Whig, condemns abolitionism and declares its adherents have no constitutional right to interfere with slavery where it is already extant. In doing so he is appealing to conservatives in both the North and South and declares, "I had rather be right than be president."

February 11

EDUCATION: The University of the State of Missouri (today's University of Missouri) is chartered at Columbia, Missouri; the first class graduates in 1843.

February 12

DIPLOMACY: Canadians logging in the disputed Aroostook region of Maine refuse to leave the disputed area and arrest land agent Rufus McIntire when he tries to expel them. Maine and New Brunswick then begin mobilizing for war, but the situation is diffused by General Winfield Scott, who is ordered to arrange a truce until a boundary commission can work out a defined border.

February 20

SOCIETAL: Dueling in the District of Columbia is outlawed by Congress.

March 3

AGRICULTURE: Congress grants $1,000 to the Patent Office to promote seed distribution, statistical research, and experimentation in the name of advancing national agriculture.

MILITARY: In light of heightened tensions along the Maine–New Brunswick border, Congress passes an act authorizing the recruitment of 50,000 volunteers.

1839

March 23–25
DIPLOMACY: War of 1812 veterans General Winfield Scott and Lieutenant Governor John Harvey of New Brunswick, who last met at the Battle of Lundy's Lane in 1814, agree not to introduce military force into the disputed Aroostook region of Maine. This agreement lays the basis for a peaceful resolution of the conflict.

April 11
DIPLOMACY: The United States and Mexico sign a treaty calling for the arbitration of claims made by Americans.

May 10
RELIGION: The Mormons under Joseph Smith formally establish their new headquarters in Illinois following their violent expulsion from Missouri.

June
NAVAL: The Texas navy obtains the steamship *Zavala,* among the first warships of its kind.

August 26
SLAVERY: African slaves commandeer the Spanish slave ship *Amistad* and sail it into Connecticut. There it is impounded despite calls by the Spanish government for its return. The Americans, however, take the issue to the courts and in March 1841 the Africans are released.

September 25
DIPLOMACY: France signs a treaty with the Republic of Texas, the first European nation to confer recognition.

November 13
POLITICS: A gathering of moderate abolitionists constituting the Liberty Party nominates James G. Birney of Kentucky as the abolitionist candidate for the presidency, with Pennsylvanian Thomas Earle for vice president.

December
TECHNOLOGY: In New York, Samuel F. B. Morse imports the first camera, or Daguerre, into the United States from France and also begins taking the first photographs, known as daguerreotypes. The process involves exposing copper plates, coated with silver, to iodine fumes while behind a lens.

December 4
POLITICS: A convention of Whigs at Harrisburg, Pennsylvania, nominates William Henry Harrison over Henry Clay for the presidency. The outspoken Clay has numerous enemies from his many years in office, and he withdraws after the first ballot to promote party unity. States rights advocate John Tyler also becomes a vice presidential candidate. The problem with the Whigs at this juncture is that they lack a viable platform to run on and are simply organized around their common opposition to the Democrats.

1840

LABOR: The *Beacon,* an antireligious, pro-labor publication, begins publishing in New York City.

LITERATURE: In Boston, the intellectual circle known as the Transcendentalists begins publishing their own journal, *The Dial,* with Margaret Fuller at the helm, one of the earliest female editors. It features works by such noted writers as Ralph Waldo Emerson, Henry David Thoreau, and Theodore Parker, among others.

Noted writer Richard Henry Dana publishes his *Two Years Before the Mast*, which draws upon the author's experiences in the U.S. Navy. He is especially appalled by the practice of flogging and subsequently crusades to have it abolished.

James Fenimore Cooper returns to public favor with the publication of his French and Indian War novel, *The Pathfinder*. This is the latest installment of his ongoing *Leatherstocking Series*.

Edgar Allan Poe publishes his *Tales of the Grotesque and Arabesque*, which includes his classic story "The Fall of the House of Usher"; it is critically well-received but the author fails to acquire a wide readership.

MEDICAL: Dr. Willard Parker initiates the first clinic attached to a medical college at the Philadelphia College of Physicians and Surgeons.

Dr. Chapin Aaron Harris founds the Baltimore College of Dental Surgery in Baltimore, Maryland; it is subsequently incorporated into the University of Maryland.

Intent upon making dentistry a recognized profession, Dr. Horace A. Hayden founds the American Society of Dental Surgeons in New York City.

MILITARY: Captain Gabriel J. Rains, campaigning against the Seminole Indians in Florida, hits upon the idea of buried explosive charges triggered by a passerby; this is the origin of antipersonnel weapons or land mines.

POPULATION: The latest census reveals a population of slightly more than 17 million inhabitants, reflecting a 30 percent growth over the previous decade.

PUBLISHING: In his pamphlet *An Essay on a Congress of Nations*, William Lash calls on Congress to establish guidelines and principles for international law and an international court.

RELIGION: Joseph Smith ventures to England and addresses 4,000 potential Mormon converts who gradually immigrate to his colony at Nauvoo, Illinois.

SCIENCE: William Cranch Boyd constructs an astronomical observatory at Harvard College to replace the device he previously used at his home in Dorchester, Massachusetts.

John William Draper of New York University takes the first crude photograph of the moon, thereby initiating the nation's pioneering role in astronomical photography.

January 8
SLAVERY: The House of Representatives reaffirms its gag rule against introducing antislavery petitions; however, the margin in favor is dwindling with a final vote of only 114 to 108

January 12
BUSINESS: The Senate again passes legislation to found an independent treasury; passage in the House is now required.

January 13
GENERAL: The steamship *Lexington* burns and sinks near Eaton's Neck, New York, killing 140 passengers.

January 19
EXPLORING: The exploring expedition under Lieutenant Charles Wilkes catches a glimpse of the southern continent Antarctica, which is promptly dubbed "Wilkes Land."
SETTLEMENT: Austin is chosen as the new capital of the Republic of Texas.

1840

March 2
EDUCATION: Bethany College is chartered in Bethany, Virginia (West Virginia), by the Disciples of Christ; the first class graduates in 1844.

March 4
EDUCATION: Richmond College (today's University of Richmond) is chartered in Richmond, Virginia, by various Baptist groups; its first class graduates in 1849.

March 31
LABOR: A 10-hour workday is established for federal employees engaged in public works by President Martin Van Buren.

April 1
POLITICS: The abolitionist Liberty Party holds its first national convention in Albany, New York, intending to draw upon the 150,000 members of abolitionist societies across America in the upcoming election. James G. Birney of Kentucky again receives the nod to run for president with Thomas Earle running as vice president.

May 5–6
POLITICS: The Democratic Party convenes at Baltimore, Maryland, for their national convention; they renominate Martin Van Buren for the presidency and also make the first ever national stance on slavery by declaring their opposition to any congressional attempts to interfere with the "peculiar institution." Their platform also espouses a strict constructionist doctrine of the Constitution and opposes a national bank and federal money for internal improvements. Significantly, this is the last Democratic convention before the Civil War to embrace principles found in the Declaration of Independence.

May 6
SETTLEMENT: The town of St. Paul is founded in present-day Minneapolis by a group of Swiss immigrants.

June 12
WOMEN: A meeting of the World Anti-Slavery Convention in London, England, convenes but excludes women delegates from its proceedings. Among the Americans snubbed are Elizabeth Cady Stanton and Lucretia Mott, who are denied seating despite the pleas of fiery abolitionist Wendell Phillips. Rejection here induces Stanton and Mott to hold a women's conference in New York at a subsequent date.

June 30
BUSINESS: The House of Representatives approves the Independent Treasury Act over continuing opposition from the Whigs.

July 4
BUSINESS: President Martin Van Buren signs the Independent Treasury Act into law, whereby the government acquires exclusive rights to manage its own monies and also creates specific depositories to hold all funds. Such institutions, or subtreasuries, are established at Boston, New York, Philadelphia, Washington, Charleston, St. Louis, and New Orleans. This is the first instance in many years whereby Northern and Southern Democrats momentarily unite to overcome bitter Whig opposition.

August 26
DIPLOMACY: The United States and Portugal conclude a treaty of commerce and navigation.

1840

November
DIPLOMACY: Canadian deputy sheriff Alexander McLeod, charged with the murder of American Amos Durfee when the schooner *Caroline* was burned, is arrested and charged with murder in New York.

November 13
DIPLOMACY: Great Britain recognizes the Republic of Texas and also concludes a commercial treaty.

December 2
POLITICS: William Henry Harrison defeats Martin Van Buren for the presidency with 234 electoral votes to 60 while John Tyler becomes vice president. The Whigs also take control of Congress; this is the first complete loss of political power by a party since 1800. This is also the first modern campaign in the sense that the Whigs pioneer the use of slogans, placards, songs, floats, and transportable log cabins to emphasize Harrison's unique frontier nature over Van Buren's aristocratic nature. "Tippecanoe and Tyler Too" had become the Whig campaign mantra.

December 13
DIPLOMACY: Henry Stephen Fox, British minister to the United States, demands that the Americans release Canadian deputy sheriff Alexander McLeod from jail in New York.

December 26
DIPLOMACY: Secretary of State John Forsyth refuses an English demand to release Canadian deputy sheriff Alexander McLeod, charged with murder, from jail in New York. British minister Henry Stephen Fox is informed that the state of New York enjoys exclusive jurisdiction over the case.

1841

INDIAN: Frontier artist George Catlin publishes his two-volume *Letters and Notes on the Manners, Customs, and Condition of the North American Indian*, which includes 300 of his engravings. He is disturbed that many Indian cultures are on the verge of disappearing.

LITERATURE: Ralph Waldo Emerson writes and publishes his first series of transcendentalist *Essays,* confirming him as a noted thinker and writer.

James Fenimore Cooper publishes *The Deerslayer*, the last installment of his *Leatherstocking Tales*. This concludes a classic series of frontier novels featuring Natty Bumpo, also known as Hawkeye, a garrulous frontier figure who is far more in tune with nature than civilization.

Henry Wadsworth Longfellow publishes *Ballads and Other Poems,* and his spirited narrative technique establishes him as a noted writer.

MILITARY: The moniker "Old Fuss and Feathers" is first applied to General Winfield Scott, long renowned for his attention toward military dress and decorum.

SETTLEMENT: A party of 48 wagons traverses the Oregon Trail, the Humbolt River, and the Sierra Nevada Mountains, to arrive safely at Sacramento, California.

SOCIETAL: A group of Transcendentalists under George Ripley establish a utopian farming community, the Brook Farm Institute of Agriculture and Education, nine miles from Boston. Members pursue a balanced life of simple living combined with high intellectual pursuits.

Catlin, George   (1796–1872)
Painter

George Catlin was born in Wilkes-Barre, Pennsylvania, on July 26, 1796, the son of a lawyer. He studied law in Connecticut and began a successful practice at home in 1819, but Catlin had always exhibited a fascination with Native Americans. By this time he had also displayed a genuine talent for painting portraits. In 1823 he stopped his legal work and decided to parley his artistic infatuation into a viable career by doing portraiture in Philadelphia and observing Native American delegations as they occasionally appeared in the city. To raise money he ventured to Albany, New York, in 1828 to paint Governor DeWitt Clinton, a wealthy sponsor, and also met Clara Bartlett Gregory, whom he eventually married. That same year he ventured to Buffalo to paint the noted Seneca orator Red Jacket and also commenced formal ethnological studies of Native Americans. In time Catlin expressed a fervent desire not only to capture Native Americans on canvas but also to help preserve their rapidly vanishing way of life. By 1830 he had amassed sufficient money to relocate to St. Louis and study Indians in detail. In this capacity he met and befriended General William Clark, governor of the new Indian Territory, who invited him along on various trips up the Mississippi and Missouri Rivers. Catlin was thus able to encounter more remote tribes such as the Blackfeet, Crow, Cree, Mandan, and Sioux, all of which he carefully documented. By 1836 Catlin had executed more than 500 superbly rendered paintings and portraits of various tribes and individuals,

foremost among them the aged Shawnee Prophet Tenskwatawa, brother of Tecumseh. The following year he established "Catlin's Indian Gallery" in New York City, whose vivacious art whetted the public's appetite for knowledge about Indians and was a great commercial success.

For the rest of the decade Catlin relocated to Europe with his wide-ranging collection and enjoyed considerable success displaying it there. As a body of work, the art is significant for preserving Indian village life, games, war dances, ceremonies, and other activities long forgotten. Catlin then returned home on a national tour but enjoyed considerably less success in Philadelphia, Boston, or an encore performance in New York. To bolster his income he next took to publishing, and his *Letters and Notes on the Manners, Customs, and Condition of the North American Indians* (1841) which, while well received, did not produce the windfall anticipated. He then tried to sell his body of work to Congress without success and later used the whole as collateral, losing them. Catlin subsequently lived in Europe from 1852 to 1857 and was commissioned by noted explorer Baron Wilhelm von Humbolt to undertake a painting expedition to South America. He returned to New York in 1870 and spent several years publishing works about his experiences among Native Americans and appealing for better treatment of them. Catlin died in Jersey City, New Jersey, on December 23, 1872, a pioneering artist and cultural anthropologist.

In Massachusetts, reformer Dorothea L. Dix begins her personal crusade to improve living conditions and treatment of the mentally ill.
SPORTS: The nation's first unofficial boxing championship unfolds with Tom Hyer defeating challenger John McCluster.

1841

Dix, Dorothea   (1802–1887)
Reformer

Dorothea Lynde Dix was born in Hampden, Maine, on April 4, 1802, the daughter of a Methodist preacher. Despite an unhappy childhood and a life of grinding poverty, she matured into a dutiful young woman with an iron will and a strict sense of morality. Dix served as headmistress of a Boston "Dame School" for young girls, but so energetically that in 1836 she was forced to visit England to recoup her health. There she encountered numerous social reformers, which inspired her to carry on similar work in the United States. To this end she began teaching at the House of Correction in East Cambridge, Massachusetts, in 1841 and three years later composed a report for the state legislature about the abuses heaped upon the mentally ill. Dix then capitalized on this success by launching a nationwide crusade to afford better treatment of insane men and women. Due to her efforts, the number of mental institution increased from 32 in 1843 to 123 by 1880. In 1845 she also collaborated with educator Horace Mann on a book entitled *Remarks on Prisons and Prison Discipline in the United States*, whose humane and farsighted suggestions were eventually adopted by penologists. However, in 1854 President Franklin Pierce vetoed legislation mandating federal involvement in mental health matters, and Dix suffered a near collapse. She then went abroad for her health while supervising reform efforts in Scotland, the Channel Islands, France, Russia, and Turkey. Dix came home in 1856 and continued her usual investigating, publishing, and lobbying on behalf of the mentally ill.

Dix was arguably one of the nation's most famous women by the advent of Civil War in April 1861, and she tendered her services to Secretary of War Edwin Stanton. Accordingly she gained appointment as chief of nurses for the Union Army and drew upon her organizational and institutional experience to recruit thousands of nurses for the war effort. She also imparted high ethical standards on prospective candidates and required them to be at least 30 years old and plain looking to weed out adventurers. However, Dix's own religious prejudices were so marked that she forbade Catholic nuns or any other religious order which she found offensive from joining. Her strident morality and despotic behavior also garnered her a reputation as "Dragon Dix," but largely through her efforts the Nurse Corps was one of the resounding success stories of the Civil War and closely paralleled the efforts of Englishwoman Florence Nightingale during the Crimean War. As an indication of her personal commitment to her charge, Dix labored the entire war without pay. Afterward, she took up the cause of caring for orphans and the blind at a national level. Dix left public life in 1881 and retired to one of the hospitals she had founded in Trenton, New Jersey, some 35 years earlier. She died there on July 17, 1887, somewhat imperious and opinionated but also a sincere champion for the ill and disadvantaged.

January 3
LITERATURE: Aspiring writer Herman Melville joins the whaler *Acushnet* at Fairhaven, England, bound for the South Seas. His experiences greatly influence his writings and ultimately inspire *Moby-Dick*, his most celebrated novel.

1841

March 4
POLITICS: William Henry Harrison is sworn in as the ninth president of the United States and the first Whig chief executive. Daniel Webster is also appointed the new Secretary of State after Henry Clay declines the post.

March 9
SLAVERY: The U.S. Supreme Court rules in favor of the 53 Africans seized when the Spanish slaver *Amistad* sailed into American waters, and they are released and allowed to return to Africa.

March 17
DIPLOMACY: The United States and Peru sign a claims convention.

April
PUBLISHING: *Graham's Magazine* commences publication in Philadelphia with Edgar Allan Poe as associate editor, who also publishes his "Murders in the Rue Morgue," the first detective story.

April 4
POLITICS: William Henry Harrison dies in office of pneumonia, becoming the first chief executive to be succeeded by his vice president.

April 9
POLITICS: President John Tyler gives his inaugural address, stressing fiscal sobriety. However, many observers question if he is simply an acting president as the Constitution makes no clear provisions for succession in office. Tyler ultimately prevails on a congressional vote to install him as president. A Democrat and a devout believer in states' rights, he is nonetheless at odds with the Whig majority over many touchstone issues.

April 10
JOURNALISM: Horace Greeley begins publishing the *New York Tribune*, a Whig-oriented penny paper. He gradually emerges as one of the nation's most influential writers and a major force behind the future Republican Party.

May
BUSINESS: Sam Houston opens the port of Houston, Texas, to stimulate trade and commerce.
SETTLEMENT: The first covered-wagon train departs Sapling Grove, Kansas, and makes for California via the Stanislaus River.

May 19
RELIGION: Theodore Parker, a noted Unitarian preacher, delivers his landmark address "On the Transient and Permanent in Christianity" in South Boston. He takes the extraordinary stance that Jesus Christ was not supernatural in nature and that the Scriptures deserve no special reverence.

June 19
MILITARY: A group of Texas irregulars and military adventurers embarks on a campaign to capture Santa Fe, New Mexico, from the Mexican Republic.

June 20
TECHNOLOGY: Samuel F. B. Morse receives a patent for his new telegraph.

Harrison, William Henry (1773–1841)
President

William Henry Harrison was born in Charles City, Virginia, on February 9, 1773, son of a leading colonial politician. He studied at Hampden-Sydney College and the University of Pennsylvania before being commissioned lieutenant in the U.S. Army in 1792. Harrison fought well under General Anthony Wayne and retired from the military in 1795 as a captain. He then functioned as secretary of the Northwest Territory before being elected to Congress in 1799. The following year President John Adams appointed Harrison territorial governor of the Indiana Territory, which he remained for the next 12 years. His tenure was marked by aggressive acquisition of Native American land, resentment of which gave rise to Tecumseh's anti-American coalition. In 1811 he won a narrow victory over the Shawnee Prophet Tenskwatawa at Tippecanoe, and in the War of 1812 he gained a major general's commission in the U.S. Army. In this capacity he withstood British and Indian forces during the siege of

William Henry Harrison *(Library of Congress)*

July 7
POLITICS: Henry Clay initiates his own fiscal proposals in the Senate to repeal the Independent Treasury Act, increase tariffs, establish a new national bank, raise higher tariff revenues, and return money accruing from federal land sales to the states. These programs are hallmarks of the Whig ideology. However, President John Tyler considers Clay's maneuver an attempt to usurp his role as nominal party leader.

July 28
POLITICS: The Senate passes Henry Clay's Fiscal Bank Bill to establish a new Bank of the United States (called the Fiscal Bank) in the District of Columbia.

August 6
BUSINESS: Whig majorities in both houses of Congress pass a bill resurrecting a new institution, the Fiscal Bank of the United States.

August 9
GENERAL: The steamship *Erie* catches fire and sinks in Lake Erie, killing 175 passengers.

1841

Fort Meigs, Ohio, in May 1813, forcing them back into Canada. Harrison subsequently took to the offensive, chased the fleeing British into western Ontario, and on October 5, 1813, he fought and won the Battle of the Thames, Ontario, where Tecumseh was killed and his confederation shattered. He then served briefly in New York before a disagreement with Secretary of War John Armstrong prompted his resignation. Harrison's status as a national war hero was nonetheless assured and in 1818 he received a congressional gold medal. In 1815 he also helped negotiate the Spring Wells Treaty with various Indian tribes, securing additional lands.

In 1816 Harrison was elected again to the House of Representatives from Ohio, and in 1825 the state legislature appointed him to the U.S. Senate. In 1828 President John Quincy Adams appointed him the first American minister to Colombia, but he clashed with President Simón Bolívar and was recalled by President Andrew Jackson the following year. Harrison returned to private life in 1829 but he resumed active campaigning following the rise of the Whig Party in 1834 and two years later he was one of several party presidential nominees, easily the most popular because of his military reputation. He subsequently lost the election to Democrat Martin Van Buren in 1836 but began planning to resume the struggle in 1840. In this he was greatly assisted by the onset of the Panic (depression) of 1837 that greatly eroded popular support for the Democrats. That year the Whigs adopted the so-called Log Cabin strategy that posited Harrison as a frontier war hero and featured campaign songs, catchy slogans, and all the trappings of the very Jacksonian democracy that Van Buren failed to take advantage of. Once coupled with John Tyler as vice president, the two men successfully campaigned under the national slogan of "Tippecanoe and Tyler, too," defeating the incumbent. In March 1841 Harrison was sworn in as the first Whig president. However, he died a month later of illness on April 4, 1841, the first chief executive to perish in office.

August 13
BUSINESS: The Independent Treasury Act is repealed by Congress at the behest of Henry Clay, and the Secretary of the Treasury resumes his responsibilities for public funds and the use of state banks for depositing funds. This measure is a necessary precondition for establishing a new national bank.

August 16
POLITICS: President John Tyler, who regards Henry Clay's Fiscal Bank Bill as unconstitutional, vetoes it. The Senate then fails to muster sufficient votes for an override. The Whigs are generally enraged by Tyler's conduct, believing that he had previously agreed to sign such legislation.

August 19
POLITICS: Congress implements a uniform system of bankruptcy so that individuals can declare bankruptcy; it endures three years and allows 33,730 individuals to claim bankruptcy.

August 29
SOCIETAL: Cincinnati, Ohio is the scene of a violent anti-black street rioting which lasts for five days.

1841

Tyler, John   (1790–1862)
President

John Tyler was born in Charles City County, Virginia, on March 29, 1790, the son of wealthy planters. He graduated from William and Mary College in 1807, studied law, and was admitted to the bar two years later. Tyler took an interest in politics and from 1811 to 1815 he served in the state legislature before being elected to the U.S. House of Representatives in 1816 as a Democratic-Republican. In 1827 he served two terms as governor before standing for a seat in the U.S. Senate as a Democrat. Politically, Tyler was an outspoken advocate of states' rights, and he also opposed both internal improvements and a second national bank as unconstitutional. In 1828 he supported the election of Andrew Jackson to the presidency but then railed against his threatened use of force during the nullification crisis of 1831. He was also highly critical of the way Jackson arbitrarily withdrew government deposits from the Bank of the United States. Tyler thus found himself

President John Tyler *(Library of Congress)*

September 3
POLITICS: Both houses of Congress adopt a second bank bill which addresses President John Tyler's constitutional concerns.

September 4
SETTLEMENT: Congress passes the Distribution-Preemption Act which allows settlers to purchase for a minimum price land they have illegally settled on. This ends a long-running dispute as to whether public land policy should focus on revenues or settlement. However, the distribution of profits to the states is rescinded should tariff rates rise beyond 20 percent.

September 9
POLITICS: Unswayed by political compromises, President John Tyler again vetoes the bill reestablishing a national bank.

September 11
POLITICS: President John Tyler's cabinet, angered by his recent veto of the bank bill, resigns from office save for Secretary of State Daniel Webster. Tyler then appoints new members for the South, thereby increasing that region's influence upon presidential decisions.

1841

in a curious alignment with Henry Clay, Daniel Webster, and other politicians of the new Whig party. However, in February 1836, the Democratic Virginia legislature ordered Tyler to remove Clay's Senate censure resolution against Jackson, and, rather than submit, Tyler resigned his seat, quit the party, and formally joined the Whigs. In this capacity he was tapped as William Henry Harrison's vice presidential running mate in the 1840 election. He provided a measure of geographical balance to the ticket even while having very little in common with Harrison. As vice president, Tyler was envisioned as an obstacle to the Whig platform as long as Harrison was in charge.

However, after only a month in power, Harrison suddenly died of illness and Tyler became the first vice president to succeed the chief executive. First he had to weather a period of political questioning of whether he was simply acting president or really president. Tyler then established the precedent that he had, in fact, been constitutionally mandated to succeed to the presidency with all the powers of that office. Despite the fact that the Whigs now controlled the government, Tyler refused to fall in line behind Clay, who was the de facto head of the party. He thus twice vetoed the rechartering of the Bank of the United States, then also rejected a revised tariff and Clay's plan to distribute revenue from land sales back to the states. This cost him the continuing allegiance of Whig members in his own cabinet, for they all resigned with the exception of Secretary of State Daniel Webster, who remained in office only long enough to conclude the famous Webster-Ashburton Treaty. Tyler then replaced his cabinet with Southerners while pushing for the annexation of Texas to appease them. When it was rejected by the Senate, the administration acquired it through a joint resolution of Congress. In 1844 Tyler threw his support behind Democrat James K. Polk, and in 1860 he attended the Washington Peace Convention to circumvent civil war. Tyler subsequently joined the Confederate House of Representatives but died on January 18, 1862 before taking his seat.

October 4
POLITICS: In Rhode Island, where only 4,000 adult males and their eldest sons can vote out of a population exceeding 100,000, disenfranchised men gather at an unauthorized convention to demand to be enfranchised. The ensuing People's Party under Thomas Dorr seeks to update the state constitution, which was approved in 1663 by King Charles II.

October 12
POLITICS: A New York court acquits Canadian sheriff Alexander McLeod of murdering Amos Durfee during the burning of the American steamship *Caroline*. This removes a major point of contention between the United States and Canada.

October 27
SLAVERY: A group of slaves being transported to New Orleans seizes control of the vessel *Creole*, sails to the British port of Nassau in the Bahamas, and is declared free. They summarily ignore all American attempts to recover them.

October 29
EDUCATION: In New York City, Catholic Bishop John Joseph Hughes urges public funding for parochial schools.

1841

November
SETTLEMENT: John Bidwell leads the first organized wagon train across the Rocky Mountains, along the Oregon Trail and into Sacramento, California. They had previously departed Sapling Grove, Kansas, with 69 adults and children.

December 16
SETTLEMENT: A bill is introduced by Missouri Senator Lewis Linn to facilitate expanded migration to the Oregon Territory by providing military escorts and land grants to males of voting age. It is not passed but heightens British awareness of American ambitions in that region.

December 27–29
POLITICS: A majority of voters approve the so-called People's Constitution to enlarge the voter franchise in Rhode Island.

1842

LABOR: The Massachusetts state supreme court decides the case of *Commonwealth v. Hunt* ruling that trade unions are lawful organizations, they are not responsible for illegal acts by individuals, and that strikes which close shops are legal. This marks a reversal of traditional judicial hostility toward organized labor.
NAVAL: Pistol manufacturer Samuel Colt begins experimenting with a submarine battery (underwater mines).
SETTLEMENT: Dr. Elijah White, newly appointed Indian agent for the Oregon Territory, conducts a party of 130 people and 18 wagons overland there from Independence, Missouri.
SLAVERY: When fugitive slave George Lattimer is seized by authorities in Boston, local abolitionists insist that he be allowed to purchase freedom from his master in Virginia.
SOCIETAL: The Sons of Temperance is founded in New York and draws heavily upon Masonic rights and rituals. For this reason it is criticized by the competing American Temperance Union for excluding its members at their meetings.
TECHNOLOGY: Samuel F. B. Morse successfully lays the first underwater telegraph cable between Castle Garden and Governor's Island, New York.

January 1
SOCIETAL: Exhibitor par excellence Phineas T. Barnum, a former newspaper editor, opens the American Museum in New York City. He employs hoaxes and extravagant, sensationalized advertising to lure an unsuspecting public inside.

January 2
ENGINEERING: The first wire suspension bridge is opened across the Schuylkill River, at Fairmount, Pennsylvania.

January 24
POLITICS: Citizens from Haverhill, Massachusetts, petition Congress to allow the Union to be peacefully disbanded; it is presented by former president John Quincy Adams.

March 1
SLAVERY: The U.S. Supreme Court decides the case of *Prigg v. Commonwealth of Massachusetts*, ruling that state law forbidding the seizure of fugitive slaves is

Barnum, P. T.   (1810–1891)
Showman

Phineas Taylor Barnum was born in Bethel, Connecticut, on July 5, 1810, and he went to work at the age of 15 when his father died. By turns a shop owner, director of lotteries, and a newspaper editor, he once spent several weeks in jail for libel and relocated to Philadelphia in search of gainful employment, There he encountered Joice Heth, an elderly African American, whom a small town huckster promoted as President George Washington's original nurse. In a flash Barnum saw an opportunity so he acquired the rights to exhibit Heth, backed by an outlandish publicity campaign, and made his reputation as a showman. In 1840 he ventured to New York and acquired John Scudder's American Museum, which he transformed from a collection of curiosities into a showcase for the bizarre. Barnum stuffed his displays with unusual and usually contrived objects, physically deformed people, and novelties such as jugglers and automated displays, backed by outlandish claims and promotions. The public, paying 25 cents a head, readily attended and apparently enjoyed such imaginative deceptions, particularly the exhibit marked "egress"—leading to the exit. For two decades Barnum cemented his reputation as "America's greatest showman" through the likes of celebrities such as 25-inch-tall "General Tom Thumb" and gained formal introduction to many heads of state, including President Abraham Lincoln, King Louis Philippe of France, and Queen Victoria of England. For all his skill at hucksterism, Barnum was a shrewd businessman and a good judge of popular taste. For that reason he invited soprano Jenny Lind, the "Swedish Nightingale," on a successful nationwide tour that also netted him a large fortune. His autobiography, first published in 1855 and repeatedly updated and reprinted, sold nearly a million copies—at least according to him.

Advancing age did nothing to inhibit Barnum's sense of adventurism and fun. He acquired a small traveling circus, expanded the routine with the usual exotic acts and claims, then successfully toured the nation touting "the Greatest Show on Earth." The public responded in droves, and in 1881 Barnum joined forces with a younger competitor, James A. Bailey, to found the famous "Barnum & Bailey's Three Ring Circus," which became a staple of family entertainment for over a century. When not engaged in his usual moneymaking schemes, Barnum turned to politics and served several terms in the Connecticut legislature. He continued pursuing his traveling circus with great energy, imagination, and personal delight until 1891, when his health began to fail. Ever the showman, when near death he reputedly asked a local newspaper to print his obituary in advance so that he could read it. The vivacious Barnum died in Philadelphia on April 7, 1891, just hours after inquiring about the daily box office receipts. Beyond being America's premier entertainer and a fine judge of public psychology, he raised the level of mass entertainment to new levels, anticipating by decades the huge response to the new motion picture industry.

unconstitutional. However, the court maintains that the actual capture of such fugitives rests entirely with the federal government and state officials need not concern themselves.

1842

March 3

LABOR: Massachusetts approves the first law restricting children in factories under the age of 12 to 10 hours of work per day.

March 4

LAW: The U.S. Supreme Court decides the case of *Dobbins v. Commissioners*, ruling that states cannot tax the salary of Federal officials.

March 7

EDUCATION: Ohio Wesleyan University is chartered in Delaware, Ohio, by the Methodists; the first class graduates in 1846.

March 21–23

SLAVERY: Abolitionist representative Joshua Giddings champions the seizure of slaves by England in the Creole case and is censured by Southerners in the House. Giddings then resigns from Congress, only to be reelected in the following May.

March 30

BUSINESS: The Tariff Act of 1842, a piece of highly protective legislation, is passed by Congress and raises tariffs to the levels authorized by the Tariff Act of 1832.

MEDICAL: The first recorded use of ether during surgery is made by Dr. Crawford W. Long of Jefferson, Georgia.

March 31

POLITICS: Henry Clay, disgusted by the Whig Party's inability to formulate programs, resigns from Congress. He intends to spend the next several years rebuilding his party from the ground up before returning to the Senate in 1849.

April 4

DIPLOMACY: British minister Alexander Baring, Baron Ashburton, presents his credentials in Washington, D.C. He is authorized to commence wide-ranging negotiations with Secretary of State Daniel Webster in a bid to head off future border disputes between America and Canada.

April 12

BUSINESS: The Mutual Life Insurance Company is chartered in New York, being the first company of its kind.

April 18

POLITICS: Dissident and disenfranchised males in Rhode Island elect Thomas W. Dorr to serve as governor while the political establishment reelects Samuel W. King to the same office. Both sides then appeal to President John Tyler for assistance.

April 25

SOCIETAL: Noted British writer Charles Dickens becomes the toast of New York City when he arrives, is feted by literary circles, and raises money for the relief of London slums. He also denounces slavery and seeks international copyright laws to protect authors everywhere.

May 2

EXPLORING: Colonel John C. Frémont begins his four-year exploration of the Rocky Mountains and Wyoming; success here will make him a national figure.

1842

Frémont, John C. (1813–1890)
Explorer

John C. Frémont was born in Savannah, Georgia, on January 21, 1813, the illegitimate son of a French emigrant and an upper class Southern woman. He was raised in Charleston, South Carolina, and briefly attended Charleston College in 1831, where he excelled at mathematics before being expelled. After holding down several minor posts, Frémont came to the attention of politician Joel R. Poinsett, who arranged for Frémont to receive his lieutenant's commission in the U.S. Army. In this capacity he accompanied French scientist Joseph N. Nicollet on a two-year expedition through the Iowa territory and finally found his calling. In 1841 he also met and married the daughter of influential Missouri Senator Thomas Hart Benton and now possessed a powerful sponsor. Consequently, between 1842 and 1849 Frémont conducted four famous expeditions throughout the American West, contesting the notions of Major Stephen H. Long that the region was entirely desert and uninhabitable. Among his many achievements was thoroughly mapping the South Pass of the Rocky Mountains, which subsequently served as an important conduit for western migration to the Pacific coast. In 1843 Frémont teamed up with noted scout Kit Carson and covered another 6,500 miles from the Great Salt lake, Utah, over the Sierra Nevada desert and into California and back. He also gained fame by publishing his reports to Congress, which became an immediate best seller and stimulated settlement. Frémont was in California when the Mexican War broke out in 1846. He helped arrange the Bear Flag revolt in California and gained appointment as governor through Commodore Robert F. Stockton but was subsequently arrested by General Stephen W. Kearny for insubordination. He still remained popularly regarded as "The Pathfinder."

Frémont was cleared of all charges at Fort Leavenworth, Kansas, but he nonetheless resigned his commission in a huff. He then gained appointment as the first U.S. senator from California. Frémont, despite his Southern roots, was an avowed abolitionist, and in 1856 he became the first candidate to run for the presidency with the new Republican Party. Aged but 43 years, he was also the youngest ever to run for such high office. Frémont, however, was badly drubbed by Democrat James Buchanan and returned to private life. When the Civil War erupted in April 1861, he was commissioned a brigadier general by President Abraham Lincoln and placed in charge of the sensitive region of Missouri. However, Frémont angered Lincoln and slaveholding Northerners alike through his unauthorized emancipation efforts of 1861 and was removed from the post. He subsequently transferred east to serve in the Shenandoah Valley of Virginia, where he was badly defeated by General Thomas J. "Stonewall" Jackson at Cross Keys in 1862. Fremont was talked out of running for the presidency in 1864 and subsequently served as territorial governor of Arizona, 1878–81. He died in New York on July 12, 1890, a celebrated frontier figure.

May 3
POLITICS: Thomas W. Dorr, elected governor of Rhode Island under the new "People's Constitution," is sworn into office over the objections of the previous executive, Samuel W. King.

1842

May 18

MILITARY: The so-called Dorr's War breaks out in Rhode Island when disenfranchised male supporters of Thomas W. Dorr try and fail to seize the local arsenal. He flees the state but subsequently returns and is arrested.

May 20

SPORTS: The Union Course on Long Island, New York, is the scene of a huge racing event between Boston, a horse from the North, and Fashion, a horse from the South. Fashion wins the event by running a four-mile course in seven minutes and 32 seconds, a new record. An estimated 50,000 racing fans are on hand to view the proceedings.

June 10

EXPLORING: Lieutenant Charles Wilkes returns to New York City after sailing 90,000 miles around the Pacific and Antarctica. This concludes the ambitious United States Exploring Expedition, although work on the published report continues until 1844 and runs to five volumes.

June 25

POLITICS: Congress passes the Reapportionment Act, requiring that Congressmen be elected by district.

June 29

POLITICS: President John Tyler vetoes a revenue bill that would maintain tariffs above the 20 percent level as per the Compromise Tariff of 1833. The legislation also mandates that the government suspend distribution of revenue surpluses from federal land sales to the states.

August 9

BUSINESS: President John Tyler vetoes a second tariff bill combining higher duties with continuing distribution of surplus revenue to the states.

DIPLOMACY: The Webster-Ashburton Treaty is concluded between Secretary of State Daniel Webster and Lord Ashburton to mitigate boundary disputes and other issues. Among other things, the Maine/New Brunswick border is finalized, the United States obtains navigation rights on the St. John River, Great Britain grants America all territory from Lake Superior to the Lake of the Woods (Minnesota), and the British government officially apologizes for the Caroline affairs. This marks a turning point in previously stiff and formal relations between the two nations.

August 20

DIPLOMACY: The Senate ratifies the Webster-Ashburton Treaty by a wide margin of 39 to nine.

August 26

BUSINESS: July 1 is defined by Congress as the start of the new fiscal year.

August 30

BUSINESS: President John Tyler signs a third Tariff Act which raises the level of duties to the levels of 1832 and also ends the distribution of surplus federal revenues when tariffs rise above a specific level.

September 11

MILITARY: In a spate of ongoing border hostility, Mexican soldiers invade and capture San Antonio from the Republic of Texas.

1842

October 3
SETTLEMENT: Marcus Whitman, determined to draw attention to the Oregon Territory, journeys to Washington and Boston in the middle of winter.

October 13
NAVAL: Commodore Lawrence Kearney and his East India Squadron begins arriving at Chinese ports to commence diplomatic and trade negotiations with Manchu dynasty officials.

October 20–21
NAVAL: Commodore Thomas ap Catesby Jones, commanding the East Pacific Squadron, mistakenly seizes the Mexican settlement of Monterrey, California, having been falsely informed that the United States and Mexico are at war. When correctly informed by the American consul, Thomas O. Larkin, he apologizes for the mistake and departs.

October 21
MILITARY: In Texas, Mexican troops attack and kill a number of Texans in the so-called Dawson Massacre.

December
SOCIETAL: Dr. Charles Frederick Ernest Minnegerode, a German political exile, sets up the first Christmas tree in the United States.

December 1
NAVAL: The only instance of mutiny aboard a U.S. Naval warship occurs when Commander Alexander S. Mackenzie hangs three individuals for allegedly plotting aboard the USS *Somers*. One individual, Midshipman Philip Spencer, is son of the present secretary of war.

December 30
SETTLEMENT: President John Tyler, at the behest of Secretary of State Daniel Webster, declares that the Hawaiian islands are off-limits to any prospective colonial powers.

1843

ARTS: Hiram Powers finishes sculpting his noted work, "Greek Slave."
BUSINESS: Benjamin T. Babbitt introduces powdered soap and markets his new product with free samples; it is tremendously successful and eventually known throughout the country.
DIPLOMACY: George Brown, American minister to the Hawaiian Islands, refuses to support attempts by France and England to secure the region's independence.
LITERATURE: Edgar Allan Poe furthers his reputation as a master of the macabre with the publication of his minor masterpiece *The Tell-Tale Heart*, a first-person narrative about psychotic delusions.
MEDICAL: Dr. Oliver Wendell Holmes publishes a highly respected essay, "The Contagiousness of Puerperal Fever," in the *New England Quarterly Journal of Medicine*.

A yellow fever epidemic strikes hard throughout the Mississippi Valley, killing 13,000 inhabitants.
MUSIC: Daniel Decatur Emmet, composer of the song "Dixie," leads the Virginia Minstrels, first known minstrel troupe to perform in New York City. His use of blackface singers sets the precedent for minstrel acts that follow.

PUBLISHING: Historian William Hickling Prescott publishes *The Conquest of Mexico*, a compelling and highly accurate narrative that sells thousands of copies.

RELIGION: German Jews living in New York City found the B'nai B'rith.

SCIENCE: The world's largest telescope is mounted at the Harvard Astronomical Observatory. The device was obtained through private subscription and marks the founding of American astronomy.

SLAVERY: The Vermont legislature votes to void the Fugitive Slave Act of 1793.

January

SOCIETAL: Reformer Dorothea Lyn Dix testifies before the Massachusetts legislature on behalf of better treatment of the insane and mentally ill. Her address, "Memorial to the Legislature of Massachusetts," excoriates long accepted practices of abuse and leads to reforms.

The Association for Improving the Condition of the Poor in New York City, an umbrella organization of many diverse charities and social groups, is founded in New York City. Its success leads to similar agencies in Brooklyn, Boston, and elsewhere.

Engraving showing underground lodgings of the poor, Greenwich Street, New York City *(Library of Congress)*

1843

January 29
GENERAL: William McKinley, the 25th president, is born at Niles, Ohio.

February 3
SETTLEMENT: The Oregon Bill of Missouri Senator Lewis Linn, intended to stimulate migration there, is approved by the Senate. This authorizes the construction of military posts to protect settlers and also land grants to prospective settlers.

February 25
DIPLOMACY: British warships raise their flags over the Hawaiian Islands.

March 3
BUSINESS: Congress repeals the Bankruptcy Law of 1841.

April
POLITICS: The Rhode Island political establishment, shaken by the outbreak of Dorr's War, writes a new constitution that incorporates an expanded voting franchise.

May
EXPLORATION: Colonel John C. Frémont commences his second exploring expedition across the Rocky Mountains, down the Snake and Columbia Rivers, and into the San Joaquin Valley of California.

May 2
SETTLEMENT: Settlers convene at Champoeg, Oregon Territory, for the purpose of establishing their own government. They eventually adopt a constitution drawn from the Iowa model.

May 8
POLITICS: Secretary of State Daniel Webster resigns from office, ostensibly over President John Tyler's intention to annex Texas; he is replaced by Abel P. Upshur.

May 22
SETTLEMENT: A wagon train with 1,000 prospective settlers departs Independence, Missouri, for the purpose of settling in the Oregon Territory. All arrive safely in October.

May 29
EXPLORING: Colonel John C. Frémont departs Kansas City, Missouri, accompanied by noted scout Kit Carson, on a march to explore the region between the Rocky Mountains and the Pacific coast. His endeavors yield a highly accurate migration route to Oregon.

June
POLITICS: The American Republic Party, an anti-Catholic, nativist organization, is founded in New York City. They intend to deny the right to vote or hold office to anybody not born in the United States. Within two years the group evolves into the Native American Party.

Several American delegates attend the World Peace Conference in London, England.

June 1
SLAVERY: Self-styled Sojourner Truth (Isabella Bomefree, later Baumfree, also Isabella Hardenbergh Van Wagenen), towering at six feet in height, commences

1843

Sojourner Truth *(Library of Congress)*

her career as a spellbinding abolitionist speaker in Brooklyn, New York.

June 15
DIPLOMACY: Mexico and the Republic of Texas agree to a truce in fighting.

June 17
POLITICS: Daniel Webster attends the dedication of the Bunker Hill Monument in Boston, Massachusetts, delivering one of his most memorable orations; President John Tyler is in attendance.

July 5
SETTLEMENT: Settlers meeting at Champeog, Oregon Territory, construct a constitution based on that of the Iowa Territory; it functions as a provisional government until the federal government accepts jurisdiction over the region.

July 12
RELIGION: Mormon prophet Joseph Smith announces a divine revelation sanctioning the practice of multiple wives, or polygamy. This practice causes a rift in the Mormon rank and file and further stirs antagonism from more traditional sects in the vicinity of Nauvoo, Illinois.

July 26
DIPLOMACY: Royal Navy warships under Admiral Richard Thomas remove the dictatorial Lord George Paulet from Hawaii, who had illegally claimed the islands for Britain, and restore King Kamehameha III to his throne.

August 14
MILITARY: Florida's Second Seminole War ends; it was the most protracted and expensive Indian conflict of United States history.

August 22
SLAVERY: At the annual National Convention of Colored Men in Buffalo, New York, speaker Henry Highland Garnett raises eyebrows by calling for a national slave insurrection.

August 23
DIPLOMACY: Mexican dictator General Antonio López de Santa Anna warns the United States not to annex the Republic of Texas—such a move would be regarded as an act of war. In light of the republic's increasing ties with European nations, the U.S. government is forced to pay more attention to the region.

August 30–31
POLITICS: The Liberty Party convenes in Buffalo, New York, and nominates abolitionist James G. Birney of Michigan for the presidency and Thomas Morris of Ohio for the vice presidency. Their platform denounces the expansion of slavery.

1843

Truth, Sojourner (ca. 1797–1883)
African-American abolitionist

Isabella Bomefee (later, Baumfree) was born a slave in Ulster County, New York, around 1797, where most of her 12 brothers and sisters were sold off. She then worked for her master, married, and watched in horror as most of her own offspring were taken and sold. In 1826 Baumfree escaped from her plantation and moved in with the Van Wagenen family, taking their name and working as a domestic until slavery was abolished the following year. Concurrently, she began experiencing religious visions and departed for New York City. There she took up residence with the family of preacher, Elijah Pierson, and commenced her own evangelical work by saving prostitutes. Around 1833 she began a close association with a religious fringe group called Kingdom of Matthias in Ossining, New York, and subsequently returned to New York in 1843. That year, while traveling and preaching on Long Island, she experienced another religious conversion and began calling herself Sojourner Truth. This marked the beginning of her celebrated career as a charismatic evangelical speaker in her own right for Truth, over six feet tall and powerfully vocal, began a personal crusade on behalf of love, brotherhood, and temperance. She relocated to a communal village in Northampton, Massachusetts, in 1843, and there befriended abolitionists Frederick Douglass, William Lloyd Garrison, and early feminist writer Olive Gilbert. In 1850 Gilbert wrote and published *The Narrative of Sojourner Truth*, which became a best seller and made the author a national celebrity. The next year Truth attended and addressed a woman's convention at Akron, Ohio, where she delivered her moving and poignant "Ain't I a woman?" speech that captivated her audience.

Truth by this time had also added abolitionism to her litany of personal crusades and she vocally supported both the Civil War and the raising of African-American regiments to wage it. She also continually addressed feminist gatherings and raised money for black soldiers through her busy lecturing schedule. In fact, one of her own sons served as a private in the famous 54th Massachusetts Infantry. In 1864 she was invited to the White House to meet with President Abraham Lincoln and also joined the National Freedmen's Bureau to help assist newly liberated slaves assimilate into society. Noted abolitionist writer Harriet Beecher Stowe lauded her as the "Libyan Sybil" for her unceasing efforts to eliminate slavery. After the war Truth actively agitated for Congress to grant free land to former slaves out west, but she was ignored. She also took issue with her former friend Douglass and opposed the Thirteenth and Fourteenth Constitutional Amendments because women's rights were still not addressed. Truth continued preaching religion and championing suffrage well into her advanced years until illness and infirmity forced her to retire to a sanatorium at Battle Creek, Michigan. She died there on November 26, 1883, receiving the largest funeral ever accorded an African-American woman.

September 29
INDIANS: Texas representatives Edward Terrant and George Terrell sign a peace accord with representatives of nine Indian tribes at Bird's Fort, North Texas.

October 16
SETTLEMENT: Secretary of State Abel P. Upshur informs Texas minister Isaac Van Zandt that the United States is interested in annexing the republic. When informed of the move, President Sam Houston declines for the time being, not wishing to be rejected in the senate by antislavery Northerners. He also desires to maintain Great Britain's diplomatic and economic support.

November 9
DIPLOMACY: The United States and France conclude an extradition convention.

December 5
NAVAL: The USS *Michigan*, which is both the first all-iron and prefabricated warship, is assembled in sections at Erie, Pennsylvania. The vessel was constructed at Pittsburgh and transported overland to Lake Erie.

December 30
EDUCATION: Cumberland University is chartered at Lebanon, Tennessee, by the Presbyterians; the first class graduates this same year.

1844

ARTS: Mathew Brady establishes his first daguerrotype studio in New York City, becoming the world's first celebrated photographer.
LITERATURE: Ralph Waldo Emerson publishes his second series of *Transcendentalist Essays,* which prove popular and confirm his position as a noted writer and philosopher.
MEDICAL: *The American Journal of Psychiatry* begins publication as the first specialized medical publication. The Association of Medical Superintendents of American Institutions for the Insane (today's American Psychiatric Association) is also founded.
PUBLISHING: The Transcendentalist publication The *Dial* is suspended after 16 issues; it is nonetheless a landmark publication for printing works by noted writers such as Ralph Waldo Emerson and Henry David Thoreau.
RELIGION: The Baptist Church splits into northern and southern denominations over the issue of slavery.

Amos Bronson Alcott, father of noted writer Louisa May Alcott, establishes a utopian community near Harvard University, Cambridge, Massachusetts.
SOCIETAL: The New York Prison Association arises to assist newly discharged prisoners in need because of their destitute condition.

January 15
EDUCATION: The University of Notre Dame is chartered at South Bend, Indiana, by Roman Catholics; its first class graduates in 1849.

January 16
DIPLOMACY: Secretary of State Abel P. Upshur assures Texas President Sam Houston that any treaty annexing Texas will pass by the necessary two-thirds vote.

February 15
POLITICS: At Nauvoo, Illinois, Mormon prophet Joseph Smith declares his candidacy for the presidency and prepares for a nationwide speaking tour.

February 23
EDUCATION: The University of Mississippi is chartered by the state legislature at Oxford, Mississippi; its first class graduates in 1851.

February 28
NAVAL: An accidental cannon burst on the steam frigate USS *Princeton* kills Secretary of State Abel P. Upshur and Secretary of the Navy Thomas Gilmer among others.

March
EXPLORING: Colonel John C. Frémont shepherds his expedition through the Sierra Nevada Mountains toward Sutter's Fort in Sacramento, California.

March 6
POLITICS: John C. Calhoun is affirmed as the new secretary of state, replacing the recently deceased Abel P. Upshur.

March 21
RELIGION: Christ fails to reappear on this day as predicted by Adventist William Miller, so he revises his date to October 22.

March 22
JOURNALISM: A letter by Andrew Jackson favoring annexation of Texas is published in the *Richmond Enquirer.*

March 27
JOURNALISM: Samuel Bowles begins editing the *Springfield Republican* in Springfield, Massachusetts.

March 29
NAVAL: Uriah Philips Levy is the first person of Jewish extraction appointed a captain in the navy.

April
SOCIETAL: German immigrants living at Milwaukee, Wisconsin, brew the first lager beer, a drink that gains in popularity throughout the region.

April 4
RELIGION: The agrarian/utopian Fouirerists sect meets in New York and elects George Ripley as their president.

April 12
DIPLOMACY: Secretary of State John C. Calhoun negotiates a treaty of annexation with the Texas minister in Washington, D.C. Once approved, it allows Texas to enter the Union as a territory, not a state.

April 18
SLAVERY: Secretary of State John C. Calhoun writes a letter to British minister Sir Richard Pakenham, strongly defending the institution of slavery.

April 22
POLITICS: A bill for the annexation of Texas, drawn up by Secretary of State John C. Calhoun, is submitted by President John Tyler to the Senate for ratification. It provides for the assumption of $10 million in Texas debts by the United States. He also warns of the risk of abolition should Great Britain be allowed to interfere with the process and seeks speedy passage.

1844

April 25
MEDICAL: Dr. John Sappington publishes his *Theory and Treatment of Fevers*, being the first medical text to advocate the use of quinine for treating malaria.

April 27
JOURNALISM: Presidential aspirants Martin Van Buren and Henry Clay publish letters opposing the contemplated annexation of Texas in the *Washington Globe* and the *National Intelligencer*, respectively, with negative effects for both. Van Buren's stance induces Andrew Jackson to endorse James K. Polk, while Clay is branded as an opportunist for subsequently stating he would support annexation if it could be accomplished without a war.

May 1
POLITICS: Henry Clay becomes the Whig nominee for the presidency while Theodore Frelinghuysen of New Jersey get the vice presidential nod. The party platform remains silent as to the issues of the annexation of Texas and a national bank.

May 6–July 8
RELIGION: Violent clashes between Protestants and Catholic immigrants in Philadelphia result in 20 deaths and around 100 injured. This affair indicates the growing strength of the nativist movement in eastern cities.

May 24
COMMUNICATIONS: Samuel F. B. Morse sends the first message "What hath God wrought!" over telegraph wires from Washington, D.C., to Baltimore, Maryland. Instantaneous communication over large areas is now technically feasible.

May 25
TECHNOLOGY: Stuart Perry of Newport, Rhode Island, receives a patent for one of the earliest gasoline-powered motors.

May 27–29
POLITICS: The Democratic nomination convention in Baltimore selects James K. Polk of Tennessee to run for the presidency and George M. Dallas of Pennsylvania for vice president after nine ballots. They run on a militant platform of annexing Texas and adopt the slogan "Fifty-Four Forty or Fight," a reference to the proposed boundary of the Oregon Territory—even at the expense of war with Great Britain. Sitting president John Tyler is also nominated by a faction within the party, but his chances of winning are virtually nil.

June 8
POLITICS: The Texas Annexation Bill fails in the Senate on a vote of 35 to 16 for fear that creation of another slave state entails a political showdown between North and South. Many Northerners also view the document as a "slaveholder's conspiracy." President John Tyler now realizes he will never muster the necessary two-thirds vote in this polarized body, so he begins pushing for a joint congressional resolution which requires only a simple majority.

June 20
BUSINESS: Samuel F. B. Morse obtains a patent for his new telegraph.

1844

Morse, Samuel F. B.   (1791–1872)

Inventor

Samuel Finley Breese Morse was born in Cambridge, Massachusetts, on April 27, 1791, son of a Calvinist minister. He studied at the elite Phillips Academy in Andover before being admitted to Yale College. Here he displayed great talent as a portrait artist before marrying and settling in New York, where Morse helped establish the National Academy of Design in 1826. Previously, Morse had impressed noted artist Washington Allston, who invited him to study at his studio in England. He then visited that country repeatedly, and Morse was touring there in 1829 when he had a chance encounter with inventor Charles Thomas Jackson, who convinced him of the practicality of sending messages with electrical impulses—a notion that subsequently dominated Morse's life. He then found work teaching art at New York University, plowing all his spare money and time into making electromagnetic communication a reality. After teaming with investors Alfred Vail and Leonard Gale in 1837, Morse finally invented a viable scheme for sending signals over a wire through a transmitter and a receiver. The mechanism also employed an ingenious series of dots and dashes, combinations of which represented numbers or letters, making it possible to decipher a message quickly. This system eventually became known as the Morse Code. All told it was a relatively simple solution to a very complex task, and it held immediate implications for the nation at large.

Morse's device had many practical applications yet it was greeted with scepticism and generated very little enthusiasm. He initially proffered it to the government in 1837, but it displayed no interest. It was not until 1844 that Congress finally appropriated $30,000—a huge sum in those days—to string up a 40-mile telegraph line between Washington, D.C., and Baltimore, Maryland. On May 24, 1844, Morse typed out the cryptic message, "What hath God wrought?" and a communications revolution began. In fact, the telegraph indelibly impacted the course of American history as it accompanied the railroads west and, through the instantaneous delivery of messages, helped conquer vast distances. For the first time in history a network of wires could connect even the most remote frontier settlement with large urban centers on the East Coast, promoting a greater sense of national unity. Telegraphs were also extensively utilized by both sides in the Civil War, proving useful in communications and intelligence work. Morse went on to found the Magnetic Telegraph Company in 1845, although the company struggled and ultimately merged with the Western Union Corporation in 1856. Within a few years this relatively simple device was being employed throughout the world. Morse eventually retired to his home in Poughkeepsie, New York, to reap a fortune in licensing fees. He died there on April 2, 1872, having ushered in a revolution in global communications.

June 25

Politics: Rhode Island rebel leader Thomas W. Dorr is tried and sentenced to life imprisonment for treason; he is paroled a year later.

June 26

Societal: President John Tyler marries Julia Gardner in New York City; he is the first chief executive to exchange vows while in office.

1844

June 27

RELIGION: Mormon prophet Joseph Smith and his brother Hyrum are killed by a mob in the Carthage, Illinois, jail after being arrested for destroying the press of a dissident Mormon.

July 1

POLITICS: Henry Clay attempts straddling the fence over Texas annexation to attract Southern votes; the ploy costs him Northern votes instead.

July 3

DIPLOMACY: The United States concludes the Treaty of Wang Hiya with China, which opens five ports to trading and grants extraterritoriality rights to Americans working and living there.

July 29

SPORTS: The New York Yacht Club, the nation's oldest, is founded in New York with steamboat magnate John Cox Stevens serving as its first commodore.

Young, Brigham   (1801–1877)
Mormon leader

Brigham Young was born in Whitingham, Vermont, on June 1, 1801, into poverty. His family of devout Methodists subsequently relocated to New York, where he worked as a house painter. In 1832 the already religious Young encountered Mormon prophet Joseph Smith, and converted to his church. Three years later he was elevated to number three in the Quorum of Twelve Apostles, an indication of the trust Smith and other church elders placed in him. At this time Mormon communities were constantly on the move owing to overt hostility from other sects, and in 1835, when Smith was jailed and the church expelled from Missouri, it was Young who helped orchestrate the mass relocation to Nauvoo, Illinois. He also functioned as a charismatic recruiter for the church, so in 1839 Smith dispatched him to England where he met with considerable success. Young returned to Illinois two years later to gain appointment as the church's fiscal agent and in 1844 had accepted Smith's

Brigham Young *(Library of Congress)*

1844

August 7
EXPLORING: Colonel John C. Frémont's expedition reaches St. Louis, Missouri, after a lengthy trek from South Pass to the Great Salt Lake, the Oregon Country, and back home across the Sierra Nevada desert.

August 8
RELIGION: Mormons in Nauvoo, Illinois, elect Brigham Young to serve as their new church leader to replace the murdered Joseph Smith.

August 13
WOMEN: A newly adopted constitution in New Jersey drops property qualifications to expand the franchise and also allows direct election of the governor. However, it also deprives women of their right to vote.

August 20
POLITICS: President John Tyler, although nominated by a faction within the Democratic Party, removes himself from the presidential race. His refusal to press for Texas annexation forces him to become the first chief executive not to seek a second term.

---

new emphasis on polygamy for church leaders, taking three wives. That year Smith also decided to run for the presidency and began touring the country. He was murdered by a mob at Carthage, Illinois, in July that year and Young hurried back from Boston to find the Mormon Church virtually leaderless and in a state of panic. Because he was such a well-known and trusted person, Young easily defeated several contenders to become the second president of the Church of Jesus Christ and the Latter Days Saints.

Young's first priority as president was to assure the safety of his followers, and he began canvassing western explorers for possible new venues of settlement. In 1846 he decided to move the entire Mormon community to the Great Salt Lake Basin (present-day Utah) and the following spring led a small group of pioneers to explore and lay the groundwork for the new state of Deseret ("Land of the Honeybee"). Young handled his charge capably and within a year 12,000 Mormon adherents had settled into their new theocracy. To these were eventually added another 70,000 converts from Europe who ultimately established 357 churches throughout the region. After the Mexican War, in which the Mormons contributed a battalion of infantry, the U.S. government began organizing the territories, and the Mormons fell into the new jurisdiction of Utah. President Franklin Pierce recognized Young's authority and appointed him territorial governor, but his successor, James Buchanan, did not agree, and he appointed non-Mormon authorities. This led to a brief outbreak of hostilities and army troops were dispatched to restore order in 1857–58. Young went into hiding but eventually accepted federal authorities. He then continued administering church matters with great success and in 1850 established the University of Deseret (today's University of Utah). Young died in Salt Lake City on August 29, 1877, one of the wealthiest and most accomplished leaders in church history and recognized for conducting one of the great mass migrations of American history.

September 19

GENERAL: William A. Burt, a government surveyor, was working on the Upper Peninsula of Michigan near Lake Superior when he noticed that his compass readings were inexplicably off by 87 degrees. Subsequent investigation discovers the Marquette iron range, one of the nation's largest.

October 22

RELIGION: Much to the disappointment of Adventist William Miller, Christ fails to make his reappearance a second time, as predicted.

November 1

POLITICS: A convention meeting in Iowa City, Iowa, adopts a new constitution to facilitate statehood.

December 3

POLITICS: By a vote of 108–80, John Quincy Adams prevails upon the House of Representatives to rescind the gag rule forbidding discussion of antislavery petitions. President John Tyler also addresses Congress this day and formally requests the annexation of Texas through a joint resolution rather than a treaty. This maneuver requires a simple majority in both houses instead of two-thirds of the Senate.

December 4

POLITICS: James K. Polk, campaigning under the bellicose slogan "54–40 or Fight," defeats Henry Clay for the presidency, winning largely on his expansionist appeals for the annexation of Texas, Oregon, and California. He is also the first dark-horse candidate to win the White House, having defeated the obvious front-runner, Martin Van Buren who opposed annexation. Clay lost New York, and hence his best chance for the White House, due to the strong showing of James G. Birney's abolitionist Liberty Party.

December 12

POLITICS: Sam Houston steps down as president of the Republic of Texas and is succeeded by Anson Jones.

1845

ARTS: Social satire on the stage unfolds with Anna Cora Mowatt's play *Fashion*, which deals with the social aspirations of a newly affluent family.

EDUCATION: The Boston school system is the first to pioneer the practice of written examinations.

LABOR: George Henry Evans begins editing the *Workingman's Advocate*, an early newspaper devoted to labor issues.

The Industrial Congress of the United States, a pioneering labor organization, is founded in New York City. Although well-intentioned, initially, it is eventually dominated by Tammany politics and corrupted.

PUBLISHING: Colonel John C. Frémont writes and publishes *The Report of the Exploring Expedition to the Rocky Mountains in the Year 1842 and to Oregon and Northern California in the Years 1843–44*, which makes him a national hero and elevates interest in the West. Moreover, the maps he incorporates in the text will guide a generation of settlers out West.

This engraving shows Irish emigrants getting ready to leave famine-stricken Ireland for the United States. *(Library of Congress)*

RELIGION: The Methodist Episcopal Church splits into Northern and Southern conferences over the issue of slavery.

SCIENCE: Alfred Beach establishes the periodical *Scientific American,* which continues today as a preeminent outlet for publication of scientific investigations.

SOCIETAL: The Great Potato Famine begins in Ireland leading to a mass influx of 1.5 million. immigrants over the next few years.

The Temple of Honor, a combination temperance society and Protestant fraternal order, is founded in New York City to promote abstinence and good moral behavior. Their ceremonies are marked by secret passwords and colorful costumes.

SPORTS: The Knickerbockers, an early baseball team, is formed using modern rules established by Alexander J. Cartwright.

1845

TRANSPORTATION: The *Rainbow*, another of the sleek and beautiful American clipper ships, is launched at New York by John W. Griffiths. Their speed and efficiency in conveying cargo is establishing the United States as a major maritime power.

WOMEN: Pioneer feminist and transcendentalist Margaret Fuller publishes her landmark tome *Woman in the Nineteenth Century*, which urges members of her gender to be more independent.

January 23

POLITICS: Congress imposes a national election day for all presidential contests; they choose the first Tuesday of November in an election year.

January 25

POLITICS: The House of Representatives approves the annexation of Texas by a vote of 120 to 98.

January 29

LITERATURE: In New York, Edgar Allan Poe publishes his collection *The Raven and Other Poems*, which garners him instant recognition as a unique and original writer.

February 1

EDUCATION: The Congress of the Republic of Texas grants a charter to the Texas Baptist Educational Society to establish a college at Independence (modern-day Baylor University).

February 3

SETTLEMENT: The House of Representatives approves a bill establishing a government in the Oregon Territory, including the disputed border region with Great

Poe, Edgar Allan   (1809–1849)
Writer

Edgar Allan Poe was born in Boston on January 19, 1809, the son of impoverished actors. His mother died during his infancy and his father abandoned his family, so he was raised by John Allan of Richmond, a wealthy benefactor. Poe briefly attended the University of Virginia in 1826 and dropped out on account of gambling. He then ventured to Boston in search of work and also published his first volume of poetry, *Tamerlane and Other Poems*, which garnered no attention. Poe then joined the U.S. Army as an artillery private, rising in this capacity to the rank of sergeant. Following the death of his foster mother in 1829, he quit the army and returned to Virginia and was again supported by his benefactor Allan. In 1830 he gained admission at the U.S. Military Academy, West Point, but had apparently lost interest in military life and was expelled for bad behavior. Listless Poe then drifted to Baltimore where his short story "MS. Found in a Bottle" won a competition sponsored by the *Baltimore Saturday Visitor*. He subsequently returned to Richmond to serve as editor of the *Southern Literary Messenger*, which profited through inclusion of short stories, poetry, and his notorious, scathing book reviews. In 1835 Poe married his 13-year-old cousin Virginia Clemm and began drinking heavily. He then lost his editorship and ventured back to New York in 1837 to publish short stories and edit various magazines. Here Poe composed

Britain. However, it makes no provisions for the legal protection of slavery, which kills its chances for passage in the Senate.

February 20
POLITICS: President John Tyler vetoes a congressional bill to prevent the Treasury from paying for ships ordered by the administration.

February 27
POLITICS: The Senate approves a bill for the annexation of Texas, 27–25, with minor modifications by Senator Thomas Hart Benton.

February 28
POLITICS: Both houses of Congress pass a joint resolution for the annexation of Texas by a simple majority, a ploy which nullifies the Senate requirement of a two-thirds vote.

March 2
SETTLEMENT: President John Tyler signs the congressional joint resolution to allow the annexation of Texas, the first instance of this device used for acquiring new territory. Henceforth, Texas is to be admitted as a state, not a territory, and up to four new states can be carved from the general area.

March 3
BUSINESS: Congress passes the Postal Act, which reduces postage to five cents per half ounce for 300 miles and also confers subsidies to steamships carrying mail.
POLITICS: Florida enters the union as the 27th state; slavery is lawful, to counterbalance Iowa, a free state.

---

several significant pieces, including "The Fall of the House of Usher," which marked him as a distinct, if disturbing, writer. By 1841 he had advanced to the editorship of *Graham's Magazine* and wrote "The Murders in the Rue Morgue," which was the first detective story. This was followed by another macabre tale, "The Masque of the Red Death," after which he resumed drinking and was fired.

After several more failed attempts at writing and editing, Poe composed his most famous poem, "The Raven," which brought him instant recognition as an accomplished writer. He subsequently held down editorial positions with the *New York Evening Mirror*, the *Broadway Journal*, and *Godey's Lady's Book*, in which he wrote excoriating reviews of contemporary writers and became highly unpopular with many literary circles. Poe himself sank deeper in depression and alcoholism following the death of his young wife in 1847, all the while penning several noteworthy poems including "Ulalume," "El Dorado," and others. However, financial and emotional security continued to elude him and he drank heavily. He was found lying on a Baltimore street, was taken to a hospital in a stupor, and died there on October 7, 1849. Given the misery associated with his life, Poe demonstrated a fascination for and a mastery of conveying disturbing, dreamlike images in his writing. His melancholy attracted French poet Charles Baudelaire, who carefully translated Poe's work after his death and rendered him the first American writer to be admired in that country.

Polk, James K. (1795–1849)
President

James Knox Polk was born in Mecklenberg County, North Carolina, on November 2, 1795, and raised in Tennessee. He graduated from the University of North Carolina with honors in 1818 and commenced a legal practice two years later. By this time Polk had established his credentials as an ardent supporter of Andrew Jackson, and in 1825 he was elected to the House of Representatives as a Democrat. As a politician, he was also disciplined and focused on issues he considered important, never wavering in pursuit of them. Polk thus flourished as a party leader over the next 14 years, and by 1835 he had risen to house speaker. In this capacity he strongly embraced Jackson's fiscal policies and helped him attack the Bank of the United States. In 1839 he left Congress at the behest of the party and was elected governor of Tennessee, serving one term. Polk subsequently lost two gubernatorial races, then turned his attention back to national politics. Here he was a vocal proponent of the acquisition of the

President James K. Polk *(Library of Congress)*

Both houses of Congress override President John Tyler's veto of a bill prohibiting the payment of naval vessels; this is also the first executive veto to be dispensed with in such manner.

March 4
POLITICS: James Knox Polk is inaugurated as the 11th president; his address proclaims the "clear and unquestionable" title to the Oregon Territory, and annexation of Texas remains strictly an American prerogative. George M. Dallas is also sworn in as vice president.

March 6
DIPLOMACY: General Juan Almonte, Mexican minister in Washington, D.C., is angered by President James K. Polk's inaugural address relative to Texas and removes himself from the capitol.

March 10
NAVAL: Historian George Bancroft is appointed secretary of the navy by President James K. Polk.

1845

Oregon Territory and the annexation of Texas, positions he used to his advantage after President Martin Van Buren made known his opposition to the latter. Van Buren greatly angered Jackson and most of the Democrats, so in 1844 they made Polk the first dark horse candidate to win the party election at his expense. Polk went on to defeat the Whig candidate Henry Clay, whose last-minute endorsement of Texas annexation cost him thousands of antislavery votes in the North. He was now both the 11th president and, aged 49 years, also the youngest man to hold that office to date.

Polk came to office with four major goals in mind: the annexation of Texas, the acquisition of Oregon, the possible purchase of California from Mexico, and a lowering of tariffs. After some intense saber-rattling and a campaign slogan of "Fifty Four Forty—or Fight!" he reached a compromise with Great Britain and peacefully divided the territory along the 49th parallel. He also accepted the annexation of Texas to the United States, which led to a break in diplomatic relations with Mexico. Polk then dispatched troops under General Zachary Taylor into the disputed region between the Nueces and Rio Grande River in Texas, the Mexicans attacked an American cavalry patrol, and war was declared on May 13, 1846. The ensuing conflict proved a rout, and by the 1848 Treaty of Guadalupe Hidalgo, the United States paid Mexico $15 million for California, New Mexico, and Arizona. Previously, he also pushed the Walker Tariff Act through Congress in 1846, which lowered rates significantly. However, Polk's very success cost him political support, for the acquisition of new territory revitalized the issue of slavery expansion and heightened abolitionist cries. Polk, a tireless worker, departed Washington, D.C., in 1849, in broken health. He died at Nashville, Tennessee, three months later on June 15, 1849, a highly effective chief executive but one whose very success in expansionism laid the groundwork for the Civil War.

March 28
DIPLOMACY: The government of Mexico severs relations with the United States upon learning of the congressional resolution for annexing Texas, and American minister Wilson Shannon is also ordered home.

May
EXPLORING: Colonel John C. Frémont initiates his third expedition in the West with 60 armed men. This time he is to survey the central Rocky Mountains and the Great Salt Lake, but Frémont quickly becomes embroiled in California politics during the ensuing Mexican War.

May 14
POLITICS: A new constitution adopted by a state convention in Louisiana drops property qualifications for voting and also allows for direct election of the governor.

May 28
MILITARY: President James K. Polk dispatches American forces under General Zachary Taylor into southwestern Texas to preclude any Mexican invasions. This

is despite the fact that, by the tenets of international law, the region remains Mexican territory. This provocative act is setting the stage for armed conflict.

June 4

ARTS: *Leonora*, penned by William Henry Fry, becomes America's first grand opera and is staged at the Chestnut Street Theater in Philadelphia at the author's expense. Fry is also the first American to promote opera to the general public.

June 8

GENERAL: Andrew Jackson, War of 1812 hero and a very popular president, dies near Nashville, Tennessee.

June 15

POLITICS: Secretary of State James Buchanan assures the government of Texas of military protection once it agrees to the terms of annexation. To underscore this point, General Zachary Taylor is ordered to move his small army of 1,500 men to a point "on or near the Rio Grande" River.

June 23

SETTLEMENT: In a special session, the Texas Congress approves the move of annexation to the United States.

June 27

POLITICS: Rhode Island rebel Thomas W. Dorr, serving a life sentence for treason, is granted an amnesty by the state legislature.

July

POLITICAL: As a sign of the times, John L. O'Sullivan, editor of the *United States Magazine and Democratic Review*, coins the term *manifest destiny*, denoting America's apparent God-given right to control the destiny of North America.

July 1

LITERATURE: Henry David Thoreau commences his celebrated and solitary sojourn at Walden Pond, Massachusetts. Through his writing it subsequently becomes the most celebrated communing with nature ever recorded.

July 4

SETTLEMENT: A Texas political convention held at San Philipe de Austin approves annexation terms; specifically, that Texas will not be divided into more than four new states and would also acquire statehood immediately with a transitional period from territorial status.

July 5–7

POLITICS: The first gathering of the Native American Party meets in Philadelphia with a handful of delegates from New York and Pennsylvania. As a rule they are anti-Catholic and anti-immigrant.

July 12

DIPLOMACY: Secretary of State James Buchanan seeks to end the Oregon Territory dispute by offering to settle on a boundary running along the 49th parallel. Sir Richard Pakenham, the British minister in Washington, D.C., declines to accept without first mentioning the offer to his government.

July 19

GENERAL: New York City suffers from another huge fire that destroys $6 million in property.

July 31

MILITARY: Bolstered to a strength of 3,500 men, General Zachary Taylor marches his army to the Nueces River and assumes defensive positions near Corpus Christi.

August 28

SLAVERY: Frederick Douglass, fearful of being kidnapped from the north and returned to his master in Maryland, emigrates to England where he will confer with English abolitionists.

September 23

SPORTS: In New York, the Knickerbocker Base Ball Club is founded.

August

SOCIETAL: Martial law is declared in Delaware County, New York, after anti-patroon rioting claims the life of a local sheriff.

October 10

NAVAL: Secretary of the Navy George Bancroft initiates the formal opening of the Naval School (U.S. Naval Academy after 1850) at Annapolis, Maryland. Captain James Buchanan, a vigorous, no-nonsense disciplinarian, is appointed its first superintendent, and he effectively lays the groundwork of the first graduating class in 1854.

October 13

POLITICS: Voters in Texas approve both annexation to the United States and a new state constitution.

October 17

DIPLOMACY: Thomas O. Larkin gains appointment as U.S. consul in Monterey, California. He is instructed by President James K. Polk to entice Californians into favoring annexation to preclude any chance of intervention by a foreign power.

American minister John Black reports from Mexico City that the Mexican government would be willing to discuss the matter of Texas once American naval vessels are withdrawn from the Veracruz region.

November 10

DIPLOMACY: John Slidell is authorized to purchase Texas, New Mexico, and California from Mexico for up to $36 million. He also is to try to fix the Texas boundary at the Rio Grande River.

The United States and Belgium conclude a treaty of commerce and navigation.

December 2

POLITICS: In his first address to Congress, President James K. Polk declares that all of North America, especially the Oregon Territory, is off-limits to European colonization. He also calls for an end to the joint occupation of that region, apparently intending to claim the entire region. His heightened version of the Monroe Doctrine becomes popularly regarded as the "Polk Doctrine." Domestically, the president calls for tariff revision and an new independent treasury system.

December 16

DIPLOMACY: The Mexican government of President José Joaquin Herrera refuses to recognize special American minister John Slidell; Herrera is then overthrown by the Mexican military under Mariano Paredes y Arrillaga.

1845

December 27
DIPLOMACY: British minister Sir Richard Pakenham requests that the Americans reiterate their offer to establish the Oregon boundary along the 49th Parallel.

December 29
POLITICS: Texas is admitted to the Union as the 28th state; slavery is legal. The stage is now set for war with Mexico.

1846

LITERATURE: Herman Melville acquires a literary reputation following publication of his novel *Typee,* based upon his own experiences on exotic Pacific isles. However, the author never acquires a large following during his own lifetime, and he is not recognized for his literary genius until the 20th Century.

Margaret Fuller, America's foremost female editor and critic, publishes her *Papers on Literature and Art.*

POLITICS: To discourage further outbreaks of anti-rent rioting in New York, a new liberal constitution is adopted that substitutes perpetual leases with fee simple ones.

SCIENCE: Swiss scientist Louis Agassiz, a leading authority on zoology and geology, arrives at Boston and eventually acquires a teaching position at Harvard College.

TECHNOLOGY: The Eastern Exchange Hotel opens in Boston, being the first such public building heated by steam.

Melville, Herman   (1819–1891)
Writer

Herman Melville was born in New York City on August 1, 1819, the son of a well-to-do merchant. His father died bankrupt in 1832, forcing young Melville to quit the Albany Academy he was attending and work to support his family. Listless and unhappy as a youth, he served as a crew member on board a Liverpool-bound packet ship in 1837, and in 1841 he slipped on board a whaling ship and headed for the South Seas. There he deserted his vessel during a port call at Nuka Hive in the Pacific and lived three years among the natives with a shipmate. He experienced several adventures on other ships and among cannibals, but in 1843 he sailed to Hawaii and enlisted in the U.S. Navy as a seaman. Melville then returned home on board the frigate USS *United States* in 1844. Once ashore he settled in at Lansingburg, New York, to take up writing. At first he drew upon his own experiences in the South Seas and used them as the background for his first two romantic novels, *Typee* (1846) and *Omoo* (1847), both of which were well received. His next maritime endeavor, *Redburn* (1849) was much more ambitious, using techniques of allegory while discussing political and religious issues, and it was a commercial failure. He followed up with a straightforward adventure, *White-Jacket* (1850), an exposé of harsh and draconian life onboard an American man of war, again, based upon the author's own experiences. The following

Erastus Brigham Bigelow develops power looms capable of manufacturing intricate tapestries and carpets at his factory in Clinton, Massachusetts.

Richard M. Hoe develops the first rotary printing press, capable of printing 8,000 newspapers an hour.

January

BUSINESS: Statistician James DeBow edits and publishes *The Commercial Review of the South and Southwest*, or *DeBow's Review*, which contains revealing insights as to the economic life of this region. It enjoys the largest circulation of any magazine in the South.

January 5

POLITICS: The House of Representatives adopts a resolution for ending joint Anglo-American occupation of the Oregon Territory.

January 12

DIPLOMACY: American envoy John Slidell's report of his unsuccessful attempt to purchase territory from Mexico reaches President James K. Polk.

January 13

MILITARY: President James K. Polk orders General Zachary Taylor to increase military pressure on the Mexican government by shifting his 3,500-man "Army of Observation" further south from the Nueces River to the left bank of the Rio Grande. This move is calculated to either induce negotiations or spark an armed conflict.

---

year Melville wrote what was to become his signature work, *Moby-Dick* (1851). This was another allegorical novel set against the background of whaling, and whose dark and foreboding themes are regarded as a psychological counterpoint to the open and cheerily optimistic of historical romantic jottings of the day. The book was not critically well-received at the time, owning to its complex and radically different nature, but it has since been accepted as an American masterpiece.

Melville subsequently raised the ire of readers with his next novel, *Pierre*, another dark and disturbing tale with a violent ending. He tried to recoup his finances by contributing various short pieces to leading periodicals of the day, including *Putnam's Magazine*. He then resorted to his usual themes with a black comedy entitled *The Confidence Man* (1857), a set of stories narrating human gullibility and extortion, which failed to sell. Melville then withdrew from the commercial marketplace for contemplation and several European pilgrimages, in which he took inspiration from architecture and painting. In 1866 he accepted the position of inspector at the New York Customshouse, while he dabbled unsuccessfully in poetry. He was then deeply affected by the deaths of both his sons, quit the customshouse in 1885, and began work on a new maritime novel, *Billy Budd*. This was a tragedy whereby a single sailor is sacrificed for the benefit of all, but it was not published until 1924. Melville, a dark and disturbing genius, died in New York on September 28, 1891.

1846

January 27
EXPLORING: Colonel John C. Frémont reaches Monterey, California, with a small body of soldiers. This time, however, his "expedition" is not tasked with exploring but, rather, preparing the region for annexation.

February 3
MILITARY: General Zachary Taylor receives orders to advance his army, now risen to 3,500 men, to the banks of the Rio Grande.

February 5
EDUCATION: The University of Lewisburg (today's Bucknell University) is chartered at Lewisburg, Pennsylvania, by the Baptists; its first class graduates in 1851.

February 6
DIPLOMACY: In Mexico City, American minister John Slidell reports to superiors that the Mexican government under General Mariano Paredes is resolving to fight the United States out of the belief that Great Britain will also declare war over Oregon.

February 10
RELIGION: A mass migration of 12,000 Mormons from Nauvoo, Illinois, to Council Bluffs on the Missouri River begins in earnest. The exodus is conducted by Brigham Young, successor to the murdered Joseph Smith.

February 19
POLITICS: The Texas state government assembles in Austin for the first time, whereupon it officially transfers authority from itself to the U.S. government.

February 26
DIPLOMACY: Secretary of State James Buchanan informs U.S. Minister in London Alan McLane that he is to discuss the Oregon matter with his British opposites should they raise the issue of joint occupation.

March 3
MILITARY: Mexican General José Castro, commanding at Monterey, California, orders the small force of Colonel John C. Frémont out of the region.

March 12
DIPLOMACY: General Mariano Paredes y Arrillaga, the new president of Mexico, also refuses to receive American envoy John Slidell, at which point he returns to Washington, D.C.

March 26
EDUCATION: Madison University (today's Colgate University) is chartered in Hamilton, New York, by the Baptists.

March 27
SETTLEMENT: A bill to allow free homesteading is introduced by Representative Andre Johnson of Tennessee, but the measure is defeated.

March 28
MILITARY: General Zachary Taylor occupies the left bank of the Rio Grande River, internationally recognized as Mexican territory, while Mexican forces at Matamoros directly across from them also commence building fortifications.

April 10
EDUCATION: St. John's College (Fordham University) is chartered in the Bronx, New York, by Roman Catholics; its first class graduates in 1846.

April 12
MILITARY: Mexican General Pedro de Ampudia issues an ultimatum to General Zachary Taylor, insisting that he withdraw his forces back beyond the Nueces River lest a general engagement result.

April 13
TRANSPORTATION: The Pennsylvania Railroad Company is created for the purpose of joining an existing track from Lancaster to Harrisburg as far west as Pittsburgh.

April 23
DIPLOMACY: The joint Anglo-American occupation of Oregon is ended by Congress, although provisions are made for a possible compromise.

April 25
MILITARY: A force of 1,600 Mexican cavalry ambush a small American mounted patrol near the Rio Grande, killing 11 men, wounding five, and capturing 63. When informed, President James K. Polk uses the skirmish as a convenient pretext for war.
POLITICS: Anticipating the worst, President James K. Polk begins writing his war message to Congress, citing Mexico's refusal to receive envoy John Slidell and the government's refusal to pay of claims by American citizens.

April 26
MILITARY: General Zachary Taylor, in light of open hostility between Mexican and American forces, informs the government that "hostilities may now be considered as commenced."

April 27
DIPLOMACY: A congressional resolution to end joint Anglo-American occupation of Oregon is signed by President James K. Polk. Moreover, the president now insists that a boundary be fixed along the 49th Parallel.
MUSIC: The high-powered Christy Minstrels open at Palmo's Opera House in New York City; they are credited with bringing minstrelsy to its highest form as an entertainment art.

April 30
MILITARY: A large Mexican army surges across the Rio Grande River, forcing American troops under General Zachary Taylor to fall back 10 miles to Point Isabel. From here Taylor intends to protect his base and lines of supply.

May
NAVAL: President James K. Polk declares the coastline of Mexico, along both the Gulf of Mexico and the Pacific Ocean, under a state of blockade.

May 3
MILITARY: In a major escalation of military tensions, Mexican units bombard American-held Fort Taylor, directly opposite Matamoros, along the Rio Grande.

May 4
LAW: The Michigan legislature abolishes capital punishment for the first time in American history.

May 8

MILITARY: The Battle of Palo Alto ensues when 2,000 American troops under General Zachary Taylor engage 4,000 Mexicans commanded by General Mariano Arista. Taylor clearly prevails in what develops into a protracted artillery duel lasting three hours and Arista withdraws to better positions at Resaca de la Palma. American losses are nine dead and 47 wounded to a Mexican tally of 320 killed and 380 wounded. Among the dead was the celebrated artillerist Major Samuel Ringgold, one of the earliest heroes of the Mexican War.

May 9

MILITARY: The Battle of Resaca de la Palma is fought when General Zachary Taylor's force of 2,000 Americans attacks a larger Mexican force in a combined cavalry and infantry assault. In a celebrated charge, Captain Charles May of the dragoons seizes both a Mexican battery and General Romulo Diaz la Vega. General Arista's right flank gives way and the retreating Mexicans are then enfiladed by American artillery. Taylor's losses are 33 killed and 89 injured to a Mexican tally of around 547 dead or wounded.

POLITICS: When word of the April 25 skirmish between Mexican and American troops arrives in Washington, D. C., the cabinet of President James K. Polk votes unanimously to go to war.

May 11

POLITICS: In his war message to Congress, President James K. Polk accuses the Mexicans of invading to "shed American blood on American soil." The House then votes 174 to 14 in favor of war.

May 12

MILITARY: The Senate approves a declaration of war against Mexico, 40 to 2, and authorizes $10 million and up to 50,000 soldiers to fight it. However, its proves to be a divisive issue nationally, with Southerners supporting the conflict to gain additional slave states and Northerners opposing it.

May 13

POLITICS: The declaration of war against Mexico is signed by President James K. Polk. However, the decision is unpopular with many leading politicians; John Quincy Adams denounces it as "a most unrighteous war," while John C. Calhoun, deploring a war of aggression, abstains from voting.

May 17–18

MILITARY: American forces under General Zachary Taylor cross the Rio Grande River and occupy Matamoros.

May 21

DIPLOMACY: President James K. Polk gives the government of Great Britain one year's notice for ending the joint occupation of the Oregon Territory.

June 3

MILITARY: Colonel Stephen W. Kearny departs Fort Leavenworth, Kansas Territory, on an expedition against Santa Fe, New Mexico, and then California. There he is to be supported by naval forces under Commodore John D. Sloat, then stationed off the western coast of Mexico.

Kearny, Stephen W. (1794–1848)
General

Stephen Watts Kearny was born in Newark, New Jersey, on August 30, 1794, and in 1810 he passed through Columbia College in New York. He was commissioned a lieutenant in the 13th Infantry shortly before the War of 1812 broke out, fighting bravely at the Battle of Queenstown Heights. Wounded and captured, Kearny was exchanged in a few months but saw no additional combat. After the war he transferred over to the 2nd Infantry and performed several years of garrison duty in Missouri. In 1819 Kearny accompanied General Henry Atkinson on his famous steamboat foray up the Yellowstone River, initiating a 30-year frontier career. In 1823 he advanced to major, helped direct the Second Yellowstone Expedition, and constructed the famous Jefferson Barracks in St. Louis in 1826. He then served at various posts in Wisconsin and the Indian Territory (Oklahoma) before becoming lieutenant colonel of the newly raised 1st Dragoon Regiment in 1833. In this capacity he accompanied Colonel Henry Leavenworth on his ill-fated Pawnee expedition of 1834 and assumed command when Leavenworth died of illness en route. Kearny rose to full colonel in 1836 and also penned an important tract, *Carbine Manual, or Rules for the Exercise and Maneuvers of the U. S. Dragoons* (1837). He then rose to command the Third Military District, a region encompassing most of the Great Plains, and in 1845 he shepherded a major expedition along the Oregon Trail to South Pass, securing it as a major conduit for western migration. His final peacetime activity was establishing Fort Kearney, Nebraska, in 1846.

When the Mexican War commenced in 1846 Kearney rose to brigadier general in command of the so-called Army of the West.

He was then tasked with conquering New Mexico and installing an American government there. This he accomplished on August 10, 1846, and then departed for California with 300 dragoons. En route he encountered the noted scout Kit Carson, whom he ordered along, and learned that California had already been subdued by forces under Commodore Robert F. Stockton. Kearny then dismissed 200 of his men and proceeded westward with only 100 dragoons. However, he arrived at Los Angeles to find the city up in arms against the invaders, and on December 2, 1846, his small force was nearly defeated by a larger force of Mexican lancers at the Battle of San Pascual. Kearny was severely wounded but eventually teamed

(continues)

Stephen Watts Kearny *(Library of Congress)*

(continued)

up with Stockton to finally subdue the unruly inhabitants. After the victory, Kearny was directed by the government to establish a government, although Stockton had already done so on his own authority and appointed Colonel John C. Frémont as governor. When Frémont refused to step down Kearny had him arrested and marched back to Fort Leavenworth to face charges of insubordination. Consequently, Frémont's father-in-law, U.S. Senator Jesse Hart Benton, blocked Kearny's well-deserved promotion to major general. He died suddenly of illness on October 31, 1848, a noted frontier figure.

June 6
POLITICS: To gather additional support for his war with Mexico, President James K. Polk submits a British treaty to the Senate for a speedy resolution of the Oregon issue. This delineates the border along the 40th Parallel to Puget Sound and thence through the Juan de Fuca Strait. In return, Polk agrees to lower the tariff on certain items.

June 10
DIPLOMACY: The United States and the German kingdom of Hanover conclude a treaty of commerce and navigation.

June 14
SETTLEMENT: American settlers under William B. Ide proclaim the Republic of California at Sonoma, assisted by a small group of soldiers under Colonel John C. Frémont. Because the design of their new flag incorporates a bear, this event becomes known as the Bear Flag Revolt.

June 15
DIPLOMACY: Secretary of State James Buchanan and British minister Sir Richard Pakenham sign an accord ending the dispute over Oregon. The 49th Parallel becomes the official boundary between the United States and Canada with some minor adjustments still to be made along the Strait of Juan de Fuca and southern Vancouver Island. This is a major diplomatic breakthrough that calms the ruffled waters between the two nations.

June 17
EDUCATION: Iowa College (today's Grinnell College) is chartered in Davenport, Iowa, by Congregationalists; its first class graduates in 1854.
JOURNALISM: James Russell Lowell, a vocal opponent of the Mexican War, publishes his "Bigelow Papers" in the *Boston Courier* in protest.

June 18
DIPLOMACY: The Senate ratifies the Oregon Territory Treaty with Great Britain.

June 19
SPORTS: The first matched baseball game unfolds at Hoboken, New Jersey, when a club known simply as the New York Nine routs the Knickerbockers, 23 to 1. The rules had previously been established by Alexander J. Cartwright of the defeated team.

June 26
BUSINESS: English repeal of the Corn Laws leads to increased imports of American grain.

July 5
POLITICS: Americans living in Sonoma, California, proclaim army explorer John C. Frémont as leader of the new "Republic of California."

July 7–9
NAVAL: Commodore John D. Sloat captures Monterey, hoists the American flag, and claims California for the United States. Commander John B. Montgomery subsequently takes control of San Francisco.

July 20
DIPLOMACY: Commodore James Biddle arrives at Yedo (Tokyo) Bay and unsuccessfully tries to coax the Tokugawa shogunate into establishing diplomatic relations. This constitutes the first visit of American warships to the Land of the Rising Sun.

July 22–25
MILITARY: Colonel Stephen W. Kearny, commanding the Army of the West, marches from Fort Leavenworth, Kansas Territory, to Bent's Fort where the Santa Fe Trail and the Arkansas River meet.

July 23
NAVAL: Commodore Robert F. Stockton supersedes Commodore John D. Sloat as commander of American naval forces off the California coast.

July 24
MILITARY: At Sonora, Colonel John C. Frémont accepts command of the California Battalion.

July 31
BUSINESS: President James K. Polk signs the Walker Tariff Bill, which lowers duties on several luxury goods.

August 2
MILITARY: Colonel Stephen W. Kearny marches his Army of the West from Bent's Fort into the deserts of New Mexico.

August 6
BUSINESS: Congress approves the Independent Treasury Act, recreating government-run subtreasuries across the nation.
SETTLEMENT: A Wisconsin state government meets the approval of Congress.

August 8
POLITICS: Pennsylvania Representative David Wilmot appends the "Wilmot Proviso" to a $2 million appropriations bill for financing the war with Mexico. Drawing upon the Northwest Ordinance of 1787, this measure forbids the importation of slavery into any prospective territory acquired from Mexico. Its net effect is to pit Northern and Southern politicians against each other over this highly divisive issue.

August 10
GENERAL: The Smithsonian Institution is chartered in Washington, D.C., by Congress in honor of English scientist James Smithson, who left the institution $500,000 in 1829 for the dissemination of knowledge to society. American physicist Joseph Henry is appointed secretary general. It continues growing and supporting a number of scientific endeavors to present times.

1846

POLITICS: Congress adjourns without passing the "Two Million Bill" and its attendant Wilmot Proviso. Slavery is thus permissible in new territories acquired from Mexico.

August 13
NAVAL: Commodore David F. Stockton joins forces with Colonel John C. Frémont in a campaign to seize Los Angeles.

August 17
JOURNALISM: The first West Coast newspaper, the *California*, begins publishing at Monterey.
MILITARY: The Army of the West under Colonel Stephen W. Kearny occupies Las Vegas, New Mexico, and declares that region part of the United States. In his march Kearny has covered 1,000 miles of searing desert without the loss of a man or a single shot being fired.

August 16
DIPLOMACY: General Antonio López de Santa Anna, having reached an agreement with President James K. Polk for peace negotiations, is allowed to pass through the U.S. Navy blockade and lands at Veracruz.

August 17
POLITICS: Commodore Robert F. Stockton claims California for the United States—then declares himself acting governor.

August 18
SETTLEMENT: Having covered 800 miles of desert in an epic trek, Colonel Stephen W. Kearny occupies Santa Fe, New Mexico, and sets up a provisional government there.

August 19
MILITARY: The American army under General Zachary Taylor departs Matamoros and marches for Monterrey, capital of Nuevo Leon state. He also declares an eight-week armistice.

September 10
TECHNOLOGY: A patent is issued to Elias Howe for the first sewing machine to employ an eye-point needle.

September 14
MILITARY: Formerly disgraced General Antonio López de Santa Anna is appointed Mexican commander in chief.

September 20–25
MILITARY: The Battle of Monterrey erupts as the 6,640-man army of General Zachary Taylor attacks 5,000 Mexican troops under General Pedro de Ampudia garrisoning the city. Intense house-to-house fighting is required before the Americans flush the defenders, including the heavily fortified Bishop's Palace, at which point Ampudia requests and receives an armistice in exchange for departing the city. American losses are 120 dead and 33 injured to an estimated Mexican loss of 430, killed and wounded.

September 22–23
POLITICS: Colonel Stephen W. Kearny issues a law code for New Mexico and also appoints Charles Bent to serve as governor.

Mexicans under Captain José Maria Flores revolt against American rule, seizing control of San Diego, Santa Barbara, and Los Angeles. Flores is then appointed acting governor.

September 25

MILITARY: A column of American troops under Colonel Alexander W. Doniphan is detached from the Army of the West by Colonel Stephen W. Kearney and marches southward to join an army under General John E. Wool. Kearny himself then departs Santa Fe, New Mexico, and heads for California with 300 men.

October 6

MILITARY: Colonel Stephen W. Kearny, en route to California, encounters noted scout Kit Carson, who informs him about the conquest of California. This news encourages Kearny to send 200 of his men back to Santa Fe, New Mexico, while he continues ahead with the remaining 100.

October 8

MILITARY: At San Luis Potosi, Mexico, General Antonio López de Santa Anna drops his "understanding" with President James K. Polk regarding peace talks and begins rallying his dispirited forces to attack the American invaders.

October 13

MILITARY: The War Department informs General Zachary Taylor that his suggested eight-week armistice has been disapproved.

October 16

MEDICAL: Dr. William Thomas Morton, a Boston dentist, uses ether for the first time while performing dental surgery at Massachusetts General Hospital. The promise of painless surgery subsequently garners much national attention for anesthesia.

November 5

POLITICS: Commodore David Stockton receives orders from the Navy Department to recognize Colonel Stephen W. Kearny as governor of California, as well as commander in chief of American forces there.

November 15

NAVAL: American warships under Commodore David Connor attack and seize the Mexican city of Tampico on the Gulf Coast of Mexico.

November 16

MILITARY: Saltillo, capital of Coahuilla, Mexico, is occupied by American forces under General Zachary Taylor without a shot being fired.

November 19

POLITICS: President James K. Polk, wary that General Zachary Taylor, a Whig, does not support his policies, wishes to deflate the latter's political capital by consenting to an amphibious expedition against Veracruz by General Winfield Scott.

November 22

MILITARY: General Zachary Taylor is informed by the government that the truce with Mexico is negated.

November 23

MILITARY: General Winfield Scott is appointed commander of a large amphibious expedition intending to land on the Mexican coast and march overland to the capital of Mexico City.

1846

November 25

MILITARY: An small American column under Colonel Stephen W. Kearny advances from New Mexico into California.

December

POLITICS: Rather than pay taxes for what he considers an unjust war, poet Henry David Thoreau is arrested and spends a night in jail at Concord, Massachusetts.

December 6–10

MILITARY: The Battle of San Pascual is waged between a force of 50 dragoons commanded by General Stephen W. Kearny and 200 lancers under Major Andreas Pico. The Americans rashly charge superior numbers and are handily repelled, although Pico does not use his manpower to any advantage. At length the Mexicans attack and withdraw several times until reinforcements arrive and the Americans keep the field with 30 percent losses.

December 12

DIPLOMACY: The United States and New Granada (Colombia) sign a treaty that affords the Americans transit rights across the Isthmus of Panama. New Granada is also assured of its sovereignty over the area.

MILITARY: American forces under Colonel Stephen W. Kearny occupy San Diego, California, then march northward toward Los Angeles.

December 14

MILITARY: Colonel Alexander W. Doniphan and 1,000 volunteers from the Army of the West depart Santa Fe, New Mexico, and march south to Chihuahua to rendezvous with General John E. Wool.

December 25

MILITARY: A column of American volunteers under Colonel Alexander W. Doniphan defeats 1,200 Mexican cavalry under Lieutenant Colonel Ponce de Léon at the Battle of Las Cruces, securing New Mexico for the United States.

December 27

MILITARY: American forces under Colonel Alexander W. Doniphan defeat Mexican forces at El Brazito, then occupy the town of El Paso.

December 28

POLITICS: Iowa joins the Union as the 29th state with its capital at Iowa City; slavery is outlawed. Its admission balances off the previous addition of Florida, a slave state.

December 29

MILITARY: General Zachary Taylor's army occupies Victoria, capital of Tamaulipas state, Mexico.

1847

ARTS: Robert Ball Hughes casts the first life-size bronze statute in America, a likeness of mathematician Nathaniel Bowditch, which is then placed over his grave in Cambridge, Massachusetts.

The Astor Place Opera House, with a seating capacity of 1,500, opens in New York City. It is the largest such building in America and hosts Verdi's *Ernani* as its opening show.

BUSINESS: Cyrus McCormick opens a new factory in Chicago to mass-produce his highly successful grain reapers.

LABOR: The New Hampshire legislature restricts the working day to 10 hours.

LITERATURE: Henry Wadsworth Longfellow writes and publishes *Evangeline*, a romantic, narrative poem of French settlers expelled from Acadia.

MUSIC: Noted songwriter Stephen Foster pens a catchy tune entitled "Oh, Susannah," based upon African-American music he encountered at church meetings.

WOMEN: The cause of women's rights advances slightly when the Vermont legislature allows them to keep full ownership of their property at the time of marriage; however, wives still require a husband's permission in order to transfer ownership of their property.

January

MILITARY: A battalion of 300 Mormons, recently recruited in Utah, arrives in California to bolster the American garrison but does not see any fighting.

January 3

MILITARY: General Winfield Scott, preparing for a major amphibious assault against Veracruz, Mexico, commandeers 9,000 soldiers from the army of General Zachary Taylor at Carmago in northern Mexico. Taylor, whose forces now consist of raw and unreliable volunteers, is then ordered to remain on the defensive at Monterrey.

January 8

MILITARY: A force of sailors, U.S. Marines, and U.S. Dragoons under Commodore Robert F. Stockton and General Stephen W. Kearny engage a larger Mexican force of infantry and lancers at San Gabriel, California. The Americans form a square and beat back repeated cavalry attacks, then advance up nearby heights and drive off the enemy infantry.

January 10

MILITARY: Newly promoted General Stephen W. Kearny captures Los Angeles from insurgents, ending active resistance to American rule.

January 13

DIPLOMACY: Mexican forces under Major Andreas Pico conclude the Treaty of Cahuenga with Colonel John C. Frémont, which formally brings fighting in California to an end. This concludes 25 years of Mexican rule and ushers in a period of American dominance.

January 14

MILITARY: General Zachary Taylor receives new instructions from the War Department ordering him to maintain defensive positions while 9,000 of his best soldiers are siphoned off for a forthcoming amphibious expedition. He correctly deduces that Democrat President James K. Polk is determined to deflect his political mettle as a Whig presidential candidate.

January 16

POLITICS: Commodore Robert F. Stockton, still believing that he enjoys civil authority in California, appoints Colonel John C. Frémont as governor. This sets both men on a collision course with General Stephen W. Kearny, who also has orders making him governor.

The House of Representatives passes a bill authorizing a territorial government for Oregon, which also excludes slavery.

January 18
EDUCATION: Fort Wayne Female College (Taylor University) is chartered at Fort Wayne, Indiana, by the Methodists.

January 19
MILITARY: Governor Charles Bent is killed at Taos, New Mexico, by insurgents.

January 22
POLITICS: General Zachary Taylor, a presidential aspirant, fears he is being unfavorably manipulated by President James K. Polk and criticizes the commander in chief in the *New York Morning Express*. Five days later he is reprimanded by Secretary of War William L. Marcy.

February 1
PUBLISHING: Noah Webster's *Speller* is the first title ever published in the Oregon Territory.

February 4
MILITARY: Missouri troops under Colonel Sterling Price recapture Taos, New Mexico, from Mexican rebels.

February 5
MILITARY: Defying the orders of both the government and General Winfield Scott, General Zachary Taylor marches west from Monterrey and toward Saltillo. His army then consists mostly of 5,000 raw volunteers stiffened by a handful of regular troops under General John E. Wool.

February 8
POLITICS: Supporters of President James K. Polk in the House of Representatives introduce a bill for $3 million for the possible acquisition of territory from Mexico. The final bill has a "Wilmot Proviso" outlawing slavery attached.

February 13
POLITICS: General Stephen W. Kearny receives orders to establish a government in Monterey, California, while Colonel John C. Frémont still considers himself governor at Los Angeles.

February 16
EDUCATION: The University of Louisiana (Tulane University) is founded as a state institution at New Orleans, Louisiana, and absorbs the Medical College of Louisiana.

February 18
MILITARY: At Tampico, Mexico, General Winfield Scott establishes a civil administration for occupied territory and leaves most political matters in the hands of local officials. This is the first such system practiced by the United States.

February 19
GENERAL: A relief expedition finally rescues the Donner party, stranded in the Sierra Nevada Mountains all winter. Accusations of cannibalism emerge.
SLAVERY: The Senate adopts the wartime appropriations bill—minus the Wilmot Proviso to exclude slavery from any territory acquired from Mexico. When the House subsequently approves the bill as written, the issue of slavery in the territo-

ries remains unaddressed. However, John C. Calhoun introduces four resolutions to protect slavery as an institution no matter where it may be instituted–unofficially negating the Missouri Compromise of 1820. Moreover, Calhoun insists that the government has no business making laws which deprive states of their rights under the Constitution. His argument subsequently serves as the basis for secession in 1861.

February 22–23

MILITARY: The Battle of Buena Vista is waged when 15,000 Mexican troops under General Antonio López de Santa Anna attack General Zachary Taylor's force of 5,000 men, strongly arrayed on good defensive terrain. The enemy, exhausted after a 250-mile march through the desert, makes several strong but uncoordinated attacks upon Taylor's lines and is beaten back piecemeal by the adroit tactics of General John E. Wool. A desperate charge by Colonel Jefferson Davis of the Mississippi Rifles also saves some American cannon from imminent capture. After two days of fighting, the demoralized Mexicans retreat to Mexico. This is Taylor's finest hour; he suffers 264 dead and 450 wounded to a Mexican toll estimated at 2,000.

February 25

EDUCATION: The State University of Iowa (University of Iowa) is chartered by the state's first general assembly; its first class graduates in 1858.

February 28

MILITARY: The expedition of Colonel Alexander W. Doniphan defeats a Mexican force at Rio Sacramento and then occupies the city of Chihuahua.

March 1

POLITICS: The Senate accepts the "Three Million Bill" for the war with Mexico, although it drops the Wilmot Proviso; this version then passes the House on a vote of 115 to 81.

March 3

BUSINESS: The first adhesive-style postage stamps are approved by Congress; previously postage was paid in cash upon receipt of the mail.
SETTLEMENT: The Senate tables the House version of the Oregon Bill, excluding slavery from the region.
TECHNOLOGY: Congress approves funding to provide gas lighting of the Capitol grounds.

March 9

MILITARY: The Battle of Veracruz unfolds when the army of General Winfield Scott, covered by American warships under Commodore David Conner, storms ashore at nearby Collado Beach with 10,000 men. Once a lodgement is secure, the American advance begins siege preparations to convince the large garrison of Castle San Juan de Ulua to surrender.

March 27

MILITARY: The fortified city of Veracruz under General Juan José Landero surrenders 3,000 troops to American forces under General Winfield Scott, who has sustained a loss of only 13 dead and 55 wounded. The city subsequently serves as a vital supply base throughout the ensuing drive against Mexico City.

1847

April
MILITARY: With Veracruz to their rear, General Winfield Scott's army of 9,000 men commence marching down the National Road toward Mexico City. The Americans depart hurriedly to beat the oncoming yellow fever season. Meanwhile General Antonio López de Santa Anna, desperate to save his capitol, musters every available soldier to stop the Americans.

April 15
DIPLOMACY: President James K. Polk appoints State Department veteran Nicholas P. Trist to negotiate a peaceful end to the Mexican War.

April 16
RELIGION: Brigham Young departs Council Bluffs on the Missouri River and marches with a small group of Mormons into the west, looking for a suitable place to settle.

April 17–18
MILITARY: General Winfield Scott wins the Battle of Cerro Gordo by attacking 14,000 Mexican soldiers under General Antonio López de Santa Anna. In a series of slashing maneuvers the Americans inflict 1,100 casualties and seize 3,000 prisoners and 40 cannon at a cost of 64 dead and 350 wounded. The advance upon Mexico City resumes in earnest.

April 19
MEDICAL: In Poughkeepsie, New York, James Smith invents and markets the first cough drops.

April 26
COMMUNICATIONS: Samuel F. B. Morse founds the Magnetic Telegraph Company to commence telegraph service between Baltimore and Washington, D.C.
POLITICS: The Mexican War is denounced as "wanton, unjust, and unconstitutional" by the Massachusetts legislature.

May 1
SCIENCE: Princeton Physicist Joseph Henry is appointed first director/secretary of the newly opened Smithsonian Institution in Washington, D.C.

May 7
MEDICAL: The American Medical Association is organized in Philadelphia, Pennsylvania, under Dr. Nathan Smith Davis.

May 31
POLITICS: General Stephen W. Kearny arrests Colonel John C. Frémont when he disobeys a direct order to step down as governor of California. Kearny then appoints Colonel Richard B. Mason to serve in his place before transporting the unruly Frémont back to Washington, D.C., to face a court martial.

June 6
DIPLOMACY: Nicholas P. Trist, chief clerk of the Department of State, begins peace negotiations with Mexico through British minister Charles Bankhead.

July 1
BUSINESS: The U.S. Post Office Department issues its first stamps in five- and ten-cent denominations with the likenesses of Benjamin Franklin and George Washington, respectively. These are also the first stamps to employ an adhesive backing.

1847

July 21–24

SETTLEMENT: Brigham Young and a small group of Mormon followers reach the Great Salt Lake in present-day Utah after an arduous trek from Council Bluffs, Iowa. The first wave consists of 143 men, three women, and two children. Young subsequently founds the state of Deseret with himself as governor.

July 26

TECHNOLOGY: A miniature electric train is built by Moses Gerrish of Dover, New Hampshire; this consists of two cars, one with the motor and batteries and one for passengers.

August 6

MILITARY: General Winfield Scott's army is reinforced at Puebla by troops under General Franklin Pierce. Thus augmented, the Americans launch their final drive against the Mexican capital.

August 19–20

MILITARY: The army of General Winfield Scott edges closer to Mexico City by defeating General Antonio López de Santa Anna at Contreras and Churubusco. The Mexican position was very strong and included Irish-American deserters of the San Patricio Battalion. A stiff fight ensues for the deserters realize that capture means execution by hanging, but at length the Americans force the Mexican position. Scott's losses are around 1,000 while Santa Anna sustains 3,000 killed and wounded. The advance upon Mexico City continues.

August 24

DIPLOMACY: Mexican and American armies observe the Armistice of Tacubaya while Nicholas P. Trist, chief clerk of the Department of State, engages Mexican officials in peace negotiations.

August 27

DIPLOMACY: Mexican and American emissaries begin peace negotiations but are slated for failure.

September

POLITICS: The Native American Party convenes in Philadelphia and nominates General Zachary Taylor for the presidency and Henry A. S. Dearborn of Massachusetts to become vice president.

September 6

DIPLOMACY: The Armistice of Tacubaya fails after Mexican officials reject American peace proposals, which included the ceding of all land north of the Rio Grande River.

September 8

MILITARY: The Battle of Molino del Rey unfolds as General Winfield Scott's 8,000 troops attack and carry strong Mexican positions manned by 10,000 soldiers with artillery and cavalry. The initial charge by General William J. Worth is bloodily repulsed, but the Americans regroup and gradually force the defenders back. General Antonio López de Santa Anna suffers more than 2,000 casualties and 685 captured while Scott suffers 117 dead, 653 wounded, and 18 missing. Among the first American officers to enter the captured town is Lieutenant Ulysses S. Grant.

1847

September 11
ARTS: The Thespian is the first theater to open in the Hawaiian Islands.

September 12–13
MILITARY: The Battle of Chapultepec is waged as 8,000 men under General Winfield Scott attack a like number of Mexicans directed by General Antonio López de Santa Anna. Among the defenders are 60 military cadets, many who lose their lives and are enshrined as national heroes. The American carry the city after stiff fighting and lose 450 men killed and wounded; Mexican losses are around 1,800.

September 14
MILITARY: The victorious army of General Winfield Scott occupies Mexico City after a brilliant campaign of maneuver. In England, the famous Duke of Wellington pronounces Scott "the greatest living soldier."

September 16
MILITARY: General Winfield Scott promulgates General Order No. 20, which establishes military rule through occupied Mexico. He eventually assesses Mexico $3 million to support the occupation.
POLITICS: General Antonio López de Santa Anna resigns as president of Mexico and makes preparations to leave the country. His tenure in that capacity has proven disastrous to the nation.

October 1
SCIENCE: In Nantucket, Massachusetts, Maria Mitchell, a librarian and amateur astronomer, discovers a new comet. She is subsequently rewarded by a gold medal from the king of Denmark and membership within the American Academy of Arts and Sciences.

November
POLITICS: Members of the abolitionist-minded Liberty Party convene in New York and nominate John P. Hale of New Hampshire for president and Leicester King of Ohio for vice president.

November 16
DIPLOMACY: Peace commissioner Nicholas P. Trist is ordered back to Washington, D.C.

November 19
GENERAL: Steamboats *Talisman* and *Tempest* collide on the Ohio River, killing 100 passengers.

November 22
DIPLOMACY: American envoy Nicholas P. Trist learns that the new government of Mexico under Manuel de la Pena is ready to negotiate peace terms. General Antonio López de Santa Anna has since been dismissed as head of Mexican forces and fled. He also ignores the order for his recall.
GENERAL: The steamship *Phoenix* catches fire and sinks on Lake Michigan, killing 200 Dutch immigrants.

November 26
MILITARY: General Zachary Taylor leaves northern Mexico for the United States.

1847

November 29
MILITARY: Marcus Whitman and 13 settlers are killed by Cayuse Indians at their mission in the Oregon Territory.

December 3
JOURNALISM: Former slave Frederick Douglass begins editing and publishing the abolitionist newspaper *North Star*.
MILITARY: General Zachary Taylor arrives at New Orleans to thunderous applause. Rumors also abound that the conquering hero intends to parley his national popularity into a political career.

December 5
RELIGION: Brigham Young is formally elected president of the Mormon Church at Winter Quarters, Nebraska. Young, who is savvy at both business and politics, proves a fortuitous choice to replace the murdered Joseph Smith.

December 6
POLITICS: An obscure frontier lawyer named Abraham Lincoln takes his seat in the U.S. House of Representatives.

December 12
DIPLOMACY: The government of New Granada (Colombia) agrees to a treaty with the United States to guarantee the neutrality of the Panamanian isthmus. Both sides are fearful that a European power might seize the isthmus for their own use and build a canal.

December 14
SLAVERY: The notion of "popular sovereignty," the ability of territorial legislatures to decide the question of slavery on their own, is introduced by Senator D. S. Dickinson of New York.

December 22
POLITICS: Abraham Lincoln, in his first address to the House of Representatives, denounces the outbreak and objectives of the Mexican War.

December 29
POLITICS: Presidential aspirant Lewis Cass of Michigan endorses the concept of "popular sovereignty" to allow territorial legislatures to decide whether or not to allow slavery. This approach allows skittish politicians to sidestep the emotional issue altogether.

1848

LABOR: The first Chinese laborers to reach America, three men, disembark at San Francisco, California.
SETTLEMENT: President James K. Polk offers to purchase Cuba from Spain for $100 million; he is politely refused.
SLAVERY: The Vermont legislature passes a resolution that calls for outlawing slavery in the new territories and abolishing it in Washington, D.C.
SOCIETAL: The Revolution of 1848 in Germany leads to a mass influx of German immigrants and political refugees into the United States.
WOMEN: In a major boost to women's rights, the New York legislature grants women equal property rights.

January 2
DIPLOMACY: Despite the fact that he has been ordered home, peace commissioner Nicholas P. Trist initiates peace negotiations with Mexican officials.

January 3
EDUCATION: Girard College is founded by financier Stephen Girard in Philadelphia, Pennsylvania, who stipulates that only white orphaned males may enroll there.

January 10
SLAVERY: Illinois Senator Stephen A. Douglas introduces a resolution forbidding the introduction of slavery into the Oregon Territory until such a time that the local legislature deems otherwise.

January 24
SETTLEMENT: James W. Marshall, then building a sawmill in the American River near Sutter's Fort, California, unearths a gold nugget. Word of his discovery triggers a wild stampede into the region by those seeking an easy fortune, better known as the "Gold Rush."

January 31
MILITARY: Colonel John C. Frémont is court-martialed for disobedience by General Stephen W. Kearny, found guilty, and cashiered from the military. President James K. Polk approves of the sentence but eventually restores him to duty. Upon further reflection, Frémont resigns his commission anyway to prospect for gold out West.

February 2
DIPLOMACY: American peace commissioner Nicholas P. Trist and Mexican officials conclude the Treaty of Guadalupe Hidalgo, ending the Mexican War. The Americans secure 500,000 square miles of new territory encompassing the new states of Texas, California, Arizona, New Mexico, Nevada, Utah, Wyoming, and Colorado. In return the Mexicans receive $15 million in compensation and an addition $3.2 million in damage claims. The burgeoning republic is now a transcontinental world power stretching from the Atlantic to the Pacific, although heated conflict over the issue of slavery accelerates.

February 15
ARTS: The play *A Glance at New York* by Benjamin Baker sets off a rage for theater productions depicting city life.

February 18
MILITARY: General Winfield Scott retires as commander of American forces in Mexico.

March 1
SOCIETAL: John Humphreys Noyes establishes a utopian farming community called "Perfectionist" in Oneida, New York.

March 10
DIPLOMACY: The Senate ratifies the Treaty of Guadalupe Hidalgo with a vote of 38 to 14 and also approves the wartime appropriations bill, minus the divisive Wilmot Proviso.
EDUCATION: Augustinian College (Villanova University) is chartered at Villanova, Pennsylvania, by the Augustinian Fathers.

1848

March 15
JOURNALISM: News of the discovery of gold in California first breaks in a San Francisco newspaper, but initially few readers actually notice.

March 23
POLITICS: Former president John Quincy Adams dies in the U.S. House of Representatives.

March 29
GENERAL: John Jacob Astor, one of America's first entrepreneurs, dies in New York at the age of 84. At this time he has a net worth of $20 million and is the nation's richest individual.

April
BUSINESS: The Pacific Mail Steamship Company is formed to handle the increased traffic in mail to the West Coast.

April 24
BUSINESS: The Chicago Board of Trade becomes the nation's first such institution to facilitate trade in agricultural products.

May
JOURNALISM: A group of six New York newspapers headed by Moses Beach agree to subsidize the cost of relaying foreign news by telegraph from Boston, the first port of call for most transatlantic vessels; this is the genesis of the Associated Press. Previously they had experimented with carrier pigeons to scoop competitors.

May 22–26
POLITICS: The Democrats' national convention convenes in Baltimore to select Lewis Cass of Michigan as their candidate for the presidency and William O. Butler of Kentucky for the vice presidency. The party platform militates against any attempt to debate the slavery question in Congress.

May 29
POLITICS: Wisconsin joins the Union as the 30th state; slavery is outlawed.

May 31
GENERAL: The papers of former president James Madison are purchased for the Library of Congress.

June 2
POLITICS: The abolitionist Liberty League gathers in Rochester, New York, to nominate Gerrit Smith of that state for the presidency and Charles E. Foot of Michigan for the vice presidency.

June 3
DIPLOMACY: The United States concludes a treaty with the Republic of New Granada whereby the United States gains right of way to cross the Isthmus of Panama in exchange for guaranteeing the region's neutrality.

June 7–9
POLITICS: The Whig Party convenes in Philadelphia to select General Zachary Taylor as its presidential candidate and Millard Fillmore of New York as vice president. Taylor's success in the recent Mexican conflict and his reputation as "Old Rough and Ready" makes him a genuine national hero.

1848

June 12
MILITARY: The American army ends its successful occupation of Mexico City.

June 13
POLITICS: Various labor organizations meet in Philadelphia and nominate Gerrit Smith of New York and William S. Waitt of Illinois to serve as candidates for president and vice president, respectively.

June 22
POLITICS: A group of progressive, antislavery former Democrats known as "Barnburners" convenes at Utica, New York, selecting Martin Van Buren for president and Henry Dodge of Wisconsin for vice president.

June 27
SLAVERY: When Indiana Senator John D. Bright issues an amendment to the Oregon Bill that extends the line drawn for the Missouri Compromise through to the Pacific, it is immediately opposed by John C. Calhoun of South Carolina. He insists that neither Congress nor territorial legislatures can deny the constitutional right to own slaves.

TECHNOLOGY: The first public use of air conditioning occurs at the Broadway Theater in New York City. This device, invented by J. E. Coffee, is powered by steam and pushes 3,000 feet of cool air per minute.

July 4
ARCHITECTURE: The cornerstone for the Washington Monument is laid in Washington, D.C.

July 18–19
WOMEN: Lucretia Mott and Elizabeth Cady Stanton organize the first women's rights convention at Wesleyan Methodist Church, Seneca Falls, New York. Resolutions are passed stipulating that women should enjoy equal rights, should be educated in the laws, and should be able to vote and speak in public without suffering indignities.

July 26
EDUCATION: The University of Wisconsin is chartered in Madison, Wisconsin, as a state institution; its first class graduates in 1854.

August 9
POLITICS: Diverse antislavery groups meeting in Buffalo, New York, form the new Free-Soil Party. They then nominate Martin Van Buren for the presidency with Charles Francis Adams of Massachusetts as vice president. As a group they are uniformly opposed to slavery or its expansion into new territory, and support internal improvements and free homesteads to settlers. Their slogan: "free soil, free speech, free labor, free men."

August 10
MILITARY: In New York, explosive bullets are patented by Walter Hunt.

August 14
POLITICS: A bill organizing the Oregon Territory—without slavery—is signed by President James K. Polk with the support of Southern legislators, apparently with the understanding that other regions may include the "peculiar institution."

Stanton, Elizabeth Cady (1815–1902)

Feminist leader

Elizabeth Cady was born in Johnstown, New York, on November 12, 1815, the daughter of a successful attorney and judge. Attentive as a child, she became distraught upon hearing her father repeatedly tell female clients that they had no rights to their own property or even their own children in the event of divorce. Early on she resolved to change this. Cady was well-educated by contemporary standards, having taught herself Greek and Latin, and subsequently attended Emma Willard's Female Seminary in Troy, New York. As she matured she became increasingly drawn into social causes such as temperance and abolitionism. In 1839 she married abolitionist leader Henry Stanton, but only after insisting he strike the word *obey* from the traditional wedding vows. The following year the couple visited the World Anti-Slavery Convention in London as delegates, and Stanton was furious when she was not allowed in on account of her gender. However, there she encountered the noted Quaker activist Lucretia Mott, and the two resolved to sponsor a convention for women's rights once they returned to the United States. Stanton, fully preoccupied with raising several children, was unable to orchestrate such a gathering until 1848, when it met in her hometown of Seneca, New York. Forceful and determined, she penned the "Declaration of Sentiments" calling for women's suffrage–the right to vote. This seminal event is considered the birth of American feminism which gathered greater momentum toward the end of the century. Stanton, an excellent writer and speaker, then lobbied New York legislators for reforms that would benefit women, and in 1860 women were granted guardianship of children and property in divorce cases.

The onset of the Civil War deepened Stanton's resolve to support abolition, although she decried President Abraham Lincoln as too accommodating toward slavery. Afterward she stridently insisted that the Fourteenth and Fifteenth Amendments to the U.S. Constitution, which extended freedom and voting rights to former African-American slaves, also be extended to women. Stanton, however, had underestimated resistance to female suffrage and equal rights, especially in light of the Reconstruction period's emphasis on black emancipation. Her unrelenting stance caused a split in the feminist movement with the more conservative-minded American Woman Suffrage Association declining

(continues)

Elizabeth Cady Stanton *(Library of Congress)*

(continued)

to uphold the principle of equal rights. Yet Stanton, strongly supported by her friend and associate Susan B. Anthony, insisted on both, and in 1869 they founded the more radical National Woman Suffrage Association. The ensuing schism split the feminist movement for more than two decades, and it was not until 1890 that the breech was mended. That year Stanton was elected president of the combined organizations, and she also found time to work on the Women's Bible, which was edited to remove all derogatory references to women. Stanton died in New York on October 26, 1902, one of the most talented female leaders of her generation.

August 19

JOURNALISM: The discovery of gold in California is first reported in the *New York Herald*, triggering a literal stampede to the West by hordes of ambitious fortune seekers.

August 24

GENERAL: More than 200 Americans die when the ship *Ocean Monarch* catches fire off Caernarvonshire, Wales.

September

SCIENCE: Science in the United States receives a major boost through founding of the American Association for the Advancement of Science, jointly sponsored by a group of American and Canadian scientists.

November 1

EDUCATION: Reformer Samuel Gregory opens the Boston Female Medical School as the nation's first medical institute for women; there are 12 students in the first class.

November 7

POLITICS: Whig candidate Zachary Taylor wins the presidential election with Millard Fillmore as his vice president, defeating their Democratic opposites Lewis Cass and William O. Butler. Taylor, though Southern-born and a slave owner himself, is not especially committed to the expansion of slavery into other areas. Furthermore, his quest has been facilitated by Free Soil candidate Martin Van Buren, who received 291,263 votes at the Democrats' expense. This is also the first election simultaneously held in every state.

December 5

SOCIETAL: President James K. Polk authenticates the recent discovery of gold deposits in California, which further fans the flames of western migration in search of easy gains.

December 15

DIPLOMACY: The United States and Great Britain conclude a postal treaty in London.

December 22

POLITICS: Southern congressmen caucus in Congress on the issue of slavery and how best to protect it as an institution.

1848

1849

ARTS: New York City hosts the Great Chinese Museum, depicting various aspects of everyday life in the Middle Kingdom.

BUSINESS: The American Horologe Company, the first factory to build watches in America, is founded in Roxbury, Massachusetts.

MEDICAL: In Geneva, New York, Elizabeth Blackwell becomes the first female college student to receive a degree in medicine anywhere in the world.

PUBLISHING: Henry David Thoreau publishes his essay "Civil Disobedience" to justify his refusal to pay taxes to support the Mexican War. He also advocates an activist citizenry to protest government misbehavior.

TRANSPORTATION: The Pacific Railroad, intending to link St. Louis to Kansas City, is chartered.

Stagecoach service commences between Independence, Missouri, and Santa Fe, New Mexico.

January

POLITICS: A gathering of 69 Southern congressmen meets again in Washington, D.C., to discuss their grievances against the North and plan strategy.

PUBLISHING: The *Lily*, the first women's rights journal, is published under the aegis of Amelia Bloomer. She also pioneers a loose set of clothing known as "Bloomers" to promote better health and movement, but they fail to catch on.

January 22

POLITICS: John C. Calhoun pens the "Address of Southern Delegates," signed by 47 Southerners, which rails against Northern transgressions against the South with respect to the preservation of slavery.

February 7

LAW: The Supreme Court disallows New York and Massachusetts from levying a tax upon newly entered aliens.

SPORTS: Tom Hyer, the de facto American heavyweight boxing champion, defeats Englishman Yankee Sullivan by knocking him out. He then retires from the ring undefeated for want of a challenger.

February 13

EDUCATION: Otterbein University is chartered in Westerville, Ohio, by the United Brethren; its first class graduates in 1857.

February 27

EDUCATION: William Jewel College is chartered in Liberty, Missouri, by the Baptists; its first class graduates in 1855.

February 28

SOCIETAL: The vessel *California* drops anchor in San Francisco harbor, and the first wave of gold seekers clambers ashore. Others arrive from China and Australia, and by years's end they are joined by 100,000 like-minded fortune hunters.

March 3

BUSINESS: Congress authorizes issuance of the gold dollar and the $20 Double Eagle coin.

POLITICS: The Home Department is established by Congress for the purpose of establishing Indian policy, sale of public land, and assisting those who wish

This 1849 print, *The Way They Go to California*, lampoons the rush to California by gold seekers, many of whom went to outlandish lengths to get there and stake a claim before the next person. *(Library of Congress)*

to develop their holdings out West. It eventually becomes known as the U. S. Department of the Interior.

March 4
SETTLEMENT: An act establishing the Minnesota Territory is signed by President James K. Polk.

March 5
POLITICS: Zachary Taylor is inaugurated as the second and final Whig president; Millard Fillmore is sworn in as vice president.

March 10
SLAVERY: The Missouri legislature votes in favor of "popular sovereignty" to decide the issue of slavery in the new territories.

April 12
BUSINESS: The first mail service from the Atlantic, overland across Panama, and then up the Pacific coast is achieved.

May 10
ARTS: A riot ensues at the Astor Place Opera House in New York when British actor George Macready impugns his American audience for rudeness; 22 people die and 36 are wounded before the militia restores order.

May 17
GENERAL: More than 400 buildings and 27 steamships are destroyed or damaged by a fire in St. Louis, Missouri.

1849

Taylor, Zachary   (1784–1850)
Soldier, president

Zachary Taylor was born in Montebello, Virginia, on November 24, 1784, son of an army officer. He was raised on a plantation in Kentucky, joined the army in 1808, and distinguished himself in the War of 1812 at Fort Harrison and other occasions. He resigned briefly in 1815 but won reappointment through President James Madison and served the next 21 years on the western frontier. In 1832 Taylor fought as a colonel in the Black Hawk War and five years later marched to Florida to fight against the Seminole. On December 25, 1837, he soundly defeated them at Okeechobee Swamp, winning promotion to brigadier general. By this time he had also acquired the colorful but appropriate nickname of "Old Rough and Ready." In 1846 President James K. Polk ordered Taylor's army to occupy part of Texas in anticipation of war with Mexico, and in 1846 he defeated Mexican armies in three successive battles at Palo Alto, Resaca de la Palma, and Monterrey. Taylor suspected that Polk and other Democrats were trying to derail his political ambitions when they stripped his army of soldiers for a new invasion by General Winfield Scott. Taylor then disregarded orders to remain on the defensive, advanced southward, and defeated a Mexican force four times his size at Buena Vista in February 1847. This victory made him a national hero and he began receiving serious consideration as a potential Whig candidate in the upcoming presidential election. Taylor, a slave-owning nationalist, had never voted in a presidential election before and knew relatively little about politics, yet was viewed as potentially attractive to voters in both the North and South. The party convention that year confirmed this belief when he edged out better known contenders such as Henry Clay, Daniel Webster, and Winfield Scott to win the nomination.

Fortunately for Taylor and the Whigs, the Democratic opposition had split into two warring factions with party regulars backing Lewis Cass while dissidents favored Martin Van Buren of the Free Soil Party. This feud allowed Taylor to win the essential state of New York and, with it, the White House. The garrulous old general was somewhat tactless in office and determined to remain aloof from partisanship and above politics. However, the nation was being riven by the prospect of extending slavery into territories acquired from Mexico. Taylor, Southern himself and a slave owner, firmly opposed this and wished to allow California into the Union as a free state. Fellow Southerners dissented for it would upset the delicate balance

(continues)

Zachary Taylor *(Library of Congress)*

(continued)

of power between free and slave states in the Senate, but whenever they mentioned secession Taylor threatened to hang anyone attempting it. He only reluctantly agreed to the "Compromise of 1850" allowing territorial legislatures to decide if they were to permit slavery or not. His administration also oversaw the Clayton-Bulwer Treaty with Great Britain, for joint control of any canal built in Panama. Taylor died suddenly of illness in office on July 9, 1850, before his effectiveness was fully established.

June 15

GENERAL: Former president James K. Polk dies suddenly in Nashville, Tennessee.

July

SLAVERY: Harriet Tubman escapes from slavery in Maryland and becomes an active member of the slowly forming "underground railroad."

August 11

POLITICS: President Zachary Taylor forbids American citizens from participating in armed incursions, or filibusters, against Cuba.

September 1–October 13

SETTLEMENT: A constitutional convention meets at Monterey, California, at the behest of General Bennett Riley, and an antislavery provision is adopted.

November 4

MEDICAL: Elizabeth Blackwell, who is blind in one eye, becomes the first female graduate of Geneva College, New York, with a medical degree.

November 13

POLITICS: A new constitution is approved by a constitutional convention in Monterey, California, and a formal application for statehood is made.

November 14

ENGINEERING: The world's longest suspension bridge opens for traffic across the Ohio River at Wheeling (West Virginia), Virginia.

November 22

EDUCATION: Austin College is chartered in Huntsville, Texas, by the Presbyterians; its first class graduates in 1850.

December 4

POLITICS: President Zachary Taylor asks Congress to allow California in as a new state. However, Southerners are riled at the prospect of creating another free state which will leave them in the minority. When Senator John C. Calhoun begins floating the idea of secession, Taylor warns any such attempt will be crushed even if he has to command troops in person.

December 22

POLITICS: As a sign of growing regionalism and partisan division, Georgian Howell Cobb is finally voted speaker of the House of Representatives after three weeks of turmoil and 63 ballots.

1849

December 20
DIPLOMACY: The United States and the kingdom of Hawaii conclude a treaty of friendship, navigation, and trade.

1850

AGRICULTURE: In an attempt to control caterpillars, New York City imports eight pairs of English sparrows which prove highly successful.

ARTS: Emanuel Leutze, an American expatriate artist living in Germany, renders his famous painting, "Washington Crossing the Delaware." It is currently displayed on the wall of the west staircase in the U.S. House of Representatives.

BUSINESS: At mid-century, the textile industry is the first manufacturing sector to achieve relatively large scale, nationally. The North boasts 564 factories, principally in New England, while the South possesses 166. Moreover, the Northern establishments rely heavily upon a mostly female workforce.

JOURNALISM: The *Weekly Oregonian* (Portland) and the *Deseret News* (Salt Lake City) are the first newspapers published in the far west.

LITERATURE: Nathaniel Hawthorne publishes *The Scarlet Letter*, and it becomes an immediate best seller for touching upon the long suppressed subject of adultery. More than 4,000 copies sell in the first 10 days.

Herman Melville publishes *White-Jacket*, which graphically describes the harsh treatment endured by sailors onboard U.S. warships.

MUSIC: American composer and pianist Louis Moreau Gottschalk tours France and Switzerland with positive reviews.

POLITICS: Tammany Hall, long a force in New York City politics, reaches new heights of influence under the aegis of Fernando Wood. He institutes charitable services for poor immigrants who then support this growing political machine.

POPULATION: The new census reveals a population of 23.2 million residents.

PUBLISHING: *Harper's Monthly Magazine* begins publishing in New York City, intending to bring condensed versions of great literary masterpieces to its American readership.

Photographer Mathew Brady breaks new artistic ground by publishing his compilation *Illustrious Americans*.

SOCIETAL: Anti-Catholic biases manifest in the newly founded Supreme Order of the Star Spangled Banner, which subsequently serves as a progenitor of the anti-immigrant Know-Nothing Party.

TECHNOLOGY: John E. Heath invents the first agricultural binder for tying grain.

TRANSPORTATION: The first federal land grant specifically granted for railroad construction is awarded to a proposed line running from Chicago, Illinois, to Mobile, Alabama.

The American clipper ship *Stag Hound*, designed by noted shipwright Donald McKay, sets a speed record of 13 days from Boston to the equator. McKay goes on to build some of the fastest vessels of his age.

January 2
DIPLOMACY: The United States concludes its first commercial treaty with El Salvador.

January 29
POLITICS: Henry Clay, still striving to preserve the Union from secession and armed conflict, returns to the Senate after a seven-year hiatus. He then issues a

McKay, Donald (1810–1880)
Shipwright

Donald McKay was born in Nova Scotia, Canada, on September 4, 1810, the son of farmers. In 1827 he relocated to study the art of shipbuilding in New York and worked as an apprentice shipwright at the firm of Isaac Webb. His good performance attracted the attention of another shipbuilder, William Currier, who induced McKay to move to Wiscasset, Maine, and Newburyport, Massachusetts, and ply his trade. He did so in 1841 and proved so successful that he was able to form a partnership with William Pickett to construct packet ships. His designs proved both beautiful and functional, so in 1845 he was invited by noted merchant Enoch Train to move again to East Boston and construct vessels for his forthcoming Boston-to-Liverpool packet line. Bewteen 1845 and 1853 McKay designed and constructed no less than 49 packet ships for Train and other maritime concerns. His ships universally won plaudits for their handsome lines, rugged construction, and speeds that were usually higher than rival designs. However, the discovery of gold in California and Australia, combined with the opening of new markets in Japan and China, required a new class of vessels that were both larger and faster than the contemporary packets. This new emphasis on speed gave rise to an entirely new school of design, the magnificent clipper ship, which would dominate seaborne commerce for several decades.

In time McKay proved himself to be the world's greatest designer of clippers. He constructed his first vessel, the *Stag Hound*, in 1850, and it was a radical departure from commercial vessels extant. Long, low, with raking lines, it sported very tall masts and very wide canvass sails by contemporary standards. *Stag Hound* was thus not only larger than its competitors but also much faster even when fully loaded. McKay's most famous design, the *Flying Cloud*, was another beautiful example of the shipwright's art. Huge at 1,800 tons, it was nonetheless the fastest clipper ever built and established a world speed record of only 89 days between New York, around Cape Horn, and thence to San Francisco. His follow-on design, *Sovereign of the Seas*, was not as speedy but much larger at 2,421 tons and mounting masts 93 feet high that carried 12,000 square feet of canvas. McKay's masterpiece, the *Great Republic*, was larger still, displacing 4,500 tons and boasting four huge masts. However, this vessel caught fire and burned while under construction and McKay incurred great financial loss. The emergence of new steamships meant that the heyday of clipper ships had ended, and he visited England in order to study steam propulsion. There he became convinced of the superiority of ironclad, steam driven warships and came home to construct several for the U.S. Navy during the Civil War. McKay died at Hamilton, Massachusetts, on September 20, 1880, having constructed some of the most lovely, legendary vessels in maritime history. The last sailing ship he constructed, *Glory of the Seas*, remained in active service until 1923.

series of resolutions known as the Compromise of 1850. Through them California is admitted into the Union as a free state, based on the free will of the population, although with the understanding that all territory acquired from Mexico is subject to the same conditions.

1850

February 5–6
POLITICS: Deliberation intensifies over Henry Clay's proposed Compromise of 1850, with an ailing John C. Calhoun insisting that the North "cease agitation of the slavery question." Clay, meanwhile, warns the South not to seek secession as a solution to their problems.

February 22
GENERAL: The Library of Congress purchases the manuscript of George Washington's Farewell Address.

March 4
POLITICS: In his final appearance in the U.S. Senate, ailing John C. Calhoun is too weak to read an address so it is presented by a colleague. In it he attacks Henry Clay's recent compromise for failing to provide the South with guarantees.
SOCIETAL: The home of Wisconsin politician John B. Smith is destroyed by a mob angered by his legislation taxing whiskey and beer.

March 7
POLITICS: Daniel Webster, a longtime opponent of Clay and a strident opponent of slavery, agrees that to preserve the Union, Northerners must accept that "peculiar institution" for the time being. This causes a decided downturn in his popularity and occasions some righteous indignation from noted poet John Greenleaf Whittier.

March 11
EDUCATION: The Women's Medical College of Pennsylvania, the first such institution designated for females, is incorporated in Philadelphia.

March 12
POLITICS: California formally applies for statehood.

March 31
POLITICS: John C. Calhoun, the "Cast Iron Man" of South Carolina and a formidable spokesman-philosopher of the South, dies at 69.

April 19
DIPLOMACY: The United States and Great Britain conclude the Clayton-Bulwer Treaty, pledging that any canal across Panama will be neutral, no attempt will be made to control Central American countries, and both countries are sworn to help defend it.

April 27
TRANSPORTATION: The Collins Line, an American concern, embarks on head-to-head competition with the famous British Cunard Line with the launching of its new steamship liner *Atlantic*.

May 8
POLITICS: After much haggling, Henry Clay's Compromise of 1850 becomes two compromise bills; the first covers the territories while the second outlaws the slave trade in the District of Columbia.

May 25
SETTLEMENT: The inhabitants of New Mexico begin forming their own state government, which does not include provisions for slavery, despite Congressional nonaction.

1850

June 3

INDIAN: Settlers in Oregon hang five Cayuse Indians accused of perpetrating the massacre of the Whitman party; this is the first use of capital punishment in the territory.

June 3–12

SLAVERY: Southern leaders convene in Nashville, Tennessee, for a conference on slavery and state's rights. Secession is openly advocated by some delegates, but in the end the moderates prevail and only modest resolutions are passed. Among them is the suggestion that slavery be continued as far as the Pacific along lines established by the Missouri Compromise.

June 17

GENERAL: The steamship *Griffith* catches fire on Lake Erie, killing 300 passengers.

July 1

BUSINESS: Monthly overland mail service is initiated between Independence, Missouri, and Salt Lake City, Utah.

July 8

RELIGION: The Mormon colony on Beaver Island, Lake Michigan, crowns James Jesse Starng as its king; continuing tension with mainlanders in 1856 leads to the colony's disbandment.

SETTLEMENT: To date 42,300 immigrants have passed through Fort Laramie, Wyoming, en route to California in search of easy fortune.

July 9–10

GENERAL: President Zachary Taylor dies of cholera and is succeeded by Millard Fillmore.

July 25

SETTLEMENT: The discovery of gold along the Rogue River, Oregon, provides impetus to a new wave of fortune seekers.

May 22

EXPLORING: Lieutenant Edwin Jesse De Haven takes the ships *Advancer* and *Rescue* from New York on an Arctic expedition to locate the lost British explorer Sir John Franklin, missing since 1845. The effort is underwritten by Henry Grinnell, a wealthy New York merchant and philanthropist.

August 21

TRANSPORTATION: The Collin Line transport steamer *Atlantic* sets a new transatlantic record by reaching Liverpool in only 10 days, four and a half hours.

September

POLITICS: A Whig convention held at Syracuse, New York, is divided over the Compromise of 1850, which leads Francis Granger and his conservative element to gradually take control.

September 6–17

POLITICS: Congress passes five bills largely inspired by Henry Clay's Compromise of 1850; California gains admittance as a free state, slavery in Utah and New Mexico remains unrestricted, Texas is reimbursed $10 million for land lost to New Mexico, the slave trade is abolished in the District of Columbia, and a strengthened Fugitive Slave Act is adopted. All five bills are signed into law by

Fillmore, Millard (1800–1874)
President

Millard Fillmore was born in Cayuga, New York, on January 7, 1800, the son of impoverished farmers. While helping on the family farm he studied law and was admitted to the state bar in 1823. In this capacity Fillmore befriended influential editor Thurlow Weed and joined the Anti-Masonic Party in 1828, gaining election to the state legislature. His most notable accomplishment there was abolition of imprisonment for debt. In 1833 Fillmore was elected to the first of three terms in the U.S. House of Representatives, where he served intermittently until 1843. He also left the Anti-Masonic Party and joined the new Whigs to counter the policies of President Andrew Jackson. In this capacity he became a close ally of Speaker Henry Clay, although in 1844 Fillmore lost the presidential party nomination along with a race for the New York governorship. Undaunted, he employed Clay's support to become the Whig vice-presidential candidate with Zachary Taylor in the victorious 1848 election. The following spring he was sworn into office and, while largely marginalized by Taylor, made clear his opposition to Taylor's rigid stance against extending slavery into the territories. However, further disagreement between the two leaders ended following Taylor's death in office on July 9, 1850, and Fillmore took his oath as the 13th president. Thus situated, he broke ranks with the radical abolitionist Whigs such as Weed and New York Senator William H. Seward and joined forces with moderates such as Daniel Webster, whom he appointed secretary of state.

The Fillmore administration was a marked departure in policy from that of his predecessor, James K. Polk. Whereas Polk was strongly expansionist, Fillmore sought to avoid conflict and placed a premium on cooperation and preservation of the Union. To this end he readily agreed to sign Clay's Omnibus Bill—the "Compromise of 1850"—which included the notorious Fugitive Slave Act. For this he was roundly condemned by Whigs and Northerners, but his strong enforcement placated Southerners at a critical juncture of national history. Fillmore, while he did not approve of slavery, felt it was a necessary evil and had to be enforced to gain Southern compliance on other pressing issues. Perhaps his most significant accomplishment was the dispatching of a naval squadron under Commodore Matthew C. Perry in 1854 which opened up the cloistered government of Japan for the first time in nearly 300 years. However, Fillmore's decision to strongly

(continues)

Millard Fillmore (*Library of Congress*)

1850

(continued)

enforce the Fugitive Slave Act created anger in the North and cost him the party nomination in 1856. He therefore ran for re-election with the nativist Know-Nothing Party, appealed for national unity, and finished third behind James Buchanan and John C. Frémont. Fillmore then returned to Buffalo, New York, where he helped found the University of Buffalo, an academy of arts, and a historical society. He died there on March 8, 1874, still defending his attempts to keep the country intact despite the row over slavery.

President Millard Fillmore. The Fugitive Slave Act , in particular, rapidly escalates the bitterness and acrimony between slave owners and abolitionists.

September 12
ARTS: In a major coup for promoter P. T. Barnum, noted soprano Jenny Lind, the "Swedish Nightingale," successfully debuts at the Castle Garden in New York City. Barnum is charging up to $1,000 for tickets and has booked Lind for 150 sold-out shows.

September 20
TRANSPORTATION: Senator Stephen A. Douglas successfully lobbies for a federal land grant to build a rail line from Chicago, Illinois, to Mobile, Alabama. This is the first land grant of its kind.

September 27
ARTS: Edwin Booth, a great American actor of the 19th century, debuts in New York at the age of 16; his brother John Wilkes Booth, gains notoriety as President Abraham Lincoln's assassin.

September 28
NAVAL: Flogging is banned from the U.S. Navy and merchant marine as a form of punishment. However, corporal punishment is still routinely administered in schools to keep students in line.
POLITICS: President Millard Fillmore appoints Mormon leader Brigham Young to serve as territorial governor of Utah.

October 21
SLAVERY: In Chicago, Illinois, a city council refuses to endorse the new Fugitive Slave Act.

October 23–24
WOMEN: The first national women's rights convention is held in Worcester, Massachusetts (the first women's convention of any kind was held at Seneca Falls, New York, in 1848). More than 1,000 delegates from 11 states are in attendance, and they approve plans to create political and educational committees.

November 11–18
POLITICS: Southern politicians meet again in Nashville, Tennessee, where secession from the Union is openly discussed. However, moderate states like Georgia seek to remain in the Union provided the recent compromise is not violated.

1850

December 13–14

POLITICS: A Georgia state convention declares its willingness to remain in the Union but will, in fact, secede if Northern states do not honor the Compromise of 1850.

December 21

DIPLOMACY: Chargé d'affaires Chevalier Hulseman writes a letter to Secretary of State Daniel Webster protesting American aid being sent to rebels in Hungary during the 1848 uprising against Austria and Russia. Webster responds that the United States has a vested interest in European revolutions, particularly those invoking the same principles upon which America was founded.

1851

ARCHITECTURE: Designer Thomas W. Walter is commissioned to enlarge the U.S. Capitol in Washington, D.C., and he adds new wings in the Greek revival style, even through it has run its course and is considered passé.

JOURNALISM: Horace Greeley publishes Karl Marx's *Revolution and Counter Revolution* as a serial in the New York *Tribune*.

John B. L. Soule, editor of the *Terre Haute Express*, prints an editorial entitled "Go West Young Man." When Horace Greeley, editor of the *New York Tribune*, prints the column in full, he becomes indelibly associated with the slogan. However, as he always insisted, it originated with Soule.

LITERATURE: Herman Melville publishes his novel *Moby-Dick*, a quintessential American masterpiece relating the struggle of man against nature, good against evil. It remains one of literature's greatest accomplishments. However, it is little understood by contemporaries and fares badly at the hands of reviewers.

Nathaniel Hawthorne publishes *The House of Seven Gables*, which centers around a curse leveled against a house during the Salem witch trials.

MUSIC: Stephen Foster's catchy song "Old Folks at Home" (Swanee River) becomes a sentimental favorite in America and Europe.

POLITICS: Sixty American delegates attend a European peace conference in London.

American concert pianist Louis Moreau Gottschalk tours Spain giving performances and is favorably received.

PUBLISHING: Historian Francis Parkman publishes the first installment of his epic work on the French and Indian War, *The Conspiracy of Pontiac*.

RELIGION: The Young Men's Christian Association (YMCA) is founded in Cleveland, Ohio, the outgrowth of informal Bible meetings by groups of young men.

SLAVERY: The Supreme Court decides the case of *Strader v. Graham*, ruling that slaves returning to Kentucky via Ohio are still subject to Kentucky laws.

Abolitionist Frederick Douglass splits with William Lloyd Garrison over the strategy to deal with slavery; Douglass wants to preserve the Union and end slavery directly while Garrison wishes to dissolve the Union and have free states distance themselves from slave-owning ones.

SOCIETAL: The Asylum for Friendless Boys is founded in New York to provide care for abused, neglected, or exploited children; this is the first serious challenge to a father's supremacy in determining child welfare.

The ongoing potato famine leads to a record 250,000 Irish immigrants to America.

Greeley, Horace (1811–1872)
Journalist

Horace Greeley was born in Amherst, New Hampshire, on February 3, 1811, into a poor household. His education proved scanty, but early on he developed what became a lifelong passion for journalism and in 1826 Greeley served as an printer's apprentice. He relocated to New York City in 1831 seeking full-time work, functioned capably as a journalist, and by 1834 was able to found his own publication, the *New York*. He also became politically active and in 1838 began contributing essays and editorials to the *Daily Whig*. Greeley acquired the reputation as an effective, opinionated, and hard-hitting editor, so in 1840 Thurlow Weed appointed him editor in chief of the *Log Cabin*, a successful political newspaper that did much to promote the presidential campaign of William Henry Harrison. A year later Greeley founded his most important paper, the *New York Tribune*, with himself as editor in chief. In it he filled the pages with a zeal for social, moral, and political reform on a variety of contemporary issues. Foremost among these was abolition, for which he excoriated North and South alike for their complicity in perpetuating what he considered pure evil. Greeley, however, proved not so selective in the stances he championed, and he invariably allowed free space for the socialist-oriented Fourierists and even regularly corresponded with German revolutionary Karl Marx. Nonetheless, the *New York Tribune* set new and high standards for journalism, principally through such talented writers as Charles A. Dana and woman's suffrage champion Margaret Fuller.

With the approach of the Civil War, Greeley waxed highly indignant over political expedients such as the Compromise of 1850 and the Kansas-Nebraska Act of 1854. He also championed the free soil movement along the frontier, and his slogan "Go West young man" epitomized his belief in the democraticizing opportunities of that region. In 1854 Greeley finally broke with the dying Whigs and was a charter member of the new Republican Party with their uncompromising stand against slavery. However, Greeley proved lukewarm in his endorsement of Abraham Lincoln for president, owing to the latter's intention to restrict slavery, not end it, and in 1864 he only supported the president's reelection at the last minute. That year he also conducted a one-man peace mission to the Confederate capital in an attempt to reach a negotiated settlement. Greeley's postwar stances on a variety of issues also proved controversial and cost him many readers. In 1867 he sought to promote national reconciliation by signing a bail bond for imprisoned Confederate president Jefferson Davis and he also advocated a full civil rights agenda for newly freed African Americans. In 1872 he also ran for the presidency as a Democrat and was soundly trounced by Ulysses S. Grant. Greeley died at Pleasantville, New York, on November 29, 1872, the most effective journalist and newspaper editor of his generation.

TECHNOLOGY: Dr. William P. Channing and Moses Gerrish install the first American electric fire alarm in Boston

January 23
SETTLEMENT: The name Portland, Oregon, is chosen for a newly incorporated city on the basis of a coin toss; the other contending name was Boston.

1851

January 28

EDUCATION: North Western University (Northwestern University) is chartered in Evanston, Illinois, by the Methodists; the first class enters in 1855.

January 29

EDUCATION: Brockway College (modern Ripon College) is chartered in Ripon, Wisconsin, by Congregationalists and Presbyterians; the first class graduates in 1867.

February 1

DIPLOMACY: France drops demands that the Hawaiian Islands pay homage to France once the latter submits to American protection.

February 13

EDUCATION: The University of Minnesota is chartered by the territorial legislature, but classes will not commence until 1869.

Heidelberg College is chartered in Tiffin, Ohio, by the German Reformed Church; the first class graduates in 1854.

February 15

SLAVERY: A mob of angry African Americans rescues Shadrack, an escaped slave, from a Boston jail in defiance of the new Fugitive Slave Act. The new law is the source of much bitterness in the North and widens the growing rift with the South.

February 18

EDUCATION: Westminister College is chartered in Fulton, Missouri, by Presbyterians; its first class graduates in 1855.

SLAVERY: President Millard Fillmore cautions citizens of the North to obey the new Fugitive Slave Law, even though emotions and resistance are running high.

March 3

BUSINESS: Congress drops the postage rates to three cents for a half-ounce carried up to 300 miles.

The coining of three-cent silver pieces is authorized by Congress.

March 25

EXPLORING: Major James Savage, while pursing a band of renegade Indians, stumbles onto the Yosemite Valley, California.

April 25

POLITICS: President Millard Fillmore, angered by the presence of Southerners in armed filibusters against Spanish-held Cuba, speaks of "palpable violations" of American neutrality and warns citizens to not to participate.

May 3

GENERAL: San Francisco suffers from a major fire which consumes 2,500 buildings and inflicts damage estimated at $12 million.

PUBLISHING: *Gleason's Pictorial Drawing Room Companion*, the nation's first illustrated weekly, debuts in New York City.

May 6

TECHNOLOGY: Dr. John Gorrie receives a patent for one of the earliest ice-making machines, although he dies of exhaustion four years later while attempting to raise money to manufacture it. The device is originally intended to cool the rooms for patients suffering from fever.

1851

May 15
TRANSPORTATION: The Erie Railroad, connecting Pierpont and Dunkirk, New York, opens for business. It is 483 miles long, making it the world's longest railroad line.

May 19
TRANSPORTATION: In a significant milestone, the first train to complete all 483 miles of the Erie Railroad stops at Dunkirk, New York, from New York City. This signifies that New York and the Great Lakes are linked by rail.

May 29
WOMEN: The second Women's Rights Convention convenes at Akron, Ohio; delegates are entranced by the tall, gaunt figure of Sojourner Truth, who is a charismatic speaker.

June 2
SOCIETAL: The Maine legislature forbids the manufacture and sale of alcoholic liquors throughout the state.

June 3
SPORTS: The New York Knickerbockers become the first baseball team in history to wear uniforms, in this instance, straw hats, white shirts, and blue trousers.

June 5
JOURNALISM: In Washington, D.C., Harriet Beecher Stowe's antislavery story *Uncle Tom's Cabin* begins as a serial in the abolitionist paper *National Era*.

June 9
LAW: A crime wave hits burgeoning San Francisco, California, so leading citizens encourage fellow citizens to band together and enforce the laws—by force.

July 10
EDUCATION: California Wesleyan College (The College of the Pacific) is chartered in Santa Clara, California, by the Methodists; its first class graduates in 1858.

July 23
INDIAN: The United States and the Sioux nation conclude the Treaty of Traverse des Sioux, whereby the tribe surrenders all land in Iowa and most of the holdings in Minnesota.

August 11–12
MILITARY: Cuban refugee Narciso López leads a force of American filibusters to commence a revolt against the island's Spanish rulers. This is in direct violation of President Millard Fillmore's declaration against such activities.

August 12
TECHNOLOGY: Isaac Merritt Singer receives a patent for his revolutionary sewing machine, which employs a continuous stitching action. He is then promptly sued by Elias Howe, who earlier produced a similar device.

August 16
MILITARY: Spanish authorities capture and execute 51 American filibusters found assisting Cuban rebels; a further 80 are imprisoned until Congress agrees to pay Spain $80,000 for their release.

August 21
POLITICS: Riots break out in New Orleans and the Spanish consulate is sacked after word of the execution of 51 Southern filibusters arrives.

1851

August 22

SPORTS: The United States yacht *America* under Commodore John C. Stevens defeats 14 British competitors and wins a prestigious race sponsored by the Royal Yacht Club of England. Such racing prowess confirms a growing national reputation for designing and constructing world-class vessels. The trophy, taken back to the United States, becomes known as the America's Cup and is successfully defended until the Australians take it in 1984.

August 31

TRANSPORTATION: Donald McKay's beautiful 225-foot clipper ship, *Flying Cloud,* sets a record sailing from New York to San Francisco in 89 days and eight hours; the record for this class of vessel is never bettered.

September 18

JOURNALISM: The *New York Daily Times* (*New York Times* after 1857) debuts in New York City with Henry Jarvis Raymond as its editor.

October 8

TRANSPORTATION: The Hudson Railroad, connecting New York City with Albany, formally opens.

October 22

POLITICS: For a third time, President Millard Fillmore warns fellow Americans not to become embroiled in filibustering expeditions, in this instance against Mexico.

December

LAW: The U.S. Supreme Court decides *Cooley v. Board of Wardens of the Port of Philadelphia,* ruling that states may regulate their own local commerce.

December 1

POLITICS: Unionist candidates, buoyed by the compromise of 1850, win several Congressional seats in Mississippi, Alabama, and South Carolina. The South is not yet ready for secession, but radical abolitionists score a coup with the selection of Senator Charles Sumner of Massachusetts.

December 5

GENERAL: Failed Hungarian revolutionary Louis Kossuth arrives in New York City, receiving tumultuous applause.

December 16

TECHNOLOGY: Hiram Hayden of Waterbury, Connecticut, receives a patent for a process designed to shape brass bowls.

December 24

GENERAL: A huge fire guts the Library of Congress, destroying two-thirds of its collection of 35,000 volumes, including many volumes sold by Thomas Jefferson in 1815.

December 29

ARTS: In New York City, notorious Irish beauty and adventurer Lola Montez (Marie Gilbert) wows an American audience in the play *Betley, the Tyrolean.*

1852

EDUCATION: The Massachusetts legislature passes the nation's first compulsory school attendance law; students between eight and 14 are required to attend at least 12 weeks of school per year. Many of the bill's supporters also oppose children laboring in the textile mills.

JOURNALISM: A new western newspaper, the *Missouri Democrat*, is founded and calls for the abolition of slavery.

LABOR: The National Typographical Union is founded in Cincinnati, Ohio.

PUBLISHING: *Godey's Lady's Book* under Sarah Josepha Hale begins publishing articles about women in the workforce, especially in the heretofore male-dominated world of business and industry.

SLAVERY: To counter a rising tide of abolitionist literature, pro-slavery advocates publish *The Pro Slavery Argument* in defense of their position.

SOCIETAL: Massachusetts, Vermont, and Louisiana, expressing alarm over alcoholic consumption, pass prohibition ordinances.

TECHNOLOGY: Alexander Bonner Latta designs and constructs the first truly effective steam fire engine for the fire department in Cincinnati, Ohio. Its highly efficient boiler can shoot as many as six jets of water.

TRANSPORTATION: The Pennsylvania Railroad is completed, linking Pittsburgh and Philadelphia by rail. However, it employs a different track gauge from the competing Erie Railroad of New York to prevent its expansion through Pennsylvania to Ohio.

January

DIPLOMACY: President Millard Fillmore agrees to dispatch Commodore Matthew C. Perry and a squadron of modern warships to the closed nation of Japan to open diplomatic relations. This is no mean feat as the ruling Tokugawa shogunate has sealed Japan off from the world since the 17th century.

POLITICS: A new Democratic splinter group, "Young America," gradually appears with its own mouthpiece, the *Democratic Review*. They espouse nationalist, expansionist viewpoints and are openly sympathetic to European and South American revolutionaries.

January 5

DIPLOMACY: President Millard Fillmore announces the release of several Americans captured by Spain in Cuba, and he urges Congress to pay reparations for damages inflicted upon the Spanish consulate at New Orleans by irate citizens.

BUSINESS: A large gathering of Southern businessmen from 11 states convenes at New Orleans to review economic conditions throughout their region.

January 15

MEDICAL: The Jew's Hospital is founded in New York City by Simon Sampson; it is subsequently known as Mt. Sinai Hospital.

January 28

SLAVERY: Radical abolitionist Wendell Phillips declares that "Eternal vigilance is the price of Liberty" while addressing the Massachusetts Anti-Slavery Society.

February 6

LAW: The Supreme Court decides the case of *Pennsylvania v. Wheeling Bridge*, ruling that Virginia does not have a right to bridge a stream or river within another state's boundaries.

February 20

TRANSPORTATION: The Michigan Southern Railroad is completed, enabling train service between the east and Chicago, Illinois.

Phillips, Wendell   (1811–1884)
Abolitionist

Wendell Phillips was born in Boston, Massachusetts, on November 29, 1811, the scion of one of that state's most distinguished families. Well educated at the Boston Latin School, Phillips was admitted to Harvard where he received his law degree in 1833. By dint of his patrician lineage and background, he was expected to enjoy an accomplished career in law and public service. However, Phillips reached a turning point in 1835 when he witnessed a mob accost radical abolitionist William Lloyd Garrison and drag him through the street by a rope. He was so outraged by the event that thereafter he dedicated himself to the cause of civil liberties and social justice. Two years later, following the murder of abolitionist Elijah Lovejoy in Illinois, Phillips issued the first of his stirring orations in Lovejoy's memory, gaining instant recognition as a leading abolitionist spokesman. This position was further reinforced in 1837 when he married the wealthy Ann Terry Greene, who induced him to abandon his law practice and become a full-time abolitionist. Within a few years he gained national renown as one of the movement's most impassioned speakers after Garrison. He also started to champion the rights of Irish Catholics, whom he viewed as another exploited class. Phillips was quickly sought after as a speaker and earned considerable fees for each engagement. By dint of his acerbic wit and thunderous delivery, he found his niche as the nation's most sought after political agitator. Phillips also spoke on a number of nonpolitical, cultural issues, and one speech, "The Lost Arts," was publicly rendered more than 2,000 times. He took the unusual position of urging that the Union be dissolved rather than compromise its moral integrity by being associated with slave states.

The onset of Civil War in April 1861 only further enhanced Phillips's reputation as a radical abolitionist. He openly attacked the U.S. Constitution for its tolerance of slavery and refused to support President Abraham Lincoln for his measured approach to the problem. In fact, Phillips condemned the president for what he perceived as Lincoln's political accommodation of that "peculiar institution." After 1865 Phillips ended his long association with Garrison, who withdrew from politics, and replaced him as head of the American Anti-Slavery Society, now dedicated to civil rights for newly freed African Americans. He also used his high public visibility to push for women's suffrage and other social issues. Even at this late date, Phillips captivated and entertained his audiences through clever use of invective, which simultaneously demonized and insulted the opposition. He also relied heavily on his wife Ann's advice, freely admitting that she was usually ahead of him with respect to social issues. Toward the end of his long career, Phillips began espousing labor rights, especially an eight-hour workday. He also rushed to the defense of newly arrived Chinese immigrants to stop their exploitation and abuse. Phillips died in Boston on February 2, 1884, one of the most memorable orators in American history and a strident advocate for change.

March 13
PUBLISHING: America's first comic publication, *Diogenes, His Lantern*, debuts in New York.

1852

This illustration idealizes slavery; the reality was that picking cotton for long hours, six days a week, was grueling work. *(Library of Congress)*

March 19

LABOR: Ohio is the first state to protect women and children working in factories, restricting both to 10-hour workdays.

March 20

PUBLISHING: Harriet Beecher Stowe's novel, *Uncle Tom's Cabin, or Life Among the Lowly*, is published in Boston and sells 1.2 million copies in 16 months. This critical rendition of slavery arouses intense feelings in both the North and South, although it is denounced in some quarters as inaccurate. She subsequently compiles a *Key to Uncle Tom's Cabin* to demonstrate her veracity.

May 9

RELIGION: The Cathedral in Baltimore, Maryland, is the site of the first Roman Catholic Church Council held in America.

June 1–6

POLITICS: The Democratic National Convention meets in Baltimore and nominates Franklin Pierce of New Hampshire for the presidency after 49 ballots, along with William R. King of Alabama for the vice presidency. Their platform opposes further congressional discussion of the slavery issue and posits the Compromise of 1850 as the best possible solution.

1852

Stowe, Harriet Beecher (1811–1896)
Writer

Harriet Elizabeth Beecher was born in Litchfield, Connecticut, on June 14, 1811, into a prominent Calvinist family. From her preacher father she inherited a strict Calvinist sense of intellect, piety, and morality that characterized her subsequent life. Beecher was well educated by attending the Litchfield academy and subsequently studied and taught at her sister's school in Hartford. In 1832 she accompanied her family to Cincinnati, where her father functioned as president of Lane Theological Seminary, and taught at the Western Female Institute. In 1936 she married fellow teacher Calvin E. Stowe and also began writing short stories for several magazines. Her first collection, *The Mayflower*, appeared in 1843 and, with her husband's encouragement, she continued refining her style. Around this time Stowe had an opportunity to visit the South, where she was repulsed by the institution of slavery and dedicated herself to abolitionism. The Stowes found the newly passed Fugitive Slave Act of 1850 equally repugnant. Her experiences thus moved her to compose a serial story initially published in the abolitionist newspaper *National Era* in 1851, and the following year it was published as a book entitled *Uncle Tom's Cabin*. This novel, released in two volumes, proved a national sensation and was an immediate best seller. It sold 1.2 million copies within a year with even larger numbers sold in England and Europe. Stowe's story focused on the harshness of slavery and equally condemned North and South for their complicity in its perpetuation. Not unexpectedly, Southern reviewers reviled the book and in some regions it became positively dangerous to own a copy. Stowe's moving epic provided a badly needed jolt to the fractured abolitionist movement, which saw her as their new literary champion. In 1856 Stowe wrote and published another antislavery novel, *Dred*, which also sold in large numbers.

In 1853 Stowe, an international celebrity, ventured to England on a speaking tour and received an antislavery petition signed by half a million women. Back home, and despite her antislavery sentiments, however, she never firmly aligned herself with abolitionists, whom she regarded as too extreme, and sought abolition through moral suasion, as per her Calvinist background. To confront the rising tide of Southern criticism toward her work Stowe also complied and

(continues)

Harriet Beecher Stowe *(Library of Congress)*

(continued)

published *A Key to Uncle Tom's Cabin* to document the abuses mentioned. President Abraham Lincoln, upon meeting the author in 1862, reputedly exclaimed, "So this is the little lady who started our big war!" After the Civil War ended, Stowe resumed writing and changed her topic matter to nostalgia and New England life. In 1869 she visited England again and endured a spate of controversy by suggesting that the celebrated poet Lord Byron had committed adultery with his half sister—an assertion now believed as true—which cost her much of her European readership. Stowe died in Hartford on July 1, 1896, indelibly associated with the most famous novel of the century.

June 16–21
POLITICS: The Whig Party convenes at Baltimore and finally nominates General Winfield Scott for the presidency after 49 ballots. William A. Graham of North Carolina is also selected for vice president while their platform reaffirms the Compromise of 1850 states' rights, and internal improvements.

June 29
GENERAL: Henry Clay, a leading national figure for nearly half a century, dies in Washington, D.C., of tuberculosis.

July 3
BUSINESS: Congress establishes a branch of the U.S. Mint in San Francisco, reflecting the tremendous growth that region has experienced since 1848.

July 4
SLAVERY: At Rochester, New York, noted abolitionist Frederick Douglass addresses an audience and questions if it is appropriate for African Americans to celebrate the Fourth of July, since many are held in bondage throughout the South.

August 2
SPORTS: The first-ever intercollegiate contest is held between competing rowing teams from Yale and Harvard at Lake Winnepesaukee, New Hampshire; hard-rowing Harvard wins by four lengths.

August 11
POLITICS: The Free-Soil Party meets in Pittsburgh, Pennsylvania, and nominates John P. Hale of New Hampshire for the presidency and George W. Julian of Indiana for vice president. Their party platform condemns both slavery and the Compromise of 1850, while also supporting free homesteads and fewer restrictions on immigration.

September 22
ARTS: Actor and playwright George L. Aiken does a stage adaptation of Harriet Beecher Stowe's *Uncle Tom's Cabin* in Troy, New York, and dramatically recreates the brutality and injustice of slavery, furthering hardening Northern attitudes against it. The play runs for 100 consecutive nights.

October
RELIGION: In New York, Reverend Thomas Gallaudet founds St. Ann's Church to minister to the deaf.

1852

October 24
GENERAL: Daniel Webster, a great political figure of the century, dies at Mansfield, Massachusetts.

October 26
POLITICS: Abolitionist Senator Charles Sumter aggressively denounces the Fugitive Slave Act in a four-hour diatribe and then submits a resolution against it.

November 2
POLITICS: Democrat Franklin Pierce defeats Whig General Winfield Scott for the presidency by a count of 254 electoral votes to 54. Whig power has been diluted politically as Union-oriented Southerners have shifted their allegiance over to the Democrats. Free Soil candidate John P. Hale also receives a paltry 156,000 votes, a good indication of his own party's decline.

November 5
TECHNOLOGY: The American Society of Civil Engineers is founded in New York City.

November 21
EDUCATION: Union Institute (Duke University) is chartered in Randolph County, North Carolina, by the Methodists; its first class graduates in 1853.

December
POLITICS: With the Whigs and Free-Soilers in irreversible decline, the new American, or Nativist, Party is gaining strength and popularity. It is somewhat secretive originally and acquires the nickname "Know Nothing" Party as members profess to know nothing about its machinations. It is also anti-Catholic and anti-immigrant in persuasion.

1853

ARCHITECTURE: The 1853 exhibition in New York City is housed in the brand new Crystal Palace, constructed entirely from cast iron and glass, and features the largest dome in the United States.

LAW: The police force in New York becomes the first in the nation to don blue uniforms.

MEDICAL: New Orleans is stricken by a yellow fever epidemic that kills 11,000 inhabitants.

MUSIC: Henry Steinway (Heinrich Steinweg) opens his piano factory in New York City.

PUBLISHING: Sara Payson Willis, writing under the *nom de plume* Fanny Fern, publishes a volume of sentimental verse entitled *Fern Leaves from Fanny's Portfolio*, which sells 70,000 copies in one year.

RELIGION: The Norwegian Evangelical Church of America is founded in Wisconsin by immigrants.

The Kong Chow Temple of San Francisco becomes America's first Buddhist temple.

SPORTS: A local sports rivalry commences when the all-New York baseball team beats the all-Brooklyn team in a series play-off, winning two games to one.

TRANSPORTATION: The New York Central Railroad is formed following the merger of 10 smaller railroad lines.

1853

WOMEN: Amos Bronson Alcott and his wife present a petition to the Massachusetts Constitutional Convention requesting that the voting franchise be extended to women.

January 8
ARTS: The first bronze equestrian statue of General Andrew Jackson is unveiled in New Orleans, Louisiana, to commemorate the 38th anniversary of his victory over the British. The artist, Clark Mills, does a masterful job balancing the horse on its rear legs, and Congress ultimately paid him $32,000.

January 12
EDUCATION: Willamette University is chartered at Salem, Oregon, by the Methodists; its first class graduates in 1859. It is also the first institution of higher learning west of the Rocky Mountains.

February
PUBLISHING: *Una*, a woman's suffrage magazine, is published by Pauline Wright Davis and Caroline H. Dall in Washington, D.C.

February 11
MUSIC: The 24-year-old concert pianist Louis Moreau Gottschalk debuts at Niblo's Garden in New York City to rave reviews. He is rapidly becoming the nation's first musical celebrity.

February 12
EDUCATION: Illinois Wesleyan University is chartered in Bloomington, Illinois, by the Methodists; its first class graduates in 1853.

February 21
BUSINESS: The Coinage Act of 1833 is passed by Congress, reducing the amount of silver used in coins smaller than one dollar. $3 gold pieces are also put in circulation.

February 22
EDUCATION: Eliot Seminary (Washington University) is chartered in St. Louis, Missouri, by the Unitarians; its first class graduates in 1862.

February 25
SETTLEMENT: Voters choose Sacramento to serve as the new capital of California.

March 2
SETTLEMENT: Congress divides the Oregon Territory by creating the new Washington Territory.

March 4
MILITARY: The Army Appropriation Act passed by Congress contains $150,000 for a national survey of the best transcontinental railroad routes; it is incumbent upon the War Department to select the most viable one.
POLITICS: Democrat Franklin Pierce becomes the 14th president of the United States and the fourth Democrat. He is the first executive to deliver his inaugural address from memory and pledges to uphold the Compromise of 1850. Vice President William R. King is administered the vice presidential oath in Cuba, an island Pierce aspires to seize.

Pierce, Franklin (1804–1869)

President

Franklin Pierce was born in Hillsborough, New Hampshire, on November 23, 1804, the son of a prominent Democratic politician who served as state governor. After passing through Bowdoin College in 1827, Pierce studied law, was admitted to the state bar three years later, and successfully stood for a seat in the state legislature. In 1833 he was elected to the U.S. House of Representatives, served two terms, and won appointment to the Senate. He then left national politics to return home and serve as the attorney general of New Hampshire while also remaining active in local Democratic politics. When the Mexican War broke out in 1846 Pierce was commissioned a brigadier general of volunteers and campaigned with General Winfield Scott at the battles of Contreras, Churubusco, and Mexico City. Despite years of public service, Pierce was relatively unknown to most Americans, a factor which stood him in good stead as the 1852 presidential election approached. Because leading candidates Lewis Cass, James Buchanan, and Stephen A. Douglas were national figures and unpalatable to large sections of the nation due to their stand on slavery and other controversial issues, Pierce won the party nomination as a compromise candidate. That year he defeated Whig candidate General Scott for the presidency by only 50,000 votes, becoming the 14th president.

Once in power, Pierce sought to function as a nationalist and brought a number of talented Northerners and Southerners into his cabinet, including William L. Marcy of New York and Jefferson C. Davis of Mississippi. He also sought to enforce provisions of the so-called Compromise of 1850, especially the Fugitive Slave Law, to placate the South and possibly end all further debate on the topic. This stance, however, only further roiled the political waters and gave greater impetus to the rising tide of abolitionism. Pierce enjoyed greater success in terms of territory and in 1853 he orchestrated the Gadsden's Purchase from Mexico, which finished the outline of the continental United States. His sought after domestic tranquility, but received a major jolt with the passage of the Kansas-Nebraska Act of 1854, which he readily signed, despite the fact that it negated the earlier Missouri Compromise of 1820 and allowed slavery to expand into the territories. This resulted in a small-scale but de facto civil war in Kansas, and various attempts to establish a legal government there ended farcically. In 1854 his administration was further embarrassed by the Ostend Declaration issued by James Buchanan in Europe, which declared that if Spain did not sell Cuba to the United States it might be seized by force. By this time Pierce was viewed as politically inept and in 1856 he lost the Democratic nomination to Buchanan. He then retired to New Hampshire to defend his record, and throughout the Civil War he attacked the policies of Abraham Lincoln until his death in Concord on October 8, 1869. The well-intentioned Pierce is regarded as one of the least effective presidents of American history.

March 7

MILITARY: After resigning his senate seat in protest of the Compromise of 1850, Jefferson Davis of Mississippi is appointed the new secretary of war by President Franklin Pierce. He proves surprisingly effective in this role.

March 15
ARTS: A stage adaptation of *Uncle Tom's Cabin* opens at Purdy's Theater in New York City, with provisions for "respectable" African Americans to attend in separate seating.

March 31
EDUCATION: The Louisiana State Seminary of Learning and Military Academy (Louisiana State University) is chartered in Alexandria, Louisiana; its first class graduates in 1869.

April 1
EDUCATION: Ohio Wesleyan Female College is chartered in Delaware, Ohio.

April 13
EDUCATION: Loyola College is chartered in Baltimore, Maryland, by Roman Catholics; the first degrees are awarded this year.

April 18
GENERAL: Vice President William R. King dies of tuberculosis in office; President Franklin Pierce continues to function without a vice president for most of his term in office.

May
TECHNOLOGY: Gail Borden obtains a patent for a process he developed which creates evaporated milk in a vacuum. This ensures a steady and safe supply of milk to city-dwelling children.

May 19
DIPLOMACY: President Franklin Pierce instructs special envoy James Gadsden to negotiate with Mexico for the purchase of additional land from Mexico, suitable for railroad passage from Texas to California. This is done at the behest of Southern interests, eager to have a train route to the Pacific coast.

May 31
SCIENCE: Dr. Elisha Kent Kane conducts the Second Grinnell Arctic Expedition from New York City onboard the brig *Advance,* still searching for the lost party of Sir John Franklin. The party becomes icebound in Kane Basin two years later and finally makes its way overland to Upernivik, Greenland, in 1855.

June
DIPLOMACY: To better project the image of the United States as a democracy, Secretary of State William Marcy orders all American diplomats abroad to dress modestly.

June 3
EDUCATION: Central College is chartered in Pella, Iowa, by the Baptists; its first class graduates in 1861.

June 8
DIPLOMACY: The expedition of Commodore Matthew C. Perry enters Yedo (Tokyo) Bay, Japan. The United States is anxious to open regular commercial and diplomatic relations as well as secure coaling and repairing rights. They also seek to end the cruel practice of either killing or abusing shipwrecked sailors who wash up on Japanese soil. The xenophobic Japanese distrust the Americans but are impressed by their steam-powered warships.

1853

Perry, Matthew C. (1794–1858)
Naval officer

Matthew Calbraith Perry was born in South Kingston, Rhode Island, on April 10, 1794, a younger brother of Oliver Hazard Perry, victor of the Battle of Lake Erie. He joined the U.S. Navy as a midshipman in 1809 and saw some active duty in the War of 1812 under Captains John Rodgers and Stephen Decatur. Over the next three decades Perry fulfilled numerous positions at sea and ashore which established him as one of the foremost naval officers of his generation. The Czar of Russia was reputedly so impressed by his commanding demeanor that he was tendered a commission in the Russian navy. He rose to captain in 1837 and assumed command of the USS *Fulton*, the navy's first side-paddle steamship. This assignment convinced Perry of the need to modernize the fleet, and thereafter he pushed superiors into the wholesale adoption of steam technology. In 1839 Perry assumed command of the navy's first gunnery school off Sandy Hook, New Jersey, handled his responsibilities adroitly, and rose to commodore in June 1841. In this capacity he served as commandant of the Brooklyn Navy Yard and oversaw construction of two superb steam frigates, the USS *Missouri* and *Mississippi*, which further demonstrated his mastery of this technology. During the War with Mexico, Perry next replaced Commander David F. Conner as commander of the Gulf Coast Squadron and directly assisted the landing of General Winfield Scott's army at Veracruz. He then sailed back to New York in 1848 before accepting one of the most dramatic and significant diplomatic missions in American history.

In 1853 President Millard Fillmore ordered Perry to take a squadron of the latest steam warships across the Pacific to establish diplomatic relations with Japan. That nation had been hermetically sealed off from the world by the Tokugawa shogunate in 1630 and isolated for nearly 250 years. Perry's orders were to establish friendly relations, open several cities to American trade, and have the Japanese stop cruelly treating shipwrecked American sailors washing up on their shores. Perry's four vessels appeared suddenly in Edo Bay (Tokyo) on July 8, 1853, and the awestruck Japanese christened them the "Black Ships" because of their color. The commodore, a tall, dignified figure, then met with panic-stricken Japanese couriers, handed them a letter from President Fillmore, and then departed, promising to return in several months. The Americans then sailed back to Edo in February 1854, and found Japanese officials willing to negotiate with these technologically advanced strangers. Perry was painfully polite to his new hosts and even showered them with numerous gifts, including a miniaturized steam locomotive, won them over, and laid the groundwork for the Treaty of Kanagawa to commence trade and diplomatic relations. Perry then came home to a hero's greeting to serve on the navy's efficiency board. He died at New York City on March 4, 1858, one of the most accomplished naval diplomats and officers in American history.

July 4

Women: Women's rights crusader Amelia Bloomer creates a sensation in Hartford, Connecticut, by wearing her Turkish style pants called "Bloomers." A political and fashion statement, they fail to catch on.

1853

July 6

SOCIETAL: The National Council of Colored People is founded at Rochester, New York, and votes to encourage vocational training for African Americans.

July 14

DIPLOMACY: In Japan, Commodore Matthew Perry presents the Tokugawa shogunate with a letter from President Millard Fillmore, inviting them to open diplomatic relations. He then departs, granting them several months to deliberate and reply.

August 29

MUSIC: Dazzling French orchestra conductor Louis-Antoine Jullien employs a giant drum in his concerts at Castle Garden in New York City.

September

EDUCATION: Nonsectarian Antioch College, Ohio, headed by former education supervisor Horace Mann, opens its doors to both male and female students.

September 10

INDIAN: In Oregon, settlers conclude the Treaty of Table Rock with nearby Indians to obtain land in exchange for $60,000; the sum is never paid.

September 15

SOCIETAL: Charles Jewett, librarian of the Smithsonian Institution, oversees the nation's first librarians' convention in New York City, which convenes at the City College of New York.

October 15

SPORTS: Englishman Yankee Sullivan is declared heavyweight boxing champion on a technicality when his opponent, John C. Morrissey, departs the ring for a few moments to confront spectators who heckled him.

November 3

MILITARY: A group of American filibusters under former attorney William Walker capture the Mexican town of La Paz, Lower California, which he proclaims as an independent republic. Officials at San Francisco repudiate his actions and refuse to send him supplies as requested.

December 24

GENERAL: The steamship *San Francisco* catches fire and sinks off the California coast, killing 240 out of 700 passengers.

December 30

DIPLOMACY: Special envoy James Gadsden concludes a treaty with the Mexican government for the purchase of 29,640 square miles of desert along southern Arizona and New Mexico at a cost of $15 million. The terrain in question is flat and ideal for a railroad to the Pacific. This is also the final territorial acquisition by the continental United States, or Lower 48, and the border remains fixed today.

1854

EDUCATION: Farmer's High School of Pennsylvania (Pennsylvania State College) is chartered at University Park, Pennsylvania, by the state legislature. It is the first Pennsylvania state school.

LITERATURE: Henry David Thoreau publishes his famous memoir entitled *Walden*, which holds that freedom is only possible once man rediscovers him-

Thoreau, Henry David   (1817–1862)
Philosopher

Henry David Thoreau was born in Concord, Massachusetts, on July 12, 1817, to very modest circumstances. After passing through the Concord Academy he attended Harvard College on a scholarship. Ironically, he graduated the same week that noted writer Ralph Waldo Emerson gave his landmark "American Scholar" address, although their lives would not intersect for some time. Thoreau originally taught at his brother's school, where he pioneered what became a personal trademark–long field trips through the woods to study nature. He quit after two years to work in his father's pencil factory but finally became acquainted with Emerson by attending the Transcendentalist Club and began writing and editing for the group's magazine, *The Dial*. In 1843 Thoreau departed for Staten Island, New York, to serve as a tutor at the home of Emerson's brother, but he soon lost interest and returned to Concord. After working in his father's factory he saved enough money to conduct a personal sojourn at nearby Walden Pond, where he lived for two years in relative isolation. This experience indelibly impacted Thoreau and helped crystallize his emerging philosophy. Whereas most Transcendentalists remained somewhat indifferent to a relationship to God and nature, Thoreau immersed himself in nature, proffering it as a panacea for living in a modern world corrupted, as he saw it, by materialism and greed. Hereafter he saw nature not simply as an object of beauty to behold but also as a means of discovering one's self, and the inner peace this would convey. He had tried selling publishers on this radical notion through titles like *A Week on the Concord and Merrimack Rivers* (1849) and *Walden* (1854), both of which he ended up printing himself. At the time these and other publica-

tions gathered very little attention for either the author or his philosophy.

In addition to ruminating about nature, Thoreau was also becoming drawn into the world of politics. A profound abolitionist, in 1846 he refused to pay a poll tax levied to support the Mexican War and spent a night in jail for it. His subsequent essay

(continues)

Title page of *Walden,* by Henry David Thoreau
(Library of Congress)

(continued)

"Resistance to Civil Government" became a classic study of political resistance and inspired such diverse admirers as Mahatma Gandhi and Martin Luther King. In 1859 Thoreau also broke with his usual placidity to strongly defend and laud radical abolitionist John Brown for his failed attempt to seize Harper's Ferry and incite a slave rebellion. For the most part, however, Thoreau was content to live simply in his single room to expound upon nature and the utter necessity of making peace with it. He continued writing and publishing philosophical tracts and essays about the harmonizing effect of nature until his death at Concord on May 6, 1862. While he lived Thoreau never gained, or even sought, recognition for his immensely original philosophical thinking. That celebrity arrived later in the 20th century, when he was hailed as one of America's most vital and influential intellectuals, an exponent of freedom through personal awareness.

self through simplicity and nature and should not be obsessed by material pursuits.

MUSIC: Noted composer Stephen Foster scores another popular hit with the sentimental "Jeanie with the Light Brown Hair."

PUBLISHING: Mary Jane Holmes, soon to be America's most widely read novelist, publishes *Tempest and Sunshine, or, Life in Kentucky*. By 1905 she has written 39 books with a total of two million copies sold.

SOCIETAL: Both the Boston Public Library and the Astor Library, New York City, open their doors to the public.

The Children's Aid Society constructs a lodging house in New York City for boys. They offer an integrated program including work in an industrial school coupled with religious training.

TECHNOLOGY: In Boston, the firm of Horace Smith and Daniel Wesson invents a hand gun with a faster mechanism for rotating the cylinder which holds the bullets. They also try to fashion ammunition that utilizes brass cartridges instead of paper ones.

January 1

EDUCATION: Ashmun University (Lincoln University) is chartered at Chester, Pennsylvania, as the first free college for African Americans.

January 4

SLAVERY: Illinois senator Stephen A. Douglas seeks to divide the central plains region into the Kansas and Nebraska territories. Moreover, he embraces the notion of "popular sovereignty" to allow either one to settle the issue of allowing slavery or forbidding it on their own. However, this arrangement negates the 1819 Missouri Compromise as both territories lie above the antislavery line adopted by that act. The ensuing debate invigorates and stokes both pro- and anti-slavery sentiments in Congress. Douglas earnestly believes in self-governance but also seeks to cement Southern support for his political ambitions.

January 13

EDUCATION: Tualatin Academy and Pacific University (today's Pacific University) is chartered in Forest Grove, Oregon, by Presbyterian and Congregationalist groups; its first class graduates in 1863.

Douglas, Stephen A.   (1813–1861)
Politician

Stephen Arnold Douglas was born in Brandon, Vermont, on April 23, 1813, the son of a doctor. Well educated but restless, he studied law briefly then drifted west in 1833, finally settling down in Jacksonville, Illinois, where he gained admission to the local bar. Douglas, a decidedly short but highly energetic individual, found his calling in politics and became a moving force behind the state Democratic Party. After holding down several state and federal positions, Douglas was elected to the U.S. House of Representatives in 1843, where he proved an outstanding proponent of Manifest Destiny, national expansion, Texas annexation, and war with Mexico. In 1846 he was especially critical of President James K. Polk for not pressing the boundary of Oregon to the 54th parallel, and instead settling with Great Britain for a new border along the 49th. Though not a slaveholder himself, Douglas was willing to tolerate the "peculiar institution" to keep Northern and Southern factions of the party acting in harmony. After the successful war with Mexico, 1846–48, of which Douglas was a vocal proponent, the new territory kindled a national debate over whether or not slavery should be allowed to expand there. Because Douglas had been elected to the U.S. Senate in 1847 and now chaired the Committee on Territories, his various decisions were at the very center of the controversy.

Douglas sought out an intelligent compromise about slavery that would satisfy both Northern and Southern Democrats. He helped put through the Compromise of 1850 to win Southern support for his much-touted Illinois Central Railroad Act, which in turn allowed the issue to be resolved on the basis of "popular sovereignty," or the territorial legislature. This bought the nation a few years of peace on the subject, but in 1854 Douglas helped promulgate the Kansas Nebraska Act, which expanded the potential for slavery previously excluded by the Missouri Compromise of 1820. Douglas, despite his best efforts to placate both sides, now opened a Pandora's box of national acrimony, particularly over the admittance of Kansas as a slave state. Still, in 1852 and 1856 he was a serious contender for the Democratic presidential nomination but lost twice. In 1857 he broke politically with fellow Democrat James Buchanan over the illegally adopted Lecompton Constitution, which legalized slavery, and whose stance cost him his Southern base. In 1858 he engaged Republican challenger Abraham Lincoln to a series of celebrated debates over the issue of slavery; although Douglas, long hailed as the "Little Giant," was reelected by the state legislature, Lincoln garnered national attention for his uncompromising position on slavery. Douglas became the Democratic nominee in 1860, although he had lost Southern support within his party which went to Kentucky's John C. Breckinridge. Lincoln won the election and, after the Civil War began, Douglas roundly condemned Southern secession and sought to keep the Union intact. He died in Chicago on June 3, 1861, a skillful party operator.

January 16–17

SLAVERY: Senators Archibald Dixon of Kentucky and Charles Sumner of Massachusetts sponsor competing resolutions intending to repeal and reaffirm the 1819 Missouri Compromise, respectively.

January 18
DIPLOMACY: American filibusterer William Walker sets himself up as president of the new republic of Sonora, crafted from uniting the existing Mexican states of Sonora and Baja, California.

January 24
POLITICS: A group of Democrats come out against the impending Kansas-Nebraska Act, which they condemn as a "slaveholder's plot." They also publish an appeal that helps organize the new Republican Party.

February
EDUCATION: The Iowa Conference Seminary (Cornell College) is chartered at Mt. Vernon, Iowa, by the Methodists; its first class graduates in 1858.

February 13
NAVAL: The squadron of Commodore Matthew C. Perry anchors off Yokohama, Japan, and awaits the Emperor's reply toward establishing trade and diplomatic relations with the United States. The Tokugawa shogunate's inability to effectively deal with foreign "barbarians" in this instance will lead to its ultimate downfall in 1868.

February 28
DIPLOMACY: Spanish officials in Havana, Cuba, seize the American vessel *Black Warrior* and levy a fine for an error in the ship's papers. The United States, eager to acquire that island, begins using the episode as a convenient pretext for war.

POLITICS: Various antislavery groups assemble at Ripon, Wisconsin, to discuss the creation of a new political organization to replace the by-now defunct Whigs. Thereafter, the new Republican Party begins emerging in various northern states.

March 31
DIPLOMACY: Commodore Matthew C. Perry concludes the Treaty of Kanagawa with the Tokugawa shogunate of Japan, whereby the ports of Shimoda and Hako-date are opened to American trade. American seamen shipwrecked in Japanese waters are also afforded protection. Perry then impresses his hosts with several examples of advanced Western technology, including a miniature steam railway engine, which are given as gifts.

April 4
DIPLOMACY: Secretary of State William Marcy inquires of David Gregg, American envoy in Hawaii, if King Kamehameha III is receptive to annexation by the United States.

April 26
SETTLEMENT: In response to the Kansas-Nebraska Act, Eli Thayer begins the Emigrant Aid Society to encourage abolitionists to settle in Kansas and allow it to become a free state. Its success triggers formation of various other secret societies to ensure that Kansas enters the Union as a slave state.

May 6
BUSINESS: Cyrus W. Field receives a company charter and a 50-year monopoly to lay a transatlantic cable; the device will not actually be laid until 1866.

1854

Burns, Anthony   (1829–1862)
Fugitive slave

Anthony Burns was most likely born in Stafford County, Virginia, in 1829, the son of African-American slaves. As such he was denied all formal education but managed to acquire some literacy from playing with white children. He subsequently converted to the Baptist Church and served as an itinerant preacher among fellow slaves. However, at one point he injured his right hand and was incapable of hard labor. Burns, then fearing deportation into the Deep South, escaped with the aid of a white sailor and made his way to Boston in March 1854. There, on May 24, 1854, he was arrested by federal authorities at the behest of his former master and under terms of the controversial Fugitive Slave Act of 1850. This act reaffirmed slaves as rightful property, mandated prompt return to their owners, and carried stiff penalties for failing to do so. However, word of Burns's arrest and his impending deportation thoroughly aroused the abolitionist-minded inhabitants of Boston who staged a mass protest outside of Faneuil Hall. The crowd was being addressed by Wendell Philips when a riot broke out in an attempt to free Burns from captivity and a sheriff was killed. During court proceedings, Burns was represented by noted attorney Richard Henry Dana, who called vigorously but futilely for his release. Crowds still thronged the courthouse so the militia had to be called out to escort the prisoner from his cell. On May 26, 1854, Burns was escorted by armed troops to a Boston dock, where he boarded a vessel and was shipped back to Virginia. The entire episode is estimated to have cost the federal government $15,000–an enormous sum at the time–for the return of this one fugitive slave.

Burns was imprisoned for five months following his return and was also sold by his original owner to David McDaniel, a speculator. McDaniel had meanwhile been contacted by a group of Bostonians who offered to purchase the man's freedom for $1,500. His owner agreed and Burns returned North in March 1855 as a free man, publicly hailed as the "Lion of Boston." Continuing donations allowed Burns to attend the Preparatory Department of Oberlin College, where he studied theology and was formally ordained a Baptist preacher. Burns preached briefly at Indianapolis, Indiana, before the climate of racial hostility forced him to relocate to St. Catherine's, Ontario, as pastor of the fugitive slave community there. He died in that capacity on July 27, 1862, without further notice. Burns's notoriety may have been brief but also decisive; in the wake of his ordeal, no other fugitive slaves were forcibly repatriated from the North. Moreover, the entire episode added greater moral and political impetus to the rising tide of abolitionism. No less than eight northern states subsequently passed "personal liberty laws" to further infringe upon compliance with the Fugitive Slave Act. In turn, Southerners pointed to the episode as proof that there was a Northern conspiracy to deny them the right to slavery, an issue that would be settled by civil war.

May 26
Politics: After a contentious session, the Kansas-Nebraska Act passes through Congress. The bill creates two new territories with "popular sovereignty" to decide the issue of slavery. Many Northerners openly denounce the act and threaten to ignore the Fugitive Slave Act of 1850 as it applies to the territories.

1854

SLAVERY: In Boston an abolitionist mob led by Wendell Phillips attacks a Federal courthouse where fugitive slave Anthony Burns is imprisoned. They subsequently arrange for Burns to purchase his freedom.

May 31
DIPLOMACY: President Franklin Pierce again entreats fellow Americans to refrain from fighting in illegal filibustering expeditions, such as has happened in Mexico.

June 5
DIPLOMACY: The United States and Great Britain conclude the Reciprocity Treaty which allows American vessels the right to fish along the Atlantic coast of Canada while Canadian ships can do the same as far south as the 36th Parallel. Duty-free entry for crops and other goods are also allowed.

June 29
DIPLOMACY: The Senate ratifies the so-called Gadsden Purchase between the United States and Mexico, although at the reduced price of $10 million.

July
SETTLEMENT: A federal land office opens in the Kansas Territory to sell property to competing pro- and anti-slavery factions vying for political control.

July 6–13
POLITICS: A group of antislavery politicians, including former Whigs, Free Soilers, and abolitionist Democrats, convene in Jackson, Michigan, and officially found the new Republican Party. Its platform unequivocally denounces both the Kansas-Nebraska Act and the Fugitive Slave Law, demands their repeal, and supports the end of slavery within the District of Columbia.

July 19
SLAVERY: In Wisconsin the state supreme court rules that the Fugitive Slave Act is unconstitutional and frees a citizen accused of assisting a runaway.

August 3
SETTLEMENT: Congress passes the Graduation Act to sell off remaining public lands at reduced prices ranging from 12 cents to $1 per acre.

September 15
JOURNALISM: The *Kansas Weekly Herald* begins publishing at Leavenworth as the first newspaper in the Kansas Territory.

October 4
POLITICS: Abraham Lincoln, a little-known congressman, delivers a major address at Springfield, Illinois, wherein he condemns the Kansas-Nebraska Act, supports gradual emancipation of African slaves, and also acknowledges the political rights of Southerners. In light of the heightened awareness of the issue of slavery, Lincoln begins garnering greater national attention from those who oppose it.

October 7
POLITICS: Pennsylvania Democrat Andrew H. Reeder is appointed territorial governor of Kansas by President Franklin Pierce.

October 16
SLAVERY: In Peoria, Illinois, Abraham Lincoln denounces the Kansas-Nebraska Act and demands the eventual emancipation of African Americans held in bondage. "No man is good enough to govern another man without that other's consent," he insists.

1854

October 18
DIPLOMACY: American ministers to Spain, Great Britain, and France confer in Ostend, Belgium, and issue the so-called Ostend Manifesto. This declaration demands that Spain sell Cuba to the United States before the latter simply seizes it. It is indicative of President Franklin Pierce's expansionist tendencies and causes renewed dissension among antislavery Northerners.

November
POLITICS: Members of the Protestant-oriented Know-Nothing Party gather at Cincinnati, Ohio, for their national convention. There they design a platform calling for the exclusion of Roman Catholics and immigrants from public office, along with a 21-year residency requirement for citizenship.

November 13
GENERAL: The emigrant ship *New Era* is shipwrecked off the New Jersey coast, killing 300 passengers.

November 29
POLITICS: J. W. Whitfield of Kansas is elected to the House of Representatives after 1,500 pro-slavery border ruffians from Missouri cross the state line to vote for him.

December 30
BUSINESS: The Pennsylvania Rock Oil Company of New Haven, Connecticut, becomes America's first oil corporation.

1855

EDUCATION: The Elmira Female College opens its doors at Elmira, New York, as one of the earliest institutions of higher education to grant college degrees to women.

The *American Journal of Education* commences publishing with Henry Barnard as its first editor; this is the first magazine dedicated to the teaching profession.

JOURNALISM: The *Daily News*, a mouthpiece for New York City's Tammany machine, begins publishing.

LITERATURE: Herman Melville's latest novel, *Israel Potter: His Fifty Years of Exile*, tells the tale of an American Revolutionary War veteran. Its naval aspects are vividly rendered in highly dramatic style.

Walt Whitman debuts by self-publishing his first collection of poems, *Leaves of Grass*, which is almost completely ignored. However, Ralph Waldo Emerson is favorably impressed and congratulates the author "at the beginning of a great career."

Henry Wadsworth Longfellow publishes his epic poem *The Song of Hiawatha*; overall this is part of a larger literary trend seeking to portray Native Americans as noble savages.

PUBLISHING: Former slave and abolitionist orator Frederick Douglass publishes his autobiography, *My Bondage, My Freedom*, in response to charges that a man exhibiting his eloquence could never have been raised a slave.

Josiah Bartlett edits and publishes the first edition of his *Famous Quotations*, updated versions of which remain standard library reference books to the present day.

The publishing firm D. Appleton & Company obtains the rights and plates to Noah Webster's *A Grammatical Institute of the English Language*, more commonly known to generations of school children as the *Blue-back Speller*. This

Whitman, Walt   (1819–1892)
Poet

Walt Whitman was born in West Hills, Long Island (New York), on May 31, 1819, the son of poor farmers. After completing his primary education he worked as a printer's devil at the age of 12 with various newspapers in and around the city. Whitman also taught school for added income while contributing minor literary pieces to leading magazines such as *Brother Jonathan*, *American Review*, and *Democratic Review*. Whitman advanced to editor of the newspaper *Brooklyn Eagle* in 1846, then lost his job two years later because of his overtly "Free-Soil" sympathies. He then drifted to New Orleans to work briefly for the *New Orleans Crescent*, returned to New York, and sold real estate with his father to make a living. However, Whitman was indelibly touched by what he saw while traveling and it inspired him to experiment with poetry constructed from radically differing verse forms. In this sense he had been influenced by writers such as Ralph Waldo Emerson, and he began writ-

Walt Whitman *(Library of Congress)*

ing about and celebrating robust individualism in his youthful democratic nation.

change of ownership does nothing to reduce the primer's immense popularity; over the next 40 years it sells one million copies annually.

RELIGION: In Utah, Mormon leader Brigham Young declares that so much as a single drop of African blood is sufficient grounds for denying men to serve in the church priesthood.

SLAVERY: Salmon P. Chase, a committed abolitionist, is elected governor of Ohio.

SOCIETAL: Point Loma, San Diego, California, constructs the first lighthouse employed on the Pacific coast.

TRANSPORTATION: A noted suspension bridge is built over the Niagara River by John Augustus Roebling.

WOMEN: Sarah Josepha Hale begins a long campaign to eliminate the word *female* when referring to women in public life.

January 9
DIPLOMACY: The United States is awarded $119,330 in compensation from Great Britain for its role in emancipating African-American slaves from the shipwrecked *Creole* in 1841.

1855

All told, Whitman's writing "style" was distinctly rambling and almost disjointed–he was never beholden to conventional norms of rhythm and rhyme. In 1855 he collected 12 poems and published them at his own expense under the title *Leaves of Grass*. The book was a critical failure but did gather a favorable and congratulatory response from Emerson. Whitman published a failed second edition in 1856, despite the fact that Emerson's praise was engraved on the cover. This was followed by a third edition in 1860, by which time Whitman's unique and experimental forms with free verse had begun attracting critical notice abroad, particularly in England.

The Civil War represented a turning point in Whitman's fortunes, for in 1862 he departed for Virginia to search out his wounded brother and subsequently took up residence in Washington, D.C. There he worked incessantly as a male nurse and invariably brought small gifts to dying soldiers, regardless of whether they were Union or Confederate. The experience of war and death seared Whitman emotionally, and in 1865 he published a significant body of poems entitled *Drum Taps* which included, among other things, a touching eulogy to the late president Abraham Lincoln. From that point on Whitman held down several administrative posts with the government, being fired from several on account of some of his more scandalous, sexually-charged poems. In 1873 he suffered a stroke and departed from Camden, New Jersey, to live with a brother. In 1892 he published his final and definitive version of *Leaves of Grass*, which finally sold well, along with two significant prose works, *Democratic Vistas* (1871) and *Specimen Days* (1882). Whitman died at Camden on March 26, 1892, an undefinable commodity in his day, but a hero and inspiration to the "beat" generation of poets during the later half of the 20th century. He also enjoyed considerable popularity throughout Europe, where his poems were translated into several languages.

January 16
POLITICS: The first Nebraska territorial legislature convenes in Omaha City.

January 25
EDUCATION: Iowa Wesleyan College is chartered at Mt. Pleasant, Iowa, by the Methodists; its first class graduates in 1856.

February 6
EDUCATION: Eureka College is chartered in Eureka, Illinois, by the Disciples of Christ; its first class graduates in 1860.

SLAVERY: Ralph Waldo Emerson addresses the Anti-Slavery Society in New York City, suggesting that $200 million would be sufficient money to purchase slaves from their owners.

February 10
EDUCATION: Kalamazoo College is chartered in Kalamazoo, Michigan, by the Baptists; its first class graduates in 1855.

SOCIETAL: Congress extends citizenship to children born in the United States, and to foreign-born women who marry U.S. citizens.

1855

February 24
LAW: President Franklin Pierce signs a bill creating the first U.S. Court of Claims, thereby eliminating the prior method of petitioning Congress for claims against the government.

March 3
DIPLOMACY: The inflammatory Ostend Manifesto, threatening to annex Cuba to the United States, is published and a public uproar ensues. Secretary of State William Marcy declines to support its assertions in any way.
MILITARY: Secretary of War Jefferson Davis suggests that Congress appropriate money for the importation of 333 camels as an experiment for traversing the deserts of the Old Southwest; total cost for the effort is $30,000.

March 30
POLITICS: The Kansas territorial legislature is marred by pro-slavery candidates when 5,000 Missouri border ruffians cross over state lines to vote on their behalf; they thus win the election. Newly appointed governor Andrew H. Reeder remains wary of an outbreak of violence.

April 28
EDUCATION: Santa Clara College (the University of Santa Clara) is chartered at Santa Clara, California, by Roman Catholics; its first class graduates in 1857.
SOCIETAL: Boston outlaws racial segregation in all public schools.

April 30
EDUCATION: The College of California is chartered at Oakland, California, by Congregationalists and Presbyterians; its first class graduates in 1864. This is also the first West Coast institution to offer a large and varied curriculum based on colleges in the East.

May 9
SLAVERY: John Mercer Langston, the first African American elected to public office, addresses a meeting of the Anti-Slavery Society in Brownhelm County, Ohio.

May 21
SLAVERY: The Massachusetts legislature enacts a personal liberty law to circumvent enforcement of the Fugitive Slave Act.

June 5
POLITICS: The anti-Catholic, anti-immigrant Native American Party (or Know-Nothing Party) renames itself the American Party during its national convention in Philadelphia.

July 2
POLITICS: The pro-slavery Kansas territorial legislature, convening in Pawnee, passes extremely pro-slavery ordinances and then expels all abolitionist legislators from that body.

July 31
POLITICS: President Millard Fillmore removes Governor Andrew H. Reeder as territorial governor of Kansas for illegal land speculation and appoints Wilson Shannon of Ohio in his stead.

1855

August
SLAVERY: In Kansas, newly arrived John Brown and his son join the antislavery militia.

August 4
DIPLOMACY: President Franklin Pierce appoints Townshend Harris to serve as the first American consul to Japan.

POLITICS: Abolitionist politicians and supporters meet at Lawrence, Kansas, to hold their own constitutional convention and to protest the fraudulently elected legislature in Pawnee.

August 6
SOCIETAL: Nativist violence flares in Louisville, Kentucky, as mobs attack and kill 20 Irish and German immigrants at the behest of the local Know-Nothing Party.

September 3
DIPLOMACY: Notorious American filibuster William Walker establishes himself as dictator of Nicaragua in Central America.

September 5
POLITICS: Antislavery societies convene at Big Springs, Kansas, and ask Congress to admit the territory as a free state. They also declare the existing territorial legislature illegal, and therefore null and void. This move coincides with the arrival of numerous arms shipments to the territory, whereby an antislavery militia, the Free State Forces, begins to coalesce.

September 17
SOCIETAL: The Boston Public Library, the first such institution in Massachusetts, formally opens its doors to the public. In addition to its valuable book collection, the library has since become famous as a depository for important historical manuscripts.

September 28
SOCIETAL: Many Chinese flee the vicinity of Seattle, Washington, after the Anti-Chinese Congress convenes in Puget.

October 1
POLITICS: With the help of "border ruffians," the pro-slavery Kansan J. W. Whitfield is again returned to the House of Representatives.

October 9
POLITICS: Not to be outdone, antislavery settlers in Kansas elect Andrew W. Reeder, the former governor, to serve as their congressman.

TECHNOLOGY: Joshua C. Stoddard of Worcester, Massachusetts, receives a patent for a steam calliope.

October 17
RELIGION: Reform Rabbi Isidor Kalisch convenes the first conference of Jewish rabbis at the Medical College in Cleveland, Ohio.

October 23
SLAVERY: Free-Soilers gather at Topeka, Kansas, and adopt a constitution which is not only antislavery but forbids African Americans from entering the territory altogether. Battle lines are now starkly drawn between pro-slavery and abolitionist factions, and an undeclared guerrilla war erupts across the frontier.

1855

November 3

SOCIETAL: A white mob led by the mayor, the sheriff, and other elected officials attacks the Chinese district of Tacoma, Washington, and violently evicts the residents.

November 9

MILITARY: U.S. Army troops arrive at Tacoma, Washington, and arrest many of those involved in anti-Chinese violence.

November 26 – December 7

POLITICS: The so-called Wakarusa War erupts when 1,500 "border ruffians" from Missouri cross into Kansas intending to attack the abolitionist settlement at Lawrence. However, after appraising the town's strong defenses, manned by Free State forces, they balk and withdraw.

December 8

DIPLOMACY: President Franklin Pierce officially denounces William Walker's filibustering efforts in Nicaragua.

December 15

POLITICS: Free-Soilers in Kansas ratify the so-called Topeka Constitution which outlaws slavery.

December 29

MILITARY: Resentful Seminoles under Chief Billy Bowlegs attack the army patrol of Lieutenant George Hartstuff at Big Cyprus Swamp, Florida, killing several soldiers and precipitating the Third Seminole War.

1856

BUSINESS: After a four-year hiatus, the whaling vessel *E. L. B. Jenny* returns to New Bedford, Massachusetts, with 2,500 barrels of spermaceti in its hold. This voyage marks the beginning of a resurgent whaling industry based in New England.

Economic editor and author Freeman Hunt publishes *Wealth and Worth*, which posits that business is a significant enough activity to be considered part of the national culture. He therefore predicts that business education will one day rival similar programs already established for medicine and law.

COMMUNICATIONS: The Western Union Telegraph Company is founded and begins stringing up an extensive network of telegraph wires around the country. Thanks to the inventiveness of Samuel F. B. Morse, large segments of the nation will soon be capable of instantaneous communication.

EDUCATION: A German language kindergarten opens in Watertown, Wisconsin, the first such facility in the United States. At this time progressive German educator Friedrich Froebel wields increasing influence on the course of American education.

LITERATURE: John Greenleaf Whittier's poem "The Barefoot Boy" is published, becoming one of his most endearing and enduring compositions.

Harriet Beecher Stowe publishes *Dred, A Tale of the Great Dismal Swamp* to highlight the economic and moral evils of slavery; it sells well but fails to achieve the notoriety of *Uncle Tom's Cabin.*

Ralph Waldo Emerson publishes his *English Traits*, a bemusing collection of character and personality sketches drawn while he visited England in 1833 and 1847.

The romantic novel *Lena Rivers* by Mary Jane Holmes sells one million copies in a single year, affirming her position as America's best-selling authoress.

PUBLISHING: Commodore Matthew C. Perry publishes his *Narrative of the Expedition of an American Squadron to the China Sea and Japan Performed in the Years 1852, 1853, and 1854,* which contributes to growing awareness of the Far East and its potential as a market.

SLAVERY: Governor James H. Adams of South Carolina, fearing that his farmers lack sufficient numbers of slaves, proposes suspending the 1807 law prohibiting the slave trade.

TECHNOLOGY: Swedish expatriate John Ericsson invents the caloric engine, driven by hot air; large and heavy, it is too cumbersome for applications beyond factory work.

TRANSPORTATION: The Illinois Central Railroad is completed and commences running from Galena and Chicago to Cairo, making it the longest continuous route in the nation. It also has the economically valuable effect of linking Lake Michigan to the Mississippi and Ohio Rivers.

January 15

POLITICS: In Kansas, Free-Soilers elect their own governor, Charles Robinson, along with their own legislature.

January 24

POLITICS: President Franklin Pierce denounces the efforts of free soil Kansans to elect their own governor and legislature as the existing territorial governor, Wilson Shannon, has already certified the pro-slavery legislature.

SLAVERY: Georgia Senator Robert A. Toombs ventures to Boston, Massachusetts, and gives a speech at the Tremont Temple defending slavery.

February 2

POLITICS: As Congress becomes more polarized over the issue of slavery it is becoming harder to find consensus candidates to serve in leadership positions; after a two-month fracas Democrat Nathaniel Banks is finally elected speaker of the House of Representatives.

February 11

POLITICS: President Franklin Pierce orders pro-and antislavery elements in the Kansas Territory to stop fighting.

February 22

INDIANS: In the Oregon Territory, Yakima Indians kill members of the Geisel family and hold several others hostage.

POLITICS: The American Party (formerly the Know-Nothings) convenes and nominates Millard Fillmore for the presidency and Andrew J. Donelson of Tennessee as vice president. Their platform retains its anti-Catholic, anti-immigrant stances.

The new Republican Party holds its first national convention in Pittsburgh, Pennsylvania, and there decides to convene a presidential nominating convention the following June.

February 22

TRANSPORTATION: The first California railroad is built and runs from Sacramento to Folsom.

1856

March 1

MUSIC: American composer George F. Bristow debuts his *Second Symphony in D Minor* with the New York Philharmonic. This is one of a handful of scores written by native-born composers.

March 4

POLITICS: Congress is petitioned by the antislavery government in Topeka, Kansas, for statehood; Illinois senator Stephen A. Douglas subsequently submits a bill that would admit the state only after a new constitutional convention.

March 26

TRANSPORTATION: Steam-powered street trains run for the first time between Boston and Cambridge, Massachusetts.

April 1

COMMUNICATION: Western Union Telegraph is established to handle telegraphic business in the far West.

April 3

EDUCATION: St. Lawrence University is chartered at Canton, New York, by the Universalists; its first class graduates in 1863.

April 21

TRANSPORTATION: The first railroad bridge across the Mississippi River is constructed between Rock Island, Illinois, and Davenport, Iowa.

April 29

MILITARY: The first shipment of camels arrives in Texas as part of a U.S. Army experiment in desert travel.

May

MUSIC: Boston is the scene of a very large music festival featuring a chorus of 600 and a full symphony orchestra.

May 1

GENERAL: Pro-slavery border ruffians attack and burn underground railroad stations in Lawrence, Kansas, killing one man. This inflames abolitionist passions and incites radicals to violence.

May 21–25

GENERAL: After pro-slavery elements attack and kill a Free-Soiler at Lawrence, Kansas, radical abolitionists under John Brown murder five pro-slavery men at Pottawatomie Creek. This initiates a period in territorial history known as "Bleeding Kansas."

May 22

POLITICS: In response to a heated diatribe delivered in the Senate against Andrew P. Butler of South Carolina, Charles Sumner of Massachusetts is accosted and caned by Congressman Preston Brooks for insulting his uncle. The attack results in serious injuries for Sumner and renders him an abolitionist martyr throughout the North.

June 2–5

POLITICS: The Democratic National Convention meets in Cincinnati, Ohio, and nominates James Buchanan to be their presidential candidate while John C. Breckinridge of Kentucky emerges as the vice presidential nominee. The party platform again endorses the Compromise of 1850 as the most rational way of dealing with the slavery issue.

June 2
POLITICS: The antislavery wing of the American Party (Know-Nothings) nominates John C. Frémont for the presidency and W. F. Johnson of Pennsylvania for vice president.

June 17–19
POLITICS: The Republican Party convenes its first presidential convention in Philadelphia, Pennsylvania, and chooses John C. Frémont as its standard bearer with William L. Dayton for vice president. Their platform opposes "popular sovereignty," insists that Congress has authority to regulate slavery, favors admitting Kansas as a free state, and favors construction of a railroad that would reach the Pacific coast.

July 3
POLITICS: The House of Representatives votes to admit Kansas as a free state, but the bill dies in the Senate, and the issue remains unresolved until after the general election.

July 4
ARTS: Henry Kirke Brown's equestrian statue of George Washington is unveiled at Union Square, New York City; money for this impressive sculpture was gathered from subscriptions.
MILITARY: U.S. Army troops, dispatched from Fort Leavenworth, force the Free State Legislature in Topeka to disband.

July 17
GENERAL: A Sunday school outing near Philadelphia, Pennsylvania, ends in a railroad disaster that takes the lives of 66 children.

July 20
RELIGION: The so-called Handcart Migration begins as a mass migration of Mormons from Nebraska to Salt Lake, Utah.

August
BUSINESS: In Milwaukee, Wisconsin, Joseph Schlitz takes control of the August Krug Brewery, renames it after himself, and begins catering to the large German populace there.

August 1
POLITICS: In light of the turmoil in "Bleeding Kansas," the U.S. House of Representatives refuses to seat delegates from either pro-slavery or abolitionist factions.

August 10
GENERAL: Hurricane winds and tides lash Last Island, Louisiana, killing 400 people.

August 18
POLITICS: When Governor Shannon of Kansas resigns from office, John W. Geary is appointed by President Franklin Pierce to succeed him.

August 30
MILITARY: A band of 300 pro-slavery militia arrack John Brown's abolitionists in the town of Osawatomie, Kansas, and are repulsed.
POLITICS: Congress adjourns without resolving the issue of "Bleeding Kansas," which the Republicans intend to make a campaign issue.

1856

September 15
MILITARY: Newly appointed Kansas territorial governor John W. Geary calls upon U.S. Army troops to prevent 2,500 "border ruffians" from Missouri from invading his charge.

September 17
POLITICS: Remnants of the Whig Party gather in Baltimore and endorse the American Party candidates Millard Fillmore and Andrew P. Donelson for president and vice president, respectively. Their platform also cautions against the increasingly strident and sectionalized nature of national politics.

September 21
TRANSPORTATION: The newly completed Illinois Central Railroad commences running trains between Chicago and Cairo, Illinois; at 700 miles it is the longest stretch of track in the nation. Construction of the system consumed the energies of 10,000 workmen.

October 7
TECHNOLOGY: Cyrus Chambers of Pennsylvania invents the first functional device able to fold book and newspaper sheets; it also proves an excellent device for folding the heavy gauge paper associated with almanacs of the day.

November 4
POLITICS: Democrat James Buchanan defeats Republican John C. Frémont for the presidency in a contest decided largely along regional lines, North against South. The vote in the electoral college is 174 to 111; former president Millard Fillmore, now running as the candidate of the American and Whig parties, captures only a single state. Hereafter the Whigs cease exerting political influence at the national level.

December 20
EDUCATION: Newberry College is chartered in Newberry, South Carolina, by the Lutherans; its first class graduates in 1866.

December 28
GENERAL: Woodrow Wilson, the 28th president, is born in Staunton, Virginia.

1857

BUSINESS: The Pennsylvania Railroad obtains a transportation monopoly in that state by purchasing the main canal system there.

The John Deere Factory in Moline, Illinois, is producing and selling 10,000 steel plows a year.
EDUCATION: Peter Cooper founds Cooper Union in New York City to provide education for the working class.
POLITICS: Irish expatriate John O'Mahoney forms the secret Fenian Movement in New York City. They function as revolutionaries dedicated to removing British rule from Ireland and Canada.
PUBLISHING: Hinton Rowman publishes *The Impending Crisis in the South*, which postulates that slavery has impoverished great numbers of whites in the region; it is immediately banned throughout the South.

The influential journals *Atlantic Monthly* under James Russell and *Harper's Weekly* under George William Curtis make their debut.
SOCIETAL: The Mardi Gras celebrations held at New Orleans feature large, decorative floats for the first time.

SPORTS: The America's Cup, won in an English boating race, is installed in the New York Yacht Club by the crew of the winning vessel *America* under Commodore John C. Stevens.

The rules of baseball are further refined in Chicago, Illinois, with games now restricted to nine innings.

TECHNOLOGY: The first passenger elevator is employed at the Haughwout Department Store in New York City.

TRANSPORTATION: New York and St. Louis are finally connected by rail once the last length of track is laid.

January 12–15

POLITICS: Kansas territorial governor John W. Geary vetoes a bill passed by the pro-slavery legislature calling for a census and a constitutional convention. He remains determined to establish fair and impartial elections.

January 15

SLAVERY: Radical abolitionist William Lloyd Garrison calls for dismemberment of the United States to preclude any association, political or otherwise, with slave states. The slogan for the Disunion Convention meeting at Worcester, Massachusetts, is "No Union With Slaveholder."

February 21

BUSINESS: Congress invalidates foreign coins as legal tender.

March 3

BUSINESS: The Tariff Act of 1857 passes through Congress, which mandates a lowering of duties by 20 percent and also expands the list of duty-free imports.

COMMUNICATIONS: Congress appropriates $70,000 for Cyrus Field to lay the first transatlantic cable from Newfoundland to Ireland. After several mishaps, the project is finally completed on August 5, 1858.

March 4

POLITICS: James Buchanan is sworn in as the 15th president of the United States and the fifth Democrat. His inaugural speech reflects familiar themes of popular sovereignty and noninterference with slavery, although he condemns the outbreak of violence in Kansas. John C. Breckinridge of Kentucky also takes his oath as vice president.

March 6

LAW: The Supreme Court decides the seminal case of *Dred Scott v. Sanford*. In this case the slave Dred Scott, who had been taken by his master from Missouri to Illinois—a free state—and then back, sued for his freedom. However, the Court, under Chief Justice Roger B. Taney, rules that Scott, as a slave, was at no time a citizen and, hence, lacks the legal ability to sue. This decision enforces the precedent that Congress cannot interfere with people's property, including slaves, anywhere in the United States. The Missouri Compromise of 1820 is thus negated and the Court's ruling sparks a new wave of outrage in the North.

May

SOCIETAL: The plight of poverty-stricken women in Boston, Massachusetts, is partly alleviated with the opening of Channing House, under the aegis of Harriet Ryan Albee.

May 1

POLITICS: Massachusetts adopts a literacy test as a requirement for voting.

1857

Buchanan, James   (1791–1868)
President

James Buchanan was born in Lancaster, Pennsylvania, on April 23, 1791, a son of farmers. He graduated from Dickinson College in 1809, studied law, and in 1814 he won a seat in the U.S. House of Representatives as a Federalist. He switched over to the new Democratic Party after 1828 and in 1834 was elected to the U.S. Senate. Buchanan was a masterful politician, gaining reelection three times, and in 1846 his name was frequently mentioned as a presidential candidate. However, that year he lost out to James K. Polk, who appointed him secretary of state. In this capacity Buchanan agreed perfectly with Polk's expansionist sentiments, and he negotiated a treaty with England for the acquisition of Oregon along the 49th Parallel without a war. He also opposed the treaty of Guadalupe Hidalgo, which ended the Mexican War, 1846–48, in preference to annexing even larger swaths of territory. Buchanan, a Southern sympathizer and essentially pro-slavery, also

James Buchanan, 15th president of the United States *(Library of Congress)*

May 21

DIPLOMACY: In Nicaragua, William Walker's regime is overthrown by forces working for Cornelius Vanderbilt.

May 26

POLITICS: Robert J. Walker of Mississippi succeeds John W. Geary as governor of the Kansas Territory, and he pledges to have any new constitution proffered by a convention ratified by a fair, popular vote.

Dred Scott, the slave at the epicenter of a recent Supreme Court ruling, is freed by his owner.

June 2

TECHNOLOGY: James Ethan Allen Gibbs of Mill Point, Virginia, receives a patent for his twisted-loop, rotary hook sewing machine.

June 16

MILITARY: Camels imported to Texas for the U.S. Army are ridden overland to California as a test of their viability as livestock. The soldiers find them smelly and ill-tempered.

pushed Spain hard to sell the island of Cuba, which would then be brought in as a slave state. He maintained his presidential aspirations in 1848 and 1852, although he was passed over twice, and President Franklin Pierce appointed him ambassador to England. In this capacity he helped craft the Ostend Manifesto of 1856, which basically declared that if Spain did not sell Cuba to the United States it might be annexed by force. His obvious pro-Southern stances endeared him to Southern Democrats, and in 1856 they helped him secure the party nomination. Buchanan handily defeated John C. Frémont, the first Republican candidate, and was sworn in as the 15th chief executive.

Once in power, the Buchanan administration was immediately buffeted by mounting national discord over the issue of slavery. On March 6, 1857, the Supreme Court handed down its infamous Dred Scott decision, which nationalized slavery and outraged many Northerners. Buchanan hoped that this ruling would settle the slavery issue once and for all, but it escalated the rhetoric and sectional antagonism instead. He then compounded his problems by assuming a pro-slavery stance over the issue of Kansas, its pro-slavery constitution, and whether or not it must gain admittance into the Union as a slave state. Here he ran afoul of Senator Stephen A. Douglas, the most powerful Democratic senator, who denounced his decision as against popular sovereignty. By 1858 he was dealing with a hostile, Republican-dominated Congress, who were dead set against the expansion of slavery into new territory. Buchanan's final crisis was in the fall of 1860, following the victory of Abraham Lincoln as president, which induced South Carolina to secede from the Union. He roundly condemned the decision but took no strenuous actions against the rebels and left the White House a thoroughly discredited man. Buchanan spent the rest of his life defending his administration before his death at Lancaster on June 1, 1868. His politically indecisive nature proved a major cause behind the civil strife he sought so earnestly to avoid.

June 18

DIPLOMACY: The United States and Japan reach an accord whereby American vessels are allowed to trade at the port of Nagasaki, which has hosted Dutch merchants for two hundred years.

June 23

TECHNOLOGY: William Kelley receives a patent for his process of steel manufacturing, which entails blowing cold air through molten iron. Ironically, Henry Bessemer of England also arrived at the same process independently. Steel, which is much harder than the iron it replaces and rust resistant, marks an important advance as a building block of a modern technological base and infrastructure.

June 27

SCIENCE: In the first conservationist discourse, an essay in *Scientific American* warns that the population of whales is seriously declining owing to the insatiable appetite for whale oil to light lamps.

July 31

SETTLEMENT: Alfred Cumming arrives in Utah to replace Brigham Young as territorial governor; his arrival sparks dissent and the brief "Mormon War."

1857

August 14
COMMUNICATION: British and American ships anchor at Valentia Bay, Ireland, to begin to lay down the first transatlantic cable.

August 24
BUSINESS: The panic of 1857 begins after a New York branch of the Ohio Life Insurance and Trust Company fails, the first of 4,932 firms to go under this year. Over-speculating in railway securities and real estate are the cause of the crash.

September 11
RELIGION: After President James Buchanan orders Brigham Young removed as governor of the Utah Territory, Mormon fanatic John D. Lee encourages nearby Indians to murder 120 California settlers in the Mountain Meadows Massacre.

September 15
GENERAL: William Howard Taft, the 27th president, is born in Cincinnati, Ohio.

October 4
MILITARY: In Utah, Mormons of the Nauvoo Legion attack a U.S. Army supply train, inflicting no losses but burning several wagons.

October 5
POLITICS: Governor Robert Walker of the Kansas Territory authorizes strictly monitored elections within his charge. Several thousand fraudulent ballots are discarded in consequence, and the Free State Party wins control of the legislature.

October 6
SPORTS: The American Chess Association is organized in New York City during the first American Chess Congress. There, 20-year-old Paul C. Morphy of New Orleans, Louisiana, easily wins the American Championship. He subsequently tours Europe, defeating all players opposing him, and reigns as the nation's first international chess master.

October 19–November 8
POLITICS: Pro-slavery delegates meeting in Lecompton, Kansas, adopt a new constitution which legalizes slaves as property. When Governor Robert Walker objects, President James Buchanan approves of the convention to promote Democratic Party unity.

November
DIPLOMACY: Notorious filibuster William Walker tries returning to Nicaragua but is arrested by the U.S. Navy en route and sent back to the United States.

December 8
POLITICS: In his first address to Congress, President James Buchanan seeks to employ U.S. Army troops to restore order in Utah and also voices his support for the new pro-slavery constitution in Kansas.

December 9
POLITICS: Democrat Stephen A. Douglas, a presidential aspirant, denounces the Kansas pro-slavery constitution in the Senate, which places him at odds with President James Buchanan.

1857

December 21
POLITICS: The pro-slavery constitution is approved by voters once the Free State Party members boycott the convention.

1858

ARCHITECTURE: Frederick Law Olmstead begins designing Central Park in New York City.

Work begins on St. Patrick's Cathedral in New York City; this is an expression of Gothic revival style as interpreted by architect James Renwick.
ARTS: Pioneering photographer Matthew Brady establishes studios in New York and Washington, D.C.
BUSINESS: The Panic of 1857 continues into the new year with another 4,222 businesses failing.

The first Macy's store opens for business in New York City, which pioneers a fixed price policy, now an established retail custom.
EDUCATION: John Gorham Palfrey, formerly editor of the *North American Review*, publishes his *History of New England*; it establishes new critical standards in historiography.
PUBLISHING: Lowell Mason's musical compilation, *Carmina Sacra*, first published in 1841, has sold 500,000 copies to date and is the most popular music text in America.
RELIGION: A religious revival begins in New York and Philadelphia this year and begins sweeping the nation. It is characterized by daily prayer meetings and is probably brought on by hardships occasioned by the panic of 1857.
SCIENCE: The first dinosaur skeleton, a plant-eating *Hadrosaur*, is unearthed in Haddonfield, New Jersey.
SOCIETAL: Birth control, heretofore a taboo subject publicly, is openly discussed in H. C. Wright's book *The Unwelcomed Child; of the Crime of an Undesigned and Undesired Maternity*.
SPORTS: The National Association of Baseball Players convenes its first-ever meeting and adopts rules pioneered by the New York *Knickerbockers*.
TECHNOLOGY: Richard Esterbrook manufactures steel pens for the first time in his factory at Philadelphia.
TRANSPORTATION: George M. Pullman designs and builds the first sleeper cars; these are initially used on the Chicago and Alton Railroad.
WOMEN: The Ladies Christian Association is founded in New York.

January 4
POLITICS: The pro-slavery constitution comes up for a second vote in Lecompton, Kansas, and this time is defeated by the majority of Free State Party members.

January 6
EDUCATION: The University of the South is chartered in Sewanee, Tennessee, by the Episcopalians; its first class graduates in 1873.

February 2
POLITICS: President James Buchanan asks Congress to admit Kansas into the Union as a slave state, even though the majority of convention members have rejected the pro-slavery Lecompton constitution.

February 3

POLITICS: Illinois Democratic senator Stephen A. Douglas leads a revolt by Northern Democrats against President James Buchanan over the latter's stance on Kansas as a pro-slavery state; he regards it as a violation of popular sovereignty.

March 23

POLITICS: The Senate votes to allow Kansas into the Union as a slave state. This is despite the dubious legality of the Lecompton constitution, which had already been rejected by the voters there.

March 27

INDIAN: The Second Seminole War ends when Chief Billy Bowlegs visits Washington, D.C., and signs a peace treaty authorizing the removal of his band from Florida to Oklahoma.

April 1

POLITICS: The House of Representatives adds a provision to the Kansas bill whereby the Lecompton constitution is to be submitted to a new popular vote.

April 6

POLITICS: In an angry message, President James Buchanan insists that Mormons are defying federal law and "Levying war against the United States."

April 12

SPORTS: Fireman's Hall, Detroit, is the scene of the first U.S. billiards championship, when Michael J. Phelan defeats John Seereiter in a grueling, nine-hour match. Among the "genteel" audience in attendance were several ladies.

May 4

POLITICS: In a compromise move, moderate Democrat William B. English of Indiana proposes to allow Kansas into the Union if the pro-slavery constitution is ratified by the inhabitants.

May 11

MILITARY: A force of 100 Texas rangers under Rip Ford surprise and attack a hostile Comanche village in Oklahoma, routing the defenders and killing several braves along with Chief Iron Jacket.

POLITICS: Minnesota enters the Union as the 32nd state; slavery is outlawed.

May 17

MILITARY: U.S. soldiers are defeated in an engagement with Nez Perce Indians at Rosalia, Washington Territory.

June 13

GENERAL: The steamship *Pennsylvania* explodes on the Mississippi River, killing 160 passengers.

June 16

POLITICS: The Illinois Republican Party nominates Abraham Lincoln to challenge Democratic incumbent Stephen A. Douglas for his seat in the U.S. Senate. Douglas has angered many on both sides of the slavery debate by straddling the issue, but Lincoln's stance is refreshingly unequivocal: "A house divided against itself cannot stand.... I believe that this government cannot endure permanently half-slave and half-free."

1858

June 18
DIPLOMACY: The United States and China conclude a treaty of peace, friendship, and commerce.

June 26
MILITARY: A column of U.S. Army troops under no-nonsense Colonel Albert S. Johnston occupies Salt Lake City, Utah, finding it largely deserted by the Mormons.

July 20
SPORTS: A showdown between baseball teams from New York and Brooklyn is also the first baseball game for which an admission fee—50 cents—is charged. Onlookers throng the Fashion Race Course on Long Island to watch Brooklyn lose, 22–18.

July 29
DIPLOMACY: American consul to Japan Townsend Harris finalizes a sweeping treaty with the Tokugawa shogunate of Japan, which opens additional ports to trade, grants resident rights to Americans, and formalizes diplomatic representation in both nations.

August 2
POLITICS: Voters in Kansas reject the Lecompton pro-slavery constitution for a third time and, with it, their bid for statehood. The entire issue has split the Democratic Party, encouraged Southern extremists, and handed the Republicans a significant campaign issue.

August 16
COMMUNICATION: President James Buchanan exchanges salutations with Queen Victoria of England over the new transatlantic cable.

August 21–October 15
POLITICS: The gaunt, gangly Abraham Lincoln takes on shorter, stouter Stephen A. Douglas, the "Little Giant," in a series of seven energetic debates. Lincoln castigates slavery outright while Douglas, if not exactly defending that "peculiar institution," reiterates that all Americans living in territories have the right to vote their preference. In the end Lincoln wins the popular vote but Douglas is subsequently reelected by the Democratically controlled legislature. Lincoln nevertheless emerges as a national spokesman for the antislavery movement.

September
POLITICS: A professor and several students from Oberlin College, Ohio, rescue a fugitive slave named John and convey him safely to Canada.

September 2
COMMUNICATION: The much vaunted transatlantic cable, 3,000 miles long, breaks down after only 28 days of operation owing to faulty insulation.

September 24
INDIAN: In the Oregon Territory, the Yakima War ends with a treaty signed between Colonel George Wright and several tribal representatives.

October 7
TRANSPORTATION: A stagecoach belonging to the Overland Mail Company arrives in Los Angeles, California, from St. Louis, Missouri, covering 2,600 barren miles of deserts and plains in only 24 days.

1858

October 16

LITERATURE: Henry Wadsworth Longfellow's epic poem "The Courtship of Miles Standish" is published. This fictitious account of the love triangle between Standish, his friend John Alden, and Priscilla proves a best seller in England, selling 10,000 copies in a single day. To date Longfellow has sold an estimated 300,000 volumes, making him of one the most popular poets of his generation.

October 25

POLITICS: New York senator William H. Seward, a presidential aspirant, delivers an important address at Rochester, presciently predicting armed conflict over the issue of slavery.

October 27

GENERAL: Theodore Roosevelt, the future 26th president, is born in New York City.

December 6

POLITICS: In his annual message, President James Buchanan implores Congress to grant him the authority to purchase Cuba and also place northern Mexico under a "temporary protectorate."

1859

ARTS: A group sculpture called "Slave Auction" is dramatically rendered by artist John Rodgers.

BUSINESS: The Great Atlantic and Pacific Tea Company (A&P) has its origins in a general store that opens on Vesey Street in New York City.

EDUCATION: The Massachusetts Institute of Technology is founded in Cambridge, Massachusetts.

JOURNALISM: The *Democrat*, published at Sioux Falls, becomes South Dakota's first newspaper.

MEDICAL: Dr. Elias Samuel Cooper founds the first medical college on the West Coast as part of the University of the Pacific.

SOCIETAL: George Washington's former home at Mount Vernon, Virginia, is declared a national monument.

TECHNOLOGY: The Fifth Avenue Hotel, New York City, boasts the first hotel passenger elevator installed in America.

January 5

POLITICS: The Illinois state senate reelects Stephen A. Douglas to the U.S. Senate, although Abraham Lincoln's performance in the race has captured national attention.

February 14

POLITICS: Oregon joins the Union as the 33rd state; slavery is outlawed.

March 7

LAW: The U.S. Supreme Court overturns a verdict by the Wisconsin State Supreme Court in the case of *Ableman v. Booth,* involving Sherman Booth, an abolitionist editor jailed for violating provisions of the 1850 Fugitive Slave Act. The state court, viewing the act as manifestly unconstitutional, freed Booth, but the Supreme Court, noting that states cannot negate federal laws, orders him imprisoned again. The Wisconsin legislature then passes a resolution defending its state sovereignty.

March 26
Music: American composer George F. Bristow performs his *Third Symphony in F* with the New York Philharmonic Orchestra; he is emerging as the most notable of native-born classical composers.

April 4
Music: Dan D. Emmett's infectious air *Dixie* is performed for the first time by Bryant's Minstrels at Mechanics Hall, New York City. As events unfold this seemingly innocuous song becomes the de facto—if unofficial—national anthem of the Confederate States of America.

April 9
Literature: Samuel Clemens (the future Mark Twain) begins working on the Mississippi River as a steamboat pilot.

April 23
Journalism: The *Rocky Mountain News* begins publication at Auraia (Denver) as Colorado's first newspaper; it sells for 25 cents in either coin or gold dust.

May 9–19
Business: The annual Southern commercial convention meets in Vicksburg, Mississippi, and passes several resolutions demanding the repeal of all government restrictions upon slavery, in effect reopening the slave trade. The delegates feel that it is incumbent upon the federal government to protect private property, no matter what its form.

May 12
Women: In New York City, the Ninth Annual Women's Rights Convention is addressed by Susan B. Anthony, who denounces the power of white males over women and African Americans.

June
Business: The Comstock Lode, a huge deposit of silver, is uncovered near present-day Virginia City, Nevada, and precipitates another stampede of fortune seekers throughout the region. Over the next two decades $300 million in gold and silver is extracted.

June 30
Sports: French daredevil Charles Blondin crosses Niagara Falls on a tightrope for the first time, observed by 25,000 spectators. Subsequent stunts of his include crossing while blindfolded, with a wheelbarrow, with a man on his back, and on stilts.

July 1
Sports: Students from Williams College and Amherst College, Massachusetts, square off in the first intercollegiate baseball game in nearby Pittsfield. Amherst stomps the competition, 66–32.

July 5–29
Politics: Another constitutional convention unfolds at Wyandotte, Kansas, and a new document is drafted which specifically prohibits slavery.

July 26
Sports: A rowing team from Harvard prevails in the first intercollegiate regatta held at Lake Quinsigamond, Massachusetts, by defeating contenders from Yale and Brown universities.

1859

August 27

BUSINESS: Oil is struck near Titusville, Pennsylvania, by Edwin L. Drake, who goes on to erect the nation's first oil well—and the rise of a vital industry. Drake's initial output is only 20 barrels per day, but within three years 128 million gallons have been extracted. The kerosene derived from oil quickly replaces whale oil as a fuel for lamps.

September

BUSINESS: Farmers in need of better ways of rapidly shipping their grain stocks to markets back east form the Merchants Grain Forwarding Association in Chicago.

September 1

TRANSPORTATION: The first modern sleeping car is built and operated by George M. Pullman.

October 3

SPORTS: The United States loses an international cricket match to an English team at Hoboken, New Jersey; the contest lasts three days before a winner is declared.

October 4

POLITICS: The antislavery Wyandotte Constitution is approved by voters in Kansas by a two-to-one margin.

Engraving of the Harper's Ferry (as it was then known) insurrection depicting the U.S. Marines storming the engine house while John Brown and his followers fire through holes in the doors. (*Library of Congress*)

1859

October 16–18
SLAVERY: Radical abolitionist John Brown leads a mixed group of blacks and whites who seize the federal arsenal at Harper's Ferry, Virginia, in a failed attempt to establish a separate "country" for African Americans in the Appalachian Mountains. However, their quixotic quest dies when a detachment of U.S. Marines under Army Colonel Robert E. Lee storms their position and forces their surrender.

November 24
MUSIC: Adelina Patti, a European-born, American-trained coloratura soprano, debuts in New York City. She subsequently becomes one of Europe's most highly regarded singers, and one of the most highly paid entertainers of her day.

Brown, John   (1800–1859)
Abolitionist

John Brown was born in Torrington, Connecticut, on May 9, 1800, the son of a tanner. He matured in a very religious household and embraced his parent's strident abolitionist views toward slavery. Despite his religious fervor, Brown proved something of a misfit in the business world, continually failing at driving cattle, tanning, farming, and selling wool. This inability to secure gainful employment meant that his 20 children from two marriages always endured a hardscrabble existence. However, by 1849, Brown found his calling as part of the rising abolitionist movement in the northeast. After living in a community established for free African Americans in North Elba, New York, he relocated his family to Ohio, where he served as a conductor with the "Underground Railroad." Brown, fired by intense religiosity, always expressed the belief that the demon of slavery could only be exorcized by bloodshed—and he gradually believed he was chosen as the instrument of God's wrath. As such, in the wake of the Kansas-Nebraska Act of 1854, which allowed the issue of slavery to be settled by "popular sovereignty," Brown moved once

again to Kansas to combat the pro-slavery factions moving into the territory. He was

(continues)

Issued in the North during the Civil War, this melodramatic portrayal of John Brown meeting a slave mother and her child on his way to execution was symbolic and used for propaganda purposes. *(Library of Congress)*

1859

(continued)

an active participant in violence between the two groups, and in May 1856 he and his sons murdered five settlers suspected of pro-slavery beliefs. Over the next three years, he also became transfixed by a scheme to instigate an armed slave uprising throughout the south and repeatedly traveled back east to seek financial support to establish a guerrilla base in the mountains of modern-day West Virginia.

On October 17, 1859, Brown and a group of 21 followers, including several free African Americans, attacked and captured the U.S. Government arsenal at Harper's Ferry, Virginia. Several men were killed in the process, and the guerrillas took several hostages while waiting for the insurrection to foment. Instead, the raiders were surrounded and attacked by a company of U.S. Marines commanded by Colonel Robert E. Lee. In the fighting that followed, 10 of Brown's party were killed and he was cap-

tured along with six others. The following November he was tried at Charles Town on charges of murder, conspiracy, and treason, found guilty, and sentenced to death. Brown seemed to welcome his fate, realizing that his sacrifice would transform him from a violent religious zealot into an abolitionist martyr. He was executed on December 2, 1859, having roiled the national polity into fury over his actions, both pro and con. Northerners came to see him as a selfless hero sacrificing himself in a noble cause while Southerners castigated him as proof of a Yankee plot intended to end slavery. Within two years, Brown fulfilled his wish with the advent of the Civil War, through which slavery was finally expunged through blood and fire. In light of his role in precipitating the crisis, he was immortalized in the North through the popular song "John Brown's Body," a hymn frequently sung by Union armies marching south.

December
BUSINESS: A new gold rush in the vicinity of Pike's Peak, Colorado, brings an estimated 100,000 prospectors into the region.

December 2
SLAVERY: Radical abolitionist John Brown, convicted of criminal conspiracy and treason, is publicly hung at Charles Town, Virginia. Southerners note with alarm how many Northerners, while disagreeing with his tactics, approve his goals. Brown, moreover, waxes philosophical over his defeat; having failed to incite an insurrection, he hopes that his execution and martyrdom will ignite a civil war that will kill off slavery as an institution. As writer Henry David Thoreau presciently and prophetically observed, "This is sowing the wind to reap the whirlwind, which will soon come."

December 5
POLITICS: As an indication of mounting and rampant sectionalism, the U.S. House of Representatives spends two months trying to select a compromise speaker and finally settles upon William Pennington of New Jersey.

Charles Sumner of Massachusetts resumes his seat in the U.S. Senate after his caning by Congressman Preston Brooks of South Carolina.

December 14
SLAVERY: The Georgia legislature, eager to preserve its slave population at present levels, enacts a new law which forbids deeds or wills from manumitting slaves after the death of their owner.

December 17
SLAVERY: The Georgia legislature votes to have any African American indicted on vagrancy be sold into bondage.

December 19
SLAVERY: President James Buchanan, in his message to Congress, rails against the foreign slave trade, yet pledges to protect American vessels from searches at sea by ships of the Royal Navy.

1860

EDUCATION: In Boston, educator Elizabeth Peabody opens an experimental English-speaking kindergarten based on the successful German model.
LITERATURE: Nathaniel Hawthorne publishes The *Marble Faun*, his last romantic novel.

Ralph Waldo Emerson publishes his essay *The Conduct of Life*, which touches upon science, culture, faith, and morality.
MEDICAL: Dr. Abraham Jacobi becomes the first physician of children's diseases at New York Medical College.
POPULATION: The latest census reveals a population of 31 million inhabitants, including 4 million slaves.
RELIGION: Olympia Brown becomes the first woman admitted to a theological school when she matriculates at St. Lawrence University, New York.
SPORTS: San Francisco sponsors its first baseball games.

February 1
POLITICS: After 44 ballots, Democrat William F. Pennington emerges as speaker and takes his chair in the U.S. House of Representatives. He does so only after the withdrawal of fellow Democrat John Sherman, whose own candidacy was hobbled by his prior endorsement of an antislavery tract. The contest highlights growing factionalism within the Democrats over that "peculiar institution."

February 2
POLITICS: Mississippi senator Jefferson Davis introduces extreme resolutions defending the legality of slavery in both slave states and the territories that guarantee the return of fugitive slaves to rightful owners.

February 15
EDUCATION: The Illinois Institute (Wheaton College) is founded in Wheaton, Illinois, by the Methodists.

February 22
LABOR: A successful work stoppage by 22,000 shoe workers in Lynn and Natick, Massachusetts, leads to higher wages. The strike is the most significant of the period and also notable in that it involved large number of women workers.

February 23
POLITICS: The Kansas Territorial Legislature re-adopts the antislavery Wyandotte Constitution over the veto of Governor Samuel Medary.

February 27
ARTS: Presidential aspirant Abraham Lincoln poses for photographer Mathew Brady in New York City; Lincoln later attributes his election victory to this effective portrait.

POLITICS: Illinois attorney Abraham Lincoln speaks at New York's Cooper Union, delivering his first memorable address in the East. Here he strongly denounces the extremism of "popular sovereignty" and remains conciliatory toward the South. However, he remains adamantly opposed to the extension of slavery into the territories.

March 6
LABOR: Hundreds of Massachusetts shoemakers, including scores of women, march out from their workplaces in protest. At nearby New Haven, Connecticut, candidate Abraham Lincoln expresses his support for the strikers.

March 9
DIPLOMACY: Niimi Masaoki, the first Japanese ambassador dispatched abroad, arrives at San Francisco onboard the warship USS *Powhatan*.

March 19
WOMEN: Suffragette Elizabeth Cady Stanton testifies before the New York State legislature in Albany to obtain her right to vote.

March 20
EDUCATION: St. Stephen's College is chartered in Annandale, New York, by the Episcopalian Church; its first class graduates in 1861.

April 3–13
COMMUNICATION: The first deliver of the noted "Pony Express" mail service commences a year ahead of the first transcontinental telegraph; riders need only 11 days to traverse the 157 separate stations, each seven miles apart, between St. Joseph, Missouri, and Sacramento, California. In this instance Tom Hamilton arrives with a satchel stuffed with 49 letters and three newspapers.

April 23–May 3
POLITICS: In the face of a mounting sectional schism, the Democratic Party holds its nominating convention at Charleston, South Carolina. However, when the majority fails to approve a territorial slave code, representatives from Alabama, Arkansas, Florida, Georgia, Louisiana, and South Carolina withdraw in protest on April 30. The remaining participants, unable to muster a two-thirds majority behind any one candidate, vote instead to adjourn and reassemble on June 18.

April 30
SLAVERY: The American warship USS *Mohawk* seizes the Spanish slave trader *Wildfire* off the coast of Florida.

May 9–10
POLITICS: Baltimore, Maryland, is the site of the Constitutional Whig Party nominating convention; this entity is drawn from remnant of the American and

Brady, Mathew B. (ca. 1823–1896)

Photographer

Mathew B. Brady was born in Warren County, New York, around 1823, the son of Irish immigrants. By 1839 he had become infatuated with portraiture and ventured to New York City to study under noted artist Samuel F. B. Morse. Morse, however, had recently returned from France, and he brought back samples of the new technology known as "daguerreotype," a primitive form of photography employing silver-coated copper plates. Brady took readily to the new medium and opened up his own studio in 1844. In practice, he proved himself a visual virtuoso by pioneering new techniques of lighting, composition, and use of makeup on his subjects. Brady gained renown as one of the nation's foremost portrait artists and acquired a loyal and well-heeled clientele. In 1845 he also commenced a personal project entitled *Illustrious Americans*, a compilation of 24 noted citizens artfully photographed which he finally published in 1850. The title was particularly well-received in England, earning him a medal. Success here led to collaboration with other noted photographers, especially Alexander Gardner, who introduced Brady to the new "wet plate" process. This innovation created a negative on glass, allowing an endless number of reproductions to be printed from the original. Such was Brady's renown that in 1860 presidential aspirant Abraham Lincoln sat for him in New York City; Lincoln considered the resulting photo so flattering that he attributed his election victory to it. In time Lincoln became one of Brady's most frequently covered subjects, who masterfully captured both his profound intellect and intense sadness on film.

The onset of the Civil War in 1861 prompted Brady to expand his reputation by become history's first combat photographer. He outfitted a specially darkened wagon that followed the Union army in the field, and he shot thousands of photographs covering generals, landscapes, troop formations, and battlefield dead. He also hired noted photographers such as Gardner and Timothy O'Sullivan, but was not above claiming credit for their own excellent work.

(continues)

Mathew B. Brady *(Library of Congress)*

(continued)

Still, the thousands of haunting images captured on glass by Brady constitute the first modern photograph coverage of a major conflict and part of the nation's historical record. Unfortunately, Brady's quest for coverage proved his own undoing, and by war's end he was seriously in debt. He was forced to sell his entire collection of 6,176 negatives for a paltry $2,840—a fraction of his original investment. In 1875 the government paid him an additional $25,000 for exclusive rights to the photos, most of which ended up in either the Library of Congress or the National Archives. Brady, however, remained a ruined man and took to drinking. He managed to maintain a small studio in New York, a mere shadow of his former business, and died in poverty on January 15, 1896. Still, he made indelible contributions to the advancement and aesthetics of photography through his pioneering techniques, and his reputation as America's most famous photographer endures.

Whig parties. They then chose John Bell of Tennessee as their candidate for the presidency with Edward Everett of Massachusetts as his vice president. They also strongly denounce sectionalism and secessionism.

May 16
POLITICS: The Republican Party convenes its nominating convention in Chicago, Illinois. The leading candidate, William H. Seward, is regarded as too radical on the issue of abolitionism, so he succumbs on the third ballot to Abraham Lincoln of Illinois. Hannibal Hamlin of Maine is then chosen as vice president. Lincoln triumphs by positing himself as a moderate on the subject of slavery; he opposes its expansion into the territories but pledges not to interfere where it already exists.

May 24–25
POLITICS: The U.S. Senate, controlled 36–24 by the Democrats, adopts Senator Jefferson Davis's pro-slavery resolutions. However, the acrimony this engenders only widens rift between Northern and Southern delegates, particularly within the Democratic Party.

June 9
PUBLISHING: *Malaeska: The Indian Wife of the White Hunter* by Ann Sophie Stevens debuts in New York City as the first of the Irwin P. Beadle "Dime Novel" series. These prove immensely popular in their day.

June 11
POLITICS: Southern Democrats who abandoned the party convention in Charleston, South Carolina, assemble in Richmond, Virginia, in a strategy session. They vote to reconvene again in Baltimore on the 28th.

June 18–23
POLITICS: The Democratic Party reconvenes its nominating convention in Baltimore, Maryland, in the absence of many Southern delegates. They nonetheless nominate Stephen A. Douglas for president with Herschel V. Johnson of Georgia as his vice presidential running mate. Their platform endorses the notion of "popular sovereignty" in the territories.

June 20
POLITICS: President James Buchanan vetoes the Homestead Bill, believing that Congress lacks the constitutional authority to grant land to individuals.

June 28
POLITICS: Southern delegates, who had previously absented themselves from the Democratic Party convention, convene in Baltimore, Maryland, as the National Democratic Party. They nominate former vice president John C. Breckinridge of Kentucky as their standard bearer with Joseph Lane of Oregon as vice president, while the party platform unequivocally supports the expansion of slavery into the territories.

August 6
MILITARY: American filibusters under William Walker attack and seize Trujillo, Honduras, storming a customhouse whose revenues are property of the British government. Walker is soon after compelled to surrender to a British warship and is taken captive.

August 31
DIPLOMACY: Secretary of State Lewis Cass, alarmed by a major French incursion into Mexico, warns the government of Napoleon III that a military occupation of that country is unacceptable to the United States.

September 8
GENERAL: The steamer *Lady Elgin* collides with the lumber vessel *Augusta* on Lake Michigan and sinks; 300 passengers are killed.

September 12
GENERAL: Notorious filibuster William Walker is turned over to Honduran authorities by the British, tried, and executed by firing squad.

September 17
GENERAL: The large steam vessel *Commonwealth* is destroyed by fire at Groton, Connecticut.

November 6
POLITICS: Abraham Lincoln and Hannibal Hamlin win the presidential contest by carrying 18 free states with 1,866,452 popular votes and 180 electoral votes—none of them from southern states. The Northern Democratic ticket of Stephen A. Douglas and Herschel V. Johnson registers second with 1,376,957 votes and 120 electoral votes while the competing National Democratic ticket of John C. Breckinridge and Joseph Lane are third with 11 slave states, 849,781 votes, and 72 electoral votes. Finishing fourth is the Constitutional Unionist ticket of John Bell and Edward Everett with 588,879 popular votes and 39 electoral votes. Lincoln's triumph proves short-lived and precipitates secessionist tremors throughout the South.

November 7
POLITICS: Defiant authorities in Charleston, South Carolina, take umbrage over Abraham Lincoln's recent victory; they raise the traditional palmetto flag over city hall and detain a federal army officer caught in the act of transferring military supplies from the Charleston arsenal to Fort Moultrie.

1860

November 8
MUSIC: Noted minstrel writer Stephen C. Foster copyrights the song "Old Black Joe," which differs from previous compositions by not using African-American dialects in the lyrics and expressing genuine sentimentality.

November 9
POLITICS: President James Buchanan summons a very divided cabinet to discuss the mounting secession crisis. Northerners Lewis Cass, Jeremiah S. Black, and Joseph Holt strongly favor preserving the federal union by force if necessary, while Southerners Howell Cobb, Jacob Thompson, and John B. Floyd oppose military intervention of any kind.
MILITARY: Partisans in Charleston, South Carolina, attempt to seize federal arms stored at Fort Moultrie.

November 10
POLITICS: The South Carolina legislature reacts to Abraham Lincoln's victory by authorizing a convention to contemplate secession from the Union. In Washington, D.C., South Carolina senators James Chestnut and James H. Hammond also resign their seats and return home.

November 13
POLITICS: The South Carolina legislature authorizes raising 10,000 volunteers to defend the state from a possible Northern invasion.

November 14
POLITICS: Georgia congressman Alexander H. Stephens addresses the state legislature at Milledgeville and implores members to oppose secession and uphold constitutional law.

November 15
MILITARY: Major Robert Anderson, U.S. Army, himself a slave-owning Southerner, is ordered to take command of the federal garrison at Fort Moultrie in Charleston harbor, South Carolina.
NAVAL: Lieutenant Thomas A. Craven, commanding the naval installation at Key West, Florida, orders landing parties to secure nearby Forts Taylor and Jefferson against possible seizure by "Bands of lawless men."

November 18
POLITICS: The Georgia legislature, following South Carolina's lead, procures $1 million to purchase arms and begin training troops.

November 19
ARTS: Adelina Patti, soon touted as the nation's foremost opera star, debuts at the French Opera House in New Orleans, Louisiana.

November 20
POLITICS: President James Buchanan is advised by Attorney General Jeremiah S. Black of his obligation to protect public property from illegal seizure, but also of the necessity of refraining from use of military force unless violence is first instigated by the secessionists. He is further counseled not to wage offensive warfare against rebellious states, but rather to rely upon the courts to uphold the law.

November 23
MILITARY: Major Robert Anderson reports on the defensive weaknesses of Fort Moultrie, Charleston harbor, and suggests transferring his garrison to nearby Fort Sumter, offshore.

November 30
POLITICS: The Mississippi state legislature begins drawing up articles of secession.

December 1
POLITICS: The Florida legislature convenes to ponder and debate the growing secession crisis.

December 3
POLITICS: The 36th Congress convenes its second session in Washington, D.C.
SLAVERY: A public memorial to abolitionist John Brown, organized in Boston, Massachusetts, by Frederick Douglass, is disrupted by pro-slavery agitators.

December 4
POLITICS: President James Buchanan delivers his final State of the Union address to Congress, noting with trepidation that different sections of the country were "now arrayed against each other." He attributes the mounting secession crisis to the machinations of free states and questions the constitutionality of using military force to interfere with that process. Buchanan nonetheless opposes secession despite his strong sympathies for the South.

December 5
POLITICS: President-elect Abraham Lincoln strongly disputes the conclusions of President James Buchanan's recent State of the Union address.

December 6
POLITICS: The House of Representatives appoints the Committee of Thirty-Three, with one member from each state, to discuss the present crisis and suggest possible solutions.

December 8
POLITICS: Secretary of the Treasury Howell Cobb, a Georgian, feels that is inevitable at this juncture and tenders his resignation. He is briefly succeeded by Philip F. Thomas of Maryland.

President-elect Abraham Lincoln approaches his political rival William H. Seward and asks him to serve as secretary of state in his new administration. Seward readily agrees, although less out of altruism than a sense than the "incompetent" Lincoln needs an experienced politician to serve as his de facto "prime minister."

December 10
POLITICS: A delegation of South Carolinians meets with President James Buchanan in Washington, D.C., assuring him that federal troops and installations will not be disturbed in the event of secession. The president remains unconvinced and begins mobilizing military resources for action. Furthermore, Buchanan continues wrestling with the issue of eventually dispatching reinforcements to the South.

The South Carolina legislature endorses a secession convention, set to convene in Columbia on December 17.

1860

December 11

MILITARY: Major Don Carlos Buell arrives at Fort Moultrie, Charleston harbor, with instructions from the War Department for Major Robert Anderson. Apparently, Secretary of War John B. Floyd, a Virginian, refuses to dispatch reinforcements there to avoid provoking a confrontation.

December 12

POLITICS: Secretary of state Lewis Cass, furious over President James Buchanan's unwillingness to forward military reinforcements to protect military installations in Charleston, South Carolina, resigns from office in protest.

The Committee of the Thirty-three, meeting in the U.S. House of Representatives, offers more than 30 well-intentioned suggestions for avoiding civil war and secession—none of them viable.

December 13

POLITICS: President James Buchanan finally decides not to send reinforcements to Fort Sumter, Charleston harbor, despite the urging of several cabinet members.

In Washington, D.C., seven senators and 23 representatives from across the South sign a manifesto encouraging secession from the Union.

December 14

POLITICS: The Georgia state legislature entreats Alabama, Florida, Mississippi, and South Carolina to appoint delegates to a forthcoming secession convention. All willingly comply.

December 17

POLITICS: The Secession Convention convenes in Columbia, South Carolina.

Attorney General Jeremiah S. Black, a close confidant of President James Buchanan, is temporarily appointed secretary of state to succeed Lewis Cass. However, even Black cannot prevail upon Buchanan to reinforce military posts; the president is convinced that the South will be more pliable if troops are withheld.

December 18

POLITICS: In an attempt to stave off violence and conciliate Southerners, Senator John J. Crittenden of Kentucky promulgates the "Crittenden Compromise," which restricts slavery to the boundaries of the old Missouri Compromise (1819) and also extends that line across the continent. Slavery is thus precluded from Northern territories but otherwise left intact. Significantly, President-elect Abraham Lincoln opposes the measure.

December 19

POLITICS: Delegates to the South Carolina Convention declare that no Federal soldiers can be sent to the forts in Charleston harbor.

December 20

POLITICS: In light of the mounting sectional crisis, the U.S. Senate appoints the Committee of Thirteen to investigate state affairs and seek possible solutions to avert civil war.

Democrat Edward M. Stanton is appointed attorney general to replace Jeremiah S. Black.

The South Carolina state convention meeting at Charleston votes 169 to 0—unanimously—to secede from the United States, declaring all prior associations

1860

with that entity null and void. This single act sets in motion a chain of events culminating in a mammoth military confrontation between North and South. Charleston's inhabitants nonetheless slip into near-delirious celebrations.

December 22

POLITICS: The South Carolina state convention demands that the federal government yield control of Forts Moultrie and Sumter, along with the U.S. Arsenal in Charleston, to state authorities. Three commissioners are then dispatched to Washington, D.C., to present those demands.

December 24

POLITICS: Governor Francis W. Perkins of South Carolina declares his state free and independent of the United States, consistent with the "Declaration of Immediate Causes" issued by the convention.

In Washington, D.C., Senator William J. Seward proffers a last-minute constitutional amendment mandating that Congress must not interfere with slavery as it exists in the states. He also seeks jury trials for any fugitive slaves apprehended in free states.

December 26

MILITARY: Major Robert Anderson, commanding the Union garrison at Fort Moultrie, South Carolina, remains cognizant of the dangers facing his command. Henceforth, under the cover of darkness and upon his own initiative, he surreptitiously transfers his soldiers from the mainland to the more defensible post of Fort Sumter in nearby Charleston harbor.

December 27

MILITARY: South Carolina state forces occupy Fort Moultrie and Castle Pinckney in Charleston harbor. This constitutes the first act of overt military aggression against the U.S. government.

NAVAL: South Carolina forces seize the U.S. revenue cutter *William Aiken* in Charleston harbor.

POLITICS: President James Buchanan expresses his surprise and regrets to southern congressmen that the garrison in Charleston slipped away to Fort Sumter, but he refuses ordering them back to the mainland.

December 28

POLITICS: A South Carolina delegation arrives in Washington, D.C., demanding that President James Buchanan removes all Federal troops from Charleston. He receives the delegates only as private citizens and again declines all demands for removing U.S. troops. Meanwhile, General in Chief Winfield Scott opposes abandoning the fort and urges Secretary of War John B. Floyd to dispatch immediate supplies and reinforcements.

December 29

POLITICS: President James Buchanan requests and receives the resignation of Secretary of War John B. Floyd after he insists on removing Federal forces from Charleston, South Carolina.

December 30

MILITARY: The U.S. Arsenal at Charleston, South Carolina, is seized by state forces. They also occupy all remaining Federal property in the city save for Fort Sumter in the harbor.

1860

POLITICS: The continuing seizure of Federal property by South Carolina authorities prompts threats of additional resignations among President James Buchanan's cabinet if he fails to take more forceful action.

December 31

POLITICS: Postmaster general Joseph Holt is appointed acting secretary of war following the resignation of John B. Floyd. President James Buchanan also refuses another demand by Southern Commissioners to withdraw Federal troops from Charleston. Finally, upon the repeated insistence of Secretary of State Jeremiah S. Black, he reluctantly orders the Army and Navy Departments to mobilize troops and ships for the relief of Fort Sumter. Lines are being inexorably drawn in the sand and must be crossed soon by one side or the other.

In the U.S. Senate, the Committee of Thirteen fails to reach accord on any possible political solutions, including the so-called "Crittenden Compromise."

1861

ARTS: The play *East Lynne* by English authoress Mrs. Henry Wood enjoys great success as a stage play and a novel, despite its reputation for rather crude melodrama.

Antonio Pastor debuts on Broadway with his new format of "Vaudeville" shows, which are fast-paced yet suitable for the entire family. By the turn of the century, Vaudeville is the leading form of popular entertainment.

BUSINESS: The U.S. Postal Service begins delivering goods along with letters for the first time.

EDUCATION: Yale University becomes the first institute of higher learning to establish doctorates of philosophy (Ph.D.) degrees along the German model.

SPORTS: The *New York Clipper*, a local newspaper, offers the first baseball trophy.

Deerfoot, a Seneca tribal runner, handily defeats all opponents in running matches staged throughout Great Britain.

January 2

MILITARY: The defense of Washington, D.C., is entrusted to Colonel Charles P. Stone, who begins organizing the District of Columbia militia.

POLITICS: President James Buchanan refuses a letter from the South Carolina commissioners. The nominally sympathetic chief executive then orders preparations to get underway for reinforcing the garrison at Fort Sumter, South Carolina. General Winfield Scott prevails upon the president to employ a civilian steamer, rather than a military transport, which would arrive quicker and draw less attention.

January 3

MILITARY: Fort Pulaski, near the mouth of the Savannah River, is peacefully occupied by Georgia state forces upon the orders of Governor Joseph E. Brown.

POLITICS: The War Department summarily cancels instructions from former Secretary of War John B. Floyd to transfer heavy cannon from Pittsburgh, Pennsylvania, to various points throughout the South.

The South Carolina commission departs Washington, D.C., deeming its mission a failure.

The Delaware legislature, although permitting slavery, votes unanimously to remain with the Union.

Florida's State Convention assembles in Tallahassee to weigh the matter of secession.

January 4

MILITARY: The U.S. Arsenal at Mount Vernon, Mobile, is peacefully occupied by Alabama state forces under orders from Governor Andrew B. Moore.

January 5

NAVAL: The supply vessel *Star of the West* departs New York for Fort Sumter, South Carolina, carrying food supplies and soldiers as reinforcements. The warship USS *Brooklyn*, originally intended for the mission, is not used by General Winfield Scott, who feels that a civilian vessel will appear less provocative.

POLITICS: Senators from seven Southern states, Alabama, Arkansas, Florida, Georgia, Louisiana, Mississippi, and Texas, confer in Washington, D.C., over the possibility of secession. They ultimately urge slave states to leave the Union and establish a confederacy of their own.

January 6

POLITICS: Governor Thomas H. Hicks of Maryland, despite being governor of a slave state, endorses the Union and wades in heavily against secession.

January 7

POLITICS: The U.S. House of Representatives approves Major Robert Anderson's recent and unauthorized transfer of Federal forces to Fort Sumter, South Carolina.

State conventions in Mississippi and Alabama begin debating secession from the Union.

January 8

POLITICS: President James Buchanan urges Congress to consider adopting the "Crittenden Compromise."

Secretary of the Interior Jacob Thompson, the last remaining Southerner in President James Buchanan's cabinet, tenders his resignation over the *Star of the West*'s departure. Before leaving Washington, D.C., he cables authorities in Charleston, South Carolina, of that vessel's departure.

January 9

MILITARY: Artillery manned by South Carolina state forces at Fort Moultrie and Morris Island fires upon the transport *Star of the West* as it approaches Charleston harbor. No damage is inflicted and it retires back to New York unscathed. Technically speaking, these are the first hostile shots of the Civil War, and Major Robert Anderson, commanding Fort Sumter's garrison, protests the action to Governor Francis W. Pickens. However, Anderson orders his men to stand down and make no attempt to interfere.

POLITICS: The Mississippi State Convention meeting in Jackson votes to secede on a vote of 84 to 15–becoming the second state to depart.

January 10

MILITARY: Federal troops under Lieutenant Adams J. Slemmer, garrisoning at Fort Barancas at Pensacola, Florida, spike their cannon and retire offshore to Fort Pickens on nearby Santa Rosa Island. Local forces soon confiscate the navy yard, but Fort Pickens remains in Union hands for the duration of hostilities.

1861

The U.S. Arsenal and Barracks at Baton Rouge, Louisiana, are confiscated by state forces under Braxton Bragg under the orders of Governor Thomas O. Moore. **POLITICS:** Senator Jefferson Davis addresses the U.S. Senate, requesting immediate action on and approval of Southern demands. However, he decries using force and seeks to resolve the crisis through constitutional means.

William H. Seward gains appointment as secretary of state.

Florida's state convention adopts secession on a 62 to 7 vote, becoming the third state to secede.

January 11

MILITARY: South Carolina governor Francis W. Pickens demands the surrender of Fort Sumter, Charleston harbor; Major Robert Anderson politely yet curtly declines.

POLITICS: The Mississippi delegation to the U.S. House of Representative walks out of Congress.

The New York legislature underscores its determination to uphold the Union by passing several government resolutions in its favor.

The Alabama State Convention approves secession on a 61 to 39 vote, becoming the fourth state to leave the Union.

January 12

POLITICS: The Ohio legislature votes overwhelmingly to support continuation of the Union.

January 13

MILITARY: An unofficial truce emerges between South Carolina authorities and the garrison at Fort Sumter, in Charleston harbor.

POLITICS: President James Buchanan entertains an envoy dispatched from South Carolina Governor Francis W. Pickens and declares that Fort Sumter will not be surrendered to state authorities. The president also receives a communiqué from Major Robert Anderson, who alerts him of his worsening situation.

January 14

POLITICS: The House of Representatives Committee of Thirty-Three fails to agree upon any compromise solution to stave off civil war. Chairman Thomas Corwin next proposes a constitutional amendment to protect slavery where it exists; it passes but is never ratified by any state.

The South Carolina legislature summarily declares that any Union attempt to reinforce Fort Sumter is tantamount to war.

January 15

MILITARY: Major Robert Anderson receives a second summons to surrender Fort Sumter, Charleston harbor; again he politely refuses.

January 16

POLITICS: The U.S. Senate effectively defeats the "Crittenden Compromise," insisting that the U.S. Constitution must be obeyed, not amended.

January 18

EDUCATION: Vassar Female College is founded in Poughkeepsie, New York, to offer women an education comparable to that received by men.

MILITARY: South Carolina officials make their third demand for the surrender of Major Robert Anderson and Fort Sumter, Charleston harbor, which is again respectfully declined.

POLITICS: Former postmaster general Joseph Holt becomes secretary of war to replace Virginian John B. Floyd.

The Massachusetts legislature votes to offer the Federal government men, money, and matériel in its struggle to preserve the Union.

January 19

POLITICS: The Georgia State Convention in Milledgeville approves secession on a 208 to 89 vote, becoming the fifth state to secede from the Union.

The Virginia General Assembly entreats all states to send delegates to a National Peace Convention in Washington, D.C.

January 21

POLITICS: Jefferson Davis of Mississippi, accompanied by Clement C. Lay and Benjamin Fitzpatrick of Alabama, and Stephen R. Mallory and David L. Yulee of Florida, make dramatic farewell addresses in the U.S. Senate chamber in Washington, D.C., then depart for home. Davis in particular is deeply troubled by the course of events and is said to pray for peace that evening.

The New York legislature votes to uphold the Union by force, if necessary.

Rabid abolitionist Wendell Phillips hails the decision of slave states to secede, feeling that their continued presence is detrimental to the remaining free states.

January 22

POLITICS: New York Governor Edwin Morgan orders all weapons and gunpowder supplies previously sold to Georgia impounded. This prompts a sharp rebuke from Governor Joseph E. Brown, who seizes several Northern vessels in retaliation.

The Wisconsin legislature votes to concur with New York's stand on preserving the Union.

January 23

NAVAL: Commander John A. B. Dahlgren removes cannon and ammunition from the Washington Navy Yard in the event of a possible attack, storing much of the latter in the attic of a building.

POLITICS: The Massachusetts legislature votes in agreement with New York's pledge to uphold the Union.

January 26

POLITICS: At Baton Rouge, the Louisiana State Convention approves secession on a vote of 113 to 17, becoming the sixth state to secede.

January 29

POLITICS: Following a congressional vote, Kansas joins the Union as its 34th state; significantly, its constitution explicitly outlaws slavery.

January 31

MILITARY: Louisiana officials orchestrate the seizure of the U.S. Branch Mint and Customs House at New Orleans, along with the U.S. Revenue schooner *Washington*.

February

LITERATURE: South Carolina poet Henry Timrod publishes his ode "Ethnogenesis," which calls for a distinctly Southern civilization. For this and subsequent war poems he is lauded as the "Laureate of the Confederacy."

1861

February 1

POLITICS: The Texas State Convention, convening in Austin, votes 166 to 7 in favor of secession, becoming the seventh state to secede. A public referendum is also scheduled to approve the measure.

February 3

POLITICS: Louisiana senators Judah P. Benjamin and John Slidell withdraw from the U.S. Senate and return home.

February 4

POLITICS: The Peace Convention, summoned by Virginia, assembles in Washington, D.C., under former president John Tyler. It consists of 131 members from 21 states, but none of the seceded states are represented.

Representatives from Alabama, Florida, Georgia, Louisiana, Mississippi, and South Carolina assemble in Montgomery, Alabama, and form a Provisional Congress of the Confederate States of America with Howell Cobb of Georgia functioning as president.

February 5

POLITICS: President James Buchanan reiterates to South Carolina officials his determination that Fort Sumter, Charleston harbor, will not be yielded to state authorities.

The Peace Conference in Washington, D.C., votes to earnestly resolve the outbreak of sectional violence both diplomatically and constitutionally.

February 7

INDIAN: The Choctaw Nation declares its allegiance with the Confederate States of America.

POLITICS: The Secession Convention at Montgomery, Alabama, begins formally drafting plans for a provisional government in the form of a confederacy of states.

February 8

POLITICS: President James Buchanan authorizes a $25 million loan for current expenditures and redemption of treasury notes.

Southern delegates at Montgomery, Alabama, proffer and unanimously approve the Provisional Constitution of the Confederate States of America—thereby founding the Confederacy. This document, while quite similar to its U.S. equivalent, explicitly declares and protects the right to own slaves. While the importation of slaves remains banned, the existing Fugitive Slave Law is strengthened.

February 9

POLITICS: Jefferson Davis of Mississippi, who is absent from the constitutional convention in Montgomery, Alabama, is unanimously elected provisional president of the Confederate States of America. Alexander H. Stephens of Georgia becomes provisional vice president. Moreover, the Provisional Confederate Congress pledges that all laws extant under the U.S. Constitution, which do not conflict with its Confederate counterpart, will be upheld.

Voters in Tennessee roundly defeat a move to convene a secession convention, 68,282 to 59,449.

February 10
POLITICS: A rather surprised Jefferson Davis is alerted by telegram of his election to the Confederate presidency. He had been anticipating a military commission of some kind but nonetheless agrees to the appointment.

February 11
POLITICS: President-elect Abraham Lincoln departs Springfield, Illinois, and wends his way toward Washington, D.C. He will not return alive.

Davis, Jefferson (1808–1889)
President, Confederate States of America

Jefferson Davis was born in Christian County, Kentucky, on June 3, 1808, and raised in Mississippi. After briefly attending Transylvania University he applied to the U.S. Military Academy in 1825 and graduated four years later in the middle of his class. As a second lieutenant in the 1st U.S. Infantry, he fought briefly in the Black Hawk War of 1832 under General Zachary Taylor and conducted Sauk Chief Black Hawk into confinement at Jefferson Barracks, Missouri. In May 1834 he married the daughter of General Taylor, but withdrew from society for a decade following her untimely death. It was not until 1844 that Davis emerged to successfully run for a seat in Congress. He resigned two years later to fight in the Mexican war he had so strenuously advocated, and successfully commanded the 1st Mississippi Rifle Regiment at the battles of Monterrey and Buena Vista. Davis returned to Mississippi a hero and subsequently won appointment to complete an unfinished term in the U.S. Senate in 1853, until President Franklin Pierce appointed him secretary of war. In this capacity, Davis displayed considerable foresight and innovation. In the spring of 1857 Davis was easily reelected to the Senate, where he continually and eloquently championed states rights and slavery. On January 21, 1861, he delivered an anguish-ridden farewell speech to the Senate before departing to tender his services to the emerging Confederate States of America. Once home Davis fully expected to become a major general of state forces,

(continues)

Jefferson Davis *(National Archives)*

(continued)

but on February 9, 1861, he was genuinely surprised to learn that the secessionist congress, meeting in Montgomery, Alabama, nominated him to serve as president.

Davis was inaugurated in the spring of 1861 at Montgomery, then transferred the seat of Confederate government to Richmond, Virginia, to shore up support from that state. In this capacity the problems Davis encountered as Confederate commander proved insurmountable. He clashed repeatedly with talented yet headstrong leaders like Pierre G. T. Beauregard and Joseph E. Johnston, periodically relieving them at inopportune times. As Confederate fortunes waned, Davis lacked the authority to decisively shift manpower from one theater to the next owing to resistance from state governments. He was thus forced to invoke measures like conscription, taxation, and confiscation to strengthen the overall Confederate position. When he and his entourage were seized by General James H. Wilson's cavalry at Irwinville, Georgia, on May 10, 1865, the Confederate States of America had reached its denouement. Davis, who never applied for a pardon and never renewed his citizenship, died in poverty at Beauvoir, Mississippi, on December 6, 1889. For many decades thereafter, in the minds of many fellow Southerners, he remained the embodiment and symbol of the Confederacy's proud and defiant "Lost Cause."

Jefferson Davis travels from his plantation in Brierfield, Mississippi, to attend inauguration ceremonies at Montgomery, Alabama.

February 12
POLITICS: The Provisional Congress of the Confederacy at Montgomery, Alabama, votes to establish a Peace Commission to the United States.

February 13
MILITARY: A detachment of U.S. Army troops under Colonel Bernard J. Dowling defeats a band of Chiricahua Apache at Apache Pass, Arizona; in July 1894 he receives the Congressional Medal of Honor for this action.

POLITICS: The electoral college counts the requisite votes and declares Abraham Lincoln the new chief executive.

February 16
POLITICS: Confederate president-elect Jefferson Davis arrives at Montgomery, Alabama, amid thunderous applause.

February 18
MILITARY: In an act widely condemned as treasonous, General David E. Twiggs surrenders all U.S. Army installations in Texas.

POLITICS: Jefferson Davis of Mississippi is inaugurated as provisional president of the Confederate States of America, declaring, "Obstacles may retard, but they can not long prevent the progress of a movement sanctified by its justice and sustained by a virtuous people." Alexander H. Stephens of Georgia, who initially opposed secession, becomes vice president. The glittering assembly is then serenaded by military bands that strike up the catchy air popularly known as "Dixie," which becomes the unofficial national anthem of the Confederacy.

February 19
POLITICS: The Confederate Convention in Montgomery, Alabama, elects Judah P. Benjamin of Louisiana as attorney general, Christopher G. Memminger of South Carolina as secretary of the treasury, John H. Reagan of Texas as postmaster general, Robert Toombs of Georgia as secretary of state, and Leroy P. Walker of Alabama as secretary of war.

February 20
POLITICS: The Provisional Confederate Congress declares the Mississippi River open to navigation and commerce. They also pass legislation creating a Confederate Department of the Navy.

February 21
NAVAL: Stephen R. Mallory, the former U.S. senator from Florida, is chosen as the Confederate secretary of the navy.
POLITICS: President Jefferson Davis receives a missive from South Carolina governor Francis W. Pickens requesting immediate action on Fort Sumter. Pickens regards the continuing presence of the Federal garrison as an affront to "honor and safety."

February 22
POLITICS: Passing through Baltimore, Maryland, president-elect Abraham Lincoln is warned of a possible attempt upon his life and finishes his journey to Washington, D.C., on board a secret train.

February 23
POLITICS: President-elect Abraham Lincoln arrives in Washington, D.C., amid a sense of mounting national consternation and foreboding over the fate of the nation.

Texas voters affirm secession by a three-to-one margin.

February 25
POLITICS: Judah P. Benjamin takes his oath as Confederate attorney general; this multitalented individual will hold several positions within the new government, excelling in all.

February 27
NAVAL: Congress authorizes the Navy Department's request for seven heavily-armed steam sloops to augment existing naval strength.
POLITICS: As a continuing gesture of averting hostilities, President Jefferson Davis appoints three commissioners for possible peace negotiations with Washington, D.C.

The Peace Commission meeting in Washington, D.C., proposes no less than six constitutional amendments to forestall the outbreak of cession and violence. None of them prove viable.

February 28
POLITICS: The House of Representatives adopts an amendment proposed by Thomas Corwin which reaffirms slavery's status where it already exists. President-elect Abraham Lincoln fully concurs with the legislation.

Calls for a state convention to weigh the possibility of secession are narrowly defeated by a popular vote in North Carolina.

The Confederate Congress agrees to a $15 million domestic loan.

The Colorado Territory is formed from the western half of the Kansas Territory, and William Gilpin gains appointment as governor.

1861

March 1

MILITARY: Pierre G. T. Beauregard is commissioned brigadier general, C.S.A.

Major Robert Anderson alerts the government that the garrison at Fort Sumter, Charleston harbor, must be either supplied and reinforced or evacuated without further delay. His provisions dwindle rapidly and he will soon have to capitulate by default.

POLITICS: President-elect Abraham Lincoln appoints Pennsylvania politician Simon Cameron to be his new secretary of war.

The Provisional Confederate States of America assumes formal control of events at Charleston, South Carolina.

March 2

BUSINESS: Congress passes the Morrill Tariff Act, which raises duties from five to 10 percent to protect American manufacturers.

POLITICS: The U.S. Senate refuses compromise solutions advanced by the Peace Convention in Washington, D.C., over the objections of Kentucky Senator John J. Crittenden. This ends all attempts at political accommodation.

Lincoln, Abraham   (1809–1865)
President

Abraham Lincoln was born near Hodgenville, Kentucky, on February 12, 1809, the son of a backwoods family. He endured childhood poverty while living on the frontiers of Indiana, becoming essentially self-taught. Lincoln eventually settled upon a career in law in Springfield, Illinois, and served as a militia captain during the brief Black Hawk War of 1832. The future commander in chief saw no combat save for, in his own words, "many bloody battles with mosquitoes." Lincoln subsequently acquired a taste for politics, joined the Whig Party, and in 1847 won a seat in the U.S. House of Representatives. In this capacity he stridently opposed both the Mexican War and the expansion of slavery into newly acquired territories. In 1858 Lincoln ran unsuccessfully as a Republican for the U.S. Senate against Democrat Stephen A. Douglas, and he captured national attention through a series of lively debates. Consequently, the gaunt and gangly attorney saw his political capital

Abraham Lincoln *(Library of Congress)*

soar and in 1860 he handily won the party's nomination for the presidency. He ran—and

President James Buchanan admits the new territories of Nevada and Dakota.

March 3

MILITARY: President Jefferson Davis appoints General Pierre G. T. Beauregard as commander of Confederate forces in the vicinity of Charleston, South Carolina. He is instructed to prepare for military action against the Federal garrison marooned at Fort Sumter in the harbor.

POLITICS: President-elect Abraham Lincoln dines with his cabinet for the first time and tours the Senate. Meanwhile, General Winfield Scott, commanding general of the U.S. Army, dourly informs Secretary of State William H. Seward that mounting a relief expedition to recuse Fort Sumter, Charleston harbor, appears impractical.

March 4

NAVAL: The Navy Department, which currently operates 42 warships, recalls all but three from foreign stations to assist in the impending crisis.

POLITICS: Abraham Lincoln is formally inaugurated as the 16th president of a less-than-united United States and is sworn in by Chief Justice Roger B. Taney.

won—on a platform dedicated to halting the expansion of slavery, not its abolition. However, Lincoln's ascension was construed as a direct threat to the South's "peculiar institution," and in December 1860 South Carolina seceded from the Union. This defiance induced other Southern states to follow and a new entity, the Confederate States of America, was already extant by the time Lincoln took his oath of office.

No newly sworn-in chief executive ever confronted a more daunting, dangerous situation than did Lincoln in the spring of 1861, with a small standing army and the Southern third of the nation up in arms against the Federal government. Despite his prior lack of military training, Lincoln displayed an astonishing grasp of strategy based on the North's overwhelming preponderance in terms of manpower and industry. Commencing at Bull Run, the Federal war effort remained beset by a secession of hesitant, if not outright blundering, leaders. Generals George B. McClellan, John Pope, Ambrose E. Burnside, and Joseph Hooker all tried and failed to defeat the Army of Northern Virginia under General Robert E. Lee. It was not until the spring and early summer of 1864 that the redoubtable General Ulysses S. Grant pinned Lee's army within its works at Richmond, while General William T. Sherman advanced upon him from behind. Lee then surrendered to Grant at Appomattox on April 9, 1865, effectively ending military operations in the East. All the while Lincoln took to the podium and pleaded for lenience toward the former Confederates and national reunification without vindictiveness. The president never lived to see the country reunited as on April 14, 1865, he was assassinated by John Wilkes Booth at Ford's Theater in Washington, D.C. Lincoln, the awkward, intensely sad-looking leader who had labored so intently and successfully at keeping the nation whole, became the first chief executive assassinated in office.

1861

His first address declares that the Union is "perpetual" and cannot be undone by secession. Moreover, he reiterates his belief that slavery cannot be allowed in the territories but is willing to leave it intact where it already exists. He remains conciliatory, assures the South it will not be attacked, and appeals to "the better angels of our nature." Hannibal Hamlin of Maine also becomes vice president, with William H. Seward as secretary of state, Salmon P. Chase as secretary of the treasury, and Edward Bates as attorney general.

The Confederate Convention, assembled at Montgomery, Alabama, officially adopts the "Stars and Bars" flag of seven stars and three stripes as its official symbol.

March 5

POLITICS: President Abraham Lincoln discusses the plight of Major Robert Anderson at Fort Sumter, South Carolina. The major telegraphs him that his supplies are due to run out within four to six weeks, after which he will have little recourse but surrender. Furthermore, both Anderson and General Winfield Scott concur that the post cannot be successfully held by less than 20,000 troops. Time is running out for a peaceful resolution, but Lincoln continues to try to deal with the delicate situation in a nuanced way.

March 6

POLITICS: The Confederate Congress authorizes recruitment of 100,000 volunteers for 12 months. President Jefferson Davis appoints Martin J. Crawford, John Forsyth, and A. B. Roman as special commissioners to deal with Republican officeholders in Washington, D.C., seeing that President Abraham Lincoln refuses to acknowledge their credentials.

March 7

NAVAL: Gideon Welles, a former Connecticut newspaper editor, is sworn in as the 24th secretary of the navy.

POLITICS: The Missouri State Convention displays a strong pro-Union streak and votes against secession, yet also considers the "Crittenden Compromise" a possible avenue for averting war.

March 9

POLITICS: At Montgomery, Alabama, the Confederate Convention authorizes the raising of military forces. They also pass a coinage bill and issuance of treasury notes in denominations ranging from $50 to $1 million.

March 11

POLITICS: The Constitution of the Confederacy is unanimously adopted by the Confederate Convention at Montgomery, Alabama, and passed along to constituent states for ratification. It is based primarily upon the existing U.S. Constitution but differs in explicitly condoning the practice of slavery.

March 13

MILITARY: Captain Nathaniel Lyon, a pugnacious, aggressive officer by nature, is appointed commander of the U.S. Arsenal at St. Louis, Missouri.

POLITICS: Despite pressure from within his own cabinet, President Abraham Lincoln directly orders Secretary of States William H. Seward not to receive Confederate peace emissaries. Through this expedient he avoids any appearance of legitimizing the Confederate government in Montgomery. He also dispatches former navy officer Gustavus V. Fox on a mission to Fort Sumter, South Carolina, to evaluate the possibility of succoring the garrison.

March 15

POLITICS: President Abraham Lincoln inquires of his cabinet whether or not a relief attempt ought to be mounted to resupply the garrison at Fort Sumter, South Carolina. The majority, especially Secretary of State William H. Seward, deems such a move as provocative and advises against it.

The Confederate Congress thanks the state of Louisiana for enriching its coffers with $536,000 appropriated from the U.S. Mint at New Orleans.

March 16

DIPLOMACY: President Jefferson Davis appoints three special ministers, William L. Yancey, Pierre A. Yost, and Dudley Mann, to visit Europe in the quest for diplomatic recognition. They are instructed to use cotton as economic leverage, whenever possible, for securing such support.

POLITICS: The Arizona (Territory) State Convention at Mesilla votes in favor of secession.

March 18

DIPLOMACY: President Abraham Lincoln appoints Charles Francis Adams as minister to Great Britain.

POLITICS: The Arkansas State Convention defeats a motion to secede on a vote of 39 to 35, then schedules a public referendum on the issue that summer.

Governor Sam Houston of Texas, having refused to take an oath of allegiance to the Confederacy, is forced to retire from office.

March 21

NAVAL: Former navy officer Gustavus V. Fox, pursuant to orders from President Abraham Lincoln, reconnoiters Fort Sumter and Charleston harbor, South Carolina, with a view toward relieving the garrison there.

March 22

POLITICS: Governor Claiborne F. Jackson of Missouri fails to convince his constituents to join the Confederacy, after which the state's citizens sharply divide into pro- and anti-Federal camps.

March 28

POLITICS: To break the impasse, President Abraham Lincoln resolves to mount a seaborne expedition to succor the Federal garrison at Fort Sumter, Charleston harbor, and orders it dispatched no later than April 6, 1861. His cabinet also divides on the matter, three to two in favor with Secretary of War Simon Cameron abstaining. In effect, the wily Illinois attorney is subtly maneuvering his Southern counterpart into firing the first shot.

March 31

POLITICS: President Abraham Lincoln orders a second relief expedition, this time to assist the federal garrison at Fort Pickens, Florida, which guards the entrance to Pensacola harbor.

April 1

POLITICS: Secretary of State William H. Seward strongly recommends that President Abraham Lincoln abandon Fort Sumter, South Carolina, while more defensible posts along the Gulf of Mexico be fortified. He further suggests that a war with Europe would serve as a "panacea" to unify the North. Lincoln courteously thanks the secretary for his sage advice—then declares he intends to run his own administration.

April 3

NAVAL: Confederate artillery on Morris Island, Charleston harbor, opens fire on the Union vessel *Rhoda H. Shannon* in the second instance of hostile shots being fired.

April 4

POLITICS: President Abraham Lincoln approves the strategy outlined by Gustavus V. Fox and informs Major Robert Anderson at Fort Sumter, Charleston, of an impending relief expedition. However, he still grants that officer discretionary authority to respond to any attack the Southerners may launch.

The Virginia State Convention in Richmond rejects an ordinance of secession, 89 to 45.

April 6

POLITICS: South Carolina governor Francis W. Pickens is advised by President Abraham Lincoln that an expedition is underway to supply—not reinforce—the Federal garrison at Fort Sumter, Charleston harbor. Moreover, if no resistance is mounted he pledges that no additional soldiers will be dispatched.

April 7

MILITARY: To increase pressure upon Major Robert Anderson, General Pierre G. T. Beauregard forbids any further communication between Fort Sumter, Charleston harbor, and the shore.

April 8

MILITARY: In response to the relief expedition dispatched toward Fort Sumter, Charleston harbor, Confederate authorities begin undertaking military preparations and planting artillery batteries.

April 10

NAVAL: The steamer *Baltic* departs New York in a second attempt to relieve the garrison at Fort Sumter, Charleston, with naval agent Gustavus V. Fox on board. En route it is joined by the USS *Pawnee* off Hampton Roads, Virginia.

Lieutenant John L. Worden arrives at Pensacola, Florida, on official business and receives permission from General Braxton Bragg to visit Fort Pickens.

April 11

MILITARY: As a sovereign state, the South cannot tolerate the impending approach of a Union supply vessel to victual Fort Sumter; assist constitutes an egregious affront to their self-proclaimed independence. General Pierre G. T. Beauregard is therefore ordered by Confederate authorities to demand the immediate capitulation of Fort Sumter, Charleston harbor. Anderson again flatly refuses their request but, as a sop to Southern sensitivities, he informs Beauregard that he is nearly out of supplies and must yield the palm by April 15 regardless. The Confederates nevertheless give Anderson 24 hours to strike his colors or they will commence bombarding.

POLITICS: Three Confederate peace emissaries depart Washington, D.C., having failed to reach an acceptable solution with Secretary of State William H. Seward. Meanwhile, Federal troops are ordered into the nation's capital, seeing that it is completely surrounded by potentially hostile territory.

April 12

MILITARY: The Civil War, a monumental struggle in military history and a defining moment for the United States, is about to unfold. At 4:30 A.M. the shoreline of Charleston harbor erupts in flame as 18 mortars and 30 heavy cannon, backed by 7,000 troops, commence a withering bombardment on Fort Sumter. Major Robert Anderson, commanding only 85 men, 43 civilian engineers, and 48 cannon, weathers the storm of shells and waits until daybreak before responding with six cannon of his own. To Captain Abner Doubleday goes the honor of firing the first Union shot of the war.

NAVAL: The USS *Pawnee*, the U.S. Revenue Cutter *Harriet Lane*, and the steamer *Baltic*, commanded by Gustavus V. Fox, arrive in Charleston harbor with food supplies for Fort Sumter. Having arrived too late to assist the garrison, they remain passive spectators while the bombardment continues.

April 13

MILITARY: After 34 hours of continuous shelling, a lucky Confederate shot slices through Fort Sumter's flagstaff at 12:48 P.M. and Major Robert Anderson decides that the wiser course is to surrender. He therefore raises the white flag at 2:30 P.M. and the firing ceases while surrender ceremonies are planned for the following day. Curiously the garrison is unhurt despite being hit by an estimated 4,000 shells. However, the affair is perceived as an overt act of Southern aggression, helps galvanize the heretofore tepid sentiments throughout the North, and grants President Abraham Lincoln the moral authority necessary for waging war against his countrymen.

NAVAL: Relief ships under Gustavus V. Fox continue loitering outside Charleston harbor, South Carolina, unwilling to approach closer in the face of hostile fire.

His mission completed, Lieutenant John L. Worden returns to Washington, D.C., from Fort Pickens, Florida. En route he is arrested by Confederate authorities near Montgomery, Alabama, and imprisoned.

April 14

MILITARY: Major Robert Anderson formally capitulates at Fort Sumter, South Carolina, to Confederate authorities. The only casualties he sustains in 24 hours of fighting are two killed and four wounded, who ironically fall when a pile of ordnance accidently ignites during a 100-gun salute to the American flag. The captives are then rowed ashore and subsequently entertained by the cream of Charleston society before departing with Gustavus V. Fox and his ad hoc squadron. "We have met them and we have conquered," Governor Francis W. Pickens crows as the first act in a long and bloody drama concludes.

SETTLEMENT: Mormons found Franklin, the first permanent settlement of the Oregon Territory; prior attempts have wilted in the face of harsh Native American resistance.

April 15

POLITICS: In a move designed to deny the Confederacy diplomatic recognition, President Abraham Lincoln declares not war but rather a state of insurrection in the South and calls for 75,000 three-month volunteers to suppress it. However, service by African Americans is declined. Lincoln also requests a special meeting of Congress to convene on July 4–Independence Day. Not surprisingly, the call to arms is denounced and ignored by the governments of North Carolina, Kentucky,

1861

Interior view of Fort Sumter on April 14, 1861, after its evacuation. *(National Archives)*

and Virginia. By contrast, the New York legislature militantly endorses the Union causes and votes $3 million to support war efforts.

April 16

POLITICS: Virginia governor John Letcher informs President Abraham Lincoln that his state will not furnish troops for what he considers the "subjugation" of the South.

April 17

NAVAL: The USS *Powhatan* under Lieutenant David D. Porter arrives at Fort Pickens, Florida, and debarks an additional 600 troops to bolster the sailors and marines already there. Thus the best harbor of the Gulf of Mexico is retained by the Union for the remainder of the war.

POLITICS: Secessionists gather at Baltimore in large numbers.

The Virginia State Convention, reacting strongly to President Abraham Lincoln's call to arms, votes 88 to 55 for secession. The proposal is then forwarded to the public for ratification.

President Jefferson Davis begins soliciting applications for Confederate letters of marque and reprisal, in effect establishing a force of Southern privateers.

The governments of Missouri and Tennessee refuse to raise the requested number of militia forces.

April 18

MILITARY: The 6th Massachusetts Infantry rides the rails from New York to Baltimore, Maryland, en route to Washington, D.C.

Colonel Robert E. Lee declines an offer from President Abraham Lincoln to command all Union forces.

Lieutenant Roger Jones orders his command of 50 men to burn the U.S. Armory at Harper's Ferry, western Virginia, thereby preventing its tooling facilities from falling into enemy hands. Fire destroys the buildings along with 15,000 rifled muskets, but the local population extinguishes the flames before the valuable factory tools, dies, and equipment are destroyed.

April 19

MILITARY: The 6th Massachusetts, transferring between railroad stations in Baltimore, Maryland, is violently attacked by pro-Southern rioters. Shots are exchanged, resulting in four soldiers killed and 36 wounded. These are the first Union casualties, while 11 civilians are also slain. Seething secessionists also begin cutting rail and telegraph lines leading toward the capital. For several anxious days Washington, D.C., remains temporarily cut off from the rest of the Union.

NAVAL: To interrupt any flow of food or war materiels from abroad, President Abraham Lincoln declares a naval blockade of the Confederate coastline. This effort encompasses all the ports of South Carolina, Georgia, Alabama, Florida, Mississippi, Louisiana, and Texas and so overwhelms the relatively small U.S. Navy that its implementation is gradual. In time the blockade intensifies to stranglehold proportions and emerges as a major factor in the economic collapse of the Confederacy.

April 20

AVIATION: Balloonist Thaddeus S. C. Lowe makes a record flight of more than 90 miles from Cincinnati, Ohio, to the coast of South Carolina in only nine hours.

MILITARY: Colonel Robert E. Lee tenders his resignation from the U.S. Army.

To obstruct the passage of Federal troops to Washington, D.C., secessionist mobs burn several raillines out of Baltimore. This requires reinforcements to arrive by water and then rebuild the tracks as they proceed on foot, slowing their progress.

NAVAL: Captain Charles S. McCauley hurriedly and prematurely orders the Gosport Navy Yard in Norfolk, Virginia, burned and evacuated. The resulting destruction is less-than complete and the dry docks become operative again in a few weeks. The Confederates also retrieve no less than 1,200 heavy naval cannon which they implant at fortifications as far west as Vicksburg, Mississippi. McCauley's badly botched withdrawal from Norfolk proves an embarrassing windfall for the Confederacy.

The venerable USS *Constitution*, "Old Ironsides" of War of 1812 fame, is towed to safety from Annapolis, Maryland, by a steamship.

The U.S. Naval Academy at Annapolis is abandoned and transferred north to Newport, Rhode Island, for the duration of the war while the campus buildings serve as barracks for Union troops.

April 21

NAVAL: Confederate forces reoccupy Gosport Navy Yard, Virginia, and salvage the old steam frigate USS *Merrimack*; in a few months this vessel is reincarnated as the ironclad CSS *Virginia*.

POLITICS: Rioting and civil disorder continue in Baltimore, Maryland, including sabotage of nearby railroad lines.

Pro-Union delegates meeting in Monongahela County in western Virginia discuss a secession movement of their own from the Confederacy.

SLAVERY: The USS *Saratoga* captures the cargo vessel *Nightingale*, which is found laden with 961 African slaves. The U.S. government has officially banned trafficking in human cargo since 1808.

April 22

NAVAL: Captain Franklin Buchanan, commanding the Washington Navy Yard, tenders his resignation in anticipation of Maryland's apparent impending secession—he is not reinstated once his state remains loyal and he ultimately joins the Confederacy. Buchanan is succeeded by Captain John A. B. Dahlgren, another distinguished officer.

April 23

MILITARY: General Robert E. Lee becomes commander of the Virginia state forces.

POLITICS: President Jefferson Davis offers aid to Confederate sympathizers in Missouri if they would attack and seize the U.S. Arsenal in St. Louis.

An assembly of free African Americans in Boston, Massachusetts, demands that Federal laws preventing their enrollment in the state militia be repealed.

April 25

MILITARY: The 8th Massachusetts under General Benjamin F. Butler defiantly parades through Washington, D.C., following its lengthy march around Baltimore, Maryland.

In a daring raid, Union Captain James H. Stokes arrives at St. Louis, Missouri, by steamer, where he removes 12,000 rifled muskets from the U.S. arsenal there. The weapons are then deposited at Alton, Illinois, for militia use, which proves a critical blow to Confederate sympathizers gathering in the region.

April 26

MILITARY: General Joseph E. Johnston arrives and receives command of Confederate forces in Virginia then guarding the capital of Richmond.

POLITICS: Georgia governor Joseph E. Brown orders all debts owned to Northern firms repudiated.

April 27

NAVAL: President Abraham Lincoln extends the Union blockade to encompass the coasts of Virginia and North Carolina following their secession. Secretary of the Navy Gideon Welles also authorizes the interdiction of Confederate privateers at sea.

POLITICS: President Abraham Lincoln authorizes suspension of writs of habeas corpus for security matters between Philadelphia, Pennsylvania, and Washington, D.C. General Winfield Scott is entrusted with adjudicating all incidents arising from this crackdown.

The Virginia Convention proffers its capital of Richmond as an alternative to Montgomery, Alabama.

April 29

POLITICS: The Maryland House of Delegates decisively votes down secession by a margin of 53 to 13.

The Provisional Confederate Congress convenes its 2nd session at Montgomery, Alabama, granting President Jefferson Davis war powers and authority to raise volunteers, make loans, issue letters of marque, and command land and naval forces. This is done in direct reaction to President Abraham Lincoln's insurrection declaration and his call for volunteers.

WOMEN: Elizabeth Blackwell, the nation's first female doctor, establishes the Women's Central Association for Relief to better coordinate the myriad of smaller war-relief groups arising. Her organization serves as the precursor for the much larger U.S. Sanitation Commission.

April 30

MILITARY: Colonel William H. Emory evacuates Fort Washita in the Indian Territory (Oklahoma) and heads north towards Fort Leavenworth, Kansas. His withdrawal renders the nearby Five Civilized Tribes (Cherokee, Chickasaw, Cree, Choctaw, and Seminole) vulnerable to Confederate influence.

May 1

MILITARY: Soldiers killed in the Baltimore riots are interred with full military honors in Boston, Massachusetts.

General Robert E. Lee orders additional Confederate forces concentrated in the vicinity of Harper's Ferry, Virginia, presently commanded by Colonel Thomas J. Jackson.

Governor Samuel W. Black of the Nebraska Territory calls out volunteer forces to assist the Union.

May 3

MILITARY: President Abraham Lincoln issues a call for 42,000 three-year volunteers, with 10 new regiments for the U.S. Army and an additional 18,000 personnel for the navy. This brings existing manpower ceilings to 156,000 soldiers and 25,000 sailors.

General Winfield Scott, the senior American commander, unveils his so-called Anaconda Plan for defeating the Southern rebellion to President Abraham Lincoln. Basically, it entails a gunboats' support drive down the Mississippi River by 60,000 troops, which commences at Cairo, Illinois, and ends at New Orleans, Louisiana. Concurrently, the U.S. Navy will tightly blockade the Confederate coast to strangle all trade with Europe. Derided at the time by younger officers favoring a swift and decisive military campaign, Scott's strategy is not formally enacted until 1864, and then in slightly modified form. Lincoln spends the next three years looking for a general to execute it forcefully.

May 6

MILITARY: The Confederate-leaning Missouri State Guard under General Daniel M. Frost establishes a training camp near St. Louis at the behest of Governor Claiborne F. Jackson. Meanwhile, Captain Nathaniel Lyon, commanding the Federal garrison at St. Louis, refuses all demands to remove his troops from the city.

NAVAL: The Confederate Congress mandates the issuance of letters of marque and reprisals to privateers.

POLITICS: President Jefferson Davis signs a bill passed by the Confederate Congress declaring a state of war with the United States.

The state legislature in Arkansas approves a secession ordinance by 69 to 1, becoming the ninth state to depart while the Tennessee legislature votes 66–25 to become the 10th. The latter also authorizes a public referendum on the issue, before the decision is finalized.

May 7

MILITARY: President Abraham Lincoln appoints newly repatriated Major Robert Anderson to recruiting duties in his native state of Kentucky.

NAVAL: The U.S. Naval Academy staff, students, and supplies finally board the steamer *Baltic* and the venerable frigate USS *Constitution*, prior to locating to a new venue at Newport, Rhode Island.

POLITICS: Once the Tennessee legislature formally endorses secession, riots erupt between pro- and anti-Union sympathizers in Knoxville. The eastern half of the state remains a strong Unionist enclave throughout the war and a region of concern to the Confederacy.

May 9

NAVAL: Confederate Secretary of the Navy Stephen R. Mallory orders Commander James D. Bulloch to England as the Confederacy's naval agent. There he engages in a battle of wits with American minister Charles Francis Adams while clandestinely acquiring ships, guns, and ammunition.

POLITICS: President Jefferson Davis authorizes enlisting upwards of 400,000 volunteers for three years or the duration of the war. The quotas are enthusiastically met at first.

May 10

MILITARY: General Robert E. Lee is made commander of all Confederate forces in Virginia, along with states' forces.

Violence erupts in St. Louis, Missouri, between Southern sympathizers and U.S. Army troops backed by a large German-speaking population. Around two dozen civilians and two soldiers die in fighting as Captain Nathaniel Lyon energetically rounds up General Daniel Frost and 625 Missouri State Guard troops at Camp Jackson. However, his rashness drives many undecided civilians into the enemy's ranks and an additional 30 are killed in subsequent rioting.

NAVAL: Confederate Secretary of the Navy Stephen R. Mallory alerts the Committee of Naval Affairs in Congress that the acquisition of a heavily armored stem vessel is "a matter of the first necessity."

May 11

MILITARY: Continuing secessionist unrest in St. Louis, Missouri, results in seven additional civilian deaths at the hands of the 5th Reserve Regiment. Colonel William S. Harney also arrives back in town and succeeds Captain Nathaniel Lyon as garrison commander.

May 13

DIPLOMACY: In a move which antagonizes the Lincoln administration, the government of Great Britain recognizes both North and South as belligerents. This is a discrete nod in terms of recognizing the Confederacy as an equal partner in the upcoming struggle, but Queen Victoria's adherence to strict neutrality otherwise dashes Southern hopes for immediate recognition and military intervention on their behalf.

MILITARY: Baltimore is secured by Federal forces under General Benjamin F. Butler, who both occupies Federal Hill and imposes martial law without prior authorization.

General George B. McClellan is appointed commander of the Department of the Ohio.

POLITICS: Virginia delegates from the western portion of the state, who disagree with secession, convene a convention of their own in Wheeling and discuss joining the Union as a new state.

May 14

DIPLOMACY: U.S. Minister Charles F. Adams arrives in London, England, where it is expected that his pristine abolitionist credentials will resonate favorably at the Court of St. James.

MILITARY: John C. Frémont, a popular explorer and one-time presidential candidate, becomes a major general in the U.S. Army. Irvin McDowell and Montgomery C. Meigs are appointed brigadier generals.

General Benjamin F. Butler consolidates his grip upon Baltimore, Maryland, and arrests noted secessionists including Ross Winans, who had previously invented a steam cannon. Governor Thomas H. Hicks also issues calls for four regiments to defend both the city and the national capital.

Major Robert Anderson is instructed by President Abraham Lincoln to assist Kentucky Unionists wherever possible, despite that state's avowed neutrality.

May 15

MILITARY: Major Robert Anderson, defender of Fort Sumter and the first Northern war hero, is promoted several ranks to brigadier general, U.S. Army.

Union General Benjamin F. Butler relinquishes command of the Department of Annapolis and arrives at Fortress Monroe, Virginia, where he gains promotion to major general of volunteers. He is succeeded by General George Cadwalader.

Colonel William S. Harney, commanding St. Louis, Missouri, implores citizens to ignore secessionist attempts to raise militia. However, he takes no steps to interfere with secessionist activities.

May 16

POLITICS: Tennessee is formally admitted into the Confederacy under Governor Isham Harris.

May 17

INDIAN: Chief John Ross declares neutrality for Cherokee throughout the Indian Territory, although the tribe continues splintering into pro- and anti-secessionist factions.

POLITICS: President Jefferson Davis agrees to a $50 million loan to the Confederate government along with the distribution of treasury notes. He also signs legislation admitting North Carolina into the Confederacy.

May 18

POLITICS: Arkansas formally joins the Confederate States of America.

Politician Francis P. Blair contacts President Abraham Lincoln concerning his suspicions about Colonel William S. Harney, commanding officer at St. Louis.

May 20

POLITICS: The Provisional Confederate Congress elects to relocate itself from Montgomery, Alabama, to Richmond, Virginia, where it will remain until 1865. This move is calculated to shore up the Old Dominion's ties to the Confederacy, but it also shifts the strategic locus of the war northward.

At the behest of Governor Beriah Magoffin, the legislature of the strategic state of Kentucky declares neutrality in the upcoming struggle.

1861

The North Carolina State Convention in Raleigh votes to become the 10th state to secede and also ratifies the Confederate Constitution.

May 21

DIPLOMACY: A bellicose Secretary of State William H. Seward issues Dispatch No. 10 for Minister Charles F. Adams in London, which threatens war with England. In light of prevailing military and political realities, Adams simply ignores it.

MILITARY: Colonel William S. Harney, commanding Federal forces in Missouri, enters into a convention with Missouri State Guard commander General Sterling Price. Harney agrees not to introduce Federal troops into the state if the Southerners can maintain order. Both Francis P. Blair and Captain Nathaniel Lyon condemn the agreement, regarding it as treasonous.

May 23

POLITICS: A popular vote for secession in Virginia is 97,750 in favor and 32,134 against. However, efforts continue on the 50 western counties of the state to remain with the Union.

SLAVERY: General Benjamin F. Butler, commanding Fortress Monroe, Virginia, refuses to hand over three runaway slaves to their owners by declaring them "contraband of war." This establishes an important precedent for allowing thousands of slaves to escape to Union lines and freedom.

May 24

MILITARY: General Samuel P. Heintzelman's 13,000 Federal soldiers occupy Alexandria and Arlington Heights, Virginia, bolstering the defenses of Washington, D.C. However, when 24-year-old Colonel Elmer E. Ellsworth of the 11th New York Regiment (Fire Zouaves) removes a Confederate flag from a hotel in Alexandria, he is shot by innkeeper James T. Jackson, who is then himself killed. Ellsworth enjoys the melancholy distinction of becoming the North's first officer fatality.

May 25

LAW: Secessionist John Merryman is imprisoned by Union authorities in Baltimore, Maryland, for recruiting Confederate troops and sabotaging railroad lines and bridges. Supreme Court Chief Justice Roger B. Taney, acting in the capacity of a Federal circuit court judge, issues a writ of habeas corpus on Merryman's behalf to release him, but the local commanding officer recognizes no authority other than the commander in chief's. Taney subsequently writes that only Congress possesses the power to suspend habeas corpus.

POLITICS: President Abraham Lincoln attends the funeral of Colonel Elmer E. Ellsworth after his remains lay in state at the White House. "So much of promised usefulness to one's country, and of bright hopes for one's self and friends," a somber Lincoln writes, "have rarely been so suddenly dashed, as in his fall."

May 26

COMMUNICATION: U.S. Postmaster General Francis P. Blair announces the suspension of all mail service to the Confederate states.

MILITARY: General George B. McClellan orders three columns of Union forces to advance on Grafton in western Virginia in order to secure the Baltimore & Ohio Railroad. This rail line constitutes the strategic link between the capital and the western states.

May 27

POLITICS: Supreme Court Justice Roger B. Taney again declares the suspension of the writ of habeas corpus unconstitutional, which President Abraham Lincoln promptly ignores in light of circumstances.

May 28

MILITARY: General Irvin McDowell is appointed commander of the Department of Northwestern Virginia, including newly acquired Alexandria.

POLITICS: The American Peace Society fails to achieve a quorum at its annual meeting, proof that it message is completely out of touch with prevailing sentiments.

May 29

WOMEN: Dorothea L. Dix approaches Secretary of War Simon Cameron and offers to assist organizing hospital services for Federal forces.

May 30

SLAVERY: Secretary of War Simon Cameron instructs General Benjamin F. Butler at Fortress Monroe, Virginia, that fugitive slaves crossing into Union lines are not to be returned but, rather, fed and given work around military installations.

May 31

MILITARY: General John C. Frémont supercedes General William S. Harney as Union commander in Missouri. The latter's agreement with General Sterling Price over the introduction of Federal troops in the region is also abrogated.

June 1

DIPLOMACY: In a major defeat for Confederate privateering, the government of Great Britain forbids armed vessels of either side from bringing prizes into English ports. However, this stance does not prevent British shipyards from clandestinely constructing warships for use by the Confederate Navy.

June 3

MILITARY: Indiana troops under General Thomas A. Morris surprise and easily defeat a Confederate detachment under Colonel George A. Porterfield at Philippi in western Virginia. This "victory," greatly exaggerated in the press as the "Philippi Races," clears the Kanawha Valley of Southerners and provides greater impetus for breaking with the Confederacy altogether.

POLITICS: Democrat Stephen A. Douglas, the "Little Giant" who defeated Abraham Lincoln in his bid for the Senate, dies in Chicago at the age of 48. The North loses one of its most eloquent and forceful spokesmen.

June 8

POLITICS: Tennessee voters approve a secession ordinance by 109,913 votes to 47,238, and they join the Confederacy as the 11th and final state to do so. However, the eastern counties remain active in the Union cause.

June 9

MILITARY: General Benjamin F. Butler decides to dislodge Confederate forces gathered at Big Bethel, Virginia, only eight miles from his main position at Hampton. The transit, however, goes badly with many units becoming lost. Worse, the 5th New York Infantry (Zouaves), resplendent in their gray uniforms, are mistaken for Confederates and fired upon, sustaining 21 casualties.

POLITICS: The Sanitary Commission is organized to provide nursing, sanitation, and other support functions for Union forces.

1861

June 10

MILITARY: Federal troops under General Ebenezer Pierce number 4,400, attack 1,500 Confederates led by General John B. Magruder at Big Bethel, Virginia. The green, inexperienced Union soldiers are committed piecemeal against enemy entrenchments by their commander; then are beaten back, principally by the well-trained 1st North Carolina under Colonel Daniel H. Hill.

Federal Captain Nathaniel Lyon, reappointed to command the St. Louis garrison, storms out of negotiations with pro-Southern governor Claiborne F. Jackson and Missouri State Guard commander General Sterling Price. He then "declares war" on the state of Missouri and prepares to deal with his opponents by force.

NAVAL: Confederate Lieutenant John M. Brooke, a gifted naval engineer, receives orders to convert the former steam frigate USS *Merrimack* into the ironclad CSS *Virginia*.

WOMEN: Dorothea L. Dix becomes Superintendent of Woman Nurses to help supervise medical services within the U.S. Army.

June 11

MILITARY: Colonel William W. Loring resigns his commission as commander of the New Mexico Territory and is succeeded by Colonel Edward R. S. Canby.

POLITICS: Pro-Union delegates meeting at Wheeling, Virginia, form an alternate government in the western-most reaches of that state and elect Francis H. Pierpont as governor, along with two U.S. Senators.

June 13

POLITICS: President Abraham Lincoln lends officials to the U.S. Sanitation Commission to assist sick and injured soldiers, as well as render assistance to their families.

June 14

MILITARY: Robert E. Lee is promoted to full general, C.S.A.

June 15

MILITARY: Federal troops under Captain Nathaniel Lyon forcibly occupy the capital of Jefferson City, Missouri, while 1,500 poorly armed and trained Confederate sympathizers under Governor Claiborne F. Jackson encamp at nearby Booneville.

June 16

COMMUNICATION: Congress passes the Pacific Telegraph Act which authorizes construction of a new telegraph line reaching from Missouri to California.

MILITARY: Confederate forces under General Robert S. Garnett seize Laurel Hill in western Virginia and subsequently occupy strong positions at Rich Mountain. Badly outnumbered by troops of the nearby Department of the Ohio under General George B. McClellan, he initiates a series of raids to keep larger Union forces off balance.

June 17

AVIATION: President Abraham Lincoln is treated to a demonstration of new balloon technology by Professor Thaddeus S. C. Lowe. Military observers present appreciate the potential use of such craft as battlefield reconnaissance platforms.

DIPLOMACY: The government of Spain declares its neutrality but, taking England's lead, recognizes the Confederacy as a belligerent power.

MILITARY: General Nathaniel Lyon and 1,700 Federal troops aggressively pursue up the Missouri River retreating Missouri State Guard forces under Governor Claiborne F. Jackson. After a 20-minute stand they flee to the southwestern corner of the state. More importantly, Union forces now control the lower Missouri River, and Lyon warns all inhabitants in the region of stern punishment for possible acts of treason.

POLITICS: Union delegates meeting in Wheeling, Virginia, unanimously declare their independence from the Confederacy.

Pro-Union inhabitants of Greeneville, Tennessee, rally to keep their region of the state out of Southern hands.

June 19

INDIAN: Cherokee Chief John Ross repeats his stance of neutrality and reminds fellow tribesmen of previous obligations to the United States.

POLITICS: Pro-Union delegates gathered at Wheeling, Virginia, elect Francis H. Pierpont to be provisional governor of the western portion of that state.

June 20

POLITICS: The governor of Kansas calls upon citizens to organize and repel any pro-secessionist attacks emanating from Missouri.

June 22

POLITICS: Pro-Union sympathizers gather in Greenville, Tennessee, vote to formally declare their allegiance to the United States.

June 23

AVIATION: Professor Thaddeus S. C. Lowe rises in his balloon to observe Confederate deployments at Falls Church, Virginia. This is one of the earliest American reconnaissance flights.

NAVAL: Armored conversion of the CSS *Virginia* (née USS *Merrimack*) continues apace at Norfolk, Virginia, under the direction of John Mercer Brooke.

PUBLISHING: Congress founds the U.S. Government Printing Office in Washington, D.C.; today it is the largest printing concern in the world.

June 27

NAVAL: A major strategy session unfolds in Washington, D.C., with representatives of the army, navy, and coast survey in attendance. The newly created Blockade Strategy Board includes Captain Samuel F. Du Pont, Commander Charles H. Davis, and other military notables, and it becomes a key planning body whose policies remain in effect throughout the war.

Confederates repel an attempt to land forces at Mathias Point, Virginia, by gunboats USS *Pawnee* and *Thomas Freeborn*. Commander James H. Ward, a former superintendent of the U.S. Naval Academy, dies in action, becoming the Navy's first officer fatality.

June 28

BUSINESS: To facilitate construction of a transcontinental railway, the Central Pacific Railroad Company is incorporated at Sacramento, California.

NAVAL: The Blockade Strategy Board resolves to seize a port in South Carolina or Georgia to serve as a coaling station and help sustain the blockade effort offshore.

June 29

MILITARY: Amid mounting war fever, President Abraham Lincoln is briefed on military strategy by generals Winfield Scott and Irvin McDowell. However, Scott protests against committing raw soldiers to combat at this stage of the conflict and argues–unsuccessfully–against seeking victory in a single, decisive battle.

June 30

NAVAL: Captain Raphael Semmes, commanding the CSS *Sumter*, evades the USS *Brooklyn* off New Orleans, Louisiana, and commences his celebrated career as a commerce raider.

July

ARTS: Matthew Brady is commissioned to make a carefully documented photographic record of the Civil War, backed by a team of 20 talented associates. This is the first war so documented and the results are truly impressive, but it ultimately leads to his financial ruin.

July 1

POLITICS: The War Department decrees that military volunteers will be recruited from both Kentucky and Tennessee, despite the former's neutrality and the latter's secession.

July 2

POLITICS: The new pro-Union legislature of western Virginia convenes at Wheeling.

President Abraham Lincoln confers with General John C. Frémont over strategy in the vital and sensitive region of Missouri, which is wracked by secessionist unrest.

July 4

POLITICS: President Abraham Lincoln addresses a special session of the 37th Congress and pleads for $4 million and an additional 400,000 men. Having exhausted all avenues for a peaceful settlement, he makes clear his intention of waging war solely against the Confederate government–and not the South itself. He also explains and justifies his recent suspension of habeas corpus as strictly a wartime expedient.

July 5

MILITARY: Colonel Franz Sigel, leading a detachment of 1,100 German-speaking volunteers, advances upon a larger force of 4,000 Missouri militia under Governor Claiborne F. Jackson near Carthage. The Confederates decide to attack Union lines, which are posted upon a hilltop, at which point Sigel, badly outnumbered, falls back.

July 6

MILITARY: General George B. McClellan, commanding the Department of the Ohio, prepares to order an Indiana brigade under General Thomas A. Morris to advance upon Confederate troops gathered at Laurel Hill in western Virginia. He intends to simultaneously lead the main body of three brigades in a similar movement against enemy forces at nearby Rich Mountain.

NAVAL: Confederate raider CSS *Sumter* under Captain Raphael Semmes docks at Havana, Cuba, with six Northern prizes in tow.

July 7

MILITARY: General Nathaniel Lyon, commanding Union forces at Springfield, Missouri, is reinforced by troops under Major Samuel D. Sturgis. He now possesses 7,000 men, but remains outnumbered two-to-one by the recently invigorated Confederates.

July 8

NAVAL: While cruising the Potomac River, the screw tug *Resolute* espies and retrieves two mysterious looking objects—which turn out to be the first confederate "torpedoes" (mines) encountered in the war.

July 9

POLITICS: The U.S. House of Representatives resolves not to oblige Union soldiers to return fugitive slaves.

July 10

INDIAN: The Creek Nation concludes a peace treaty with agent Colonel Albert Pike of the Confederacy.

MILITARY: Having reconnoitered enemy positions, General George B. McClellan commences his offensive in western Virginia by dispatching General William S. Rosecrans to dislodge enemy troops from Rich Mountain, while another force under General Thomas A. Morris advances upon Confederates gathered at Laurel Hill.

POLITICS: General Abraham Lincoln assures General Simon B. Buckner, head of the Kentucky militia, that Union forces will not violates his state's neutrality.

July 11

MILITARY: General William S. Rosecrans and 2,000 Union troops defeat Colonel John Pegram's 1,300 Confederates at Rich Mountain in western Virginia, after marching all night through a heavy downpour. Victory here places Union forces astride General Robert S. Garnett's lines of communication, and he begins withdrawing from Laurel Hill while pursued by the main force under General George B. McClellan.

POLITICS: The U.S. Senate formally expels absent members from Arkansas, North Carolina, Texas, and Virginia. One senator from Tennessee is also ejected but Andrew Johnson, a loyalist from the eastern region of that state is allowed to retain his seat.

July 12

INDIAN: Colonel Albert Pike arranges treaties between the Confederacy and the Choctaw and Chickasaw tribes residing in the Indian Territory (Oklahoma).

MILITARY: Colonel John Pegram surrenders 555 Confederates to General William S. Rosecrans at Beverly, western Virginia, which is subsequently occupied by the main Union force under General George B. McClellan. Southerners under General Robert S. Garnett, anxious to escape a closing pincer movement, hurriedly march from Kaler's Ford on the Cheat River to nearby Corrick's Ford.

July 13

MILITARY: General Robert S. Garnett's Confederates are defeated at Corrick's Ford (Carricksford) in western Virginia, by General Thomas A. Morris's Indiana brigade. Union losses are variously reported as from 10 to 53 in number, while the Confederates admit to 20. Significantly, Garnett is the first general officer on either side killed in action.

POLITICS: The House of Representatives expels Missouri member John Clark on a vote of 94 to 45.

July 14

MILITARY: Command of Southern forces in western Virginia reverts to General Henry R. Jackson. Meanwhile, a Union push under General Robert Patterson stalls south of Harper's Ferry after encountering a stiff defense by General Joseph E. Johnston. Patterson's timidity and hesitancy to fight occasions him the unflattering nickname of "Granny" from his troops.

July 16

MILITARY: Anxious to maintain the strategic initiative on the heels of good progress in western Virginia, General Irvin McDowell orders his 32,000 men toward Manassas Junction. "On to Richmond!" becomes the national mantra—despite the fact that McDowell's recruits only cover six miles to Fairfax Court House. Another two days are required to reach Centreville, 22 miles distant from the capital, and his dilatoriness grants Confederate forces under General Pierre G. T. Beauregard a badly needed respite to collect and reposition themselves to meet him.

NAVAL: In a reversal of fortunes, the Confederate prize crew aboard the captured *S. J. Waring* is overpowered by its crew—led by William Tilghman, an African-American sailor. The ship subsequently arrives in New York six days later.

July 17

MILITARY: President Jefferson Davis orders General Joseph E. Johnston to reinforce General Pierre G. T. Beauregard in Virginia. For this first time in military history large numbers of troops are strategically shuttled from one front to another by train, bringing Confederate numbers at Manassas Junction to nearly match Union strength.

July 18

DIPLOMACY: Secretary of State William H. Seward instructs American ministers in England and France to endorse the previously rejected 1856 Declaration of Paris, which outlawed privateering. However, this move is scuttled when the government of neither European nation will apply it to the Confederacy.

MILITARY: General Irvin McDowell dispatches a reconnaissance in force under General Daniel Tyler toward Confederate forces collected at Centreville, Virginia. These soldiers skirmish with Southerners posted across a creek for an hour before the 12th New York makes an ill-advised charge and is blasted back by heavy rifle fire emanating from the dense woods.

July 19

MILITARY: Newly arrived General John Pope warns the inhabitants of northern Missouri that treasonable activity would be punished promptly, "without awaiting a civil process."

NAVAL: The Captain-General of Cuba orders all the Northern prizes brought into Havana by Captain Raphael Semmes of the CSS *Sumter* released.

July 20

JOURNALISM: The New York *Tribune* is the first newspaper to adopt the political pejorative "Copperhead" (a poisonous snake found in the South) for any Northern politician opposing the war effort.

1861

MILITARY: General Joseph E. Johnston arrives at Manassas Junction, Virginia, with reinforcements and succeeds General Pierre G. T. Beauregard as senior commander, although he allows the latter to retain overall command. General Irvin McDowell, meanwhile, decides that the Confederate right is too strong to assail frontally and seeks an unguarded crossing point nearer to Beauregard's left flank. All told, McDowell conceives a viable enough battle plan but entrusts it to men and officers too inexperienced to execute it properly.

POLITICS: The third session of the 1st Provisional Confederate Congress convenes in Richmond, Virginia, for the first time. President Jefferson Davis declares that Arkansas, North Carolina, Tennessee, and Virginia have allied themselves to the Confederacy and that the new capital is now permanently established at Richmond.

July 21

MILITARY: A momentous day unfolds with the predawn movement of General Daniel Tyler's division, which begins groping through the darkness at 2:00 A.M. Four hours later his cannon begin lobbing shells on Confederate positions behind the stone bridge across Bull Run. After two hours of heavy fighting the Southerners give way in confusion and the Federals resume advancing in the direction of Henry House Hill. A brigade of five Virginia regiments under General Thomas J. Jackson deploys in their path, assisted by several batteries, and ferociously resists a Union onslaught by 18,000 men. Jackson's aggressive defense greatly inspires the Southerners and, sensing victory and the exhausted state of their antagonists, Beauregard orders a sudden advance across the entire line with the trademark "Rebel yell." McDowell's tired, demoralized soldiers withdraw in confusion and headlong into a well-dressed throng of civilians gathered by the roadside to witness their anticipated "victory." The first major engagement of the Civil War ends in a tactical triumph for the Confederacy with Southern losses of 1,982 to a Union tally of 2,896.

NAVAL: The U.S. Marine Corps receives its baptism of fire when a battalion commanded by Major John Reynolds loses nine killed, 19 wounded, and 16 missing.

July 22

MILITARY: The three-month enlistment of many Union volunteers begins expiring, allowing many of them to be discharged. President Abraham Lincoln counters by signing two bills authorizing one million three-year volunteers.

General George B. McClelland is ordered to succeed the now-disgraced General Irvin McDowell.

POLITICS: Consistent with the "Crittenden Compromise," the House of Representatives votes for war to preserve government under the Constitution and save the Union, while preserving the status quo over slavery. The measure is likewise taken up for consideration by the Senate.

The Missouri State Convention, meeting at Jefferson City, votes overwhelmingly in favor of the Union and also relocates the capital to St. Louis. Secessionist governor Claiborne F. Jackson, however, declares himself the only legitimate political authority in that state.

July 24

MILITARY: General Jacob D. Cox engages and disperses Southerners under General Henry A. Wise at Tyler Mountain in western Virginia. The town of Charleston is subsequently evacuated in the face of mounting Union pressure and the Kanawha Valley is soon free of Confederates.

POLITICS: Congress authorizes the position of assistant secretary of the Navy, along with legislation "for the temporary increase in the navy."

July 25

POLITICS: Congress authorizes the recruitment of volunteers, offering those serving two years a $100 bonus.

Tennesseean senator Andrew Johnson moves to adopt the "Crittenden Compromise" in the U.S. Senate and it passes 30 to five. This mandates and reaffirms that the war is being waged to preserve both the Constitution and the Union, and not to abolish slavery.

Confederate Secretary of State Robert Toombs, having resigned to join the military, is replaced by Robert T. Hunter.

July 27

POLITICS: President Abraham Lincoln confers with newly arrived General George B. McClellan in Washington, D.C. The chief executive urges a strategic offensive with advances into Tennessee by way of Virginia and Kentucky. McClellan, who is not as easily stampeded into action as his predecessor, respectfully demurs.

July 28

MILITARY: In light of the deteriorating situation in western Virginia and the death of General Robert Garnett at Carricksford, the little-known General Robert E. Lee is ordered to take command of Confederate forces there.

July 29

POLITICS: Horace Greeley, previously the hawkish editor of the New York *Tribune*, writes to President Abraham Lincoln and suggests peace negotiations to end the fighting.

July 30

POLITICS: The Missouri State Convention votes 56–25 to declare the gubernatorial seat open, thereby deposing Confederate-leaning Claiborne F. Jackson as chief executive.

SLAVERY: General Benjamin F. Butler seeks clarification in his orders from the War Department as to policies respecting the great number of escaped African Americans in his camp.

July 31

MILITARY: President Abraham Lincoln elevates a heretofore obscure army officer, Ulysses S. Grant, to brigadier general of volunteers in Illinois. This turns out to be one of the most decisive military appointments of the war and a harbinger of victory in the war.

POLITICS: Pro-Union forces in Missouri are bolstered by the election of Hamilton R. Gamble as governor.

August 1

MILITARY: President Jefferson Davis urges General Joseph E. Johnston to maintain the strategic initiative with further offensive actions against Union forces still in Virginia.

NAVAL: Gustavus V. Fox, a former naval officer, gains appointment as assistant secretary of the Navy.

August 2
MILITARY: Union forces under General Nathaniel Lyon and Confederates under General Ben McCulloch clash at Dug Springs, Missouri. Lyon, badly outnumbered, orders his men back to Springfield to regroup.
POLITICS: Congress approves virtually all President Abraham Lincoln's acts and appropriations deemed necessary to pursue the war effort, along with issuances of bonds and tariff increases to raise revenue. To better fund the war effort, Congress also passes its first-ever national income tax of 3 percent on incomes over $800.

August 3
AVIATION: In another early application of aerial reconnaissance, John LaMountain lifts off the deck of the USS *Fanny* in a balloon while anchored off Hampton Roads, Virginia, and observes Confederate gun positions at Sewell's Point.
NAVAL: Congress directs the Department of the Navy to design and construct three ironclad prototypes. They also institute an "Ironclad Board" to study and recommend the acquisition and deployment of ironclad warships.
POLITICS: Governor Isham G. Harris of Tennessee seeks to visit with authorities in Richmond, Virginia, and discuss ways of shoring up tenuous Confederate authority in his state.

August 5
BUSINESS: President Abraham Lincoln signs legislation authorizing the first national income tax of three percent on all incomes over $800.
POLITICS: The first session, 37th Congress, concludes its monumental, 34-day special session and adjourns.

August 6
SLAVERY: President Abraham Lincoln signs the First Confiscation Act, which emancipates all African-American slaves found in the employ of Confederate armed forces, either as laborers or soldiers.

August 7
NAVAL: The U.S. government authorizes construction of seven ironclad gunboats under engineer James B. Eads of St. Louis, Missouri, for riverine service: USS *Cairo, Carondelet, Cincinnati, Louisville, Mound City, Pittsburgh,* and *St. Louis.* These vessels gradually emerge as the nucleus of Union naval power along strategic western water routes.

August 8
MILITARY: General Ulysses S. Grant takes command of Union forces at Ironton, Missouri.
SLAVERY: Secretary of War Simon Cameron declares that citizens are not obliged to obey the Fugitive Slave Law as it pertains to secessionists. He further orders General Benjamin F. Butler not to return escaped slaves to their Confederate owners.

August 9
MILITARY: A force of 12,000 Confederates under generals Ben McCulloch and Sterling Price converge upon Springfield, Missouri, and encamp near Wilson's Creek, 10 miles to the southwest. The aggressive General Nathaniel Lyon, rather than abandon the town without a fight, musters his 4,200 Federals and prepares to launch a preemptive strike of his own.

August 10

MILITARY: Union General Nathaniel Lyon initiates the Battle of Wilson's Creek by storming Confederate campsites at 5:30 A.M. General Franz Sigel, meanwhile, stealthily advances upon the Southern camp from below and rousts Confederate cavalry deployed there. General Ben McCulloch, however, reacts quickly to this threat and dispatches troops that drive Sigel off, securing the Confederate rear area. Lyon, unaware of Sigel's debacle, holds his ground as Price commits two frontal assaults in superior force and he is killed. The Federals consequently draw off in orderly fashion. Losses at Wilson's Creek proved nearly equal with the Union suffering 1,317 casualties to a Southern tally of 1,230.

August 11

JOURNALISM: Citing aid and comfort to the enemy, the government suspends postal privileges to the New York *Daily News* for the next 18 months. This is the first of five Northern newspapers silenced for alleged Confederate views.

August 14

MILITARY: General Charles C. Frémont declares martial law in St. Louis, Missouri, and begins confiscating the property of suspected Confederate sympathizers.

August 15

MILITARY: General Robert Anderson, formerly commander at Fort Sumter, assumes control of the Department of the Cumberland (Tennessee and Kentucky). However, his health is compromised by bouts of nervous exhaustion attributed to his recent ordeal and he retires from active duty soon afterward.

In view of Confederate successes in Missouri, General John C. Frémont pleads with the War Department for immediate reinforcements. President Abraham Lincoln, cognizant of the threat to this vital border state, authorizes an immediate transfer of troops.

POLITICS: President Jefferson Davis orders all remaining Northerners out of Confederate territory within 40 days.

August 16

POLITICS: President Abraham Lincoln reiterates that the South remains in a state of insurrection and declares all commercial intercourse between loyalist and rebellious states prohibited.

August 17

MILITARY: Henry W. Halleck is promoted to major general, U.S. Army.

August 18

JOURNALISM: New York newspapers *Journal of Commerce*, *Daily News*, *Day Book*, and *Freeman's Journal* are summarily banned from publishing for alleged disloyalty.

August 19

JOURNALISM: The Southern-leaning editor of the *Essex County Democrat* (Massachusetts) is accosted by a mob, tarred, and feathered. Newspaper offices in Easton and West Chester, Pennsylvania, are also accosted by pro-Union mobs over their suspected Southern sympathies.

POLITICS: Pro-slavery expatriates from Missouri petition for their state to join the Confederacy even while driven from office.

August 20

MILITARY: General George B. McClellan formally assumes control of the newly constituted Department and Army of the Potomac. This vaunted force becomes a permanent fixture in the struggle for Virginia over the next four years.

August 24

DIPLOMACY: President Jefferson Davis appoints James M. Mason of Virginia to be special commissioner to Great Britain, John Slidell of Louisiana as special commissioner to France, and Pierre A. Rost of Louisiana as special commissioner to Spain. Each man is specifically instructed to seek diplomatic recognition for the Confederacy and, with it, the ability to acquire arms and ammunition.

NAVAL: A combined Union expedition assembles at Hampton Roads, Virginia, under Commodore Silas H. Stringham. This powerful force mounts 143 rifled cannon while Stringham, a capable veteran of many years with the Mediterranean Squadron, is well-versed in the latest fort-reducing tactics perfected during the Crimean War.

Captain Andrew H. Foote is appointed to replace Captain John Rodgers as commander of the gunboat flotilla on the western waters.

POLITICS: President Abraham Lincoln informs Governor Beriah Magofin of Kentucky of his refusal to withdraw Union troops already in Kentucky, regardless of its professed neutrality.

August 27

NAVAL: The naval expedition under Commodore Silas Stringham anchors off Hatteras Inlet, North Carolina, and prepares to attack and land troops to storm nearby forts Clark and Hatteras. These are garrisoned by 350 men of the 7th North Carolina under Colonel William F. Mountain and are poorly situated to resist such a powerful force.

August 28

NAVAL: To seal off Pamlico Sound, an important blockade-running route, a combined expedition of eight warships and two transports under Commodore Silas Stringham takes up bombardment positions off Hatteras Inlet, North Carolina. Around 10 A.M. he forms his vessels into a fast moving circle offshore which continuously bombards Confederate positions with a heavy, plunging fire.

August 29

MILITARY: General Benjamin F. Butler lands 900 soldiers and occupies Forts Hatteras and Clark at Hatteras Inlet, North Carolina. The Union thus secures its first toehold in Southern territory, and the inlet performs useful service throughout the war as a coaling and resupply station for the blockading squadron offshore.

August 30

MILITARY: Without prior authorization, General John C. Frémont proclaims a conditional emancipation declaration in Missouri and frees all slaves belonging to Confederate sympathizers. President Abraham Lincoln, after learning of his actions, declares them dictatorial and potentially alienating for slave-owning Unionists in the region.

August 31

MILITARY: General William S. Rosecrans takes three brigades of Ohio troops, 6,000 strong, and marches south from Clarksburgh, western Virginia, intending to attack Confederates under General John B. Floyd at Carnifex Ferry.

NAVAL: The Navy Department abolishes the daily rum ration for sailors.

September 1

EDUCATION: Mary Chase, an African-American freedwoman, starts the first school for contrabands (escaped slaves) in Alexandria, Virginia.

MILITARY: General Ulysses S. Grant arrives at Cape Girardeau, Missouri, and takes nominal command of Union forces throughout southeastern Missouri.

September 2

POLITICS: President Abraham Lincoln, eager to placate slaveholding border states, instructs General Charles Frémont in Missouri to "modify" his emancipation proclamation—in effect, countermand it.

September 3

MILITARY: In a major development, General Leonidas K. Polk orders Confederate forces to violate Kentucky neutrality and preempt any possible Union advances there. General Gideon Pillow responds by occupying Hickham, Clark Cliffs, and Columbus, establishing a continuous war front now stretching from Missouri to the Atlantic Ocean.

September 5

MILITARY: General Ulysses S. Grant prepares his forces gathered at Cairo, Illinois, for an immediate occupation of Paducah, Kentucky, at the strategic confluence of the Tennessee and Ohio Rivers. The mouth of the Cumberland River is also nearby.

NAVAL: Captain Andrew H. Foote reports for duty at St. Louis, Missouri, replacing Commander John Rodgers.

September 6

DIPLOMACY: The U.S. Consul in London is alerted of the purchase of steamers *Bermuda, Adelaide*, and *Victoria* by Confederate agents.

MILITARY: Federal troops under General Ulysses S. Grant advance south from Cairo, Illinois, to Paducah, Kentucky, at the mouth of the Tennessee River, to forestall its capture by Confederates. Grant then appoints General Charles F. Smith to assume command of all Union forces in western Kentucky after he hastens back to Cairo.

NAVAL: Gunboats USS *Tyler* and *Lexington* under Commander John Rodgers provide useful support during General Ulysses S. Grant's occupation of Paducah, Kentucky, which places the mouth of the Tennessee and Cumberland Rivers under Union control.

September 9

POLITICS: President Abraham Lincoln is advised by his cabinet to relieve the erratic but popular General John C. Frémont from command in Missouri. The president nonetheless relents for the time being and instructs General David Hunter to convey additional troops there as reinforcements.

September 10

MILITARY: General Albert S. Johnston is appointed commander of all Confederate forces in the West.

General William S. Rosecrans and 6,000 Union troops attack 2,000 Confederates under General John B. Floyd at Carnifex Ferry in western Virginia. The Federals press forward into a stretch of the Gauley River and clear a heavily wooded area, capturing many Southern supplies. Floyd hastily shuttles his command across the river under the cover of darkness and destroys the nearby ferry to avoid a pursuit.

In western Virginia, General Robert E. Lee prepares his command to pass over to the offensive. He formulates a complicated plan to isolate and storm the Union outpost atop Cheat Mountain, for its possession would sever Northern communications along the Staunton-Parkersburg Turnpike.

September 11

MILITARY: General Robert E. Lee and 15,000 Confederates launch an overly complex and unsuccessful attack upon General J. J. Reynolds and his 2,000 Union troops at Cheat Mountain and Elkwater, western Virginia. The assailants are hampered from the onset by rough terrain and heavy rainfall, and then are misled by prisoners into thinking that they are outnumbered. Lee, alarmed by the supposed approach of Union reinforcements, then calls off the attack and unceremoniously withdraws, an inauspicious debut for the Confederacy's premier soldier.

POLITICS: President Abraham Lincoln orders the emancipation declaration of General John C. Frémont modified to conform with existing acts of Congress, which are far less strident on the issue of freeing slaves.

The Kentucky legislature, angered by Confederate violation of its neutrality, demands the immediate removal of all Southern forces from its territory. A similar call applying to Federal troops is defeated by pro-Unionists.

September 12

POLITICS: President Abraham Lincoln dispatches a personal emissary to St. Louis and again instructs General John C. Frémont to modify his emancipation proclamation—which he considers a potential threat to Kentucky's allegiance. He also orders Federal troops to arrest of 31 members of the Maryland legislature suspected of collusion.

September 13

MILITARY: President Jefferson Davis and General Joseph E. Johnston heatedly argue over the Confederate seniority systems respecting generals; this initiates a permanent estrangement between the two men.

General Sterling Price, seeking to maintain the strategic initiative, marches from Wilson's Creek and besieges Lexington, Missouri—midway between Kansas City and St. Louis—with 7,000 state guards.

September 14

NAVAL: Lieutenant John H. Russell fights the first pitched naval engagement of the Civil War at Pensacola, Florida, by sailing the frigate USS *Colorado* past Confederate batteries at night, then leading 100 sailors and marines on a cutting-out expedition that nets several vessels.

September 15

MILITARY: General Robert E. Lee, bested at Cheat Mountain, directs the Confederate evacuation form Virginia's westernmost counties. Consequently, he earns the unflattering sobriquet of "Granny." Recent operations reflect badly upon Lee as a military leader, and plans are afoot to transfer him to a quiet sector in South Carolina.

POLITICS: President Abraham Lincoln confers with his Cabinet about the necessity of removing the erratic General John C. Frémont as commander of Missouri.

1861

General John C. Frémont has politician Frank P. Blair, his most vocal critic, arrested in St. Louis, Missouri.

September 16

MILITARY: Confederate general Sterling Price is reinforced and tightens his grip around Lexington, Missouri, while Union defenders under Colonel James A. Mulligan, 23rd Illinois, await promised assistance from St. Louis. Unbeknownst to him, General John C. Frémont fails to assist the beleaguered garrison.

NAVAL: The Ironclad Board recommends to Secretary of the Navy Gideon Welles the construction of three new ironclad warships—*Monitor*, *Galena*, and *New Ironsides*. The former is a revolutionary new turreted design promoted by Swedish émigré engineer John Ericsson.

September 18

MILITARY: General Sterling Price's Confederates fiercely assail the Union perimeter at Lexington, Missouri, and cut the garrison off from their water supply. At day's end, with few losses to either side, Price calls off the attack and allows the intense heat to do its work.

POLITICS: The Kentucky legislature authorizes the use of force to expel Confederate forces from its territory.

September 19

MILITARY: Advancing Confederates under General Felix Zollicoffer attack and drive Union troops from Barboursville, Kentucky. The Southerners then commence erecting strong defensive positions across Cumberland Gap, Bowling Green, and Columbus.

NAVAL: The North Atlantic Blockading Squadron under Commodore Louis M. Goldsborough is ordered to commence operating off the coasts of North Carolina and Virginia.

September 20

MILITARY: Colonel James Mulligan, 23rd Illinois, surrenders 2,800 Union troops at Lexington, Missouri, to General Sterling Price after a nine-day siege. Price's men ingeniously employed dampened bales of hemp as movable breastworks, which they rolled ahead of their advance. General John C. Frémont's unwillingness or inability to lift the siege causes many in St. Louis and Washington, D.C., to question his competence.

September 25

MILITARY: President Jefferson Davis and General Joseph E. Johnston engage in another heated contretemps, this time over Southern strategy and the allocation of resources.

SLAVERY: The Navy Department authorizes employment of African-American "contrabands" onboard naval vessels. They will begin drawing pay at the rank of "boy," $10 per month and one ration per day.

September 27

MILITARY: President Abraham Lincoln and General George B. McClellan engage in protracted debate as to resuming offensive operations in Virginia. The general feels that his Army of the Potomac is not yet ready for field operations whereas Lincoln is taking political heat over its perceived inactivity.

Ericsson, John   (1803–1889)
Shipwright

John Ericsson was born in Langsbansbytten, Sweden, and he joined the corps of mechanical engineers as a cadet at the age of 14. He then served in the Swedish army as a lieutenant of topographical engineers, where he remained until emigrating to England in 1827. Ericsson was a confirmed tinkerer, and in 1829 he designed and built the experimental locomotive *Novelty* for his English hosts. This device was capable of reaching then unheard of speeds of 30 miles per hours. Ericsson also dabbled in marine engineering, designing a viable screw propeller for steam warships to replace the clumsy side paddles. The conservative British admiralty expressed no interest in the device, but Ericsson had a chance encounter with U.S. Navy Captain Robert F. Stockton, who convinced him to move to America. Stockton subsequently used his political influence to have Ericsson design and build the navy's first steam frigate, the USS *Princeton*, and in 1844 this became the world's earliest propeller-driven warship. Beyond propulsion, its many innovations included placement of the engines below the waterline to avoid hostile fire, and two new 12-inch diameter cannons, one designed by Stockton and one by Ericsson, on the deck. After an unfortunate explosion killed Secretary of the Navy Abel P. Upshur, Ericsson found himself blacklisted and was unable to find work with the Navy for the next 15 years. He simply turned his attention to applying the new steam technology to domestic merchant vessels.

It was not until the advent of the Civil War in April 1861 that Ericsson found favor with the Navy Department again. The government was concerned that the Confederates were building new classes of iron warships and accepted bids for Union ironclads to counter them. Ericsson trumped the competition by submitting designs for a radical new warship, the USS *Monitor*, which was a low-lying vessel with a single revolving turret housing two cannon. Though often derided as looking like a "cheese box on a raft," this ship was the world's first modern warship. On March 9, 1862, the *Monitor*, under Lieutenant John L. Worden, successfully confronted the Confederate ironclad CSS *Virginia* off Hampton Roads, Virginia, fighting the larger vessel to a draw and preserving the Union blockade of Norfolk. The success of Ericsson's design led to several new classes of warships, hereafter known generally as monitors, for the U.S. Navy, and they became the focus of American ship construction. Ericsson, for his part, patriotically turned over his unpatented plans to other engineering firms to facilitate rapid construction. By war's end ships of his design proved instrumental in blockading the South, leading to its ultimate demise. After the war Ericsson continued designing new warships for the navy, including the high speed *Destroyer* of 1878. He died in New York on March 8, 1889, one of the most influential shipwrights of history. At the behest of the Swedish government, his remains were returned home, carried there on a monitor-class vessel he helped pioneer.

October 1

AVIATION: Inventor and balloonist Professor Thaddeus S. C. Lowe is appointed head of the Union Army's nascent aeronautical section.

MILITARY: President Abraham Lincoln appoints General Benjamin F. Butler to command the Department of New England, created largely for the purposes of raising and training new troops for future operations. He also requests action on a large naval expedition to the South Atlantic coast to carve out a coaling station.

At Centreville, Virginia, President Jefferson Davis and generals Joseph E. Johnston and Pierre G. T. Beauregard continue arguing over strategy. At length they agree to consolidate their positions and restrain from launching offensive operations into Northern territory until at least the following spring.

NAVAL: Secretary of the Navy Gideon Welles opposes issuing letters of marque and reprisal against the South as it inadvertently implies recognition of national sovereignty.

October 2

POLITICS: Governor Andrew B. Moore of Alabama warns tradesmen against charging exorbitant prices for their goods and services.

October 3

DIPLOMACY: Louisiana Governor Thomas O. Moore summarily bans cotton exports in a move to force England and France to recognize Confederate independence.

MILITARY: General Joseph J. Reynolds advances from Cheat Mountain with 5,000 men to dislodge a Confederate force gathered at Camp Bartow, along the southern fork of the Greenbrier River, western Virginia. Unable to turn their flank, Reynolds simply withdraws back to Cheat Mountain and an impasse settles in over the region.

October 4

INDIAN: The Confederacy concludes a treaty with the Shawnee, Seneca, and Cherokee in the Indian Territory.

NAVAL: President Abraham Lincoln approves a contract for constructing the U.S. Navy's first ironclad warships; among them is John Ericsson's revolutionary USS *Monitor*.

October 7

NAVAL: The steam-powered ironclad CSS *Virginia* (née USS *Merimack*), completely armored and redesigned by Confederate naval engineer John M. Brooke, makes its brief but ominous debut off Hampton Roads, Virginia.

POLITICS: President Abraham Lincoln dispatches Secretary of War Simon Cameron with a letter to General Samuel R. Curtis and inquires if General John C. Frémont should be replaced as commanding officer in Missouri.

October 9

MILITARY: General Braxton Bragg orders 1,000 Confederates under General Richard H. Anderson across Pensacola Bay to attack Union-held Fort Pickens on Santa Rosa Island, Florida. The attack stalls and a quick sweep by the Federal garrison nets several stragglers as the Southerners withdraw.

October 10

SLAVERY: President Jefferson Davis, writing to General Gustavus W. Smith, briefly ponders the use of African-American slaves as laborers for the Confederate army.

October 12

NAVAL: Newly launched Confederate ram CSS *Manassas* under Commodore George N. Hollis departs New Orleans, Louisiana, and ventures down the Mississippi River accompanied by the armed steamers *Ivy* and *James L. Day*. A stiff

Sailors relaxing on the deck of the USS *Monitor.* *(Library of Congress)*

engagement develops in which Hollis rams the USS *Richmond* and *Vincennes,* running them aground.

October 14
LAW: To discourage treasonable activity, President Abraham Lincoln orders General Winfield Scott to suspend writs of habeas corpus anywhere in the region from Washington, D.C., to Maine.

SLAVERY: Secretary of War Simon Cameron orders General Thomas W. Sherman to organize and arm fugitive slaves into military squads at Port Royal, South Carolina.

October 16
POLITICS: President Jefferson Davis denies requests by Confederates to return home and serve in their state militia in lieu of regular army service.

October 17
NAVAL: After some deliberation, Commodore Samuel F. Du Pont informs Secretary of the Navy Gideon Welles that Port Royal, South Carolina, is an inviting target and would constitute an important asset to the blockading effort.

October 18

POLITICAL: President Abraham Lincoln meets with his Cabinet over continuing dissatisfaction with General in Chief Winfield Scott and his probable retirement. He also experiences problems prying troops from the armies of generals William T. Sherman and George B. McClellan for the upcoming Port Royal expedition.

October 20

MILITARY: General George B. McClellan, eager to test Confederate responses and pressured by radical Republicans to resume the offensive, orders politician-turned-soldier Colonel Charles P. Stone to dispatch troops from Poolesville, Maryland, and demonstrate along enemy lines near Leesburg, Virginia.

October 21

MILITARY: Acting upon faulty intelligence, Colonel Edward D. Baker ferries 1,700 men of his brigade across the Potomac River at Ball's Bluff, Virginia, beneath a 100-foot-high ledge overlooking that waterway. He does so without proper reconnaissance and remains unaware strong Confederate forces under Colonel Nathan G. Evans are posted in the woods above him. An unequal battles ensues for three and a half hours until Baker is killed and his command succumbs to panic. The Federals lose nearly 1,000 men, mostly drowned or captured.

October 22

MILITARY: General Thomas J. "Stonewall" Jackson is ordered to lead Confederate forces into the Shenandoah Valley of western Virginia.

October 23

NAVAL: Crew members of the captured Confederate privateer *Savannah* are tried in New York on charges of piracy and threatened with execution. Though convicted, their sentences are never carried out.

October 24

COMMUNICATION: The vaunted "Pony Express" is finally disbanded after being made obsolete by the first transcontinental telegraph service. It nonetheless provided valuable service by informing the far western states of recent political and military events back East. The new telegraph is something of a technological marvel, having taken the past 16 months to span 3,000 miles between Washington, D.C., and San Francisco, California.

POLITICS: President Abraham Lincoln relieves General John C. Frémont of command in Missouri and replaces him with General David Hunter. He also attends funeral services for Colonel Edward D. Baker, a close friend, recently killed at Ball's Bluff, Virginia.

October 25

NAVAL: Swedish inventor and engineer John Ericsson begins constructing his revolutionary, one-turret warship USS *Monitor* at Greenpoint, New York.

October 28

MILITARY: General Albert S. Johnston arrives and relieves General Simon B. Buckner as commander of the Confederate Army Corps of Kentucky at Bowling Green.

October 29

NAVAL: A huge combined expedition of 17 warships, 25 supply vessels, and 25 transports under Commodore Samuel F. Du Pont, conveying General Thomas

W. Sherman and 13,000 Federal troops, departs Hampton Roads, Virginia. This force, the largest American armada assembled to date, is intending to capture Port Royal, South Carolina, and make a Union lodgment midway between Charleston and Savannah, Georgia.

October 30
MILITARY: President Jefferson Davis complains to General Pierre G. T. Beauregard about publishing excerpts from his report on the Battle of First Manassas (Bull Run) "to exalt yourself at my expense." The two leaders are never reconciled.

October 31
MILITARY: The ailing, 75-year-old General in Chief Winfield Scott, once the premier officer of his era, voluntarily resigns as head of Union forces. He then retires in virtual isolation to the U.S. Military Academy at West Point, New York, for the remainder of the war.

POLITICS: Secessionist-leaning Missouri legislators meet at Neosho and again vote to join the Confederacy. Thus the state remains simultaneously claimed by both belligerents.

November 1
MILITARY: Thirty-four-year-old General George B. McClellan gains appointment as the new general in chief to succeeded the ailing Winfield Scott. In light of his youth, dash, and reputation, much is expected of him.

General Ulysses S. Grant arrives at Cairo, Illinois, to take charge of the District of Southeast Missouri. Rumpled and nondescript in appearance, he proves himself aggressively disposed and begins formulating plans to evict Confederate forces from their strong point along the bluffs at Columbus, Kentucky.

November 2
MILITARY: Incorrigible General John C. Frémont is relieved of command of the Department of the West at Springfield, Missouri, and is temporarily replaced by General David Hunter.

November 4
NAVAL: The huge naval expedition of Commodore Samuel F. Du Pont anchors off Port Royal, South Carolina. Meanwhile, Confederate vessels under Commodore Josiah Tattnall fire upon the Coast Survey ship *Vixen* and USS *Ottawa* as they reconnoiter the two-mile-wide channel entrance.

POLITICS: President Jefferson Davis, frustrated in his inability to reach an agreement with General Pierre G. T. Beauregard over strategy, solicits advice from senior generals Samuel Cooper and Robert E. Lee. He is also increasingly aware of rumors accusing him of political ineptitude.

November 5
MILITARY: General Robert E. Lee assumes responsibilities as head of the newly constituted Department of South Carolina, Georgia, and East Florida.

General John C. Frémont, still commanding the Department of the West, orders General Ulysses S. Grant on a diversionary attack against Columbus, Kentucky. He anticipates this maneuver will keep Confederate forces occupied and unable to cross the Mississippi River into Missouri.

1861

November 6

POLITICS: President Jefferson Davis is formally reelected chief executive of the Confederate States of America and slated to serve a six-year term. Vice President Alexander H. Stephens likewise remains in office, as do members of the first permanent Confederate Congress.

November 7

MILITARY: Approximately 3,000 Union troops under General Ulysses S. Grant debark at Hunter's Farm, three miles above his objective at Belmont, Missouri. His opponent, General Gideon Pillow, commands 2,500 men and Grant's enthusiastic soldiers storm into their camp. Despite entreaties from Grant and other officers, order breaks down and they embark on a headlong plundering spree, which allows Pillow to be reinforced by Confederates under General Leonidas K. Polk. Grant has little choice but to cut his way through enemy lines to the riverbank and escape, but the affair demonstrates his willingness to undertake offensive missions.

NAVAL: The South Atlantic Blockading Squadron of 77 vessels under Commodore Samuel F. Du Pont debarks the 16,000 Federal troops of General Thomas W. Sherman off Port Royal Sound, South Carolina, halfway between Charleston and Savannah, Georgia. The Union thus acquires a second lodging on the Confederate coastline; in time Port Royal/Hilton Head emerges as a major supply center for the blockading squadron.

November 8

NAVAL: The screw sloop USS *San Jacinto* under Captain Charles Wilkes boards the British mail packet *Trent* in Old Bahama Channel and forcibly removes Southern envoys James M. Mason and John Slidell. This is an egregious violation of international law and threatens to embroil the United States in a new war with Great Britain.

November 9

MILITARY: Federal troops under General Thomas W. Sherman, assisted by gunboats, advance from Port Royal, South Carolina, and capture the city of Beaufort on the Broad River. Confederate department commander General Robert E. Lee expresses concern to superiors in Richmond over the Union's ability to land troops anywhere, at will.

In a major shake-up of command, General Henry W. Halleck becomes head of Federal troops in the newly designated Department of Missouri (Missouri, Arkansas, Illinois, and western Kentucky), while General Don Carlos Buell replaces General William T. Sherman as head of the Department of the Cumberland.

November 11

AVIATION: Professor Thaddeus S. C. Lowe, Union chief of army aeronautics, rides an observation balloon launched from the gunboat *G. W. Custis* while anchored in Chesapeake Bay. Meanwhile, a torchlight parade unfolds in Washington, D.C., in honor of General George B. McClellan, now hailed as the savior of the Republic.

MILITARY: General George B. Crittenden assumes command of Confederate troops in the District of Cumberland Gap, Tennessee. His chief subordinate, General Felix K. Zollicoffer, is assigned to hold southeastern Kentucky but also not to expose his men by remaining south of the Cumberland River.

November 12

NAVAL: The British-built steamer *Fingal* arrives at Savannah, Georgia, with a store of military supplies. The vessel is subsequently taken into Confederate service as the CSS *Atlanta*.

November 13

POLITICS: George B. McClellan contemptuously snubs President Abraham Lincoln, when the latter calls upon his headquarters, by retiring to bed. Henceforth, the general will be summoned to the White House when consultations become necessary.

November 15

INDIAN: A mixed force of 1,400 Texans under Colonel Douglas H. Cooper and allied Cherokee, Choctaw, and Chickasaw Indians arrive at Canadian Creek, Indian Territory (Oklahoma), intending to fight the 1,000 Union-leading Creeks gathered there under Chief Opothleyahola. However, they discover that the enemy has slipped away, so Cooper orders a pursuit toward nearby Round Mountain.

MILITARY: President Abraham Lincoln and his cabinet begin focusing their attention upon the city of New Orleans, Louisiana, the Confederacy's second largest city and a port of strategic significance. In choosing an experienced leader to spearhead an amphibious expedition and capture it, Secretary of the Navy Gideon Welles selects Captain David G. Farragut, a 60-year-old Tennessean known for his aggressive tactics.

NAVAL: The USS *San Jacinto* under Captain Charles Wilkes arrives at Fortress Monroe, Virginia, with captured Confederate emissaries James M. Mason and John Slidell. This is the government's first inkling of what had transpired at sea, and Wilkes is hailed in the press as a hero.

RELIGION: The U.S. Christian Commission is organized as a wartime extension of the Young Men's Christian Association (YMCA). They are designated to forward supplies and other forms of assistance to Union troops.

November 16

NAVAL: Confederate Secretary of the Navy Stephen R. Mallory accepts bids for four heavily armed ironclad vessels.

POLITICS: To preclude a potentially ruinous war with Great Britain, Postmaster General Montgomery Blair and Senator Charles Sumner of Massachusetts urge the immediate release of Confederate envoys James M. Mason and John Slidell.

November 18

INDIAN: A detachment of the 9th Texas under Colonel Douglas H. Cooper, assisted by allied Indians, skirmish with Creek warriors under Opothleyahola at Round Mountain, Indian Territory (Oklahoma). The Federal Indians are driven off yet skillfully extricate themselves and retire.

NAVAL: Commodore David D. Porter is tasked with acquiring and supplying numerous gunboats for the long anticipated campaign against New Orleans, Louisiana.

POLITICS: Confederate Kentuckians gather at Russellville and adopt a secession ordinance. Like Missouri, this state has separate legislatures in both Northern and Southern camps.

A convention of North Carolina loyalists meets at Hatteras to both denounce secession and reaffirm their allegiance to the Union. Marble Nash Taylor is then elected provisional governor of captured portions of the state.

November 20

MILITARY: General George B. McClellan, a superb organizer and disciplinarian, reviews 70,000 men of the Army of the Potomac near Washington, D.C. In contrast to the amateurish forces hastily gathered the previous summer, visitors favorably comment on the military deportment and martial ardor of all ranks.

SLAVERY: General Henry W. Halleck, newly arrived at the Department of Missouri in St. Louis, declares General Order No. 3, which excludes all African Americans from army camps within his jurisdiction.

November 21

MILITARY: Confederate General Lloyd Tilghman becomes commander of strategic Forts Henry and Donelson on the Tennessee and Cumberland Rivers, respectively. These are lynchpins of Confederate defense in the central theater and their retention is critical to the Southern war effort.

POLITICS: The Confederate Cabinet is reorganized with Judah P. Benjamin succeeding LeRoy P. Walker as secretary of war.

November 24

MILITARY: Confederate Colonel Nathan B. Forrest mounts a prolonged cavalry raid against Caseyville and Eddyville, Kentucky, initiating what becomes a spectacular career.

NAVAL: The USS *San Jacinto* under Captain Charles Wilkes drops anchor in Boston, Massachusetts, whereupon captured Confederate envoys James M. Mason and John Slidell are imprisoned at Fort Warren.

November 25

MILITARY: Confederate Secretary of War Judah P. Benjamin orders pro-Union guerrillas captured in Tennessee to be tried and executed if found guilty of burning bridges.

November 26

NAVAL: A banquet honoring Captain Charles Wilkes is held in Boston as diplomats begin weighing the international ramifications of his actions.

POLITICS: A constituent convention gathers at Wheeling, Virginia, and adopts a resolution of secession against Virginia to establish an independent state.

November 27

DIPLOMACY: National indignation runs high in Great Britain once word of the *Trent* Affair circulates. Signs and editorials declaring an "outrage on the British flag" appear as war with America seems in the offing.

November 28

POLITICS: The Confederate Congress inducts Missouri as the 12th Confederate state.

November 29

GENERAL: In an act of defiance, farmers in the vicinity of Charleston, South Carolina, and Savannah, Georgia, burn their cotton crops rather than see them confiscated by Union forces.

November 30

DIPLOMACY: The British cabinet headed by Foreign Secretary Lord John Russell, greatly incensed by the Trent Affair, demands both a formal apology and the immediate release of Confederates James M. Mason and John Slidell. The British minister to the United States, Lord Lyons, is also instructed to depart Washington, D.C., if a satisfactory response is not forthcoming in one week.

December 1

DIPLOMACY: The British cabinet prepares for war with the United States by dispatching 6,000 troops to Canada and sending Admiral Sir Alexander Milne to Halifax, Nova Scotia, with 40 vessels mounting 1,273 cannon.

POLITICS: Secretary of War Simon Cameron reports to President Abraham Lincoln as to what should be done about the thousands of African-American slaves flocking into Union lines. Lincoln agrees with the report but, desperate to maintain the allegiance of slave-owning border states like Delaware, Maryland, Kentucky, and Missouri, orders all mention of emancipation or military service removed. He prefers to have Congress address both issues.

December 2

LAW: General Henry W. Halleck is authorized to suspend writs of habeas corpus within the Department of Missouri.

MILITARY: Secretary of War Simon Cameron reveals that U.S. forces comprise 20,334 soldiers and 640,637 volunteers.

December 3

POLITICS: President Abraham Lincoln, in his message to Congress, suggests that slaves appropriated from Southern owners be allowed to emigrate northward. He also reiterates his belief that the Union must be preserved by every means at the government's disposal.

December 4

DIPLOMACY: Queen Victoria of England forbids all exports to the United States, especially materials capable of being used for armaments.

MILITARY: From his headquarters in St. Louis, Missouri, General Henry W. Halleck condones and authorizes all punitive measures against Confederate sympathizers within his jurisdiction. These include the death penalty for any citizen caught assisting rebel guerrillas.

POLITICS: The U.S. Senate expels former vice president John C. Breckinridge from its ranks on a vote of 36 to 0. Since the previous November Breckinridge has been serving as a Confederate major general.

RELIGION: Southern Presbyterians gather in Augusta, Georgia, to separate themselves from their Northern brethren. They then found the Assembly of the Presbyterian Church in the Confederate States of America.

December 5

POLITICS: Congress entertains petitions and bills intended to abolish slavery throughout the land.

December 6

JOURNALISM: Pro-Union newspaper editor William G. Brownlow is arrested by Confederate authorities on charges of treason in Knoxville, Tennessee.

December 7

NAVAL: The USS *Santiago de Cuba* under Commander Daniel B. Ridgley accosts the British ship *Eugenia Smith* at sea and removes Confederate purchasing agent J. W. Zacharie of New Orleans, Louisiana. Coming on the heels of the *Trent* affair, this act exacerbates tensions between the two nations.

1861

December 8

INDIAN: Pro-Union Creek leader Opothleyahola and 1,000 warriors arrive at Bird Creek (Chusto-Talasah), Indian Territory (Oklahoma), and assume defensive positions. The chief then dispatches a messenger to the hostile tribes indicating that he does not wish to spill blood, but his determination to fight unsettles many of Colonel Douglas H. Cooper's Indians and they begin deserting him.

RELIGION: The American Bible Society begins distributing up to 7,000 Bibles a day to Union soldiers and sailors.

December 9

INDIAN: Pro-Confederate Cherokee, Chickasaw, and Choctaw, assisted by the 9th Texas under Colonel Douglas H. Cooper, attack Pro-Union Creek under Opothleyahola at Bird Creek (Chusto-Takasah) in the Indian Territory (Oklahoma). Resistance is fierce initially, but gradually the Creek flanks retreat and Opothleyahola's center also falls back. However, the Confederates remain dogged by supply shortages and prove unable to pursue the fleeing Creek.

POLITICS: In light of recent military disasters at Bull Run and Ball's Bluff, Congress votes 33 to three to establish an oversight committee to monitor military events. This becomes infamously known as the Joint Committee on the Conduct of the War and proves to be the bane of many senior Union leaders.

December 10

POLITICS: The Confederate Congress admits the expatriate "government" of Kentucky into the Confederacy as its 13th state. It thus joins Missouri as having representatives in both belligerent camps.

December 11

GENERAL: Charleston, South Carolina, is ravaged by a destructive fire that consumes half of the city.

December 13

MILITARY: Newly appointed General Robert H. Milroy elects to attack Confederate positions atop nearby Allegheny Mountain in western Virginia. Laboring up the heavily wooded slopes he is handily repulsed, at which point the rebels counterattack downhill and scatter their Union antagonists.

December 14

MILITARY: General Henry H. Sibley assumes control of Confederate forces along the Upper Rio Grande River, along with the New Mexico and Arizona Territories. He begins military preparations for an offensive to secure the region.

December 16

POLITICS: Congressman Clement Vallandigham of Ohio, soon vilified as a "Copperhead," introduces a resolution commending Captain Charles Wilkes for his role in the *Trent* affair.

December 17

DIPLOMACY: Armed forces of Great Britain, France, and Spain attack and occupy Veracruz, Mexico, ostensibly seeking reparations for unpaid debts. However, once Napoleon III begins maneuvering to seize political control of that nation, the two other belligerents remove their troops. The French emperor seeks to take advantage of America's preoccupation with civil war for his own gain.

RELIGION: Commodore Henry H. Foote institutes regular Sunday services on board his fleet of gunboats on the Cumberland River.

December 19

DIPLOMACY: Lord Lyons, British minister to the United States, informally alerts Secretary of State William H. Seward of his instructions, namely, that the Americans must unconditionally release Southern commissioners James M. Mason and John Slidell, who have been illegally removed from the British vessel *Trent.* The American government has one week to respond satisfactorily, after which time Great Britain is withdrawing its ambassador in anticipation of war.

December 20

POLITICS: The influential Joint Committee on the Conduct of the War is formally instituted in the U.S. Congress following the disastrous rout at Ball's Bluff in the previous October. It is comprised mainly of Radical Republicans like Benjamin F. Wade and Zachariah Chandler of Michigan, and tasked with closely scrutinizing the conduct of the president and his senior commanders throughout the war.

December 21

POLITICS: The U.S. Congress institutes the Navy Medal of Honor as the nation's highest military award granted to that service. Initially it is intended for enlisted ranks, and officers are not eligible to receive it until 1915.

December 22

MILITARY: General Henry W. Halleck reiterates orders that any individuals found sabotaging Union railroads or telegraph lines will be immediately shot without civil trial.

December 23

DIPLOMACY: British ambassador Lord Lyons formally presents Secretary of State William H. Seward his ultimatum for the release of the two imprisoned Confederate commissioners.

December 24

EDUCATION: Waco University is established in Waco, Texas, by the Baptists.

December 25

POLITICS: President Abraham Lincoln celebrates Christmas with his family and later that day confers with legal authorities over the disposition of the imprisoned Confederate envoys.

SLAVERY: General Ulysses S. Grant orders the expulsion of fugitive African Americans from Fort Holt, Kentucky.

December 26

DIPLOMACY: An international crisis is averted when President Abraham Lincoln's cabinet concurs that the seizure of James M. Mason and John Slidell is illegal and that the two captives should be released and allowed to continue on to Europe. Secretary of State William H. Seward then orders their release from confinement at Fort Warren, Boston, blaming the entire matter on a "misunderstanding" by Captain Charles Wilkes.

December 27

DIPLOMACY: Secretary of State William H. Seward alerts House and Senate Foreign Relations Committees as to President Abraham Lincoln's decision to free

Confederate agents James M. Mason and John Slidell from detention at Fort Warren, Boston. He also provides British minister Lord Lyon with a lengthy diplomatic note—not an apology—explaining the American response.

December 28

MILITARY: Colonel Nathan B. Forrest leads a detachment of 300 Confederate cavalry toward Sacramento, Kentucky. En route he encounters a smaller force of 168 Union troopers under Major Eli Murray. The Federals charge headlong into twice their number of Southerners, then are assailed on both flanks and scattered. Triumphant in the first of his many scrapes, the future "Wizard of the Saddle" returns to Greeneville, hotly pursued by 500 cavalry under Union Colonel James Jackson, 3rd Kentucky Cavalry.

December 31

MILITARY: Noting the inactivity of Union forces in the East, a despondent President Abraham Lincoln anxiously cables General Henry W. Halleck in St. Louis, Missouri, and hopes to hear of offensive operations in that theater at least. "Are you and General Buell in concert?" he inquires.

1862

ARCHITECTURE: Alexander T. Stewart builds the nation's largest retail store in New York City, eight stories tall and constructed from steel and stone.

EDUCATION: The State College of Agriculture and Mechanics (today's University of Maine) is founded at Orono, Maine.

JOURNALISM: A little-known writer, Samuel Langhorne Clemens, begins working as a journalist in Virginia City, Nevada, under the nom de plume Mark Twain.

The *Golden Age* of Lewiston becomes the first newspaper published in the Idaho Territory.

MEDICAL: Dr. Louis Elsberg opens the first public clinic for throat diseases at the Medical College of New York.

PUBLISHING: Noted painter and artist Winslow Homer accompanies Union armies into the field, creating many notable illustrations for *Harper's Weekly* magazine.

William G. Brownlow publishes his anti-Southern diatribe, *The Rise, Progress, and Decline of Secession*, which sells 100,000 copies in the North. He had previously been imprisoned by Confederate authorities in Knoxville, Tennessee, for displaying overt Unionist sympathies.

SPORTS: The first fully enclosed baseball fields are constructed at Union Grounds, Brooklyn, New York.

January 1

DIPLOMACY: Confederate agents James M. Mason and John Slidell board the HMS *Rinaldo* off Provincetown, Massachusetts, and sail for Great Britain via Halifax.

MILITARY: General in Chief George B. McClellan remains sidelined by illness as President Abraham Lincoln frets over his continuing military inactivity.

General Thomas J. Jackson, eager to secure the lightly defended town of Romney, western Virginia, orders 8,500 Confederates under General William W. Loring, from their winter quarters at Winchester. However, no sooner do they depart than temperatures plunge to freezing and the men, lacking heavy overcoats, suffer severely.

January 6

MILITARY: President Abraham Lincoln ignores cries by Radical Republicans to replace General George B. McClellan, then ill with typhoid fever, over allegations of military inactivity. Lincoln also continues urging General Don Carlos Buell, commanding the Army of the Ohio in Kentucky, to assume an offensive posture.

NAVAL: In response to critical shortages of trained manpower, Commodore Andrew H. Foote suggests drafting soldiers to serve on the gunboat fleet. The army proves reluctant to comply, and General Ulysses S. Grant suggests that guardhouses be emptied to assist the navy.

January 8

POLITICS: President Jefferson Davis contacts fugitive Missouri governor Claiborne F. Jackson and assures him that his state is not being neglected by the Confederate government. He also presses the governor to raise additional troops to offset Union advantages in manpower.

January 9

NAVAL: Commodore David G. Farragut of the USS *Hartford* formally takes charge of the Western Gulf Blockading Squadron. Thus situated, he is tasked with orchestrating the capture of New Orleans, Louisiana, an essential aspect of overall Union strategy. Farragut, cognizant of the dire necessity for utmost secrecy, instructs his wife to burn any correspondence she receives from him.

January 10

MILITARY: President Abraham Lincoln expresses alarm to Secretary of War Simon Cameron over the apparent lack of military activity in the West.

Believing themselves heavily outnumbered, Union forces abandon strategic Romney, western Virginia, to advancing Confederates under General William W. Loring. That leader also enters into a bitter contretemps with General William L. Loring over charges he abused his soldiers by marching them during bitterly cold weather.

POLITICS: Confederate-leaning Missourians Waldo P. Johnson and Trusten Polk are expelled from the U.S. Senate.

January 11

POLITICS: Secretary of War Simon Cameron resigns from office amid charges of corruption and mismanagement. President Abraham Lincoln subsequently nominates former attorney general Edwin M. Stanton, a confidant of General George B. McClellan, as his successor. The appointment proves fortuitous as Stanton infuses military administration with energy and efficiency.

NAVAL: Commodore Louis M. Goldsborough assembles a large naval expedition of 100 vessels off Hampton Roads, Virginia.

January 12

NAVAL: The naval expedition of Commodore Louis M. Goldsborough sails from Hampton Roads, Virginia, in preparation for an attack upon strategic Roanoke Island, North Carolina. He is also conveying 15,000 Union troops under General Ambrose Burnside.

January 13

MILITARY: President Abraham Lincoln again urges generals Henry W. Halleck and Don Carlos Buell to initiate offensive operations in the western theater.

1862

General George B. McClellan refuses to consult with either the president or other officials as to his impending plan of operations. Moreover, he disagrees with the president's strategy of attacking along a broad front.

NAVAL: Lieutenant John L. Worden, still convalescing from months of Confederate captivity, is appointed commander of the revolutionary new vessel USS *Monitor*, then under construction on Long Island, New York.

Commodore Louis M. Goldsborough and his 100-ship expedition arrive off Hatteras Inlet, North Carolina. Once on station he reiterates orders that gunners must be completely trained and familiar with the new Bormann fuses fitted to 9-inch shrapnel shells.

January 16

MILITARY: General Felix K. Zollicoffer disobeys orders from General George B. Crittenden by positioning Confederate troops north of the Cumberland River, Kentucky, where they must fight with a river at their backs. Shortly after Crittenden arrives with reinforcements, he concludes that the water is running too high to safely recross. He thus intends to make the most of his subordinate's mistake by attacking an oncoming Union column at Logan's Cross Roads.

January 17

NAVAL: Federal gunboats USS *Conestoga* and *Lexington* conduct a preliminary reconnaissance of the Tennessee River past Confederate-held Fort Henry. The detailed information they convey helps formulate plans for its capture.

January 18

GENERAL: Former president John Tyler dies in Richmond, Virginia, at the age of 62.

MILITARY: General George H. Thomas, having enticed Confederate troops north of the Cumberland River to attack him, encamps 4,000 Union troops at Mill Springs, Kentucky. Reconnaissance parties dispatched toward the river confirm that General George B. Crittenden's Confederates are approaching and will strike the Federals at dawn.

January 19

MILITARY: A force of 4,000 Confederates under General Felix K. Zollicoffer and William H. Carroll attack the Union encampment at Logan's Cross Roads, Kentucky. Braving heavy rain and mud, the Southerners overrun the Union pickets at daybreak and drive them headlong into the main defensive line commanded by General George H. Thomas. The Confederates charge one more time but Thomas, expecting the move, stations the newly arrived brigade of General Samuel P. Carter obliquely, and his men catch the Southerners in a deadly enfilade. Zollicoffer then mistakenly gallops toward the Union position in a fog and is shot dead from the saddle. Crittenden's men then break and flee back to Beech Grove with Thomas in pursuit. Confederate losses are 125 killed, 309 wounded, and 99 missing to 40 Union dead, 207 wounded, and 15 missing.

January 20

NAVAL: At the behest of Secretary of the Navy Gideon Welles, the Union Gulf Blockading Squadron is reorganized into two distinct formations: the East Gulf Blockading Squadron and the West Gulf Blockading Squadron, with the latter commanded by Commodore David G. Farragut. His fleet consists of 17 steam warship and 19 mortar boats under his foster brother, Commander David D. Porter.

January 23
MILITARY: As General Thomas J. Jackson leads his Stonewall brigade out from Romney, western Virginia, General William W. Loring feels that his own command has been deliberately left in an exposed position only 20 miles from Union lines. Loring and other officers then violate the chain of command by petitioning friends in the Confederate Congress for a change in orders.

January 26
MILITARY: General Pierre G. T. Beauregard transfers from the Eastern Theater to the West, where he is subordinate to General Albert S. Johnston. Meanwhile, command in Virginia remains with General Joseph E. Johnston.

January 27
DIPLOMACY: Emperor Napoleon III of France declares that the American conflict infringes upon trade relations with France, but that he will observe a policy of strict neutrality.

POLITICS: President Abraham Lincoln, exasperated by the lack of initiative displayed by Union commanders, issues General Order No. 1. This mandates a general offensive against the Confederacy from various points along the line. February 22–George Washington's birthday–is selected as the deadline to commence combined operations by both army and navy forces.

January 28
NAVAL: Commodore Andrew H. Foote advises General Henry W. Halleck to begin riverine operations against Forts Henry and Donelson soon before the water levels of the Tennessee and Cumberland Rivers begin subsiding.

January 30
DIPLOMACY: Recently released Confederate envoys James M. Mason and John Slidell arrive at Southampton, England, and are cordially received.

MILITARY: General Henry W. Halleck, at St. Louis, Missouri, finally authorizes combined operations against Confederate strong points at Forts Henry and Donelson. General Ulysses S. Grant, eager to assume the offensive, brooks no delay putting his command in motion.

NAVAL: John Ericsson's revolutionary ironclad USS *Monitor*, derided by many onlookers as "a cheese box on a raft," is launched at Greenpoint, Long Island, amid thunderous applause. Trial runs begin immediately.

January 31
DIPLOMACY: Queen Victoria of England further dampens Southern hopes by reiterating her stance of observing strict neutrality in matters of war. Nonetheless, the British advise Confederate agents of their displeasure over having Southern ports blocked by obstacles.

MILITARY: Confederate Secretary of War Judah P. Benjamin orders General Thomas J. Jackson to relocate those portions of his command from Romney, western Virginia, to Winchester. Jackson, now aware that General William W. Loring has violated the chain of command behind his back, sullenly complies–then resigns from the army. Fortunately for the Confederacy, President Jefferson Davis refuses to accept it and, assisted by Virginia governor John Lechter, he persuades Jackson to remain in uniform.

POLITICS: President Abraham Lincoln finally issues his Special War Order No. 1, which requires an advance on Manassas Junction, Virginia, by the Army of the Potomac, no later than February 22, 1862. General George B. McClellan, however, simply ignores the directive and continues training his recruits to a fine edge.

SLAVERY: Radical Republicans demand that General George B. McClellan attack Southern positions immediately, along with deliberately freeing slaves and enlisting them in the army. The general, however, steadfastly declines to turn a war to save the Union into a social crusade to free African Americans held in bondage.

TRANSPORTATION: Congress passes the Railways and Telegraph Act, empowering the president to commandeer any rail facility deemed essential for the war effort.

February 1

MILITARY: Confederate forces under General Henry H. Sibley advance from El Paso, Texas, into New Mexico, intending to conquer that region for the South.

February 2

MILITARY: General Ulysses S. Grant departs Cairo, Illinois, on his campaign against Confederate-held Fort Henry on the Tennessee River. He embarks 17,000 troops on river transports, accompanied by Commodore Andrew H. Foote's gunboats. Grant intends to land near Panther Creek west of the fort and cut the garrison's escape.

February 3

MILITARY: President Abraham Lincoln and General George B. McClellan continue at loggerheads over an exact timetable for resuming offensive operations into Virginia. They also differ on strategy, with the president leaning toward a direct, overland campaign while the general wishes to sidestep Confederate defenses by landing on the enemy's coast.

NAVAL: The Federal government resolves to treat Confederate privateersmen as prisoners of war rather than prosecute them as pirates. This forestalls any chance that Union naval personnel might be hanged in retaliation.

February 4

NAVAL: The gunboat squadron of Commodore Henry H. Foote begins sounding out Confederate defenses at Fort Henry on the Tennessee River. Several moored mines ("torpedoes") have also been worked free by the fast current and are examined closely by naval personnel.

SLAVERY: Members of the Confederate Congress at Richmond, Virginia, debate the virtues and vices of utilizing free African Americans for service in the Confederate army. Such a commonsense remedy to address endemic manpower shortages is never seriously entertained, however.

February 5

DIPLOMACY: Queen Victoria lifts all restrictions against transporting guns, ammunition, and other military stores to Southern ports.

MUSIC: The poem "Battle Hymn of the Republic" by Julia Ward Howe debuts in an issue of *Atlantic Monthly*. It is subsequently arranged to the popular tune "John Brown's Body."

Howe, Julia Ward (1819–1910)

Author

Julia Ward was born in New York City on May 27, 1819, the daughter of a wealthy banker. Family affluence enabled her to receive an excellent education, including the Classics, languages, geometry, history, and literature. Consequently, she always exhibited a scholarly streak, and in 1839 she visited Boston on her own to confer with noted female author Margaret Fuller. She then married Dr. Samuel Gridley Howe, a noted philanthropist, in 1843, and settled in Boston. In addition to raising her family, she actively edited her husband's abolitionist newspaper, *The Commonwealth*, for many years. She also began dabbling in fiction and poetry against her husband's wishes. After her first volume, *Passion Flowers*, was published in 1854, the couple separated. Howe nonetheless continued writing and publishing and also became active in abolitionist and woman suffrage issues. Though pacifist by nature, she strongly supported President Abraham Lincoln and the Civil War. In 1862, after visiting troops in the field, she reputedly wrote her most famous composition, "Battle Hymn of the Republic," while sleeping in a tent. It was first published in the *Atlantic Monthly* in 1862, then the poem was set to the traditional tune of "John Brown's Body," becoming in time the unofficial anthem of the Union Army. This celebrated composition rendered her national recognition as one of the country's most talented female writers.

After the war, Howe parleyed her talents and energies into the woman suffrage move-ment. In 1868 she founded the New England Woman's Club in Boston which evolved into the larger American Woman Suffrage Association. While Howe supported women's rights, she frowned upon the gender-exclusive feminists like Elizabeth Cady Stanton and Susan B. Anthony, who maintained that men were an obstacle to progress, and also delved into other social issues at hand. Howe, by contrast, welcomed male participation in her organization and restricted her activities to women's rights. In the end her conservative strategy triumphed with the founding of the National American Woman Suffrage Association, when the competing schools of thought merged and were reconciled. Howe was also ardently pacifistic and she was horrified by the carnage associated with the Franco-Prussian War of 1870–71. She published an international appeal to women in 1870 and the following year presided over the new Woman's International Peace Association. Howe also found the time to continue writing poetry, fiction, and a biography of her heroine Margaret Fuller. Advancing age notwithstanding, Howe reached her peak of social activism in 1888 when she conducted a lengthy speaking tour of the West Coast. She retained her recognition as one of America's most influential women and in 1908 was the first female inducted into the prestigious American Academy of Arts and Sciences and was also made its president. She died while serving in this capacity in Newport, Rhode Island, on October 17, 1910.

February 6

MILITARY: General Ulysses S. Grant commences his strategic flanking movement with a concerted drive against Confederate-held Fort Henry on the Tennessee River. Meanwhile, Southern general Lloyd Tilghman hurriedly evacuates his 3,400-man garrison to Fort Donelson, 10 miles distant on the Cumberland River, before his escape is blocked.

1862

NAVAL: Commodore Andrew H. Foote leads a flotilla of four ironclads and three wooden gunboats against Fort Henry on the Tennessee River, and opens fire at a range of 1,700 yards. General Lloyd Tilghman remains behind with 100 artillerists and 17 cannon to mount an "honorable defense" while his garrison escapes intact.

February 7

MILITARY: General Ulysses S. Grant, having secured Fort Henry, maps out his strategy for attacking Fort Donelson, Tennessee, on the Cumberland River. Unlike Fort Henry, this is a spacious, well-sited position encompassing 100 acres within its outer works, being both amply garrisoned and armed with heavy cannon.

NAVAL: A large naval expedition under Union captain Louis M. Goldsborough departs its anchorage at Hatteras Inlet, North Carolina, steams into Croatan Sound, and attacks Roanoke Island. Inexplicably, this strategic point is under-manned and poorly situated to receive an attack of this magnitude.

February 8

MILITARY: Three Union brigades under generals Jesse Reno, John G. Parke, and John G. Foster, totaling 10,000 men, advance upon Confederate defensive works on the northern end of Roanoke Island, North Carolina. Southern positions crumble under the onslaught and surrender. Moreover, possession of Roanoke Island impedes communications with Norfolk, Virginia, leading to its eventual abandonment.

The recent fall of Fort Henry, Tennessee, prompts General Albert S. Johnston to order Confederate forces under General William J. Hardee to depart the south bank of the Tennessee River and march for Nashville.

POLITICS: In light of the Roanoke disaster, the Confederate Congress tasks an investigative committee to explore the behavior of General Henry A. Wise along with allegations of incompetence against General Benjamin Huger, overall theater commander. Secretary of War Judah P. Benjamin is slated for some scrutiny. Moreover, as the administration of President Jefferson Davis reels from the fall of Fort Henry, a pervasive sense of gloom settles upon the Confederacy.

February 9

WEST: General Gideon J. Pillow supercedes generals Bushrod J. Johnson and Simon B. Buckner as commander of Confederate-held Fort Donelson, Tennessee.

February 10

NAVAL: Captain Franklin Buchanan complains that he still lacks the neces-sary trained crewmen to render his nearly completed steam ram CSS *Virginia* operational.

WEST: Union general Samuel R. Curtis, commanding the 12,000-man Army of the Southwest, departs Rolla, Missouri, and marches against the Missouri Home Guard under General Sterling Price. He intends to drive them into Arkansas to preclude any interference with the main Union thrust underway down the Mississippi River.

February 11

MILITARY: Union forces under generals John A. McClernand and Charles F. Smith begin marching 15,000 men overland from Fort Henry to Fort Donelson on the Cumberland River, Tennessee, despite heavy rains. The fort's garrison, mean-while, receives a new commander, General John B. Floyd.

TRANSPORTATION: The U.S. Military Rail Roads are established by Secretary of War Edwin M. Stanton. These are adopted to insure the safe and efficient coordination of military transport along thousands of miles of rail line, nationwide. Consequently, rail-borne Union logistics achieve a degree of effectiveness unmatched by its Southern counterpart.

February 12

MILITARY: General Ulysses S. Grant directs 15,000 Union troops marching overland to invest Fort Donelson on the Cumberland River, Tennessee, now defended by 21,000 Confederates under General John B. Floyd. The Federals are directed to begin siege operations under the watchful eyes of generals John A. McClernand and Charles F. Smith, in concert with various gunboats offshore.

February 14

NAVAL: At 3:00 P.M. Commodore Andrew H. Foote's gunboat flotilla commences bombarding Fort Donelson on the Cumberland River, Tennessee, at one point closing to within 400 yards. However, the Confederate guns, situated on a 150-foot-high bluff overlooking the river, are well served and subject the Union fleet to a plunging fire.

POLITICS: President Abraham Lincoln seeks to pardon all political prisoners consenting to take a loyalty oath.

February 15

MILITARY: At 6:00 A.M., Confederate defenders under generals John B. Floyd and Gideon J. Pillow suddenly sortie from Fort Donelson, Tennessee, in a bid to escape. Their attack penetrates the division of General John A. McClernand, but then stalls as the Confederate leaders argue among themselves what to do next. Meanwhile, General Ulysses S. Grant, who is on the river conferring with Commodore Henry H. Foote, hastily repairs back to camp and organizes a sharp counterattack that drives the Southerners back into their post.

General Albert S. Johnston arrives in Nashville, Tennessee, to coordinate the rapidly crumbling Confederate line. As a precaution, Governor Isham Harris removes all his state papers and flees south.

A Confederate column of 3,000 men under General Henry H. Sibley march from Mesilla, New Mexico Territory, and against Union-held Fort Craig. That post is presently garrisoned by 1,000 regulars under Colonel Edward R. S. Canby.

February 16

MILITARY: The Confederate bastion of Fort Donelson, Tennessee, surrenders to General Ulysses S. Grant. Previously, generals John B. Floyd and Gideon J. Pillow abandon their command and ignominiously flee, leaving General Simon B. Buckner to capitulate. The victorious Grant takes 15,000 Southerners captive, along with 20,000 stands of arms, 48 field pieces, 57 heavy cannon, and considerable supplies. For winning the first significant land action of the West, he is lionized in the newspapers as "Unconditional Surrender" Grant and subsequently gains promotion to major general.

The Confederate column of General Henry H. Sibley arrives outside Fort Craig, New Mexico Territory. Sibley, however, considers it too strong to attack directly and decides to bypass it, possibly luring the garrison out into the open on nearby floodplains.

1862

February 17
NAVAL: The formidable ironclad ram CSS *Virginia* is commissioned–with the equally redoubtable Captain Franklin Buchanan at the helm.

February 18
POLITICS: The first-ever elected Confederate Congress convenes in Richmond, Virginia.

February 19
MILITARY: The Confederate Congress in Richmond, Virginia, orders the release of 2,000 Federal prisoners.

Union troops under General Charles F. Smith seize and occupy Clarksville, Tennessee, along with nearby Fort Defiance.

General Henry H. Sibley orders his Confederate column of 3,000 men across the Rio Grande River at Valverde Ford, five miles north of Union-held Fort Craig, New Mexico. As anticipated, Colonel Edward R. S. Canby sorties his own 2,000-man garrison–mostly untrained New Mexico volunteers, and marches hard to prevent the Southerners from crossing.
NAVAL: Commodore Andrew H. Foote's gunboats assist in the capture of Fort Defiant and Clarksville, Tennessee, which Confederates hastily evacuate upon his approach. The commodore then urges General William F. Smith to advance quickly upon Nashville while the Cumberland River is running high.

February 20
GENERAL: President Abraham Lincoln's 12-year-old son William Wallace ("Willie") Lincoln dies at the White House of typhoid fever.
NAVAL: Commodore David G. Farragut arrives at Ship Island, Mississippi, and prepares to launch what Secretary of the Navy Gideon Welles has deemed, "the most important operation of the war,"–the expedition against New Orleans, Louisiana.

In light of the twin disasters of Forts Henry and Donelson, the Confederate government sanctions an evacuation of Southern troops from Columbus, Kentucky.

Tennessee governor Isham Harris relocates the Confederate state capital to Memphis once Nashville is threatened by advancing Union forces.

February 21
MILITARY: Union troops under Colonel Edward R. S. Canby engage General Henry H. Sibley's marauding Confederates at Valverde, New Mexico Territory, five miles north of strategic Fort Craig. After a stout but indecisive fight, Canby disengages and marches back to the fort, which is still a menace to Confederate lines of communication.
POLITICS: Colonel Charles P. Stone is removed from command and arrested on orders from the Committee on the Conduct of the War. He is blamed with betraying troops defeated at Ball's Bluff, Virginia, the previous October and is imprisoned 189 days without trial.
SLAVERY: Nathaniel Gordon, a convicted slave trader, is hanged in New York City; this is the first application of capital punishment for the outlawed practice.

February 22
POLITICS: In Richmond, Virginia, President Jefferson Davis is inaugurated as the first elected head of state of the Confederate States of America. His presidential

address places blame for the present hostilities squarely on the North and considers their stance against states' rights in violation of principles established by the American Revolution. Alexander H. Stephens continues on as his vice president. From this point on, the Southerners consider their constitution and government as permanent, not provisional.

February 23

MILITARY: General Benjamin F. Butler is tapped to serve as commander of the new Department of the Gulf.

General Albert S. Johnston takes command of the Confederate Central Army at Murfreesboro, Tennessee, and begins marshaling his forces.

General John Pope becomes commander of the Army of the Mississippi at Commerce, Missouri.

POLITICS: President Abraham Lincoln appoints Senator Andrew Johnson of Tennessee to serve as military governor of the pro-Union eastern portion of his state.

February 24

NAVAL: Captain Franklin Buchanan of the CSS *Virginia* is ordered by Confederate Secretary of the Navy Stephen R. Mallory to sortie his James River Squadron against Union vessels anchored off Hampton Roads, Virginia, as soon as practicable.

February 25

BUSINESS: The Legal Tender Act is approved by President Abraham Lincoln. This is the nation's first government-sponsored paper money system. The new currency, known popularly as greenbacks, is intended only as a wartime expedient to allow the Treasury Department to pay its bills. Ultimately, $400 million are in circulation by war's end.

COMMUNICATION: The War Department is authorized to commandeer all telegraph lines and services to facilitate and prioritize military communications.

MILITARY: Union General William Nelson, assisted by the gunboat USS *Cairo*, bloodlessly occupies Nashville, Tennessee. This is the first Southern state capital and a significant industrial center captured by the North. Thereafter it serves as a base of operations and supply center for the Army of the Ohio under Don Carlos Buell.

NAVAL: The new Union ironclad USS *Monitor* is commissioned at Long Island, New York, with Lieutenant John L. Worden commanding. It is a revolutionary design featuring a single, rotating turret housing two 11-inch Dahlgren smoothbore cannon. Being mostly underwater, it also employs a forced draft ventilation system for the crew.

February 27

POLITICS: Like his northern counterpart, President Jefferson Davis finds it necessary to suspend writs of habeas corpus as a wartime expedient. He then declares martial law in Norfolk and Portsmouth, Virginia, as Union forces begin approaching in force.

February 28

POLITICS: An anxious President Jefferson Davis advises General Joseph E. Johnston, commanding Confederate forces in Virginia, to formulate contingency plans for evacuating men and materiel to safety, if necessary.

March 1

MILITARY: Confederate General Pierre G. T. Beauregard begins distributing troops along an arc stretching from Columbus, Kentucky, past Island No. 10 on the Mississippi River, and Fort Pillow, Tennessee, as far south as Corinth, Mississippi. General Albert S. Johnston also starts moving his command from Murfreesboro, Tennessee, toward an eventual rendezvous with Beauregard at Corinth.

March 2

MILITARY: Confederate forces under General Leonidas K. Polk finally abandon their strong point at Columbus, Kentucky, and withdraw south. The garrison and its 140 cannon are subsequently relocated across the Mississippi River to New Madrid, Missouri, and Island No. 10, under General John P. McCown.

March 3

NAVAL: A naval expedition under Commodore Samuel F. Du Pont attacks and captures Cumberland Island and Sound, Georgia, along with Fernandina and Amelia Islands, Florida. Fort Clinch, seized by a crew from the USS *Ottawa*, is the first Federal installation retaken during the war.

March 4

POLITICS: The U.S. Senate confirms Senator Andrew Johnson as military governor of Tennessee with a rank of brigadier general.

MILITARY: General Earl Van Dorn marches 16,000 men from the Boston Mountains, Arkansas, toward the Missouri border. He is determined to engage the smaller Union army of General Samuel R. Curtis somewhere in the extreme northwest corner of Arkansas.

March 6

MILITARY: General Samuel R. Curtis and 10,000 Union troops entrench along Sugar Creek, near Pea Ridge and Elkhorn Tavern, Arkansas, in anticipation of a major Confederate assault. General Earl Van Dorn then arrives and begins testing the Northern position, finding it too strong to be assailed frontally. He then orders his men on a night march around Curtis to cut him off from Missouri and attack from behind.

POLITICS: President Abraham Lincoln urges Congress to offer monetary compensation to any state which willingly abolishes slavery. The measure is roundly rejected by several state legislatures.

The Confederate Congress allows military authorities to destroy any cotton, tobacco, or other stores deemed of use to the enemy if they cannot be safely relocated.

March 7

MILITARY: Confederate forces under General Earl Van Dorn conduct a complicated night march around Pea Ridge, Arkansas, to catch the Union Army of the Southwest from behind. However, General Samuel R. Curtis quickly perceives the danger and simply orders his entire command to perform an "about face." This move immediately negates whatever advantage Van Dorn's wearying maneuver sought to achieve. The action commences across the line when General Sterling Price's Missourians launch two desperate charges and are heavily repelled. A final assault at sunset pushes the Union line back 800 yards but fails to break it.

March 8

MILITARY: Fighting resumes at Pea Ridge, Arkansas, once Confederate artillery bombards the position of General Samuel R. Curtis, who then constricts and consolidates his line. Curtis then deduces that the Southerners are nearly out of ammunition and attacks, driving Van Dorn's force off in confusion. Pea Ridge is the first major Union victory in the far West and thwarts Confederate hopes of invading Missouri for two years.

NAVAL: The ironclad ram CSS *Virginia* under Captain Franklin Buchanan sorties from Norfolk, Virginia, and engages wooden vessels of the Union blockading squadron off Hampton Roads. Buchanan slams into the sloop USS *Cumberland,* then riddles the *Congress* at close range with heavy gunfire. A third ship, the *Minnesota,* grounds itself in anticipation of being attacked. Buchanan, who is wounded by gunfire from the shore, then breaks off the action.

The USS *Monitor* under Lieutenant John L. Worden, having survived a perilous transit from New York, arrives off Hampton Roads, Virginia, in the evening.

POLITICS: President Abraham Lincoln issues General Order No. 2, which reorganizes the Army of the Potomac into four corps. It also stipulates that one of these corps be detached for the purpose of defending Washington, D.C., and the assignment falls upon General Irvin McDowell's command.

March 9

NAVAL: Around 9:00 A.M. Lieutenant Catesby ap Roger Jones takes the ironclad ram CSS *Virginia* out of Norfolk, intending to finish off the grounded USS *Minnesota* off Hampton Roads. Approaching his quarry, he is startled to see the low-lying and strange-looking *Monitor* sail directly in his path. Over the next four hours the iron giants duel at close range before thousands of spectators. Both vessels, heavily armored, fire repeatedly yet fail to inflict serious damage on each other before the contest subsides. This dramatic but inconclusive engagement heralds the dawn of iron warships in naval warfare and the passing of wooden vessels.

March 10

POLITICS: President Abraham Lincoln pays a bedside visit to Lieutenant John L. Worden, wounded in the eye during the clash between USS *Monitor* and CSS *Virginia.*

March 11

MILITARY: General Henry W. Halleck is appointed commander of all Union forces in the West through an amalgamation of the Departments of Kansas, the Missouri, and the Ohio into a new Department of the Mississippi.

POLITICS: President Abraham Lincoln, disillusioned by General George B. McClellan's lack of aggressiveness, issues War Order No. 3. This removes the reluctant leader as general in chief, although he retains command of the Army of the Potomac. Henceforth, all generals are to report directly to Secretary of War Edwin M. Stanton.

President Jefferson Davis refuses to accept the reports of generals John B. Floyd and Gideon J. Pillow concerning the fall of Fort Donelson, and he unceremoniously removes both from command.

March 13

MILITARY: General George B. McClellan convenes a war conference at Fairfax Court House, Virginia, and finalizes his strategy against Richmond. Rather than

1862

Buchanan, Franklin (1800–1874)

Confederate admiral

Franklin Buchanan was born in Baltimore, Maryland, on September 17, 1800, and in January 1815 he commenced his naval career by becoming a midshipman. He completed several Mediterranean cruises, handled his affairs competently, and by 1841 had risen to the rank of commander. That year he took command of the new steam frigate USS *Mississippi* until 1844, when Secretary of the Navy George Bancroft tasked him with drafting plans for a proposed naval academy. Buchanan complied and his scheme so impressed Bancroft that when the academy opened at Annapolis, Maryland, in 1845, Buchanan gained appointment as its first superintendent. In this capacity he proved himself a tough, no-nonsense administrator that placed the fledgling school on a firm footing. Buchanan then sought a combat command, and in 1846 he received command of the sloop USS *Germantown* for use in the Mexican War. Seven years later he commanded the steam frigate USS *Susquehanna*, Commodore Matthew C. Perry's flagship, on the expedition to open Japan. Buchanan made captain in 1855 and spent the next several years commanding the Washington Navy Yard. However, in April 1861, fearing that his native state of Maryland would secede and join the Confederacy, he tendered his resignation. That state remained loyal to the Union, however, but when Buchanan applied for reinstatement the Navy Department refused. He dithered for months pondering his fate before finally visiting Richmond, Virginia, and tender-ing his service to the Confederate States of America.

In September 1862 Buchanan became a captain in Confederate service and was posted as chief of the Bureau of Orders and Details. He performed well as always but chafed in an administrative role and sought out a more active command. Then, in February 1862, he took charge of the Chesapeake Squadron and spent several weeks converting the captured Union steam frigate USS *Merrimac* into the Confederate ironclad CSS *Virginia*. On March 8, 1862, Buchanan made history by sailing down to Hampton Roads and sinking several wooden warships belonging to the Union blockading squadron. The age of modern naval warfare had dawned, but Buchanan exposed himself recklessly, was wounded, and consequently missed the dramatic engagement with the Union ironclad USS *Monitor* on the following day. After several months of convalescence, Buchanan assumed command of Confederate naval forces at Mobile, Alabama, including the giant ironclad CSS *Tennessee*. On August 5, 1864, he bravely waged a losing battle with Admiral David G. Farragut and was captured. Buchanan was subsequently exchanged a few weeks later but saw no more active duty. Afterward he served as president of Maryland Agricultural College before dying at his home in Talbot County on May 11, 1874. Aggressive and hard-hitting, Buchanan was the ideal candidate to usher in the age of modern, heavily armored warships.

campaign overland from Urbana on the Rappahannock River, he elects to shift his Army of the Potomac by boat up the York and James Rivers to outflank strong Confederate defenses.

General Ambrose E. Burnside lands three brigades of 12,000 Union troops at Slocum's Creek on the Neuse River, North Carolina, supported by 13 gunboats. His objective is New Bern, the state's second-largest city and an important railhead.

A heavy bombardment from General John Pope's siege guns at Point Pleasant, Missouri, induces Confederate forces under General John P. McCown to evacuate their base at New Madrid for Island No. 10 in the Mississippi River. He abandons tons of valuable supplies in the process.

POLITICS: President Abraham Lincoln approves of plans of operation along the Virginia coast by General George B. McClellan's Army of the Potomac. He urges that leader, "at all events, move such remainder of the army at once in pursuit of the enemy."

SLAVERY: New army regulations forbid officers from returning fugitive African-American slaves to their owners. Failure to comply is punishable by court-martial.

March 14

MILITARY: General Ambrose E. Burnside leads 12,000 Union troops through mud and rain on an advance toward New Bern, North Carolina, the former colonial capital. Confederate defenders under General Lawrence O. Branch resist doggedly for several hours until a militia unit in his center suddenly flees. New Bern is then occupied by Burnside's victorious Federals that afternoon. The loss in matériel to the Confederacy proves significant, and the Union gains another base for projecting military strength further inland.

March 15

MILITARY: General Ulysses S. Grant is exonerated of misconduct by General Henry W. Halleck, and he resumes command of Union forces in Tennessee.

NAVAL: Commodore Andrew H. Foote's flotilla of six gunboats and 121 mortar boats unleashes a preliminary bombardment of Confederate defenses on Island No. 10 in the Mississippi River.

March 16

MILITARY: Federal troops under General John Pope, in concert with Commodore Henry H. Foote's gunboat flotilla, initiate combined operations against Confederate positions on Island No. 10 in the Mississippi River. This post, well sited and heavily armed, presents a formidable obstacle to all river navigation.

March 17

MILITARY: The Army of the Potomac—105,000 strong—begins embarking at Alexandria, Virginia, for an amphibious transit to Fortress Monroe on the York and James Rivers. Through this maneuver General George B. McClellan hopes to outflank strong Confederate defenses guarding the capital of Richmond.

NAVAL: The CSS *Nashville* slips past blockading vessels USS *Cambridge* and *Gemsbock* off Beaufort, North Carolina. The Navy Department is quite embarrassed by its failure to stop the raider, and Assistant Secretary Gustavus V. Fox pronounces it "a Bull Run for the Navy."

March 18

POLITICS: President Jefferson Davis appoints Confederate Secretary of War Judah P. Benjamin as his new secretary of state to replace outgoing Robert M. T. Hunter, who has been elected to the Senate in Richmond.

March 20
MILITARY: General Benjamin F. Butler assumes command of the Department of the Gulf at Ship Island, Mississippi, prior to operations against New Orleans, Louisiana.

March 21
MILITARY: Colonel Turner Ashby alerts General Thomas J. Jackson that General Nathaniel P. Banks is withdrawing two divisions of Union troops from Winchester in the Shenandoah Valley. Jackson, fearing that these soldiers are en route to reinforce the Army of the Potomac's drive against Richmond, determines to lure them back.

March 22
MILITARY: General Manfield Lovell, commanding the Confederate garrison at New Orleans, Louisiana, reports that he has six steamers available for the city's defenses, but the inhabitants are dismayed once the bulk of Confederate naval assets are deployed upriver.

Confederate cavalry under Colonel Turner Ashby mistakenly report to General Thomas J. Jackson that Union strength at Kernstown, western Virginia, is about 4,000 strong, the same as his own. In fact General James Shields commands at least twice as many men, with most of them hidden in nearby copses.
NAVAL: The future CSS *Florida*, presently disguised as the British steamer *Oreto*, departs Liverpool for Nassau. There the vessel is to be renamed and outfitted with four 7-inch cannon. This is the first such English vessel constructed for the Confederate navy, and it is clandestinely secured through the efforts of naval agent James D. Bulloch.

March 23
MILITARY: General Thomas J. Jackson concludes an impressive two-day march by covering 41 miles in two days and then attacks at Kernstown, Virginia. However, Union General Nathan Kimball continuously feeds more men into the fray and fights the Southerners to a draw. Once increasing numbers of Federals surge forward, Jackson's entire line falls back in semi-confusion out of town. Kernstown, while a Confederate tactical defeat, harbors immense strategic implications, for President Abraham Lincoln orders General Irvin McDowell's I Corps detained at Washington, D.C., thereby depriving the Army of the Potomac of their services in the upcoming Peninsula Campaign. It also heralds the start of Jackson's sizzling Shenandoah Valley Campaign, one of the Civil War's most legendary undertakings, which affirms his reputation for tactical wizardry.

Union soldiers commence digging a 12-mile long, 50-foot wide canal astride the Mississippi River to allow Union gunboats to bypass strong Confederate defenses on Island No. 10.

March 24
SLAVERY: The continuing unpopularity of emancipation is underscored in Cincinnati, Ohio, when radical abolitionist Wendell Phillips is pelted by eggs.

March 25
MILITARY: Major John M. Chivington of the 1st Colorado Volunteers is ordered to attack a Confederate force lodged near Santa Fe, New Mexico Territory. He arrives at the far end of Glorietta Pass that evening, capturing several sentinels, and prepares to storm the enemy camp at dawn.

NAVAL: Confederate Secretary of the Navy Stephen R. Mallory orders Commodore Josiah Tattnall to replace the wounded Captain Franklin Buchanan at Norfolk, Virginia.

March 26

MILITARY: In an early morning raid, Colonel John M. Chivington, 1st Colorado Volunteers, advances through Glorietta Pass, New Mexico Territory, and attacks Confederates under Major Charles L. Pryon encamped at Johnson's Ranch. A last minute charge by Union cavalry against the Southern rear guard nets several prisoners, then Chivington orders his men back to Kozlowski's Ranch to regroup.

March 27

MILITARY: Colonel William R. Scurry's 4th Texas arrives at Johnson's Ranch, New Mexico Territory, to reinforce a Confederate detachment under Major Charles L. Pryon. The Southerners then brace themselves for an anticipated Union attack and, once it fails to materialize, Scurry resumes the offensive by marching through Glorietta Pass.

NAVAL: Secretary of War Edwin M. Stanton informs naval engineer Charles Ellet to commence building numerous steam rams at Pittsburgh, Pennsylvania, and Cincinnati, Ohio, capable of thwarting the new Confederate ironclad known to be under construction at Memphis, Tennessee.

March 28

MILITARY: Union troops at Johnson's Ranch near Glorietta Pass, New Mexico, are reinforced by a detachment under Colonel John P. Slough. Major John M. Chivington, 1st Colorado Volunteers, then leads his force back through Glorietta Pass and happens upon the lightly guarded Confederate baggage train at Johnson's Ranch, which is captured. This spells the end of General Henry H. Sibley's Confederate offensive and he withdraws back to Texas.

March 29

MILITARY: General Albert S. Johnston assembles his Army of Mississippi at Corinth, Mississippi, by amalgamating the armies of Kentucky and Mississippi into a single structure with General Pierre G. T. Beauregard as his second in command, and generals Leonidas K. Polk (I Corps), Braxton Bragg (II Corps), William J. Hardee (III Corps), and George B. Crittenden (Reserve).

Confederate General William W. Mackall arrives and replaces the disgraced General John P. McCown as commander of New Madrid, Missouri, and Island No. 10 in the Mississippi River.

April 2

MILITARY: Confederate spy Rose Greenhow is expelled from Washington, D.C., by Federal authorities.

Skirmishing continues between opposing pickets around Pittsburg Landing, Tennessee, as General Pierre G. T. Beauregard conceives an overly complex order of battle that places all three Confederate corps in three distinct waves of attacks, a tactic exacerbating mass confusion in the swirl of battle.

April 3

MILITARY: President Abraham Lincoln remonstrates General George B. McClellan over his failure to assign a corps of 20,000 men to man the defenses of

Washington, D.C. He reiterates his demand that the I Corps of General Irvin McDowell be assigned the task of defending the national capital.

General George B. McClellan makes final preparations to direct his massive Army of the Potomac on its drive against Richmond, Virginia. A talented disciplinarian and organizer, he commands 112,000 well-trained men.

Massed Confederate forces under General Albert S. Johnston decamp from Corinth, Mississippi, and begin groping toward Union positions at Pittsburg Landing, Tennessee. Their movement is dogged by driving rain and poor marching discipline that many commanders feel might alert the defenders of their approach.

SLAVERY: The U.S. Senate abolishes slavery in the District of Columbia on a 29 to 14 vote.

April 4

MILITARY: With his army of 112,000 men assembled on the York Peninsula, Virginia, General George B. McClellan finally begins his long-awaited campaign against Richmond. In contrast to the slapdash Union forces of the previous year, the Army of the Potomac is well-trained, well-led, and eager to prove its mettle in combat.

NAVAL: Covered by darkness and rain, the ironclad USS *Carondelet* under Commander Henry Walke dashes past Confederate batteries on Island No. 10 on the Mississippi River. The Southerners are now cut off from reinforcements from downstream while Union forces under General John Pope can safely cross the Mississippi River to the Tennessee shore.

April 5

MILITARY: The Army of the Potomac begins marching in the direction of Yorktown, Virginia, then defended by 15,000 Confederates under General John B. Magruder. Magruder conducts elaborate ruses like erecting false "Quaker guns" along his line while continually marching his men around to give an impression of greater numbers. General George B. McClellan is completely taken in by the deception and pauses to commence siege operations.

Massed Confederates under General Albert S. Johnston prepare to strike Union positions at Pittsburg Landing, Tennessee. Despite entreaties from General Pierre G. T. Beauregard and others to relent, Johnston determines to hit the invaders hard next day, declaring "I would fight them if they were a million."

POLITICS: General Andrew Johnson, military governor of his home state of Tennessee, suspends several city officials in Nashville when they refuse to take an oath of allegiance to the Union.

April 6

MILITARY: On this momentous day the Battle of Shiloh erupts at dawn as 44,000 Confederates under General Albert S. Johnston surprise 39,900 Union troops under General Ulysses S. Grant. Grant is then at his headquarters in nearby Savannah, Tennessee, seven miles distant, and actual leadership devolves on General William T. Sherman. However, General Johnston is fatally injured while directing combat from his saddle. General Pierre G. T. Beauregard then assumes tactical control of events and orders up 62 cannon to blast Federal defenders in the so-called Hornet's Nest. Meanwhile Grant returns to camp once fighting commences and begins organizing a coherent defense, backed by gunboats on the Tennessee River. Beauregard briefly tests Grant's new position, judges it to be too well defended to be carried by his exhausted soldiers, and the fighting ceases.

NAVAL: Throughout the bloody fighting at Shiloh, heavy and accurate gunfire from Federal gunboats USS *Tyler* and *Lexington* assist the last-ditch Union defenses.

April 7

MILITARY: General Ormsby M. Mitchel recruits Union spy James J. Andrews for a clandestine raid behind enemy lines to sabotage railroad lines between Atlanta, Georgia, and Chattanooga, Tennessee. Andrews then solicits 22 volunteers from General Joshua W. Sill's Ohio brigade and gradually infiltrates them by small teams into Marietta, Georgia, where the scheme is to commence.

The struggle at Shiloh resumes at 7:30 A.M. as Union forces under General Ulysses S. Grant, newly reinforced, mount a spirited counterattack to regain ground lost in the previous day's fighting. The Confederates under General Pierre G. T. Beauregard resist gamely but slowly yield to superior numbers. Casualties at Shiloh stun both North and South alike due to their sheer enormity. Grant, with 65,000 men engaged, loses 13,047 while the 44,000 Confederates sustain losses of 10,694. The reality of modern warfare has tellingly hit the contestants.

NAVAL: The Federal gunboat USS *Pittsburgh* slips past Island No. 10 on the Mississippi River and joins the *Carondelet* in covering General John Pope's army as it is ferried to the Tennessee shore. The noose is tightening around the Confederate defenders.

SLAVERY: The U.S. government concludes a new agreement with Great Britain for a more aggressive suppression of the slave trade.

April 8

MILITARY: General William W. Mackall surrenders 4,500 Confederates on Island No. 10 in the Mississippi River to General John Pope. Considering the difficult terrain and tricky currents to be surmounted, Pope performed well. Moreover, his victory constitutes the latest in a series of disasters for the Confederacy in the West. President Abraham Lincoln subsequently assigns Pope to command the newly organized Army of Virginia.

Federal troops under General Ulysses S. Grant advance from Pittsburg Landing, Tennessee, in pursuit of General Pierre G. T. Beauregard's withdrawing Confederates. General William T. Sherman engages them briefly but is capably contained by the rear guard directed by Confederate General Nathan B. Forrest.

NAVAL: Commodore David G. Farragut runs the last of his West Gulf Blockading Squadron vessels over the Southwest Pass bar and into the Mississippi River. He then assembles his 24 warships, mounting 200 large-caliber cannon, along with 19 mortar ships under Commander David D. Porter, and makes for Head of Passes.

POLITICS: President Jefferson Davis proclaims martial law in East Tennessee to suppress the activities of pro-Union inhabitants.

April 9

NAVAL: Confederate Secretary of the Navy Stephen R. Mallory, convinced that the biggest threat to New Orleans, Louisiana, is the Mississippi River Squadron of Commodore Andrew H. Foote, refuses to allow Confederate vessels at Fort Pillow, Tennessee, to shift southward.

POLITICS: President Abraham Lincoln, frustrated by General George B. McClellan's lack of aggressiveness, confers with Cabinet members over what to do. The chief executive then suggests several lines of attack for the Army of the Potomac and entreats McClellan to attack immediately, insisting, "But you must act."

The Confederate Congress approves a conscription measure over the protest of many politicians who feel this is a violation of the states' rights and personal liberties.

April 10

MILITARY: General Joseph E. Johnston assumes command of Confederate forces in the Peninsula district of Virginia, and reinforcements gradually raise Southern manpower to 34,000. Johnston nevertheless waxes pessimistic about resisting the Army of the Potomac, thrice his size, for long.

After weeks of methodical preparation, Union artillery commanded by Captain Quincy A. Gillmore commences shelling Fort Pulaski on Cockspur island, Savannah harbor. His highly accurate, rifled Parrott cannons fire penetrating shells that systematically decimate the fort's defenses. The engagement is a test for the Union's new ordnance against traditional masonry fortifications.

SLAVERY: President Abraham Lincoln signs a joint congressional resolution stipulating gradual emancipation of African-American slaves. It is aimed primarily at the border states and grants "pecuniary aid" in exchange for voluntary compliance.

April 11

MILITARY: Fort Pulaski, Georgia, surrenders to Union Captain Quincy A. Gillmore following a heavy bombardment of 5,725 shells from nearby Tybee Island. This battle also marks the first employment of long-range, rifled ordnance with impressive results against older, masonry defenses.

General Henry W. Halleck replaces General Ulysses S. Grant at Pittsburg Landing, Tennessee, over allegations of Grant's drunkenness, although he remains in charge of the District of West Tennessee. Command of the Army of the Tennessee temporarily reverts to General George H. Thomas.

SLAVERY: Following the Senate's cue, the House of Representatives votes 93 to 39 to gradually abolish slavery in the District of Columbia.

April 12

MILITARY: Major James J. Andrews and 22 Union volunteers steal the Confederate locomotive named *General* and three freight cars at Big Shanty, Georgia, then head northward toward Chattanooga, Tennessee. Their mission is to destroy railroad bridges leading to the city but the plan is thwarted by rainy weather. Once the *General* finally runs out of steam and is abandoned, the spies flee into the woods where the majority are captured. Andrews and seven volunteers are executed as spies on June 7, 1862, but eight men eventually escape captivity and the rest are exchanged. The raiders become the U.S. Army's first recipients of the Congressional Medal of Honor in March 1863. The episode has entered Civil War folklore as the "Great Locomotive Chase."

April 13

SLAVERY: General David Hunter, commanding the vicinity of Fort Pulaski, Georgia, declares his region free of slavery and begins unilaterally manumitting all African Americans under his jurisdiction.

April 14
MILITARY: A high-level war meeting convenes in Richmond, Virginia, where General Joseph E. Johnston pleads with superiors to abandon the Yorktown–Warwick River line before General George B. McClellan attacks in overpowering strength. However, President Jefferson Davis and his chief military adviser, General Robert E. Lee, balk at the suggestion, observing that it necessitates the abandonment of Norfolk.

NAVAL: Federal mortar boats under Commodore Andrew H. Foote commence bombarding Fort Pillow, Tennessee, astride the Mississippi River. This fortification lays 60 miles south of Island No. 10 and guards the northern approaches to Memphis. The exchange of fire is intermittent over the next seven weeks.

April 15
MILITARY: At a special war council held in Richmond, Virginia, President Jefferson Davis breaks the strategic impasse by ordering General Joseph E. Johnston to move his army to Yorktown on the Peninsula and reinforce General John B. Magruder's troops holding the line there.

April 16
MILITARY: With Union forces only 10 miles from his capital and an endless stream of bad news from the West, President Jefferson Davis authorizes conscription to maintain existing Confederate manpower levels. Consequently, all white males aged 18 to 35 become eligible for three years of service. This is also the first coercive military conscription in American history.

NAVAL: Commodore David G. Farragut begins massing the 17 warships of his West Gulf Blockading Squadron, including the gunboats of Commodore David D. Porter, below Forts Jackson and St. Philip, Louisiana. These aged structures, one on either side of the Mississippi River, are situated 12 miles above Head of Passes, mount 90 cannon, and are further backed up by a "mosquito squadron" of small warships under Captain George N. Hollis.

SLAVERY: President Abraham Lincoln signs a bill outlawing slavery in the District of Columbia on a compensatory basis—$300 per slave. However, African Americans escaping from masters still loyal to the Union remain subject to the existing Fugitive Slave Act and must be returned.

April 17
MILITARY: Confederate reinforcements bring the strength of General Joseph E. Johnston's force along the Yorktown–Warwick River line up to 53,000 men. He nonetheless remains largely outumbered by the Army of the Potomac, which fields roughly twice that number.

April 18
NAVAL: Commodore David G. Farragut dispatches Commander David D. Porter with 20 mortar boats to bombard Forts Jackson and St. Philip on the Mississippi River. Porter, convinced he can neutralize these positions through firepower alone, begins pelting them with 200-pound mortar for the next five days.

April 21
MILITARY: To offset manpower advantages enjoyed by the North, the Confederate government authorizes creation of special guerrilla formations by passing the Partisan Ranger Act, then adjourns its first session.

1862

Farragut, David   (1801–1870)
Admiral

David Farragut was born in Campbell's Station, Tennessee, on July 5, 1801, the son of a U.S. Naval officer. He was orphaned at New Orleans and adopted into the family of Captain David Porter, a noted American sailor. Farragut accompanied his stepfather on the frigate USS *Essex* as a midshipman during its heroic sortie around Cape Horn and into the Pacific Ocean, where it decimated the British whaling fleet. He subsequently survived Porter's defeat in February 1814 at the hands of British warships HMS *Phoebe* and *Cherub* and returned to the United States on board a cartel (exchange) vessel. Over the next 45 years he functioned capably in various grades and capacities, rising to captain in 1855. In this capacity he served in California constructing naval facilities at Mare Island in San Francisco Harbor. Farragut was residing with his family in Norfolk, Virginia, when the Civil War erupted in April 1861, forcing him to relocate to New York City. However, on account of his

David G. Farragut *(National Archives)*

April 24
NAVAL: Commodore David G. Farragut, impatient for success and concluding that the bombardment of Forts Jackson and St. Philip has been ineffectual, determines to run his entire fleet past them in the dark. At 2:00 A.M. in the predawn darkness, his 17 vessels steam by the forts in three divisions. Confederate defenders under General Johnson K. Duncan unleash a heavy cannonade but inflict very little damage. With Porter's single, decisive stroke, the fate of New Orleans, Louisiana, is decided.

April 25
MILITARY: Federal artillery under General John G. Parke commence bombarding Fort Macon on Bogue Banks Island off Beaufort, South Carolina. At length Colonel Moses J. White surrenders, and his garrison of 300 Confederates pass into captivity.

NAVAL: The Union flotilla under Commodore David G. Farragut captures the city of New Orleans, Louisiana, following a brief exchange with Confederate gunners at English Turn. The Mississippi River is running high at the time and enables the fleet to point its cannon directly over the levee and toward the city. The Confederacy thus loses its largest and wealthiest seaport, while the North acquires a splendid base for operations farther upstream.

Southern origins, he was not entirely trusted by the Navy Department and was restricted to supervising a retirement board. It took the intercession of his stepbrother, Captain David Dixon Porter, to secure command of the West Gulf Blockading Squadron in January 1862. In this capacity Farragut successfully ran Confederate defenses at Forts Jackson and St. Philip on the Mississippi River on the night of April 24, 1862, then sailed on and forced the important Confederate city of New Orleans to surrender. This decisive victory placed Union forces at the mouth of the Mississippi River and allowed for armed forays directly into the Confederate heartland.

Farragut subsequently ran numerous Southern defenses on the Mississippi River, bombarded Vicksburg, Mississippi, but was unable to capture it with army troops. After additional good service back in the Gulf of Mexico, Farragut was worn out and he returned home to New York to recuperate, receiving a hero's welcome. On August 5, 1864, he confronted his greatest naval challenge by attacking heavily guarded Mobile, Alabama, the last remaining gulf port of the Confederacy. To accomplish this his fleet had to run a gauntlet of minefields, took some losses, then exclaimed, "Damn the torpedoes! Full speed ahead!" This advance brought him into contact with the large Southern ironclad CSS *Nashville* under Admiral James Buchanan, which he subdued after an intense battle. When Mobile finally surrendered on August 23, 1864, Farragut gained promotion as the first vice admiral in U.S. history. Failing health precluded his participation at the capture of Fort Fisher, North Carolina, and he spent the rest of the Civil War performing blockade duty on the James River. In 1866 Farragut advanced to full admiral, another distinction, and commanded the European Squadron on an extended goodwill tour from 1867 to 1868. Farragut died while inspecting the Portsmouth, New Hampshire, Navy Yard, on August 14, 1870. He is distinct in becoming America's first admiral and among the most effective combat officers of naval history.

April 26

DIPLOMACY: President Abraham Lincoln pays a courtesy call upon the French warship *Gassendi*, anchored at the Washington Navy Yard.

April 27

NAVAL: U.S. Naval forces accept the surrender of Fort Livingston on Bastian Bay, Louisiana, and crewmen from the USS *Kittatinny* hoist the Stars and Stripes over its ramparts. Nearby forts Quitman, Pike, and Wood also capitulate later that afternoon.

April 28

MILITARY: The Confederate garrisons of Forts Jackson and St. Philip, on the Mississippi River, mutiny against General Johnson K. Duncan and surrender 900 prisoners to Union forces under Commander David D. Porter.

NAVAL: The British steamer *Oreto* anchors at Nassau, the Bahamas, and waits to be manned by Confederate sailors. It is eventually impressed into Southern service as the CSS *Florida*.

April 29

MILITARY: In Virginia, a skittish General Joseph E. Johnston, painfully cognizant of the vast array of Union siege artillery before him along the Yorktown–Warwick

River line informs superiors that he is withdrawing inland as soon as practicable. He does so rather than be bombarded into submission.

POLITICS: In Louisiana, city officials formally surrender New Orleans to Federal authorities. However, raising the American flag over the customs house occasions outbursts of anger and indignation from the populace.

April 30

MILITARY: Confederate forces under General Thomas J. Jackson advance from Elk Run, western Virginia, toward Staunton in driving rain. This proves one of the war's most impressive forced marches and bequeaths to troops involved the sobriquet "Jackson's foot cavalry."

General Henry W. Halleck finalizes his reorganization of the Armies of the Mississippi with General Ulysses S. Grant as second in command, George H. Thomas and the Army of the Tennessee (right wing), John Pope and the Army of the Mississippi (left wing), John A. McClernand (reserve wing), and Don Carlos Buell and the Army of the Ohio acting independently.

May

AVIATION: Pioneering balloonist Professor Thaddeus S. C. Lowe becomes the first man to make military reconnaissance photographs while flying above Confederate lines near Richmond, Virginia. He takes no less than 64 overlapping pictures and is also the first man to transmit military intelligence by telegraph while airborne.

May 3

MILITARY: General Joseph E. Johnston begins withdrawing 55,000 Confederates from Yorktown, Virginia, before heavy Union siege ordnance can commence firing. The Army of the Potomac, stalled a month while planting siege guns, can now begin moving up the Peninsula in pursuit.

May 4

MILITARY: General George B. McClellan's Army of the Potomac occupies the Yorktown–Warwick River line recently abandoned by Confederate forces. As the Southerners under General Joseph E. Johnston funnel through Williamsburg in retreat, McClellan advances after them in pursuit and in great number, but also cautiously. Movement on either side is hampered by continual downpours that turn the roads to mud.

Confederate forces evacuate Tucson, New Mexico Territory, ahead of the "California column" of Colonel James H. Carleton. Meanwhile, the main Southern army under General Henry H. Sibley straggles into El Paso, Texas, following their arduous campaign in the West.

May 5

AGRICULTURE: Congress authorizes creation of the Department of Agriculture, headed by a commissioner. As such, it will not be accorded cabinet rank until 1889.

MILITARY: A Union force of 41,000 men commanded by General Edwin V. Sumner confronts a determined Confederate rear guard numbering 32,000 at Williamsburg, Virginia. The Southerners are posted at Fort Magruder under General James Longstreet, in the center of their line, and they rebuff an attack by General Joseph Hooker's division. On the Confederate left, General Winfield

S. Hancock's Union brigade suddenly appears behind enemy lines around 3:00 P.M. and begins shelling the surprised Southerners with cannon fire. Confederate brigades under generals Jubal A. Early and Daniel H. Hill try to outflank the intruders and are repelled in turn. Sumner fails to take advantage of the situation and an impasse settles across the battlefield. Williamsburg, the first pitched battle of the Peninsula Campaign, proves both indecisive and characterized by heavy casualties: Union losses are 2,239 while the Confederates sustain 1,703.

POLITICS: President Abraham Lincoln and Secretary of War Edwin M. Stanton board the steamer *Miami* and sail to Hampton Roads, Virginia, to prod General George B. McClellan to greater efforts.

May 7

MILITARY: Confederate General Thomas J. Jackson nudges his footsore host from Staunton, western Virginia, toward the outskirts of McDowell. As the 10,000 Confederates deploy to engage the next morning, Union reinforcement arrives in the form of General Robert C. Schenk's brigade, giving the defenders 6,000 rank and file.

NAVAL: President Abraham Lincoln tours the ironclad USS *Monitor* off Fortress Monroe, Virginia.

May 8

MILITARY: At 4:30 P.M., General Thomas J. Jackson leads 10,000 Confederates in an attack against 6,000 Federals under General Robert H. Milroy at McDowell in western Virginia. Union troops nonetheless charge up the heavily wooded hill, firing into an open copse where the Southerners had deployed, and inflict heavy losses. Confederate General Edward Johnson and his Army of the Northwest grimly repulse every attack as Jackson labors to rush up additional troops. At length Milroy orders a retreat while Confederate troopers under Colonel Turner Ashby pursue and round up numerous stragglers.

May 9

MILITARY: President Abraham Lincoln diplomatically admonishes General George B. McClellan for not moving more vigorously upon the Confederate capital at Richmond, Virginia, seemingly within his grasp.

NAVAL: The ailing Confederate commodore Andrew H. Foote, wounded at the capture of Fort Donelson, is relieved by Captain Charles H. Davis above Fort Pillow, Tennessee.

SLAVERY: General David Hunter declares that all African-American slaves in his newly created Department of the South (Florida, Georgia, South Carolina) are emancipated. Willing slaves are also welcomed to be armed and incorporated into the army.

May 10

MILITARY: The Gosport Navy Yard at Norfolk, Virginia, is occupied by Union forces under General John E. Wool, whose movements are partially directed from offshore by President Abraham Lincoln. The mighty steam ram CSS *Virginia* is now deprived of a berth as it draws too much water to be concealed further up the James River.

NAVAL: The scratch-built Confederate River Defense Fleet of eight converted steam rams under Captain James E. Montgomery bravely sorties at Plum Run Bend on the Mississippi River, just north of Fort Pillow, Tennessee. He fiercely engages seven U.S. Ironclads under Commodore Charles H. Davis in one of the few squadron actions of the Civil War. Once the formidable USS *Carondelet* moves into firing range it punishes the Confederates with rifled cannon fire and Montgomery withdraws to the safety of Fort Pillow.

May 11

NAVAL: Because the large ironclad ram CSS *Virginia* draws too much water to operate further up the James River, Commodore Josiah Tattnall unceremoniously scuttles it off Craney Island, Virginia, to prevent capture. The Northern Blockading Squadron now enjoys unfettered access up the James as far as Drewry's Bluff.

May 12

MILITARY: The Army of the Potomac under General George B. McClellan advances to White House, Virginia, looming to within 22 miles of the Confederate capital Richmond.

NAVAL: Crewmen of the former CSS *Virginia* gather under Lieutenant Catesby ap Roger Jones at Drewry's Bluff on the James River, where they man an artillery battery. This is a formidable position rising 100 feet above the river and is only seven miles from Richmond, Virginia, so its defense is imperative.

POLITICS: President Abraham Lincoln declares the captured ports of Beaufort, North Carolina, Port Royal, South Carolina, and New Orleans, Louisiana, open to trade. He hopes that the resumption of commercial life will encourage and strengthen their political bonds to the North.

Pro-Union sympathizers hold a convention in Nashville, Tennessee, under the watchful gaze of Federal troops.

May 13

SLAVERY: Harbor pilot Robert Smalls and eight African-American coconspirators abscond with the Confederate steamer *Planter*, sail from Charleston Harbor, South Carolina, and surrender to the USS *Onward* offshore.

SOCIETAL: The seemingly inexorable approach of the Army of the Potomac places the Confederate capital at Richmond, Virginia, in a panic. President Jefferson Davis sends his wife Varina out of the city for safety.

May 15

NAVAL: Commodore John Rodgers leads the ironclads USS *Monitor*, *Galena*, and *Nauguatuck* up the James River until they encounter the formidable Confederate defenses along Drewry's Bluff, seven miles below Richmond, Virginia. The ensuing battle is one-sided as the Union ships, outgunned and unable to circumvent obstacles in their path, take a pounding. Rodgers then limps back to Norfolk, and Richmond is saved.

POLITICS: Rude behavior by New Orleans women toward Union occupiers prompts an angry General Benjamin F. Butler to issue his infamous General Order No. 28, the so-called Woman Order. This stipulates that any female disrespectfully disposed toward Federal troops will be arrested and treated as a prostitute. The act offends Southern sensibilities and triggers indignation across the Confederacy.

May 17

MILITARY: Union troops under General Jacob D. Cox commence moving across the Flat Top Mountains of western Virginia, with a view toward severing the

Virginia & Tennessee Railroad. To prevent this General Humphrey Marshall plans to attack from the east on the following day while General Henry Heath's division is ordered to strike from the south. Cox, fearing himself out numbered, withdraws completely.

NAVAL: The USS S*ebago* and *Currituck* escort troop transport *Seth Low* several miles down the Pamunkey River, Virginia, forcing Confederates to burn or scuttle 17 vessels to prevent capture. However, the river at this point is so narrow that the vessels are obliged to run backwards for several miles before turning their bows around.

May 18

NAVAL: Commander Stephen D. Lee demands the surrender of Vicksburg, Mississippi, but Confederate General Martin L. Smith refuses. A year will elapse before the "Gibraltar of the West" succumbs to Union forces.

May 19

SLAVERY: President Abraham Lincoln countermands General David Hunter's unauthorized emancipation order as it relates to his Department of the South (South Carolina, Georgia, and Florida).

May 20

MILITARY: Confederate General Thomas J. Jackson's rapidly moving command swells to 17,000 men with the arrival of General Richard S. Ewell's contingent in the Luray Valley, western Virginia. Jackson is determined to prevent General Nathaniel P. Banks from reinforcing the Army of the Potomac.

SETTLEMENT: Congress passes the Homestead Act, which insures settlers 160 acres of land if they remain on the land for five years and cultivate their plots. Southerners heretofore opposed the measure, fearing that it would attract overwhelming numbers of abolitionist homesteaders to the territories. Three million acres is ultimately distributed among 25,000 citizens by war's end, which facilitates the coming tide of western settlement.

May 21

MILITARY: Stalled eight miles from the Confederate capital of Richmond, Virginia, and ignoring his numerical superiority over the Confederates, General George B. McClellan calls for reinforcements. To that end, the I Corps of General Irvin McDowell prepares to march overland from Washington, D.C., to join him.

Confederates under General Thomas J. Jackson move northward in the Luray Valley via passes in the Massanutten Mountains and approach the isolated Union outpost at Front Royal. His movements are effectively masked by cavalry under Colonel Turner Ashby, who completely confounds Union General Nathaniel P. Banks.

May 23

MILITARY: A force of 23,000 Confederates under General Thomas J. Jackson bursts upon a rather surprised Union garrison at Front Royal, Virginia. En route General Richard Taylor is hailed by notorious spy Belle Boyd, who relays useful intelligence as to Union dispositions about the town. Thus informed, Jackson pushes forward men of his 1st Maryland, C.S.A., to clear Front Royal and prevent Union forces from burning two valuable bridges. Front Royal quickly succumbs to the Southern onslaught and the Federals retreat.

May 24

MILITARY: Pursuing Confederates under General Thomas J. Jackson maneuver to intercept retreating Federals under General Nathaniel P. Banks at Newtown, western Virginia, but are slowed by the delaying actions of cavalry commanded by General John P. Hatch. Jackson's alarming progress, however, induces President Abraham Lincoln to order General Irvin McDowell's I Corps halted at Fredericksburg and redirected back into the Shenandoah Valley.

POLITICS: The defeat at Front Royal stings Union authorities into action, and President Abraham Lincoln orders General John C. Frémont to gather up his forces and drive the Confederates from the Shenandoah Valley. He also advises General George B. McClellan that promised reinforcements are not forthcoming at this time.

May 25

MILITARY: President Abraham Lincoln, chafing over the stalled Union offensive outside Richmond, Virginia, again urges General George B. McClellan to resume his advance. "I think the time is near when you must either attack Richmond or give up the job and come to the defense of Washington," he declares.

The Army of the Potomac, reduced to a crawl before Richmond, Virginia, becomes divided by the Chickahominy River, with three Union corps lodged on its north bank and two below. This situation prompts General Joseph E. Johnston to contemplate an offensive stroke against the commands of generals Edwin V. Sumner, William B. Franklin, and Fitz John Porter, and possibly defeat them.

Having prevailed over Union forces below Winchester, General Thomas J. Jackson hurriedly marches his weary men toward another engagement in that town. General Richard S. Ewell's division advances against General Nathaniel Banks's troops on the right, while the Louisiana Brigade of General Richard Taylor simultaneously strikes their right. Banks's tactical ineptitude costs him 2,019 casualties while the Southerners sustain barely 400. Over the past three days Jackson's command has netted 3,030 prisoners, 9,000 firearms, and such a trove of quartermaster stores that the Confederates jocularly refer to their defeated adversary as "Commissary Banks."

General Pierre G. T. Beauregard decides to abandon Corinth, Mississippi, to superior Union forces and preserve his own army of 50,000 men. He then concocts a number of clever stratagems to convince General Henry W. Halleck that the Confederates are actually being reinforced and intend to fight.

POLITICS: President Jefferson Davis expresses disappointment that General Joseph E. Johnston has not commenced his offensive battle against the much larger Army of the Potomac. Nonetheless, he insists "We are steadily developing for a great battle, and under God's favor I trust for a decisive victory."

May 28

MILITARY: Confederate cavalry under General J. E. B. Stuart arrives at Richmond, Virginia, with intelligence that the much-feared approach of General Irvin McDowell's I Corps from Fredericksburg will not transpire. This development further prods General Joseph E. Johnston, commanding Confederate forces in Virginia, to cancel his impending lunge at three Union corps north of the Chickahominy River in favor of attacking the remaining two corps on the south bank.

Roughly 50,000 Union troops under generals Irvin McDowell, John C. Frémont, and Nathaniel P. Banks begin concentrating in the vicinity of Harper's

Ferry, western Virginia, to cut off and possibly annihilate marauding Confederates under General Thomas J. Jackson. All are encouraged by an anxious President Abraham Lincoln, who urges them "Put in all the speed you can."

May 30

MILITARY: General Joseph E. Johnston makes a close reconnaissance of Union forces looming within 10 miles of Richmond, Virginia, and observes how they are physically divided by the rain-swollen Chickahominy River. He elects to concentrate 51,000 men against the combined III and IV Corps of General Samuel P. Heintzelman and Erasmus D. Keyes, unsupported on the south bank. However, Johnston's execution is compromised by overreliance on verbal commands, which further complicates matters for his inexperienced officers and men.

Confederates under General Thomas J. Jackson withdraw from Winchester, Virginia, to avoid encirclement by three converging Union columns. General Turner Ashby's cavalry is left behind to constitute a rear guard, and the town is subsequently secured by Federal troops under General James Shield.

Union forces under General Henry W. Halleck secure 2,000 Confederates prisoners at Corinth, Mississippi, following the withdrawal of General Pierre G. T. Beauregard. Halleck thus secures a vital transportation link and severs the vital Memphis & Charleston, and Mobile & Ohio Railroads but is nonetheless criticized for his dilatory pace. In truth, it has taken the glacial Halleck 30 days to cover only 22 miles from Pittsburg Landing.

May 31

MILITARY: Federal troops under General George B. McClellan continue their glacial advance upon Richmond, Virginia, but topography requires him to further split his forces along either bank of the rain-swollen Chickahominy Creek. This deployment prompts General Joseph E. Johnston to destroy the isolated III and IV corps under generals Samuel P. Heintzelman and Eramus D. Keyes at Fair Oaks on the south bank. The impending Confederate onslaught, though well-planned, is hobbled from the onset from poor staff work and overreliance on verbal orders. Hard fighting manages to oust the division of General Silas Casey from its position and captures several batteries, but the Federals promptly re-form and establish new lines to the rear.

Johnston's secondary attack at nearby Seven Pines fares little better. Union troops under redoubtable Phil Kearny fiercely resist General W. H. C. Whiting's advance and repulse him. A second attack mounted by Whiting also falters, at which point General Joseph E. Johnston arrives to personally supervise matters. Johnston is then seriously wounded by a ball in the shoulder and succeeded by a dithering General Gustavus W. Smith, who orders his remaining forces from the field.

June 1

MILITARY: Confederate forces resume their offensive by striking the Army of the Potomac at Seven Pines, Virginia. The Southerners deliver their charges fiercely, but in piecemeal fashion, and they are driven off in disarray. At length General Robert E. Lee gallops up from Richmond to succeed General Gustavus W. Smith and he orders the fighting stopped at 1 P.M. The Confederates, who did most of the attacking, lose 6,134 men to a Union tally of 5,031. President Jefferson Davis next assigns Lee to succeed the tottering Smith as field commander. Unknown at

1862

the time, a corner had been turned in the military course of events—and a brilliant new chapter was about to unfold.

POLITICS: An anxious President Abraham Lincoln telegrams and implores General George B. McClellan to "Hold all your ground, or yield any inch by inch in good order."

June 3

NAVAL: Prolonged bombardment by Federal gunboats on the Mississippi River convinces Confederate defenders to abandon Fort Pillow, Tennessee. The nearby city of Memphis is likewise poorly garrisoned, save for a weak naval squadron.

June 5

POLITICS: In another deft blow against slavery, the United States recognizes the largely black nations of Liberia and Haiti; President Abraham Lincoln formalizes the process by appointing diplomatic ministers to both nations.

June 6

NAVAL: At 4:20 A.M. Union gunboats under Commander Charles H. Davis weigh anchor off Island No. 45, two miles north of Memphis, Tennessee, and make

---

Lee, Robert E.   (1807–1870)
General

Robert E. Lee *(National Archives)*

Robert Edward Lee was born at Stratford, Westmoreland County, Virginia, on January 19, 1807, a son of famed Revolutionary War hero "Light Horse Harry" Lee. He entered the U.S. Military Academy in 1825 and graduated four years later second in his class—without a single demerit. Lee then received his second lieutenant's commission in the elite Corps of Engineers and joined the staff of General Winfield Scott during the Mexican War, 1846–48. He ended the war as a brevet lieutenant colonel and between 1852 and 1855 also served as superintendent of cadets at West Point. Lee next served in Texas until 1859 and then, during a furlough at home, commanded a detachment of U.S. Marines that captured abolitionist John Brown at Harper's Ferry, Virginia. In 1860 the gathering war clouds induced General-in-Chief Scott to tender Lee a ranking position within the Federal army, but he respectfully declined and joined the Confederacy. By March 1862 Lee

directly for the city. A small Confederate squadron of steam rams under Captain James E. Montgomery sorties to confront them as thousands of spectators line the riverbanks to observe. Davis feigns a retreat and Montgomery pursues until he is surprised in midstream by Union rams sailing four abreast. Confederate losses in the ensuing rout total around 100 with another 100 captured. Davis, having dispensed with his adversary, brooks no delay in making Memphis his prize. All western Tennessee is not firmly in Union hands, and this latest acquisition, the Confederacy's fifth largest city, subsequently functions as a vital staging area for operations against Vicksburg, Mississippi.

June 8

MILITARY: The main portion of the Army of the Valley under General Thomas J. Jackson camps at Port Republic, western Virginia, prior to advancing against Union forces commanded by General James Shields. Seven miles away General Richard S. Ewell's force of 5,000 men assumes defensive positions at Cross Keys, anticipating a major thrust there by General John C. Frémont's forces. At length Frémont approaches Ewell's position with 12,000 men but, before serious fight-

---

was at Richmond acting as a senior military adviser to President Jefferson Davis. He then launched an audacious series of hard, pounding attacks on General George B. McClellan–the Seven Days' Battles–which drove him back from the gates of Richmond. Lee then audaciously gambled upon an invasion of Union territory, carried the war directly into Maryland, and waged another hard-fought clash with McClellan at Antietam on September 17, 1862, which nearly proved disastrous until Lee was rescued by the sudden appearance of General Ambrose P. Hill's division.

Shortly afterward, the Army of the Potomac attacked Lee as he sat entrenched behind strong field fortifications at Fredericksburg on December 13, 1862. The result was a lopsided slaughter with 13,000 Federal losses to a Confederate tally of 5,300. In the spring of 1863, General Joseph Hooker led a reconstituted Army of the Potomac across the Rapidan River but Lee's ensuing attack brilliantly crushed Hooker's flank and induced him to retreat. In the summer of 1863 Lee sought to maintain the strategic initiative by reinvading Northern territory. His plan quickly went awry when General J. E. B. Stuart led his cavalry on a spectacular ride into Pennsylvania–which deprived the Army of Northern Virginia of its reconnaissance capabilities. Consequently, when Lee collided with Union forces under General George G. Meade at Gettysburg, Pennsylvania, on July 1–3, 1863, Lee's bloody defeat marked the high tide of Confederate military fortunes. His next contest of strength occurred in the late spring of 1864 against General Ulysses S. Grant, conqueror of Vicksburg. Over the next year Grant pinned Lee within his fortifications at Richmond while another Army under General William T. Sherman advanced upon him from Georgia. Lee, having fought magnificently, finally surrendered on April 9, 1865. After the war he spurned lucrative offers of employment to serve as president of Washington College in Lexington, Virginia. Lee died at Lexington on October 12, 1870, an iconic figure of the Civil War.

ing can develop, he suddenly disengages and falls back down the Keezletown Road.

June 9

MILITARY: Confederates under General Thomas J. Jackson cross a narrow wagon bridge over the North River to attack General Erasmus B. Tyler's brigade at Port Republic, western Virginia. Tyler arrays his 3,000 men in a line anchored by a seven-gun battery, and Jackson orders General Richard Taylor's Louisiana brigade against the Union left to storm it. By 11:00 A.M. Tyler, heavily outnumbered, orders a withdrawal which degenerates into a rout. Union losses amount to 1,108, including 558 prisoners, while the Southerners incur roughly 800 casualties, dead and wounded.

Port Republic is the sixth and final rout of Jackson's remarkable Shenandoah Valley Campaign. Since the previous March his famous "foot cavalry," whose strength peaked at 17,000 men, have slogged 676 miles, won four pitched battles and several skirmishes while defying all attempts by 60,000 Federals to snare them. Most importantly, Jackson's endeavors repeatedly siphoned off valuable Union manpower that might have been better employed before Richmond. "God has been our shield," Jackson modestly concludes, "and to His name be all glory."

June 10

MILITARY: General Henry W. Halleck authorizes General Ulysses S. Grant, John Pope, and Don Carlos Buell to resume independent command of their respective armies. Grant, as the senior officer present, acts again as theater commander, and the tempo of events in the West once again escalates.

June 11

DIPLOMATIC: In a sternly worded missive to Minister Charles F. Adams in London, British prime minister Lord Palmerston protests the behavior of General William F. Butler toward civilians at New Orleans.

June 12

MILITARY: At 2:00 A.M. General J. E. B. Stuart bursts into his headquarters, declaring "Gentlemen, in ten minutes every man must be in the saddle." His 1,200 Virginian troopers then commence their dramatic and celebrated ride from Richmond, Virginia, and around the Army of the Potomac. Stuart is tasked with verifying rumors that General George B. McClellan's right flank is "up in the air" to facilitate a new offensive envisioned by new commander General Robert E. Lee.

June 13

MILITARY: General J. E. B. Stuart's cavalry reaches a threshold after filing through Old Church, Virginia, on the right flank of General George B. McClellan's army. No Confederate unit had ever penetrated Union lines this far but, rather than retrace his steps, Stuart boldly plunges ahead and begins his circular ride to fame.

June 14

MILITARY: General J. E. B. Stuart's cavalry destroys the bridge over the Chickahominy River at Forge Site to prevent a Union pursuit and completes its ride around the Army of the Potomac's left flank. Previously, the Confederates had been pursued by Federal cavalry under Colonel Philip St. George Cooke, Stuart's father-in-law.

June 15

MILITARY: General J. E. B. Stuart gallops into Richmond, Virginia, ahead of his troopers, with important military intelligence about the Army of the Potomac.

His 100-mile jaunt brings General Robert E. Lee welcome information about the dispositions of the Union V Corps under General Fitz John Porter, presently unsupported on the north bank of the river. Lee, eager to break the impasse near Richmond, begins concocting a plan for Porter's defeat.

POLITICS: With amazing perspicacity, President Abraham Lincoln informs a worried General John C. Frémont that Confederate reinforcements, seemingly headed for the Shenandoah Valley, are most likely a ruse to mask General Thomas J. Jackson's transfer to Richmond, Virginia.

June 16

MILITARY: At 2:00 A.M. Union general Henry W. Benham rouses the divisions of generals Horatio Wright and Isaac I. Stevens and orders them to attack Confederate emplacements at nearby Secessionville, South Carolina. The local Southern commander, Colonel Thomas G. Lamar of the 1st South Carolina Artillery, is apprised of Benham's intentions and prepares a two-mile-long position, crowned by heavy cannon, to receive him. The ensuing battle is a minor disaster for the Federals, and Benham loses 107 killed, 487 wounded, and 80 captured to a Confederate tally of 52 killed, 144 injured, and 8 missing.

June 17

MILITARY: General Braxton Bragg, a close friend and confidant of President Jefferson Davis, succeeds the ailing General Pierre G. T. Davis as commander of the Confederate Western Department. Bragg is a capable strategist and an accomplished logistician, but his garrulous disposition and fits of indecision alienate all but the most faithful subordinates.

June 19

NAVAL: Commander Matthew F. Maury reports to Confederate Secretary of the Navy Stephen R. Mallory on mining operations along the James River. He also broaches the use of galvanic batteries and the CSS *Teaser*, the first naval vessel to be outfitted as a minelayer; it also carries the first Confederate observation balloon.

SLAVERY: President Abraham Lincoln signs legislation outlawing slavery in all the territories.

June 23

MILITARY: General Robert E. Lee assembles his commanders at the Dabb's House near Richmond, Virginia, and outlines his offensive against the Army of the Potomac's right wing under General Fitz-John Porter. He plans to concentrate no less than 55,000 men against Porter's 30,000-strong V Corps by throwing the combined weight of generals Thomas J. Jackson, James Longstreet, Daniel H. Hill, and Ambrose P. Hill in a single, coordinated strike.

POLITICS: President Abraham Lincoln, disillusioned by General George B. McClellan's fabled cautiousness, ventures to West Point, New York, to confer with former general in chief Winfield Scott.

June 25

MILITARY: The Army of the Potomac edges to within six miles of the Confederate capital at Richmond, Virginia, the closest Union forces will approach in three years. General George B. McClellan, desiring to place heavy cannon on the city's outskirts to bombard it, orders Oak Grove, a section of swampy wooded terrain to his front, wrested from the enemy. Union forces acquire Oak Grove at the cost of 626 men while the Confederates suffer 441 casualties, but no one could have anticipated that the strategic initiative is passing suddenly and irretrievably over to the South.

June 26

MILITARY: Throughout the morning three Confederate divisions under generals James Longstreet, Daniel H. Hill, and Ambrose P. Hill march and concentrate 47,000 men in the vicinity of Mechanicsville, Virginia. Opposing them were 30,000 Federal troops of General Fitz-John Porter's V Corps, strongly entrenched behind Beaver Dam Creek. The aggressive General A. P. Hill orders a frontal assault against Porter but his well-positioned soldiers have little difficulty blasting back the enthusiastic Confederates. Lee's battle plan misfires spectacularly and with a loss of 1,484 Confederates to 361 Federals. His sudden pugnaciousness perplexes and unnerves General George B. McClellan, who orders Porter to abandon his strong position. McClellan also begins shifting his base of operations from the Pamunkey River to Harrison's Landing on the James River. This is the first stirring of what many participants on either side ridicule as the "Great Skedaddle."

June 27

MILITARY: The Union V Corps under General Fitz-John Porter retires four miles southeast from Mechanicsville, Virginia, and establishes a new defensive perimeter along a swampy plateau near Gaines's Mill. Confederates under General Robert E. Lee pursue smartly, and he determines to make another concerted attack on the new position. The charge is spearheaded by 4,000 fresh troops, but fighting is intense and bloody before Union forces finally abandon their strong plateau. Porter then withdraws in good order toward Chickahominy Creek and closer to General George B. McClellan's main force. Gaines's Mill is the most costly of the so-called Seven Days' Battles, with Confederate losses of 7,993 to a Union tally of 6,837.

General Braxton Bragg directs 3,000 men of General John P. McCown's division to transit by rail from Tupelo, Mississippi, to Chattanooga, Tennessee, to join the army of General Edmund Kirby-Smith. The movement takes six days and proceeds smoothly, which convinces Bragg that larger transfers of men and supplies could be shuttled there before Union forces can respond effectively.

POLITICS: President Abraham Lincoln formally accepts the resignation of the controversial explorer, soldier, and politician John C. Frémont.

June 28

MILITARY: General George B. McClellan withdraws from Richmond, Virginia, and bitterly concludes he is losing the campaign for want of promised reinforcements. General Robert E. Lee, meanwhile, having analyzed McClellan's temperament, orders his army on an intricate move down four different roads in an attempt to surround and possibly cripple his timid opponent.

NAVAL: At 2:00 A. M., Admiral David G. Farragut and Commander David D. Porter slip their respective squadrons past heavy Confederate gun emplacements at Vicksburg, Mississippi, suffering 15 killed and 30 wounded—trifling considering the amount of ordnance poured upon them.

June 29

MILITARY: General John B. Magruder, advancing east from Williamsburg, Virginia, with 11,000 men, cautiously probes the region for Union forces. Contact with the Federals is finally established at Allen's Farm around 9:00 A.M., although Magruder suddenly finds himself confronting the entire II Corps of 26,000 men under General Edwin V. Sumner, backed by 40 cannon. Thus far Magruder's "pursuit" availed him little beyond 626 casualties. Sumner's mishandling of affairs cost him 919 men and he also abandons 2,500 sick and injured soldiers. Overnight the II Corps withdraws to new positions at White Oak Swamp and Glendale.

June 30

MILITARY: General Robert E. Lee, intent upon destroying at least a portion of General George B. McClellan's Army of the Potomac, issues another set of complicated attack plans to catch the fleeing Federals in a pincer at Glendale. By 4:00 P.M. that afternoon an exasperated Lee can only count on 19,000 men of generals James Longstreet and Ambrose P. Hill, and they charge the center of the Union line, then strongly posted behind White Oak Swamp Creek. General George A. McCall is captured, but before the Southerners can exploit their breakthrough and seize vital crossroads, they are evicted by savage, hand-to-hand fighting and the combat draws down with nightfall. Lee's losses at White Oak are 3,673 while McClellan sustains 3,797.

July 1

MILITARY: Having failed to destroy the Army of the Potomac at White Oak Swamp the previous day, General Robert E. Lee maneuvers to deliver one last and possibly crushing blow against them at Malvern Hill, a 150-foot-high rise flanked by swamps and other obstacles, and ably manned by General Fitz-John Porter's V Corps. Porter's secure flanks promise to funnel any Confederate attack directly up the center of his waiting line, which is crowned by 100 pieces of field artillery. Lee nevertheless commits his army to several costly and futile assaults and then relents after suffering 5,650 casualties to a Union tally of 3,007.

The Seven Days' Campaign reaches its bloody conclusion with Union forces pushed far from the Southern capital of Richmond, Virginia. The Confederacy is thus preserved for another three-and-a-half years at a cost of 20,141 casualties. The Army of the Potomac, which handled itself well under excruciating circumstances, loses 15,849. Most important of all, the campaign defines General Robert E. Lee as an assertive and offensive-minded battle captain, much given to calculated risks. Warfare in the Eastern Theater now largely revolves around him.

Union forces under Colonel Philip H. Sheridan engage a large force of 4,700 Confederates under General James R. Chalmers at Booneville, Mississippi, 20 miles south of Corinth. Chambers presses hard against Sheridan's pickets, who are carrying the latest Colt revolving rifles, and is repelled. Sheridan's aggressive handling of troops also catches the eye of General Henry W. Halleck, who arranges his promotion to brigadier general.

NAVAL: The Western Flotilla under Commodore Charles H. Davis unites with the naval expedition of Admiral David G. Farragut above Vicksburg, Mississippi. This commingling of fresh and saltwater squadrons represents an impressive effort by both.

POLITICS: To meet mounting wartime expenditures, President Abraham Lincoln raises the federal income tax to three percent on all incomes over $600 per annum. (The first income tax passed in 1861 was never enforced.) The Bureau of Internal Revenue is founded to collect all monies.

RELIGION: An anti-polygamy act, aimed at Mormons of the Utah Territory, is passed by Congress.

TRANSPORTATION: Congress passes the Pacific Railroad Act, authorizing construction of the first transcontinental railroad. This will be accomplished by the Union Pacific Railroad laying down a track from Nebraska to Utah, where it will meet another line constructed from California by the Central Pacific Railroad.

July 2

EDUCATION: President Abraham Lincoln signs the Land-Grant College Act (or Morrill Act), which transfers 30,000 acres of public land to educational institutions throughout the North, for the purpose of promoting studies relating to agriculture, engineering, and military science.

POLITICS: President Abraham Lincoln authorizes the "ironclad test oath" to extract loyalty from all Federal employees, and it is eventually extended to include government contractors, attorneys, jurors, and passport applicants. Furthermore, citizens in Federal-occupied regions of the South are likewise required to pledge their allegiance.

July 7

MILITARY: President Abraham Lincoln visits General George B. McClellan at Harrison's Landing, Virginia, to discuss recent events. The general blames his recent setback upon a lack of promised reinforcements, and he also urges the president to adopt a more conservative approach to strategy—and abolition.

Photograph showing a construction train on the Union Pacific Railroad (*Library of Congress*)

July 10
MILITARY: The newly designated Army of Virginia under General John Pope positions itself in the Shenandoah Valley and reminds inhabitants of their obligation to assist Union efforts. He also promises swift justice for any treasonable or harmful deeds against military personnel.

July 12
MILITARY: The Congressional Medal of Honor, established in 1861 to honor naval personnel, is expanded to include soldiers.
NAVAL: Faced with falling water levels on the Yazoo River, the large Confederate ironclad CSS *Arkansas* under Lieutenant Isaac N. Brown sorties into the Mississippi River and heads south toward Vicksburg, Mississippi.

July 13
POLITICS: President Abraham Lincoln seeks congressional action to compensate states willing to voluntarily abolish slavery. He also informs Secretary of State William H. Seward and Secretary of the Navy Gideon Welles of his intention to draft an initial "emancipation proclamation" for the Cabinet to examine.

July 14
MILITARY: General John Pope exhorts his Army of Virginia by declaring that "The strongest position a soldier should desire to occupy is one from which he can most easily advance against the enemy." He then deploys his men between Washington, D.C., and Confederate forces to draw their attention away from General George B. McClellan's Army of the Potomac.
POLITICS: President Abraham Lincoln approves legislation for a Federal pension system to assist all widows and children of Union soldiers killed in the war. Meanwhile, 20 representatives from border states announce their opposition to the president's compensated emancipation plan.

July 15
MILITARY: Apaches under Mangas Coloradas and Cochise engage California troops under Colonel James H. Carleton at the Battle of Apache Pass, New Mexico Territory (Arizona).
NAVAL: Union vessels under Commodore Charles H. Davis attack the newly built Confederate ironclad CSS *Arkansas* under Lieutenant Isaac N. Brown as it churns down the Mississippi River. Both sides sustain damage but the *Arkansas* escapes intact and remains a menace to Union shipping throughout the region.

July 16
NAVAL: David G. Farragut is formally appointed rear admiral by Congress, the first officer in the U.S. Navy to hold such rank. President Abraham Lincoln also signs legislation conferring promotions to all serving flag officers.

July 17
POLITICS: President Abraham Lincoln approves the Second Confiscation Act, which mandates freedom for any African-American slaves reaching Union lines. Those wishing to emigrate outside the United States will also receive assistance. Various kinds of property useful to the Confederate war effort are also subject to seizure. However, escaped slaves in loyal border states remain subject to return under the Fugitive Slave Act.

July 19

POLITICS: Horace Greeley, editor of the New York *Tribune*, composes a letter to President Abraham Lincoln and calls upon him to free the slaves as a means of weakening the Confederacy.

July 21

ARTS: James Sloan Gibbons publishes his noted poem "We Are Coming Father Abraham" in the *New York Evening Post*; it is subsequently set to music by Stephen Foster and Luther O. Emerson.

POLITICS: President Abraham Lincoln discusses with his cabinet the possible employment of African-American soldiers, but no action is taken at this time.

July 22

MILITARY: Colonel Nathan B. Forrest and 1,000 Confederate cavalry capture Murfreesboro, Tennessee, defeating a Union garrison of 1,200 men. He does so by overrunning the camps of the 9th Michigan and 7th Pennsylvania Cavalry, then bluffing the still intact 3rd Minnesota to surrender.

Confederate raiders under Colonel John H. Morgan return to Livingston, Tennessee, after a spectacular raid through Kentucky. The Federals also learn that a Confederate operative working for Morgan had tapped into their telegraph lines and intercepted army dispatches for the past 12 days.

NAVAL: The USS *Essex* under Captain William B. Porter, accompanied by the ram *Queen of the West*, resumes attacking the Confederate ironclad CSS *Arkansas* off Vicksburg, Mississippi. Both Union vessels are driven off without seriously damaging their opponent, which defiantly steams past Vicksburg's batteries and challenges the Federals to fight.

POLITICS: President Abraham Lincoln unveils a draft of his Emancipation Proclamation to his Cabinet, which frees all African Americans held in bondage throughout the South. However, he heeds Secretary of State William H. Seward's suggestion to postpone its unveiling until after a significant military victory by the North. Secretary of War Edwin M. Stanton then announces that the army can appropriate personal property for military purposes and also employ freed African Americans as paid laborers.

Federal and Confederate officials reach an agreement on a method for exchanging prisoners of war. It functions effectively until the fall of 1863, when Union complaints over the treatment of African Americans results in its cancellation.

July 23

MILITARY: General Henry W. Halleck, newly arrived general in chief in Washington, D.C., discusses the possibility of joint operations between generals George B. McClellan and John Pope.

Union cavalry under Colonel Hugh J. Kilpatrick, advancing from Fredericksburg, Virginia, raids Confederate supplies gathered at Carmel Church until driven off by General J. E. B. Stuart.

General John Pope tightens restrictions upon the inhabitants of the Shenandoah region by insisting that all military-age males take an oath of allegiance or face deportation to the South.

General Braxton Bragg begins skillfully transferring 31,000 Confederate troops from Tupelo, Mississippi, to Chattanooga, Tennessee—a distance of 776 miles—in one of the largest Southern rail movements of the war. However, Bragg leaves behind two independent and feuding leaders: generals Sterling Price at Tupelo and Earl Van Dorn at Vicksburg, each commanding 16,000 men.

July 24

NAVAL: Falling water levels on the Mississippi River and rising sickness induce Admiral David G. Farragut to remove his squadron from below Vicksburg, Mississippi, to New Orleans, Louisiana, following a two-month hiatus. Moreover, his experience outside Vicksburg convinces him that the city will never be taken by naval forces alone.

POLITICS: Martin Van Buren, the eighth president of the United States, dies in Kinderhook, New York.

July 29

MILITARY: Federal authorities arrest Confederate spy mistress Belle Boyd at Warrenton, Virginia, and she is sent to the Old Capital Prison in Washington, D.C.

The first elements of the Confederate Army of Mississippi arrive at Chattanooga, Tennessee, concluding a strategic transfer of resources from the Deep South back to the center. General Braxton Bragg skillfully cobbles together a force of 30,000 men for an impending offensive into Kentucky.

NAVAL: Ship "209," christened *Enrica*, departs Liverpool, England, ostensibly for sea trials. It actually heads for Nassau, the Bahamas, for service with the Confederate navy as the infamous commerce raider CSS *Alabama*.

July 31

DIPLOMACY: U.S. Minister Charles F. Adams badgers Foreign Secretary Lord Russell not to allow the newly launched *Enrica* (the future CSS *Alabama*) to leave port. The British government dithers five days before Lord Russell issues the requisite orders, but beforehand Confederate agents slip aboard and sail it away, ostensibly for conducting sea trials. Ultimately, this vessel accounts for the destruction of 60 Union merchant ships.

MILITARY: Generals Braxton Bragg and Edmund Kirby-Smith confer at Chattanooga, Tennessee, and hammer out a strategy for the upcoming Kentucky campaign. The former, while senior, fails to exert his authority over Kirby-Smith, who insists upon a virtually independent command.

POLITICS: President Jefferson Davis directs that any Union officer captured from General John Pope's Army of Virginia is to be treated like a felon. This is in retaliation for any Southern citizens shot for treason under Pope's draconian administration of the Shenendoah Valley.

August 2

DIPLOMACY: Secretary of State William H. Seward orders American Minister to England Charles F. Adams to ignore any British offers of mediation between North and South.

August 4

POLITICS: President Abraham Lincoln issues a call for 300,000 drafted militia to serve nine months; this levy is never enacted. Yet, despite persistent manpower shortages, he declines the services of two African-American regiments from Indiana, suggesting instead that they be employed as laborers.

August 5

MILITARY: General John C. Breckinridge is ordered by General Earl Van Dorn to attack the Union enclave at Baton Rouge, Louisiana, with his 2,600 Confederates and accompanied offshore by the ironclad CSS *Arkansas*. The Union garrison of 2,500 soldiers under General Thomas Williams deploys to receive him, and a sharp action erupts in very dense fog around 4:30 P.M. Fighting finally subsides around six hours later when Breckinridge concedes defeat and orders his command back to Vicksburg, Mississippi.

NAVAL: The large Confederate ironclad CSS *Arkansas* under Lieutenant Henry K. Stevens steams down the Mississippi River to assist the expedition against Baton Rouge, Louisiana. His mission is to neutralize Union gunboats, but his craft sustains a broken propeller shaft en route and proves unable to effectively support the military effort ashore.

August 6

INDIAN: A starving band of Mdewkanton Santee (Sioux) Indians arrives at the Lower Agency, Minnesota, where Chief Little Crow (Taoyateduta) pleads with agent Andrew F. Myrick for promised foodstuffs. However, war activities delay the arrival of treaty payments from Washington, D.C., and local authorities refuse to give Little Crow the credit necessary to feed his people. Despite desperate entreaties for help, Myrick rebuffs the Indians, declaring "So far as I am concerned, if they are hungry, let them eat grass." The chief and his entourage angrily depart, incensed at white indifference to their plight.

NAVAL: A Federal naval flotilla under Commander David D. Porter of the USS *Essex* attacks and further damages the large ironclad CSS *Arkansas* near Baton Rouge, Louisiana. That vessel has a broken propeller shaft and, when it runs aground, Lieutenant Henry K. Stevens orders it scuttled to prevent capture.

August 7

MILITARY: A force of 24,000 Confederates under General Thomas J. Jackson decamps from Gordonsville, Virginia, and marches north to Orange Court House. However, because General Ambrose P. Hill completely misinterprets his orders and fails to leave camp, the usually hard-marching Confederates cover only eight miles.

August 8

LAW: Secretary of War Edwin M. Stanton suspends writs of habeas corpus throughout the country to facilitate cases against treason and draft evasion.

MILITARY: Federal authorities again release and parole Confederate spy Belle Boyd from Old Capitol Prison, in Washington, D.C., citing lack of evidence to detain her further.

August 9

MILITARY: Aware that Confederates under General Thomas J. Jackson are converging upon his position near Cedar Mountain, Virginia, General Nathaniel P. Banks deploys 9,000 Federal troops at its base to confront Jackson, who then attacks without proper reconnaissance with two divisions, but at 4:30 P.M. Banks commits his entire reserves to battle, which outflank the Confederates and threaten to roll up their line. However, Jackson is rescued in timely fashion as the first elements of General A. P. Hill's division come trudging up the road and his line is stabilized. Banks then withdraws his men and the Southerners retain

Little Crow   (ca. 1820–1863)
Sioux chief

Little Crow (Taoyateduta) was born into the Mdewkanton (Santee) band of the Sioux nation around 1820, near present-day St. Paul, Minnesota. His father was a hereditary chief and around 1834 Little Crow assumed control of the band. Contact with white settlers in this remote region was increasing, but the chief seems to have been amicably disposed toward them. In 1846, after he was injured in an altercation with his brothers over the use of alcohol, Little Crow approached the Indian agency at nearby Fort Snelling about sending missionaries among the Indians to promote temperance. In 1851 he was a signatory to the Treaty of Mendota, whereby the Santee ceded most of their territory to settlers and moved onto reservations. Resentful Indians perpetuated the Spirit Lake Massacre in 1857, at which point Little Crow volunteered to help pursue those responsible. The following year he ventured to Washington, D.C., with a tribal delegation to further negotiations and secure an annuity of goods and food to assist his people. However, by 1861, the government was absorbed by the Civil War and the Indian Department neglected its responsibilities of feeding the Indians as promised. By the summer of 1862 the Santee were reduced to eating their own horses to survive, and when Little Crow angrily remonstrated to agent Andrew Myrick that stockpiled supplies were deliberately being withheld, Myrick told him and his people to eat grass. Tensions then flared when angry Santee braves murdered five white settlers and Little Crow, sensing the inevitability of conflict, began orchestrating an armed uprising.

On August 18, 1862, armed Sioux swooped down on unsuspecting white settlements, killing upwards of 400 men, women, and children. The defiant Myrick was among those slain, and his mouth was then stuffed with grass. The Indians continued on a rampage until a force under General Henry H. Sibley could organize itself and counterattack. The Sioux were then decisively beaten at Wild Lake on September 23, 1862, and many prisoners were seized. President Abraham Lincoln spared most of them from the hangman's noose, but on December 26, 1862, 38 braves went to the scaffold in the largest mass execution in American history. For his part, Little Crow escaped capture and made his way to Canada, but British authorities refused to help. He then returned to Minnesota the following year with a small band of warriors and resumed depredations against settlements. However, on July 3, 1863, he was shot and killed by farmers while picking berries. Little Crow's remains were then flung upon a garbage heap, where they remained for several months, although his skeleton eventually made its way into the collections of the Minnesota Historical Society. In 1971 the bones were turned over to his descendants and interred at a Sioux burial ground in South Dakota. For the time it was fought, Little Crow's uprising was one of the bloodiest Indian conflicts in American history and initiated removal of the Sioux from their ancestral homelands.

possession of the field. Jackson loses 1,334 men to a Union tally of 2,353, which leads participants to dub the engagement "Slaughter Mountain."

August 13
MILITARY: General Robert E. Lee begins advancing his Army of Northern Virginia from the Peninsula and toward Gordonsville, Virginia. He begins by dispatching

30,000 men under General James Longstreet by rail, where they are scheduled to link up with the corps of General Thomas J. Jackson.

August 14

POLITICS: President Abraham Lincoln confers with a delegation of free African Americans at the White House and suggests Central America as a possible venue for colonization. The suggestion is badly received by many black leaders, especially Frederick Douglass, who accuses the president of "contempt for Negroes."

August 16

MILITARY: General Edmund Kirby-Smith departs Knoxville, Tennessee, with 10,000 men and plunges headlong through the Cumberland Gap and into Kentucky. This action initiates a concerted Southern effort to reclaim that state for the Confederacy.

August 17

INDIAN: Half-starved Sioux tribesmen stage an uprising in southwest Minnesota by killing five settlers on their farm in Acton Township. Chief Little Crow, when informed of the action, realizes that war with the whites is unavoidable and takes to the warpath. The result is a savage, six-week conflict claiming upwards of 600 lives.

August 18

INDIAN: Rampaging Sioux warriors attack the Upper and Lower Indian Agencies, Minnesota, killing 20 people including Agent Andrew J. Myrick, whose mouth is then stuffed with the very grass he told the Indians to eat. A detachment of 46 soldiers under Captain John Marsh, 5th Minnesota, advancing to rescue the settlers is then ambushed at Redwood Ferry and nearly annihilated with the loss of 24 soldiers.

POLITICS: President Jefferson Davis, addressing the newly convened second session of the Confederate Congress in Richmond, Virginia, excoriates the behavior of General Benjamin F. Butler at New Orleans, Louisiana.

August 20

INDIAN: A large gathering of Mdewkanton Santee (Sioux) warriors under Chief Little Crow attack Fort Ridgely, Minnesota, and are repulsed by 180 soldiers and three cannon under Lieutenant Timothy Sheehan. The garrison loses six killed and 20 wounded while Santee casualties are considerably heavier. The Indians draw back but continue the siege while awaiting reinforcements.

JOURNALISM: New York *Tribune* editor Horace Greeley pens his "Prayer of Twenty Millions" in an unabashed plea for the abolition of slavery.

August 21

POLITICS: Confederate military authorities issue a directive to execute any Northern officers found commanding African-American troops. Generals David Hunter and John W. Phelps, in particular, are likewise to be treated as felons if captured for their roles in arming slaves to fight in the Union army.

August 22

INDIAN: Chief Little Crow of the Mdewkanton Santee (Sioux) is joined by another 400 warriors of the Sisseton and Wahpeton bands, for a total of nearly 800. These then make another aborted attack upon the 180-man garrison of Fort Ridgely, Minnesota, and are again repulsed with 100 casualties. Federal troops sustain three killed and 13 wounded.

JOURNALISM: President Abraham Lincoln responds to *New York Tribune* editor Horace Greeley and candidly admits he intends to neither preserve nor destroy that "peculiar institution." Lincoln is in a bind to keep slave-owning border states loyal to the North out of military considerations. "My paramount objective is to save the Union," he insists.

August 23

INDIAN: The town of New Ulm, Minnesota, is attacked by 400 rampaging Mdewkanton Santee (Sioux) under Chief Little Crow. The town, stoutly defended by civilians under Judge Charles Flandreau, is nearly consumed by fire but the Indians are repulsed and withdraw. The whites lose 36 dead and 23 wounded; Sioux losses are unknown but presumed to be as heavy.

MILITARY: General J. E. B. Stuart attacks Catlett's Station, Virginia, headquarters of General John Pope. He thus seizes 300 captives, Pope's personal baggage and uniform, along with his military correspondence. General Robert E. Lee is thereby informed of Union strategy to unite Pope's 51,000-man Army of Virginia with the 100,000-strong Army of the Potomac under General George B. McClellan. Lee begins formulating a plan to crush Pope before the two forces can merge.

August 24

MILITARY: In a stunningly bold maneuver, General Robert E. Lee divides the Army of Northern Virginia by detaching 25,000 men under General Thomas J. Jackson's corps on a rapid march to destroy the Orange & Alexandria Railroad, thereby cutting General John Pope's supply line. Meanwhile, his remaining 30,000 men under General James Longstreet remain in place until Pope takes the bait.

NAVAL: Having received its armament, CSS *Alabama* is commissioned into Confederate service off Terceria, Azores, under celebrated raider Raphael Semmes.

August 25

MILITARY: General Thomas J. Jackson's corps detaches itself from the Army of Northern Virginia and advances to the Rappahannock River. By dint of hard slogging the Southerners cover 56 miles in only two days—one of the most impressive performances of the entire war—and arrive behind General John Pope's Army of Virginia. Jackson also manages to interpose himself between Pope and the Union capital at Washington, D.C.

POLITICS: To placate Radical Republicans and alleviate manpower shortages, Secretary of War Edwin M. Stanton authorizes the recruitment of up to 5,000 African-American soldiers. Orders are then cut for General Rufus Saxton, military governor of the South Carolina Sea Islands, to raise five regiments of black troops for military service in the field. Much is anticipated from this pilot program.

August 26

MILITARY: In a surprise move, Confederate forces led by General Isaac Trimble storm into Manassas Junction, Virginia, capturing General John Pope's main supply base. The malnourished Confederates of General Thomas J. Jackson, looking more like scarecrows than soldiers, gleefully gorge themselves.

NAVAL: Captain Franklin Buchanan is promoted to rear admiral for his conduct on the CSS *Virginia* on March 8, 1862, the first Confederate naval officer so honored.

August 27

INDIAN: A relief column of 1,400 soldiers under Colonel Henry H. Sibley arrives at Fort Sibley, Minnesota, from distant Fort Snelling. Meanwhile, a detachment of troopers under Major Joseph R. Brown is ambushed at Birch Coulee, losing 16 killed and 44 wounded.

MILITARY: General John Pope, stung by the capture of his supply base at Manassas Junction, hurriedly marches from behind the Rappahannock River in search of Confederates under General Thomas J. Jackson. Jackson, meanwhile, is staying along the Warrenton Turnpike to await the arrival of General James Longstreet's corps. The most perilous part of General Robert E. Lee's gambit is about to be launched.

August 28

MILITARY: Generals Robert E. Lee and James Longstreet force a passage through Thoroughfare Gap, Virginia, to engage the main Union army. In the process they encounter and brush aside a division under General James B. Ricketts and cavalry forces commanded by General John Buford.

Two Confederate divisions of General Thomas J. Jackson surprise and attack a force of 2,800 Union troops under General Rufus King at Groveton, Virginia. However, as the heady Southerners advance anticipating an easy victory they charge headlong into the "Black Hat" brigade of General John Gibbon at Brawner's Farm. A fierce fight of two hours ensues before both sides withdraw exhausted and depleted. Jackson loses 1,200 men out of 4,500 committed while Union forces sustain 1,100 casualties out of 2,800 present.

General Braxton Bragg's Confederate Army of Mississippi, soon to be redesignated the Army of Tennessee, proceeds northward from Chattanooga and into Kentucky proper, several days behind a second column under General Edmund Kirby-Smith.

POLITICS: Congress founds the Department of Engraving and Printing with five employees.

August 29

MILITARY: General Thomas J. Jackson assumes defensive positions along an unfinished railroad berm near Groveton, Virginia, as Union forces under General John Pope mass 65,000 men for an attack. The Second Battle of Manassas begins as generals Franz Sigel and Joseph Hooker assail Jackson's line while the V Corps under General Fitz-John Porter detects the approach of General James Longstreet's 30,000 Confederates on Pope's left flank. Porter immediately notifies his superior as to the danger confronting his army, but Pope nonetheless orders him to attack Jackson's position at once. Porter disobeys and prepares to face Longstreet; his insubordination costs him his career but probably spared the Army of Virginia from annihilation.

August 30

MILITARY: The Second Battle of Manassas resumes as Union troops, ordered by General John Pope to pursue supposedly defeated Confederates, find them still occupying string defensive position instead. Regardless, General Fitz-John Porter's V Corps surges forward and assails Jackson's right, and waves of blue-coated infantry surge forward. Suddenly a massed charge, spearheaded by General John B. Hood's Texan Brigade, begins rolling up the Union left. Jackson, seeing his

Federal opponents suddenly waver, orders his own men forward in front and Pope's army dissolves. Losses at Second Manassas are severe with Pope reporting 16,054 men lost while Lee sustained 9,197. Moreover, the Southerners are in no position to take the war northward into Maryland.

General Mahlon D. Manson, bolstered by the arrival of troops under General Charles Cruft, pours 6,500 Federal soldiers—mostly new recruits—into defensive positions six miles below Richmond, Kentucky. General Patrick R. Cleburne's Confederates then attack and dislodge the defenders, who fall back in confusion through the streets of Richmond. Southern losses are 98 killed, 492 wounded, and 10 missing while Manson suffers 206 killed, 844 wounded, and 4,303 captured. The Southern invasion of Kentucky is off to a productive start.

August 31
MILITARY: The Union Army of Virginia under General John Pope regroups and rallies at Centreville, Virginia, as General Robert E. Lee dispatches the fast moving command of General Thomas J. Jackson on a forced march around the Union left to possibly cut their retreat from Washington, D.C.

September 1
MILITARY: Confederates under General Thomas J. Jackson, resting around Ox Hill and Chantilly, Virginia, are suddenly accosted by Union forces from General Joseph Hooker's division. Fighting commences around 4:00 P.M. when additional Federals under General Isaac I. Stevens, IX Corps, advance down Warrenton Pike and charge. These are then bolstered by the appearance of General Philip Kearny's brigade, which laces into advancing Confederates and closes a gap in Union lines. However, Kearny, while conducting a personal reconnaissance ahead of his troops, stumbles into Confederate pickets and is shot dead. Losses in this brief but intense encounters are estimated at 500 Confederates and 700 Federals.

September 2
INDIAN: A detachment of soldiers is attacked in camp at Birch Coulee, Minnesota, by Santee warriors under Big Eagle (Wambdi Tanka). They manage to keep their attackers at bay for the next 31 hours.

MILITARY: President Abraham Lincoln, ignoring the advice of his Cabinet, restores General George B. McClellan as head of the Army of the Potomac, a decision widely hailed by soldiers in the ranks. The bumbling and recently disgraced General John Pope, meanwhile, continues on without an official command.

September 3
MILITARY: General John Pope complains to General in Chief Henry W. Halleck that his recent debacle is due to General Fitz-John Porter's refusal to obey orders and General George B. McClellan's inability to provide timely support.

POLITICS: Kentuckian Joseph Holt is appointed judge advocate general of the United States.

September 4
MILITARY: The Army of Northern Virginia under General Robert E. Lee moves 40,000 men across the Potomac River at White's Ford, Virginia, and filters into Maryland. The invasion of the North commences.

NAVAL: The CSS *Florida* under Lieutenant Joseph N. Maffit plunges past Union vessels and enters Mobile Bay, Alabama. His success results in an official rebuke for local Union commanders and demands for better management of the blockade effort.

September 5
MILITARY: General John Pope is formally relieved of command and ordered back to Washington, D.C., for reassignment. General in Chief Henry W. Halleck then orders that his Army of Virginia is to be consolidated within the Army of the Potomac under General George B. McClellan.

September 6
MILITARY: General John Pope accepts the military equivalent of Siberian exile by assuming command of the Department of the Northwest (Wisconsin, Iowa, Minnesota, and the Nebraska and Dakota Territories). There he is primarily concerned with ending a deadly Sioux uprising.

September 7
MILITARY: The Union capital at Washington, D.C., panics as Confederate forces under General Robert E. Lee occupy Frederick, Maryland—within striking distance. General George B. McClellan, newly reappointed as commander of the Army of the Potomac, sallies forth from the capital to engage them.

September 8
MILITARY: General Robert E. Lee issues a proclamation to the inhabitants of Maryland, assuring them that "We know no enemies among you, and will protect all, of every opinion." Regardless, public attitude toward the invaders remains tepid.

NAVAL: Commodore John Wilkes assembles the West India Squadron (a mobile or "flying" squadron) and is tasked with halting depredations by Confederate raiders CSS *Alabama* and *Florida*.

September 9
MILITARY: As the Army of Northern Virginia passes through Frederick, Maryland, General Robert E. Lee expresses concern about the sizable Union garrison holding Harper's Ferry, as it could threaten his rear. He therefore issues Special Order No, 191 which detaches the corps of General Thomas J. Jackson back into the Shenandoah Valley to capture that strategic post while General James Longstreet's corps advances toward Hagerstown. Lee has again daringly—and dangerously—split his army in two.

September 10
MILITARY: The Confederate corps of General Thomas J. Jackson, accompanied by the divisions of generals Lafayette McLaws and John G. Walker, depart their cantonment near Frederick, Maryland, and execute a converging movement against Harper's Ferry in western Virginia. Meanwhile, General James Longstreet continues marching toward Hagerstown, leaving the Army of Northern Virginia badly dispersed and subject to defeat.

September 13
MILITARY: Private Barton W. Mitchell of the 27th Indiana accidently finds a copy of General Robert E. Lee's Special Order No. 191 wrapped around a discarded cigar. Once informed, General George B. McClellan suddenly realizes that the Southerners are scattered and subject to defeat. Inexplicably, he waits 16 hours before putting the army in motion while his golden opportunity ebbs.

Harper's Ferry in western Virginia is being enveloped by a three-pronged Confederate maneuver. General Lafayette McLaws' division occupies neighboring Maryland Heights across the river while General John G. Walker positions his force on nearby Loudoun Heights. The 12,000-man Union garrison under Colonel Dixon S. Miles is thus speedily trapped by 23,000 Confederates now enjoying superiority in both numbers and position.

September 14

MILITARY: General George B. McClellan sorties his entire Army of the Potomac, intending to catch the dispersed Confederates of General Robert E. Lee before they can regroup. He orders the IX Corps under General Jesse L. Reno and the I Corps of General Joseph Hooker to march their respective ways through Fox and Turner's Gaps near South Mountain, but they encounter General James Longstreet's command. Longstreet then feeds the brigades of generals Robert Rodes and John B. Hood into the fray, and they slowly give ground. The Federals clear South Mountain by 10 P.M., with 28,500 men pushing back 17,850 Confederates. Losses in this severe engagement amount to 2,325 Union to 2,685 Confederate. The Federal noose is slowly drawing shut.

Cognizant of General Robert E. Lee's dispersed Army of Northern Virginia, General George B. McClellan dispatches the VI Corps of General William B. Franklin to advance with all haste through Crampton's Gap, Maryland. They encounter a smaller Confederate force yet their two divisions of 12,800 men take nearly all day to batter their way up the hillside and flush the defenders from the heavily wooded slopes. By 6:00 P.M. the exhausted Southerners begin streaming down the mountainside in confusion and Franklin is finally positioned to pitch full force into General Lafayette McLaws' division at Harper's Ferry. However, he overestimates the size of Confederate forces opposing him and encamps for the night.

Confederate artillery ringing Harper's Ferry, western Virginia, begins bombarding Union positions to force the garrison of Colonel Dixon S. Miles into submission. The shelling is intense and intimidating, but relatively few injuries result. Worse, in light of the Battle of South Mountain, Jackson must seize the town no later than the next morning, lest General Robert E. Lee be forced to cancel his invasion of Maryland.

General Sterling Price occupies Iuka, Mississippi, with 15,000 soldiers prior to uniting with General Braxton Bragg in Kentucky. General Ulysses S. Grant, however, sees a opportunity to trap and destroy the exposed Confederates. He therefore orders columns under generals William S. Rosecrans and Edward O. Ord to approach Iuka from different directions and catch the defenders in a pincer movement.

September 15

MILITARY: General Robert E. Lee instructs his Army of Northern Virginia, presently strung out along the hills of Sharpsburg, Maryland, to begin consolidating to thwart a possible attack by superior Union forces. He also recalls the army of General Thomas J. Jackson from the Shenandoah Valley immediately.

After a prolonged bombardment in which Colonel Dixon A. Miles is mortally wounded, General Julius White surrenders the Union garrison at Harper's Ferry, western Virginia, to General Thomas J. Jackson. For a loss of 39 dead and 247 injured, the Southerners kill 44, wound 173, and seize 12,520 prisoners, a like number of small arms, 73 cannon, tons of supplies and equipment, and innumerable livestock. This is the largest Federal capitulation of the Civil War; Jackson quickly rounds up his prize and proceeds back to Antietam, Maryland, with alacrity.

September 16
MILITARY: General Robert E. Lee, buoyed by the recent seizure of Harper's Ferry, western Virginia, determines not to leave Maryland without a fight and positions his army along a series of low hills at Sharpsburg (Antietam), He initially musters only 18,000 troops, but lethargic movements by the Army of the Potomac allow two divisions of General Thomas J. Jackson's corps to arrive and deploy on the Confederate left. Jackson's final division under General Ambrose P. Hill is still at Harper's Ferry, 17 miles distant, and under orders to join the main body at once.

September 17
MILITARY: The Battle of Antietam commences at 5:30 A.M. when 12,000 soldiers of General Joseph Hooker's I Corps advance against the Confederate left under General Thomas J. Jackson. Hooker makes good progress against the first row of defenders in a cornfield until General John B. Hood's Texas brigade bursts onto the scene and drives him back. Jackson then counterattacks across the line and is himself heavily repulsed in turn. In the Confederate center General Daniel H. Hill leads 5,000 men slung along the length of a sunken road which acts as a trench. Heavily pressed, Hill is forced to retire though a deadly enfilade dropping men in clumps and bequeaths his position a nickname of "Bloody Lane." The locus of combat then shifts over to the Confederate right where General Ambrose Burnside's men make repeated and ineffectual attempts to cross the stone bridge over Antietam Creek. He finally succeeds at 3:00 P.M. and advances, but Burnside's own left is suddenly assailed by General Ambrose P. Hill's "Light Division," and the Federals are driven back to their starting point. McClellan, with 75,000 present (although 25,000 were not engaged), suffers 12,410 casualties while Lee, who could ill-afford such attrition, loses 11,172. The combined total of 3,500 dead and 17,100 wounded renders this the single bloodiest day in American military history.

General Braxton Bragg's Confederates capture 4,000 Union troops under Colonel John T. Wilder at Munsford, Kentucky, but only after a curious play of chivalry unfolds. Wilder, an amateur soldier, arrives at General Simon B. Buckner's headquarters under a flag of truce and seeks his advice as a gentleman. The general willingly obliges his visitor by taking him on a tour of Confederate lines to highlight their superiority in numbers. Wilder, finally convinced, agrees to lay down his arms.

SLAVERY: The failure of General Robert E. Lee at Antietam grants President Abraham Lincoln the military pretext he sought to announce his Emancipation Proclamation.

September 18
MILITARY: General Robert E. Lee disengages and begins ferrying the Army of Northern Virginia across the Potomac River at Blackford's Ferry, Maryland, and back into Virginia. He departs having sustained thousands of casualties, but superior forces under General George B. McClellan fail to intervene or even actively pursue.

September 19

MILITARY: Union columns of 9,000 men each under generals William S. Rosecrans and Edward O. C. Ord march west and south of Iuka, Mississippi, attempting to crush 15,000 Confederates under General Sterling Price between them. However, Price's cavalry alerts him of their approach and he prepares to attack Rosecrans before the two forces can unite. General Henry Little's division then spearheads the Southern assault, which crumples the Union left and seizes nine cannon of the 11th Ohio battery. Price abandons his tactic by nightfall and elects to join up with Confederate forces under General Earl Van Dorn, who is himself planning an attack upon Corinth. Casualties are 86 Southerners killed, 408 wounded, and 200 captured to a Union tally of 141 men dead, 613 injured, and 36 missing.

September 20

MILITARY: A Confederate division under General Ambrose P. Hill advances against two Union brigades crossing Boetler's Ford into Virginia. As he deploys to attack, his men come under severe fire from 70 Union field pieces posted across the river. The Confederates nonetheless advance and drive the Federals back across the stream into Maryland.

NAVAL: Admiral Samuel F. du Pont warns Assistant Secretary of the Navy Gustavus V. Fox of the perils facing any contemplated attack upon Charleston, South Carolina. "It is a cul-de-sac," he declares, "and resembles a porcupine's hide turned outside in than anything else, with no outlet—you go into the bag—no running forts as at New Orleans." His warnings go unheeded by the Navy Department.

September 22

SLAVERY: The Emancipation Proclamation is unveiled by President Abraham Lincoln and which promises freedom for all African Americans currently held as slaves in secessionist states. However, it carefully skirts the issue as it pertains to liberating blacks in northern border states. Public reaction is decidedly mixed and ranges from euphoria in New England to angry protest elsewhere, but Lincoln's stance also lessens chances that either England or France will intervene on the Confederacy's behalf and shed blood to preserve the institution of slavery, long banned in Europe.

September 23

INDIAN: As Little Crow's band of 800 Mdewkanton Santee (Sioux) warriors flee up the Minnesota Valley, they are pursued by 1,600 volunteers and troops under Colonel Henry H. Sibley. Sibley then encamps for the evening at Lone Tree Lake (reported as Wood Lake) and Little Wolf suddenly turns and springs on his pursuers, attacking at dawn. Fortunately for Sibley, when several of his men try to desert they run headlong into the Indians and the entire camp is thus alerted. The Santee are subsequently repulsed by artillery; Chief Mankato and 30 warriors are killed. Sibley then presses ahead and the bulk of the Santee surrender en masse. The soldiers then rescue 269 white hostages while taking 2,000 Native Americans prisoner, many of whom are slated for execution for their earlier atrocities against settlers.

JOURNALISM: President Abraham Lincoln's Emancipation Proclamation appears in the Northern press for the first time; reactions are mixed and range between antipathy and admiration.

September 24
POLITICS: President Abraham Lincoln authorizes suspension of all writs of habeas corpus as sought by Secretary of War Edwin M. Stanton. Furthermore, military trials are now required for all persons suspected of dodging the draft or encouraging disloyal practices.

A three-day conference of Union governors convenes in Altoona, Pennsylvania, at the behest of Governor Andrew G. Curtin. They gather to pledge continuing support for the president and sound out new ideas as to how best prosecute the war.

The Confederate Congress adopts the seal of the Confederacy.

September 27
POLITICS: The Second Confederate Conscription Act is enacted, mandating that all males between 35 and 45 years of age be subject to military service. It also makes allowances for religious-based conscientious objectors, provided they pay a $500 exemption tax.
SLAVERY: The first regiment of former African-American slaves, the *Chasseurs d'Afrique*, musters into Union service at New Orleans, Louisiana, at the behest of General Benjamin F. Butler.

September 28
MILITARY: The armies of Confederate generals Sterling Price and Earl Van Dorn unite at Ripley, Tennessee, prior to launching offensive operations against the vital railroad junction at Corinth, Mississippi. Van Dorn, who enjoys seniority over the resentful Price, is regarded as nominal commander.

September 30
MILITARY: A strong detachment of 4,500 Union and territorial troops under General Edward Salomon skirmishes with a small Confederate detachment at Newtonia, Missouri. Newly arrived Southerners under Colonel Douglas H. Cooper are roughly handled by Cooper's men and are only rescued by the timely appearance of Colonel Joseph O. Shelby's 5th Missouri cavalry, accompanied by several mounted battalions of Cherokee, Chickasaw, and Choctaw. Salomon consequently orders a retreat in the direction of Sarcoxie, accomplished under close pursuit.

October 1
MILITARY: The 50,000-man Army of the Ohio under General Don Carlos Buell departs Louisville, Kentucky, in four columns; three of these will concentrate at Perryville while a fourth is ordered to move toward Confederate-held Frankfort. Their movements are complicated by incessant heat and shortages of water.

In a fateful move, General John C. Pemberton arrives at Vicksburg, Mississippi, superceding General Earl Van Dorn as commander of the Department of Mississippi and East Louisiana.
NAVAL: All army vessels of the Western Gunboat Fleet are formally transferred from the U.S. War Department to the Navy Department. Command of the newly designated Mississippi Squadron now devolves upon Captain David D. Porter, who replaces less aggressive Commodore Charles H. Davis.

October 2
POLITICS: In a less-than subtle hint, President Abraham Lincoln sets up his tent right next to General George B. McClellan's headquarters in an attempt to spur that officer to greater efforts.

October 3

MILITARY: Confederate forces numbering 22,000 troops under generals Earl Van Dorn and Sterling Price Attack 23,000 Union troops commanded by General William S. Rosecrans at Corinth, Mississippi. The latter deploys his men in several, mutually supporting lines of defense with all intervals between them covered by carefully sited cannon. The impetuous Van Dorn encounters the first line of Union earthworks around 9:30 A.M., after which the Confederates, with great gallantry and heavy losses, grind the defenders back toward their second line of entrenchments. That night Van Dorn redeploys his army in a semicircle around the town and its chain of five lunettes (batteries).

October 4

MILITARY: At 4:00 A.M., confederates under General Earl Van Dorn resume attacking General William S. Rosecrans's defensive works at Corinth, Mississippi. By dint of hard fighting and heavy sacrifice, part of General Martin E. Green's division storms and seizes the Robinson lunette (battery) while his remaining brigades actually force their way into the town. Van Dorn finally concedes defeat around 1:00 P.M. and orders a withdrawal to Ripley. Federal casualties are put at 2,520 while Van Dorn sustains 4,233—losses the Confederacy can ill afford in this theater.

POLITICS: In the Confederate-held capital of Frankfort, Kentucky, Governor Richard Haws takes his oath of office with General Braxton Bragg in attendance. However, the attendant festivities are suddenly canceled when word arrives of 20,000 approaching Union troops.

October 5

DIPLOMACY: British Prime Minister Lord Palmerston and Foreign Secretary Lord Russell have up to this point leaned in favor of recognizing the Confederacy, a position facilitated by embarrassing Union defeats of the spring and summer. Their plans are derailed by word of Antietam and the Emancipation Proclamation for the British government would never condone fighting to preserve the institution of slavery.

MILITARY: General Earl Van Dorn's Confederates retreat from Corinth, Mississippi, and onto Holly Springs and are intercepted by Union troops under General Edward O. C. Ord along the Hatchie River, Tennessee. An intense but indecisive clash erupts and the Southerners continue retreating.

October 6

MILITARY: A frustrated President Abraham Lincoln orders General Henry W. Halleck to prod dithering General George B. McClellan into action. "The President directs that you cross the Potomac and give battle to the enemy or drive him south," Halleck's telegram read, "Your army must move now while the roads are good." McClellan, true to character, largely ignores the directive.

October 7

MILITARY: The III Corps of General Charles C. Gilbert, Army of the Ohio, trudges down the Springfield Road near Perryville, Kentucky, and his arrival prompts the Confederate Army of Mississippi under General Braxton Bragg to begin massing its 16,000 men for an attack. However, due to poor cavalry reconnaissance, he is unaware that two more corps under General Don Carlos Buell arrive that evening, raising Federal totals to 25,000.

1862

October 8

MILITARY: General Don Carlos Buell arranges his 25,000 men for battle near Perryville, Kentucky. At 10:00 A.M., General Braxton Bragg arrives at the front and orders the Confederates forward against the Union left. General William J. Hardee is also directed to mass his troops along the center to keep Union forces at bay. At 2:00 P.M., General Leonidas K. Polk's command, infiltrating through an unguarded ravine, suddenly turns the Union left and violently drives it back. In the reformed center, the Union III Corps handily repels a Southern attack by Colonel Samuel Powell's brigade, and troops under General Philip H. Sheridan begin pressing their lines. Fighting rages on until darkness and Bragg, while he had won a tactical victory, finally perceives he is badly outnumbered and withdraws in good order back to Harrodsburg. The Battle of Perryville proves a costly encounter for both sides: Buell records 4,211 casualties while Bragg sustains 3,405.

October 10

MILITARY: General J. E. B. Stuart leads his force of 1,800 Confederate troopers out of Darkesville, Virginia, and fords the Potomac River near Black Creek, Maryland. His orders are to destroy the Cumberland Valley railroad bridge near Chambersburg, Pennsylvania, a major supply artery for the Army of the Potomac.

POLITICS: President Jefferson Davis encourages the Confederate Congress to draft 4,500 African Americans for the purpose of constructing fortifications in and around Richmond, Virginia.

October 11

NAVAL: Confederate raider CSS *Alabama* under Captain Raphael Semmes captures and burns the Union vessel *Manchester*. Semmes learns from reading captured New York newspapers the dispositions of several U.S. Navy warships looking for him.

POLITICS: President Jefferson Davis modifies the draft law to exempt all persons owning 20 or more slaves. This rule serves to heighten a pervasive sense of class conflict, and many Southerners accuse Davis of waging "a rich man's war and a poor man's fight."

October 12

NAVAL: Confederate commander and noted oceanographer Matthew F. Maury pilots the *Herald* past the Union blockade off Charleston, South Carolina, then sails for England to purchase additional warships for the South.

October 13

MILITARY: President Abraham Lincoln again urges General George B. McClellan to resume offensive operations. "Are you not being over-cautious when you assume that you can not do what the enemy is constantly doing?" he pointedly inquires. McClellan nevertheless refuses to budge and spends several days reorganizing and resting the Army of the Potomac.

Defeated Confederates under General Braxton Bragg and Edmund Kirby-Smith filter back through the Cumberland Gap into Tennessee. Their heralded invasion of Kentucky, representing the high tide of Confederate fortunes in the center region, dismally fails.

October 14

Politics: Elections held in Pennsylvania, Iowa, Ohio, and Indiana result in Democratic Party gains. The new members largely oppose emancipation and favor peaceful accommodation with the Confederacy.

October 16

Military: The Department of the Tennessee is resurrected with General Ulysses S. Grant as commander. He begins marshaling men and resources for an immediate campaign against Vicksburg, Mississippi.

October 17

Military: Colonel John H. Morgan takes 1,800 cavalry and departs from his Confederate camp, 25 miles southeast of Richmond, Kentucky, on his second major raid of the war. He the gallops for the lightly defended town of Lexington, intending to take it by storm.

October 20

Military: President Abraham Lincoln instructs former politician-turned-general John A. McClernand to command the newly formed Army of the Mississippi, then mount an expedition with troops from Indiana, Illinois, and Iowa, against Vicksburg, Mississippi. This action complicates and infringes upon efforts already underway by General Ulysses S. Grant.

October 21

Politics: President Abraham Lincoln urges elections in Tennessee for new state and congressional officials.

President Jefferson Davis advises General Theophilus H. Holmes of Confederate plans for an offensive to clear Tennessee and Arkansas of Federal forces.

October 24

Military: General Don Carlos Buell is sacked as commander of the Army of the Ohio for failing to aggressively pursue General Braxton Bragg's defeated army, now safely resting at Knoxville and Chattanooga, Tennessee.

October 25

Military: President Abraham Lincoln again urges General George B. McClellan to commit the Army of the Potomac to offensive operations in Virginia. When McClellan informs the president of his fatigued horses, an angry chief cables back, "Will you pardon me for asking what the horses of your army have done since the battle of Antietam that fatigue anything?"

October 26

Military: After continual prodding, General George B. McClellan finally crosses the Potomac River back into Virginia, but so cautiously that General Robert E. Lee's Confederates easily interpose themselves between the invaders and Richmond. President Abraham Lincoln is nonetheless "rejoiced" at the news.

The Union Army of the Mississippi under General John A. McClernand is disbanded and reassigned, largely through the machinations of General Ulysses S. Grant.

October 29

Politics: The steady stream of bad news from the West convinces President Jefferson Davis that the Confederacy lacks the manpower and arms to defend everything. "Our only alternatives are to abandon important points," he cautions, "or to use our limited resources as effectively as circumstances will permit."

October 30
DIPLOMACY: The Emperor Napoleon III suggests that France, Russia, and Great Britain conduct a joint mediation effort to end the American war. Failing that, he recommends recognizing the Confederacy.
NAVY: The U.S. Navy Department announces a $500,000 reward for the capture of Confederate raider "290" (CSS *Alabama*). A dozen warships, better employed elsewhere, are unnecessarily sent off in pursuit.

October 31
NAVAL: To compensate for its lack of warships, the Confederate Congress authorizes a Torpedo Bureau under General Gabriel J. Rains and an embryonic Naval Submarine Battery Service headed by Lieutenant Hunter Davidson. The numerous devices they test and deploy prove menacing to Union vessels at sea, in harbors, and especially on rivers—ultimately sinking 40 ships.

November 1
SLAVERY: General Benjamin F. Butler, commanding the garrison at New Orleans, Louisiana, imposes new restrictions on movement in and out of the city. In another controversial move, he also emancipates all African-American slaves from non-loyal owners.

November 4
POLITICS: Northern Democrats win significant elections in New York, New Jersey, Illinois, and Wisconsin, but Republican victories in California and Michigan offset these losses and the party retains control of the House of Representatives.
TECHNOLOGY: In Indianapolis, Indiana, Richard J. Gatling receives a government patient for his revolutionary, multibarreled, rapid-fire Gatling gun, a precursor to modern machine guns. Functional models are developed by the end of the war but are rarely committed to combat operations.

November 5
POLITICS: President Abraham Lincoln, exasperated by General George B. McClellan's dilatoriness, finally orders him replaced as head of the Army of the Potomac by General Ambrose E. Burnside.

November 8
MILITARY: After a stormy and controversial tenure commanding the Department of the Gulf at New Orleans, Louisiana, General Benjamin F. Butler is replaced by General Nathaniel P. Banks. To preempt any celebrations by the populace, Butler peremptorily closes all breweries and distilleries within his jurisdiction.

November 9
MILITARY: General Ambrose E. Burnside assumes command of the Army of the Potomac, a position he never sought and tried twice to refuse. Acting upon his instructions, Union cavalry under Colonel Ulric Dahlgren dashes spectacularly through Confederate positions at Fredericksburg, Virginia, taking 54 prisoners. This feat proves that the town's defenses are weak, and Burnside plans for an offensive there.

November 10
MILITARY: General Joseph Hooker replaces General Fitz-John Porter as V Corps commander in the Army of the Potomac. Porter is slated to undergo court-martial proceedings for his role in the Second Battle of Manassas.

November 14
MILITARY: Newly installed General Ambrose E. Burnside, commanding the Army of the Potomac, effects a major reorganization of his charge by placing generals Joseph Hooker, Edwin V. Sumner, and William B. Franklin as Commanders of the new Right, Central, and Left Grand Divisions, respectively. These new formations consist of two corps apiece.

November 15
MILITARY: General Ambrose E. Burnside initiates an advance upon Falmouth, Virginia, by first feinting toward Warrenton. An excellent organizer, his troops cover 40 miles in two days of hard slogging and arrive opposite the town of Fredericksburg on the Rappahannock River. Burnside's alacrity also left the Confederate high command perplexed as to his location and intentions.
NAVAL: President Abraham Lincoln and several Cabinet members narrowly escape injury when an experimental Hyde rocket accidentally explodes during a demonstration at the Washington Navy Yard.

November 17
MILITARY: The Union Right Grand Division under General Edwin V. Sumner deploys at Falmouth, Virginia, directly across from Fredericksburg on the Rappahannock River. This concludes an impressive, 40-mile march by the usually plodding Army of the Potomac, orchestrated by General Ambrose E. Burnside. This maneuver proves so stealthy that General Robert E. Lee temporarily loses contact with his adversary.

November 18
MILITARY: The Army of the Potomac under General Ambrose E. Burnside continues occupying Falmouth, Virginia, behind the Rappahannock River and directly opposite the heights of Fredericksburg. However, the general takes no offensive actions over the next three weeks, allowing Confederates under General James Longstreet to arrive.

November 21
MILITARY: General Ambrose E. Burnside demands that the mayor of Fredericksburg, Virginia, surrender. When he refuses, Burnside advises him to evacuate women and children from the town.

November 22
MILITARY: General Ambrose E. Burnside reverses himself and assures the mayor of Fredericksburg, Virginia, that he will not fire into the town. In exchange, he expects no hostile actions on behalf of its inhabitants.
POLITICS: Secretary of War Edwin M. Stanton releases the majority of political prisoners still in army custody.

November 24
MILITARY: President Jefferson Davis elevates General Joseph E. Johnston to commander of Confederate troops in the west, succeeding generals John C. Pemberton

1862

and Braxton Bragg. He is specifically tasked with guiding Pemberton in the defense of Vicksburg, Mississippi.

November 26

MILITARY: President Abraham Lincoln confers with General Ambrose E. Burnside at Aquia Creek, Virginia, over his prospective assault upon Fredericksburg. The general seeks a direct attack while the president argues for a multipronged approach. At length the general's view prevails.

November 28

MILITARY: In a preemptive strike, Union General James G. Blunt and 5,000 men attack 2,000 Confederate cavalry under General John S. Marmaduke at Cane Hill, Arkansas. The Southerners are driven into the Boston Mountains, but Blunt declines to pursue for fear of becoming surrounded. However, his presence induces General Thomas C. Hindman to attack his isolated column anyway.

November 29

MILITARY: General John B. Magruder arrives to take charge of the District of Texas, New Mexico, and Arizona. He makes recapturing the port city of Galveston an immediate Confederate priority and begins marshaling the requisite men and ships necessary for a surprise attack.

NAVAL: General John B. Magruder orders the Confederate steamers *Bayou City* and *Neptune* outfitted with bales of cotton "armor" and transformed into "cotton-clads." They will figure prominently in the upcoming attack upon Galveston, Texas.

November 30

MILITARY: After incessant delays, pontoons and other bridging equipment requested three weeks earlier by General Ambrose E. Burnside arrive at Falmouth, Virginia. The Army of the Potomac is now enabled to cross the Rappahannock River to Fredericksburg, but during this interval General Robert E. Lee rushes 35,000 men under General James Longstreet to fortify the heights above the city.

December 1

SLAVERY: President Abraham Lincoln proffers a plan for compensated emancipation to the 37th Congress, but it elicits little enthusiasm. "In giving freedom to the slave, we assure freedom to the free," he insists. Lincoln also promises to assist those willing to be colonized elsewhere.

December 3

MILITARY: General Thomas C. Hindman marches his Confederate Army of the Trans-Mississippi, 11,000 strong, from Van Buren, Arkansas, in bitter, winter weather. His goal is to strike and destroy the outnumbered Union division of General James G. Blunt at Cane Hill. However, Blunt is alert to the danger and appeals to General Francis J. Herron at Springfield, Missouri, for immediate assistance.

General Joseph E. Johnston arrives to coordinate military operations of General John C. Pemberton at Vicksburg, Mississippi, and General Braxton Bragg at Nashville, Tennessee. This additional level of authority, however, further complicates an already Byzantine command structure.

December 5

INDIAN: President Abraham Lincoln pardons the bulk of 303 Santee (Sioux) warriors slated for execution for their role in a bloody uprising. The final number condemned to be hanged is 38.

December 6
MILITARY: In one of the most amazing forced marches of the entire Civil War, two Union divisions from the Army of the Frontier under General Francis J. Herron slog 100 miles from Springfield, Missouri, and miraculously arrive at Fayetteville, Arkansas, to reinforce General James G. Blunt at Cane Hill. This is a remarkable accomplishment that preserves the Union war effort in Arkansas.

December 7
MILITARY: General John H. Morgan and 2,400 Confederate cavalry surprise and capture Hartsville, Tennessee, along with 1,800 Union soldiers under Colonel Absalom B. Moore.

General Thomas C. Hindman commences the Battle of Prairie Grove, Arkansas, by advancing upon the footsore host of General Francis J. Herron, eight miles from Fayetteville. He possesses 11,000 men and outnumbers his opponent but, having achieved strategic surprise, Hindman inexplicably assumes defensive positions. Fighting commences around 9:30 A.M., when the aggressive Herron attacks what he perceives to be a small Confederate force. He is badly repelled in a series of charges while subsequent Confederate advances are likewise driven back by superior Union artillery. General James G. Blunt then hurriedly marches to Prairie Grove with his own fresh troops, and fighting continues until nightfall. Union forces totaling 8,000 men sustain 1,251 casualties while 11,000 Confederates endure 1,317. Hindman, short on supplies, has little option but to withdraw.

December 8
ARTS: Augustin Daly debuts his production of the German play *"Leah" the Forsaken* by S. H. Von Mosenthal; he subsequently produces scores of plays translated from German, French, and other languages.
POLITICS: President Abraham Lincoln recommends Captain John L. Worden for a vote of thanks from the U.S. Congress over his role in commanding the USS *Monitor* at Hampton Roads.

December 10
POLITICS: The U.S. House of Representatives approves a bill creating the new state of West Virginia on a vote of 96 to 55.

December 11
MILITARY: The Army of the Potomac under General Ambrose E. Burnside begins bridging its way across the Rappahannock River to Fredericksburg, Virginia. However, as the fog lifts his engineers receive heavy sniper fire from General William Barksdale's Mississippi brigade. Burnside then orders his artillery to bombard Fredericksburg in retaliation, which inflicts considerable damage but fails to dislodge the snipers. At length seven boatloads of volunteers row themselves across the river under fire and finally flush the Southerners from the town.

Ambrose E. Burnside *(National Archives)*

1862

Confederate General Nathan B. Forrest rides with 2,500 troopers out of Columbia, Tennessee, intending to harass Union lines of communication. His goal is to wreck portions of the Mississippi Central and Mobile & Ohio Railroads. Forrest's first objective, however, is the nearby town of Lexington.

December 12

MILITARY: While vengeful troops of the Army of the Potomac are preoccupied with a looting binge at Fredericksburg, Virginia, General Robert E. Lee hastily summons the corps of General Thomas J. Jackson from positions further downstream and he occupies the right flank of Lee's line. By nightfall General Ambrose E. Burnside has finished crossing the Rappahannock River and deploys 112,000 men below Confederate positions.

NAVAL: The Federal ironclad USS *Cairo* under Commander Thomas O. Selfridge strikes a Confederate "torpedo" (mine) on the Yazoo River, Mississippi, and sinks. This is the first of 40 Union vessels lost to new, submerged Confederate ordnance.

December 13

MILITARY: The Battle of Fredericksburg, Virginia, commences at 10:00 A.M. A dense fog suddenly lifts and reveals to Southerners under General Robert E. Lee an awe-inspiring sight of serried ranks of blue-coated infantry advancing up the slopes toward them. The first thrust is committed against Lee's right when

Battle of Fredericksburg, Virginia, December 13, 1862. Lithograph by Currier & Ives *(Library of Congress)*

General William B. Franklin commits generals George G. Meade and John Gibbon to strike General Thomas J. Jackson's corps. Despite an early breakthrough, Jackson's riposte proves decisive: he dispatches the divisions of Jubal A. Early and Daniel H. Hill to slash at both Union flanks and they chase the Federals back down the slope with loss. Burnside's main attack then unfolds against the Southern center, up a steep hill called Marye's Heights, ably manned and defended by General James Longstreet. General Edwin V. Sumner's Grand Division, assisted by part of General Joseph Hooker's command, 60,000 men in all, bravely charge Confederate positions uphill and are mowed down with great slaughter. Fighting eases by nightfall after Burnside sustains 12,653 casualties while the well-protected Confederates endure 5,377. Lee aptly remarks "It is well that war is so terrible. We should grow too fond of it."

December 14
MILITARY: The Army of the Potomac under General Ambrose E. Burnside begins withdrawing back across the Rappahannock River as Confederates under General Robert E. Lee continue strengthening their defenses. Lee summarily ignores General Thomas J. Jackson's suggestion to counterattack across the line and possibly destroy the entire Union force.

December 15
MILITARY: The Army of the Potomac completes withdrawing across the Rappahannock River, covered by darkness and heavy rainfall. Prior to retreating, General Ambrose E. Burnside sent a flag to General Robert E. Lee requesting a temporary truce to retrieve the Union dead—and those still alive after two days of exposure to the cold. Lee magnanimously grants his request.

December 16
MILITARY: The Army of the Potomac reoccupies Falmouth, Virginia, where General Ambrose E. Burnside issues a directive accepting full responsibility for the disaster at Fredericksburg.

December 17
POLITICS: Radical Republicans precipitate a cabinet crisis for President Abraham Lincoln by demanding the resignation of Secretary of State William H. Seward and replacing him with Treasury Secretary Salmon P. Chase. Highly insulted, Seward tenders his resignation to the president, who summarily refuses to accept.

RELIGION: General Ulysses S. Grant issues General Order No. 11, expelling the Jews from his theater of operations. "The Jews, as a class violating every regulation of trade established by the Treasury Department, and also department orders," it read, "are hereby expelled from the department within twenty-four hours from the receipt of this order." In a few weeks Grant is ordered to rescind the directive.

December 18
MILITARY: General Nathan B. Forrest and 2,500 Confederates attack a Union cavalry detachment under Colonel Robert G. Ingersoll that is defending the town of Lexington, Tennessee. Forrest's men clatter across an unburned bridge on the Lower Road, flanking a portion of the defenders. Ingersoll manages to repel three headlong charges by the Confederates but is eventually overrun and surrenders.

December 20

MILITARY: The XIII Corps, consisting of 32,000 Union troops in four divisions under General William T. Sherman, embarks on transports at Memphis, Tennessee, and sails down the Mississippi River. Sherman intends to flank Confederate defenses at Vicksburg, Mississippi, and pin down reinforcements at Grenada to prevent them from reaching the city.

In a spectacularly effective move, Confederate cavalry under General Earl Van Dorn captures a primary Union stockpile at Holly Springs, Mississippi, netting $1.5 million worth of supplies and 1,500 prisoners. He does do by utilizing superb marching discipline, which keeps Union forces unsure as to his intentions and objective. Van Dorn then orders the bulk of supplies burned, tracks torn up, and telegraph wires cut. Holly Springs is one of the most devastating cavalry raids of the war and has dire consequences for General Ulysses S. Grant.

December 21

MILITARY: General Ulysses S. Grant, having lost his main supply base at Holly Springs, Mississippi, to rampaging Confederate cavalry under General Earl Van Dorn, evacuates Oxford and marches back to Memphis, Tennessee. This withdrawal terminates his first attempt to attack the Confederate citadel at Vicksburg, Mississippi.

December 23

POLITICS: President Jefferson Davis excoriates Union General Benjamin F. Butler for his treatment of civilians in New Orleans, Louisiana, and threatens to hang him if caught.

December 26

INDIAN: Federal authorities at Mankato, Minnesota, simultaneously hang 38 Santee (Sioux) Indians for their complicity in a bloody uprising. This remains the largest mass execution in American history.

MILITARY: The 43,000 Army of the Cumberland under General William S. Rosecrans begins advancing from Nashville, Tennessee, and toward General Braxton Bragg's Confederates at Murfreesboro. However, the advance is dogged by cold, wet weather and effective resistance by Southern troopers under General Joseph Wheeler.

The XIII Corps under General William T. Sherman disembarks 32,000 men at Johnson's Plantation near the mouth of the Yazoo River. This places Union forces on the northern outskirts of Vicksburg, Mississippi, and only six miles from the city. However, the 6,000 defenders already present are speedily being reinforced by troops from nearby Grenada to a total strength of 14,000.

NAVAL: The Federal gunboat under Commodore David D. Porter, having escorted General William T. Sherman's expedition up the Yazoo River, begins shelling the Confederate defenses on nearby Hayne's Bluff to cover the landing of troops.

December 27

MILITARY: Confederate cavalry under General John H. Logan captures 600 Union prisoners in a surprise attack upon Elizabethtown, Kentucky. He then begins uprooting tracks and trestles belonging to the Louisville & Nashville railroad, a vital supply line.

Union forces under General William T. Sherman encounter increasing Confederate resistance north of Vicksburg, Mississippi. They still press southward, traversing nearly impassible terrain, bayous, and swampland before reaching their objective at Chickasaw Bluffs. Sherman gradually discovers only four practical approaches to the bluffs, all of which are amply covered by well-sited Confederate batteries.

December 28

MILITARY: A column of Confederate cavalry under General J. E. B. Stuart successfully tangles with Federal cavalry near Selectman's Fort on Occoquan Creek, taking 100 captives. He then gallops off for Burke's Station, only 12 miles from Washington, D.C., and telegraphs a humorous message to Quartermaster General Montgomery C. Meigs as to the poor quality of Union mules.

General Earl Van Dorn, commanding 3,500 Confederate cavalry, safely slips through Union lines, crosses the Tallahatchie River, and arrives safely back at Grenada, Mississippi. His spectacularly successful raid covers 500 miles in two weeks and completely cripples the impending Federal attack upon Vicksburg.

Outside Chickasaw Bluffs, Mississippi, General Frederick Steele's 4th Division makes a preliminary probe of Confederate defenses near Blake's Levee but is halted by heavy artillery fire and defensive works erected in his path. General William T. Sherman remains determined to attack in force but is still uninformed of the Union disaster at Holly Springs, which allowed Southern troop strength to rise to 14,000 men.

POLITICS: In an attempt to diffuse rising class tensions, the Confederate Congress strikes a clause in its Conscription Act which allows draftees to hire substitutes to take their place.

December 29

MILITARY: The 32,000 Union troops of XIII Corps under General William T. Sherman attack prepared Confederate defenses along Chickasaw Bluffs, six miles north of Vicksburg, Mississippi. They withstand a maelstrom of Southern rifle and artillery fire from the heights and are bloodily repelled. Further attack serves only to lengthen the casualty lists so Sherman suspends the action at nightfall. Union losses in this lopsided affair total 1,776 to a Confederate tally of 207. The defeat also ends the first Federal attempt to capture Vicksburg.

December 30

MILITARY: General William S. Rosecrans and 43,000 men of his Army of the Cumberland trudge into Murfreesboro, Tennessee, from Nashville, having taken three days to cover 30 miles in bad weather. He then establishes his line running roughly running north to south behind Stone's River, across which sat 37,000 Confederates of the Army of Tennessee under General Braxton Bragg. Both leaders intend to attack the following day by hitting their opponent's right flank.

December 31

MILITARY: At 6:00 A.M., the Confederate Army of Tennessee under General Braxton Bragg launches an all-out assault against the Union Army of the Cumberland along Stone's River near Murfreesboro, Tennessee. Fleeing Federals withdraw nearly three miles before General Alexander McCook organizes new defensive lines. General William S. Rosecrans then energetically visits all threatened points along his line, brings up new units, and consolidates his defenses. Bragg, meanwhile, remains far behind at headquarters, relying solely on reports to stay abreast of battlefield developments and, hence, the fresh division of General John C. Breckinridge remains uncommitted. This proves a grave mistake for, had they been deployed earlier, they might have tipped the balance in favor of the South. Bragg is nonetheless convinced that he has won the contest and telegraphs word of his "victory" to authorities in Richmond, Virginia. Moreover, he fully expects to find the Federals gone and in full flight from their positions by daybreak.

General Nathan B. Forrest and 1,200 Confederate cavalry engage the 2nd Union Brigade under Colonel Cyrus L. Dunham at Parker's Cross Roads, Tennessee. However, Forrest's plans are suddenly overturned by the sudden and unexpected appearance of John W. Fuller's 3rd Brigade, which surprises the Confederates from behind. In the ensuing confusion, Forrest orders his men to charge through Union lines and cut themselves an avenue of escape. Parker's Cross Roads proves a rare setback for Forrest, and his sheer survival adds further luster to his reputation.

Naval: The famous ironclad USS *Monitor*, en route from Hampton Roads, Virginia, to Beaufort, North Carolina, sinks in a gale off Cape Hatteras while under tow. Sixteen crewmen perish and 47 are rescued by the USS *Rhode Island*.

Politics: President Abraham Lincoln approves an act establishing West Virginia as the 35th state.

1863

Arts: The painting *The White Girl* by artist James McNeill Whistler causes a sensation in Paris art circles.

Business: John D. Rockefeller founds his first petroleum refinery in Cleveland, Ohio.

The Travelers Insurance Company, which offers the first such coverage to travelers, is founded by James G. Batterson.

Ebenezer Butterick begins offering stylish clothing patterns cut from paper templates by children, and they prove an immediate success with homemakers.

Labor: The Brotherhood of Railway Locomotive Engineers forms.

Fincher's Trades Review, an influential trade paper, begins publishing in Philadelphia, Pennsylvania.

Literature: Henry Wadsworth Longfellow publishes his *Tales of a Wayside Inn*, a collection of six narrative tales.

January

Religion: In a letter to the commanding general of Missouri, President Abraham Lincoln announces that all Southern Churches behind Federal lines are to be exempted from any kind of interference.

Sports: Roller-skating becomes all the rage in many Northern cities. The four-wheeled device had been invented by James L. Plimpton.

A new rule in the still evolving game of baseball mandates that both balls and strikes are to be called.

January 1

Military: Combat at Murfreesboro, Tennessee, is suspended as both sides redress ranks and attend to their wounded. At daybreak General Braxton Bragg is flummoxed to find that the Union Army of the Cumberland stands its ground defiantly before him. Both sides then gird themselves for renewed combat next day.

A surprise attack is mounted by General John B. Magruder upon Galveston, Texas. In the predawn darkness he quickly moves 1,500 men and several cannon onto Galveston Island and attacks a Union garrison consisting of 250 men of Colonel Isaac Burrell's 42nd Massachusetts. The Confederates prevail in stiff fighting and the garrison surrenders.

NAVAL: A sortie by Confederate "cotton-clads" *Bayou City* and *Neptune* under Major Leon Smith pitches into the Union blockading squadron under Commander William B. Renshaw off Galveston, Texas. Both sides lose men and vessels but Renshaw, perceiving the battle lost, orders his squadron into deeper water. He and 12 other Union sailors perish when demolition charges explode prematurely. Galveston remains a Southern enclave for the rest of the war.

POLITICS: "I do order and declare that all persons held as slaves within designated states, and parts of states, are, and henceforth shall be free," President Abraham Lincoln declares. His Emancipation Proclamation becomes law, although it liberates only African Americans in Confederate territory. Slaves in Union-held area strategic border states of Maryland, Kentucky, and Missouri are exempt

Thomas Nast's engraving celebrates the emancipation of the Southern slaves with the end of the Civil War. *(Library of Congress)*

1863

and remain in bondage for the time being. As anticipated, Lincoln's Proclamation appeals to the governments of France and England, further diminishing European sympathy for the South, and with it the likelihood of military intervention on their behalf.

January 2

MILITARY: General Braxton Bragg, after surveying the new line held by General William S. Rosecrans along Stones River, Tennessee, decides to renew the struggle. He then commits his remaining intact formation, the Kentucky division under General John C. Breckinridge, to strike the Union left flank partially anchored along the river. Breckinridge moves forward, charges directly into the teeth of massed Union artillery posted across the river, and is bloodily repelled with 1,700 casualties. His defeat signals the end of the battle and many senior Confederate leaders, including General Leonidas K. Polk, implore Bragg to retreat. Rosecrans holds the field and claims a narrow tactical victory, but at the horrendous cost of 13,249 casualties among 41,000 men present. Confederate losses of 10,266 out of 34,739 engaged, while smaller numerically, are proportionately larger and represent attrition that the Confederacy cannot sustain in this theater.

January 4

RELIGION: General in chief Henry W. Halleck orders General Ulysses S. Grant to rescind his controversial Order No. 11, which expelled all Jews from his jurisdiction.

January 7

JOURNALISM: An editorial in the Richmond *Inquirer* denounces the Emancipation Proclamation as "the most startling political crime, the most stupid political blunder, yet known in American history."

POLITICS: The Democratically controlled Illinois State Legislature roundly condemns President Abraham Lincoln's Emancipation Proclamation and excoriates the chief executive for turning the war from a conflict to save the Union into a crusade to liberate African Americans.

January 10

MILITARY: In a celebrated court-martial, General Fitz-John Porter is cashiered and dropped from the army list for disobeying orders at the Battle of Second Manassas. Not only does this action deprive the Union army of a highly capable leader but the verdict itself remains in contention until finally being overturned in 1879.

January 11

MILITARY: A force of 32,000 Union troops under General John A. McClernand and Admiral David D. Porter attack and capture Confederate Fort Hindman (Arkansas Post) under General Thomas J. Churchill. Churchill realizes the hopelessness of his position and capitulates that evening. McClernand captures 4,791 Confederates, who also lose two dead and 81 wounded, along with 17 cannon, thousands of weapons, and tons of ammunition.

NAVAL: The paddle steamer USS *Hatteras,* cruising 30 miles off Galveston, Texas, is approached at night by a mysterious vessel. It turns out to be the Confederate raider CSS *Alabama* under Captain Raphael Semmes, which sinks the *Hatteras* in a fierce engagement of only 13 minutes. Semmes rescues the entire crew whereupon Union vessels redouble their efforts to track down this elusive foe.

Federal gunboats under Admiral David D. Porter effectively shell the strong Confederate works of Fort Hindman (Arkansas Post) on the Arkansas River. Naval fire proves devastatingly effective at reducing both batteries and fortifications, and Porter notes, "No fort ever received a worse battering, and the highest compliment I can pay to those engaged is to repeat what the rebels said, "You can't expect men to stand up against the fire of those gunboats."

January 12
POLITICS: The 3rd Session of the 1st Confederate Congress convenes at Richmond, Virginia, where President Jefferson Davis addresses them, still hoping for eventual European recognition. Davis also sharply criticizes the Union's recent Emancipation Proclamation.

January 13
SLAVERY: In South Carolina, Union Colonel Thomas W. Higginson begins recruiting former African-American slaves for his 1st South Carolina Volunteer Infantry.

January 17
POLITICS: President Abraham Lincoln signs legislation allowing for the immediate payment of military personnel. He also asks Congress for currency reforms to halt mounting inflation throughout the North.

January 18
MILITARY: Acting upon the orders of General Henry Heth, the 64th North Carolina under Colonel James A. Keith sweeps through Shelton Laurel, western North Carolina, looking for Northern sympathizers. At length he nets 15 male captives, most of whom are not involved in bushwhacking operations; these are subsequently executed and buried in shallow graves. Southerners are outraged by the atrocity, and an investigation ensues.

January 20
MILITARY: The Army of the Potomac under General Ambrose E. Burnside begins its infamous "mud march." No sooner does his turning maneuver commence than inclement weather begins and troops, supplies, and the all-important pontoon bridges bog down on muddy roads.

January 21
MILITARY: The march of the Army of the Potomac under General Ambrose E. Burnside is stymied by heavy rain and inclement conditions during its attempted flank march to the Rappahannock River, Virginia. His columns are bedeviled by roads so choked with mud that supply wagons sink up to their axles.
POLITICS: President Abraham Lincoln endorses revocation of the infamous "Jew Order" of General Ulysses S. Grant because it "proscribed an entire religious class, some of whom are fighting in our ranks."

January 22
MILITARY: General Ambrose E. Burnside's offensive across the Rappahannock River into Virginia stumbles and finally ends on account of heavy rains and impassible mud. After heated consultation with subordinates, Burnside cancels his "master stroke" and orders the men back into camp at Falmouth, Virginia.

1863

January 23

MILITARY: A demoralized—and rather soggy—Army of the Potomac settles back into winter quarters at Falmouth, Virginia, directly across from Fredericksburg. General Ambrose E. Burnside, agitated by the performance of subordinates, issues General Order No. 8, which peremptorily strips generals Joseph Hooker, Edwin V. Sumner, and William B. Franklin of their respective commands.

January 25

MILITARY: General Ambrose E. Burnside is removed as commander of the Army of the Potomac and replaced by boisterous General "Fighting Joe" Hooker, one of his loudest critics. Generals Edwin V. Sumner and William B. Franklin, however, remain relieved of duties pending a court of inquiry.

POLITICS: Massachusetts Governor John A. Andrew authorizes recruitment of the 54th Massachusetts Infantry, composed entirely of African Americans and led by white officers.

January 27

INDIAN: In response to Shoshone attacks upon settlers and miners in the Great Basin region, Colonel Patrick E. Connor of the 1st California Cavalry leads 300 soldiers on an expedition against the encampment of Chief Bear Hunter on the Bear River, Idaho Territory. After a raging conflict of several hours, Bear Hunter and 224 Indians are slain, with an additional 124 women and children taken prisoner. Federal losses are 21 dead and 46 wounded.

JOURNALISM: Philadelphia journalist A. D. Boileau is arrested for allegedly publishing anti-Union editorials in his *Journal*.

NAVAL: The ironclad monitor USS *Montauk* under Captain John L. Worden spearheads a Federal assault upon Fort McAllister on the Ogeechee River, Georgia. Admiral Samuel F. du Pont, who orders the attack, is disappointed by the results, especially the inaccuracy and slow rate of fire of his vessels. "If one ironclad cannot take eight guns," he reasons, "how are five to take 147 guns in Charleston Harbor." Again, the Navy Department ignores his warning.

January 28

POLITICS: President Jefferson Davis warns General Theophilus Holmes of the dangers confronting his Trans-Mississippi Department. "The loss of either of the two positions—Vicksburg or Port Hudson—would destroy communication with the Trans-Mississippi Department," he writes, "and inflict upon the Confederacy an injury which I am sure you have not failed to appreciate."

January 29

POLITICS: The Confederate Congress authorizes a loan of $15 million from French financiers.

A pensive President Jefferson Davis inquires of General John C. Pemberton at Vicksburg, Mississippi, "Has anything or can anything be done to obstruct the navigation from the Yazoo Pass down?"

January 30

MILITARY: General Ulysses S. Grant, officially placed in charge of western operations at Milliken's Bend, Louisiana, begins formulating a new strategic campaign against Vicksburg, Mississippi.

NAVAL: Admiral David D. Porter's squadron begins sweeping the Yazoo River for supplies of cotton to deprive the Confederacy of this valuable commodity. Captured bales are also employed as additional "armor" on his ships.

January 31
NAVAL: Obscured by a thick haze, the Confederate steam rams CSS *Palmetto State* and *Chicora,* under commanders Duncan R. Ingraham and John R. Tucker briefly sortie against the South Atlantic Blockading Squadron off Charleston, South Carolina. The Confederate vessels then withdraw to Charleston after a stiff fight, having dented—but not broken—the Union blockade.

February 1
BUSINESS: By this period of the war inflation erodes the Confederate dollar to where it has the purchasing power of 20 cents.
NAVAL: The ironclad USS *Montauk* under Captain John L. Worden, assisted by *Seneca, Wissahickon, Dawn,* and mortar boat *C. P. Williams,* again attack Fort McAllister on the Ogeechee River, Georgia. *Montauk* sustains 48 hits in the four-hour exchange, none of them critical. However, little damage is inflicted on the enemy.

February 2
AGRICULTURE: Congress appropriates $3,000 to distribute cotton and tobacco seed throughout the Union.

February 3
DIPLOMACY: Secretary of State William H. Seward receives an offer through the French embassy in Washington, D.C., to mediate the war. His response will be forthcoming.
POLITICS: The U.S. Congress votes Captain John L. Worden its thanks for services rendered as captain of the USS *Monitor* at the Battle of Hampton Roads in 1862.

February 5
DIPLOMACY: Queen Victoria outlines her reasons to Parliament for refusing to get involved with mediation efforts between the North and South, namely because the South's prospects for success are dwindling.
MILITARY: General Joseph Hooker reorganizes the Army of the Potomac and dispenses with his predecessor's "grand divisions" scheme. A new nine-corps structure is then imposed under generals John F. Reynolds (I), Darius N. Couch (II), Daniel E. Sickles (III), George G. Meade (V), John Sedgwick (VI), William F. Smith (IX), Franz Sigel (XI), Henry W. Slocum (XII), and George Stoneman (U.S. Cavalry Corps).

February 6
DIPLOMACY: Secretary of State William H. Seward unilaterally rejects a French offer to mediate hostilities.

February 8
JOURNALISM: Alleged disloyal statements lead the Chicago *Times* to be temporarily suspended from publication.

1863

February 10

GENERAL: Despite the ongoing drama of Civil War, promoter P. T. Barnum manages to grab headlines by arranging the marriage between the diminutive "General Tom Thumb" (Charles S. Stratton, only two feet, five inches tall) to the equally tiny Mercy Lavinia Warren at Grace Church, New York. The wedding is well-attended.

February 11

DIPLOMACY: In London, Confederate agent James M. Mason addresses the Lord Mayor's banquet over the desirability of recognizing the Confederacy.

February 16

POLITICS: The U.S. Congress authorizes the Conscription Act, affecting all men aged between 20 and 45, to address the inadequacies of voluntary enlistment. However, substitutes can still be hired for $300.

February 17

JOURNALISM: The order suspending publication of the Chicago *Times* is rescinded by General Ulysses S. Grant.

February 18

POLITICS: Union troops break up and disperse a convention by Democrats in Frankfort, Kentucky, whose activities they construe as pro-Confederate.

February 19

JOURNALISM: Federal troops convalescing in a hospital at Keokuk, Iowa, angered by antiwar sentiments expressed in the local newspaper *Constitution,* hobble over and ransack the news office.

POLITICS: President Jefferson Davis contacts General Joseph E. Johnston, noting anxiously how little confidence General Braxton Bragg solicits from his senior subordinates. "It is scarcely possible in that state of the case for him to possess the requisite confidence of the troops," Davis notes. However, the president is not disposed toward removing his old friend and confidant from command, a reluctance with fatal consequences for the South.

February 23

DIPLOMACY: Pennsylvanian Simon Cameron, former secretary of war, resigns his post as minister to Russia.

February 24

NAVAL: Confederate vessels CSS *William H. Webb* and *Beatty,* assisted by the newly captured *Queen of the West,* attack and repeatedly ram the ironclad USS *Indianola* below Warrenton, Mississippi. Outnumbered and outmaneuvered by the faster craft, *Indianola* sustains serious damage and Commander George Brown surrenders.

February 25

NAVAL: The USS *Vanderbilt* captures the British merchant vessel *Peterhoff* off St. Thomas in the Caribbean, sparking a diplomatic row over the disposition of mail found onboard. Eventually, President Abraham Lincoln orders the craft and all confiscated mail returned to their rightful owners.

POLITICS: The U.S. Congress approves a national banking system drawn up by Secretary of the Treasury Salmon P. Case, whereby participating institutions reserve up to one-third of their capital in U.S. securities. These, in turn, serve as a basis for issuing national bank notes (currency) to the public to facilitate long-term financing of the war effort. This system lasts with little change until the establishment of the Federal Reserve in 1913. The Confederacy, which operates without such fiscal safeguards, is forced to issue more than $1 billion in paper money and endures crippling inflation.

February 26

INDIAN: Upon further reflection, the National Council of Cherokee Indians abolishes slavery, renounces its prior affinity for the Confederacy, and rejoins the Union.

March 2

MILITARY: Congress authorizes four new major generals and nine new brigadiers for the U.S. Army, with an additional 40 major generals and 200 brigadiers for the volunteers. Conversely, 33 senior military officers are dismissed from the service for a variety of reasons.

TRANSPORTATION: Congress establishes the standard railroad gauge (width) at four feet, eight and one half inches; this has since become a world standard for most railways.

March 3

BUSINESS: Jay Cooke is named Federal agent tasked with promoting the sale of war bonds.

DIPLOMACY: Congress passes a resolution condemning offers of mediation as "Foreign intervention."

INDIAN: Congress agrees to subsidize the removal of all Native Americans from Kansas.

POLITICS: President Abraham Lincoln signs the Enrollment or Federal Draft Act, whereby all able-bodied males from 20 to 46 years of age are eligible for military service. This is the first such legislation enacted by the government.

Congress approves a loan of $300 million for the year 1863. It also formally and finally suspends writs of habeas corpus as a wartime expedient.

SCIENCE: The National Academy of Sciences, a private, nonprofit organization, is founded for the purpose of promoting science and research.

SETTLEMENT: The Idaho Territory is formed by Congress, culled from parts of the adjoining Washington and Dakota Territories, and incorporating present-day Montana and Wyoming.

March 5

JOURNALISM: In Columbus, Ohio, rampaging Union troops gut the editorial offices of the newspaper *Crisis* for allegedly printing pro-Southern editorials.

MILITARY: General Earl Van Dorn advances with 6,000 Confederates against the Union position at Thompson's Station, Tennessee. The defenders consist of 2,857 Federal soldiers and cavalry, supported by six cannon, under Colonel John Coburn. A final charge by Colonel Nathan B. Forrest breaks Union resistance and Coburn surrenders.

March 8

MILITARY: A sudden raid by Captain John S. Mosby and his Confederate rangers captures General Edwin H. Stoughton in his headquarters at Fairfax County

Court House, Virginia, along with 32 prisoners and 58 horses. The general was then asleep in his bed only to be rudely awakened by a slap to his backside—delivered by Mosby himself.

March 10

LAW: In the Prize Cases, the Supreme Court approves the legality of the Union naval blockade on a 5–4 vote. They do so by legitimizing the blockade of a sovereign state while simultaneously denying that the Confederate States of America actually exists as a nation. The Court also rules that while only Congress has the authority to declare war, Lincoln, as commander in chief, has the authority to suppress a rebellion through military means.

POLITICS: President Abraham Lincoln signs a general amnesty for all soldiers, presently absent without leave (AWOL), to rejoin their units by April 1, 1863.

March 14

MILITARY: General Nathaniel P. Banks advances 30,000 men of his Army of the Gulf upon Port Hudson, Louisiana. It is now painfully apparent to Union authorities that this position, second in strength only to Vicksburg, Mississippi, itself, must be reduced by assault in the near future.

NAVAL: Admiral David G. Farragut's squadron of seven ships runs past Confederate batteries at Port Hudson, Louisiana, at 11:00 P.M. His flagship, the USS *Hartford*, is lashed alongside the *Albatross*, weathers a storm of shot and shells, and makes the final passage intact, but accompanying vessels *Monongahela* and *Richmond* are turned back, thus Farragut is cut off from part of his force for several weeks.

Union Admiral David D. Porter pushes his gunboats, mortar boats, and four tugs up the Yazoo River to secure Steele's Bayou above Vicksburg, Mississippi.

March 16

NAVAL: Federal gunboats of the Yazoo River Expedition engage Fort Pemberton at Greenwood, Mississippi, whereupon the ironclad USS *Chillicothe* receives eight direct hits, suffers 22 casualties, and drifts helplessly. Failure here terminates General Ulysses S. Grant's second attempt to circumvent the northern defenses of Vicksburg.

March 17

SOUTH: A force of 2,100 Union cavalry and six guns under General William W. Averell advance from Morrisville, Virginia, then cross the Rappahannock River intending to surprise Confederate cavalry stationed at Kelly's Ford. The startled Southerners then advance to meet the intruders with 800 men. Averell lines up his five regiments abreast behind a stone wall, lets the Confederates gallop to within close range, then rakes them with intense artillery and carbine fire. Charges and countercharges ensue throughout the afternoon before Averell ends the contest and withdraws across the river in good order. Though indecisive, Kelly's Ford alerts Southern horsemen to the growing proficiency of their Northern counterparts. The youthful Southern gunner John "Gallant Pelham" is also mortally wounded.

March 18

POLITICS: The Democratically controlled state legislature of New Jersey passes a number of peace resolutions condemning all aspects of the war effort and demanding a negotiated ending. This prompts a sharp rebuke from state regiments in the field, who pass resolutions of their own condemning the legislature's activities as "wicked" and "cowardly."

March 21

MILITARY: General William T. Sherman's expedition to Steele's Bayou gropes along the tree-choked riverbanks, much harassed by snipers and man-made obstacles in its path. Progress remains slow but determined as they proceed to rescue Admiral David D. Porter's gunboat squadron, then trapped at Deer Creek.

March 25

MILITARY: General Nathan B. Forrest and his Confederate cavalry column attack Union troops at Brentwood, Tennessee, consisting of 520 men of the 22nd Wisconsin under Colonel Edward Bloodgood and 230 men of the 19th Michigan posted south of the town. Both Federal detachments surrender but, as the Southern marauders withdraw, they are set upon by a third force of Union cavalry under Colonel Green C. Smith and lose some wagons and supplies.

March 26

POLITICS: The Confederate Congress in Richmond, Virginia, approves the Impressment Act, authorizing government agents to seize slaves and foodstuffs to supply the military establishment. Waste and abuse in its enforcement lead several state governments to condemn this practice.

SLAVERY: Voters in the new state of West Virginia approve the gradual emancipation of all African Americans.

March 27

INDIAN: President Abraham Lincoln entertains numerous Native American leaders at the White House and implores them to take up agriculture. "I can see no way in which your race is to become as numerous and prosperous as the white race," he lectured, "except by living as they do, by the cultivation of the earth."

March 30

POLITICS: President Abraham Lincoln announces that April 30, 1863, will be designated a national day of fasting and prayer.

April 1

NAVAL: The USS *Tuscumbia* under Admiral David D. Porter hosts Generals Ulysses S. Grant and William T. Sherman on a grand reconnaissance of the Yazoo River as far as Hayne's Bluff. The nature of the terrain and other imposing natural obstacles convince Grant to turn his attention to operations below the city.

April 2

MILITARY: General Ulysses S. Grant meets with Admiral David D. Porter to promulgate a final plan of operations against Vicksburg, Mississippi. They decide that while forces under General William T. Sherman mount a large-scale diversion along Hayne's Bluff to the north, the bulk of the army under Grant will march south down the west bank of the Mississippi River. There they will embark and be carried across to the Confederate shore by Porter's fleet.

POLITICS: Richmond, Virginia, is the scene of an infamous "bread riot." That morning a small crowd of women and boys announce that they are marching from the capitol square to obtain bread. Numerous onlookers gradually swell the procession's ranks to 1,300 people, who grow unruly and demand action. Full-scale rioting and looting then erupt, with many businesses being ransacked.

President Jefferson Davis, upon hearing of the outbreak of violence, bravely races over and demands that the crowd disperse or be fired upon by the militia.

April 4

DIPLOMACY: American minister Charles F. Adams loudly protests the impending departure of the vessel *Alexandria,* destined for eventual service with the Confederate navy.

April 5

POLITICS: President Abraham Lincoln meets with General Joseph Hooker at Fredericksburg, Virginia, to discuss strategy. At that time both leaders concur that the object of future military operations should center upon the destruction of General Robert E. Lee's army, with Richmond, Virginia, a secondary concern.

April 6

DIPLOMACY: The British government seizes the newly completed vessel *Alexandria* to placate the U.S. government. However, it is eventually released by the courts to the Confederacy.

April 7

NAVAL: Admiral Samuel F. du Pont's ironclad squadron launches its long anticipated attack against Charleston, South Carolina. His slow firing monitors are only able to loose 139 rounds while 77 well-handled Confederate cannon pour in 2,000 shells upon them. Consequently, all nine vessels are struck repeatedly with the USS *Keokuk* suffering 90 hits near or below the waterline, which renders it nearly uncontrollable. Du Pont, who had anticipated much worse, suspends the action at nightfall, thankful that the day was "a failure instead of a disaster," although defeat here will cost him his command.

April 8

NAVAL: The badly battered ironclad USS *Keokuk* sinks outside of Charleston, South Carolina. However, its signal book is eventually recovered by the Confederates, who can now decipher the squadron's communications.

April 10

POLITICS: President Jefferson Davis exhorts his countrymen to forego the planting of cotton and tobacco in favor of foodstuffs desperately needed by Confederate forces. "Let fields be devoted exclusively to the production of corn, oats, beans, peas, potatoes, and other food for man and beast," he lectures, "and all your efforts be directed to the prompt supply of these articles in the districts where our armies are operating."

April 12

MILITARY: President Abraham Lincoln is informed by General Joseph Hooker that he wishes to swing around General Robert E. Lee's flank and threaten Richmond, Virginia. The president reminds the general that the destruction of Lee's army remains a paramount objective.

The XIX Corps of Union General Nathaniel P. Banks, numbering 16,000 men in three divisions, marches up the Teche River toward Irish Bend on Bayou Teche, Louisiana, to capture Fort Bisland. Banks moves two divisions overland while directing the 4,500 men of General Curvier Grover's division to land north and cut their retreat.

1863

April 13

MILITARY: At Irish Bend, Louisiana, Confederate forces gird themselves to deliver an early morning strike against superior forces under General Nathaniel P. Banks. General Richard Taylor, rather than be crushed between Banks and General Curvier Grover, determines to attack at dawn and allow the fort's garrison to escape. His men carefully skirt Union positions along the riverbank, assume an offensive posture, and prepare to strike the Federals at dawn to allow the garrison to escape.

April 14

MILITARY: Confederates under General Richard Taylor abandon Fort Bisland, Louisiana, and then attack the Union encampment of General Curvier Grover. The Southerners get the best of it and manage to escape while Grover remains in camp and his force sustains 600 casualties. Taylor then withdraws to safety, although he is forced to scuttle the recently recaptured CSS *Diana*. Fort Bisland, meanwhile, is occupied by General Nathaniel P. Banks.

April 15

MILITARY: Union General John G. Foster sails down the Pamlico River, North Carolina, to relieve the siege of New Bern, forcing Confederates under General Daniel H. Hill to withdraw.

General Ulysses S. Grant masses 45,000 troops at Milliken's Bend, Louisiana, 10 miles north of the Confederate bastion of Vicksburg, Mississippi. He then orders General James B. McPherson's corps down the west bank of the river to New Carthage, while additional forces under General William T. Sherman begin forming before Chickasaw Bluff.

NAVAL: Confederate raider CSS *Alabama* under Captain Raphael Semmes captures and burns the Union whalers *Kate Cory* and *Lafayette* off Fernando de Noronha, Brazil.

April 16

MILITARY: Union forces under General John G. Foster advance inland from Washington, North Carolina, and tangle with the rear guard of General Daniel H. Hill at nearby Kinston.

NAVAL: A gala ball held at Vicksburg, Mississippi, is rudely interrupted by the river squadron of Admiral David D. Porter, who passes 12 transports past Confederate batteries posted on nearby bluffs. The action lasts two and a half hours but, despite a withering cannonade, Porter succeeds brilliantly. Most of his vessels sustain light damage but the steamer *Henry Clay* is sunk and the gunboat *Forest Queen* is disabled. The squadron then berths off New Carthage, Mississippi, and prepares to transport the army of General Ulysses S. Grant over to the Confederate shore.

POLITICS: President Jefferson Davis signs legislation permitting minors under 18 to hold military commissions.

April 17

MILITARY: Union Colonel Benjamin H. Grierson embarks on an ambitious, 16-day diversionary raid from La Grange, Tennessee, down through the heart of Mississippi and thence to Baton Rouge, Louisiana. To complete this 600-mile sojourn, he takes with him 1,700 troopers of the 6th and 7th Illinois Cavalry, the 2nd Iowa, and a horse battery.

April 18
MILITARY: The Federal gunboat USS *Stepping Stones* under Lieutenant William B. Cushing, carrying 270 soldiers, suddenly raids Confederate-held Fort Huger on the Nansemond River, Virginia. Before the garrison can react, the Federal forces charge into the fort, seizing 137 prisoners and five cannon, then depart.
POLITICS: The Confederate Congress authorizes a volunteer navy to encourage the outfitting of privateers at private expense.

April 20
POLITICS: President Abraham Lincoln declares that the new state of West Virginia be established from the westernmost counties of Virginia as of June 20, 1863.

April 21
MILITARY: Union cavalry under Colonel Benjamin H. Grierson skirmishes with Confederates at Palo Alto, Mississippi. Grierson, hotly pursued by Southerners, cleverly splits his column by sending Colonel Edward Hatch and the 2nd Iowa off to threaten the Mobile & Ohio Railroad. The Confederates, as anticipated, take the bait and mistakenly chase after Hatch, leaving Grierson to complete his raid through Mississippi almost unopposed.
NAVAL: A convoy of additional Union army transports passes the batteries at Vicksburg, Mississippi, at night and under fire. These then join the main fleet at New Carthage and prepare to transport the army of General Ulysses S. Grant across the river en masse. This feat proves one of the most decisive improvisations of the war.

April 24
BUSINESS: To combat spiraling inflation, the Confederate Congress levies a 10 percent "tax in kind" on all produce harvested throughout the South. This move is greatly resented by the agrarian sector, which is already subject to requisition by the Confederate commissary and quartermaster offices.
MILITARY: The combined Army of the Tennessee under General Ulysses S. Grant reaches Hard Times Plantation, Louisiana, on the left bank of the Mississippi River. There he immediately orders the troops ferried on transports directly across to Bruinsville, Mississippi, on the Confederate shore.

Colonel Benjamin H. Grierson's Union cavalry storms into Newton Station, Mississippi, seizing a newly arrived ammunition train and tearing up miles of valuable track belonging to the Southern Mississippi Railroad. This places the raiders only 100 miles east of the Confederate bastion of Vicksburg, and General John C. Pemberton orders his reserve force of five infantry and artillery regiments from Jackson to intercept them.
POLITICS: President Abraham Lincoln authorizes General Order No. 100, the so-called Liber Code, an early attempt to codify and standardize laws pertaining to the conduct of war.

April 27
MILITARY: At Falmouth, Virginia, the 134,000-man Army of the Potomac is put into motion by General Joseph Hooker. Hooker takes 75,000 men down the banks of the Rappahannock River, intending to deploy them in the region known as the Wilderness, 10 miles behind Confederate lines. No previous Union com-

mander has enjoyed such a numerical preponderance over General Robert E. Lee before.

April 29

MILITARY: General John Stoneman's Union cavalry division crosses the Rappahannock River into Virginia and commences a major raid. However, not only does this endeavor prove largely ineffectual, it also strips the Army of the Potomac of its cavalry and, with it, the ability to scout and reconnoiter densely wooded terrain.

NAVAL: Admiral David D. Porter's gunboat squadron bombards Confederate batteries on the Mississippi River at Grand Gulf, Mississippi. After five hours of continuous combat, Porter's army transports skirt the remaining batteries without incident as Federal forces bypass Grand Gulf altogether.

April 30

MILITARY: The Army of the Potomac under General Joseph Hooker marches 309 miles down the banks of the Rappahannock River and crosses 10 miles behind General Robert E. Lee's position at Fredericksburg, Virginia. Considering the size and complexity of the operation, Hooker executes it brilliantly and catches the Southerners off guard.

General Ulysses S. Grant ferries the XIII Corps of General John A. McClernand and the XVII Corps of General James B. McPherson (23,000 men in all) across the Mississippi River at Bruinsburg, Mississippi. At a stroke Grant bypasses strong Confederate defenses and carves out a lodgement on the east bank of the river, only 35 miles below the bastion at Vicksburg.

NAVAL: The gunboat squadron and transports of Admiral David D. Porter cover and ferry the army of General Ulysses S. Grant across the Mississippi River at Bruinsburg, Mississippi, 10 miles below Grand Gulf. Confederate defenses at Vicksburg are laid bare and Grant is now capable of attacking that erstwhile impregnable bastion from the rear.

May 1

MEDICAL: The New York Hospital for Ruptured and Crippled Children is dedicated in New York.

POLITICS: Peace Democrat Clement L. Vallandigham gives a speech in Mount Vernon, Ohio, in which he denounces "this wicked, cruel, and unnecessary war." Such speech marks him for eventual arrest.

MILITARY: Elements of the Army of Northern Virginia under General Thomas J. Jackson arrive near Chancellorsville, Virginia, and tangle with advanced Union pickets nearby. However, this aggressive display by the Confederates unnerves General Joseph Hooker, who inexplicably orders his Army of the Potomac into the woody morass known as the Wilderness. Meanwhile, Southern cavalry under General J. E. B. Stuart skillfully discern that the Union right flank is "up in the air" and subject to be turned. General Robert E. Lee, sizing up his adversary, next orders Jackson to take 30,000 men—the bulk of his army—on a circuitous, 14-mile end run around Hooker's exposed right. He is hoping for a decisive attack that will cripple his more numerous adversary.

Advancing inland from Bruinsburg, Mississippi, General Ulysses S. Grant masses 23,000 men and attacks 8,000 Confederates under General John S. Bowen

The Battle of Chancellorsville, May 1–4, 1863. Lithograph by Currier & Ives *(Library of Congress)*

at Port Gibson. Stout fighting ensues but Union numbers prevail and the Southerners are forced from the field. With his bridgehead now secure, Grant's offensive begins to gather momentum. He also takes the bold and risky expedient of cutting his own supply line, carrying all essential impedimenta on the backs of his soldiers and foraging off the land.

SLAVERY: The Confederate Congress authorizes military tribunals to execute any white Union officers caught commanding African-American soldiers. Black soldiers seized in uniform, if not killed outright, are to be promptly sold as slaves.

May 2

MILITARY: Proceeding all night with speed and great marching discipline, 30,000 Confederates under General Thomas J. Jackson steal their way around the Army of the Potomac's right flank at Chancellorsville, Virginia. At 6:00 P.M. his men slash into the unsuspecting Federals with a vengeance while they are preparing dinner. They crumble under the Southern onslaught, reeling back two miles. Jackson, ignoring the mounting confusion around him, rides forward on a personal reconnaissance and is accidentally shot by men of the 18th North Carolina.

Federal forces under General Ulysses S. Grant bridge Bayou Pierre outside Port Gibson, Mississippi, and begin fanning out across the countryside. He next intends to seize the town of Edwards Station, 16 miles east of Vicksburg, to cut the Vicksburg & Jackson Railroad and isolate the garrison.

Union cavalry under Colonel Benjamin H. Grierson fight their final skirmish with Confederate forces at Robert's Ford on the Comite River, Louisiana, before clattering into Baton Rouge and safety. He concludes his spectacular raid with a loss of only three dead, seven injured, and nine missing; five ailing soldiers have also been left behind for treatment. Confederate losses are estimated at 100 dead, 500 captured, 2,000 weapons taken, and more than 50 miles of railroad track and telegraph lines destroyed.

May 3

MILITARY: At first light the struggle around Chancellorsville, Virginia, renews. General J. E. B. Stuart mounts 50 cannon atop Hazel Grove and bombards the Union forces of General Joseph Hooker. Hooker, though still outnumbering his opponents two-to-one, clings to his defensive posture and, suddenly stunned by a falling column, he orders the Army of the Potomac to retreat back to the Rappahannock River. This act convinces General Robert E. Lee that Union forces lack the stomach to attack, and he unhesitatingly divides his force again and marches off with General Richard A. Anderson's division to meet a new Union threat developing in his rear.

Combat at Chancellorsville occasions very heavy losses to both sides: Hooker suffers 17,287 casualties while Lee sustains 12,463. Moreover, Lee and the South are now deprived of General "Thomas J. "Stonewall" Jackson, who dies of his wounds shortly afterward. This loss irreparably shatters the most outstanding tactical duo of the Civil War, and Lee's Army of Northern Virginia, while formidable, is never quite as devastatingly effective.

General John Sedgwick's VI Corps, numbering 19,000 men, is ordered by General Joseph Hooker to storm the heights of Fredericksburg, Virginia. Resistance proves stout, and on his third charge Sedgwick orders his men to settle the issue with cold steel alone and the Confederates are ejected from their works. The VI Corps then proceeds west towards Chancellorsville until it collides with General Cadmus M. Wilcox's brigade on a high ridge, upon which sits Salem Church. Heavy fighting ensues; Sedgwick suffers 1,523 casualties to a Southern tally of 674.

Colonel Abel D. Streight surrenders 1,500 men of his "Mule Brigade" to General Nathan B. Forrest at Cedar Bluff, Alabama. Forrest, possessing only 600 troopers, surrounds his opponent and, by constantly parading them and a single battery, gives the impression of a far larger force.

NAVAL: The gunboat squadron of Admiral David D. Porter moves to engage Confederate batteries at Grand Gulf, Mississippi, and finds that the defenders have fled beforehand. "The Navy holds the door to Vicksburg," he writes to General Ulysses S. Grant.

May 4

MILITARY: The Battle of Salem Church, Virginia, continues as General John Sedgwick keeps attacking Confederate positions. However, General Robert E. Lee, having boldly divided his army again, dispatches General Richard H. Anderson's division to assist the defenders. Outnumbered and nearly outflanked, the Federals skillfully withdraw toward the Rappahannock River and entrench. Total

Union casualties for the day number 4,700; Confederate losses are unknown but presumed lighter.

May 5

POLITICS: Having denounced the war as "wicked and cruel," Clement L. Vallandigham, a Northern Democrat or "Copperhead," is arrested at his home by Union solders. As he is removed to the headquarters of General Ambrose E. Burnside at Cincinnati, Ohio, riots ensue and culminate in the burning of several pro-administration newspaper offices.

SPORTS: In Charleston, Maryland, Joe Coburn becomes the new national heavyweight boxing champion by knocking down Mike McCoole after 63 rounds.

May 8

POLITICS: President Abraham Lincoln declares that all foreigners wishing to become citizens remain eligible for military service under the draft.

May 9

POLITICS: To oversee the new national bank, Congress appoints Hugh McCulloch to be Comptroller of Currency.

May 10

MILITARY: The incomparable General Thomas J. Jackson, publicly renowned as "Stonewall" and admired by soldiers on both sides, dies of pneumonia at Guiney's Station, Virginia. His passing proves an irreparable loss to General Robert E. Lee and the Confederate war effort.

May 11

POLITICS: Testy Secretary of the Treasury Salmon P. Chase, having been disapproved on an appointment, angrily tenders his resignation to President Abraham Lincoln; it is not accepted.

May 12

MILITARY: At 9:00 A.M., General John A. Logan's 3rd Division of General James B. McPherson's XVII Corps advances upon Raymond, Mississippi, encountering strong resistance from General John Gregg's Confederates. McPherson then commits his entire corps, 12,000 strong, and cracks the Southern right wing. Gregg subsequently disengages and falls back in good order toward Jackson. General Ulysses S. Grant then alters his strategy toward Vicksburg; rather than be caught between the two fires of General John C. Pemberton to the west and General Joseph E. Johnston to the east, he intends to seek each out individually and defeat them piecemeal.

May 13

MILITARY: General Joseph E. Johnston arrives at Jackson, Mississippi, to find a small garrison of 6,000 men under General John Gregg, and declares "I am too late." He realizes two full Union Corps are presently marching up toward the city and gives orders to evacuate troops and other supplies immediately. He also instructs General John C. Pemberton at Vicksburg to take his 22,000 men and catch the Federals between the two forces.

May 14

MILITARY: General Robert E. Lee attends a high-level strategy conference in Richmond, Virginia, where he advocates a risky but potentially rewarding scheme for invading Pennsylvania and defeating Federal forces on their own soil. Such a move would further discredit the Republican Party and possibly secure European intervention on the Confederacy's behalf.

Around 9:00 A.M., the advance guard of General James B. McPherson's XVII's Corps makes contact with Confederate outposts around Jackson, Mississippi. General William T. Sherman also sends his men forward and seizes several poorly guarded cannon. Confederates under General John Gregg then disengage and escape north from the city. General Ulysses S. Grant now obtains a strategic railroad junction east of Vicksburg.

May 15

JOURNALISM: Angry Federal troops storm the offices of the newspaper *Jeffersonian* in Richmond, Indiana, and ransack it on account of its supposedly pro-Southern sentiments.

May 16

MILITARY: General John C. Pemberton places his 22,000 men along a commanding position known locally as Champion's Hill, Mississippi, roughly halfway between Jackson and Vicksburg. The 32,000-man army of General Ulysses S. Grant then arrives and deploys the XIII Corps of General John A. McClernand on his right and the XVII Corps of General James B. McPherson on his left. By 5:30 P.M., Pemberton's battered force is in full flight across Baker's creek, burning the bridge behind them. Grant, by dint of rapid marching, prevents two disparate Confederate forces from uniting against him and defeats both decisively. Union losses are 1,838 to a Southern tally of 3,840.

May 17

MILITARY: General John C. Pemberton, routed at Champion Hill the day previously, prepares to defend a bridgehead along the west bank of the Big Black River, 12 miles east of strategic Vicksburg, Mississippi. At 5:00 A.M., the first elements of General John A. McClerand's XIII Corps encounters Confederate pickets, and by 10:00 A.M. Southern forces are streaming across the Big Black in defeat. Pemberton manages to fire the remaining bridge over the river but his men do not stop running until they reach the outskirts of Vicksburg, Mississippi. Big Black River is another debacle for the South, which loses 1,751 killed, wounded, and missing, along with 18 artillery pieces. Union casualties come to 279.

May 18

DIPLOMACY: In yet another blow to Confederate aspirations, Foreign Secretary Lord Russell declares to the House of Commons that Great Britain has no intention of intervening in the American conflict.

MILITARY: Union forces under General Ulysses S. Grant cross the Big Black River and take up storming positions outside the Confederate bastion of Vicksburg, Mississippi. Southern defenses appear outwardly hopeless, but General John C. Pemberton declares his intention to fight to the last. That same day General Joseph E. Johnston frantically wires the general and warns him not to become trapped within the city.

May 19

MILITARY: A preliminary attack by General Ulysses S. Grant upon Vicksburg, Mississippi, is repelled with heavy loss.

POLITICS: To end divisive sentiments arising from the arrest and detainment of Ohio Peace Democrat Congressman Clement L. Vallandigham, Secretary of War Edwin M. Stanton orders him released and deported to Confederate lines.

May 22

MILITARY: President Jefferson Davis implores General Braxton Bragg in Tennessee to come to the aid of Vicksburg, Mississippi, if possible.

General Ulysses S. Grant again launches a frontal assault upon the defenses of Vicksburg, Mississippi, hitting a three-mile stretch of entrenched positions after a continuous and heavy bombardment. Of the 45,000 Union troops committed, 3,199 become casualties. Confederate losses appear to be less than 500. Grant then resigns himself to commencing the formal siege operations he sought to avoid, although food shortages, intense summer heat, and civilian discomfort all take their toll on the defenders.

POLITICS: The U.S. War Department establishes the Bureau of Colored Troops to better coordinate recruitment of African Americans from all regions of the country.

May 23

POLITICS: Confederate Secretary of War John A. Seddon strongly suggests to President Jefferson Davis that their forces in the Trans-Mississippi Department mount an offensive to help relieve the pressure on Vicksburg, Mississippi. Specifically, he cites the capture of Helena, Arkansas, as a possible objective.

May 27

MILITARY: At 6:00 A.M., General Nathaniel P. Banks launches his long-anticipated attack upon Confederate-held Port Hudson, Louisiana. The combined assaults on the northern breastworks by generals Christopher Auger and Godfrey Wetzel become separated in rough terrain and are defeated piecemeal. A subsequent advance by General Thomas W. Sherman is also repelled, and Banks finally suspends the attack. Union losses are 1,995 while the Confederates record 235 casualties. Port Hudson also witnesses the first large-scale employment of African-American troops, who acquit themselves well.

May 28

MILITARY: The 54th Massachusetts Infantry, composed entirely of African-American soldiers and white officers, parades through Boston under Colonel Robert G. Shaw, a wealthy Boston Brahmin and devoted abolitionist. The unit then ships out for Hilton Head, South Carolina, to serve in the siege of Charleston.

May 30

MILITARY: General Robert E. Lee reorganizes his Army of Northern Virginia into four corps: General James Longstreet (I), General Richard S. Ewell (II), General Ambrose P. Hill (III) and General J. E. B. Stuart (Cavalry Corps.

Flag of the 22nd Regiment U.S. Colored Troops depicting an African-American soldier bayoneting a fallen Confederate soldier. *(Library of Congress)*

1863

May 31
MILITARY: In a high-level strategy session at Richmond, Virginia, President Jefferson Davis openly expresses to General Robert E. Lee his disdain for General Joseph E. Johnston's handling of affairs outside of Vicksburg, Mississippi.

June 1
JOURNALISM: General Ambrose E. Burnside again closes the offices of the Chicago *Times* over their allegedly disloyal comments, creating another public uproar and a political headache for President Abraham Lincoln.

June 2
POLITICS: President Abraham Lincoln orders Peace Democrat Clement L. Vallandigham transported to Wilmington, North Carolina, for detention as an enemy alien.
SLAVERY: Harriet Tubman, guiding a force of Union troops up the Combahee River, South Carolina, helps burn a plantation and free 800 African-American slaves. She does so with the blessing of her commander, General David Hunter.

Tubman, Harriet (ca. 1820–1913)
African-American abolitionist

Aramita Tubman was born into slavery on a plantation in Dorchester County, Maryland, around 1820. She eventually adopted her mother's name of Harriet and worked many years as a domestic, and at the age of 13 she was struck violently in the head as punishment, suffering periodic seizures thereafter. In 1844 she married a free black named John but feared that her family might be broken up and sold. She thereupon fled with her brothers to Philadelphia and was rescued by Quakers working in the abolitionist movement. Rather than enjoy her newfound freedom, Tubman chose to return repeatedly to the South incognito, eventually rescuing her aged parents from enslavement. She received no help from her husband, who remarried and remained in Maryland, but over the next decade Tubman was responsible for rescuing 300 African Americans and conducting them northward to freedom along the celebrated "underground railway." This was in spite of the fact that the Fugitive Slave Law of 1850 meted out stiff punishment to any person caught aiding an escaping slave. So notorious did Tubman become that her former owners offered a $40,000 reward for her capture. She also strongly supported radical abolitionist John Brown in his attempt to foment a slave insurrection and was deeply disappointed when it failed. When the Civil War commenced in April 1861, Tubman unflinchingly offered her service to the Union army as a nurse, a scout, and a spy. She proved especially useful to abolitionist-minded General David Hunter in South Carolina, and received a travel pass usually reserved for important dignitaries. Tubman enjoyed considerable celebrity among plantation slaves throughout the war, who assisted her, fed her, and sheltered her throughout her many dangerous forays into the Confederacy.

After the war Tubman continued her activities assisting the freedmen while also caring for her elderly parents and numerous orphans. Her gallant wartime efforts

(continues)

(continued)

notwithstanding, the government refused to grant her the same pension usually allotted to white nurses–$20 a month–until the 1890s. Undaunted, Tubman became closely associated with civil rights and woman's suffrage, frequently being engaged as a public speaker at political events. She was also essential for establishing the first African Methodist Episcopal Church in upstate New York. Tubman labored in both obscurity and poverty until 1869 when Sarah Bradford published *Harriet Tubman, The Moses of Her People*, which brought in additional funds. She used the money to found the Harriet Tubman Home for Aged Negroes, which has since become a national landmark. Tubman contracted pneumonia and died on March 10, 1913, and a memorial plaque was dedicated in the town of Auburn, New York, by noted civil rights leader Booker T. Washington. On August 28, 2003, New York Governor George Pataki declared that March 10 would be celebrated as Harriet Tubman Day in honor of her selfless achievements and sacrifice.

June 3

MILITARY: General Robert E. Lee begins his second invasion of the North by moving 75,000 men of his Army of Northern Virginia from Fredericksburg, Virginia, toward the Shenandoah Valley. General Ambrose P. Hill's corps is temporarily detained near Fredericksburg until needed.

June 4

JOURNALISM: President Abraham Lincoln orders Secretary of War Edwin M. Stanton to revoke General Ambrose E. Burnside's suspension of the Chicago *Times*.

June 5

MILITARY: Fighting erupts at Franklin's Crossing on the Rappahannock River as troops of General Ambrose P. Hill's command skirmish with the Union VI Corps under General John Sedgwick. The stiff resistance encountered convinces Sedgwick that the Southerners are still present in force and he reports his findings to General Joseph Hooker. That leader, unconvinced, next orders several cavalry forays to ascertain enemy intentions.

June 6

MILITARY: At Brandy Station, Virginia, General J. E. B. Stuart holds a grand review of 8,000 Confederate cavalry for a large crowd of political dignitaries and spectators gathered onto railroad cars.

June 7

DIPLOMACY: French military forces occupy Mexico City at the behest of Emperor Napoleon III.

MILITARY: At 5:30 A.M., General Henry E. McCulloch leads 1,500 Confederates in an attack against 1,061 Federals at Milliken's Bend, Louisiana, and withdraws after three hours of heavy fighting. African-American soldiers, who suffer disproportionately high casualties, murder several captured Southerners after learning that they had killed black captives in their custody. Union losses in this affair tally 101 dead, 285 injured, and 266 missing while the Confederates sustain 44 killed, 131 wounded, and 10 missing.

June 8

MILITARY: The Army of Northern Virginia under General Robert E. Lee arrives at Culpepper Court House, Virginia, where General J. E. B. Stuart stages another elaborate cavalry review. Stuart, a jaunty, supremely confident gamecock, delights in displaying his finely honed troopers, but he is nonetheless slated to receive some rather unexpected—and unwelcome—visitors.

At Falmouth, Virginia, General Alfred Pleasonton musters his Union cavalry corps, two infantry brigades, and six light batteries, 11,000 men in all, to reconnoiter across the Rappahannock River. His mission is to locate the main body of Confederates and ascertain if they are moving north onto Union territory.

June 9

MILITARY: At 4:00 A.M., General John Buford's brigade of Union cavalry splashes across the Rappahannock River at Beverly, Virginia, while, four miles downstream, General David M. Gregg's force crosses at Kelly's Ford. General Alfred Pleasonton has thrown two columns against the known headquarters of General J. E. B. Stuart in an attempt to catch the wily trooper in a coordinated pincer movement. Stuart, with 9,500 troopers scattered over a wide area, immediately dispatches riders out to assemble the command at Brandy Station while he organizes defenses along Fleetwood Hill. Stiff and indecisive fighting erupts before Pleasonton, perceiving dust clouds on the horizon, assumes that columns of Confederate infantry are approaching. He then signals his men to withdraw and the fighting ceases. Brandy Station is the largest mounted action of the war and a tactical victory for the Confederates, who hold the field and inflict 936 Union casualties for a loss of 523 men. However, the 10-hour struggle underscores in bold relief the excellent progress Union cavalry has achieved under capable leadership.

NAVAL: Union mortar boats resume their protracted bombardment of Vicksburg, Mississippi, designed to cut off resupply efforts and undermine civilian morale. On average, they hurl 175 heavy explosive shells into the city every day while its inhabitants cower in nearby caves.

June 11

POLITICS: In an act of defiance by Ohio Peace Democrats, they nominate Clement L. Vallandigham as their gubernatorial candidate, despite the fact the Confederate government has shipped him off to Canada.

June 12

MILITARY: General Richard S. Ewell, advancing along the Blue Ridge Mountains of western Virginia, detaches General Richard E. Rodes' division and a cavalry brigade of General Albert G. Jenkins toward the town of Berryville to drive out an 1,800-man Union garrison under Colonel Andrew T. McReynolds.

June 14

MILITARY: At 4:00 A.M., General Nathaniel P. Banks hurls another assault against Confederate defenses at Port Hudson, Louisiana. This time the infantry division of General Halbert E. Payne charges the strong entrenchments at Priest Cap and, despite heroic efforts, is repelled with 1,805 casualties. The well-protected Confederate defenders lose only 22 killed and 25 wounded.

The Confederate II Corps under General Richard S. Ewell engages a Federal force under General Robert H. Milroy at Winchester, western Virginia. Milroy initially believes that the enemy to his front are simply a large foraging party, but by the time he realizes that the entire Army of Northern Virginia is bearing down on him, it is too late. The general hastily convenes a war council that elects to spike its artillery, burn its baggage trains, and evacuate Winchester under the cover of darkness. However, Ewell has anticipated such a move and he instructs General Edward Johnson to position his men along Martinburg Turnpike at Stevenson's Depot and cut off Milroy's retreat.

POLITICS: President Abraham Lincoln anxiously goads General Joseph Hooker into some kind of action to oppose this latest Confederate incursion. "If the head of Lee's army is at Martinsburg and the tail of it on the Plank Road between Fredericksburg and Chancellorsville, the animal must be very slim somewhere. Could you not break him?"

June 15

MILITARY: Confederates under General Edward Johnson successfully ambush retiring forces under General Robert H. Milroy at Stevenson's Depot, four miles north of Winchester, Virginia. Among the huge haul they capture is 2,500 prisoners, 300 wagons, 300 horses, and 23 cannon. Union combat losses add another 905 dead and 305 wounded to the tally while Johnson suffers 47 killed, 219 wounded, and three missing. This victory clears Federal forces from the Shenandoah Valley and facilitates General Robert E. Lee's impending invasion of Pennsylvania.

Confederate General Joseph E. Johnston again wires General John C. Pemberton at Vicksburg, Mississippi, that his position is hopeless and that he must evacuate the city immediately and save his army. However, Pemberton never receives the message owing to cut telegraph wires, and he remains trapped within his works by Federal forces under General Ulysses S. Grant.

POLITICS: President Abraham Lincoln calls for 100,000 militia to muster in Pennsylvania, Maryland, Ohio, and West Virginia, to thwart recent Confederate advances northward.

The approach of the Army of Northern Virginia toward Pennsylvania soil causes outbreaks of excitement and panic at Baltimore, Maryland.

June 16

MILITARY: The new Confederate offensive leads to a furious spate of telegrams between General in Chief Henry W. Halleck and General Joseph Hooker as to General Robert E. Lee's intentions. Hooker wants to rush troops north and confront Lee above Washington, D.C., while Halleck insists that he follow the Southerners and relieve the garrison at Harper's Ferry, West Virginia, en route.

June 17

MILITARY: As the Army of Northern Virginia under General Robert E. Lee advances north into Maryland, General J. E. B. Stuart is ordered to screen his right flank from prying Federal eyes. His Union opposite, General Alfred Pleasonton, is determined to uncover Confederate intentions and come to grips with his gray-coated adversaries. Colonel Thomas Munford, 5th Virginia Cavalry, is also scouting in the vicinity of Aldie, Virginia, when he brushes up against Union troopers under General Hugh J. Kilpatrick. Fighting is intense but dies down for the evening; Union losses for the day total around 300 to a Confederate tally of 100.

NAVAL: The ironclad USS *Weehawken* under Captain John Rodgers, assisted by the *Nahant*, engage Commander William A. Webb and the formidable steam ram CSS *Atlanta* in Wassaw Sound, Georgia. *Atlanta* grounds in the channel during its approach and is subsequently worked free, but its rudder is damaged and the ship steers erratically. Rodgers' vessels then slip quickly into point-blank range and pound their adversary into submission after a 15-minute struggle, another serious loss for the struggling Confederate navy.

June 18

MILITARY: General Ulysses S. Grant summarily relieves General John A. McClernand from command of the XIII Corps for insubordination and replaces him with General Edward O. C. Ord. The final straw came when McClernand issues unauthorized, laudatory statements to his men which praise them for their role in the failed assault upon Vicksburg, Mississippi, while denigrating the performance of other units.

June 20

BUSINESS: Jay Cooke oversees creation of the first National Bank in Philadelphia, Pennsylvania, and also spearheads the drive for Union war bonds. These endeavors result in the first uniform national currency for many states once banks begin issuing national bank notes.

MILITARY: Union cavalry under General Alfred Pleasonton increases pressure on the mounted screen of General J. E. B. Stuart, now left unsupported east of the Blue Ridge Mountains. He orders General David M. Gregg's division to attack General Wade Hampton's Confederates at Goose Creek, Virginia, while another force under General John Buford threatens to outflank them.

POLITICS: West Virginia joins the Union as the 35th state and a stalwart Union ally. Moreover, its constitution mandates the gradual emancipation of all African-American slaves.

June 22

MILITARY: General J. E. B. Stuart receives discretionary and somewhat vague instructions from General Robert E. Lee, ordering him to alternately raid Union supply lines while guarding the army's right flank when it advances northward into Pennsylvania.

June 23

MILITARY: The Army of Northern Virginia under General Robert E. Lee nears Chambersburg, Pennsylvania, with several disparate Union columns groping along in pursuit.

June 24

NAVAL: Admiral John A. B. Dahlgren is relieved of duties at the Washington Navy Yard, D.C., and ordered to succeed Admiral Samuel F. du Pont as the new commander of the South Atlantic Blockading Squadron.

June 25

MILITARY: General J. E. B. Stuart leads three cavalry brigades north from Salem Depot, Virginia, to join the main Confederate army north of the Potomac River. However, Stuart's interpretation of his otherwise discretionary orders ultimately

1863

draws him away from the main theater of operations, hindering Confederate intelligence-gathering abilities at a time when the whereabouts of pursuing Union forces are unknown.

June 26

NAVAL: Admiral Andrew H. Foote dies in New York City of wounds received in the siege of Fort Donelson in February 1862.

Confederate schooner CSS *Archer* under Lieutenant Charles W. Read boldly attacks and sinks the U.S. revenue cutter *Caleb Cushing* at Portland, Maine, but subsequently surrenders to the USS *Forest City* after expending his last ammunition. This concludes the dashing career of Read who, in the span of only 19 days, captures 22 vessels despite 47 Union craft on the lookout for him.

June 27

MILITARY: President Abraham Lincoln appoints General George G. Meade to replace General Joseph Hooker as commander of the Army of the Potomac.

Confederate cavalry under General J. E. B. Stuart clashes with Union forces at Fairfax Court House, Virginia, taking some prisoners. He then approaches the town, eager to secure supplies abandoned by General Joseph Hooker, but is surprised and nearly captured in a sudden charge by 86 troopers of the 11th New York Cavalry. Fortunately, Stuart and his retinue are rescued in time by the 1st North Carolina Cavalry under Colonel Laurence S. Baker, who abruptly pushes the attackers back. The dashing leader is apparently so pleased that he intends to continue raiding the Union rear, instead of joining the Army of Northern Virginia as planned.

June 28

MILITARY: General Robert E. Lee is startled to find strong Union forces gathering at Frederick, Maryland, and threatening his rear. Their exact intentions remain hazy as all of Lee's cavalry under General J. E. B. Stuart has departed on a deep raid through Union territory. Then Lee, as a precaution, orders his dispersed command to concentrate in the vicinity of Gettysburg, Pennsylvania, an important road junction.

General John C. Pemberton, defending the vital Confederate bastion at Vicksburg, Mississippi, is petitioned by his soldiers to surrender rather than see the entire force starve to death. After a seven-week siege, the final curtain is about to fall.

June 30

MILITARY: General John F. Reynolds is ordered by General George Gordon Meade to occupy the vital road junction at Gettysburg, Pennsylvania. The town is then occupied by a cavalry division under General John Buford who, cognizant of its value, prepares his command to defend it. He briefly skirmishes with part of General Henry Heth's division, sent to Gettysburg to forage for shoes, but when the latter informs General Ambrose P. Hill of the presence of Federal troops at the junction, Hill blithely dismisses the notion.

Marauding Confederate cavalry under General J. E. B. Stuart skirmishes with Union troopers under General Elon Farnsworth at Hanover, Pennsylvania. An inconclusive fight unfolds as Union reinforcements arrive under generals Hugh J. Kilpatrick and George Custer, while the Confederates receive General Fitzhugh

Lee. Rather than rejoin the Army of Northern Virginia, then concentrating at Gettysburg, Stuart now takes his command on an even wider detour around pursuing Union forces.

POLITICS: President Abraham Lincoln ignores continuing pressure to reappoint General George B. McClellan as head of the Army of the Potomac.

July 1

MILITARY: Early this morning the Confederate division of General Henry Heth forages for shoes in the vicinity of Gettysburg, Pennsylvania, when they unexpectedly encounter dismounted Union cavalry under General John Buford. Sharp fighting commences as the Southerners impulsively charge and are repelled by rapid firing Spencer carbines. Combat then intensifies as generals Oliver O. Howard and Abner Doubleday arrive with the Union XI and III Corps, respectively, as does the entire Confederate II Corps under General Richard S. Ewell. Quick maneuvering allows the rebels to roll up Howard's line and soon his troops are streaming through Gettysburg in confusion. Disaster is only averted when General Winfield S. Hancock comes galloping up at the head of his II Corps and occupies the high ground along Cemetery Hill. This act allows the Army of the Potomac to occupy excellent defensive terrain around Gettysburg that evening. Casualties for the day amount to 9,000 Federals and 6,800 Confederates.

A Confederate staff officer finally locates the elusive cavalry of General J. E. B. Stuart and orders him to repair to the main army under General Robert E. Lee at Gettysburg with all haste.

General William S. Rosencrans climaxes his successful Tullahoma Campaign by bloodlessly occupying Chattanooga, Tennessee, as Confederates under General Braxton Bragg withdraw. This is one of the most outstanding instances of strategic maneuvering during the entire Civil War.

POLITICS: The Missouri State Convention votes to end slavery on July 4, 1870.

July 2

MILITARY: At Gettysburg, Pennsylvania, 75,000 Confederates confront 85,000 Federals, whose defensive line resembles a fishhook with its right anchored on Culp's Hill to the north, then running the length along Cemetery Ridge to a large hill called Little Round Top on its extreme left. Lee determines to defeat the enemy where he finds him, over objections by General James Longstreet, and orders strong attacks on both Union flanks. At one point the Southern advance nearly carries them through the Union line, but a sharp countercharge by General Winfield S. Hancock pushes them back downhill. A crisis develops on the extreme Union left at Little Round Top as a tremendous firefight unfolds between Colonel Joshua Chambers' 20th Maine and an Alabama brigade sent to dislodge him. His ammunition failed, Chambers decides the issue with a sudden bayonet charge down the slope that routs his adversaries and saves the Union left. Meade then correctly predicts that Lee, foiled on either flank, will direct the bulk of his efforts at the Union center the next day.

Late in the afternoon, General J. E. B. Stuart stumbles into the headquarters of General Robert E. Lee at Gettysburg, Pennsylvania. An exasperated Lee, who entered the fight without accurate information for lack of mounted reconnaissance, curtly declares, "Well, General Stuart, you are here at last."

POLITICS: Confederate vice president Alexander H. Stephens writes to President Abraham Lincoln about prisoner exchanges and potential discussions to end the war. Lincoln responds that he is not interested.

July 3

MILITARY: At 1:00 P.M., General Alexander E. Porter's 140 cannon commence bombarding the Union line at Gettysburg, Pennsylvania. The Federals respond in kind with 100 cannon of their own, initiating the largest artillery duel in American history. At 3:00 P.M., Confederates from the divisions of generals George E. Pickett, Johnston Pettigrew, and Isaac Trimble advance from the nearby woods and into what amounts to a killing ground, for Union batteries are carefully sited for interlocking fields of fire. Only a handful of surviving Confederates penetrate Meade's defense but are quickly swallowed by the Union reserves. Eventually thousands of wounded and stunned survivors stream back across the field toward Seminary Ridge in abject defeat. General Robert E. Lee, surveying the carnage around him, is heard to murmur "It is all my fault, my fault."

Confederate cavalry under General J. E. B. Stuart, conspicuously absent during the first two days of fighting, is now ordered to seek out and assail the Union rear. En route he encounters Union cavalry under General David M. Gregg, who fights the Southerners to a standstill in one of the biggest mounted clashes of the war. The overworked brigade of General George A. Custer particularly distinguishes itself with repeated, headlong charges which induce Stuart to relinquish the field.

The debacle at Gettysburg represents the turning of the tide of Confederate military fortunes. Three days of ferocious combat with a determined adversary enjoying stark terrain advantages depletes the Army of Northern Virginia by an estimated 20,451 men. The actual loss may have been as high as 28,000—a horrific toll of irreplaceable, trained manpower. The Army of the Potomac is equally savaged with losses of 23,049.

Generals John C. Pemberton and Ulysses S. Grant arrange an armistice to confer about surrender terms at Vicksburg, Mississippi. Grant bluntly informs his opposite: "You will be allowed to march out, the officers taking with them their side arms and clothing, and the field, staff, and cavalry officers one horse each. The rank and file will be allowed all their clothing but no other property."

NAVAL: The onset of surrender negotiations at Vicksburg, Mississippi, signals an end to the ongoing naval bombardment of the city by Admiral David D. Porter's Mississippi River Squadron. Naval personnel had fired 16,000 rounds from a variety of ships, gunboats, and mortar craft, in addition to 13 naval guns hauled ashore.

July 4

DIPLOMACY: Confederate vice president Alexander H. Stephens rides the CSS *Torpedo* down the James River under a flag of truce and steams to Hampton Roads, Virginia. There he hopes to confer with Union officials in an attempt to spur dialogue between the two governments, but Federal authorities turn him back.

INDIAN: Chief Little Crow, who initiated the Santee (Sioux) uprising in Minnesota almost a year earlier, is shot dead by farmers while picking berries.

MILITARY: Despite pleas and entreaties from President Abraham Lincoln, General George G. Meade declines to pursue or hound the fleeing Confederates. In light of horrific casualties recently sustained by his Army of the Potomac at Gettysburg, and the disorganization this entails, his reluctance is understandable.

The Army of Northern Virginia under General Robert E. Lee withdraws in good order from Gettysburg, Pennsylvania, and marches for Williamsport, Maryland, to recross the Potomac River into Virginia. Progress is slow owing to incessant rain and a wagon train of wounded stretching 17 miles.

The Confederate citadel of Vicksburg, Mississippi, surrenders to General Ulysses S. Grant after a brutal, seven-week siege. Union losses for the entire campaign come to 800 killed, 3,900 wounded, and 200 missing out of 77,000 committed. The Southerners lost 900 dead, 2,500 wounded, 200 missing, and 29,491 captured. The Confederacy is now completely cut in two along the Mississippi River. "Grant is my man," an ebullient President Abraham Lincoln beams, "and I am his the rest of the war."

Union forces defending Helena, Arkansas, under General Benjamin M. Prentiss withstand a determined Confederate attack from generals Theophilus H. Holmes and Sterling Price. Unable to make any headway and unwilling to withstand a withering cannonade, the Southerners concede defeat and withdraw after losing 380 dead, 1,100 wounded, and 1,100 captured out of 7,600 present. The Federals sustain only 239 killed, wounded, and missing.

July 5

MILITARY: General William T. Sherman marches from Vicksburg, Mississippi, at the head of 40,000 troops divided among the corps of generals Frederick Steele, Edward O. C. Ord, and John G. Parke. His missions is to recapture Jackson by driving General Joseph E. Johnston out from behind the Big Black River.

July 6

NAVAL: Admiral John A. B. Dahlgren relieves Admiral Samuel F. du Pont as commander of the South Atlantic Blockading Squadron off Port Royal, South Carolina. Du Pont's removal is as much about friction with Secretary of the Navy Gideon Welles as it is his failure before Charleston.

July 8

MILITARY: General John H. Morgan crosses the Ohio River at Cumming's Ferry, Kentucky, and begins raiding Indian and Southern Ohio. His appearance stimulates some anxiety over the rekindling of pro-Confederate "Copperhead" activities throughout that region.

July 9

MILITARY: Confederate General Franklin Gardner surrenders Port Hudson, Louisiana, to the Army of the Gulf under General Nathaniel P. Banks. The Southerners lost roughly 146 killed, 447 wounded, and 6,400 captured while Union casualties topped 708 dead, 3,336 injured, and 319 missing. Victory here removes the last Confederate obstacle on the Mississippi River, now freely navigable as far as St. Louis, Missouri, for the first time in two years.

July 10

MILITARY: The siege of Charleston, South Carolina, begins as General Quincy A. Gilmore lands 3,700 Federal troops of General George C. Strong's brigade on Morris Island, overpowering Confederate forces stationed there. Gilmore next begins preparing to overrun Battery Wagner commanded by General William B. Taliafero.

NAVAL: Admiral John A. B. Dahlgren initiates a second naval siege of Charleston, South Carolina, by bombarding Confederate positions on Morris Island. The ironclads USS *Nahant*, *Weehawken*, *Catskill*, and *Montauk* are subsequently damaged by Confederate shore batteries, none seriously.

July 11

DIPLOMACY: American minister to England Charles F. Adams denounces the British practice of building ironclads and outfitting blockade runners for use by the Confederacy. He makes it clear to Foreign Secretary Earl John Russell that American patience with such transgressions is running out.

MILITARY: A determined Union assault upon Battery Wagner, Charleston harbor, South Carolina, is launched by General Quincy A. Gilmore. However, Gilmore is unaware that the garrison has been recently enlarged to 1,200 men and his attack is easily rebuffed with losses of 49 killed, 123 wounded, and 167 missing. The Southerners sustain only six dead and six wounded.

July 12

MILITARY: Troops under generals William T. Sherman and Joseph E. Johnston spar in the vicinity of Clinton, Mississippi. Union forces unleash a prolonged bombardment of Confederate positions when suddenly a brigade commanded by Colonel Isaac Pugh attacks Southern redoubts defended by General John C. Breckinridge. Pugh, his advance unsupported, loses 500 men out of 800.

July 13

JOURNALISM: President Abraham Lincoln admonishes General John M. Schofield, commanding in Missouri, for his arrest of William McKee, editor of the St. Louis *Democrat*, for alleged antiwar activity.

SOCIETAL: Violent antidraft riots erupt in New York City shortly after the first names are read for induction. At length a seething mob of 50,000 Irish émigrés attacks the draft office, burning it to the ground. Over the next four days violence escalates until Federal troops arrive to restore order. More than 1,000 people, principally African Americans targeted by the mob, are either killed or injured.

July 14

MILITARY: The Army of Northern Virginia steadily evacuates Williamsport, Maryland, behind two divisions under General Henry Heth that act as a rear guard. However, General George A. Custer's cavalry brigade sweeps into nearby Falling Waters, rounding up several stragglers. General John Buford's division is also approaching but General Hugh J. Kilpatrick simply orders two companies of the 6th Michigan Cavalry to charge the Confederates. The Federals capture 719 prisoners, three battle flags, and two cannon, but Southern losses would have been even greater had Kilpatrick waited until he had his entire force.

POLITICS: President Abraham Lincoln, disillusioned by General George G. Meade's lax pursuit of retreating Confederates, indelicately informs him, "Your golden opportunity is gone and I am distressed immeasurably because of it."

July 15

MILITARY: After the Arkansas River becomes fordable, Union General James G. Blunt assembles 3,000 men (mostly Native Americans and African Americans) and two batteries for a preemptive strike against 6,000 Confederates gathering at Elk Creek, Indian Territory (Oklahoma). He intends to disperse General Douglas H. Cooper's command before he is reinforced by an additional 3,000 Confederates under General William L. Cabell.

POLITICS: Stricken by news of Gettysburg, Vicksburg, and Port Hudson, a somber President Jefferson Davis intones, "The clouds are truly dark over us."

July 16

MILITARY: General Joseph E. Johnston begins a nighttime evacuation of Jackson, Mississippi, rather than face envelopment by General William T. Sherman. He accordingly falls back across the Pearl River covered by darkness and withdraws 30 miles eastward.

July 17

INDIAN: General James G. Blunt, leading 3,000 Union troops, attacks 6,000 Confederate Creek, Choctaw, Cherokee, and Texans under General Douglas H. Cooper at Honey Springs, Indian Territory (Oklahoma). The aggressive Blunt outflanks Douglas twice before his Indians mount a whooping counterattack that grants him time to cross the Elk River to safety. Blunt's prompt action saves the Indian Territory for the Union. This is also the first time that Native Americans confront and fight large numbers of African Americans.

July 18

MILITARY: A second Federal assault upon Battery Wagner, Charleston harbor, South Carolina, is courageously spearheaded by Colonel Robert G. Shaw's 54th Massachusetts Infantry, recruited entirely from African Americans, which clambers up the fort's parapet and plants its flag despite heavy fire. Consequently, Sergeant William H. Carney becomes the first black soldier to win the Congressional Medal of Honor, despite a bloody repulse. Union casualties total 1,515 while the Confederates sustain 36 dead, 133 injured, and five missing.

NAVAL: Admiral John A. B. Dahlgren's ironclad squadron lends heavy supporting fire during the failed assault against Battery Wagner, Charleston harbor. His vessels close to within 300 yards of Confederate works, but the moment they cease fire to allow the Union infantry assault, the defenders suddenly emerge to repel them.

July 22

BUSINESS: The New York Chamber of Commerce releases figures stating Union losses at sea to Confederate raiders at 150 vessels worth $12 million. This is stark testimony to the effectiveness of oceanic raiders like CSS *Alabama*, *Florida*, and *Georgia*.

July 26

MILITARY: After a continuous running fight of several days, Confederate General John H. Morgan and his

Rear Admiral John A. Dahlgren standing by a Dahlgren gun on the deck of the USS *Pawnee*. *(Library of Congress)*

1863

remaining 364 troopers surrender at Salineville, Ohio. Morgan is slated for confinement at the Ohio State Penitentiary in Columbus.

POLITICS: Kentucky Senator John J. Crittenden, author of the "Crittenden Compromise" of 1860, dies at Frankfort, Kentucky.

Former Texas governor Sam Houston, who refused to take an oath to the Confederacy and was driven from office because of it, dies at his ranch at the age of 70.

July 29

DIPLOMACY: Queen Victoria informs Parliament that she sees "No reason to depart from the strict neutrality which Her Majesty has Observed from the beginning of the contest." This is the latest blow against Confederate hopes for recognition and direct military assistance.

July 30

POLITICS: President Abraham Lincoln threatens to execute captured Confederate officers and subject Southern soldiers to hard labor if captured Union officers are harmed in any manner for leading African-American troops, or if former slaves now wearing a Federal uniform are sold back into bondage.

August 1

MILITARY: Noted Confederate spy Belle Boyd is again arrested at Martinsburg, West Virginia, and sent to Washington, D.C., for internment.

NAVAL: Admiral David D. Porter formally succeeds Admiral David G. Farragut as commander of all naval forces and operations along the Mississippi River. Farragut, worn out and ailing, is preparing to go on extended leave to recover his health.

POLITICS: To ameliorate mounting desertion problems, President Jefferson Davis offers an amnesty to all ranks presently without leave, warning them that they have no choice but "victory, or subjugation, slavery, and utter ruin of yourselves, your families, and your country." To that end he announces a pardon to all Confederate army deserters who rejoin their units within the next 20 days.

A throng of an estimated 3,000 Democrats at Mattoon, Illinois, gathers to hear Peace Democrat John R. Eden denounce the administration of President Abraham Lincoln. Cole County remains a hotbed of antiwar agitation for the rest of the struggle.

August 3

POLITICS: To discourage continuing violence, New York Governor Horatio Seymour asks President Abraham Lincoln to suspend conscription in his state. The president flatly refuses.

August 6

POLITICS: President Jefferson Davis assures a jittery Governor Milledge L. Bonham of South Carolina of his continuing support for the defense of Charleston "which we pray will never be polluted by the footsteps of a lustful, relentless, inhuman foe."

August 8

MILITARY: General Robert E. Lee tenders his resignation to President Jefferson Davis over his recent failure at Gettysburg, Pennsylvania, but Davis refuses to accept it.

August 10

POLITICS: At a meeting with President Abraham Lincoln, abolitionist Frederick Douglass stridently protests the inequity of pay between black and white soldiers, despite assurances from recruiters that they would be paid the same.

August 12

NAVAL: The experimental submarine CSS *Hunley* arrives at Charleston, South Carolina. This novelty consists of an iron steam boiler that has been waterproofed and fitted with tapered bow and stern sections. The *Hunley* is 40 feet long and only 3.5 feet in diameter, being propelled by five men operating a crankshaft-driven propeller. General Pierre G. T. Beauregard, commanding the city's defenses, is intrigued by the device and seeks to impress it into active service as soon as testing is completed.

August 16

MILITARY: After considerable prodding from the government, General William S. Rosecrans pushes his Army of the Cumberland out of Chattanooga and toward the Georgia border. Due to mountainous terrain before him, he plans to spread out into three widely spaced columns to cover all three passes, a risky ploy that endangers his command with utter defeat.

August 18

TECHNOLOGY: Intrigued by new weapons, President Abraham Lincoln test fires a new, rapid-fire Spencer carbine at Treasury Park, Washington, D.C. This weapon gives Federal cavalry units a decided edge in firepower over Confederate units still armed with muzzle-loading rifles.

August 20

INDIAN: Colonel Kit Carson commences his "scorched earth" policy against the Navajo in the New Mexico Territory, being further assisted by Ute, Zuni, and Mescalero Apache tribesmen. All captives taken are then transferred to a new reservation at Bosque Rendondo for resettlement.

August 21

MILITARY: William C. Quantrill and 450 Confederate irregulars and partisans storm into Lawrence, Kansas, a noted abolitionist center and hotbed for Union "jayhawker" activities. Over the next four hours they systematically round up and execute 180 men and boys, then set fire to 185 buildings. It is the largest single atrocity of the Civil War.

August 25

MILITARY: General Thomas Ewing, commanding the Union Border District in Missouri, issues General Order No. 11. This controversial measure forces 20,000 residents of Bates, Cass, Jackson, and parts of Vernon Counties, long suspected of collaborating with Confederate guerrillas, to abandon their homes. These structures are then peremptorily burned in retaliation for the Lawrence massacre.

August 26

MILITARY: Union cavalry under General William W. Averill skirmishes heavily with Confederate forces at White Sulphur Springs, West Virginia. His 2,000 troopers dash headlong into a like number of Confederates under Colonel George S. Patton, attack repeatedly across densely wooded terrain, and are defeated.

Carson, Kit   (1809–1868)
Frontier scout

Christopher ("Kit") Carson was born in Madison County, Kentucky, on December 24, 1809, and in 1811 he accompanied his family to Boone's Lick, Missouri. Carson, who was barely educated and semiliterate his whole life, briefly apprenticed himself to a saddler, but he ran away at the age of 16 to join an expedition to Santa Fe, New Mexico. He then found his calling in exploring and trapping along the vast western frontier, which occupied him for the rest of his life. Carson proved himself particularly adept at trapping and Indian fighting and made several forays in and out of the Mojave Deserte region by 1831. That year he was badly wounded in a skirmish against the Blackfeet and subsequently married an Arapaho woman in an Indian ceremony. His reputation as a scout received a decided boost after encountering Lieutenant John C. Frémont on a riverboat near St. Louis. Frémont prevailed upon Carson to serve as his scout during an army exploring expedition, June–October, 1842, and he effectively discharged his duties. Frémont then published the results of his efforts, which gained Carson national recognition. He subsequently accompanied Frémont on two more expeditions, 1834–44 and 1845 and was in California when the war with Mexico erupted in 1846. Carson campaigned actively for the conquest of Los Angeles and was traveling east with dispatches when he encountered the cavalry column of Colonel Stephen W. Kearny. Kearny impressed Carson into his expedition as a scout, where he fought well at the disastrous skirmish of San Pascual, December 6, 1846. He then rode to Washington, D.C., with dispatches and was commissioned a lieutenant in the elite Regiment of Mounted Riflemen by President James K. Polk. The appointment was blocked by enemies in the Senate, however, and Carson returned to Taos, New Mexico, to live as a private citizen.

In the postwar period Carson found useful work as a government Indian agent and worked exclusively with the Ute tribe. In this capacity he accused Territorial Governor David Meriwether of insensitivity toward Native Americans, which led to his arrest, but he was later restored. When the Civil War broke out in April 1861, Carson joined the 1st New Mexico Volunteer Infantry as its colonel, and he fought well against Confederate forces at the Battle of Valverde on February 21, 1862. He then served under the harsh General James H. Carleton in administering Indian affairs throughout New Mexico and Arizona, which spawned outright war among uncooperative Apache and Navaho tribesmen. Carson ignored Carleton's orders to liquidate the offending tribes but did conduct a harsh, scorched-earth policy that drove them into submission and led to their relocation onto reservations. On March 13, 1865, Carson was brevetted to brigadier general for good service, and the following year he assumed command of Fort Garland, Colorado. He died on May 23, 1868, shortly after resuming duties as an Indian agent.

August 29

NAVAL: The experimental submarine CSS *Hunley*, under Lieutenant John A. Payne, tragically sinks on a trial run in Charleston harbor, South Carolina, killing all six crew members. The vessel apparently foundered in the wake of the steamer *Etiwan* after its hatches were opened for better ventilation.

1863

September 1
NAVAL: Admiral John A. B. Dahlgren leads his ironclad force in a five-hour night action against Confederates at Fort Sumter, Charleston Harbor, South Carolina. The vessels steam to within 500 yards of the embattled fortress before firing, and they receive 70 hits from shore batteries before the action is suspended at daybreak.

September 2
SLAVERY: To curtail mounting manpower shortages, the Alabama state legislature considers arming slaves to serve in the army.

September 3
INDIAN: Union troops under General Alfred Sully attack a hostile Santee (Sioux) village at Whitestone Hill, Dakota Territory, killing an estimated 200 inhabitants. The Americans then burn the village and withdraw with 156 captives.

September 5
DIPLOMACY: After being prodded by American minister Charles F. Adams, British Foreign Secretary Lord Russell confiscates two "Laird rams" before they can be seized by Confederate agents in England. Previously, Adams warned his hosts in no uncertain terms that "it would be superfluous for me to point out to your lordship that this is war." Government seizure of these heavily armed vessels ends a prolonged diplomatic sore point between London and Washington.

September 6
MILITARY: Confederate forces manning batteries Wagner and Gregg on Morris Island, Charleston Harbor, South Carolina, are secretly evacuated by General Pierre G. T. Beauregard. This final act concludes 60 days of near continuous bombardment by Union land and naval forces—one third of the 900 defenders have become casualties.

September 7
MILITARY: A small Confederate battery of 42 men under 20-year-old Lieutenant Richard W. Dowling, 1st Texas Heavy Artillery, engages a 4,000-man amphibious expedition under General William B. Franklin at the mouth of the Sabine River. Dowling allows the vessel to approach to within close range before opening fire with his masked batteries at 4:00 P.M. Within minutes two Union gunboats are forced to strike their colors and the rest dejectedly sail back to New Orleans.
NAVAL: Admiral John A. B. Dahlgren demands the surrender of Fort Sumter in Charleston harbor, South Carolina, and once it refuses he conducts a personal reconnaissance in force with the ironclads USS *Weehawken* and *New Ironsides*. After *Weehawken* grounds in the channel, the *New Ironsides* interposes itself between Fort Moultrie and the stricken vessel, taking 50 hits. Both vessels eventually return to safety.

September 9
DIPLOMACY: The British government formally initiates steps to prevent the two "Laird rams" from leaving the country or entering Confederate service.
MILITARY: General James Longstreet's I Corps of 15,000 veteran troops begins loading into trains in Virginia for a nine-day trek to Lafayette, Georgia, to reinforce General Braxton Bragg in Tennessee.

The strategic city of Chattanooga, Tennessee, surrenders to the Army of the Cumberland under General William S. Rosecrans without a shot being fired. General Braxton Bragg and the Army of Tennessee then fall back 28 miles to Lafayette, Georgia, to await reinforcements form the east.

NAVAL: Admiral John A. B. Dahlgren launches a nighttime assault against Fort Sumter, Charleston harbor, South Carolina, with 413 sailors and U.S. Marines under Commander Thomas H. Stevens. The Southerners, having earlier recovered a codebook from the sunken USS *Keokuk,* decipher Union signals and anticipate their attack. The Federals are consequently rebuffed with a loss of 100 prisoners.

September 10

MILITARY: Confederate forces under General Sterling Price evacuate Little Rock, Arkansas, for nearby Rockport, whereupon General Frederick Steele's Federals advance and establish a pro-Union administration there. This is the latest blow to the Confederacy, still reeling from the loss of Vicksburg, and it imperils the Trans-Mississippi Department under General Edmund Kirby-Smith.

September 11

POLITICS: President Abraham Lincoln authorizes General Andrew Johnson, military governor of Tennessee, to form a civilian government. Lincoln also declines to accept General Ambrose E. Burnside's latest attempt to resign.

September 13

MILITARY: General Braxton Bragg orders General Leonidas K. Polk to attack and overwhelm the isolated Union XXI Corps under General Thomas L. Crittenden at Lee and Gordon's Mills in northern Georgia. Polk, however, dithers and fails to maneuver in a timely fashion, so this part of the widely scattered Army of the Cumberland escapes annihilation. General William S. Rosecrans finally recognizes the danger and orders his army to concentrate.

September 18

MILITARY: The Army of the Cumberland and the Army of Tennessee confront each other across Chickamauga Creek, Georgia. For once Confederate forces outnumber the Federals, having massed 68,000 men to a Union tally of 58,000. General Braxton Bragg seeks to impose himself between General William S. Rosecrans and his main supply base at Chattanooga, Tennessee, but skirmishes with Union cavalry along Reed's and Alexander's bridges delay the move a full day.

September 19

MILITARY: The Battle of Chickamauga begins once advanced elements of General George H. Thomas's XIV Corps encounter Confederate cavalry under General Nathan B. Forrest. As fighting escalates both General Braxton Bragg and General William S. Rosecrans cancel their respective plans for the day and continually feed new units into an ever-expanding fray. The day's combat occasioned serious losses to both sides and little else. That evening, following the arrival of General James Longstreet's veteran I Corps, Bragg appoints him to command his left wing while General Leonidas K. Polk leads the right.

September 20

MILITARY: General Braxton Bragg intends to renew combat at Chickamauga at dawn, but confusion and delays preclude any Confederate action before 9:00

A.M. The pattern of fighting resembles that of the previous day, and another bloody stalemate appears in the offing until fate intervenes. General William S. Rosecrans is mistakenly informed that a gap has developed in the center of his line so he orders General Thomas J. Wood's division to plug it. No sooner does Wood redeploy than General James Longstreet's I Corps burst through, arrayed six brigades deep. This unexpected onslaught completely sweeps away the Union center and right, carrying off Rosecrans and several ranking leaders in a tumultuous retreat. Only the XIV Corps of General George H. Thomas, which assumed strong defensive positions along Snodgrass Hill, holds its ground against steep odds. This is the bloodiest day of the war in the West with Union casualties of 16,179 to a Southern tally of 17,804. Bragg's lackluster leadership causes further rifts in an already fractious chain of command.

September 21

POLITICS: President Abraham Lincoln repeatedly orders General Ambrose E. Burnside at Knoxville, Tennessee, to reinforce General William S. Rosecrans's shattered army at Chattanooga, but he refuses to budge.

September 22

MILITARY: General William S. Rosecrans continues rallying the Army of the Cumberland at Chattanooga, Tennessee, while General Ulysses S. Grant dispatches three divisions of the XV Corps from Vicksburg, Mississippi, to assist him. Meanwhile, the Confederate Army of Tennessee leisurely occupies the high ground around the city to commence a siege.

September 24

DIPLOMACY: The Confederate government appoints Ambrose D. Mann its special agent to the Holy See in Rome.

NAVAL: A total of eight Russian warships gradually arrive and visit New York City. They are seeking refuge in American ports as Great Britain and France are threatening war over the Polish insurrection, although the move is widely interpreted throughout the North as a sign of diplomatic support. Another squadron of six vessels eventually anchors in San Francisco, California, and the Russians are warmly received by the political establishment.

September 25

POLITICS: President Abraham Lincoln castigates General Ambrose E. Burnside at Knoxville, Tennessee, for not reinforcing Union forces besieged at Chattanooga. "Having struggled," he write, "to get you to assist General Rosecrans, and you have repeatedly declared you would do it, and yet you steadily move to the contrary way." Upon further reflection the letter is not sent.

September 27

MILITARY: President Abraham Lincoln again implores General Ambrose E. Burnside at Knoxville, Tennessee, to forward reinforcements to assist General William S. Rosecrans at Chattanooga. "My order to you meant simply that you should save Rosecrans from being crushed out, believing if he lost his position, you could not hold East Tennessee in any event."

General Braxton Bragg, determined to starve out the Army of the Cumberland from Chattanooga, Tennessee, orders General Joseph Wheeler's cavalry to raid tenuous Union lines of communication throughout the 60-mile-long Sequatchie Valley.

October 1
POLITICS: President Abraham Lincoln instructs General John M. Schofield, commanding Union forces in Missouri, to place renewed emphasis on the restoration of civilian rule and domestic tranquillity. "Your immediate duty, in regard to Missouri, now is to advance the efficiency of that establishment and to so use it, as far as practicable, to compel the excited people there to leave one another alone."

October 3
POLITICS: President Abraham Lincoln designates the last Thursday in November Thanksgiving Day.
SLAVERY: Secretary of War Edwin M. Stanton authorizes liberated African-American slaves to enlist in Maryland, Tennessee, and Missouri.

October 5
NAVAL: The CSS *David*, a torpedo boat with an especially low silhouette and equipped with an exploding spar, steams out of Charleston Harbor, South Carolina, at night and intends to fatally jab USS *New Ironsides* below the waterline. That vessel is struck and sustains heavy damage while the *David*, its boilers extinguished by the blast, drifts helplessly alongside its victim for several minutes before escaping.

October 6
MILITARY: Confederate guerrillas under William C. Quantrill attack what they thought was an isolated Union outpost at Baxter Springs, Kansas. Dressed in captured blue uniforms, they trot over to a column of 100 men and several wagons before shooting. Only General James G. Blunt and a third of his command manage to escape; the remainder are captured and then murdered.

October 9
DIPLOMACY: The British government apprehends the so-called *North Carolina* and *Mississippi*, the two formidable "Laird rams" nearing construction at Birkenhead, England, rather than risk a possible war with the United States.
MILITARY: General Joseph Wheeler ends his spectacular dash through the Sequatchie Valley by recrossing the Tennessee River at Muscle Shoals, Alabama. In a week he guts Union supply lines, inflicts 2,000 casualties, captures more than 1,000 wagons, burns five bridges, tears up miles of track, and ruins millions of dollars in equipment. This spectacular raid nearly throttles the Army of the Cumberland, already on half-rations.

October 10
MILITARY: President Jefferson Davis arrives at Chattanooga, Tennessee, to confer with General Braxton Bragg over military strategy. He is also there to quell seething unrest between Bragg and many senior subordinates.

October 13
POLITICS: Republican governors prevail during elections held in Indiana, Iowa, and Ohio. Foremost among these is Andrew Curtin, Pennsylvania's pro-war administrator and staunch ally of President Abraham Lincoln. By contrast, Peace Democrat Clement L. Vallandigham, who ran for the Ohio governorship while exiled in Canada, is roundly trounced by a pro-war Republican.

October 14

MILITARY: General Ambrose P. Hill, tramping through Warrenrton, Virginia, perceives the rearguard of General George G. Meade strung out and fording the Broad Run at Bristoe Station. He decides to attack at once, unaware that the entire II Corps of General Gouverneur K. Warren lays in wait behind a railroad embankment at right angles to his approach. The Confederate attack, thoroughly enfiladed, collapses after 40 minutes with a loss of 1,361 men. The Federals suffer only 548 casualties.

October 15

NAVAL: The day before it is to be committed to combat, the experimental Confederate submarine CSS *Hunley* disastrously founders a second time in Charleston harbor, killing all seven crew members including Horace L. Hunley, its inventor. Nonetheless, General Pierre G. T. Beauregard orders the craft recovered and refitted.

October 16

MILITARY: President Abraham Lincoln, acting through the offices of General in Chief Henry W. Halleck, urges General George G. Meade to attack General Robert E. Lee's forces, but he continues resisting such prodding. Lee, meanwhile, falls back and assumes strong defensive positions along the Rappahannock River in Virginia.

October 17

MILITARY: General William S. Rosecrans is formally relieved of command from the Army of the Cumberland and succeeded by General George H. Thomas. The new commander calmly reviews the perilous situation of his army at Chattanooga, Tennessee, and declares "We will hold the town 'till we starve."

October 19

MILITARY: As anticipated, Confederate cavalry under General J. E. B. Stuart is attacked by General Hugh J. Kilpatrick's Union troopers at Warrenton, Virginia. Just as fighting commences, General Fitzhugh Lee's 2nd Virginia Cavalry suddenly strikes the flank and rear of General George A. Custer's brigade while Stuart leads the 1st North Carolina forward at the charge. The Federals rapidly about face and run with vengeful Confederates hotly pursuing them. This embarrassing affair became jocularly known as the "Buckland Races."

October 23

MILITARY: General Ulysses S. Grant arrives at Chattanooga, Tennessee, and, accompanied by General George H. Thomas, he advances to within gunshot range of Confederate lines below Lookout Mountain for a peek at enemy dispositions. His curiosity satisfied, Grant next orders a new supply route established from Bridgeport to the beleaguered garrison, the so-called "Cracker Line."

POLITICS: President Jefferson Davis relieves General Leonidas K. Polk as corps commander of the Army of Tennessee, to end tensions with his superior, General Braxton Bragg. He is replaced by General William J. Hardee.

October 27

MILITARY: General Joseph Hooker commences operations to reopen the Tennessee River and thus facilitate the flow of Union supplies to Chattanooga, Tennessee. He also posts a force under General John W. Geary, XII Corps, at Wauhatchie Station to guard his line of communications.

1863

October 29

MILITARY: A predawn Confederate attack unfolds against Union positions at Wauhatchie Station, Tennessee. General Micah Jenkins's division of four brigades hits the Union camp hard in the darkness, but Federal troops under General John W. Geary rally and, by firing at muzzle flashes, resist stoutly. By 3:00 A.M., Jenkins has retreated back to Lookout Mountain; the all-important "Cracker Line" survives intact.

November 2

POLITICS: A Pennsylvania committee, tasked with organizing festivities surrounding the dedication of a Union cemetery for soldiers fallen in the Battle of Gettysburg, invites President Abraham Lincoln to attend the ceremony, scheduled for November 19. To their delight and surprise, the chief executive accepts the invitation, and he begins working on a short speech to codify his justification for the war effort.

November 3

MILITARY: At Bayou Borbeau, Louisiana, three Federal divisions of General William B. Franklin's XIX Corps encamp carelessly and beyond mutual supporting distance. General Richard Taylor, though outnumbered two-to-one, masses his Confederates for a sudden attack upon General Stephen G. Burbridge's exposed division. Burbridge, unable to reform his crumbling line, falls back three miles to the camp of General George F. McGinnis for support.

November 5

SLAVERY: President Abraham Lincoln rebukes General Nathaniel P. Banks for his tardy efforts at reestablishing civilian government in Louisiana which, he insists, must assure African Americans "On the question of permanent freedom."

November 7

MILITARY: The Army of the Potomac pushes two bridges over the Rappahannock River, Virginia, and runs into stiff fights at Kelly's Ford and Rappahannock Station. General William H. French, commanding the I, II, and III Corps, proceeds across the River at Kelly's Ford en masse, catching the Confederate division of General Robert Rodes by surprise. North Carolina troops guarding the ford are overwhelmed by the sudden attack and largely captured, leaving Union forces now firmly established on the south bank of the Rappahannock.

Five miles upstream, General John Sedgwick moves his V and VI Corps rapidly against Rappahannock Station, defended by the celebrated "Louisiana Tigers" of Colonel Harry T. Hays and a division under General Robert Hoke. Heavy fighting stops at nightfall, and General Robert E. Lee somewhat naturally assumes that the enemy would not attack further that night, so he declines to reinforce the bridgehead. That same evening, through a driving downpour, Sedgwick unleashes his 6th Maine in a bayonet charge that completely startles the "Tigers." The Confederate defenders are crushed with 1,600 prisoners taken, forcing Lee to withdraw to Culpeper Court House.

November 11

POLITICS: President Jefferson Davis, ever concerned about the situation before Chattanooga, Tennessee, cautions General Braxton Bragg to "not allow the enemy

1863

to get up reinforcements before striking him, if it can be avoided." Defeat here might lead to another thrust into the Confederate heartland.

November 14

MILITARY: General James Longstreet's 15,000 Confederates begin crossing the Tennessee River at Loudoun, Tennessee, en route to Knoxville. Meanwhile, General Ambrose E. Burnside gallops into the town beforehand to personally evacuate the 5,000 Union troops stationed there and shepherds them back to Knoxville. A curious parallel race unfolds as the two forces—almost within gunshot of each other—slog through ankle-deep mud to reach the city first.

November 15

MILITARY: The I Corps of General James Longstreet and a division of Union troops under General Ambrose E. Burnside march on through driving rain and deep mud to reach Knoxville, Tennessee, first. Throughout their arduous ordeal the contestants are separated only by one mile and a bend in the Tennessee River. Burnside, anxious to avoid being trapped outside the city, redoubles his efforts to reach Campbell's Station ahead of the enemy. Longstreet, meanwhile, dispatches General Lafayette McLaw's division to capture the crossroads ahead of him.

November 16

MILITARY: The Confederate corps of General James Longstreet and a retiring Union division under General Ambrose E. Burnside depart Lenoir, Tennessee, in the early morning darkness. Burnside, feeling he is losing the race, orders his baggage burned to pick up speed. The Union column fortuitously reaches Campbell's Station just 15 minutes ahead of the Confederates and deploys to give battle. Longstreet then dispatches the brigade of General Evander M. Law around the Union position to strike it from behind while another division under General Lafayette McLaw strikes Burnside's right. Both attacks are repelled in heavy fighting, and Longstreet finally concedes.

November 18

POLITICS: President Abraham Lincoln, somewhat depressed over the illness of his son Tad, boards a special train that whisks him to Gettysburg, Pennsylvania, for the purpose of dedicating a military cemetery.

November 19

MILITARY: As Union forces of General Ambrose E. Burnside race to fortify the city of Knoxville, Tennessee, he orders a cavalry brigade of 700 men under General William P. Sanders to contest the Confederate advance under General James Longstreet. Sanders does exactly that and contains his antagonists for several hours before being killed, the only Southern-born Union general to fall. Fort Loudoun is subsequently renamed Fort Sanders in his honor.

POLITICS: A gathering of 15,000 citizens at Gettysburg, Pennsylvania, is harangued by stirring oratory by Edward Everett over the course of two hours. Onlookers are next greeted by the spectacle of a gaunt, towering President Abraham Lincoln striding over to the podium. In only two minutes he completes his "Gettysburg Address," one of the most seminal political speeches in all history. "Four score and seven years ago our fathers brought forth, upon this continent, a new nation, conceived in liberty, and dedicated to the proposition that all men are created equal," it began. The audience listened in raptured silence, applauding lightly and not fully comprehending the import of what they had just heard, but in only 272 words, Lincoln codifies the ideals of the American republic and the absolute necessity for preserving it.

November 20

POLITICS: Unhappy over his recent address at Gettysburg, Pennsylvania, President Abraham Lincoln contacts Edward Everett saying "I am pleased to know that, in your opinion, the little I did say was not a failure."

November 23

MILITARY: General Ulysses S. Grant, prior to assaulting the main Confederate defenses of General Braxton Bragg along Missionary Ridge, Tennessee, orchestrates a clever reconnaissance in force near the enemy's center. He orders General George H. Thomas to parade the IV Corps in full view of enemy positions along Orchard Knob and, at precisely 1:30 P.M., Union forces suddenly lurch forward, completely dispersing their astonished opponents. This easy success allows Grant to deploy his troops at the very foot of Lookout Mountain, and he also employs Orchard Knob as his headquarters for the remainder of the campaign.

November 24

MILITARY: At 8:00 A.M., General Joseph Hooker masses his three divisions—12,000 men—to the foot of Lookout Mountain, Tennessee, and begins scaling toward the 1,100-foot summit. Confederates under General Carter L. Stevenson, who can scarcely muster 2,693 men to oppose them, resist fiercely but ultimately yield to the Federal juggernaut. By evening Hooker has achieved all his objectives and the following morning, when a clinging fog finally disperses, Union leaders are relieved to behold the Stars and Stripes flying boldly from the summit.

November 25

MILITARY: At Chattanooga, Tennessee, the final struggle between General Ulysses S. Grant, with 64,000 men, and General Braxton Bragg, commanding 46,000, unfolds. At 10:00 A.M. General William T. Sherman takes 16,000 men on a concerted drive against the Confederate right anchored upon Missionary Ridge, but his lack of progress induces Grant to mount diversions elsewhere to prevent Bragg from shifting reinforcements to his right. General Joseph Hooker's command then attacks through Rossville gap from Lookout Mountain on Bragg's left to threaten the Southern rear, but he is delayed by the necessity of building a bridge. Grant finally orders General George H. Thomas to advance and seize Confederate rifle pits fronting their main position along Missionary Ridge. Thomas quickly overruns the defenders and then—without orders—continues charging up the slope, driving the enemy before him. The Confederate stranglehold on Chattanooga is decisively and dramatically ended through Grant's bold stroke. Union casualties are 5,335, only marginally lighter that the Confederate tally of 6,687.

November 26

MILITARY: Five corps of the Army of the Potomac under General George G. Meade successfully cross the Rapidan River, Virginia, covered by a fog. Meade is now counting on the speed and stealth of his 85,000 men to crush the widely dispersed right wing of the Army of Northern Virginia before it can concentrate to oppose him. However, events quickly go awry as the marching order breaks down, units become entangled, and valuable time is lost. The Southerners react quickly and effectively to the new threat.

November 27
MILITARY: No sooner has the Army of the Potomac successfully crossed the Rapidan River than General William H. French's III Corps takes the wrong road and spends several hours countermarching about. The delay allows the Army of Northern Virginia to deploy the division of General Edward Johnson at Payne's Farm, Virginia, and heavy fighting erupts. Elements of General Ambrose P. Hill's III Corps and General Jubal A. Early's II Corps also arrive, at which point Meade suspends the action. Confederate losses are 545 while the Union tally is not recorded.

Confederate General Patrick R. Cleburne, mustering only 4,157 men, confronts a force twice his size under General Joseph Hooker at Ringgold Gap, Georgia. The Federals are immediately blasted back with losses while a column is dispatched to ascend the mountain of Cleburne's flank. These too stumble headlong into a clever ambush and are sent scampering back down the slope. Cleburne is finally ordered by General William J. Hardee to withdraw, but his stiffly fought rear guard buys the Southerners four precious hours and inflicts 507 Union casualties. Cleburne sustains 20 dead, 190 wounded, and 11 missing.

November 29
MILITARY: At 6:00 A.M., the Confederates launch a desperate attack against Fort Sanders at Knoxville, Tennessee, despite frightfully cold weather. Three brigades of infantry go forward as ordered but, lacking ladders, prove unable to surmount the deep, ice-filled ditch surrounding the works. General James Longstreet loses 129 killed, 458 wounded, and 226 missing, while the defenders endure five killed and eight wounded.

November 30
MILITARY: President Jefferson Davis grants General Braxton Bragg's request that he be relieved of command in the Army of Tennessee at Dalton, Georgia, and he is temporarily succeeded by General William J. Hardee.

December 1
MILITARY: Notorious Southern spy Belle Boyd, suffering from typhoid fever, is again released from a Federal prison in Washington, D.C., and warned to steer clear of Union territory.
TECHNOLOGY: Samuel D. Gooddale of Cincinnati, Ohio, receives a patent for his stereoscope, which allows for three-dimensional views of photographs.

December 3
MILITARY: General James Longstreet's I Corps abandons its siege of Knoxville, Tennessee, and enters into winter quarters at nearby Greenville. From this position he is at liberty to remain in the theater or march to rejoin General Robert E. Lee's main force in Virginia.

December 7
POLITICS: The 4th Session of the First Confederate Congress gathers in Richmond, Virginia. President Jefferson Davis there acknowledges the failures of the previous year but declares "The patriotism of the people has proven equal to every sacrifice demanded by their country's need."

December 8

POLITICS: To exacerbate the growing rift in Southern politics, President Abraham Lincoln addresses the opening of the 38th Congress and proffers his Proclamation of Amnesty and Reconstruction to all Southerners willing to take a loyal oath. In it he offers to recognize the sitting government of any seceded state provided that at least 10 percent of all male voters submit to the oath and abolish slavery. This amnesty does not apply to high ranking Confederate officials or former army officers who resign to fight for the South, but Radical Republicans in Congress find its tone too conciliatory.

December 12

POLITICS: Henceforth, the Confederate government refuses to accept any supplies sent from the North to Union captives.

December 14

MILITARY: General James Longstreet attacks Bean's Station, Tennessee, at 2:00 A.M., startling but not dislodging Union cavalry under General James M. Shackleford. At length Shackleford conducts an orderly withdrawal through Bean's Gap to Blain's Cross Roads and digs in behind a rail breastwork. Fighting in harsh winter weather inflicts roughly 200 casualties on either side.

POLITICS: President Abraham Lincoln grants Mrs. Mary Todd—his sister-in-law—a general amnesty after she visits the White House and takes a loyalty oath.

December 16

MILITARY: President Jefferson Davis, forgiving past difficulties, appoints General Joseph E. Johnston to succeeded General William J. Hardee as commander of the Army of Tennessee. General Leonidas K. Polk is also promoted to head of the Army of Mississippi.

December 17

POLITICS: President Abraham Lincoln promulgates plans for a Federal Bureau of Emancipation to assist liberated African Americans. Congress, however, fails to enact the requisite legislation until March 1865.

December 18

POLITICS: President Abraham Lincoln, displeased with General John M. Schofield's handling of civilian affairs in Missouri, suggests to Secretary of War Edwin M. Stanton that he be simultaneously relieved and promoted to major general, thereby avoiding any ruffled feathers.

December 27

MILITARY: General Joseph E. Johnston arrives at Dalton, Georgia, to take charge of the Confederate Department of Tennessee and its attendant and much battered army.

December 28

POLITICS: The Confederate Congress in Richmond, Virginia, abolishes the practice of hiring draft substitutions and also modifies the detested tax in kind.

December 31

POLITICS: President Jefferson Davis appoints North Carolina senator George Davis as interim Confederate attorney general to replace outgoing Wade Keyes.

1863

1864

BUSINESS: George Presbury Rowell founds the nation's first advertising agency in Boston, Massachusetts.

CONSERVATION: George Perkins Marsh, a noted lawyer and scholar, publishes *Man and Nature, or, Physical Geography as Modified by Human Action*; this is a pioneering appeal for land conservation and geological study.

EDUCATION: The Columbia Institution for the Deaf, Dumb, and Blind is established in Washington, D.C., by Congress and at the behest of Edward Miner Gallaudet.

The University of Kansas is founded at Lawrence, Kansas.

GENERAL: The phrase "In God We Trust" appears for the first time on minted two-cent pieces.

JOURNALISM: The *Frontier Scout* is published at Fort Union, North Dakota, as that territory's first newspaper.

LABOR: Cigar makers and iron molders both form their own respective unions.

RELIGION: The Tremont Temple is established in Boston, Massachusetts, by Baptists; it features significant lay participation in all church matters.

SPORTS: Former boxing champion John Morrissey establishes the Saratoga Race Track at Saratoga, New York, and also organizes the first stakes races.

The Park Place Croquet Club of Brooklyn, New York, is the first such organization in the country.

The first recorded curve ball is thrown by William A. Cumming of the Brooklyn Stars in a game against the Brooklyn Atlantics.

TECHNOLOGY: Steel made from the British Bessemer process is introduced to the United States at Wyandotte, Michigan. The plant in question manufactures high-grade steel rails for the railroads.

TRANSPORTATION: The New York State legislature rejects Hugh B. Wilson's request for a franchise to construct the first subway system beneath New York City.

January 2

SLAVERY: Irish-born general Patrick R. Cleburne petitions for the arming of African Americans in the Confederate army to address endemic manpower shortages. Not only does President Jefferson Davis ignore the recommendation but he deliberately denies Cleburne his well-deserved promotion to lieutenant general because of it.

January 4

MILITARY: President Jefferson Davis instructs General Robert E. Lee to begin requisitioning food from civilians to feed his troops as it becomes necessary.

January 5

INDIAN: Colonel Christopher "Kit" Carson begins his protracted winter campaign against hostile Navajo in the Canon de Chelly region of the New Mexico Territory. General James H. Carleton, commanding the department, anxiously wires government officials that his numerous prisoners are suffering from want of winter clothing and requests stocks from the Indian Department.

POLITICS: More than 1,000 African-American citizens of New Orleans, Louisiana, including a handful of surviving War of 1812 veterans, petition President Abraham Lincoln for the right to vote.

January 7
POLITICS: President Abraham Lincoln, beset by a rash of army desertions, invariably commutes the death sentences of offenders and insists "I am trying to evade the butchering business lately."

January 11
SLAVERY: Senator John B. Henderson of Missouri proposes a joint resolution for the abolition of slavery, which ultimately becomes the Thirteenth Amendment to the U.S. Constitution.

January 13
MUSIC: Stephen Foster, one of the nation's most popular songwriters, dies in New York City at the age of 37. One of his last compositions was the noted and popular "Beautiful Dreamer."
POLITICS: President Abraham Lincoln instructs generals Quincy A. Gilmore in Florida and Nathaniel P. Banks in Louisiana to begin reconstituting civil authority "with all possible dispatch."

President Jefferson Davis advises General Joseph E. Johnston against falling back from his present strong position at Dalton, Georgia, declaring "I trust you will not deem it necessary to adopt such a measure."

January 19
POLITICS: The pro-Union Arkansas constitutional convention embraces antislavery provisions in its new document.

January 20
POLITICS: President Abraham Lincoln advises General Frederick Steele, commanding the District of Arkansas, to schedule free elections as soon as possible to reestablish a free civilian government.

January 21
POLITICS: A gathering of pro-Union citizens in Nashville, Tennessee, proposes a constitutional convention bent on abolishing slavery.

January 22
POLITICS: Isaac Murphy becomes governor of the free-state portions of Arkansas following a vote by the state convention.

January 23
POLITICS: President Abraham Lincoln approves a policy whereby plantation owners must recognize freedom for all former slaves and hire them on the basis of contract law.

January 26
DIPLOMACY: William L. Drayton, U.S. Minister to France, expresses embarrassment over the presence of several Confederate cruisers operating in French waters and his government's inability to deal with them at present.

January 27
POLITICS: President Jefferson Davis summons General Braxton Bragg to Richmond, Virginia, for consultation as long as his "health permits."

January 28
Military: General Jubal A. Early directs generals Edward L. Thomas and Thomas L. Rosser on a combined infantry/cavalry raiding force from New Market, Virginia, toward Union positions in the Allegheny Mountains. Their goal is to secure forage for the horses and the cattle to feed the men.

January 31
Politics: President Abraham Lincoln again urges General Nathaniel P. Banks at New Orleans, Louisiana, to begin reinstituting civilian authority, leaving him "at liberty to adopt any rule which shall admit to vote any unquestionably free state men and none others. And yet I do wish they would all take the oath."

February 1
Military: The House of Representatives resurrects the rank of lieutenant general, U.S. Army, with Ulysses S. Grant in mind.

General George E. Pickett attacks Union forces under General Innis N. Palmer at Batchelder's Creek, North Carolina, inflicting 326 casualties and forcing the Northerners back into New Bern. However, two Confederate columns under General Seth M. Baton and Colonel James Dearing perceive Federal defenses at Fort Anderson as too formidable and the attack is canceled.
Politics: President Abraham Lincoln authorizes a draft of 500,000 men to serve three years or for the duration of the conflict.

February 3
Politics: To better suppress espionage, desertion, and disloyalty, President Jefferson Davis recommends suspension of writs of habeas corpus in cases arising from such charges.

February 6
Politics: The Confederate Congress outlaws the importation of luxuries or the possession of U.S. paper money. It also mandates that half of tobacco and food exports must be surrendered to government agents before ships are allowed to clear ports.

February 7
Diplomacy: William Preston becomes the Confederate envoy to French-controlled Mexico. The Confederacy supports Napoleon III's occupation of the country and its puppet emperor Maximilian in the hope of gaining diplomatic recognition and possible military intervention.

February 9
Arts: President Abraham Lincoln sits through a photographic session; one portrait is subsequently engraved and utilized on the U.S. five-dollar bill.

February 12
Military: President Abraham Lincoln entertains General Hugh K. Kilpatrick at the White House, whereupon the latter discusses plans for a possible raid against Richmond, Virginia, to free Union prisoners kept under squalid conditions there. The president listens intently to the blustering trooper and eventually grants his approval.

February 14
Military: Meridian, Mississippi, falls without resistance to Union forces led by General William T. Sherman, who covers 150 miles in 11 days. The corps of

General Leonidas K. Polk, badly outnumbered, gives ground before it. Sherman then begins systematically destroying all buildings, supplies, and railroads in his earliest application of what becomes known as "total war." Ultimately, 155 miles of track, 61 bridges, and 20 locomotives are laid waste.

February 15

POLITICS: The Confederate Congress appropriates $5 million for a sabotage campaign based in Canada. It is to be orchestrated by Thomas C. Hines, who intends to meet with, and coordinate his actions with, the Peace Democrats from the North. Meanwhile, President Jefferson Davis evinces concern that General William T. Sherman might march from Meridian, Mississippi, and directly into Montgomery, Alabama.

February 17

NAVAL: The submarine CSS *Hunley* under Lieutenant George E. Dixon sinks the 1,934-ton Union screw sloop USS *Housatonic* under Captain Charles W. Picketing in Charleston Harbor, South Carolina. *Hunley* apparently survives the explosion long enough to signal to shore that it is returning, then inexplicably sinks, killing all hands. *Housatonic* also enjoys the melancholy distinction of being the first warship in history lost to a submarine attack.

POLITICS: The Confederate Congress suspends writs of habeas corpus as they relate to arrests made under the authority of the president or secretary of war. They also expand the draft to include all white males between the ages of 17 and 50. Another act authorizes the employment of African Americans as army laborers.

Confederate vice president Alexander H. Stephens continues protesting the suspension of habeas corpus, insisting it is "Far better that our country be overrun by the enemy, our cities sacked and burned, and our land laid desolate, than that the people should suffer the citadel of their liberties to be entered and taken by professed friends." In light of this opposition, the Georgia legislature counters with a resolution reaffirming that state's support for the war effort and all it may entail.

February 18

POLITICS: Abraham Lincoln declares the port of Brownsville, Texas, open for business and terminates the Federal blockade there.

February 19

SOCIETAL: The Knights of Pythias, a fraternal and benevolent society, is founded in Washington, D.C., by Justus H. Rathbone and 12 other associates.

February 20

MILITARY: The Battle of Olustee, Florida, transpires between generals Thomas Seymour and Joseph Finnegan, with both sides numbering roughly 5,000 men apiece. The Northerners advance upon Finnegan's force, strongly dug in behind entrenchments, but Seymour orders them to charge. The attackers are beaten back with loss and Seymour uses his remaining bridge under Colonel James Montgomery to cover his retreat. He loses 1,861 men—a staggering loss rate of 34 percent—while Finnegan sustains 946, or 20 percent. Consequently, Florida is secured for the Confederacy.

NAVAL: Admiral John A. B. Dahlgren, greatly alarmed by the loss of the USS *Housatonic* to a Confederate submarine attack, suggests to Navy Secretary Gideon Welles that the government offer a $20,000–30,000 reward for the capture or destruction of any such craft. "They are worth more to us than that," he concludes.

February 22

MILITARY: Confederate cavalry under General Nathan B. Forrest attacks and defeats a larger Union rear guard under General William Sooy Smith near Okolona, Mississippi. However, resistance stiffens as the Southerners engage the main Union body and several of Forrest's charges are bloodily repelled. Two Union countercharges likewise fail with the loss of six cannon, and Smith ultimately retreats in the direction of Pontotoc.

POLITICS: Senator Samuel Pomeroy of Kansas, viewing President Abraham Lincoln as unelectable, begins a covert attempt to have Secretary of the Treasury Salmon P. Chase drafted as the Republican Party's standard bearer for this year. However, once his "Pomeroy Circular" is printed, it creates an uproar and a backlash against Chase, who promptly ends his candidacy for the presidency. He also offers to resign but Lincoln declines to accept.

Michael Hahn is elected governor of the free-state portions of Louisiana.

February 23

POLITICS: Secretary of the Treasury Salmon P. Chase absents himself from cabinet meetings in light of disclosures surrounding the recent "Pomeroy Circular."

February 24

POLITICS: President Abraham Lincoln signs legislation to compensate slave owners in Union-controlled regions by paying them $300 for each of their slaves who enlist in the Union army.

The U.S. Senate, following the House of Representatives, votes to create the rank of lieutenant general.

February 25

MILITARY: General John M. Palmer and his XVI Corps continue probing Confederate positions at Buzzard Roost Gap, Georgia, but encounter heavy resistance. After a flanking move by General Jefferson C. Davis along the western side of the imposing ridge, Palmer calls off the attempt and withdraws for the evening. Union losses are 289 casualties to 140 Confederates, but afterward General George H. Thomas divines the strategy of sending Union troops through Snake Gap Creek, 15 miles behind Confederate lines, to outflank the defenders.

February 26

POLITICS: President Abraham Lincoln reaffirms his faith in General Benjamin F. Butler and also commutes all death sentences for desertion to imprisonment for the duration of the war.

February 27

MILITARY: Andersonville Prison, near Americus, Georgia, a 16½-acre log stockade, receives its first Union captives. Crowded and squalid from the onset, it gains infamy as the worst prison site in the Confederacy.

February 29

POLITICS: The U.S. Congress formally revives the rank of lieutenant general at the behest of President Abraham Lincoln.

1864

Ulysses S. Grant *(National Archives)*

March 1

MILITARY: A Union cavalry column under General Hugh J. Kilpatrick, meeting resistance as he approaches the Confederate capital of Richmond, Virginia, suddenly cancels the raid, veers away, and recrosses the Chickahominy Creek. Colonel Ulric Dahlgren, meanwhile, finding the James River swollen and impassible, decides to shift his attack from the east, then also suspends the attack and begins circling back to rejoin Kilpatrick.

POLITICS: President Abraham Lincoln nominates General Ulysses S. Grant for the rank of lieutenant general.

March 2

POLITICS: The U.S. Senate confers the rank of lieutenant general on Ulysses S. Grant.

March 4

POLITICS: The U.S. Senate confirms Andrew Johnson as governor of Tennessee.

Pro-Union governor Michael Hahn is sworn into office at New Orleans, Louisiana.

March 5

POLITICS: Confederate authorities issue new regulations mandating that all Southern vessels donate half their cargo capacity to government shipments. This is undertaken as much to reduce wartime profiteering as to alleviate mounting supply shortages.

March 8

MILITARY: General Ulysses S. Grant formally accepts his commission as lieutenant general in a ceremony at the White House, then meets and confers with President Abraham Lincoln for the first time. Grant thus becomes the first American military leader to hold such lofty rank since George Washington.

March 9

MILITARY: General Ulysses S. Grant succeeds General Henry W. Halleck as general in chief, with the latter being demoted to chief of staff. Furthermore, to maintain good relationships with the Army of the Potomac, Grant retains General George G. Meade as the commander of that force.

March 12

MILITARY: Sweeping leadership changes are finalized in the Union army with General Ulysses S. Grant in overall command of military operations, General Henry W. Halleck serving as chief of staff, General William T. Sherman leading the Military Division of the Mississippi, and General James B. McPherson heading both the Army and Department of the Tennessee.

NAVAL: Admiral David D. Porter leads a Union armada of 13 ironclads, four tinclads, and four wooden gunboats up the Red River, Louisiana, in concert with the Shreveport Expedition of General Nathaniel P. Banks. Meanwhile, army transports convey the 3rd Division, XVI Corps of General Andrew J. Smith up as an advanced force.

March 13
POLITICS: President Abraham Lincoln, after receiving a signed petition from African Americans in Louisiana, encourages Governor Michael Hahn to consider drafting a new state constitution that allows minorities to vote. Curiously, of the 1,000 blacks signing the document, no less than 27 had previously served under General Andrew Jackson in the War of 1812 with a promise of freedom that was subsequently reneged on.

March 15
POLITICS: Michael Hahn, newly elected governor of Louisiana, receives powers previously reserved for the military government as civilian authority is slowly revived and reinstituted. This event proves a forerunner of what ultimately transpires during Reconstruction in the postwar period.

March 18
MILITARY: General William T. Sherman formally gains appointment as commander of the Military Division of the Mississippi.
SLAVERY: Pro-Union Arkansas voters ratify a new constitution mandating the abolition of slavery.

March 19
POLITICS: The Georgia state legislature grants President Jefferson Davis a vote of confidence and, following the next significant Confederate victory, desires that peace talks be conducted with Washington, D.C, but solely on the basis of recognizing Southern independence.

March 21
POLITICS: President Abraham Lincoln approves legislation allowing the Nevada and Colorado territories to become states.

March 23
MILITARY: General Frederick Steele, ordered into the field by the War Department and beset by chronic supply shortages, reluctantly leads 10,400 Union troops out of Little Rock, Arkansas. His mission is to proceed east and link up with the Red River Expedition of General Nathaniel P. Banks. Steele objects to campaigning as the roads, such as they are, remain poor while his flanks are vulnerable to attack by hard-riding Confederate cavalry.

March 24
MILITARY: General Nathaniel P. Banks finally arrives at Alexandria, Louisiana, a week behind schedule, before leading the Union drive up the Red River toward Shreveport. He receives additional bad news in the form of declining water levels on the river itself, which jeopardizes continuing naval support from Admiral David D. Porter's gunboats. Undeterred, Banks elects to proceed.

March 25
MILITARY: General Nathan B. Forrest attacks and captures the town of Paducah, Kentucky, with his force of 2,800 troopers. Colonel Stephen G. Hicks, the garrison commander, refuses to surrender and withdraws his 665 men into the safety of

nearby Fort Anderson, where he repels a Confederate attack. Forrest then withdraws with 50 captives and 400 horses, some of which are confiscated from civilians.

March 27

MILITARY: Union prisoners begin arriving en masse at Camp Sumter in Andersonville, Georgia. Once filled to capacity, it becomes the most squalid and infamous prison camp throughout the South.

March 28

POLITICS: Charleston, Illinois, is the scene of violent antiwar rioting, aimed at Union soldiers on furlough. Throngs of Democrats gather to hear antiwar Congressional candidate John R. Eden speak, as hundreds of soldiers mill around in curiosity. Once liquor begins flowing, shots are suddenly exchanged between the two sides and Democrats under Sheriff John O'Hare begin retrieving hidden weapons from nearby wagons. Six men are killed and 20 injured by the Knights of the Golden Circle (Copperheads) before the violence is suppressed by additional troops. An additional 50 Democrats are arrested, with 29 held indefinitely by military authorities at Springfield until a clemency order from President Abraham Lincoln releases them.

March 29

POLITICS: President Abraham Lincoln prevails upon General George G. Meade to forsake a court of inquiry pertaining to his performance at the battle of Gettysburg. For several months now the general has weathered blistering attacks upon his leadership by the Northern press.

April 1

MILITARY: General Frederick Steele, having waited in vain for cavalry reinforcements under General John M. Thayer, departs Arkadelphia, Arkansas, and begins to march for the Red River, Louisiana. All men and animals under his command are already on half rations while his progress is dogged by Confederate cavalry under Joseph O. Shelby and John S. Marmaduke.

April 4

DIPLOMACY: In light of French aggression toward Mexico, the U.S. House of Representatives unanimously passes a resolution protesting the policies of Napoleon III. It reaffirms American resolve never to recognize a monarchical regime arising in the Western hemisphere at the behest of any European power, consistent with the Monroe Doctrine. The Congress also lends its moral support to rebel forces under President Benito Juarez.

April 6

MILITARY: The army of General Nathaniel P. Banks wends its way along the banks of the Red River and along a narrows toward Shreveport, Louisiana. The route is poorly chosen for Banks's army is strung out for miles in single file in the bayou wilderness and susceptible to attack by General Richard Taylor.

SLAVERY: The Convention of Louisiana, meeting in New Orleans, adopts a new state constitution abolishing slavery.

April 8

MILITARY: The Union Army of 18,000 men under General Nathaniel P. Banks moves along single file toward Mansfield, Louisiana, where it is suddenly attacked by 8,000 Confederates led by General Richard Taylor at Sabine Crossroads. Taylor observed how attenuated the Union force was and ordered his command forward.

The rebels crash through two Federal lines, overrunning Banks' artillery and wagon train, which they stop to plunder. Banks, soundly thrashed, retreats with a loss of 2,235 men. Taylor, in comparison, captures 20 cannon, 200 wagons, and 1,000 draft animals for less than 1,000 casualties.

April 9

MILITARY: Union strategy for an all-out push against the Confederacy is finalized by General Ulysses S. Grant into five major components: General Nathaniel P. Banks is to capture Mobile, Alabama; General William T. Sherman will drive deep into Georgia from Tennessee and seize Atlanta; General Franz Sigel is to advance down into the Shenandoah Valley, breadbasket of the Confederacy; and General Benjamin F. Butler will descend upon Richmond, Virginia, from the south bank of the James River. Most importantly, General George G. Meade's Army of the Potomac is to seek out and rivet their attention upon General Robert E. Lee and his Army of Northern Virginia.

POLITICS: The U.S. Senate approves the Thirteenth Amendment to the Constitution by a vote of 38 to six. The legislation, aimed at outlawing slavery, is then passed to the House of Representatives for ratification.

General Nathaniel P. Banks consolidates 15,000 men of his shaken army, soon reinforced by two veteran corps from General Andrew J. Smith's XVI Corps, along Pleasant Hill, Louisiana. General Richard Taylor then advances upon the Federals at 9:00 A.M. with 12,000 men and attacks. The rebels are soundly repulsed in stiff fighting and Taylor gradually withdraws, which rescues Banks from his previous defeat at Mansfield. Union losses are 1,506 to a Confederate tally of 1,621. The Northerners still continue retreating to Grand Ecore, spelling an end to the vaunted Red River Campaign.

April 10

MILITARY: Union forces under General Frederick Steele encounter stiff Confederate resistance from General Sterling Price at Prairie D'Ane, Arkansas, and a running battle ensues over the next four days. However, with the Red River campaign of General Nathaniel P. Banks now ignominiously defeated, Steele suddenly finds himself marooned deep behind enemy lines with few supplies and no prospect of reinforcements.

April 11

POLITICS: The pro-Union administration of Governor Isaac Murphy is inaugurated at Little Rock, Arkansas.

April 12

MILITARY: General Nathan B. Forrest leads 1,500 Confederate cavalry in an attack upon Fort Pillow, Tennessee, on the Mississippi River, then guarded by 557 Union soldiers, including 262 African Americans, under Major Lionel F. Booth. The Confederates succeed after a bloody fight, at which point many of the black soldiers are murdered. Confederate losses are 14 dead and 86 wounded, a pittance compared to the Federal tally of 231 killed, 100 wounded, and 226 captured—only 58 blacks are taken alive.

April 15

POLITICS: Governor Andrew Johnson of Tennessee delivers a speech in Knoxville endorsing the principles of emancipation.

1864

Nathan Bedford Forrest *(Library of Congress)*

April 17

MILITARY: General Ulysses S. Grant suspends all prisoner exchanges until the Confederates release identical numbers of Union captives—an impossible demand, given their restricted manpower. Confederate authorities strongly disagree with his dictates, and the practice of prisoner exchanges halts altogether, depriving the South of an important source of trained military manpower.

April 18

MILITARY: Confederate cavalry under General John S. Marmaduke detects a party of 1,170 Union soldiers near Poison Springs, Arkansas, and advances to give battle with 3,335 troopers. Southern numbers gradually assert themselves and the Federals suddenly break in panic and flee to the rear. Poison Springs is a significant Union defeat for it requires General Frederick Steele's army, at Camden, on the defensive, where it languishes on half rations.

April 19

NAVAL: The huge Confederate steam ram CSS *Albemarle* under Commander James W. Cooke attacks the Federal blockading squadron off Plymouth, North Carolina, sinking the USS *Southfield* and killing Commander C. W. Flusser. The surviving Union vessels then draw off, leaving the nearby army garrison unsupported.

POLITICS: The U.S. Congress passes legislation admitting Nebraska as a state.

April 20

MILITARY: The government reduces rations accorded to Southern prisoners of war in retaliation for mistreatment of Union captives.

General Robert F. Hoke attacks and captures 2,800 Union soldiers and a large quantity of supplies at Plymouth, North Carolina, after a three-day siege. Key to his success was the sudden appearance of the steam ram CSS *Ablemarle*, which bombarded the defenders from offshore. Confederate losses are 163 killed and 554 wounded.

April 21

POLITICS: President Abraham Lincoln confers with the governors of Ohio, Illinois, Indiana, and Iowa.

April 22

SLAVERY: President Jefferson Davis writes General Leonidas K. Polk respecting African-American prisoners. "If the negroes are escaped slaves, they should be held safely for recovery by their owners," he states, "If otherwise, inform me."

April 25

MILITARY: A force of 4,000 Confederate cavalry under General William L. Cabell surprises a Union wagon train at Mark's Mills, Arkansas, catching the armed guard of Colonel Francis M. Drake in a pincer. Cabell seizes 240 wagons and

1,700 prisoners as only 300 Federals escape back to their main force at Camden. Moreover, the enraged Southerners also murder 150 African-American slaves who had attached themselves to the column.

Outnumbered and nearly surrounded by Confederates under generals Edmund Kirby-Smith and Sterling Price, General Frederick Steele abandons Camden, Arkansas, and retreats to Little Rock. He begins methodically evacuating that night and cleverly slips past Confederate outposts without detection.

April 27
DIPLOMACY: President Jefferson Davis dispatches a special commissioner to Canada to help possibly negotiate a truce with the United States.

April 28
NAVAL: Admiral David D. Porter's flotilla remains trapped on the Red River by receding water levels. The admiral himself is resigned to the necessity of scuttling his entire squadron to prevent its capture, and he advises Secretary of the Navy Gideon Welles that "you may judge my feelings at having to perform so painful a duty."

April 29
NAVAL: Admiral David D. Porter's gunboat flotilla is almost completely stranded on the Red River near Alexandria, Louisiana, by receding waters. Fortunately, succor arrives in the form of army engineer Colonel Joseph Bailey, who proposes building a series of dams to raise the water. The result is one of the best improvisations of the entire war.
POLITICS: The U.S. Congress increases all import duties by 50 percent to better fund the war effort.

April 30
GENERAL: Five-year-old Joe Davis, son of President Jefferson Davis, dies of injuries received at a fall from the Confederate White House in Richmond, Virginia.
MILITARY: The Battle of Jenkin's Ferry, Arkansas, unfolds as Confederate cavalry under General John S. Marmaduke attacks a Union rearguard under General Samuel Rice. Meanwhile, General Frederick Steele successfully passes the bulk of his army over the Sabine River and extricates his command. Men of the 2nd Colored Infantry subsequently murder several Southern prisoners in retaliation for atrocities against them at Poison Spring in April.
NAVAL: To assist the gunboat squadron of Admiral David D. Porter, engineer Colonel Joseph Bailey begins constructing a dam of logs across the Red River. "Two or three regiments of Maine men were set to work felling trees," Porter notes, "Everyman seemed to be working with a vigor seldom equaled."
SLAVERY: President Jefferson Davis issues orders to return all captured slaves found fighting in Union ranks back to their rightful orders "on proof and payment of charges."

May 2
MILITARY: General Franz Sigel leads 6,500 Union troops out of Winchester, Virginia, and down the Shenandoah Valley Pike toward New Market. His goal is to deny the Confederacy any food or cattle grown in this highly productive region.
POLITICS: President Jefferson Davis addresses the opening session of the Second Confederate Congress, accusing Northerners of "barbarism" through their

"plunder and devastation of property of noncombatants, destruction of private dwellings, and even edifices devoted to the worship of God."

May 3

POLITICS: President Abraham Lincoln and his cabinet discuss the recent murder of African-American prisoners at Fort Pillow, Tennessee.

May 4

MILITARY: Generals Ulysses S. Grant and George G. Meade direct the Army of the Potomac across the Rapidan River, Virginia, toward the heavily forested area known as the Wilderness. They lead a veteran force of 122,000 men, divided into four commands: General Winfield S. Hancock's II Corps, the V Corps under General Gouvernor K. Warren, John Sedgwick's VI Corps, and General Ambrose E. Burnside's IX Corps.

General William T. Sherman advances his force of 110,000 men from Chattanooga, Tennessee, and against Confederate forces under General Joseph E. Johnston. The Union goal is Atlanta, Georgia, an important communications hub.

POLITICS: The U.S. House of Representatives passes the punitively worded Wade-Davis Reconstruction Bill, 73 to 59, over President Abraham Lincoln's objections. Curiously, Radical Republicans like Thaddeus Stevens find the measure far too conciliatory to their liking.

May 5

EDUCATION: The Society of Friends founds Swarthmore College near Philadelphia, Pennsylvania.

MILITARY: The Battle of the Wilderness erupts once General Gouvernor K. Warren's V Corps encounters General Richard S. Ewell's II Corps along the Orange Turnpike Road. Warren is well situated to sweep the Southerners before him, but insurmountable delays grant Ewell time to rush up reinforcements. Two miles south, General Winfield S. Hancock's II Corps engages General Ambrose P. Hill's III Corps in fierce fighting. An all-out Confederate advance surges ahead initially, but Hill is halted by General George W. Getty's division, VI Corps, who stands long enough for Hancock to bring sufficient numbers up.

NAVAL: The ironclad ram CSS *Albemarle* under Commander James W. Cooke, escorted by the smaller *Bombshell* and *Cotton Planter*, steams into Albemarle Sound off Plymouth, North Carolina, to engage the Federal squadron anchored there. However, Captain Melanchton Smith keeps the Southerners under a steady bombardment and, with *Albemarle* damaged and maneuvering badly, Cooke orders his vessel back up the Roanoke River for repairs.

May 6

MILITARY: The Battle of the Wilderness continues as General Winfield S. Hancock's II Corps, advancing down the Orange Plank Road, smashes into General Ambrose P. Hill's III Corps, nearly breaking it. Suddenly General James Longstreet makes his belated appearance with the veteran I Corps and strikes Hancock's left and rear. Longstreet is then seriously wounded by friendly fire while General Micah Jenkins, riding alongside him, is killed. Delays ensue, and when the Confederates finally sort themselves out and advance, they encounter entrenched Federal troops backed by artillery and are repulsed.

1864

Two miles away, General John Sedgwick's VI Corps renews its struggle against General Richard S. Ewell's II Corps along the Orange Turnpike. A fresh Confederate division under General John B. Gordon then manages to work its way around the Union right and charges, severely disrupting their entire line. The onset of nightfall dampens further fighting, and both sides settle in behind entrenchments. Worse, the dry vegetation and undergrowth are set ablaze by the fighting, and hundreds of wounded soldiers, unable to crawl to safety, perish in the flames.

The Wilderness is a dazzling tactical upset by General Robert E. Lee, who tackles an opponent twice his size in an area where he is least expected—and handles him roughly. Grant, who endured the ignominy of having both flanks turned, suffers frightful losses of 17,666; Confederate casualties, through not recorded, are probably in the vicinity of 8,000, but Grant is undeterred and maintains the strategic initiative by sidestepping around Lee's left flank, inching ever closer to Richmond, Virginia, and forcing the indomitable Southerners to follow.

May 7

MILITARY: The struggle for the Wilderness concludes once General Ulysses S. Grant sets a strategic precedent by ignoring his losses and slipping around the Confederate flank. He then marches 12 miles southeast to Spotsylvania Court House. General Philip A. Sheridan has only the division of General Wesley Merritt available to him, and these troops are sent trotting down the road to Spotsylvania. En route General George A. Custer's brigade runs headlong into General Fitzhugh Lee's dismounted Confederates at Todd's Tavern, skirmishing furiously. Additional cavalry units are fed into the fray, but the Southerners manage to keep their line intact and Spotsylvania remains in their hands. Union losses are around 250, the Confederates sustain possibly half as many.

The Atlanta Campaign begins. General William T. Sherman, commanding the armies of the Cumberland (General George H. Thomas), the Ohio (General John M. Schofield), and the Tennessee (General James B. McPherson), roughly 112,000 men, advances upon Dalton, Georgia. There he confronts the Army of Tennessee under General Joseph E. Johnston, who commands 62,000 Confederates. These are organized into two corps under generals John B. Hood and William J. Hardee, while a third corps under General Leonidas K. Polk is en route from Mississippi. Southern mounted troops are entrusted to the highly capable General Joseph Wheeler.

May 8

MILITARY: Thousands of soldiers from both sides file into positions along a three-mile front at Spotsylvania Court House, Virginia. General Gouvernor K. Warren's V Corps and General John Sedgwick's VI Corps then charge the Southerners headlong in their fieldworks, being heavily repulsed. That night General Robert E. Lee instructs his men to continue felling trees, digging trenches, strengthening the entire line with them.

May 9

MILITARY: General George Crook, riding at the head of 6,155 Union troops, advances into southwestern Virginia to destroy a portion of the Virginia & Tennessee Railroad. En route he encounters 2,400 Confederates and 10 cannon under

General Albert G. Jenkins at Cloyd's Mountain. A bloody impasse continues for several hours until a Union column suddenly appears on the Southern left and rolls up their line. Crook then burns the New River Bridge, thereby obtaining his objective.

May 10

MILITARY: Determined to test Confederate defenses, General Ulysses S. Grant begins organizing large-scale assaults near Spotsylvania, Virginia. He believes that General Robert E. Lee has sufficiently weakened his center by reinforcing both flanks and singles out the "Mule Shoe" in consequence. Colonel Emory Upton, who arrays his 12 regiments in a densely packed assault column, charges forward and penetrates the Mule Shoe's left flank, overturning General Richard Rodes's division and taking 1,000 prisoners. The lodgment, however, is not properly supported and ultimately fails, but Grant remains highly impressed by Upton's innovation; he vows to try the same experiment with an entire corps next day.

Three brigades of Confederate troopers under General J. E. B. Stuart arrive at Beaver Dam Station, Virginia, hotly trailing General Philip H. Sheridan's cavalry column. Though outnumbered, Stuart dispatches a brigade under General James B. Gordon to harass the Union rear while deploying generals William C. Wickham and Lunsford L. Lomax into blocking positions at the junction of Yellow Tavern, only six miles north of Richmond.

Union General James B. McPherson declines pushing ahead through Snake Gap Creek, Georgia, and commences fortifying his position. Unknown at the time, he was opposed only by a single cavalry brigade under General James Canty. McPherson then digs in and awaits developments. General Joseph E. Johnston's line of retreat thus remains intact and, when apprised of the danger, he immediate shifts his forces to safer ground.

NAVAL: Back on the Red River, the dam constructed by Colonel Joseph Bailey is deliberately breached and the ironclads USS *Mound City, Pittsburgh*, and *Carondelet* successfully shoot the rapids. Admiral David D. Porter is delighted and informs Secretary of the Navy Gideon Welles that "The passage of these vessels was a beautiful sight, only to be realized when seen."

May 11

MILITARY: Ignoring heavy losses, General Ulysses S. Grant renews the struggle at Spotsylvania Court House by attacking the Confederate center again. This time he instructs the entire II Corps of General Winfield S. Hancock drawn up into dense attack columns to spearhead the assault. Meanwhile, General Robert E. Lee carefully monitors Union movements and concludes that Grant is preparing to slip around his left flank again. He inadvertently orders all artillery removed from the Mule Shoe, rendering it more vulnerable to attack.

At 11:00 A.M., a tremendous cavalry fight erupts as 4,500 Confederates under General J. E. B. Stuart are attacked by twice their numbers under General Philip H. Sheridan at Yellow Tavern, Virginia. The attackers are repelled, but Stuart is mortally wounded in the stomach and Sheridan is forced to withdraw eastward down the Chickahominy River. Union losses are 704 men while the Southerners sustain more than 300—including the irreplaceable Stuart, who dies the following day.

May 12

MILITARY: The struggle at Spotsylvania Court House, Virginia, is renewed as General Ulysses S. Grant launches a bruising frontal assault against the center of General Robert E. Lee's line. General Winfield S. Hancock's II Corps, arrayed in dense columns, slams irresistibly into the Mule Shoe and overwhelms General Edward Johnson's "Stonewall Brigade," capturing him, 3,000 prisoners, and 20 cannon. Then a vicious, point-blank musketry duel breaks out which degenerates into hand-to-hand fighting, bayonets rasping, and rock throwing. The melee occasions such terrible carnage that the area is christened "Bloody Angle" by the survivors. At length Grant is forced to call off the attack, which affords stark testimony to the power of Confederate fieldworks, which have elevated the lowly spade to that of rifles and cannon in tactical significance. Union losses are 18,339 men to 10,000 Confederates.

May 13

NAVAL: The USS *Louisville*, *Chillicothe*, and *Ozark*, last of Admiral David D. Porter's gunboats, dash over a wing dam on the Red River, Louisiana, and float off to safety. The ingenuity of army engineers under Colonel Joseph Bailey saved an entire squadron from imminent capture or destruction.

May 14

MILITARY: The armies of generals William T. Sherman and Joseph E. Johnston confront each other in full battle array at Resaca, Georgia. The Federals muster 100,000 men and the Confederates, recently joined by a corps under General Leonidas K. Polk, number 60,000. Union troops manage to storm a line of Southern earthworks along Camp Creek, situated on some low-lying hills, a significant gain enabling them to post artillery pieces and shell the entire Confederate line. The toughest struggle, however, is waged on the Union left, where aggressive General John B. Hood successfully attacked along the Dalton-Resaca wagon road until a division dispatched by General George H. Thomas drives them back. More hard fighting is anticipated on the following day.

General Franz Sigel resumes advancing with 6,500 men toward New Market, Virginia, as 5,500 Confederates under General John C. Breckinridge assume strong defensive positions. Breckinridge then suddenly sends forward two infantry brigades linked by a dismounted cavalry force, and they sweep through the town by driving Sigel's men before them. However, when a gap forms in his line, Breckinridge is forced to commit 264 cadets (or 'Katydids") from the nearby Virginia Military Institute to fill it. At 3:00 P.M., the Confederates crown the heights and seize two cannon while the defeated Federals withdraw across the Shenandoah River to safety.

May 15

MILITARY: The Battle of Resaca resumes as Union forces under General Joseph Hooker engage the Confederates of General John B. Hood on the Union left. Meanwhile, General William T. Sherman orders a division of the XVI Corps across the Oostanaula River to seize a strategic railroad bridge in the Southern rear. General Joseph E. Johnston, his lines of communication now imperiled, expertly disengages, throws a pontoon bridge over the Oostanaula, and withdraws to safety in the predawn darkness. Losses in the two-day struggle are roughly 6,000 Union and 5,000 Confederates as Sherman continues pushing ever deeper into Georgia.

May 16
MILITARY: General Pierre G. T. Beauregard leads 18,000 Confederates in a sharp attack against General Benjamin F. Butler's Army of the James near Drewry's Bluff, Virginia. General Robert Ransom's men charge and capture General Charles A. Heckman and 400 prisoners before ammunition shortages force him to halt. Meanwhile, Southerners under General Robert F. Hoke hit the Union center but, becoming lost in the fog, his attack sputters. Butler then withdraws behind fortifications along Bermuda Hundred. Confederate losses are 2,506 while the Union sustains 4,160 casualties. The Federals are now completely corked into the Peninsula, unable to move.

May 19
GENERAL: Literary circles are saddened to hear of the death of noted New England writer and novelist Nathaniel Hawthorne at Plymouth, New Hampshire.

May 20
MILITARY: General Ulysses S. Grant directs the Army of the Potomac south and east in an attempt to outflank Confederate defenses along the Mattaponi River, Virginia. His objective is Hanover Station, 24 miles north of Richmond, where the Virginia Central Railroad intersects with the Richmond, Fredericksburg & Potomac Railroad, two major Southern supply arteries.

General Pierre G. T. Beauregard, intending to further pen up General Benjamin F. Butler's Army of the James in the Bermuda Hundred Peninsula, attacks Union positions at Ware Bottom Church, Virginia. Initially, the divisions of generals Alfred H. Terry and Adelbert Ames are hard pressed before counterattacking and driving their antagonists back to their starting positions. Union losses are roughly 800 to 700 for the Confederates, but Butler remains effectively hemmed in and unable to assist the main drive outside of Richmond, Virginia.

May 21
DIPLOMACY: Secretary of State William H. Seward instructs U.S. Minister to France John Bigelow that, while he is to remonstrate against French activities in Mexico, he must avoid outright belligerence until after the Civil War has been successfully concluded.
MILITARY: Bested by Southern fortifications around Spotsylvania, General Ulysses S. Grant begins probing Confederate lines near Milford Station, Virginia. He is surprised by the lack of strong resistance and prepares to sidestep around General Robert E. Lee's left flank and appear in force across the Anna River.

May 23
MILITARY: The II Corps of General Winfield S. Hancock deploys on the northern bank of the North Anna River at Chesterfield Ford while the XI Corps under General Ambrose E. Burnside lands at Jericho Mills. Meanwhile the V and VI Corps under generals Gouvernor K. Warren and Horatio G. Wright, respectively, fan out into the area west of Jericho Mills.

May 25
MILITARY: The XX Corps under General Joseph Hooker, advancing upon New Hope Church, Georgia, collides headlong into General John B. Hood's Confederates. The Federals are initially repulsed until Hooker masses two entire divisions and charges the troops of General Alexander P. Stewart. Stewart, however, clings

tenaciously to his ground, and at length Hooker retires with 1,600 casualties. This encounter places Union troops only 25 miles northeast of Atlanta.

May 26

SETTLEMENT: The Montana Territory is carved out of the Idaho Territory and establishes its preliminary capital at Bannock.

May 28

DIPLOMACY: Puppet Emperor Maximilian of Austria lands at Veracruz, Mexico, in order to assume his throne. A political neophyte, he is backed by the machinations of French emperor Napoleon III and opposed by Mexican politician-turned-guerrilla Benito Juarez. The United States considers his presence a violation of the long-stated Monroe Doctrine, but it is too absorbed by civil war to lodge much beyond diplomatic protests.

May 31

MILITARY: General Ulysses S. Grant's Overland Campaign to Richmond, Virginia, while a costly tactic, succeeds brilliantly at the strategic level. In one very bloody month he has forced the redoubtable Army of Northern Virginia from field positions along the Rapidan River to the very gates of the Confederate capital.

POLITICS: Radical Republicans, dissatisfied with President Abraham Lincoln, nominate former general John C. Frémont in Cleveland, Ohio, as their party candidate for the presidency. They also choose General John Cochrane of New York as vice president. Among Frémont's strongest supporters is African-American abolitionist Frederick Douglass, who feels that Lincoln is far too leniently disposed toward Southerners in his reconstruction plans.

June 2

MILITARY: At Cold Harbor, Virginia, General Ulysses S. Grant prepares his men for a frontal assault against what he perceives are weak Confederate lines. However, he cancels the operation after General Winfield S. Hancock's II Corps, exhausted by marching in hot weather, arrives in poor condition. Grant reluctantly postpones his attack another day, allowing General Robert E. Lee additional time to fortify and dig in.

June 3

MILITARY: The Battle of Cold Harbor unfolds across a continuous, seven-mile front dotted by earthen fortifications and interlocking fields of fire. The Southern position, manned by 59,000 men, confronts 108,000 Federal troops. General Ulysses S. Grant then orders his men to charge across open fields in dense columns as the defenders unleash withering torrents of bullets and canister, cutting them down in droves. Within 30 minutes 7,000 Federals are casualties, while the Confederates sustain roughly 1,500 loses. It is the biggest military blunder of Grant's career and the Northern press begins assailing him as a "butcher."

General Robert E. Lee had won his final open-field battle, for Cold Harbor also marks an end to the mobile phase of the Overland Campaign to Richmond, Virginia. Since May, both sides have absorbed tremendous losses, with Union casualties exceeding 50,000. The Southern toll exceeds 32,000 which, while numerically smaller, actually constitutes a higher percentage of their army, 46 to 41 percent. General Ulysses S. Grant, moreover, receives a constant and steady flow of reinforcements, whereas Confederate manpower resources are dwindling.

1864

June 5

MILITARY: Having advanced down the Shenandoah Valley as far as Harrisonburg before turning east, General David Hunter leads 15,000 Union troops on to engage 5,600 Confederates under General William E. Jones at Piedmont, Virginia. Charging through a gap in the Southern line, the Federals capture all of Jones's artillery and his line shatters. Jones is killed rallying his command, which loses 1,600 men to a Union tally of 780.

June 7

POLITICS: The Republican Party convenes in Baltimore, Maryland, to nominate its presidential and vice presidential candidates. Assisted by several pro-war Democrats, they are able to portray themselves as the "National Union Convention."

June 8

POLITICS: The Republican Party convention held at Baltimore, Maryland, renominates Abraham Lincoln to run for the presidency. However, sitting Vice President Hannibal Hamlin is dropped in favor of Tennessee governor Andrew Johnson, a Southern War Democrat, whose presence will broaden the ticket's appeal. Their platform calls for a military end to the rebellion and ratification of the Thirteenth Amendment to abolish slavery.

June 9

POLITICS: President Abraham Lincoln endorses a constitutional amendment to outlaw slavery.

June 10

DIPLOMACY: The Austrian prince Maximilian is crowned emperor of Mexico at the behest of France and his throne is backed by a large French army. He is competing with fugitive president Benito Juarez for the hearts of Mexicans.

MILITARY: In a display of tactical virtuosity, General Nathan B. Forrest and 3,500 Confederate cavalry rout a Union force twice its size at Brice's Cross Road, Mississippi. Forrest anticipated that General Samuel D. Sturgis would commit his cavalry to battle first, followed by his infantry, and he determined to defeat each as they came up. Eager to maintain the battlefield initiative, Forrest next unleashes simultaneous attacks that strike the Union left, right, and center while a small force maneuvers around Sturgis's rear. The tiring Federals, hit from all sides, suddenly bolt and career headfirst into their own wagon and artillery train, overturning both. Forrest, defeating twice his numbers, suffers 492 casualties and inflicts 2,240.

POLITICS: In light of a growing manpower crisis, the Confederate Congress authorizes military service for all males between the ages of 17 and 50.

June 11

MILITARY: General Philip H. Sheridan rides into Trevilian Station, Virginia, where he encounters the dismounted division of General Wade Hampton waiting for him in the woods. He quickly dispatches the Michigan brigade of General George A. Custer to turn Hampton's flank and slash his rear, which he does with aplomb. Custer then dashes in between Hampton and General Fitzhugh Lee's divisions, capturing 50 wagons, 800 prisoners, and 1,500 horses. Lee is tardy sorting his command out but then begins pressing the unsupported Custer hard. At the last minute Sheridan gallops up with reinforcements, and the Southerners retire with an additional 500 Confederate prisoners taken.

June 12

MILITARY: General Philip H. Sheridan's cavalry renews its clash with generals Wade Hampton and Fitzhugh Lee at Trevilian Station, Virginia. However, Hampton's well-positioned troopers repel seven Union charges, at which point Sheridan concludes his raid and rides back to the main Union force at Petersburg. Trevilian Station is one of the largest cavalry clashes of the entire war and among the most costly: Sheridan admits to 735 casualties while the Confederate loss is estimated at roughly 1,000.

June 14

MILITARY: In a major feat, Union engineers construct the 2,100-foot-long James River bridge from Windmill Point to Fort Powhatan, Virginia. It enables General Ulysses S. Grant to quickly shift his army across the river and threaten Petersburg. General Robert E. Lee is completely taken unawares.

June 15

POLITICS: The Thirteenth Amendment to the U.S. Constitution fails to be ratified by the House of Representatives, falling 13 votes short (95 to 66) of the two-thirds majority required for passage.

The U.S. Congress passes legislation granting equal pay to African-American soldiers. For many months black personnel refused to accept less pay than their white counterparts in protest.

Former congressman and Peace Democrat Clement L. Vallandigham arrives in Ohio following his Canadian exile. He thereupon resumes his activities for securing a negotiated peace with the Confederacy.

June 16

POLITICS: President Abraham Lincoln, addressing the Sanitation Fair in Philadelphia, Pennsylvania, declares "War, at best, is terrible, and this war of ours, in its magnitude and duration, is one of the most terrible." He assures his audience, however, stating "We accepted this war for a worthy object, and the war will end when that object is attained."

June 18

MILITARY: The siege of Petersburg, Virginia, begins in earnest once General Robert E. Lee and 50,000 bedraggled, hungry men defend a line 26 miles in circumference while simultaneously guarding the four railroads out of the city that constitute his supply line. In contrast, General Ulysses S. Grant leads 110,000 well-fed, well-equipped soldiers, backed by a steady stream of reinforcements that the Confederates cannot match. The past four days of fighting along the city's outskirts cost the Union 10,586 casualties while the Southerners lost around 4,000.

General David Hunter's 18,000 Union troops renew their attack upon Lynchburg, Virginia. However, newly arrived Confederates under General Jubal A. Early boost the defenders to 14,000, who resist tenaciously. Hunter concludes that the enemy has been reinforced overnight and outnumbers him, so he orders an ignominious retreat back up the Shenandoah Valley. Early then recaptures the strategic initiative by energetically pursuing his larger adversary.

1864

June 19

NAVAL: The USS *Kearsarge* under Captain John A. Winslow engages the CSS *Alabama* under Captain Raphael Semmes off Cherbourg, France. The Union vessel enjoys a slightly larger crew and marginally heavier armament, along with the decided advantage that *Alabama's* ammunition has deteriorated from lengthy exposure to salt air. Both vessels handle their guns well; *Kearsarge* receives 28 hits, including a potentially disastrous strike by a 100-pound shell that fails to explode. On the other hand, the Union gunnery is superb and inflicts tremendous hull damage to its adversary, puncturing the *Alabama* repeatedly. Within an hour the ship is listing and Semmes, unable to dash for the French coast, abandons ship. This action terminates the South's most celebrated commerce raider.

June 21

POLITICS: President Abraham Lincoln visits Union troops in the siege lines of Petersburg, Virginia, making a conspicuous target for snipers in his tall, stovepipe hat.

Confederate Secretary of the Treasury Christopher G. Memminger resigns over criticism of his handling of monetary affairs.

June 22

MILITARY: General Ulysses S. Grant, confronting strong Southern defenses before him at Petersburg, Virginia, tries his time-honored tactic of shifting troops around their flank in a bid to extend and weaken their lines by cutting the Weldon Railroad. General David B. Birney's II Corps and General Horatio G. Wright's VI Corps advance through dense woods to reach their objective, but General Cadmus M. Wilcox's division holds fast while generals William Mahone and Bushrod R. Johnson assail Birney's flanks. The struggle is savage and rout the veteran Union division of General John Gibbon, taking 1,600 prisoners.

General John B. Hood exceeds his orders to extend the Confederate left at Kennesaw Mountain by launching an unauthorized assault with 11,000 men against Union positions at Kolb's Farm, Georgia. General Joseph Hooker, commanding 14,000 troops and 40 cannon, is forewarned of Hood's approach and makes careful preparations to receive him. Concentrated rifle and artillery fire mow down the charging Confederates and Hood ultimately withdraws with 1,500 casualties to a Union total of 250.

June 23

MILITARY: Union generals David B. Birney and Horatio G. Wright repeat their attack upon Confederate defenses guarding the Weldon Railroad, Virginia, with their II and VI Corps, respectively. A strong initial advance recovers all ground lost on the previous day, but a stubborn defense mounted by General William Mahone blocks them from reaching the railroad. At dusk the Federals again withdraw below the Jerusalem Plank Road with 2,962 casualties.

June 24

SLAVERY: The Maryland Convention gathers and votes to abolish slavery.

June 25

MILITARY: Colonel Henry Pleasant's 48th Pennsylvania, composed mostly of miners from Schuykill County, begins tunneling beneath Confederate defenses at Petersburg, Virginia. The plan is to run a 511-foot shaft beneath a South Carolina battery positioned at Elliott's Salient and stock it with 8,000 pounds of gunpowder. Over the next month, General Ambrose E. Burnside also specially trains a division of African Americans under General Edward Ferrero to spearhead the assault once the charges have been detonated.

June 27

MILITARY: General William T. Sherman wages the Battle of Kennesaw Mountain, Georgia, against General Joseph E. Johnston. The Confederates are skillfully arrayed along high ground strewn with large boulders and trees—affording a perfect killing ground for troops advancing from below. The first Union wave consists of two divisions from General John A. Logan's XV Corps, Army of the Tennessee. General William W. Loring responds with intense rifle and artillery fire, dropping Federals in bloody clumps. The main thrust against Johnston's line occurs further south at Cheatham's Hill, stoutly defended by General William J. Hardee's corps. Up the hillside go 8,000 men from divisions under generals Jefferson C. Davis and John Newton, XIV Corps, heavily raked by fire from above which depletes their ranks. Sherman finally calls off the attack after losses of 3,000 men, including two generals killed; Johnston sustains about 750 casualties.

POLITICS: Abraham Lincoln accepts the Republican Party nomination for the presidency.

June 28

POLITICS: President Abraham Lincoln signs legislation repealing the Fugitive Slave Act, a major irritant that helped spark the present conflagration.

June 30

POLITICS: The U.S. Congress approves the Internal Revenue Act to help finance the war.

Secretary of the Treasury Salmon P. Chase tenders his resignation to President Abraham Lincoln who, much to his surprise, accepts it. "You and I have reached a point of mutual embarrassment in our official relation which seems cannot be overcome," Lincoln writes, "or longer sustained, consistently with public service."

July 1

POLITICS: President Abraham Lincoln appoints William P. Fessenden as his new secretary of the treasury.

The U.S. Senate passes the vindictive Wade-Davis plan for reconstruction 26 to three, with 20 abstaining.

July 2

POLITICS: President Abraham Lincoln, finding the Wade-Davis plan for reconstruction too harsh for his liking, weighs simply not signing it and allowing it to die by pocket veto.

TRANSPORTATION: Congress authorizes the Northern Pacific Railroad to construct a line running from Lake Superior to Portland, Oregon, and thereby facilitate new settlements.

July 4

POLITICS: President Abraham Lincoln signs legislation modifying certain aspects of the Enrollment Act of 1863, striking the clause allowing substitutes to be purchased for $300.

1864

The president also clashes with Radical Republicans over the tenor of reconstruction in the Wade-Davis Bill, which would have placed conditions solely in the hands of Congress. Lincoln specifically objects to provisions requiring loyalty oaths by 50 percent of each state's 1860 population. In the end, he simply kills the measure by not signing it.

SOCIETAL: The Bureau of Immigration is established by Congress to facilitate the importation of contract laborers.

July 5

POLITICS: New York *Tribune* editor Horace Greeley receives peace feelers from the Confederate government and he contacts President Abraham Lincoln. Lincoln allows him to meet with the individuals at Niagara Falls, New York.

July 7

MILITARY: General Ulysses S. Grant, realizing the seriousness of Confederate thrusts in Maryland, rushes General James B. Rickett's division (VI Corps) to Baltimore by rail, and from there it will march on foot to Monocacy Junction. There it will reinforce General Lew Wallace, holding the intersection with 3,000 men, who is contemplating a desperate holding action.

July 8

MILITARY: A hodgepodge of Union troops under General Lew Wallace assumes defensive positions behind the Monocacy River near Frederick, Maryland, to defend the national capital from General Jubal A. Early's advancing Confederates. On the day before battle he cobbles together a force of 6,000 men from various sources, which is all that stands in the way between the rebels and Washington, D.C.

July 9

MILITARY: The Confederate Fabian tactics of General Joseph E. Johnston, which have so infuriated General William T. Sherman, unfortunately draw the ire of President Jefferson Davis. Seeking a possible pretext to relieve Johnston, whom he personally despises, Davis dispatches General Braxton Bragg to his headquarters on a "fact-finding" mission. Johnston, meanwhile, continues withdrawing from the Chattahoochee River to Peachtree Creek, only three miles north of Atlanta, Georgia.

General Lew Wallace, with 6,000 troops, confronts 14,000 Confederates under General Jubal A. Early at Monocacy, Maryland. General James B. Rickett's veteran division easily repels two charges by General John B. Gordon as the Southerners gradually work their way around the Union left. A final charge by General William R. Terry's Virginia brigade dislodges the defenders and Wallace orders his entire force withdrawn up the Baltimore Pike in good order. Union losses are 1,800, while the Confederates sustain around 700. The road to Washington, D.C., is now wide open, but Monocacy delays Early's advance by 24 hours and grants the capital time to shore up its defenses.

July 10

MILITARY: Confederates under General Jubal A. Early file through Rockville, Maryland, to confront Union defenders at Fort Stevens, outside Washington, D.C. That post is only manned by 209 inexperienced artillerists but President Abraham Lincoln blithely exclaims "Let us be vigilant but keep cool. I hope neither Baltimore nor Washington will be sacked."

1864

July 12

MILITARY: Confederates under General Jubal A. Early withdraw from the vicinity of Washington, D.C., and are cautiously shadowed by General Horatio G. Wright's Federal forces. For a few tense moments President Abraham Lincoln, visiting the parapets, is under enemy fire, and young Lieutenant Oliver Wendell Holmes (a future Supreme Court justice) unthinkingly shouts "Get down, you fool!"

July 14

MILITARY: A force of 7,500 Confederates under generals Stephen D. Lee and Nathan B. Forrest gather to attack General Andrew J. Smith outside of Tupelo, Mississippi. Lee insists that they charge the awaiting Federals head on, and they are repeatedly decimated by concentrated rifle and artillery fire. Tupelo proves a surprising Union victory, but Forrest's command survives the debacle intact and still functioning. Union losses are 674 to a Confederate tally of 1,326.

July 16

POLITICS: A pensive President Jefferson Davis telegraphs General Joseph E. Johnston at Atlanta, Georgia, "I wish to hear from you as to your present situation and your plan of operation so specifically as will enable me to anticipate events." Johnston matter-of-factly replies, "As the enemy is double our number, we must be on the defensive. My plan of operations must therefore depend upon that of the enemy."

July 17

MILITARY: General Joseph E. Johnston is preparing to pounce on the isolated Army of the Cumberland under General George H. Thomas at Peachtree Creek, Georgia. Suddenly, a telegram arrives from President Jefferson Davis announcing his replacement by the impetuous, highly aggressive General John B. Hood. Davis's antipathy for the highly capable Johnston proves a turning point in the course of events.

July 20

MILITARY: No sooner does the 20,000-man Army of the Cumberland under General George H. Thomas cross Peachtree Creek, Georgia (three miles north of Atlanta), than it is set upon by 19,000 Confederates under newly appointed General John B. Hood. The hardest fighting occurs on the right wing where General Edward C. Walthall's Confederates lace into the divisions of generals Alpheus S. Williams and John W. Geary, XX Corps, whereby the latter is nearly surrounded and hard-pressed for over three hours. Hood's gambit ultimately fails so he suspends further fighting at 7:00 P.M. and orders a retreat. Peachtree Creek is the first of his highly audacious but ultimately futile attempts to save Atlanta, and it costs him 2,500 men to a Union tally of 1,779 killed, wounded, and missing.

July 22

MILITARY: General John B. Hood initiates the Battle of Atlanta by ordering General William J. Hardee's corps to strike at the Army of the Tennessee under General James B. McPherson. However, Hardy errs in not moving troops far enough to the east and, instead of turning McPherson's left flank, he attacks him head on. Tragedy strikes Union forces when McPherson, reconnoitering ahead of his troops, stumbles onto a Confederate picket and is shot dead. Federal reinforcements then storm across the field in turn, driving the gray coats before them and restoring their lines. Hood's second sortie proves another costly failure that depletes his army of 8,000 men while Union losses are 3,722.

POLITICS: President Jefferson Davis orders General Edmund Kirby-Smith to assist the Army of Tennessee under General John B. Hood. In light of the fact that the Mississippi River is full of Union gunboats, this proves an impossible order to fulfill.

July 23

POLITICS: The Louisiana State Convention adopts a new constitution which outlaws slavery.

July 24

MILITARY: General Jubal A. Early's 14,000 Confederates engage the smaller Union VIII Corps under General George Crook at Kernstown, Virginia. Crook's 8,500 men initially withstand several charges until they are finally flanked by General John C. Breckinridge and driven from the field. Crook's defeat would have been more costly had Early not mishandled his cavalry and he escapes intact. Unfortunately for the South, their victory here convinces the political establishment in Washington, D.C., that vigorous, new leadership is required to secure the Shenandoah region.

July 28

INDIAN: General Alfred Sully engages a large number of hostile Teton Lakota (Sioux) in their camp at Killdeer Mountain (North Dakota). Sully is looking for remnants of the Santee (Eastern Sioux) responsible for staging a bloody uprising in Minnesota two years earlier, especially their notorious chief, Inkpaduta. The latter sought refuge among his Teton brethren, who prepare to wage battle rather then turn him over. Sully takes the unusual step of deploying his 3,000 men in a hollow square and advancing in this formation upon the camp. This walking wall of firepower gradually evicts the Teton from their campsite and they flee, losing an estimated 150 warriors. Sully sustains five dead and 10 wounded.

MILITARY: General Oliver O. Howard and the Army of the Tennessee advance upon East Point, Georgia, determined to sever the last remaining rail links to Atlanta. Confederate General John B. Hood dispatches the corps of generals Stephen D. Lee and Alexander P. Stewart to hit the Union left flank at Ezra Church and roll it up. The Southerners advance as ordered but, instead of striking Howard's flank, they mistakenly veer into the front of General John A. Logan's XV Corps. By the time the Confederates depart Ezra Church they had lost upwards of 5,000 men to a Union tally of only 562. The battle dissuaded the Federals from cutting Atlanta's rail lines and so depletes Hood's army that hereafter he is forced on the defensive.

July 30

MILITARY: The Battle of the Crater unfolds as fuses to an explosive-laden tunnel, dug beneath Confederates lines at Petersburg, Virginia, are lit. At 4:45 P.M., the ground beneath Elliot's Salient erupts furiously, destroying an artillery emplacement and killing 278 North Carolina troops. The Union force pauses 15 minutes before charging into the smoking crater, which measures 1,870 feet long, 80 feet wide, and 30 feet deep. The Confederates recover more quickly than expected, rush reinforcement to the threatened point, and shoot downward into the milling Federal troops. Union losses are 3,798 while the Southerners sustain 1,491 casualties.

General George Stoneman's cavalry column departs the outskirts of Macon, Georgia, and attempts circling around the city to cross the Ocmulgee River. He advances as far as Hillsboro before being set upon by General Alfred Iverson and three brigades of Confederate troopers near Sunshine Church and surrenders with 700 men. This "raid" proves one of the biggest cavalry fiascos of the entire war and nearly paralyzes General William T. Sherman's mounted arm for several weeks.

August 4
MILITARY: General William T. Sherman, pursuant to his strategy of circling Atlanta, Georgia, from the west, orders General John M. Schofield's Army of the Ohio, reinforced by General John M. Palmer's XIV Corps, Army of the Tennessee, to storm Confederate earthworks near Utoy Creek. Success here places Union troops within two miles of the strategic railroad junction at East Point.

August 5
NAVAL: At 6:00 A.M., Admiral David G. Farragut launches an all-out attack against Confederate defenses guarding Mobile Bay, Alabama. Disaster strikes when the ironclad USS *Tecumseh* detonates a torpedo and sinks 30 seconds later with a loss of 90 crewmen. "Damn the torpedoes, full speed ahead!" is Farragut's response to the crisis as his flagship *Hartford* plunges directly through the Confederate minefield intact. He next confronts the large steam ram CSS *Tennessee* under the equally redoubtable Admiral James Buchanan, which tries repeatedly ramming the Hartford. Farragut easily dodges his slower adversary while all 17 ships of his squadron pummel it with intense cannon fire. Buchanan finally lowers his flag at 10:00 A.M., as Farragut wins another bold gamble and closes the Confederacy's last remaining port on the Gulf Coast.

POLITICS: Radical Republicans Benjamin Wade and Henry W. Davis denounce President Abraham Lincoln for pocket vetoing their reconstruction legislation and campaign openly to replace him. "The authority of Congress is paramount and must be respected," they insist.

August 6
MILITARY: General Philip H. Sheridan arrives at Harper's Ferry, West Virginia, to assume command of the Army of the Shenandoah, consisting of the VI Corps under General Horatio G. Wright, the VIII Corps under General George Crook, the XIX Corps under General William H. Emory, and three cavalry divisions led by General T. A. Tolbert.

August 7
MILITARY: General Ulysses S. Grant's choice of 33-year-old General Philip H. Sheridan to lead the Army of the Shenandoah causes consternation among President Abraham Lincoln and Secretary of War Edwin M. Stanton. Both men fear that the youthful Sheridan is too inexperienced for so delicate a mission, but Grant insists on having this aggressive, headstrong firebrand at the helm.

August 10
MILITARY: General Philip H. Sheridan leads Union forces out of Harper's Ferry, West Virginia, and into the Shenandoah Valley as Confederates under General Jubal A. Early watch warily.

1864

August 15

MILITARY: General Philip H. Sheridan withdraws toward Winchester, Virginia, inducing Confederates under General Jubal A. Early to follow. Sheridan is acting under orders to move with caution, and he is believed to be facing upwards of 40,000 Southerners. President Abraham Lincoln's precarious political fortunes preclude any embarrassing defeats this close to the national election. Early, however, misinterprets such behavior as timidity.

August 16

MILITARY: Union cavalry under General Wesley Merritt engages General Richard H. Anderson's Confederate division at Front Royal, Virginia. A swirling saber melee also erupts between Southern troopers of General William C. Wickham and Union cavalry under General Thomas C. Devlin as the former tries to ford the Shenandoah River. A decisive charge by Devlin sends his opponents scampering and he seizes two flags and 139 prisoners.

August 18

MILITARY: General Ulysses S. Grant refuses Confederate requests to resume prisoner exchanges. This act deprives the South of critically needed trained manpower, but also prolongs the hardships of Union prisoners languishing in poorly maintained Confederate prisons. In truth, the South can barely feed its own soldiers, let alone captives.

Confederate forces attack General Winfield S. Hancock's II Corps at Deep Bottom Run, Virginia, and are repelled with loss. General Ulysses S. Grant remains convinced that Southern defenses north of the James River have not been depleted, so he recalls Hancock's expedition back to Petersburg. Operations in this vicinity cost the Union 2,901 casualties to a Confederate tally of about 1,500.

At 4:00 P.M., General Gouvernor K. Warren's V Corps attacks and captures Globe Tavern and portions of the Weldon railroad outside Petersburg, Virginia. General Pierre G. T. Beauregard, commanding at Petersburg, quickly dispatches General Henry Heth's division to slash at Warren's left flank. Timely Union reinforcements from the divisions of generals Samuel W. Crawford and Lysander Cutler make a timely appearance and drive the Southerners back into the city. Still, General Robert E. Lee must take the Weldon Railroad back and intact.

August 19

MILITARY: General Gouvernor K. Warren's V Corps is reinforced at Weldon Station, Virginia, by three divisions of the IX Corps, plus General Gershom Mott's division from the II Corps. These arrive and deploy in time to meet a large Southern counterattack orchestrated by General Ambrose P. Hill. By nightfall, Warren's position has been heavily jostled, but control of this section of the Weldon Railroad remains in Union hands. Federal losses for the day are 4,455 while Confederates are thought to have sustained around 1,600.

A surprise raid by 2,000 Confederate cavalry under General Nathan B. Forrest briefly captures Memphis, Tennessee, and the local Union commander, General Cadwallader C. Washburn, only escapes in his nightclothes. Forrest then resumes raiding Federal supply lines with near impunity over the next two months. His success even elicits backhanded praise from General William T. Sherman, who refers to him as "that devil Forrest."

1864

August 23

POLITICS: President Abraham Lincoln expresses pessimism over his reelection chances, noting "It will be my duty to cooperate with the President-elect, as to save the Union between the election and the inauguration, as he will have secured his election on such ground that he cannot possibly save it afterwards."

August 25

MILITARY: At 5:00 P. M., Confederates under General Ambrose P. Hill savagely assault the Union II Corps under General Winfield S. Hancock at Ream's Station, Virginia. Hill's 10,000 men initially rebounded of the divisions of generals Nelson A. Miles and David M. Gregg, until parts of the former suddenly gave way. General John Gibbon's veteran division, exhausted from fatigue, also stumbles badly in combat and runs. Union losses in these embarrassing affairs are 2,372 while the Southerners sustain only 700 casualties.

August 26

MILITARY: A convention of African Americans in Philadelphia, Pennsylvania, advance resolutions calling for the commissioning of black military officers.

August 29

POLITICS: The Democratic National Convention convenes in Chicago, Illinois, where noted "Copperhead" Clement L. Vallandigham delivers the keynote address.

August 30

POLITICS: The Democratic Party convention in Chicago, Illinois, adopts a peace platform demanding an immediate end to hostilities with the South. Their stance is virtually the mirror opposite of that adopted by President Abraham Lincoln and the Republicans.

August 31

MILITARY: General William J. Hardee leads 20,000 Confederates against a similar-sized force under General Oliver O. Howard at Jonesboro, Georgia. The Federals are strongly positioned in a semicircle on high ground and enjoy a clear field of fire. Hardee's piecemeal attacks continually disintegrate in the face of concentrated rifle fire and he finally withdraws after suffering 2,000 casualties. Howard loses a mere 178.

POLITICS: The Democratic Party convention in Chicago, Illinois, nominates former general George B. McClellan as its candidate for president and George H. Pendleton of Ohio for vice president.

September 1

MILITARY: Confederates under General William J. Hardee are attacked by superior Union forces as the struggle at Jonesboro, Georgia, continues. General William T. Sherman designs an elaborate movement by several corps, but Union attacks are poorly coordinated and beaten off with considerable loss. Sherman's men finally penetrate Southern defenses, taking hundreds of prisoners from General Daniel C. Govin's brigade. Union losses are 1,274 out of 20,460 present; the Confederates suffer 911 out of 12,661 engaged. Hardy's heroic stand permits General John B. Hood sufficient time to slip out of Atlanta before Sherman's noose can close around it.

Sherman, William T.   (1820–1891)
General

Tecumseh Sherman was born in Lancaster, Ohio, on February 8, 1820, the son of a judge. Orphaned at an early age, he became a ward of Senator Thomas Ewing, who subsequently christened him William. Sherman, with his stepfather's patronage, then gained appointment to the U.S. Military Academy in 1836 and graduated near the top of his class four years later. He joined the third U.S. Artillery as a second lieutenant and fought in Florida's Second Seminole War until 1841. Sherman then fulfilled a long stint of garrison duty throughout the Deep South, where he thoroughly familiarized himself with the people and geography. Sherman greatly admired the South and evinced genuine affection for the Southerners, but after the Civil War commenced in 1861 he departed Louisiana

William Tecumseh Sherman *(Library of Congress)*

for St. Louis, Missouri, and sought to regain his army commission. He then commanded a brigade under General Irvin McDowell at Bull Run on July 21, 1861, being one of few officers to distinguish himself in combat. Sherman then rose to brigadier general the following August and transferred to the District of Cairo, Illinois, where he became acquainted with General Ulysses S. Grant during the campaign against Forts Henry and Donelson in February 1862. The high-strung Sherman and the low-key Grant struck up a cordial relationship that lasted the remainder of the lives. He commanded a division in Grant's Army of the Tennessee and fought conspicuously at the bloody Battle of Shiloh, April 5–6, 1862. Sherman, who had commanded the pickets that day, had been surprised by Confederates under General Albert S. Johnston, but he effectively rallied his command and contributed to the final Union victory.

Over the next two years Sherman fought capably under Grant and in the spring of 1864 succeeded him as commander of the western frontier. In this capacity he undertook his most famous endeavor, the conquest of Atlanta, Georgia, by overcoming the skilled defensive tactics of General Joseph E. Johnston and then the ferocious onslaughts of General John B. Hood. Atlanta fell on September 2, 1864, after which Sherman embarked on a campaign of "total war" against the Southern populace and burned a 60-mile swath of destruction across the South. By the time the war successfully concluded in April 1865, he had devastated large tracts of land throughout Georgia and South Carolina. Sherman rose to lieutenant general in July 1866 while heading the Division of the Missouri. Three years later newly elected President Grant appointed him commanding general of the army with four stars, becoming only the second individual in American history so honored. Over the next decade Sherman worked earnestly to improve conditions in the army and foster greater professionalism, including the wholesale adoption of German staff methods. Sherman retired from the military in November 1883 and resisted calls to enter politics as a Republican. He died in New York City on February 14, 1891.

September 2

MILITARY: "So Atlanta is ours and fairly won," General William T. Sherman telegraphs President Abraham Lincoln, after the city surrenders to the XX Corps of General Henry W. Slocum. This single act rekindles President Abraham Lincoln's sagging election prospects while exerting a distressing effect throughout the South. Over the past four months Union forces have sustained 4,432 dead and 22,822 wounded while the Confederates endure 3,044 killed and 18,952 injured.

NAVAL: Secretary of the Navy Gideon Welles receives permission to mount a large amphibious assault against Fort Fisher, Wilmington, North Carolina. Success here will close down the South's remaining seaport.

SLAVERY: To offset critical manpower shortages, General Robert E. Lee advises President Jefferson Davis of the necessity of replacing white laborers with African Americans, thereby freeing the former for military service.

September 3

POLITICS: President Abraham Lincoln, in honor of recent victories at Mobile, Alabama, and Atlanta, Georgia, declares the upcoming September 5 a day of national celebration and prayer for such events "call for devout acknowledgment to the Supreme Being in whose hands are the destinies of nations."

September 5

SLAVERY: Voters in Louisiana ratify a new constitution abolishing slavery.

September 7

MILITARY: General William T. Sherman issues Special Order No. 67 to the inhabitants of Atlanta, Georgia, requiring all 1,600 families to evacuate the city immediately. "War is cruelty and you cannot refine it," he declares to the city's mayor, "When peace does come you may call on me for anything. Then I will share with you the last cracker."

Ruins of a train depot, blown up on Sherman's departure from Atlanta, Georgia (*Library of Congress*)

September 8
POLITICS: Former general George B. McClellan accepts the Democratic Party nomination for the presidency, but rejects their peace platform and declares "The Union is the one condition of peace—we ask for no more." He nonetheless continues railing against President Abraham Lincoln's handling of the war.

September 9
MILITARY: General Joseph Wheeler, having completed his latest raid against Union supply lines in Tennessee, recrosses the Tennessee River at Florence, Alabama, and gallops home. In fact, his endeavors achieve very little for Union repair crews quickly restore damaged sections of track. The next result of Wheeler's activities are to deprive General John B. Hood of excellent cavalry during a critical phase of the Georgia campaign.

September 11
MILITARY: Generals William T. Sherman and John B. Hood conclude a 10-day truce to facilitate the evacuation of citizens and their belongings from Atlanta, Georgia. When petitioned by the inhabitants to reconsider, Sherman states "You might as well appeal against the thunderstorm as against these terrible hardships of war." The age of total war has arrived with a vengeance.

September 16
MILITARY: At dawn General Wade Hampton's cavalry charges a Union force at Coggin's Point, Virginia, completely dispersing elements of the First D.C. Cavalry and the Thirteenth Pennsylvania Cavalry. The raiders then abscond with 2,486 head of cattle—and 300 prisoners—in a line stretching seven miles long. Hampton arrives back behind Confederate lines the next day after committing the largest incident of cattle rustling in American history.

Rebecca West, a Union spy in Winchester, Virginia, observes the departure of General Joseph Kershaw's Confederate cavalry division and 12 cannon from the army of General Jubal A. Early. She manages to relay the information back to General Philip H. Sheridan, then conferring with General Ulysses S. Grant over strategy at Charlestown, West Virginia. News of the transfer induces Sheridan to attack Early immediately. Grant concurs fully, laconically stating "Go in," then departs.

September 17
POLITICS: Former general John C. Frémont withdraws his name from the election contest and urges a united Republican Party front under Abraham Lincoln. He fears that a Democratic victory might lead to either recognition of the Confederacy or the survival of slavery.

September 19
MILITARY: At 2:00 P.M., General Philip H. Sheridan's army, totaling 35,000 men, attacks the 12,000 Confederates of General Jubal A. Early at Winchester, Virginia. Heavy fighting forces Southerners under General Stephen Ramseur to give way, but generals Richard Rodes and John B. Gordon strike back in a vicious counterattack that stuns the XIX Corps. An equally desperate cavalry charge by General Fitzhugh Lee then fails to stop approaching Union troopers under generals Wesley Merritt and William W. Averill, and Confederate resistance collapses around 5:00 P.M. Union loses are 5,018 to a Confederate tally of 3,611, but Early hastily withdraws to Fisher's Hill.

POLITICS: President Jefferson Davis advises the governors of South Carolina, North Carolina, Alabama, Georgia, Virginia, and Florida that recent proclamations requiring aliens to either serve in the army or leave are depriving the Confederacy of many skilled workers. Moreover, he insists that "harmony of action between the States and Confederate authorities is essential to public welfare."

September 22

MILITARY: The Battle of Fisher's Hill erupts that afternoon when 28,000 Union troops under General Philip H. Sheridan begin probing General Jubal A. Early's line. Early, who possesses only 9,000 men, suspects that a ruse of some kind is in play and prepares to retreat. Suddenly, two divisions of Federal cavalry under General George Crook emerge screaming down the hillside on Early's left flank, sweeping aside the dismounted troopers of General Lunsford L. Lomax. Early's Confederates are thoroughly thrashed, losing 1,235 men and 14 cannon to a Union tally of 456. Sheridan declines to pursue his defeated enemy further, preferring instead to hold back and commence implementing a "scorched earth" policy to devastate the fertile Shenandoah.

POLITICS: President Jefferson Davis arrives by train at Macon, Georgia, and assures compatriots that "Our cause is not lost."

September 23

DIPLOMACY: In Japan, the Tokugawa shogunate, feeling heavy pressure from the United States and other European nations, agrees to open Yokohama and selected other ports to Western vessels.

POLITICS: President Abraham Lincoln requests the resignation of Postmaster General Montgomery Blair as a concession to Radical Republicans in the upcoming election.

September 24

MILITARY: General Philip H. Sheridan lopes down the Shenandoah Valley but, instead of pursuing defeated Southern troops, he begins burning crops to eliminate the Confederacy's breadbasket. This occurs with the complete approbation of General Ulysses S. Grant, who advises "If the war is to last another year we want the Shenandoah Valley to remain a barren waste." The single-minded Sheridan does not disappoint his superior.

POLITICS: President Abraham Lincoln appoints William Dennison the new postmaster general to replace the outgoing Montgomery Blair.

September 25

MILITARY: President Jefferson Davis arrives at Palmetto, Georgia, to confer with General John B. Hood over strategy. Because of personality clashes, Hood transfers the ornery General William J. Hardee. Davis also approves of Hood's daring strategy for invading Tennessee to strike at Union supply lines, in the hope of forcing General William T. Sherman to evacuate Georgia in pursuit.

September 27

MILITARY: Confederate guerrillas under William "Bloody Bill" Anderson ride into Centralia, Missouri, and proceed systematically plundering the town and robbing its inhabitants. He next apprehends 23 unarmed Union musicians on a train and has them summarily executed. The tragedy continues once Major A. V. E. Johnson rides into town with 158 newly recruited men of his 39th Missouri Infantry, mounted on mules. Johnson and most of his men die in an ambush, and then the guerrillas return to Centralia to kill off any remaining soldiers. By the time "Bloody Bill" completes his black deed, 116 Federals are dead.

September 29

MILITARY: Two divisions of the V Corps under General Gouvernor K. Warren strike Confederate positions along the Squirrel Level Road near Poplar Springs Church, Virginia. The defenders and their position are quickly overrun but delays by General John G. Parke's IX Corps enable General Ambrose P. Hill to rush up reinforcements and counterattack. Flanked by generals Henry Heth and Cadmus M. Wilcox, Parke abandons his gains and falls back among Warren's troops at Peeble's Farms.

General David B. Birney's X Corps of 18,000 men attacks up the slopes of New Market Heights, Virginia, spearheaded by General Charles A. Paine's division of African Americans. The black troops encounter heavy fire and dogged resistance, losing 800 men in an hour, but tenaciously forge ahead and carry the earthworks in a tremendous display of courage and sacrifice. Significantly, of 16 Congressional Medals of Honor awarded to African Americans in the Civil War, no less than 14 originate here.

General Edward O. C. Ord's XVIII Corps surges ahead against Fort Harrison, Virginia, then garrisoned by 800 inexperienced artillerists. The Federals have little experience taking their objective but beat off an attack that Confederates retreating from New Market Heights manage to launch. Union troops then begin entrenching and strengthening their lines for the inevitable Southern counterattack the following day.

September 30

MILITARY: Eager to prevent Union troops from lengthening his trench lines, General Robert E. Lee arrives at Richmond, Virginia, with eight infantry brigades to recapture Fort Harrison, Virginia. He launches the divisions of generals Robert F. Hoke and Charles Field in a bid to overwhelm the defenders, but the entrenched Federals easily repel four determined charges. Union losses over the past two days top 3,300 while the Confederates lose approximately 2,000.

October 2

MILITARY: President Jefferson Davis appoints General Pierre G. T. Beauregard as commander of the Division of the West to better coordinate the actions of generals John B. Hood and Richard Taylor. In truth, Davis regards "the little Cajun" as meddlesome and seeks to end his interference in the critical Eastern theater of operations, nor is Beauregard able to achieve much in the West.

Confederate forces at Saltville, Virginia, including guerrillas under Champ Ferguson and a Tennessee brigade led by General Felix H. Robertson, defeat a detachment of the Fifth U.S. Colored Cavalry and then execute upwards of 100 wounded soldiers. Several of their white officers are also murdered.

October 4

POLITICS: U.S. Postmaster General William Dennison joins President Abraham Lincoln's cabinet.

SOCIETAL: Syracuse, New York, is the scene of the "National Convention of Colored Citizens of the United States," with 144 delegates drawn from 18 states.

October 5

MILITARY: A division of Confederates under General Samuel O. French, numbering 3,276 men, is tasked with capturing a major Union supply depot at Alltoona Pass, Georgia. That post is defended by 2,025 Union soldiers under the recently arrived General John M. Corse, who counts on both rugged terrain and rapid-fire Henry repeating rifles to thwart the enemy. The Southerners attack from the south and west for several hours, but Corse invariably sweeps his antagonists back down the slopes. Union losses are 706 while the Confederates sustain 897.

POLITICS: President Jefferson Davis appears before cheering crowds at Augusta, Georgia, and lauds them with ringing oratory, predicting a complete Confederate victory. "Never before was I so confident that energy, harmony, and determination would rid the country of its enemy," he declares, "and give the women of the land that peace their good deeds have so well deserved."

October 6

JOURNALISM: The Richmond *Inquirer* breaks new ground by printing an essay promoting the use of African-American soldiers for the Confederacy. The idea is gaining greater currency, although President Jefferson Davis is never reconciled to it.

October 7

MILITARY: General Robert E. Lee again determines to recapture Fort Harrison, Virginia, to restore his siege lines outside Richmond. He then orders two overworked divisions under generals Robert F. Hoke and Charles W. Field to drive Union forces from the Darbytown Road. The Confederates encounter stiff opposition from General Alfred H. Terry's division, X Corps, at Johnson's Farm. Hoke also makes a tardy appearance and fails to advance, at which point Lee calls off the action. Confederate casualties are 1,350 to a Union tally of 399.

The army of General Philip H. Sheridan continues its policy of burning crops and confiscating livestock at Woodstock, Virginia. To date his men have destroyed 2,000 barns, 70 flour mills, driven off 4,000 head of cattle, and killed 3,000 sheep. Sheridan vows that when he is finished the region "will have little in it for man or beast."

NAVAL: The USS *Wachusett* under Commander Napoleon Collins decides to attack and capture the Confederate raider CSS *Florida* at Bahia, Brazil, after learning that Lieutenant Charles M. Morris and most of his crew are ashore. *Florida* surrenders after a brief struggle, having previously accounted for 37 Union prizes. However, the nature of its seizure, a blatant violation of Brazilian neutrality, results in diplomatic protests.

October 9

MILITARY: Union cavalry brigades under generals George A. Custer and Wesley Merritt engage the Confederate cavalry division of General Thomas L. Rosser at Tom's Brook, Virginia. As Custer leads 2,500 troopers to confront Rosser's 3,500 men, he recognizes his adversary as an old West Point roommate and doffs his hat before engaging. Merritt, meanwhile, crashes headlong into opposing troops, routing them while Custer ends up chasing Rosser's command for 20 miles. This is the biggest triumph of the Union mounted arm over its vaunted adversary and becomes celebrated as the "Woodstock Races."

1864

October 11

POLITICS: The recent round of elections in Pennsylvania, Ohio, and Indiana demonstrate support for President Abraham Lincoln.

October 12

GENERAL: U.S. Supreme Court Justice Roger B. Taney, head of that body since 1835, dies in Washington, D.C. He wrote the majority opinion for the infamous Dred Scott decision of 1857 which reaffirmed the status of African Americans as property, thereby exacerbating sectional tensions.

October 13

POLITICS: Maryland narrowly approves a new constitution mandating the abolition of slavery. The margin is only 30,174 to 29,799, a 375-vote margin.

October 17

MILITARY: General John B. Gordon and topographical engineer Captain Jedediah Hotchkiss steal upon the Union encampment at Cedar Creek, Virginia, ascend Massanutten Mountain, and closely examine their deployment. They discern that General Horatio G. Wright's left flank is entirely "in the air" and subject to a sudden flanking attack. This intelligence is immediately relayed to General Jubal A. Early.

October 18

MILITARY: Indomitable General Jubal A. Early, upon learning that General Philip H. Sheridan is absent from his army, plans to attack the Union encampment at Cedar Creek. Acting upon General John B. Gordon's advice, he sends three divisions along differing paths that ultimately converge behind the exposed VIII Corps of General George Crook, on their left. This march, carried out under extreme secrecy, is one of the most audacious turning movements of the entire war.

October 19

MILITARY: Lieutenant Bennett H. Young and his band of 20 Confederate Kentuckians slip across the Canadian border and attack three banks in St. Albans, Vermont, 15 miles from the border. Two citizens are shot, one fatally. After absconding with $20,000, the Southerners set fire to several buildings and try fleeing back into Canada. As word of their crime spreads, however, a nearby Union officer forms a posse and chases after them. They the catch the raiders on Canadian soil and turn them over to the proper authorities for processing and extradition.

At 5:00 A.M., the Battle of Cedar Creek erupts as the Confederate divisions of generals Clement A. Evans, Stephen Ramseur, and John Pegram plunge out of an early morning fog and pitch into the Union camp of General Horatio G. Wright. The Federal VIII and IX Corps, flanked and completely surprised, crumble before the Southern onslaught. Fortunately, General Philip H. Sheridan is returning from his strategy session in Washington, D.C., and encounters refugees as he approaches Cedar Creek. "Little Phil" then spurs his horse for 12 miles and rallies his men for a swift counterattack. The exhausted, disorganized Confederates offer little resistance and bolt from the field after suffering 2,810 casualties. Sheridan's losses are put at 5,671, but Southern resistance in the strategic Shenandoah Valley is finally broken.

October 20

POLITICS: President Abraham Lincoln decrees that the last Wednesday of every November will be celebrated as "a day of Thanksgiving and Praise to Almighty God, the beneficent Creator and Ruler of the Universe."

October 22

NAVAL: Confederate Secretary of the Navy Stephen R. Mallory writes to President Jefferson Davis, defending his decision to deploy the CSS *Tallahassee* and *Chickamauga* as commerce raiders rather then detaining them at Wilmington, North Carolina, as part of the local defenses. "A cruise by the *Chickamauga* and *Tallahassee* against the northern coasts and commerce would at once draw a fleet of fast steamers from the blockading squadron off Wilmington in pursuit of them," he reasons, "and this alone would render such a cruise expedient."

October 23

MILITARY: The Battle of Westport, Missouri, unfolds as Confederates under General Sterling Price fend off numerous Union forces. General James G. Blunt brushes up against Southern cavalry expertly led by General Joseph O. Shelby and is rebuffed. However, Price cannot spare the reserves to mount a pursuit, for General Alfred Pleasonton looms across Big Blue River, pressing upon his rear. At length General Samuel R. Curtis reinforces Blunt and they force their way across Brush Creek just as Pleasonton is closing in from behind. Price's army then bolts the field and flees in confusion toward the southwest. Casualties are roughly 1,500 apiece in this, the last major engagement of the Trans-Mississippi region.

October 26

MILITARY: Confederate outlaw William "Bloody Bill" Anderson is killed in a Union ambush at Richmond, Missouri.

October 27

MILITARY: An advance by 43,000 Union troops commences against the South Side Railroad, below Petersburg, Virginia, in the early morning rain. General Geoffrey Weitzel's main thrust is blunted while an African-American brigade under General John Holman slips around the Southern flank and charges. Holman's progress is subsequently stymied by stiff resistance offered by General William Mahone's Southerners, and Weitzel, seeing further gains as impossible, orders his men withdrawn. Union losses are 1,103 to a Confederate tally of 451.

Concurrently, an even larger operation unfolds near Hatcher's Run when the II Corps under General Winfield S. Hancock, the V Corps of General Gouverneur K. Warren, and the IX Corps under General John G. Parke march seven miles southwest of Petersburg through driving rain. Parke's command encounters heavy resistance from General Cadmus M. Wilcox's Confederate division and stops. Nightfall closes the engagement at Hatcher's Run, and the Federals retire in good order back to their lines. Hancock suffers 1,700 casualties whereas Confederate losses are estimated at 1,000. General Ulysses S. Grant subsequently concludes offensive operations and settles into winter quarters.

NAVAL: The imposing Confederate ram CSS *Albemarle* is sunk by a spar torpedo operated by 21-year-old Lieutenant William B. Cushing on the Roanoke River, North Carolina. Cushing utilized two 30-foot steam launches, each outfitted with a 14-foot-long spar torpedo, and a crew of 15. The *Albemarle* is fatally damaged

1864

and sinks, as does Cushing's own vessel, and he is forced to swim to shore. Only Cushing and one other member of the expedition make it back safely; the remaining 13 fall captive.

October 28
MILITARY: James G. Blunt's division surprises and attacks General Sterling Price's retreating army at Newtonia, Missouri. However, quick reactions by General Joseph O. Shelby and his "Iron Brigade" allow the bulk of Confederate forces to escape to safety.

October 31
POLITICS: Nevada becomes the nation's 36th state. Its two Republican-leaning U.S. senators will assist the abolitionist programs of President Abraham Lincoln and the state's three electoral votes will also support the president's reelection bid.

November 1
POLITICS: The new Maryland state constitution, abolishing slavery, is enacted.

November 2
MILITARY: Secretary of State William H. Seward informs the mayor of New York that Confederate agents arriving from Canada are planning a campaign of arson to burn the city down by election day.

November 4
NAVAL: Artillery under General Nathan B. Forrest attacks and sinks three Union paddle-wheelers on the Tennessee River near Johnsonville, Tennessee. His latest raid disrupts the flow of Union supplies and results in considerable damage; four gunboats, 14 steamers, 17 barges, 33 cannon, 150 captives, and 75,000 tons of supplies ruined. Total losses to the Union exceed $6.7 million.

November 6
POLITICS: More than 100 Copperheads and Confederate sympathizers are arrested by Colonel Benjamin Sweet in Chicago, Illinois. They are allegedly plotting to seize the polls on election day, stuff the ballots, then burn the city down. None of those apprehended are ever brought to trial.

November 7
POLITICS: The 2nd Session of the 2nd Confederate Congress convenes in Richmond, Virginia. President Jefferson Davis declares that the Confederacy still desires a negotiated settlement with the North, but only on the basis of independence. Despite the recent fall of Atlanta, Georgia, Davis assures his compatriots, "There are no vital points on the preservation of which the continued existence of the Confederacy depends."

November 8
POLITICS: The Republican ticket of Abraham Lincoln and Andrew Johnson decisively wins reelection by 2,330,552 votes to 1,835,985 for Democrat George B. McClellan. This translates into 212 Republican electoral votes to 21 for the Democrats; McClellan carries only New Jersey, Delaware, and Kentucky. This margin of 55 percent of votes cast is so large that all 81 electoral votes of the seceded states would not have altered the outcome. Moreover, Lincoln receives his highest percentage of support from soldiers and sailors fighting on the front lines.

November 9
MILITARY: The army of General William T. Sherman organizes itself into two wings under generals Oliver O. Hazard (XV, XVII Corps) and Henry W. Slocum (XIV, XX Corps) prior to marching upon Savannah, Georgia. Sherman then declares that "the army will forage liberally on the country during the march" as he intends to ignore his own lines of communication. All ranks are expected to refrain from destroying private property, if possible, but this proves an even greater application of "total war."
POLITICS: At a party celebrating his election victory, President Abraham Lincoln implores his countrymen to remain steadfast in their pursuit of final victory and reunite the country under a single banner.

November 13
MILITARY: General Jubal A. Early is ordered back to New Market, Virginia, and from there to dispatch part of his army from the Shenandoah Valley to the defenses of Petersburg. This act concludes his celebrated Valley Campaign of 1864, which involved 1,670 miles of marching and 75 pitched battles of various sizes.

November 14
POLITICS: President Abraham Lincoln accepts General George B. McClellan's resignation from the U.S. Army.

November 15
MILITARY: General William T. Sherman departs a thoroughly devastated Atlanta, Georgia, and lumbers toward Savannah and the sea with 62,000 men. Most notoriously, he also embarks on a 60-mile-wide swath of destruction across the state, destroying anything of use to the Confederacy. His unequivocal object is to "make Georgia howl," and within 21 days Sherman's "bummers" inflict damage on the South approaching $300 million, leaving a twisted, blackened landscape in their wake.

November 17
POLITICS: President Jefferson Davis dismisses outright any notion by Georgia state senators that they should conclude a separate peace treaty with the U.S. government.

November 18
MILITARY: President Jefferson Davis instructs General Howell Cobb of Georgia to mobilize the state's entire militia force to oppose the advance of General William T. Sherman. He then entrusts the whole to the command of General William J. Hardee.

November 19
POLITICS: President Abraham Lincoln lifts the blockades from Norfolk, Virginia, and Pensacola, Florida, declaring them open for business.

November 21
MILITARY: The Army of Tennessee under General John B. Hood advances 31,000 men and 8,000 cavalry from Florence, Alabama, and toward Nashville, Tennessee, to threaten Union lines of communication. However, his timetable has been delayed three weeks by General Nathan B. Forrest's absence, and during that interval General George H. Thomas enlarges the defenses of Nashville.

November 25

INDIAN: Colonel Christopher "Kit" Carson leads 200 charging cavalry through a hostile Kiowa encampment near Adobe Walls, Texas. Simultaneously, his Ute and Apache allies steal the warriors' horses. However, the survivors flee into nearby Comanche lodges with pleas for help, and soon hundreds of angry warriors begin massing to attack the intruders. Carson, suddenly confronted by the largest body of Native Americans he has ever encountered, quickly ducks behind the ruins of Adobe Walls where the fire of two 12-pound mountain howitzers keep the milling warriors at bay. Several hours of long-distance fire ensue before the Americans and their allies escape to the safety of New Mexico in the darkness. Carson suffers two dead and 10 wounded; Indian losses are between 50 and 150, due mainly to cannon fire.

MILITARY: Confederate agents dispatched from Canada set fire to 10 New York hotels in an unsuccessful attempt to burn the city down. One Southern perpetrator is caught and eventually hanged.

November 27

NAVAL: The Union steamer USS *Greyhound*, then functioning as the floating headquarters of General Benjamin F. Butler, explodes and sinks in the James River, Virginia, with a high-level conference in progress. Fortunately, Butler, General Robert Schenck, and Admiral David D. Porter escape unharmed. This accident is most likely the result of Confederate sabotage, whereby an exploding "coal torpedo" was inadvertently shoveled into the *Greyhound*'s boiler.

November 29

INDIAN: Colorado militia under Colonel John M. Chivington attack a peaceful Cheyenne camp at Sand Creek, Colorado. The Indians under Chief Black Kettle had been directed there by military authorities with the understanding that they would be safe. Nonetheless, vengeful militiamen sweep down upon the sleeping camp at dawn with artillery and then charge, killing all they encounter. Black Kettle and up to 149 Cheyenne, including women and children, are cut down and scalped. Militia losses are nine dead and 40 wounded.

November 30

MILITARY: General John M. Schofield arrives at Franklin, Tennessee, with 15,000 men of his IV and XXII Corps, and begins strengthening the city's defenses. Within hours he is accosted by 23,000 Confederates of General John B. Hood's Army of Tennessee, approaching from positions south of the town. Hood's initial charge catches two brigades of General George D. Wagner's division out in the open, sweeps them aside, and charges directly into Federal trenches beyond. The defenders are obliged to hold their fire until the cheering Southerners are nearly on top of them, then unleash a concentrated fusillade stopping men by the hundreds. Hood's men, compacted into a dense mass, resist violently but are cut down in droves by rifle and artillery fire on either flank. The Battle of Franklin costs Hood 6,252 men and six generals, including the talented Patrick L. Cleburne, while Union loses total 2,326.

December 5

NAVAL: In reporting on affairs at sea, Secretary of the Navy Gideon Welles declares "The blockade of a coastline, greater in extent that the coast of Europe from Cape Trafalgar to Cape North, is an undertaking without precedent in history."

December 6

MILITARY: General George H. Thomas is ordered by General Ulysses S. Grant to attack Confederate forces gathering outside Nashville, Tennessee, and "wait no longer for remount of your cavalry."

POLITICS: President Abraham Lincoln, in a conciliatory move, appoints Radical Republican and former secretary of the treasury Salmon P. Chase as the fifth Chief Justice of the U.S. Supreme Court to succeed the recently deceased Roger B. Taney.

December 9

MILITARY: General Ulysses S. Grant, frustrated by the perceived lack of aggressiveness by General George H. Thomas, orders General John M. Schofield to succeed him as theater commander. The directive is subsequently suspended when Thomas informs Grant that his intended attack has been canceled on account of heavy snowfall. The onset of freezing weather may have inconvenienced Thomas, but it causes the poorly clad and sheltered Confederates under General John B. Hood to shiver in their trenches.

December 10

POLITICS: President Abraham Lincoln appoints General William F. Smith and Henry Stanberry as special commissioners to report on civil and military matters west of the Mississippi River.

December 13

DIPLOMACY: Charles Coursel, a Montreal police magistrate, declares that he has no authority to detain Lieutenant Bennet Young and his 20 compatriots for their role in the raid on St. Albans, Vermont, and releases them on bond. A diplomatic uproar ensues and Secretary of State William H. Seward notifies British authorities of his intention to nullify the Rush-Bagot Agreement of 1817. This measure had previously demilitarized the U.S.–Canadian border along the Great Lakes region after the War of 1812.

NAVAL: An ailing and fatigued Admiral David G. Farragut arrives in New York City onboard the USS *Hartford,* receiving his second hero's welcome by its inhabitants.

December 14

MILITARY: The weather near Nashville, Tennessee, has moderated, and General George H. Thomas informs anxious superiors of his intention to attack General John B. Hood's Confederate camp next day. True to form, he begins methodically and unhurriedly arranging his men for battle.

December 15

MILITARY: The Battle of Nashville commences as General George H. Thomas unleashes the XVI and IV Corps against the Confederate left wing under General Benjamin F. Cheatham. Simultaneously, a large diversionary attack by General James B. Steedman's African-American troops sustains heavy loss but pins down the Confederate right. All the while General John B. Hood is furiously shifting troops around to support his overextended line but it crumbles under the weight of the Union assault. Hood is badly drubbed and should have withdrawn that evening but he defiantly elects to make another stand.

December 16
MILITARY: The Battle of Nashville resumes as General George H. Thomas, surprised that General John B. Hood's Confederates have not retreated, renews his drive against their reformed left wing. In the ensuing rout, the Federals capture General Edward Johnson and nearly all of Hood's artillery. Only the onset of darkness and the timely arrival of General Nathan B. Forrest's cavalry prevents the Army of Tennessee from completely disintegrating. Hood's losses total 5,962 while Thomas, the methodical pugilist, loses 3,057.

December 17
MILITARY: President Jefferson Davis glumly informs General William J. Hardee that he cannot reinforce the defenses of Savannah, Georgia, with units drawn from the Army of Northern Virginia.

December 18
POLITICS: President Abraham Lincoln pleads for an additional 300,000 volunteers to bolster the Union army's depleted ranks in anticipation of a final, victorious drive.

December 21
MILITARY: Savannah, Georgia, falls to Union forces under General William T. Sherman, thereby completing his 285-mile "March to the Sea." He telegrams President Abraham Lincoln, "I beg to present to you as a Christmas gift the city of Savannah with 150 heavy guns and also about 250,000 bales of cotton."

December 23
POLITICS: President Abraham Lincoln approves congressional legislation creating the rank of vice admiral; David G. Farragut becomes the first naval officer so honored, and he acquires rank equivalent to that of lieutenant general.

December 24
NAVAL: The USS *Louisiana*, packed with explosives and intended to be detonated under the guns of Fort Fisher, Wilmington, North Carolina, accidently ignites 250 yards from its objective. When this fails to appreciably damage the defenses, 60 Union warships under Admiral David G. Farragut begin a concerted bombardment which strikes the fort with 155 shells per minute.

December 25
MILITARY: An attack upon Fort Fisher, Wilmington, North Carolina, by the Army of the James under General Benjamin F. Butler, transpires. He lands 2,200 men at 2:00 A.M. and advances inland, thinking that the defenders have been silenced. Suddenly, Confederate gunners unleash a torrent of shot and shell that keeps the attackers 50 yards from their objective. Butler is so nonplussed by the stout defense that he summarily cancels the entire operation and withdraws to the fleet offshore.

December 28
MILITARY: General Ulysses S. Grant admits to President Abraham Lincoln that operations against Fort Fisher, North Carolina, are a complete fiasco, and

he insists that General Benjamin F. Butler be sacked for "Gross and culpable failure."

SOCIETAL: Congress enacts a law forbidding racial discrimination in the hiring of letter carriers.

December 30

MILITARY: President Abraham Lincoln, less politically vulnerable since his landslide reelection, relieves General Benjamin F. Butler as commander of the Army of the James.

POLITICS: Maryland politician Francis P. Blair contacts President Jefferson Davis and suggests conferring with him in Richmond, Virginia, as a peace overture to "explain the view I entertain in reference to the state of affairs of our country."

December 31

MILITARY: Union forces settle comfortably into their siege lines outside of Petersburg and Richmond, Virginia, being constantly reinforced to a strength of 110,000 men and capably led by General Ulysses S. Grant. By contrast, the once formidable Army of Northern Virginia of General Robert E. Lee withers away through illness, desertion, and combat. His 66,000 gaunt, ragged soldiers remain fierce and devoted but also perish in the cold and mud of trench warfare. The results of Grant's war-winning strategy—to pin Lee inside his works and weaken him through sheer attrition—is never more apparent.

1865

ARTS: Yale University establishes the first department of fine arts under Professor John F. Weir.

BUSINESS: John Batterson Stetson establishes a hat factory in Philadelphia, Pennsylvania, and his unique design, the "Stetson" (or "Ten-Gallon Hat") proves immediately successful throughout the West.

EDUCATION: The Indiana Agricultural College (Purdue University) is chartered at Lafayette, Indiana.

Cornell University is founded at Ithaca, New York, by Erza Cornell and Andrew Dickson White.

The Agricultural and Mechanical College of Kentucky (University of Kentucky) is founded at Lexington, Kentucky.

JOURNALISM: The San Francisco *Examiner* and the San Francisco *Chronicle*, edited by William Moss and Michael Harry DeYoung, respectively, begin publishing.

LITERATURE: Walt Whitman publishes his celebrated collection of war poems entitled *Drum Taps*.

Mary Mapes Dodge writes *Hans Brinker; or, The Silver Skates*, soon acknowledged as a children's classic.

PUBLISHING: Historian Francis Parkman continues his series on Canada with *Pioneers of France in the New World*.

SCIENCE: Swiss-born Harvard naturalist Louis Agassiz commences a 19-month expedition to Brazil and the Amazon region to study and collect indigenous fishes.

SPORTS: The National Association of Baseball now boasts a total of 91 clubs, proof of that sport's burgeoning popularity nationwide.

John Wesley Hyatt receives a patent and a $10,000 prize for perfecting a composition billiard ball to replace the more expensive ivory ones then in use.

TECHNOLOGY: The Fredonia Gas, Light, and Water Works Company of Fredonia, New York, is the first business to sell natural gas for lighting purposes.

January 2

NAVAL: Secretary of the Navy Gideon Welles contacts Secretary of War Edwin M. Stanton and expresses the dire necessity for capturing and closing Wilmington, North Carolina, "the only port by which any supplies whatever reach the rebels."

January 3

MILITARY: General Alfred H. Terry receives command of the forthcoming joint expedition against Fort Fisher, Wilmington, North Carolina. At this stage of the war even General Benjamin F. Butler's political allies cannot salvage his waning military fortunes.

January 4

NAVAL: Admiral David D. Porter begins laying out his strategy for the reduction of Fort Fisher, Wilmington, North Carolina. He intends to use a naval brigade, consisting of sailors and U.S. Marines, to hit the fort frontally while army troops work their way around the rear.

January 5

POLITICS: President Abraham Lincoln authorizes James Singleton to pass through Union lines and enter the Confederacy; his mission is to unofficially encourage peace negotiations.

January 6

POLITICS: U.S. Representative J. M. Ashley of Ohio renews the political drive to ratify the Thirteenth Amendment to the U.S. Constitution. "If slavery is wrong and criminal, as the great body of Christian men admit," he declares, "it is certainly our duty to abolish it."

President Jefferson Davis pens a caustic letter to Vice President Alexander H. Stephens and claims that Stephens' whispering campaign against him is undermining Southern morale. "I assure you that it would be a source of the sincerest pleasure to see you devoting your agenda and animated ability exclusively to upholding the confidence and animating the spirit of the people to unconquerable resistance against their foes," he lectures.

January 7

INDIAN: A large body of 1,000 Cheyenne and Sioux warriors, angered over the 1864 Sand Creek massacre, attack the frontier settlement of Julesburg and Valley Station, Colorado Territory. The Indians send a small detachment forward to lure the garrison out, and a party of the 7th Iowa Cavalry under Captain Nicholas J. O'Brien obliges them. Fortunately, the intended ambush miscarries when it is sprung too early, and the troopers scamper back to the fort and safety. The warriors, unable to overcome such strong defenses, subsequently loot and burn nearby settlements.

January 9

MILITARY: General John B. Hood straggles into Tupelo, Mississippi, with remnants of the once-proud Army of Tennessee. President Jefferson Davis intends to transfer the bulk of the survivors eastward to contest the advance of General William T. Sherman in the Carolinas.

POLITICS: President Abraham Lincoln dispatches Secretary of War Edwin M. Stanton to Savannah, Georgia, for discussions with General William T. Sherman. Among the issues raised is Sherman's alleged mistreatment of African-American refugees.

U.S. Representative Moses Odell, a New York Democrat, endorses the proposed constitutional amendment to outlaw slavery, insisting that "The South by rebellion has absolved the Democratic party in the North from all obligation to stand up longer for the defense of its 'cornerstone.'"

The Tennessee constitutional convention approves an amendment abolishing slavery and places it up for a popular vote.

January 10
POLITICS: Heated debate in the U.S. House continues as to a constitutional amendment to abolish slavery. Representative Fernando Wood of New York insists its passage negates any chance for peaceful reconciliation with the South.

January 11
MILITARY: Despite freezing weather, 300 Confederate cavalry under General Thomas L. Rosser attack a Union encampment at Beverly, West Virginia. The defenders, comprising detachments from the 8th and 34th Ohio Cavalry, are caught by surprise and overwhelmed before serious resistance is mounted. Rosser secures 583 captives, 100 horses, 600 rifles and—above all—10,000 rations to feed his hungry men.

SLAVERY: The Missouri constitutional convention approves an ordinance abolishing slavery.

January 12
NAVAL: Admiral David D. Porter arrives off Wilmington, North Carolina, with a fleet of 59 warships and 8,000 men commanded by General Alfred H. Terry. This is the largest Union armada and combined amphibious expedition of the entire war.

POLITICS: Secretary of War Edwin M. Stanton confers with African-American leaders in Washington, D.C., over how to best assimilate freed slaves into society. Garrison Frazier, the group spokesman, suggests that blacks continue farming the land until they are able to purchase it. And, despite allegations of callous indifference by General William T. Sherman toward "contrabands," Frazier states "We have confidence in General Sherman, and think that what concerns us could not be in better hands."

Senior Maryland politician Francis P. Blair confers with President Jefferson Davis in Richmond, Virginia, sounding out possible overtures for peace. To facilitate a possible rapprochement, Blair suggests mounting a joint military expedition against the French in Mexico. Davis dismisses the scheme as quixotic but acquiesces to sending Confederate representatives to confer with President Abraham Lincoln in February.

January 14
MILITARY: Union troops under General Alfred H. Terry land outside Fort Fisher, Wilmington, North Carolina, and move quickly to prevent Confederate

attempts to reinforce the garrison. Nevertheless, 350 soldiers under General H. C. Whiting make it through Union lines, and bring the fort defenders up to 2,000 men.

NAVAL: The armada of Admiral David D. Porter, mounting 627 heavy cannon, begins its reduction of Confederate defenses at Fort Fisher, Wilmington, North Carolina. Porter moves his ships to within 1,000 yards of the fort and delivers a meticulously aimed fire of 100 shells per minute. Within hours the bulk of Fort Fisher's armament has been dismounted or made useless.

January 15

MILITARY: General Alfred H. Terry commences an all-out assault on Fort Fisher, Wilmington, North Carolina, with three brigades commanded by generals Newton M. Curtis, Galusha Pennypacker, and Louis H. Bell. Resistance is fierce and all three Union brigadiers are either killed or wounded in fierce, hand-to-hand fighting lasting eight hours. Terry then commits his final brigade under General Joseph C. Abbott and the defenders are overpowered by 10:00 P.M. Combined Union losses are 1,341 while the Confederates sustain roughly 500 with an additional 1,500 taken.

NAVAL: Admiral David D. Porter orders his ironclad monitors to point-blank range of Fort Fisher, Wilmington, North Carolina, and maintains a withering bombardment of Confederate defenses. Once the fort's heavy cannon are silenced, the naval brigade goes forward in three desperate charges that are repelled but also distract the defenders from army troops circling from behind. For their role in this significant victory, no less than 35 sailors and marines win the Congressional Medal of Honor.

January 16

POLITICS: Maryland politician Francis P. Blair conveys a letter from President Jefferson Davis to President Abraham Lincoln, suggesting the commencement of peace talks "between the two nations." Lincoln, like Davis, dismisses any notion of a joint expedition against Mexico, but agrees to attend a peace conference slated for February.

The Confederate Congress, lacking confidence in President Jefferson Davis's conduct of military affairs, passes a resolution, 14 to 2, to appoint General Robert E. Lee as general in chief, and also to restore General Joseph E. Johnston as commander of the Army of Tennessee.

SLAVERY: General William T. Sherman issues Special Field Order No. 15 which confiscates land on the Georgia coast for the express purpose of settling African-American refugees. He later insists this is nothing but a temporary expedient until the refugees can be resettled inland on a more permanent basis.

January 18

POLITICS: President Abraham Lincoln hands Francis P. Blair a letter for President Jefferson Davis, demonstrating his willingness to negotiate peace for the inhabitants of "our one common country."

January 19

POLITICS: President Abraham Lincoln inquires of General Ulysses S. Grant about the possibility of finding Robert Lincoln, his eldest son, a staff position. Grant subsequently appoints him assistant adjutant general with a rank of captain.

President Jefferson Davis, intent upon shoring up support for his flagging reputation as a war leader, convinces a reluctant General Robert E. Lee to serve as general in chief of Confederate forces. Lee consents but cautions "I must state that with the addition of immediate command of the army, I do not think I could accomplish any good."

January 20
POLITICS: Secretary of War Edwin M. Stanton, recently arrived from Savannah, Georgia, confers with President Abraham Lincoln as to recent conversation he held with General William T. Sherman.

January 21
MILITARY: General William T. Sherman begins relocating his headquarters from Savannah, Georgia, to Beaufort, South Carolina. Over all, his march through the Carolinas has been plagued by heavy rains.

January 22
NAVAL: Lieutenant John Low, C.S.N., sails the steamer CSS *Ajax* from Dublin, Ireland, and makes for Nassau, the Bahamas, to receive its armament. However, adroit work by American minister Charles F. Adams dissuades the British from allowing any guns to be shipped there.

January 23
POLITICS: President Jefferson Davis, reacting to pressure from the Confederate Congress, signs the General in Chief Act which makes General Robert E. Lee supreme military commander.

January 24
MILITARY: Reversing himself, General Ulysses S. Grant now approves of renewed prisoner exchanges. This influx of new Confederate manpower is calculated to exacerbate existing food shortages.

January 27
POLITICS: President Jefferson Davis begins choosing a commission to conduct informal peace talks as suggested by Francis P. Blair. This ultimately consists of Vice President Alexander H. Stephens, Senate President Robert Hunter, and Assistant Secretary of War John A. Campbell. They are authorized to discuss political moves to arrange an armistice, although Southern independence must be the ultimate goal.

January 31
MILITARY: General Robert E. Lee is appointed general in chief of Confederate forces in light of continuing dissatisfaction over President Jefferson Davis's handling of military affairs.
POLITICS: The U.S. House of Representatives finally musters the two-thirds majority vote (119 to 56) and ratifies the Thirteenth Amendment to the U.S. Constitution to abolish slavery. This legislation was previously passed by the Senate on April 8, 1864, and is now handed off to the states for ratification.

February 1
POLITICS: Illinois becomes the first state to ratify the Thirteenth Amendment to the Constitution, which formally abolishes slavery.

John Rock, an African-American attorney from Boston, Massachusetts, becomes the first minority lawyer to argue before the U.S. Supreme Court.

Confederate Secretary of War James A. Seddon resigns due to office political pressure.

February 2

POLITICS: President Abraham Lincoln departs Washington, D.C., to meet with Confederate peace commissioners at Hampton Roads, Virginia.

Rhode Island and Michigan are the second and third states to ratify the Thirteenth Amendment.

February 3

POLITICS: President Jefferson Davis dispatches Confederate Vice President Alexander H. Stephens, John A. Campbell, and Robert M. T. Hunter to confer with President Abraham Lincoln and Secretary of State William H. Seward onboard a ship off Hampton Roads, Virginia. The meeting deadlocks since the Southerners insist on independence as a precondition for peace, while Lincoln will only accept their unconditional surrender.

Maryland, New York, and West Virginia ratify the Thirteenth Amendment for a total of six states.

February 4

MILITARY: General Ulysses S. Grant orders Union forces to cut off Southern wagon trains near Hatcher's Run, Virginia, along the Boydton Plank Road. The II Corps under General Andrew A. Humphreys, the V Corps of General Gouvernor K. Warren, and a cavalry under General John M. Gregg draw the assignment.

POLITICS: President Abraham Lincoln returns to Washington, D.C., somewhat distraught that nothing has been accomplished through direct peace negotiations. He then assures General Ulysses S. Grant, "Nothing transpired, or transpiring, with the three gentlemen from Richmond is to cause any change, hindrance, or delay of your military plans or operations."

February 5

MILITARY: General Gouverneur K. Warren's V Corps launches a renewed offensive along the Boydton Plank Road near Hatcher's Run (Dabney's Mill), Virginia, while General Andrew A. Humphrey's II Corps likewise occupies the nearby Vaughan Road. The Confederates then launch several strong attacks throughout the course of the day but are repulsed, and Humphreys is reinforced overnight by General David M. Gregg's cavalry division.

POLITICS: President Abraham Lincoln floats the idea of offering $400 million to slave states if they will surrender by April 1. His cabinet uniformly rejects the suggestion, however, so Lincoln abandons it.

February 6

MILITARY: Heavy fighting resumes along Hatcher's Run, Virginia, as Confederate forces of General John B. Gordon's division slam into the exposed V Corps of General Gouverneur K. Warren. In the course of heavy fighting Southern general John Pegram falls in action, but renewed onslaughts by General Clement A. Evans gradually force the Federals off the Boydton Plank Road.

POLITICS: In reporting to the Confederate Congress the recent conference held at Hampton Roads, President Jefferson Davis denounces President Abraham Lincoln for insisting upon unqualified submission as the sole basis for peace. He declares this unacceptable and vows that the fight for Southern independence will go on.

General and former vice president John C. Breckinridge is appointed the new Confederate secretary of war to replace outgoing James A. Seddon.

February 7
MILITARY: Fighting continues at Hatcher's Run, Virginia, as Union forces finally and successfully extend their siege lines at a cost of 1,512 casualties. Southern losses are unknown but presumed as heavy. Worse, General Robert E. Lee's defensive perimeter is now stretched to 37 miles in length just as General Ulysses S. Grant again prepares to shift his forces further leftward.
POLITICS: Maine and Kansas ratify the Thirteenth Amendment; the Delaware legislature fails to muster the necessary two-thirds majority.

February 8
POLITICS: President Abraham Lincoln signs a U.S. House resolution declaring that 11 states of the soon-to-be defunct Confederacy should not enjoy representation in the electoral college.

February 9
POLITICS: Upon the recommendation of General Robert E. Lee, now general in chief, President Jefferson Davis enacts a pardon for all Confederate deserters who report back to their units with 30 days.
SLAVERY: Unionists in Virginia ratify the Thirteenth Amendment, outlawing slavery.

February 12
POLITICS: The Electoral College meets and confirms President Abraham Lincoln's election victory on a vote of 212 to 21.

February 13
DIPLOMACY: Lord John Russell informs American diplomats in London of the government's unease over recent buildups of naval strength along the Great Lakes region, contrary to the 1817 Rush-Bagot Agreement. The British are summarily informed that the buildup is in direct response to the Confederate raid on St. Albans, Vermont, on October 19, 1864, which was launched from Canada.
POLITICS: Reacting to complaints from west Tennessee politicians, President Abraham Lincoln admonishes military authorities there, insisting that "the object of the war being to restore and maintain blessings of peace and good government, I desire you to help, and not hinder, every advance in that direction."

February 17
MILITARY: Union forces under General William T. Sherman accept the surrender of Columbia, capital of South Carolina, from city officials. Meanwhile, General Wade Hampton's cavalry burns enormous stockpiles of cotton bales before departing, sparks from which ignite several uncontrollable fires. Southerners are convinced that the city has been torched on Sherman's orders and mark it as a defining atrocity of the war.

1865

POLITICS: The U.S. Congress repudiates all debts accrued by various Confederate governments.

February 18

MILITARY: Charleston, South Carolina, is occupied by Union forces under General Alexander Schimmelfenning. For many Federals, the capture of the "fire eater" center of the Confederacy is sweet revenge.

POLITICS: General Robert E. Lee agrees in principle to the notion of arming slaves to fight for Southern independence but feels they must be fighting as free men.

February 20

POLITICS: The Confederate House of Representatives approves the use of African-American slaves as soldiers.

February 21

MILITARY: General Robert E. Lee alerts Confederate Secretary of War John C. Breckinridge that, if absolutely necessary, he will abandon Richmond, Virginia, and make all haste for Burkeville to maintain communication with Confederate forces in the Carolinas. He also requests that General Joseph E. Johnston be returned to active duty as the health of General Pierre G. T. Beauregard appears fragile.

February 22

MILITARY: Union forces under General John M. Schofield occupy Wilmington, North Carolina, closing the last remaining port of the Confederacy from the land side. The Federals are now poised to conduct military operations toward the interior of the state and, to facilitate this, Schofield orders all railroad tracks in the vicinity repaired.

SLAVERY: Tennessee voters approve a new state constitution that abolishes slavery while Kentucky legislators reject the Thirteenth Amendment.

February 23

POLITICS: The Thirteenth Amendment is ratified by Minnesota.

February 24

MILITARY: General William T. Sherman vigorously protests to General Wade Hampton the alleged murder of several Union soldiers on a foraging expedition. Hampton replies that his government authorizes him to execute any Federals caught burning private property.

February 25

MILITARY: General Joseph E. Johnston arrives at Charlotte, North Carolina, to resume command of the Army of Tennessee and all Confederate forces extant in South Carolina, Georgia, and Florida. He now leads a skeleton force of 25,000 ragged, hungry men, observing, "in my opinion, these troops form an army far too weak to cope with Sherman."

February 27

MILITARY: Generals Philip H. Sheridan and Wesley Merritt take 10,000 cavalry down the Shenandoah Valley toward Lynchburg, Virginia, intending to sever the Virginia Central Railroad and the James River Canal. They command the 1st Cavalry division of General Thomas C. Devlin and the 3rd Cavalry Division of General George A. Custer.

March 1
POLITICS: The Thirteenth Amendment is ratified by Wisconsin but rejected by New Jersey.

March 2
MILITARY: The 3rd Cavalry Division of General George A. Custer clatters up to Waynesboro, Virginia, where it observes 2,000 Confederates under General Gabriel C. Wharton's division drawn up on a ridge line, supported by a few hundred cavalry under General Thomas L. Rosser. Custer quickly perceives that Wharton lacks the manpower to cover both his flanks and dispatches three dismounted regiments to encircle the Confederate left. He sounds the advance and his flankers burst through the woods on Wharton's flank and then leads his two remaining brigades on a thunderous charge through the Confederate center. The Southerners simply dissolve under the onslaught and General Jubal A. Early and his staff flee from the field. Custer takes 1,600 prisoners, 17 flags, 11 cannon, and 200 wagons for a loss of nine dead and wounded.

March 3
BUSINESS: To better regulate finances, the U.S. Congress levies a 10 percent tax on state bank notes to drive them out of circulation. These are then replaced by bank notes drawn from institutions belonging to the national banking system. It is a move calculated to improve centralized financing for the war effort.
POLITICS: President Abraham Lincoln, acting through Secretary of War Edwin M. Stanton, instructs General Ulysses S. Grant to ignore any of General Robert E. Lee's intimations toward peace unless he surrenders first.
SLAVERY: Congress institutes the Bureau for the Relief of Freedmen and Refugees (Freedmen's Bureau) to assist former African-American slaves to find work and education and obtain land. This, in effect, constitutes the nation's first social welfare agency and is tasked with helping 4 million liberated slaves adjust to freedom.

March 4
POLITICS: President Abraham Lincoln is inaugurated for a second term in Washington, D.C. Despite the carnage and acrimony of the past four years he strikes a conciliatory tone with his adversaries. "With malice towards none; with charity for all, with firmness in the right, as God gives us to see the right, let us strive to finish the work we are in," he declares, "to bind up the nation's wounds, to care for him who shall have borne the battle, and for his widow and his orphan—to do all which may achieve and cherish a just and lasting peace, among ourselves, and with all nations." In contrast to Lincoln's stunning eloquence, newly elected Vice President Andrew Johnson delivers a rambling, incoherent speech that offends many in the audience.

Tennessee Unionist William G. Brownlow is elected governor to replace Andrew Johnson.

March 5
POLITICS: Comptroller of Currency Hugh McCulloch is appointed Secretary of the Treasury, replacing William Fessenden, who resigned after winning a seat as U.S. Senator from Maine.

March 6
MILITARY: The 600-man expedition of General John Newton encounters Confederate resistance under General William Miller at Natural Bridge, Florida. The

Federals make repeated attempts to outflank them but find Southern defenses too strong to storm. Miller is also reinforced to a strength of 1,000 men, so Newton falls back and entrenches on an open pine barren. This minor Confederate victory prevents the state capital at Tallahassee from being attacked.

March 7
POLITICS: Admiral David D. Porter testifies before Congress, proffering some salty commentary as to the leadership abilities of generals Benjamin F. Butler and Nathaniel P. Banks.

March 8
SLAVERY: The Confederate Congress authorizes African-American slaves to bear arms for military service on a vote of nine to eight.

March 9
MILITARY: General Robert E. Lee warns Confederate Secretary of War John C. Breckinridge about endemic supply shortages and "Unless the men and animals can be subsisted, the army cannot be kept together, and our present lines must be abandoned."

The Battle of Kinston, North Carolina, unfolds as General Braxton Bragg attacks soldiers of General Jacob D. Cox's XXII Corps. He does so by dispatching General Robert F. Hoke's division on a flank attack that dislodges Federals under General Samuel P. Carter, while General Daniel H. Hill undertakes a similar move against the Union right. However, neither commander can dislodge a second Union line commanded by General Thomas H. Ruger and the Southern offensive stumbles. Bragg then orders his men across the Neuse River and back into Kinston. Union loses are 1,257 while the Confederates suffer only 134.

POLITICS: President Abraham Lincoln accepts the resignation of John P. Usher as secretary of the interior and appoints Assistant William Otto to succeed him.

Vermont ratifies the Thirteenth Amendment.

March 10
MILITARY: Covered by an early morning fog, Confederate cavalry led by generals Wade Hampton and Joseph Wheeler successfully attacks sleeping cavalry of General Hugh J. Kilpatrick at Monroe's Crossroads, North Carolina. Kilpatrick, surprised and clad only in his undershirt, narrowly evades capture as the Southerners under General Matthew Butler gallop through his camp, sweeping up all in their path. The Federals gradually rally and recapture their bivouac, and Hampton withdraws in good order back to Fayetteville. Kilpatrick insists that his losses are no greater than 190, while killing 80 Confederates and taking 30 prisoner. The affair becomes popularly known on both sides as the "Battle of Kilpatrick's Pants."

March 11
POLITICS: President Abraham Lincoln declares an amnesty for all army and navy deserters returning to their units within two months. Failure to do so results in a loss of citizenship.

March 13
POLITICS: Desperate to secure additional manpower, President Jefferson Davis reluctantly signs the "Negro Soldier Law" allowing slaves to serve in the Confed-

erate army. The legislation implies that individuals who serve may be manumitted at a later date with the permission of their owner and state legislatures. Had such pragmatic measures been approved earlier the men might have mitigated continual Confederate personnel shortages and wielded a positive impact on the Southern war effort.

March 14

DIPLOMACY: Despite Southern overtures toward emancipation, Lord Palmerston declares to Confederate envoys James M. Mason and Duncan F. Kenner that English diplomatic recognition is now a closed issue, especially seeing that the war, in all likelihood, will terminate in a Union victory very shortly.

March 15

MILITARY: General William T. Sherman orders his army out of Fayetteville, North Carolina, and toward Goldsborough. Meanwhile, Union cavalry under General Hugh J. Kilpatrick advances to Averasboro and headlong into General William J. Hardee's division of 6,000 men, strongly posted with a swamp on their right and the Black River to their left. Kilpatrick backs off until additional Federal forces can come up.

March 16

MILITARY: The Battle of Averasboro erupts as General Hugh J. Kilpatrick's pushes the 8th Indiana Cavalry forward. These push back skirmishers from Colonel Alfred Rhet's brigade but then are stopped cold by the main Confederate body under General Lafayette McLaws. All four divisions of the Union XX Corps under General Henry W. Slocum then deploy on the field and drive the Southerners back into their fieldworks. Fighting continues as the Union troops attempt to flank McLaws with scant success and the battle unwinds by nightfall. General William J. Hardee subsequently orders the Confederates to fall back upon Smithville, which they accomplish without incident.

March 17

MILITARY: General Edward R. S. Canby begins his drive toward Mobile, Alabama, with 32,000 men of the XVI and XII Corps; his opponent, General Dabney H. Maury, only musters 2,000 rank and file. Canby intends to catch the city in a pincer, with one column under General Frederick Steele proceeding out of Pensacola to the east as he leads another force from the west along the shore of Mobile Bay. However, progress is slow owing to the muddy condition of the roads they must pass over, and corduroy has to be laid to allow the passage of heavy artillery.

POLITICS: The 2nd Session, 2nd Confederate Congress adjourns, although in a pique over President Jefferson Davis's insinuation of obstructionism.

March 19

MILITARY: The Battle of Bentonville, North Carolina, commences as General Henry W. Slocum orders General William P. Carlin's division, XX Corps, down the Goldsborough Road toward Cole's Plantation. En route he encounters large numbers of heavily entrenched Confederates and halts. Desperate fighting breaks out along the line as hard-charging Southerners fail to break through Union lines. The conflict winds down with nightfall as both sides bring up additional reinforcements.

March 20

MILITARY: The right wing of General William T. Sherman's army under General Oliver O. Howard marches toward Bentonville, North Carolina, to reinforce the left wing under General Henry W. Slocum. His arrival boosts Union numbers to 60,000—three times the size of his Southern opponent. Confederates under General Joseph E. Johnston, meanwhile, continue strengthening their fortifications and are especially eager to protect Mill Creek Bridge, their only escape route, from being seized.

March 21

MILITARY: The Battle of Bentonville resumes as General William T. Sherman dispatches General Joseph A. Mower's division to turn the Confederate left and rear while the main Union force demonstrates to their front. Mower makes surprisingly good progress and nearly reaches Mill Creek Bridge before being violently assailed on both flanks and driven back. However, General Joseph E. Johnston simply lacks the manpower to follow up his success and he orders the army to withdraw northwest toward Smithville. Bentonville is the last conventional clash of the Civil War and both sides perform admirably. Union casualties are 1,646 to a Confederate tally of 2,606.

March 22

MILITARY: General James H. Wilson, at the head of 13,500 Union cavalry, crosses the Tennessee River from Gravelly Springs, Tennessee, and gallops into northern Alabama. His objective is to seize the Confederate munitions center at Selma and commands the divisions of generals Edward M. Cook, Eli Long, and Emory Upton; this is also the largest cavalry force ever fielded in American military history. Wilson, determined to confuse the defenders while en route, divides his command into three columns and takes three separate but mutually supporting routes.

March 23

MILITARY: The combined forces of generals William T. Sherman and John M. Schofield, numbering in excess of 100,000 men, unite at Goldsborough, North Carolina. Thus far Sherman has covered 425 miles from Savannah, Georgia, in only 50 days and with no major mishap. It is a logistical and organizational triumph that far exceeds his better known "March to the Sea" in complexity and difficulty.

POLITICS: President Abraham Lincoln and his son Tad depart Washington, D.C., for City Point, Virginia, outside Petersburg, to confer with General Ulysses S. Grant.

March 24

MILITARY: General Robert E. Lee, in light of his slowly eroding defenses in and around Petersburg, Virginia, conceives his final tactical offensive of the war. He orders General John B. Gordon to take elements of several Confederate corps and seize a portion of nearby Union lines. A breakthough would undoubtedly force General Ulysses S. Grant to concentrate his forces near the break, thereby allowing the Army of Virginia to slip out of Petersburg and join General Joseph E. Johnston in North Carolina.

POLITICS: President Abraham Lincoln arrives at Fortress Monroe, Virginia, prior to meeting with General Ulysses S. Grant and William T. Sherman at City Point.

March 25
MILITARY: At 4:00 P.M., the Battle of Fort Stedman, Virginia, begins as Confederate pioneer companies silence outlying Union pickets and remove their abatis (defensive obstacles). Then General John B. Gordon launches 11,000 Southerners into Union trenches near Fort Stedman, surprising the defenders and capturing the fort and Batteries X, XI, and XII. However, General John Hartranft leads 4,000 men back to the trenches, recaptures Fort Stedman, and forces Gordon's veterans back. Lacking the manpower necessary to contest the Union advance, the Confederates fall back in disorder, losing 3,500 men, including 1,500 prisoners. Union casualties amount to 1,044; Lee now has little recourse but to prepare for the abandonment of Petersburg.
POLITICS: President Abraham Lincoln arrives at City Point, Virginia, and meets with General Ulysses S. Grant.

March 28
POLITICS: President Abraham Lincoln, generals Ulysses S. Grant and William T. Sherman, and Admiral David D. Porter confer on the steamship *River Queen* to discuss postwar policy toward their former adversaries. Lincoln, fearful of continuing guerrilla activity, instructs them to offer generous terms to the vanquished in order to bring them back into the fold quickly.

March 31
MILITARY: Union forces under General Philip H. Sheridan continue turning the Confederate right flank at Dinwiddie Court House, Virginia. He is suddenly assailed in the left flank by General George E. Pickett's division and violently shoved back, but Pickett, cognizant of how dangerously thin his force is stretched, withdraws to Five Forks under cover of darkness. Moreover, General Robert E. Lee fears for the precariousness of his perimeter and explicitly instructs Pickett to "Hold Five Forks at all hazards."

April 1
MILITARY: The Battle of Five Forks, Virginia, begins as General Philip H. Sheridan orders cavalry under generals George A. Custer and Thomas C. Devlin to slash at the Confederate right flank while his remaining forces engage and pin them frontally. Inexplicably, Confederate generals George E. Pickett and Fitzhugh Lee are absent as the struggle develops, being at a fish bake several miles to the rear. Sheridan then orders his cavalry to charge the entire Confederate line and it buckles and breaks. Victory at Five Forks cost the Union 986 casualties while the Confederates lost 4,400 men in addition to 11 flags and four cannon. Worse still, General Robert E. Lee has no recourse but to abandon Richmond to save his army from encirclement.

Union cavalry under generals Eli Long and Emory Upton press 1,500 Confederate cavalry under General Nathan B. Forrest at Ebenezer Church, Alabama, where he awaits the arrival of General James R. Chalmer's division. At 4:00 P. M., the first Union wave under Long gallops forward, crashes into the Confederate center, and is repulsed. Another part of Upton's men hit Forrest's center-left, held by Alabama militia, and they bolt and collapse the entire line. Federal losses amount to 12 dead and 40 wounded to a Confederate tally of 300, mostly captured.

April 2
MILITARY: General Ulysses S. Grant decisively orders an all-out assault on Confederate defenses ringing Petersburg, Virginia. At 4:30 A. M. General Horatio G.

Wright's VI Corps storms the Southern right at Fort Fisher, as far as Hatcher's Run, and fatally ruptures General Robert E. Lee's line. The XXIV Corps also charges down Boydton Plank Road, routing the defenders while redoubtable General Ambrose P. Hill dies rallying his men.

General Robert E. Lee orders the immediate evacuation of Petersburg, Virginia, and advises President Jefferson Davis to relocate the seat of Confederate government far from Richmond. Thus the siege of Petersburg, which commenced on June 15, 1864, successfully terminates with Union losses of 5,100 killed, 24,800 wounded, and 17,500 captured; Confederate losses over this same period are variously estimated at between 28,000 and 38,000.

General James H. Wilson arrives before Selma, Alabama, a heavily fortified city guarded by 5,000 men under General Nathan B. Forrest. Wilson immediately dispatches General Eli Long's division to attack the Confederate right while dismounted; the troopers cross 600 yards of open space, taking heavy losses. Wilson then decides the issue with a thundering charge down the Selma Road which finally scatters the defenders. Forrest's losses are 2,700 captured and 102 cannon seized; Union casualties are 46 dead, 300 wounded, and 13 missing.

POLITICS: As Confederate defenses around Richmond, Virginia, collapse, a greatly relieved President Abraham Lincoln telegraphs General Ulysses S. Grant, "Allow me to tender to you, and all with you, the nation's grateful thanks for this additional and magnificent success."

April 3

MILITARY: Union forces under General Godfrey Weitzel, commanding the largely African-American XXV Corps, prepares to occupy Richmond, Virginia. At 5:30 A.M., he sends forward an advance party under Major Atherton H. Stevens, which is received by civil authorities at city hall. Richmond then formally capitulates to Union forces, who promptly raise the Stars and Stripes over the state capitol. President Abraham Lincoln, visiting General Ulysses S Grant in Petersburg, happily declares "Thank God I have lived to see this. It seems to me that I have been dreaming a horrid dream for four years, and now the nightmare is gone."

POLITICS: President Jefferson Davis and his cabinet arrive by special train in Danville, Virginia.

April 4

POLITICS: President Abraham Lincoln ventures up the James River to Richmond, Virginia, aboard the USS *Malvern*. Once ashore he is escorted by Admiral David D. Porter and 10 sailors to the Confederate White House, all the while being greeted by throngs of former African-American slaves. Many of these reach out and touch Lincoln's person to convince themselves that he is not an apparition.

President Jefferson Davis, pausing momentarily at Danville, Virginia, calls on fellow Southerners not to lose hope for ultimate victory is certain from "our own unquenchable resolve."

April 5

MILITARY: General Robert E. Lee, preparing to depart Amelia Court House, Virginia, is now joined by the troops of General Richard S. Ewell, bringing his strength up to 58,000. Lee then determines to attack Union forces under generals Philip H. Sheridan and George G. Meade directly in their path at Jetersville and cut themselves free. Three divisions under General James Longstreet are readied to march, but Lee cancels the move and instead opts for a night march around the Union left flank, followed by a quick dash to Farmville where promised supplies should be waiting. Federal forces continue milling around their fortifications until 10:30 P.M. when General Ulysses S. Grant arrives to personally supervise the pursuit.

POLITICS: As President Abraham Lincoln delights sitting in Jefferson Davis's chair, he is approached by Confederate Assistant Secretary of War John A. Campbell, himself a former U.S. Supreme Court justice, who requests that the president help maintain the rule of law in Virginia.

Secretary of State William H. Seward is severely injured in a carriage accident in Washington, D.C.

April 6

MILITARY: The Battle of Sayler's Creek unfolds as the Army of the Northern Virginia, retreating from Amelia Court House to Farmsville, Virginia, inadvertently separates into three parts. Closely pursuing Union forces are thus able to exploit gaps between the commands of generals Richard S. Ewell, Richard H. Anderson, and John B. Gordon with disastrous effect. The Southerners initially repulse the Union advance as they pour over the flooded Sayler's Creek, but the division of General George W. Getty effectively flanks the defenders. Ewell's entire line is then promptly double-enveloped and surrenders 3,400 prisoners.

A similar drama develops to Ewell's right-rear, where a Union cavalry division under General Wesley Merritt attacks General Richard H. Anderson's corps. Here the weak formations of generals George E. Pickett and Bushrod Johnson dissolve in the face of a mounted charge by General George A. Custer. As Southern defenses buckle, Anderson's survivors flee into the woods and Federal troops round up another 2,600 captives, 300 wagons, and 15 cannon.

The final act to play occurs on the Confederate left where 17,000 men of General Andrew A. Humphrey's II Corps engages General John B. Gordon's rear guard, numbering only 7,000. Gordon is presently protecting a Southern wagon train bogged down in the mud and Humphrey quickly sends a strong column around his left. Gordon quickly abandons the field to save his command, although an additional 1,700 men are taken prisoner.

Sayler's Creek proves a black day for the Army of Northern Virginia, which loses 7,700 men and eight generals—one-fifth of its entire strength. Union losses amount only to 166 killed and 982 wounded. This also represents one of the largest numbers of Americans captured in battle until Bataan, 1942.

April 7

DIPLOMACY: The U.S. government, having lost millions of dollars in shipping to the English-built CSS *Alabama* and other raiders, begins a lengthy litigation process seeking restitution.

POLITICS: An anxious President Abraham Lincoln, upon hearing that General Robert E. Lee might capitulate if cornered, implores General Ulysses S. Grant to "Let the thing be pressed."

Tennessee ratifies the Thirteenth Amendment while William G. Brownlow, an unabashed Unionist, is inaugurated as governor.

April 8

MILITARY: Rather than surrender, General Robert E. Lee seeks to break through Union cavalry under General Philip H. Sheridan blocking his path at Appomattox

Court House. At a council of war held late that night, Lee and his generals agree to attack Sheridan in the morning then press onto Lynchburg.

April 9

MILITARY: Palm Sunday. General Robert E. Lee directs generals John B. Gordon and Fitzhugh Lee to attack General Philip H. Sheridan's forces at Appomattox Court House, Virginia. The Federal troopers are gradually dislodged from their position when Lee discerns Union General Edward O. C. Ord's entire Army of the James drawn up in battle formation behind them. He finally acknowledges the futility of fighting further and parleys with Union authorities to discuss surrender terms.

At 1:30 P.M., General Robert E. Lee, accompanied only by his secretary, meets with General Ulysses S. Grant and formally surrenders the Army of Northern Virginia at Appomattox Court House, Virginia. The terms proffered by Grant are generous, whereby all of Lee's 30,000 survivors are paroled and allowed to go home, officers are permitted to retain sidearms, and all horses and mules remain with their rightful owners. In a kindly gesture, Union forces issue 25,000 rations to the half-starved Confederates. The harsh and bloody Civil War, the most costly conflict in American history, reaches its humane and dignified denouement.

Fort Blakely, Mobile, Alabama, is besieged by 45,000 Federal troops once General Frederick Steele is joined by the main force under General Edward R. S. Canby. An assault force of 16,000 then attacks the Confederate defenses at noon, covered by the fire of 37 field pieces and 75 siege guns. Their success prompts General St. John R. Liddell to surrender after 20 minutes of fighting. Union losses

This painting depicts the surrender of Robert E. Lee and his army at the Appomattox Court House, Virginia, to General Ulysses S. Grant *(Library of Congress)*

are 113 killed and 516 wounded while the Southerners incur 629 casualties and 3,423 men and 40 cannon captured.

April 10

MILITARY: General Robert E. Lee issues Order No. 9 and thanks the men and officers of the Army of Northern Virginia, who had served him famously over the past three years, in victory and now defeat. "With an increasing admiration of your constancy and devotion to your country," Lee writes, "and a grateful remembrance of your kind and generous consideration of myself, I bid you an affectionate farewell."

POLITICS: President Abraham Lincoln is accosted by happy crowds in Washington, D.C., and then asks a military band to strike up *Dixie*, "one of the best tunes I have ever heard."

President Jefferson Davis, upon learning of General Robert E. Lee's capitulation, hastily departs Danville, Virginia, and makes for Greensborough, North Carolina.

News of General Robert E. Lee's surrender sparks wild celebrations in northern cities.

April 11

POLITICS: President Abraham Lincoln delivers his final public address to enthusiastic crowds gathered about the White House. He again pleas for magnanimity and peaceful reconciliation with the inhabitants of former secessionist states.

April 12

MILITARY: The vaunted Army of Northern Virginia formally capitulates at Appomattox Court House, Virginia, to General Joshua L. Chamberlain. As General John B. Gordon leads a column of weather-beaten 28,000 Southerners along the Richmond Stage Road, completely lined by Union forces, Chamberlain orders his men to present arms to the solemn procession. The salute is returned in kind.

POLITICS: President Jefferson Davis, readying to flee Greensborough, North Carolina, confers with General Joseph E. Johnston about the potential surrender of remaining Confederate forces. He then authorizes Johnston to meet with Union authorities and get the best terms possible.

April 13

POLITICS: Secretary of War Edwin M. Stanton orders the military draft suspended and also reduces supply requisitions.

April 14

MILITARY: General Robert Anderson hoists the American flag over the battered remnants of Fort Sumter, Charleston harbor, South Carolina. It is the identical standard lowered by him on April 14, 1861.

POLITICS: In his final cabinet meeting, President Abraham Lincoln reiterates his call for reconciliation with the South, and then repairs to Ford's Theater in Washington, D.C., to attend the play "Our American Cousin." At 10:15 P.M., Lincoln is suddenly shot by actor John Wilkes Booth, who then escapes. Meanwhile, Secretary of State William H. Seward, recovering in his home from a recent accident, survives an assassination attempt by Lewis Powell. Secretary of War Edwin M. Stanton declares martial law throughout the District of Columbia and initiates a massive dragnet to snare the assassins.

April 15

ARTS: In recognition of President Abraham Lincoln's death, all theaters in New York City close for the next ten days.

POLITICS: President Abraham Lincoln dies at 7:22 A.M., leaving Secretary of War Edwin M. Stanton to reputedly declare "Now, he belongs to the ages." Vice President Andrew Johnson is then sworn in as the nation's 17th chief executive by Chief Justice Salmon P. Chase; Johnson's first request is to ask members of Lincoln's cabinet to retain their offices.

President Jefferson Davis departs Greensborough, North Carolina, on horseback and rides all night towards Lexington.

April 16

MILITARY: General James H. Wilson's army occupies Columbus, Georgia, after brushing aside a hodgepodge collection of Confederates and militia, taking 1,200 captives and 52 cannon. The victorious troopers then commence burning several factories, 100,000 bales of cotton, 15 locomotives, and 200 rail cars. Another column under General Edward M. McCook seizes West Point, destroying an additional 19 locomotives and numerous railcars.

April 17

POLITICS: John Wilkes Booth, who broke his leg after assassinating President Abraham Lincoln, hides near Port Tobacco, Maryland, where he awaits transportation over the Potomac River to freedom.

The body of President Abraham Lincoln lies in state in the East Room of the White House, Washington, D.C.

President Jefferson Davis and his entourage arrive at Salisbury, North Carolina.

April 18

MILITARY: Confederate forces under General Joseph E. Johnston agree to surrender 37,000 men to General William T. Sherman at Durham Station, North Carolina. However, terms of their "Memorandum or Basis of Agreement" will be viewed in Washington, D.C., as overly generous and disavowed. Sherman will also be accused of overstepping his authority and ordered to renegotiate the pact with identical terms used at Appomattox.

April 19

POLITICS: Funeral services are held for President Abraham Lincoln in Washington, D.C., and huge crowds throng the proceedings.

President Jefferson Davis and his remaining cabinet flee to Charlotte, North Carolina.

April 20

POLITICS: Arkansas ratifies the Thirteenth Amendment.

April 21

GENERAL: A train bearing the casket of President Abraham Lincoln departs Washington, D.C., for Springfield, Illinois, as immense crowds of mourners gather along the tracks en route.

April 22
CRIME: John Wilkes Booth and his accomplice David E. Herold escape in a small rowboat from Maryland to Virginia.

April 24
CRIME: Presidential assassins John Wilkes Booth and David E. Herold make their way to Port Conway, Virginia.
POLITICS: President Andrew Johnson formally rejects the surrender agreement reached between generals William T. Sherman and Joseph E. Johnston. He then dispatches General Ulysses S. Grant to Raleigh, North Carolina, to personally inform Sherman of his displeasure.

April 25
CRIME: Union troops chase assassins John Wilkes Booth and David E. Herold to Bowling Green, Virginia, just south of the Rappahannock River. The two fugitives seek refuge in the barn belonging to farmer Richard H. Garrett.

April 26
CRIME: John Wilkes Booth is cornered in a barn near Bowling Green, Virginia, while attempting to escape from Federal troops and dies of his wounds. His accomplice, David E. Herold, is apprehended.
MILITARY: Generals Joseph E. Johnston and William T. Sherman meet again at Durham Station, North Carolina, and renegotiate a surrender agreement with identical terms to those offered at Appomattox, Virginia.
POLITICS: President Jefferson Davis departs Charlotte, North Carolina, and heads for the Trans-Mississippi region, intending to carry on a guerrilla struggle for Southern independence.

April 27
GENERAL: At 2:00 A.M., boilers on the steamer *Sultana* explode with a deafening roar, hurling crew and passengers alike into the frigid waters of the Mississippi River. By the time help finally arrives from Memphis, Tennessee, two hours later, more than 1,700 people have perished from burns and hypothermia. Only 600 are fished from the waters alive. *Sultana* remains the single biggest maritime disaster in United States maritime history and eclipses the more famous *Titanic* disaster 47 years hence.

April 28
POLITICS: The train bearing President Abraham Lincoln's casket pauses briefly at Cleveland, Ohio, where 50,000 citizens come to pay their final respects.

President Jefferson Davis accepts the resignation of Confederate Secretary of the Treasury George A. Trentholm from his cabinet.

April 29
POLITICS: President Andrew Johnson issues an executive order lifting commercial restrictions against all Southern states except Texas, still technically at war with the United States.

President Jefferson Davis and his entourage reach Yorksville, South Carolina.

April 30
MILITARY: General Edward R. S. Canby holds preliminary talks with General Richard Taylor at Mobile, Alabama, as to the latter's forthcoming capitulation.

1865

Afterward, Taylor returns to his headquarters at Meridian, Mississippi, and makes preparations.

May 1

POLITICS: President Andrew Johnson calls for a board of nine army officers to try the eight individuals accused of participating in Abraham Lincoln's assassination.

President Jefferson Davis reaches Cokesbury, South Carolina, en route to the Florida coast. There they hope to catch a fast vessel and make for Texas.

May 2

POLITICS: President Andrew Johnson accuses a fugitive Jefferson Davis of complicity in the assassination of President Abraham Lincoln and offers $100,000 for his capture.

President Jefferson Davis arrives at Abbeville, South Carolina, and heads for Washington, Georgia, escorted by four brigades of cavalry under General Basil W. Duke. Members of his cabinet begin disputing his intention of renewing their struggle through guerrilla warfare.

Confederate Secretary of Navy Stephen R. Mallory tenders his resignation to President Jefferson Davis at Washington, Georgia.

SOCIETAL: The New York legislature authorizes the first paid fire department in New York City.

May 3

POLITICS: The funeral train bearing the remains of President Abraham Lincoln pulls into Springfield, Illinois, its final stop.

Confederate Secretary of State Judah P. Benjamin resigns from President Jefferson Davis's cabinet and eventually flees to England.

May 4

MILITARY: General Richard Taylor formally surrenders all Confederate forces east of the Mississippi River to General Edward R. S. Canby at Citronelle, Alabama. He receives the identical terms proffered to General Robert E. Lee at Appomattox and is also allowed to employ steamships to send his men home.

POLITICS: Abraham Lincoln is laid to his final rest at Springfield, Illinois.

May 5

CRIME: The nation's first train heist occurs when an engine belonging to the Ohio & Mississippi Railroad is stopped and robbed at North Bend, Ohio.

POLITICS: Connecticut ratifies the Thirteenth Amendment to abolish slavery.

President Jefferson Davis and his dwindling coterie arrive at Sandersville, Georgia.

May 6

POLITICS: President Andrew Johnson appoints General David Hunter to head the military commission tasked with trying those implicated in the assassination of President Abraham Lincoln. The accused are prosecuted by Joseph Holt, Judge Advocate General, U.S. Army.

May 9

CRIME: The trial of eight suspected conspirators begins in Washington, D.C.

POLITICS: President Andrew Johnson declares the naval blockade will remain in place for two more weeks to impede any escape by fugitive Confederate leaders.

Francis H. Pierpont receives official recognition as governor of Virginia; previously he headed Unionist Virginians in the Union-controlled portion of the state.

President Jefferson Davis is reunited with his wife Varina at Dublin, Georgia.

May 10

MILITARY: Dreaded Confederate guerrilla William C. Quantrill is mortally wounded and captured in a Union ambush near Taylorville, Kentucky. He dies in prison shortly afterward.

POLITICS: President Andrew Johnson declares armed resistance "virtually at an end" although sporadic skirmishes persist in rural parts of the South.

President Jefferson Davis and his wife Varina are captured near Abbeville, Georgia, by men of the 1st Wisconsin Cavalry under Lieutenant Colonel Benjamin Pritchard—part of General James H. Wilson's command. His arrest signals the end of Confederate government.

May 12

SOCIETAL: President Andrew Johnson appoints General Oliver O. Howard to head the new Freedmen's Bureau.

May 13

MILITARY: Colonel Theodore H. Barrett arrives in Texas to take command of Union troops under Colonel David Branson and leads them into combat at Palmetto Ranch. They engage a force of Confederate cavalry under Colonel John S. Ford, who deftly outflanks the overconfident Federals. Barrett promptly falls back, pursued by the Southerners, who chase him for 17 miles. Union losses are estimated at 130 killed, wounded, and captured; the Confederates are thought to have suffered far less. Palmetto Ranch is the last pitched Civil War encounter west of the Mississippi River.

May 16

POLITICS: President Jefferson Davis, his family, and several ranking Confederate officials are placed on steamers and sent down the Savannah River, Georgia, and call at Port Royal, South Carolina.

May 22

POLITICS: President Andrew Johnson opens all Southern seaports as of July 1 with the exception of four harbors in Texas: Galveston, La Salle, Brazos Santiago, and Brownsville.

President Jefferson Davis arrives in chains at Fortress Monroe, Virginia, and will remain confined there until May 13, 1867.

May 23

MILITARY: The Grand Army of the Republic parades in a mass review at Washington, D.C., and flags are permitted to fly at full mast for the first time in four years. Sadly, not one of the 166 African-American regiments raised during the war is present during the festivities.

The army of General William T. Sherman, sporting a much looser appearance than the spit-and-polish Army of the Potomac, victoriously tramps its way through Washington, D.C. Moreover, Sherman still seethes over his contretemps with Secretary of War Edwin M. Stanton and the surrender terms imposed on General Joseph E. Johnston, so he refuses to shake Stanton's hand.

1865

POLITICS: The Piedmont government, a collection of Unionist politicians from Virginia, formally occupies the state capital at Richmond.

May 26

MILITARY: General Simon B. Buckner, representing General Edmund Kirby-Smith, surrenders to General Edward R. S. Canby's deputy General Peter J. Osterhaus at New Orleans, Louisiana. This completely dissolves all remaining Confederate forces west of the Mississippi River. General Joseph O. Shelby, however, angrily spurs 1,000 followers southward into Mexico to help found a military colony.

May 27

POLITICS: President Andrew Johnson empties the prisons of almost all Southerners still incarcerated by the military.

May 29

DIPLOMACY: In a detailed letter, American minister Charles F. Adams outlines to British foreign minister Lord John Russell that British-built Confederate warships are responsible for the destruction of 110,000 tons of American shipping—and compensation is in order. The damage wrought proves so extensive that the United States forfeits its prior status as the world's largest maritime carrier.

POLITICS: President Andrew Johnson proclaims an amnesty and pardon agreement to any former Confederates submitting to a loyalty oath. He also extends recognition to four new state governments established by his predecessor, along with plans for readmitting Southern states back into the Union. Johnson's continuation of moderate reconstruction or, as he deems it, Restoration, spells trouble at the hands of Radical Republicans who are intent on exacting a measure of revenge for the erstwhile rebels.

William H. Holden gains appointment as provisional governor of North Carolina.

June 2

DIPLOMACY: The government of Great Britain officially rescinds belligerent status from the Confederate States of America.

MILITARY: General Edmund Kirby-Smith formally surrenders Confederate forces at Galveston, Texas, to General Edmund J. Davis. The articles of capitulation are signed aboard the USS *Fort Jackson*.

POLITICS: President Andrew Johnson pardons Lambdin P. Milligan, a notorious "Copperhead" agitator, from hanging.

June 6

POLITICS: President Andrew Johnson orders all remaining Confederate prisoners of war released after they take a loyalty oath.

Voters in Missouri approve a new constitution abolishing slavery.

June 13

POLITICS: President Andrew Johnson appoints William L. Sharkey as provisional governor of Mississippi, continuing his policy of reestablishing civilian authority as quickly as possible.

June 17

POLITICS: President Andrew Johnson appoints James Johnson and Andrew J. Hamilton as provisional governors of Georgia and Texas, respectively.

June 21
POLITICS: President Andrew Johnson appoints Lewis E. Parsons to serve as provisional governor of Alabama.

June 22
NAVAL: Confederate raider CSS *Shenandoah* under Lieutenant James I. Waddell fires the last shots of the Civil War while capturing six Union whalers in the Bering Sea. Waddell hears rumors that the war has ended from his captives but disbelieves them.

June 23
INDIAN: General Stand Watie surrenders his Confederate Cherokee at Doaksville, Indian Territory (Oklahoma). He is the last ranking Confederate officer to lay down his arms.
POLITICS: President Andrew Johnson declares the Union naval blockade of all Southern states officially ended.

June 24
POLITICS: President Andrew Johnson lifts all commercial restrictions from states and territories west of the Mississippi River.

June 30
CRIME: A military commission finds all eight conspirators charged with the assassination of President Abraham Lincoln guilty. David E. Herold, Lewis Payne, George A. Atzerodt, and Mary E. Surratt are sentenced to hang while Dr. Samuel Mudd, Samuel Arnold, and Michael O'Laughlin receive life sentences. Edward Spangler receives six years in prison.

July
JOURNALISM: Edwin Lawrence Godkin founds *The Nation* in New York City, a weekly publication concerned with politics and the arts.

July 1
POLITICS: President Andrew Johnson declares all Southern ports now open to foreign commerce and shipping.
   New Hampshire ratifies the Thirteenth Amendment.

July 7
CRIME: Four individuals found guilty of the assassination of President Abraham Lincoln go to the gallows in Washington, D.C. Four others are slated to serve their sentences on the Dry Tortugas Islands, Florida.

July 13
POLITICS: President Andrew Johnson appoints William Marvin provisional governor of Florida.

July 19
POLITICS: Governor Madison J. Wells implores the inhabitants of Louisiana to take the oath of allegiance or lose their right to vote.

August 2
NAVAL: Lieutenant James I. Waddell of the CSS *Shenandoah* learns from the British vessel *Barracouta* that the Civil War has ended in a complete Union victory. Fearing that he and his crew will be charged with piracy, and ignoring protests from many sailors, Waddell orders the vessel to make way for England.

1865

August 21

POLITICS: The Mississippi state legislature negates its secessionist ordinance and also abolishes slavery.

August 28

NAVAL: Admiral David D. Porter is appointed the sixth superintendent of the U.S. Naval Academy, and he orchestrates its transfer back to Annapolis, Maryland, from Newport, Rhode Island. Porter serves four years there, rising to vice admiral.

September 1

EDUCATION: Former general Robert E. Lee becomes president of Washington College, Virginia.

September 4

JOURNALISM: A heated editorial in the New York *Times* calls for Jefferson Davis's trial so as to demonstrate that the recent failed rebellion was a crime.

September 5

POLITICS: The South Carolina legislature, once the epicenter of secession, formally nullifies its ordinance to do the same.

September 14

DIPLOMACY: Representatives of nine Native American tribes (Cherokee, Creek, Choctaw, Chickasaw, Osage, Seminole, Seneca, Shawnee, and Quapaw) gather at Fort Smith, Arkansas, to sign a treaty of loyalty to the United States.

October 2

POLITICS: Former general Robert E. Lee takes his oath of allegiance to the United States and receives a full pardon.

October 11

POLITICS: Former Confederate vice president Alexander H. Stephens and several high ranking cabinet officials are paroled by President Andrew Johnson.

October 12

POLITICS: President Andrew Johnson declares an end to martial law in Kentucky.

November 3

NAVAL: Secretary of the Navy Gideon Welles instructs all U.S. Navy vessels to render proper honors upon entering English ports. This diplomatic nicety is resumed once the British government retracts belligerent status from the now defunct Confederacy.

November 5

NAVAL: Lieutenant James I. Waddell docks the USS *Shenadoah* at Liverpool, England, after covering 58,000 miles and seizing 38 Union prizes. His is the final Confederate flag struck. Following a few days of confinement, Waddell and his crew are released by British authorities and allowed to leave.

November 9

POLITICS: The North Carolina legislature overturns its 1861 secession ordinance, outlaws slavery, and elects new members to Congress.

November 10
CRIME: Captain Henry Wirz is hanged by Union authorities for his role as commandant of notorious Andersonville Prison, Georgia. He is the only Confederate military officer so punished.

November 13
POLITICS: The South Carolina state legislature ratifies the Thirteenth Amendment.

November 18
LITERATURE: Little-known writer and social commentator Samuel Clemens ("Mark Twain") begins his celebrated literary career by publishing "The Celebrated Jumping Frog of Calaveras County" in the weekly magazine *The Nation*.

November 24
SOCIETAL: The Mississippi state legislature passes laws concerning vagrancy, labor service, and other "black codes" aimed at regulating African Americans and defining their role in greater society. Henceforth, blacks are forbidden from serving on juries, cannot testify against white persons in a court of law, cannot bear arms, and cannot assemble in large numbers. Collectively, these are an early manifestation of what becomes known as "Jim Crow" laws in the 20th century.

December 1
POLITICS: The government revokes wartime suspension of writs of habeas corpus, except in states of the former Confederacy, the District of Columbia, and the New Mexico and Arizona Territories.

December 2
POLITICS: The Alabama state legislature ratifies the Thirteenth Amendment, granting the requisite three-fourths approval by the states to render it law.

December 4
POLITICS: The 39th U.S. Congress convenes and the House of Representative institutes the Joint Committee on Reconstruction to oppose what is perceived as moderate tendencies by President Andrew Johnson. Known as the "Committee of Fifteen," it consists of nine Republicans and six Democrats, and votes consistently along party lines. Among its first actions is disputing the credentials of newly elected senators and representatives from former Confederate states, hence denying them seats in Congress. According to senator and Radical Republican Charles Sumner, the South has committed "State suicide."

The Thirteenth Amendment is ratified by North Carolina but it fails in Mississippi.

December 5
DIPLOMACY: Secretary of State William H. Seward instructs American minister to France John Bigelow to express, in no uncertain terms, American displeasure with France's occupation of Mexico.
POLITICS: The Georgia legislature ratifies the Thirteenth Amendment.

December 6
POLITICS: In his first annual message to Congress, President Andrew Johnson declares with "gratitude to God in the name of the people for the preservation of the United States."

1865

December 11
POLITICS: The Thirteenth Amendment is ratified by Oregon.

December 12
POLITICS: The U.S. Senate appoints the "Joint Committee on Reconstruction" at the behest of William P. Fessenden of Maine.

December 14
POLITICS: U.S. Representative Thaddeus Stevens of Pennsylvania, an outspoken Radical Republican, assumes the mantle of leadership within the "Committee of Fifteen."

December 18
POLITICS: Secretary of State William H. Seward declares the Thirteenth Amendment to the U.S. Constitution, approved by 27 states, as formally adopted. Thus, after two and a half contentious centuries, the incubus of slavery is finally expunged from the American polity and psyche alike. However, in many places throughout the states of the former Confederacy, it is supplanted by equally repugnant "Jim Crow" laws which are not finally eliminated until the Civil Rights Act of 1964—a century hence.

December 24
POLITICS: The Ku Klux Klan is founded in Tennessee as a secret society intent upon terrorizing newly freed African Americans. Former Confederate general Nathan B. Forrest is installed as the first Grand Wizard, although he eventually resigns once members resort to violence against blacks.

December 25
BUSINESS: The Union Stockyard opens in Chicago, Illinois, and wields a profound impact on the economic growth of the midwest and prairies by facilitating the soon-to-be thriving cattle industry.

MAPS

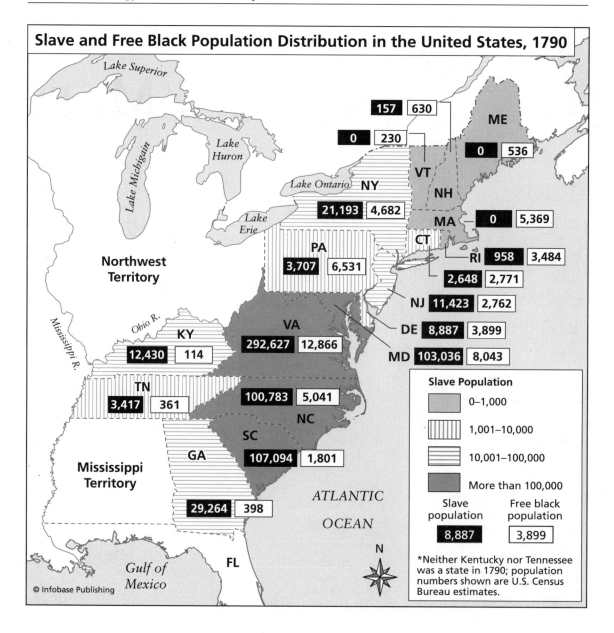

Slave and Free Black Population Distribution in the United States, 1790

Lake Superior

Lake Michigain

Lake Huron

Lake Ontario

Lake Erie

Northwest Territory

Mississippi R.

Ohio R.

157 630

0 230

ME

0 536

VT

NY

21,193 4,682

NH

MA

0 5,369

CT

RI 958 3,484

2,648 2,771

PA

3,707 6,531

NJ 11,423 2,762

DE 8,887 3,899

VA

292,627 12,866

MD 103,036 8,043

KY

12,430 114

TN

3,417 361

NC

100,783 5,041

SC

107,094 1,801

GA

29,264 398

Mississippi Territory

ATLANTIC

OCEAN

Gulf of Mexico

FL

N

© Infobase Publishing

Slave Population

0–1,000

1,001–10,000

10,001–100,000

More than 100,000

Slave population	Free black population
8,887	3,899

*Neither Kentucky nor Tennessee was a state in 1790; population numbers shown are U.S. Census Bureau estimates.

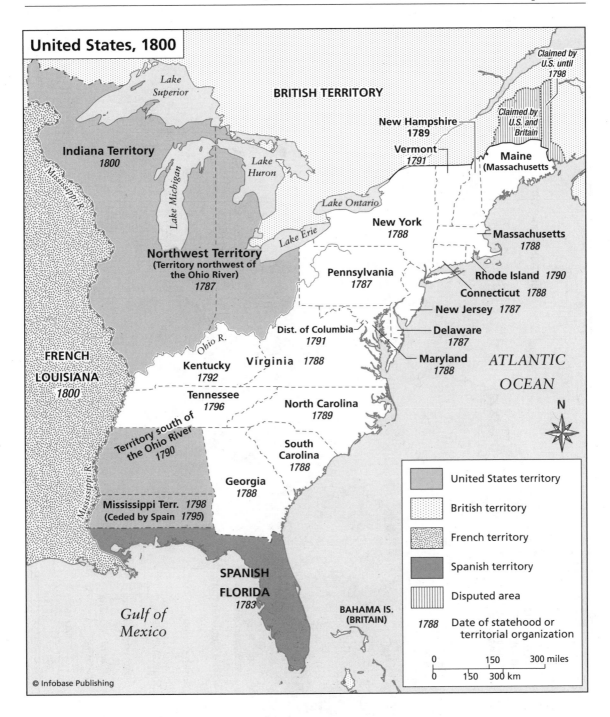

United States, 1800

BRITISH TERRITORY

Lake Superior

Claimed by U.S. until 1798

Claimed by U.S. and Britain

New Hampshire 1789

Vermont *1791*

Maine (Massachusetts

Indiana Territory *1800*

Lake Huron

Lake Michigan

Lake Ontario

Lake Erie

New York *1788*

Massachusetts *1788*

Northwest Territory (Territory northwest of the Ohio River) *1787*

Pennsylvania *1787*

Rhode Island *1790*

Connecticut *1788*

New Jersey *1787*

Dist. of Columbia *1791*

Mississippi R.

Ohio R.

FRENCH LOUISIANA *1800*

Kentucky *1792*

Virginia *1788*

Delaware *1787*

Maryland *1788*

ATLANTIC OCEAN

Tennessee *1796*

North Carolina *1789*

Territory south of the Ohio River *1790*

South Carolina *1788*

N

Georgia *1788*

Mississippi R.

Mississippi Terr. *1798* (Ceded by Spain *1795*)

SPANISH FLORIDA *1783*

BAHAMA IS. (BRITAIN)

Gulf of Mexico

United States territory

British territory

French territory

Spanish territory

Disputed area

1788 Date of statehood or territorial organization

0   150   300 miles
0   150   300 km

© Infobase Publishing

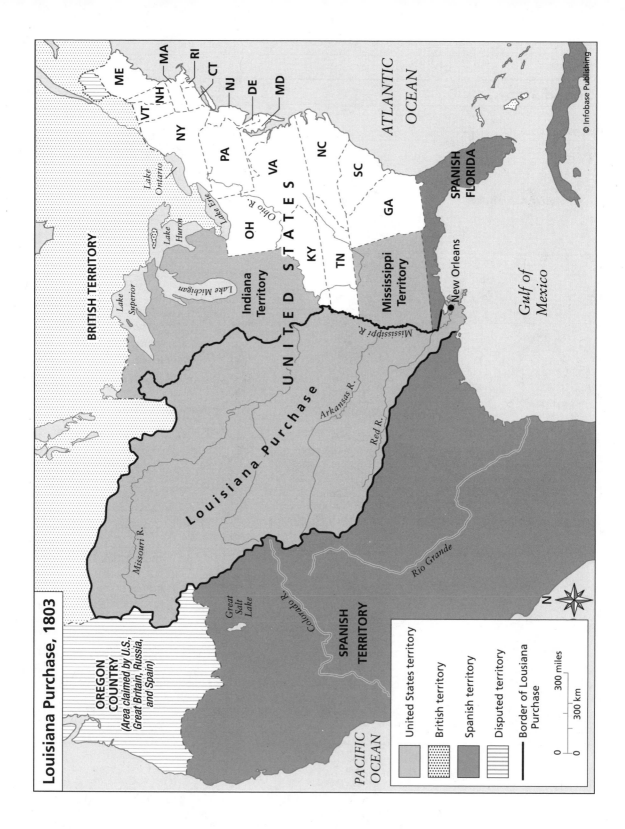

Louisiana Purchase, 1803

BRITISH TERRITORY

OREGON COUNTRY
(Area claimed by U.S., Great Britain, Russia, and Spain)

PACIFIC OCEAN

UNITED STATES

Louisiana Purchase

Indiana Territory

Mississippi Territory

SPANISH TERRITORY

SPANISH FLORIDA

New Orleans

Gulf of Mexico

ATLANTIC OCEAN

ME
VT
NH
MA
RI
CT
NY
NJ
DE
MD
PA
VA
NC
SC
GA
OH
KY
TN

Lake Ontario
Lake Erie
Lake Huron
Lake Michigan
Lake Superior

Ohio R.
Mississippi R.
Missouri R.
Arkansas R.
Red R.
Colorado R.
Great Salt Lake
Rio Grande

© Infobase Publishing

United States territory
British territory
Spanish territory
Disputed territory
Border of Lousiana Purchase

N

0   300 miles
0   300 km

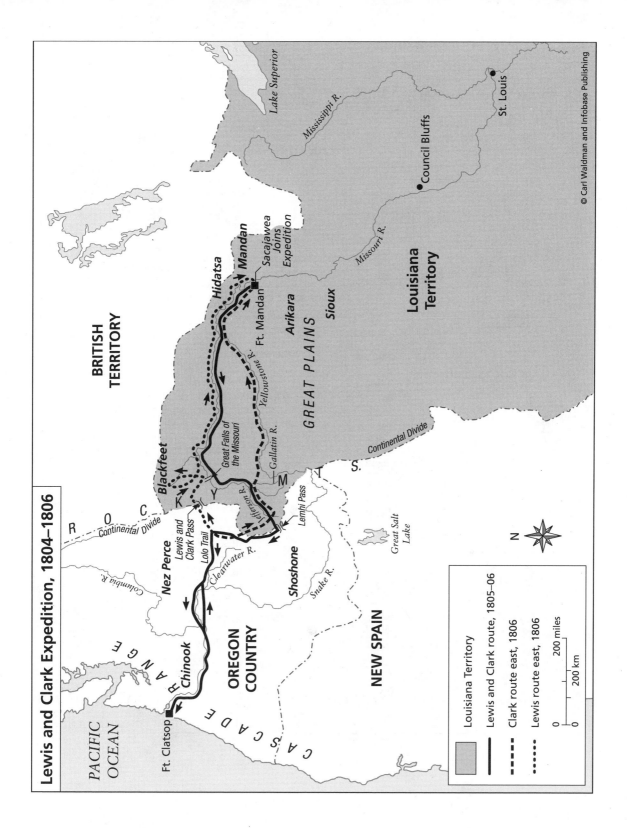

Lewis and Clark Expedition, 1804–1806

© Carl Waldman and Infobase Publishing

St. Louis

Council Bluffs

Lake Superior

Mississippi R.

BRITISH TERRITORY

Missouri R.

Louisiana Territory

Mandan

Hidatsa

Sacajawea Joins Expedition

Ft. Mandan

Arikara

Sioux

GREAT PLAINS

Yellowstone R.

Blackfeet

Great Falls of the Missouri

Gallatin R.

M

Continental Divide

Great Salt Lake

R   O   C

K

Y

Continental Divide

Jefferson R.

Lemhi Pass

S.

M   T   S.

Lewis and Clark Pass

Nez Perce

Lolo Trail

Clearwater R.

Shoshone

Snake R.

Columbia R.

NEW SPAIN

Chinook

OREGON COUNTRY

C   A   S   C   A   D   E   R   A   N   G   E

PACIFIC OCEAN

Ft. Clatsop

N

200 miles

200 km

Louisiana Territory

Lewis and Clark route, 1805–06

Clark route east, 1806

Lewis route east, 1806

0   200 miles

0   200 km

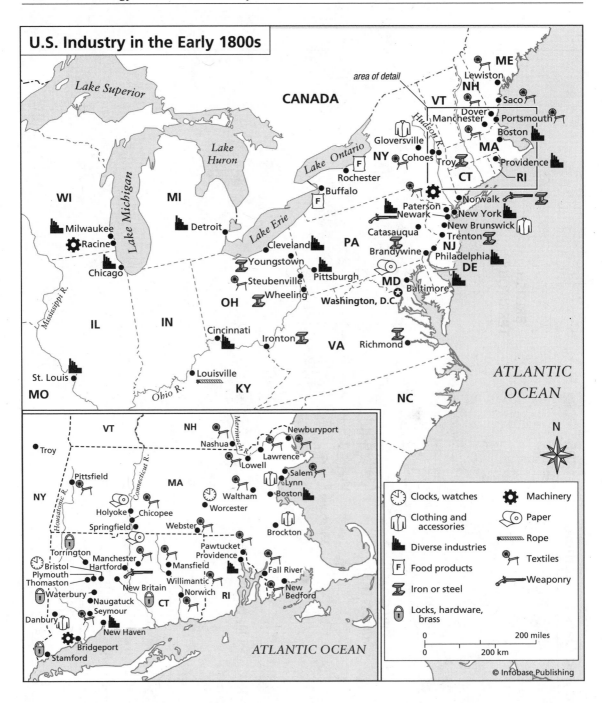

U.S. Industry in the Early 1800s

Lake Superior

CANADA

Lake Huron

Lake Michigan

Lake Ontario

Lake Erie

WI

MI

Milwaukee
Racine
Chicago

Detroit

Cleveland
Youngstown
Steubenville
Wheeling

PA

Pittsburgh

ME
Lewiston
NH
Saco
VT
Dover
Manchester
Portsmouth
Boston
MA
Gloversville
NY
Cohoes
Troy
Providence
RI
CT
Norwalk
Buffalo
Rochester
Paterson
Newark
New York
New Brunswick
Catasauqua
Trenton
NJ
Brandywine
Philadelphia
DE

area of detail

Hudson R.

St. Louis

MO

IL

IN

Ohio R.

KY

Cincinnati

Ironton

Louisville

Mississippi R.

OH

Washington, D.C.

MD
Baltimore

VA

Richmond

NC

ATLANTIC OCEAN

N

VT

NH

Troy

Pittsfield

NY

Nashua
Lowell
Lawrence
Newburyport

Merrimack R.

Holyoke
Chicopee
Springfield

MA

Waltham
Worcester

Salem
Lynn
Boston

Webster
Brockton

Connecticut R.

Housatonic R.

Torrington
Bristol
Plymouth
Thomaston
Waterbury
Danbury
Naugatuck
Seymour
New Haven
Bridgeport
Stamford

Manchester
Hartford
New Britain
Willimantic
Norwich
CT

Pawtucket
Providence
Mansfield

Fall River
New Bedford
RI

ATLANTIC OCEAN

Legend

- 🕐 Clocks, watches
- 👕 Clothing and accessories
- 🏭 Diverse industries
- F Food products
- ⚙ Iron or steel
- 🔒 Locks, hardware, brass
- ⚙ Machinery
- 📄 Paper
- Rope
- ✳ Textiles
- Weaponry

0   200 miles
0   200 km

© Infobase Publishing

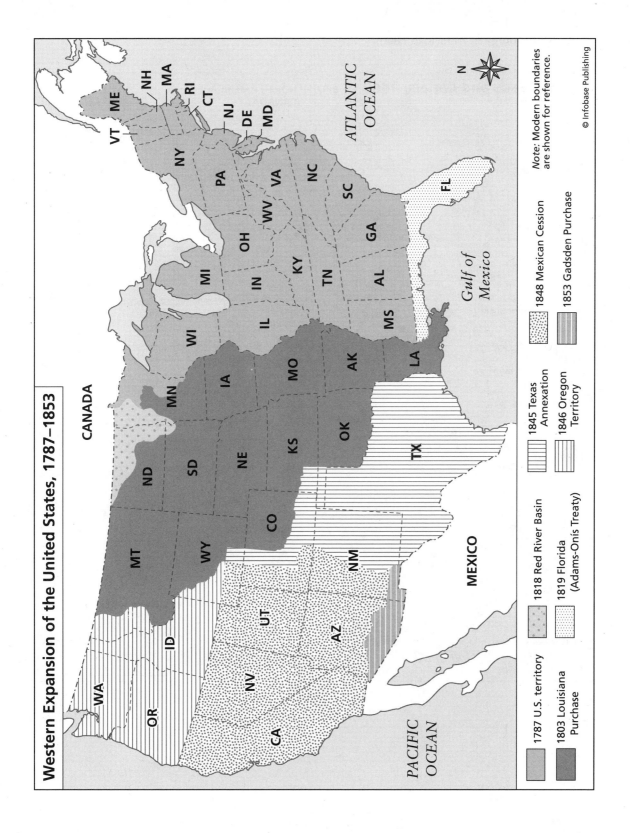

Western Expansion of the United States, 1787–1853

CANADA

ATLANTIC OCEAN

Gulf of Mexico

MEXICO

PACIFIC OCEAN

N

VT ME NH MA RI CT NJ DE MD
NY
PA
WV VA
OH NC
IN SC
IL KY TN GA
MI AL
WI MS
IA MO LA
MN AK
ND SD NE KS OK
WY CO TX
MT
ID UT NM
WA OR NV AZ
CA
FL

Note: Modern boundaries are shown for reference.

© Infobase Publishing

1787 U.S. territory

1803 Louisiana Purchase

1818 Red River Basin

1819 Florida (Adams-Onis Treaty)

1845 Texas Annexation

1846 Oregon Territory

1848 Mexican Cession

1853 Gadsden Purchase

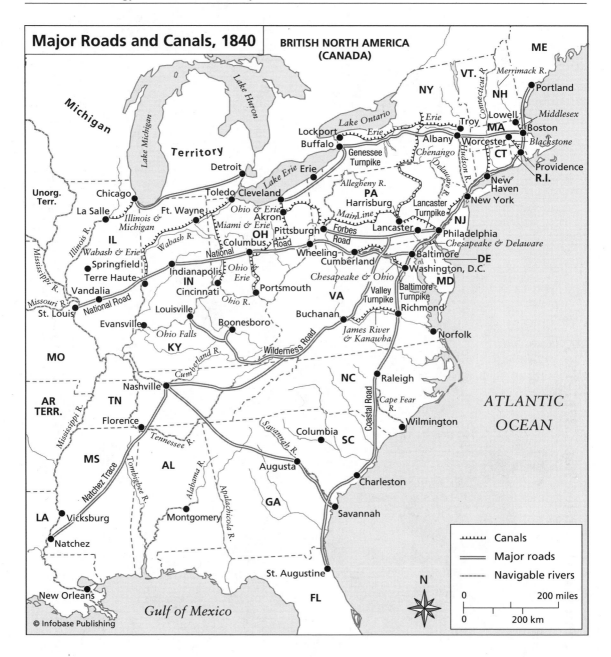

Major Roads and Canals, 1840

BRITISH NORTH AMERICA (CANADA)

ATLANTIC OCEAN

Gulf of Mexico

© Infobase Publishing

Canals
Major roads
Navigable rivers

0   200 miles
0   200 km

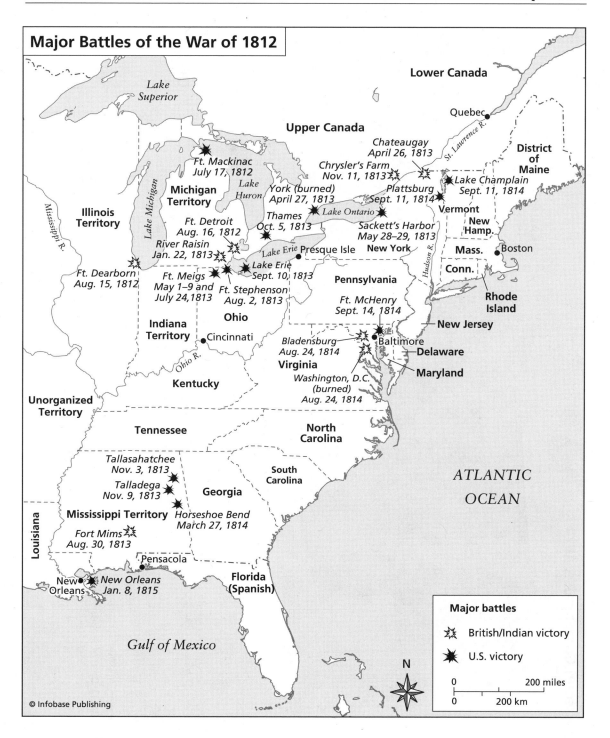

Major Battles of the War of 1812

Lake Superior

Lower Canada

Quebec

Upper Canada

St. Lawrence R.

District of Maine

Ft. Mackinac
July 17, 1812

Chateaugay
April 26, 1813

Chrysler's Farm
Nov. 11, 1813

Lake Champlain
Sept. 11, 1814

Lake Huron

Michigan Territory

York (burned)
April 27, 1813

Plattsburg
Sept. 11, 1814

Vermont

New Hamp.

Lake Michigan

Illinois Territory

Mississippi R.

Thames
Oct. 5, 1813

Lake Ontario

Sackett's Harbor
May 28–29, 1813

Ft. Detroit
Aug. 16, 1812

River Raisin
Jan. 22, 1813

Presque Isle

New York

Mass.

Boston

Ft. Dearborn
Aug. 15, 1812

Lake Erie
Sept. 10, 1813

Conn.

Lake Erie

Ft. Meigs
May 1–9 and
July 24,1813

Ft. Stephenson
Aug. 2, 1813

Pennsylvania

Rhode Island

Hudson R.

Ohio

Ft. McHenry
Sept. 14, 1814

New Jersey

Indiana Territory

Cincinnati

Bladensburg
Aug. 24, 1814

Baltimore

Delaware

Ohio R.

Virginia

Maryland

Kentucky

Washington, D.C.
(burned)
Aug. 24, 1814

Unorganized Territory

Tennessee

North Carolina

ATLANTIC OCEAN

Tallasahatchee
Nov. 3, 1813

South Carolina

Talladega
Nov. 9, 1813

Georgia

Louisiana

Mississippi Territory

Horseshoe Bend
March 27, 1814

Fort Mims
Aug. 30, 1813

Pensacola

Florida
(Spanish)

New Orleans

New Orleans
Jan. 8, 1815

Gulf of Mexico

N

Major battles

British/Indian victory

U.S. victory

| 0 | | 200 miles |
| 0 | | 200 km |

© Infobase Publishing

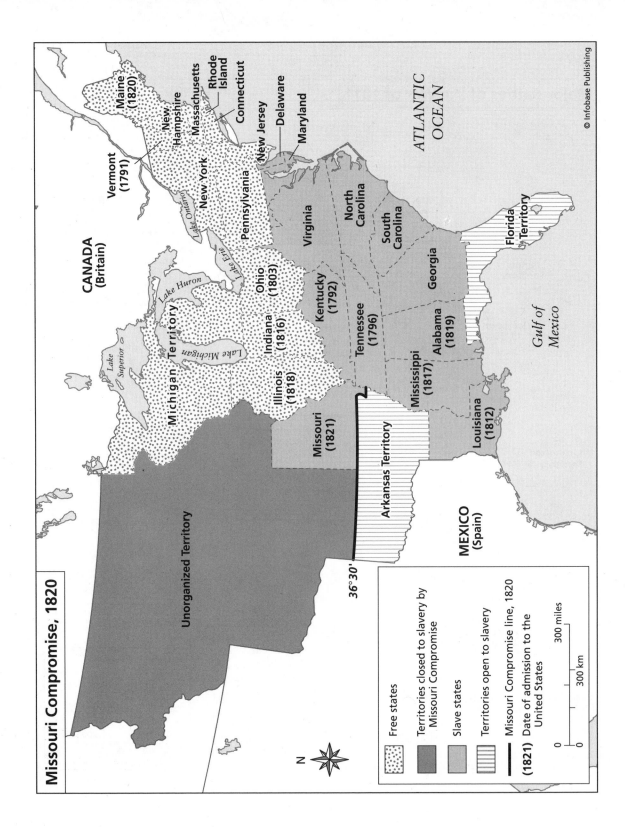

Missouri Compromise, 1820

CANADA (Britain)

ATLANTIC OCEAN

MEXICO (Spain)

Gulf of Mexico

Maine (1820)
New Hampshire
Massachusetts
Rhode Island
Connecticut
New Jersey
Delaware
Maryland
Vermont (1791)
New York
Pennsylvania
Virginia
North Carolina
South Carolina
Georgia
Florida Territory
Ohio (1803)
Indiana (1816)
Illinois (1818)
Michigan Territory
Kentucky (1792)
Tennessee (1796)
Alabama (1819)
Mississippi (1817)
Louisiana (1812)
Missouri (1821)
Arkansas Territory
Unorganized Territory

Lake Ontario
Lake Erie
Lake Huron
Lake Michigan
Lake Superior

36° 30'

N

© Infobase Publishing

Free states
Territories closed to slavery by Missouri Compromise
Slave states
Territories open to slavery
Missouri Compromise line, 1820
(1821) Date of admission to the United States

0   300 miles
0   300 km

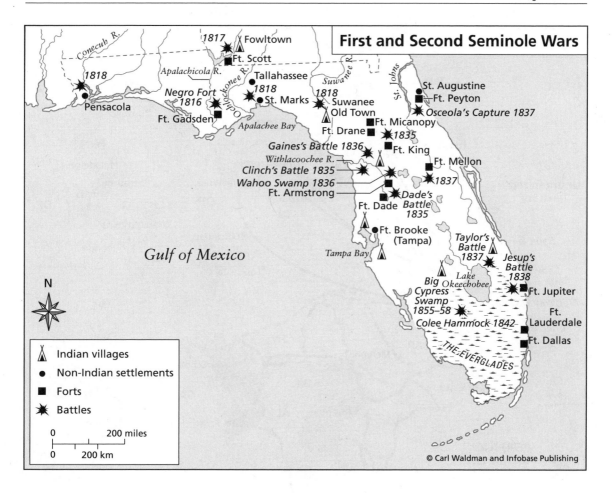

First and Second Seminole Wars

1817 ✕ Fowltown

■ Ft. Scott

Conecuh R.

Apalachicola R.

1818

● Tallahassee

1818

Negro Fort
1816 ● St. Marks

✕ Pensacola

■ Ft. Gadsden

Apalachee Bay

Ochlockonee R.

Suwanee R.

1818

✕ Suwanee
Ⓐ Old Town

St. Johns R.

● St. Augustine
■ Ft. Peyton

✕ Osceola's Capture 1837

■ Ft. Micanopy

Ft. Drane ■ ✕ *1835*

Gaines's Battle 1836 ✕ Ⓐ Ft. King

Withlacoochee R.

Clinch's Battle 1835 ✕

Wahoo Swamp 1836 ✕

Ft. Armstrong

■ Ft. Dade

Ⓐ ● Ft. Brooke
(Tampa)

✕ Dade's
Battle
1835

■ Ft. Mellon

✕ *1837*

Tampa Bay

Ⓐ

Taylor's
Battle
1837 Ⓐ

Jesup's
Battle
1838

Ⓐ Big
Cypress
Swamp
1855–58 ✕

Colee Hammock 1842

*Lake
Okeechobee*

✕ ■ Ft. Jupiter

Ft.
Lauderdale ■

■ Ft. Dallas

THE EVERGLADES

Gulf of Mexico

N

Ⓐ Indian villages

● Non-Indian settlements

■ Forts

✕ Battles

0 ——— 200 miles

0 ——— 200 km

© Carl Waldman and Infobase Publishing

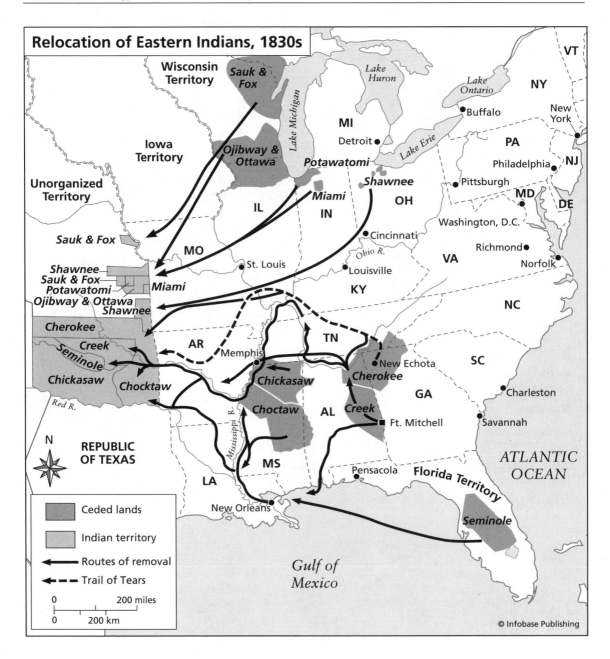

Relocation of Eastern Indians, 1830s

Wisconsin Territory

Sauk & Fox

Iowa Territory

Unorganized Territory

Ojibway & Ottawa

Potawatomi

Shawnee

Miami

IL

IN

OH

Sauk & Fox

MO

St. Louis

Shawnee
Sauk & Fox
Potawatomi
Ojibway & Ottawa
Shawnee

Miami

Cherokee

Creek

Seminole

Chickasaw

Chocktaw

Red R.

AR

Memphis

Chickasaw

Choctaw

TN

AL

Cherokee

New Echota

Creek

Ft. Mitchell

GA

SC

Charleston

Savannah

Lake Michigan

Lake Huron

Lake Ontario

Lake Erie

Detroit

Buffalo

New York

VT

NY

PA

Philadelphia

NJ

Pittsburgh

MD

DE

Washington, D.C.

Richmond

Norfolk

VA

NC

Cincinnati

Ohio R.

Louisville

KY

N

REPUBLIC OF TEXAS

Mississippi R.

LA

MS

New Orleans

Pensacola

Florida Territory

Seminole

ATLANTIC OCEAN

Gulf of Mexico

Ceded lands

Indian territory

Routes of removal

Trail of Tears

0   200 miles

0   200 km

© Infobase Publishing

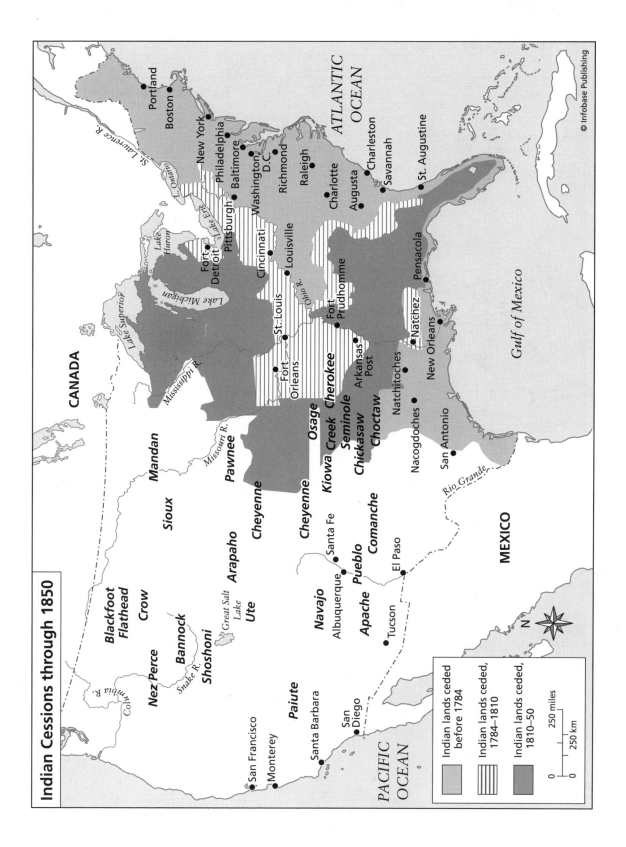

Indian Cessions through 1850

Portland
Boston
New York
Philadelphia
Baltimore
Washington, D.C.
Richmond
Raleigh
Charlotte
Augusta
Charleston
Savannah
St. Augustine

ATLANTIC OCEAN

St. Lawrence R.
L. Ontario
Lake Erie
Lake Huron
Lake Superior
Lake Michigan

Pittsburgh
Fort Detroit
Cincinnati
Louisville
Ohio R.
St. Louis
Fort Prudhomme
Fort Orleans
Arkansas Post
Pensacola
Natchez
Natchitoches
New Orleans

Mississippi R.
Missouri R.

CANADA

Mandan
Sioux
Pawnee
Cheyenne
Cheyenne

Osage
Kiowa Creek
Cherokee
Seminole
Chickasaw
Choctaw

Nacogdoches
San Antonio

Comanche

Gulf of Mexico

Blackfoot
Flathead
Crow
Bannock
Nez Perce
Shoshoni

Great Salt Lake
Ute

Arapaho

Navajo
Pueblo
Apache

Santa Fe
Albuquerque
El Paso
Tucson

MEXICO

Rio Grande

Columbia R.
Snake R.

Paiute

San Francisco
Monterey
Santa Barbara
San Diego

PACIFIC OCEAN

N

© Infobase Publishing

Indian lands ceded before 1784

Indian lands ceded, 1784–1810

Indian lands ceded, 1810–50

250 miles

250 km

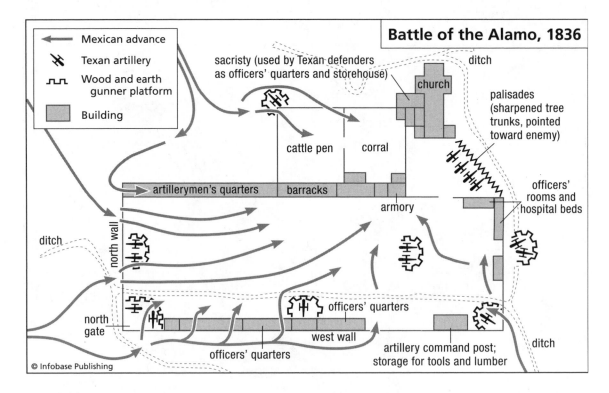

Battle of the Alamo, 1836

Mexican advance
Texan artillery
Wood and earth gunner platform
Building

sacristy (used by Texan defenders as officers' quarters and storehouse)

ditch

church

palisades (sharpened tree trunks, pointed toward enemy)

cattle pen

corral

officers' rooms and hospital beds

artillerymen's quarters

barracks

armory

ditch

north wall

north gate

officers' quarters

west wall

officers' quarters

artillery command post; storage for tools and lumber

ditch

© Infobase Publishing

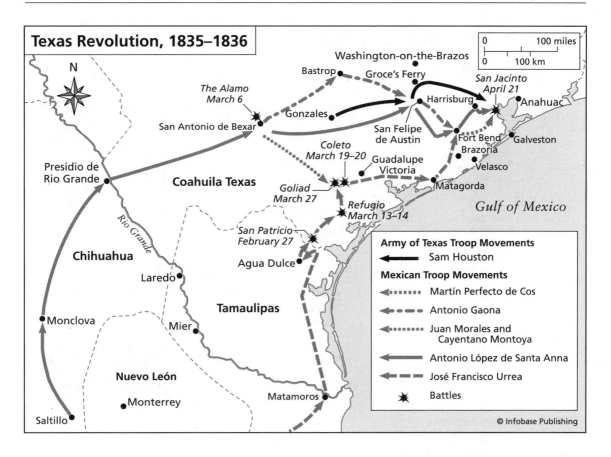

Texas Revolution, 1835–1836

N

The Alamo
March 6

Washington-on-the-Brazos

Bastrop   Groce's Ferry

San Jacinto
April 21

Harrisburg   Anahuac

Gonzales

San Antonio de Bexar

San Felipe
de Austin

Fort Bend   Galveston
Brazoria

Presidio de
Rio Grande

Coahuila Texas

Coleto
March 19–20

Guadalupe
Victoria

Velasco

Goliad
March 27

Matagorda

Gulf of Mexico

Rio Grande

Refugio
March 13–14

Chihuahua

San Patricio
February 27

Laredo

Agua Dulce

Tamaulipas

Mier

Nuevo León

Monclova

Monterrey

Matamoros

Saltillo

Army of Texas Troop Movements
Sam Houston

Mexican Troop Movements
Martín Perfecto de Cos

Antonio Gaona

Juan Morales and
Cayentano Montoya

Antonio López de Santa Anna

José Francisco Urrea

Battles

© Infobase Publishing

0   100 miles
0   100 km

Mexican-American War, 1846–1848

Sutter's Fort
San Francisco
Monterey
Santa Barbara
Los Angeles Jan. 10, 1847
San Gabriel Jan. 8, 1847
San Pasqual Dec. 6, 1846
San Diego

Fort Leavenworth
Pueblo   Bent's Fort
Santa Fe Aug. 18, 1846
Las Vegas
Albuquerque

UNITED STATES

Colorado R.
Arkansas R.
Red R.

Disputed Area

Tucson
El Paso
Gila R.

Sabine R.

Texas
San Antonio
San Jacinto
Corpus Christi

Rio Bravo

Sacramento Feb. 28, 1847
Chihuahua

Monclova   Laredo
Mier
Palo Alto May 8, 1846
Resaca de la Palma May 9, 1846
Matamoros

PACIFIC OCEAN

Gulf of California

MEXICO

Parras
Buena Vista Feb. 22–23, 1847
Monterrey Sept. 21–25, 1846

Gulf of Mexico

Mazatlán
Victoria

San Luis Potosí
Tampico

Molino del Rey Sept. 8, 1847
Mexico City captured Sept. 8–14, 1847
Chapultepec Sept. 13, 1847
Cerro Gordo April 18, 1847
Veracruz
Puebla March 22–29, 1847
Contreras and Churubusco Aug. 22, 1847

Acapulco

American military advances
◄—·—·— Alexander Doniphan
◄········· Stephen Kearny
◄‑ ‑ ‑ ‑ Winfield Scott
◁——— John Sloat
◁‑‑‑‑ Robert F. Stockton
◀——— Zachary Taylor
◄—··—··— John Wool
✴ Battles

0   300 miles
0   300 km

N

© Infobase Publishing

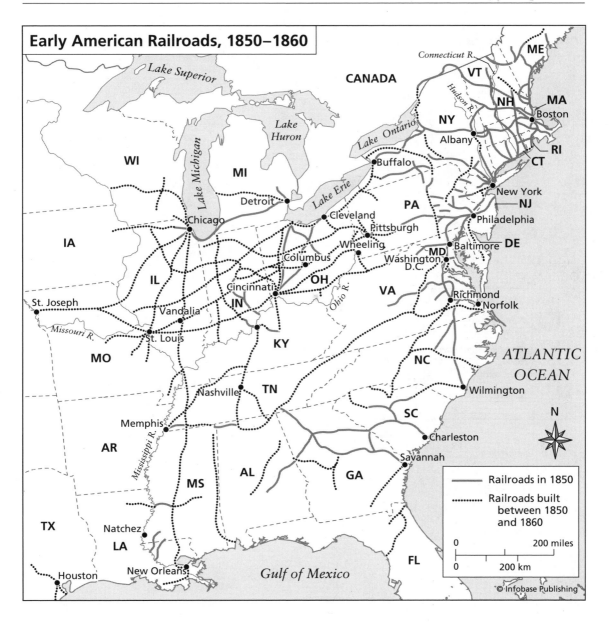

Early American Railroads, 1850–1860

Railroads in 1850

Railroads built between 1850 and 1860

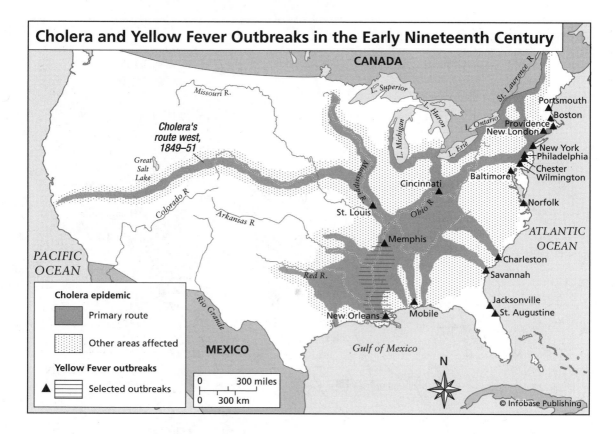

Cholera and Yellow Fever Outbreaks in the Early Nineteenth Century

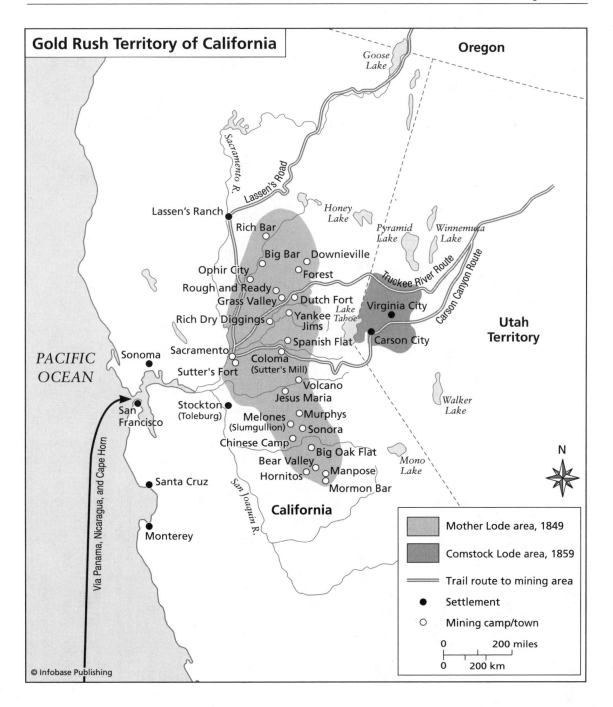

Gold Rush Territory of California

Oregon

Goose Lake

Sacramento R.

Lassen's Road

Lassen's Ranch

Rich Bar

Honey Lake

Pyramid Lake

Winnemucca Lake

Big Bar   Downieville

Ophir City   Forest

Rough and Ready   Truckee River Route

Grass Valley   Dutch Fort

Lake Tahoe   Virginia City

Rich Dry Diggings   Yankee Jims

Carson Canyon Route

Utah Territory

Spanish Flat   Carson City

Sacramento

PACIFIC OCEAN   Sonoma

Sutter's Fort   Coloma (Sutter's Mill)

Volcano

Jesus Maria

Walker Lake

Stockton (Toleburg)   Murphys

San Francisco   Melones (Slumgullion)   Sonora

Chinese Camp   Big Oak Flat   *Mono Lake*

Bear Valley

Santa Cruz   Hornitos   Manpose

San Joaquin R.   Mormon Bar

Via Panama, Nicaragua, and Cape Horn

Monterey   **California**

N

Mother Lode area, 1849

Comstock Lode area, 1859

Trail route to mining area

● Settlement

○ Mining camp/town

0   200 miles

0   200 km

© Infobase Publishing

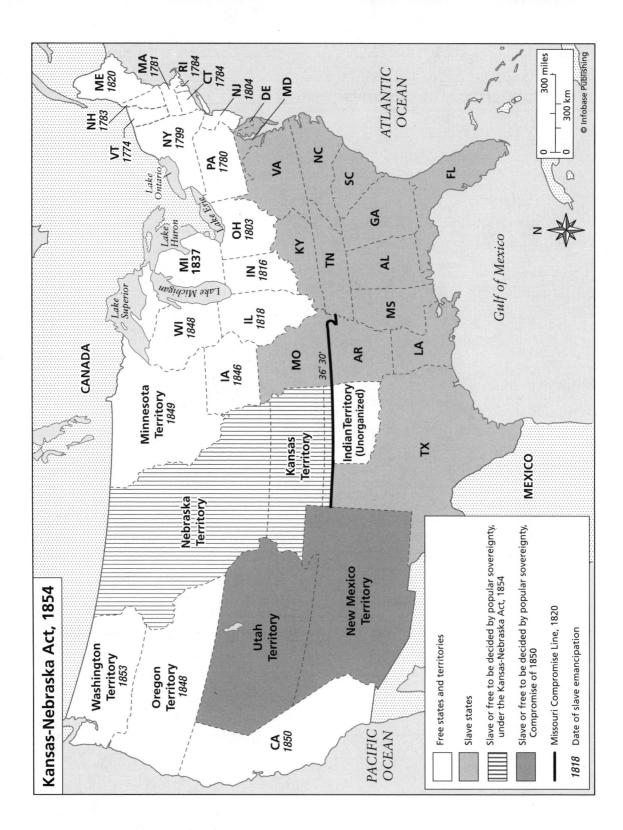

Kansas-Nebraska Act, 1854

MA *1781*
RI *1784*
CT *1784*
ME *1820*
NH *1783*
NJ *1804*
DE
MD
VT *1774*
NY *1799*
PA *1780*

ATLANTIC OCEAN

VA
NC
SC
GA
FL

KY
TN
AL
MS
LA

OH *1803*
IN *1816*
IL *1818*
MI 1837
WI *1848*
IA *1846*
MO
AR
TX

36° 30'

Indian Territory (Unorganized)

Gulf of Mexico

MEXICO

Lake Ontario
Lake Erie
Lake Huron
Lake Michigan
Lake Superior

CANADA

Minnesota Territory *1849*

Kansas Territory

Nebraska Territory

Washington Territory *1853*

Oregon Territory *1848*

Utah Territory

New Mexico Territory

CA *1850*

PACIFIC OCEAN

N

300 miles
300 km
0
0

© Infobase Publishing

Free states and territories

Slave states

Slave or free to be decided by popular sovereignty, under the Kansas-Nebraska Act, 1854

Slave or free to be decided by popular sovereignty, Compromise of 1850

Missouri Compromise Line, 1820

1818 Date of slave emancipation

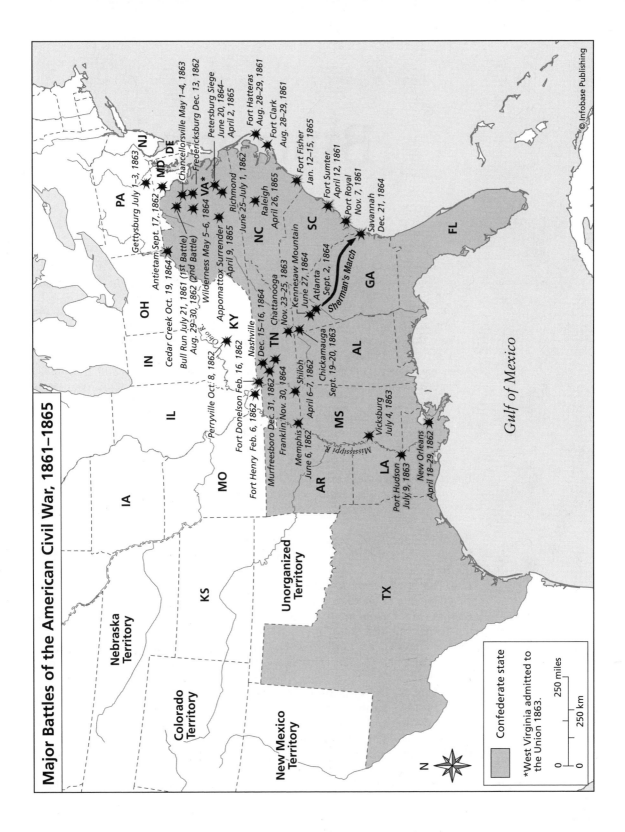

Major Battles of the American Civil War, 1861–1865

Gettysburg July 1–3, 1863

Antietam Sept. 17, 1862

Chancellorsville May 1–4, 1863

Fredericksburg Dec. 13, 1862

Petersburg Siege June 20, 1864– April 2, 1865

Fort Hatteras Aug. 28–29, 1861

Fort Clark Aug. 28–29, 1861

Fort Fisher Jan. 12–15, 1865

Fort Sumter April 12, 1861

Port Royal Nov. 7, 1861

Richmond June 25–July 1, 1862

Raleigh April 26, 1865

Wilderness May 5–6, 1864 *VA*

Appomattox Surrender April 9, 1865

Cedar Creek Oct. 19, 1864

Bull Run July 21, 1861 (1st Battle)
Aug. 29–30, 1862 (2nd Battle)

Perryville Oct. 8, 1862

Fort Donelson Feb. 16, 1862

Fort Henry Feb. 6, 1862

Nashville Dec. 15–16, 1864

Chattanooga Nov. 23–25, 1863

Murfreesboro Dec. 31, 1862

Franklin Nov. 30, 1864

Kennesaw Mountain June 27, 1864

Atlanta Sept. 2, 1864

Chickamauga Sept. 19–20, 1863

Shiloh April 6–7, 1862

Memphis June 6, 1862

Savannah Dec. 21, 1864

Sherman's March

Vicksburg July 4, 1863

Port Hudson July 9, 1863

New Orleans April 18–29, 1862

Ohio R.

Mississippi R.

PA

NJ

MD

DE

OH

IN

KY

IL

TN

NC

SC

GA

AL

MS

AR

LA

TX

FL

MO

IA

KS

Nebraska Territory

Colorado Territory

New Mexico Territory

Unorganized Territory

Gulf of Mexico

N

250 miles

250 km

0

0

Confederate state

*West Virginia admitted to the Union 1863.

© Infobase Publishing

BIBLIOGRAPHY

Adair, Douglass G. *The Intellectual Origins of Jeffersonian Democracy: Republicanism, the Class Struggle, and the Virtuous Farmer*. Lanham, Md.: Lexington Books, 2000.

Allgor, Catherine. *A Perfect Union: Dolley Madison and the Creation of the American Nation*. New York: Henry Holt, 2006.

Allison, Robert J. *Stephen Decatur: American Naval Hero, 1779–1820*. Amherst: University of Massachusetts Press, 2005.

Angevine, Robert G. The *Railroad and the State: War, Politics, and Technology in Nineteenth-Century America*. Stanford, Calif.: Stanford University Press, 2004.

Ayers, Edward L. *Crucible of the Civil War: Virginia from Secession to Commemoration*. Charlottesville: University of Virginia Press, 2006.

——. *What Caused the Civil War?: Reflections on the South and Southern History*. New York: Norton, 2005.

Baker, Anne. *Heartless Insanity: Literature, Culture, and Geography in Antebellum America*. Ann Arbor: University of Michigan Press, 2007.

Baker, Jean H. *Sisters: The Lives of America's Suffragists*. New York: Hill and Wang, 2005.

Baker, Jennifer J. *Securing the Commonwealth: Debt, Speculation, and Writing in the Making of Early America*. Baltimore, Md.: Johns Hopkins University Press, 2005.

Ball, Durwood. *Army Regulars on the Western Frontier, 1848–1861*. Norman: University of Oklahoma Press, 2001.

Banner, Stuart. *How the Indians Lost Their Land: Law and Power on the Frontier*. Cambridge, Mass.: Belknap Press of Harvard University Press, 2005.

Basker, James G., ed. *Early American Abolitionists: A Collection of Anti-Slavery Writings, 1760–1820*. New York: Gilder Lehrman Institute of America, 2005.

Beck, Paul N. *The First Sioux War: The Grattan Fight and Blue Water Creek, 1854–1856*. Lanham, Md.: University Press of America, 2004.

Belko, W. Stephen. *The Invincible Duff Green: Whig of the West*. Columbia: University of Missouri Press, 2006.

Berube, Claude, and John A. Rodgaard. *A Call to the Sea: Captain Charles Stewart of the USS Constitution*. Dulles, Va.: Potomac, 2005.

Blackman, Ann. *Wild Rose: The True Story of a Civil War Spy*. New York: Random House, 2005.

Blair, Jayne E. *The Essential Civil War: A Handbook to the Battles, Armies, Navies, and Commanders*. Jefferson, N.C.: McFarland, 2006.

Blake, David H. *Walt Whitman and the Culture of American Celebrity*. New Haven, Conn.: Yale University Press, 2006.

Bohan, Ruth L. *Looking into Walt Whitman: American Art, 1850–1920*. University Park: Pennsylvania State University Press, 2006.

Bowling, Kenneth R., and Donald R. Kennon, eds. *Establishing Congress: The Removal to Washington, D.C., and the Election of 1800*. Athens: Ohio University Press, 2005.

Braden, Bruce, ed. *"Ye Will Say I am no Christian": The Thomas Jefferson/John Adams Correspondence on Religion, Morals, and Values*. Amherst, N.Y.: Prometheus Books, 2006.

Brands, H. W. *Andrew Jackson: His Life and Times*. New York: Doubleday, 2005.

Bratt, James D. *Antirevivalism in Antebellum America: A Collection of Religious Voices*. New Brunswick, N.J.: Rutgers University Press, 2006.

Brown, Kent M. *Retreat from Gettysburg: Lee, Logistics, and the Pennsylvania Campaign*. Chapel Hill: University of North Carolina Press, 2005.

Brown, Susan M. "U.S. Soldiers and Veterans in War, Peace, and Politics during the Revolutionary War and State-Formation Period." Unpublished Ph.D. diss., New School University, 2005.

Buel, Richard. *America on the Brink: How the Political Struggle over the War of 1812 Almost Destroyed the Young Republic*. New York: Palgrave, 2005.

——. *Historical Dictionary of the Early American Republic*. Lanham, Md.: Scarecrow Press, 2006.

Buell, Lawrence, ed. *The American Transcendentalists: Essential Writings*. New York: Modern Library, 2006.

Buinicki, Martin T. *Negotiating Copyright: Authorship and the Discourse of Literary Property Rights in Nineteenth-Century America*. New York: Routledge, 2006.

Burin, Eric. *Slavery and the Peculiar Solution: A History of the American Colonization Society*. Gainesville: University Press of Florida, 2005.

Burnstein, Andrew. *Jefferson's Secrets: Death and Desire at Monticello*. New York: Basic Books, 2005.

Butts, Michele T. *Galvanized Yankees on the Upper Missouri: The Face of Loyalty*. Boulder: University Press of Colorado, 2003.

Calonius, Erik. *The Wanderer: The Last American Slave Ship*. New York: St. Martin's Press, 2006.

Campbell, Robin D. *Mistresses of the Transient Hearth: American Army Officers' Wives and Material Culture, 1840–1880*. New York: Routledge, 2005.

Carey, Charles W. *The Mexican War: "Mr. Polk's War."* Berkeley Heights, N.J.: Enslow, 2002.

Carmichael, Peter S. *The Last Generation: Young Virginians in Peace, War, and Reunion*. Chapel Hill: University of North Carolina Press, 2005.

Carroll, Lorraine. *Rhetorical Drag: Gender, Impersonation, Captivity, and the Writing of History*. Kent, Ohio: Kent State University Press, 2006.

Cashin, Joan E. *First Lady of the Confederacy: Varina Davis's Civil War*. Cambridge, Mass.: Belknap Press of Harvard University Press, 2006.

Casto, William R. *Foreign Affairs and the Constitution in the Age of Fighting Sail*. Columbia, S.C.: University of South Carolina, 2006.

Cawardine, Richard. *Lincoln: A Life of Purpose and Power*. New York: Alfred A. Knopf, 2006.

Chhibber, Pradeep K., and Ken Pollman. *The Formation of National Party Systems: Federalism and Party Competition in Canada, Great Britain, India, and the United States*. Princeton, N.J. : Princeton University Press, 2004.

Clinton, Catherine, and Nina Silber, eds. *Battle Scars: Gender and Sexuality in the Civil War*. New York: Oxford University Press, 2006.

Cogliano, Francis D. *Thomas Jefferson: Reputation and Legacy*. Charlottesville: University of Virginia Press, 2006.

Cohoon, Lorinda B. *Serialized Citizenships: Periodicals, Books, and American Boys, 1840–1911*. Lanham, Md.: Scarecrow Press, 2006.

Colaiaco, James A. *Frederick Douglass and the Fourth of July: Speaking Truth to America*. New York: Palgrave Macmillan, 2006.

Corps, Terry. *Historical Dictionary of the Jacksonian Era and Manifest Destiny*. Lanham Md.: Scarecrow Press, 2006.

Coski, John M. *The Confederate Battle Flag: America's Most Embattled Emblem*. Cambridge, Mass.: Belknap Press, 2005.

Crapol, Edward P. *John Tyler: the Accidental President*. Chapel Hill: University of North Carolina Press, 2006.

Creighton, Margaret S. *The Colors of Courage: Gettysburg's Forgotten History, Immigrants, Women, and African Americans in the Civil War's Defining Battle*. New York: Basic Books, 2005.

Cunningham, Noble E. *Jefferson vs Hamilton: Confrontations that Shaped a Nation*. New York: St. Martin's Press, 2000.

Currie, David P. *The Constitution in Congress: Democrats and Whigs, 1829–1861*. Chicago, Ill.: University of Chicago Press, 2005.

Daehnke, Joel. *In the Works of Their Hands is Their Prayer: Cultural Narrative and Redemption on the American Frontiers, 1830–1930*. Athens: Ohio University Press, 2003.

Davis, Clark. *Hawthorne's Shyness: Ethics, Politics, and the Question of Engagement*. Baltimore, Md.: Johns Hopkins University Press, 2005.

Davis, David B. *Inhuman Bondage: The Rise and Fall of Slavery in the New World*. New York: Oxford University Press, 2006.

DePalma, Margaret C. *Dialogue on the Frontier: Catholic and Protestant Relations, 1793–1883*. Kent, Ohio: Kent State University Press, 2004.

Derks, Scott. *The Value of a Dollar: Colonial Era to the Civil War, 1600–1865*. Millerton, N.Y.: Grey House Publishing, 2005.

Dershowitz, Alan M. *America on Trial: Inside the Legal Battles that Transformed Our Nation*. New York: Warner Books, 2004.

Deyle, Steven. *Carry Me Back: The Domestic Slave Trade in American Life*. New York: Oxford University Press, 2005.

Doolen, Andy. *Fugitive Empire: Locating Early American Imperialism*. Minneapolis: University of Minnesota Press, 2005.

Doutrich, Paul R. Shapers of the Great Debate on Jacksonian Democracy: A Biographical Dictionary. Westport, Conn.: Greenwood Press, 2004.

Dudley, Wade G. *Splintering the Wooden Wall: The British Blockade of the United States, 1812–1815.* Annapolis, Md.: Naval Institute Press, 2003.

Earle, Peter. *The Pirate Wars.* New York: Thomas Dunn Books/St. Martin's Press, 2005.

Edling, Max M. *A Revolution in Favor of Government: Origins of the U.S. Constitution and the Making of the American State.* New York: Oxford University Press, 2003.

Einhorn, Robin L. *American Taxation, American Slavery.* Chicago, Ill.: University of Chicago Press, 2006.

Eisenberg, John. *The Great Match Race: When North met South in America's First Sports Spectacle.* Boston: Houghton Mifflin, 2006.

Elazar, Daniel J., and John Kincaid, eds. *The Covenant Connection: From Federal Theology to Modern Federalism.* Lanham, Md.: Lexington, 2000.

Elkin, Stephen L. *Reconstructing the Commercial Republic: Constitutional Design After Madison.* Chicago, Ill.: University of Chicago Press, 2006.

Emerson, W. Eric. *Sons of Privilege: The Charleston Light Dragoons in the Civil War.* Columbia: University of South Carolina Press, 2005.

Escott, Paul D. *Military Necessity: Civil-Military Relations in the Confederacy.* Westport, Conn.: Praeger Security International, 2006.

Etcheson, Nicole. *Bleeding Kansas: Contested Liberty in the Civil War Era.* Lawrence: University Press of Kansas, 2004.

Fazio, Michael W. *The Domestic Architecture of Benjamin Henry Latrobe.* Baltimore, Md.: Johns Hopkins University Press, 2006.

Finkleman, Paul, ed. *Encyclopedia of the New American Nation: The Emergence of the United States, 1754–1829.* 3 vols. Detroit, Mich.: Charles Scribner's Sons, 2005.

Finseth, Ian F., ed. *The American Civil War.* New York: Routledge, 2006.

Foletta, Marshall. *Coming to Terms with Democracy: Federalist Intellectuals and the Shaping of an American Culture.* Charlottesville: University of Virginia Press, 2001.

Foos, Paul. *A Short, Offhand, Killing Affair: Soldiers and Social Conflict during the Mexican-American War.* Chapel Hill: University of North Carolina Press, 2002.

Ford, Lacey K., ed. *A Companion to the Civil War and Reconstruction.* Malden, Mass.: Blackwell, 2005.

Fowler, Damon L., ed. *Dining at Monticello: In Good Taste and Abundance.* Charlottesville, Va.: Thomas Jefferson Foundation, 2005.

Francaviglia, Richard V., and Douglas W. Richmond, eds. *Duel Eagles: Reinterpreting the U.S.–Mexican War, 1846–1848.* Fort Worth: Texas Christian University Press, 2000.

Frazier, Harriet C. *Runaway and Freed Missouri Slaves and Those Who Helped Them, 1763–1865.* Jefferson, N.C.: McFarland, 2004.

Fresonke, Kris. *West of Emerson: The Design of Manifest Destiny.* Berkeley: University of California Press, 2003.

Furstenberg, François. *In the Name of the Father: Washington's Legacy, Slavery, and the Making of a Nation.* New York: Penguin Press, 2006.

Gabler-Hover, Janet, and Robert Sattelmeyer, eds. *American History Through Literature, 1820–1870.* 3 vols. Detroit, Mich.: Charles Scribner's Sons, 2005.

Gaff, Alan D. *Bayonets in the Wilderness: Anthony Wayne's Legion in the Old North West*. Norman: University of Oklahoma Press, 2004.

Gaido, Daniel. *The Formative Period of American Capitalism: A Materialist Interpretation*. New York: Routledge, 2006.

Garvey, T. Gregory. *Creating the Culture of Reform in Antebellum America*. Athens: University of Georgia Press, 2006.

Gershenson, Harold P. *America the Musical, 1776–1899: A Nation's History through Music*. Greensboro, N.C.: Kindermusik International, 2005.

Giertz, John B. "The Lincoln-Douglas Campaign of 1858: A Constitutive Theoretical Analysis." Unpublished Ph.D. diss., Regent University, 2005.

Gilje, Paul A. *The Making of the American Republic, 1763–1815*. Upper Saddle River, N.J.: Pearson Prentice Hall, 2006.

Ginzberg, Lori D. *Untidy Origins: A Story of Women's Rights in Antebellum New York*. Chapel Hill: University of North Carolina Press, 2005.

Goldschmidt, Henry, and Elizabeth McAlister, eds. *Race, Nation, and Religion in the Americas*. New York: Oxford University Press, 2004.

Goodrich, Thomas. *The Darkest Dawn: Lincoln, Booth, And the Great American Tragedy*. Bloomington: Indiana University Press, 2005.

Goudie, Sean X. *Creole America: The West Indies and the Formation of Literature and Culture in the New Republic*. Philadelphia: University of Pennsylvania Press, 2006.

Gough, Barry. *Fighting Sail on Lake Huron and Georgian Bay: The War of 1812 and Its Aftermath*. Annapolis, Md.: Naval Institute Press, 2002.

Graber, Mark A. *Dred Scott and the Problem of Constitutional Evil*. New York: Cambridge University Press, 2006.

Grant, James. *John Adams: Party of One*. New York: Farrar, Straus, & Giroux, 2005.

Grant, Susan-Mary, and Peter Parish, eds. *Legacy of Disunion: The Enduring Significance of the American Civil War*. Baton Rouge: Louisiana State University Press, 2003.

Greenberg, Amy S. *Manifest Manhood and the Antebellum American Empire*. New York: Cambridge University Press, 2005.

Grenier, John. *The First Way of War: American War Making on the Frontier, 1607–1814*. New York: Cambridge University Press, 2005.

Griffin, John C. *Abraham Lincoln's Execution*. Gretna, La.: Pelican Publishing Co., 2006.

Groom, Winston. *Patriotic Fire: Andrew Jackson and Jean Laffite at the Battle of New Orleans*. New York: Alfred A. Knopf, 2006.

Gunn, Giles, ed. *A Historical Guide to Herman Melville*. New York: Oxford University Press, 2005.

Guttridge, Leonard F. *Our Country, Right or Wrong: The Life of Stephen Decatur, the U.S. Navy's Most Illustrious Commander*. New York: Forge, 2006.

Hagedorn, Ann. *Beyond the River: The Untold Story of the Heroes of the Underground Railroad*. New York: Simon & Schuster, 2002.

Hankins, Barry. *The Second Great Awakening and the Transcendentalists*. Westport, Conn.: Greenwood Press, 2004.

Hannings, Bud. *Forts of the United States: An Historical Dictionary, 16th through 19th Centuries*. Jefferson, N.C.: McFarland, 2005.

Hart, Gary. *James Monroe*. New York: Times Books, 2005.

Harris, Sharon M. *Executing Race: Early American Women's Narratives of Race, Society, and the Law*. Columbus: Ohio State University Press, 2005.

Helton, Tina L. "The Literary Frontier: Creating an American Nation (1820–1840)." Unpublished Ph.D. diss., Louisiana State University, 2005.

Henkin, David M. *The Postal Age: The Emergence of Modern Communications in Nineteenth-Century America*. Chicago, Ill.: University of Chicago Press, 2007.

Hess, Earl J. *Field Armies and Fortifications in the Civil War: The Eastern Campaigns*. Chapel Hill: University of North Carolina Press, 2005.

Hessinger, Rodney. *Seduced, Abandoned, and Reborn: Visions of Youth in Middle-Class America, 1780–1850*. Philadelphia: University of Pennsylvania Press, 2005.

Hewett, Elizabeth. *Correspondence and American Literature, 1770–1865*. New York: Cambridge University Press, 2004.

Holtz, Jeffrey. *Divergent Visions, Contested Spaces: The Early United States Through the Lens of Travel*. New York: Routledge, 2006.

Holzer, Harold. *Lincoln at Cooper Union: The Speech that Made Abraham Lincoln President*. New York: Simon and Schuster Paperbacks, 2005.

Homestead, Melissa J. *American Woman Authors and Literary Property, 1822–1869*. New York: Cambridge University Press, 2005.

Horn, James, Jan Ellen Lewis, and Peter S. Onuf, eds. *The Revolution of 1800: Democracy, Race, and the New Republic*. Charlottesville: University of Virginia Press, 2002.

Horton, James O., and Lois Horton. *Slavery and the Making of America*. New York: Oxford University Press, 2005.

Hutson, James L. *Stephen A. Douglas and the Dilemma of Democratic Equality*. Lanham, Md.: Rowman and Littlefield, 2006.

Hyslop, Stephen G. *Bound for Santa Fe: The Road to New Mexico and the American Conquest*. Norman: University of Oklahoma Press, 2002.

Janin, Hunt. *Claiming the American Wilderness: International Rivalry in the Trans-Mississippi West, 1528–1803*. Jefferson, N.C.: McFarland, 2006.

Johnson, Odai. *Absence and Memory in Colonial American Theater: Fiorelli's Plaster*. New York: Palgrave Macmillan, 2006.

Johnson, Paul E. *The Early American Republic, 1789–1829*. New York: Oxford University Press, 2007.

Kagan, Robert. *Dangerous Nation*. New York: Alfred A. Knopf, 2006.

Kaplan, Amy. *The Anarchy of Empire in the Making of U.S. Culture*. Cambridge, Mass.: Harvard University Press, 2005.

Kastor, Peter J. *The Nation's Crucible: The Louisiana Purchase and the Creation of America*. New Haven, Conn.: Yale University Press, 2004.

Kaufmann, J. E., and H. W. Kaufmann. *Fortress America: The Forts that Defended America, 1600 to the Present*. Cambridge, Mass.: Da Capo Press, 2005.

Ketchum, Ralph, ed. *Selected Writings of James Madison*. Indianapolis, Ind.: Hackett Pub., 2006.

Keyssar, Alexander. *The Right to Vote: The Contested History of Democracy in the United States*. New York: Basic Books, 2000.

King, Desmond. *The Liberty of Strangers: Making the American Nation*. New York: Oxford University Press, 2005.

Knetsch, Joe. *Florida's Seminole Wars*. Charleston, S.C.: Arcadia, 2003.

Knudson, Jerry W. *Jefferson and the Press: Crucible of Liberty*. Columbia: University of South Carolina Press, 2006.

Kohn, Denise, Sarah Meer, and Emily B. Todd. *Transatlantic Stowe: Harriet Beecher Stowe and European Culture*. Iowa City: University of Iowa Press, 2006.

Kopper, Kevin P. "Arthur St. Clair and the Struggle for Power in the Old Northwest, 1763–1803." Unpublished Ph.D. diss., Kent State University, 2005.

Lambert, Frank. *The Barbary War: American Independence in the Atlantic World*. New York: Hill and Wang, 2005.

Lanning, Michael L. *The Civil War 100: The Stories Behind the Most Influential Battles, People, and Events in the War Between the States*. Naperville, Ill.: Sourcebooks, 2007.

Larkin, Jack. *Where We Lived: Discovering the Places We Once Called Home: The American Home from 1790 to 1840*. Newtown, Conn.: Taunton Press, 2006.

Larson, John, and Michael Morrison, eds. *Whither the Early Republic: A Forum on the Future of the Field*. Philadelphia: University of Pennsylvania Press, 2005.

Lause, Mark A. *Young America: Land, Labor, and Republican Community*. Urbana: University of Illinois Press, 2005.

Leiner, Frederick C. *The End of Barbary Terror: America's 1815 War Against the Pirates of North Africa*. New York: Oxford University Press, 2006.

Lenner, Andrew C. *The Federal Principle in American Politics, 1790–1833*. New York: Rowman and Littlefield, 2001.

Leonard, Gerald. *The Invention of Party Politics: Federalism, Popular Sovereignty, and Constitutional Development in Jacksonian Illinois*. Chapel Hill: University of North Carolina Press, 2002.

Leonard, Thomas M. *James K. Polk: A Clear and Unquestionable Destiny*. Wilmington, Del.: Scholarly Resources, 2000.

Levine, Bruce C. *Confederate Emancipation: Southern Plans to Free and Arm Slaves during the Civil War*. New York: Oxford University Press, 2005.

——. *Half Slave and Half Free: The Roots of Civil War*. New York: Hill and Wang, 2005.

Levinson, Irving W. *War within War: Mexican Guerrillas, Domestic Elites, and the United States of America, 1846–1848*. Fort Worth: Texas Christian University Press, 2005.

Link, William A. *Roots of Secession: Slavery and Politics in Antebellum Virginia*. Chapel Hill: University of North Carolina Press, 2003.

Longacre, Mark G. *Rhetoric and the Republic: Politics, Civic Discourse, and Education in Early America*. Tuscaloosa: University of Alabama Press, 2007.

Lundin, Roger. *There Before Us: Religion and American Literature from Emerson to Eliot*. Grand Rapids, Mich.: William B. Eerdmans, 2006.

Malcomson, Robert. *A Very Brilliant Affair: The Battle of Queenstown Heights, 1812*. Toronto, Ont.: Robin Brass Studio, 2002.

McAfee, Thomas B. *Inherent Rights, the Written Constitution, and Popular Sovereignty*. Westport, Conn: Greenwood Press, 2000.

McCaffrey, James M. *The Army in Transformation, 1790–1860.* Westport, Conn.: Greenwood Press, 2006.

McCarthy, Timothy P., and John Stauffer, eds. *Prophets of Protest: Reconsidering the History of American Abolitionism.* New York: New Press, 2006.

McDonald, Robert M. S., ed. *Thomas Jefferson's Military Academy: Founding West Point.* Charlottesville: University of Virginia Press, 2004.

McDougall. *Freedom Just Around the Corner: A New American History, 1585–1828.* New York: Perennial, 2005.

McNutt, Donald J. *Urban Revelations: Images of Ruin in the American City, 1790–1860.* New York: Routledge, 2006.

McWilliams, John. *New England's Crises and Cultural History: Literature, Politics, History, Religion, 1620–1860.* New York. Cambridge University Press, 2004.

Mason, Matthew. *Slavery and Politics in the Early American Republic.* Chapel Hill: University of North Carolina Press, 2006.

Matson, Cathy D. *The Economy of Early America: Historical Perspectives & New Directions.* University Park: Pennsylvania State University Press, 2006.

May, Robert E. *Manifest Destiny's Underworld: Filibustering in Antebellum America.* Chapel Hill: University of North Carolina Press, 2002.

Mayo, Louise A. *President James K. Polk.* New York: Nova Science Publishers, 2006.

Meyer, David R. *Networked Machinists: High-Technology Industries in Antebellum America.* Baltimore, Md.: Johns Hopkins University Press, 2006.

Meyers, Karen. *Colonialism and the Revolutionary Period: Beginnings to 1800.* New York: Facts On File, 2005.

Milder, Robert. *Exiled Royalists: Melville and the Life We Imagine.* New York: Oxford University Press, 2006.

Miller, Susan A. *Coacoochee's Bones: A Seminole Saga.* Lawrence: University Press of Kansas, 2003.

Mills, Bruce. *Poe, Fuller, and the Mesmeric Arts: Transition States in the American Renaissance.* Columbia: University of Missouri Press, 2006.

Missall, John, and Mary Lou Missall. *The Seminole Wars: America's Longest Indian Conflict.* Gainesville: University Press of Florida, 2004.

Mitton, Steven H. "The Free World Confronted: The Problem of Slavery and Progress in American Foreign Relations, 1833–1844." Unpublished Ph.D. diss., Louisiana State University, 2005.

Monroe, Dan. *Shapers of the Great Debate on the Civil War: A Biographical Dictionary.* Westport, Conn.: Greenwood Press, 2005.

Morrisey, Will. *Self-Government, the American Theme: Presidents of the Founding and Civil War.* Lanham, Md.: Lexington Books, 2004.

Moser, Harold D. *Daniel Webster: A Bibliography.* Westport, Conn.: Praeger Publishers, 2005.

Nabers, Deak. *Victory of the Law: the Fourteenth Amendment, the Civil War, and American Literature, 1852–1867.* Baltimore, Md.: Johns Hopkins University Press, 2006.

Neely, Mark E. *The Boundaries of American Political Culture in the Civil War Era.* Chapel Hill: University of North Carolina Press, 2005.

Neff, John R. *Honoring the Civil War Dead: Commemoration and the Problem of Reconciliation.* Lawrence: University Press of Kansas, 2005.

O'Brien, Sean-Michael. *In Bitterness and Tears: Andrew Jackson's Destruction of the Creeks and Seminoles*. Westport, Conn.: Greenwood Press, 2003.

Olegario, Rowena. *A Culture of Credit: Embedding Trust and Transparency in American Business*. Cambridge, Mass.: Harvard University Press, 2006.

Oliver, Sandra L. *Food in Colonial and Federal America*. Westport, Conn.: Greenwood Press, 2005.

Onuf, Nicholas G. *Nations, Markets, and War: Modern History and the American Civil War*. Charlottesville: University of Virginia Press, 2006.

Onuf, Peter S., and Leonard J. Sadosky. *Jeffersonian America*. Malden, Mass.: Blackwell, 2002.

Osborne, William M. *The Wild Frontier: Atrocities during the American-Indian War from Jamestown to Wounded Knee*. New York: Random House, 2000.

Pacheco, Josephine F. *The Pearl: A Failed Slave Escape on the Potomac*. Chapel Hill: University of North Carolina Press, 2005.

Pasley, Jeffrey L. *"The Tyranny of Printers": Newspaper Politics in the Early American Republic*. Charlottesville: University of Virginia Press, 2001.

Patterson, Benton R. *The Generals: Andrew Jackson, Sir Edward Pakenham, and the Road to New Orleans*. New York: New York University Press, 2005.

Paul, R. Eli. *Blue Water Creek and the First Sioux War, 1854–1856*. Norman: University of Oklahoma Press, 2004.

Pennell, Melissa M. *Masterpieces of American Romantic Literature*. Westport, Conn.: Greenwood Press, 2006.

Person, Leland S. *A Historical Guide to James Fenimore Cooper*. New York: Oxford University Press, 2006.

Peterson, Anna L. *Seeds of the Kingdom: Utopian Communities in the Americas*. New York: Oxford University Press, 2005.

Pfau, Michael. *The Political Style of Conspiracy: Chase, Sumner, and Lincoln*. East Lansing: Michigan State University Press, 2005.

Phillips, Jerry. *Romanticism and Transcendentalism: 1800–1860*. New York: Facts On File, 2005.

Portnoy, Alisse. *Their Right to Speak: Women's Activism in the Indian and Slave Debates*. Cambridge, Mass.: Harvard University Press, 2005.

Preston, Daniel, and Marlena C. DeLong, eds. *The Papers of James Monroe*. 2 vols. Westport, Conn.: Greenwood Press, 2003–2004.

Prushankin, Jeffrey S. *A Crisis in Confederate Command: Edmund Kirby Smith, Richard Taylor, and the Army of the Trans-Mississippi*. Baton Rouge: Louisiana State University Press, 2005.

Reid, Brian H. *Robert E. Lee: Icon for a Nation*. London: Weidenfield and Nicolson, 2005.

Reid, Stuart. *The Secret War for Texas*. College Station: Texas A & M University Press, 2007.

Remini, Robert V. *Andrew Jackson and His Seminole Wars*. New York: Viking, 2001.

Resendez, Andres. *Changing National Identities at the Frontier: Texas and New Mexico, 1800–1850*. New York: Cambridge University Press, 2005.

Reynolds, David S. *John Brown, Abolitionist: The Man Who Killed Slavery, Sparked the Civil War, and Seeded Civil Rights*. New York: Alfred A. Knopf, 2005.

—— *Walt Whitman*. New York: Oxford University Press, 2005.

Richards, Jeffrey H. *Drama, Theater, and Identity in the American New Republic*. New York: Cambridge University Press, 2005.

Riss, Arthur. *Race, Slavery, and Liberalism in Nineteenth-century American Literature*. New York: Cambridge University Press, 2006.

Roberts, David. *A Newer World: Kit Carson, John C. Frémont, and the Claiming of the American West*. New York: Touchstone Books, 2000.

Robertson, Andrew W. *The Language of Democracy: Political Rhetoric in the United States and Britain, 1790–1900*. Charlottesville: University of Virginia Press, 2005.

Robertson, Lindsay G. *Conquest by Law: How the Discovery of America Dispossessed Indigenous Peoples of Their Lands*. New York: Oxford University Press, 2005.

Robinson, Armistead L. *Bitter Fruits of Bondage: The Demise of Slavery and the Collapse of the Confederacy, 1861–1865*. Charlottesville: University of Virginia Press, 2005.

Rosen, Fred. *Gold! The Story of the 1848 Gold Rush and How It Shaped a Nation*. New York: Thunder's Mouth Press, 2005.

Rossignol, Marie-Jeanne. *The Nationalist Ferment: The Origins of U.S. Foreign Policy, 1789–1812*. Columbus: Ohio State University Press, 2004.

Rothman, Adam. *Slave Country: American Expansion and the Origins of the Deep South*. Cambridge, Mass.: Harvard University Press, 2005.

Rugemer, Edward B. "The Problem of Emancipation: The United States and Britain's Abolition of Slavery." Unpublished Ph.D. diss., Boston College, 2005.

Saillant, John. *Black Puritan, Black Republican: The Life and Thought of Lemuel Haynes, 1753–1833*. New York: Oxford University Press, 2003.

Schroeder, John H. *Commodore John Rodgers: Paragon of the Early American Navy*. Gainesville: University Press of Florida, 2006.

Schweitzer, Ivy. *Perfecting Friendship: Politics and Affiliation in Early American Literature*. Chapel Hill: University of North Carolina Press, 2006.

Seefeldt, Douglas, Jeffrey L. Hantman, and Peter S. Onuf, eds. *Across the Continent: Jefferson, Lewis and Clark, and the Making of America*. Charlottesville: University of Virginia Press, 2005.

Shankman, Andrew W. *Crucible of American Democracy: The Struggle to Fuse Egalitarianism and Capitalism in Jeffersonian Pennsylvania*. Lawrence: University Press of Kansas, 2004.

Siddali, Silvana R. *From Property to Person: Slavery and the Confiscation Acts, 1861–1862*. Baton Rouge: Louisiana State University Press, 2005.

Siemers, David J. *Ratifying the Republic: AntiFederalists and Federalists in Constitutional Time*. Stanford, Calif.: Stanford University Press, 2002.

Silber, Nina. *Daughters of the Union: Northern Women Fight the Civil War*. Cambridge, Mass.: Harvard University Press, 2005.

Silbey, Joel H. *Storm Over Texas: The Annexation Controversy and the Road to Civil War*. New York: Oxford University Press, 2005.

Silverstone, Scott A. *Divided Union: The Politics of War in the Early American Republic*. Ithaca, N.Y.: Cornell University Press, 2004.

Singer, Jane. *The Confederate Dirty War: Arsons, Bombings, and Plots for Chemical and Germ Attacks on the Union*. Jefferson, N.C.: McFarland, 2005.

Sizer, Lyde Cullen, and Jim Cullen, eds. *The Civil War Era*. Malden, Mass: Blackwell, 2005.

Skaggs, David C. *Thomas Macdonough: Master of Command in the Early U.S. Navy*. Annapolis, Md.: Naval Institute Press, 2003.

Smith, Adam I. P. *No Party Now: Politics in the Civil War North*. New York: Oxford University Press, 2006.

Smith, Craig. *Daniel Webster and the Oratory of Civil Religion*. Columbia: University of Missouri Press, 2004.

Smith, David A., comp. *Presidents from Adams through Polk, 1825–1849: Debating the Issues in pro and con Primary Documents*. Westport, Conn.: Greenwood Press, 2005.

Smith, Joshua. *Borderland Smuggling: Patriots, Loyalists, and Illicit Trade in the Northeast, 1783–1820*. Gainesville: University Press of Florida, 2006.

Smith, Roy C. *Adam Smith and the Origins of American Enterprise: How the Founding Fathers Turned to a Great Economist's Writings and Created the American Economy*. New York: St. Martin's Press, 2004.

Smith, Thomas T. *The Old Army in Texas: A Research Guide to the U.S. Army in Nineteenth Century Texas*. Austin: Texas State Historical Association, 2000.

Soodalter, Ron. *Hanging Captain Gordon: The Life and Trial of an American Slave Trader*. New York: Atria Books, 2006.

Spencer, Mark D. *David Hume and Eighteenth-Century America*. Rochester, N.Y.: University of Rochester Press, 2005.

Stadler, Gustavus. *Troubling Minds: The Cultural Politics of Genius in the United States, 1840–1890*. Minneapolis: University of Minnesota Press, 2006.

Stauffer, John. *The Black Hearts of Men: Radical Abolitionists and the Transformation of Race*. Cambridge, Mass.: Harvard University Press, 2002.

Sugden, John. *Blue Jacket: Warrior of the Shawnees*. Lincoln: University of Nebraska Press, 2000.

Sutton, Robert P. *Federalism*. Westport, Conn.: Greenwood Press, 2002.

Taylor, Andrew, and Eldrid Herrington, eds. *The Afterlife of John Brown*. New York: Palgrave Macmillan, 2005.

Thiesen, William H. *Industrializing American Shipbuilding: The Transformation of Ship Design and Construction, 1820–1920*. Gainesville: University Press of Florida, 2006.

Towers, Frank. *The Urban South and the Coming of the Civil War*. Charlottesville: University Press of Virginia, 2004.

Tucker, Spencer. *Stephen Decatur: A Life Most Bold and Daring*. Annapolis, Md.: Naval Institute Press, 2005.

Tulloch, Hugh. *The Routledge Companion to the American Civil War*. New York: Routledge, 2006.

Tushnet, Mark, ed. *Arguing Marbury v. Madison*. Stanford, Calif.: Stanford Law and Politics, 2005.

Vandervort, Bruce. *Indian Wars of Canada, Mexico, and the United States*. New York: Routledge, 2005.

Volo, James M. *The Antebellum Period*. Westport, Conn.: Greenwood Press, 2004.

Wallace, William J. "The Medieval Specter: Catholics, Evangelicals, and the Limits of Political Protestantism, 1835–1860." Unpublished Ph.D. diss., University of Virginia, 2005.

Wallenstein, Peter, and Bertram Wyatt-Brown, eds. *Virginia's Civil War*. Charlottesville: University Press of Virginia, 2005.

Warshauer, Matthew. *Andrew Jackson and the Politics of Martial Law: Nationalism, Civil Liberties, and Partisanship*. Knoxville: University of Tennessee Press, 2006.

Watkins, William J. *Reclaiming the American Revolution: The Kentucky and Virginia Resolutions and Their Legacy*. New York: Palgrave Macmillan, 2004.

Watson, Harry L. *Liberty and Power: The Politics of Jacksonian America*. New York: Hill and Wang, 2006.

Wayne, Tiffany K. *Encyclopedia of Transcendentalism*. New York: Facts On File, 2006.

Weber, Jennifer L. *Copperheads: The Rise and Fall of Lincoln's Opponents in the North*. New York: Oxford University Press, 2006.

Weddle, Kevin J. *Lincoln's Tragic Admiral: The Life of Samuel Francis Du Pont*. Charlottesville: University of Virginia Press, 2005.

Weierman, Karen W. *One Nation, One Blood: Interracial Marriage in American Fiction, Scandal, and Law, 1820–1870*. Amherst: University of Massachusetts Press, 2005.

Weitz, Mark A. *More Damning than Slaughter: Desertion in the Confederate Army*. Lincoln: University of Nebraska Press, 2005.

Wertheimer, Eric. *Underwriting: The Poetics of Insurance in America, 1722–1872*. Stanford, Calif.: Stanford University Press, 2006.

Widmer, Edward L. *Martin Van Buren*. New York: Times Books, 2005.

Wilentz, Sean. *Andrew Jackson*. New York: Times Books, 2005.

——. *The Rise of American Democracy: Jefferson to Lincoln*. New York: Norton, 2005.

Williams, Heather A. *Self-Taught: African American Education in Slavery and Freedom*. Chapel Hill: University of North Carolina Press, 2005.

Williams, Patrick G., Charles Bolton, and Jeannie M. Whayne, eds. *A Whole Country in Commotion: The Louisiana Purchase and the American Southwest*. Fayetteville: University of Arkansas Press, 2005.

Williams, Susan S. *Reclaiming Authorship: Literary Women in America, 1850–1900*. Philadelphia: University of Pennsylvania Press, 2006.

Wills, Garry. *Negro President: Jefferson and Slave Power*. Boston: Houghton Mifflin, 2005.

——. *Henry Adams and the Making of America*. Boston: Houghton Mifflin, 2005.

Winders, Richard B. *Crisis in the Southwest: The United States and the Struggle over Texas*. Wilmington, Del.: SR Books, 2002.

Wood, John H. *A History of Central Banking in Great Britain and the United States*. New York: Cambridge University Press, 2005.

Wooton, David, Ed. *The Essential Federalist and Anti-Federalist Papers*. Indianapolis, Ind.: Hackett, 2003.

Wright, Daniel S. *The First Cause Is to Our Sex: The Female Moral Reform Movement in the Antebellum Northeast, 1834–1848*. New York: Routledge, 2006.

Wright, Gavin. *Slavery and American Economic Development*. Baton Rouge: Louisiana State University Press, 2007.

Wright, Robert E. *The US National Debt, 1787–1900*. 4 vols. London: Pickering & Chatto, 2006.

Young, Jeffrey R. *Proslavery and Sectional Thought in the Early South, 1740–1829*. Columbia: University of South Carolina Press, 2006.

Young, Michael P. *Bearing Witness Against Sin· The Evangelical Birth of the American Social Movement*. Chicago, Ill.: University of Chicago Press, 2006.

Zacks, Richard. *The Pirate Coast: Thomas Jefferson, the First Marines, and the Secret Mission of 1805*. New York: Hyperion, 2005.